An Introduction to
the Modern Middle East

An Introduction to

THE MODERN
MIDDLE EAST

*History, Religion,
Political Economy, Politics*

DAVID S. SORENSON

Air War College

Westview
PRESS

A Member of the Perseus Books Group

Published by Westview Press,
A Member of the Perseus Books Group

Find us on the World Wide Web at www.westviewpress.com.

Westview Press books are available at special discounts for bulk purchases in the United States by corporations, institutions, and other organizations. For more information, please contact the Special Markets Department at the Perseus Books Group, 2300 Chestnut Street, suite 200, Philadelphia PA 19103, or call (800) 255-1514, or e-mail special.markets@perseusbooks.com.

DESIGNED BY JEFF WILLIAMS

Library of Congress Cataloging-in-Publication Data
Sorenson, David S., 1943-
  An introduction to the modern Middle East : history, religion, political economy, politics / David S. Sorenson.
    p. cm.
  Includes bibliographical references and index.
  ISBN-13: 978-0-8133-4399-0
  ISBN-10: 0-8133-4399-2
  1. Middle East—Politics and government. 2. Religion and politics—Middle East. 3. Middle East—Economic conditions. I. Title.
  DS44.S67 2007
  956—dc22

                                                                    2007030942

10 9 8 7 6 5 4 3

CONTENTS

Preface and Acknowledgments   *vii*
Glossary   *xiii*

Introduction:
Thinking about the Middle East   1

SECTION I
The Historical, Religious, Economic, and Political Foundations of the Middle East   9

1 The Modern History of the Middle East   11
2 Religion in the Middle East   42
3 The Political Economy of the Middle East   73
4 Politics in the Middle East   94

SECTION II
The Countries of the Arabian Peninsula and Arabian Gulf Area   123

5 Saudi Arabia   127
6 The Persian Gulf Emirates   146
7 Yemen   175

8 Iran   190

9 Iraq   211

 SECTION III
The Countries of the Eastern Mediterranean   229

10 Egypt   233

11 Turkey   254

12 Syria   276

13 Lebanon   292

14 Israel   307

15 Jordan   331

16 Palestine   347

SECTION IV
The Countries of North Africa   365

17 Tunisia   369

18 Libya   382

19 Morocco   394

20 Algeria   411

Notes   *425*

Index   *501*

PREFACE AND
ACKNOWLEDGMENTS

The purpose of this book is to introduce and explain the politics of the modern Middle East, which (in this book) includes the countries of the Persian (or Arabian) Gulf, the eastern Mediterranean countries, and North Africa. The countries in each geographical grouping are:

Persian Gulf	Eastern Mediterranean	North Africa
Saudi Arabia	Egypt	Tunisia
Bahrain	Turkey	Libya
Kuwait	Syria	Morocco
Qatar	Lebanon	Algeria
United Arab Emirates	Israel	
Oman	Jordan	
Yemen	Palestine	
Iran		
Iraq		

The book opens with themes allowing a comparison of countries and follows with sections on the individual countries. It begins with an introductory chapter on thinking about Middle Eastern politics; a chapter summarizing the post–World War I history of the Middle East follows. While the entire period of Middle Eastern and North African history is both significant and interesting, the book emphasizes the period following World War I because it marks the beginning of the modern state system in the region. The next three chapters cover significant themes in politics, religion, and political economy. The thematic chapters focus on the three sections that follow, covering the major geographical regions that make up the Middle East: the Arabian (or Persian) Gulf region, the eastern Mediterranean, or Levant, and North Africa, or the Maghreb. Each section contains individual chapters on the countries discussed there.[1]

While the book emphasizes politics, it starts with a chapter on modern history, and each country chapter contains an introductory section on its history or political foundations. This is because present political conditions cannot be understood when divorced from their past. Present-day actors carry out their functions in an environment where the past shapes their political latitudes. Their own understanding of their history similarly shapes their own beliefs and values. This is true in every country in the world, but it may be particularly true of countries in the Middle East.

Images.   Readers will find short vignettes at the beginning of most sections and chapters called "images," drawn from observations by the author that led to personal reflection. Perhaps they will do the same for the reader.

Arabic Spellings.   Arabic is a unique language written in an alphabet that does not easily transliterate into English or other alphabetic languages. There are, for example, a number of ways in Arabic to render the English letter *a,* and no Arabic equivalent of the English *p* exists, so *b* substitutes. There are "hard" and "soft" renditions of several letters (*g, h,* for example). Thus there is no consensus on how to transliterate Arabic into English, and consequently words may be spelled differently but have the same meaning. For example, the US media normally spell the name of the Iraqi leader as Saddam Hussein, but it is also correctly spelled "Husayn." The announcements of the election of a new Palestinian president in January 2005 read "Mahmoud" Abbas in the *New York Times* and "Mahmud" Abbas in *al-Jazeera.* In 2001, the Associated Press decided to change the spelling from "Mohammed" to "Muhammad," and "Koran" to "Quran," because such spellings are closer to Arabic pronunciations. But there are variations; for example, the king of Morocco spells his name "Mohamed." This book also uses those spellings. It uses the most familiar method of spelling Arabic words in English, so the name of the late Egyptian President "Nasser" is used rather than the more correct "Nasir," "Hussein" instead of "Husayn," and "sheik" instead of "shaykh." The formal name "Said" is properly written "Sa'id" and pronounced "Sayyid." The indefinite article *al* will be provided the first time a word associated with it is used, but eliminated thereafter, unless its use is common (for example, the name of the Egyptian resort town Sharm al-Sheikh). The article *al* (the) will be in lower case and connected to the following word.

Names.   The structure of names in the Arab world varies from country to country. The more formal naming system in some of the Arabian Peninsula countries uses name structure that identifies both father and family. The term ibn or bin means "son of" the name that follows, and bint means daughter of the father whose name follows. Al refers to the family name. Thus the king of Saudi Arabia is Fahd ibn Abdul Aziz al-Saud, meaning that his first name is Fahd, he is the son of King ibn Saud (the first king of Saudi Arabia), and he is of the Saud family. A second bin or bin with a name following means "grandson of." In the less traditional Arab countries, and in Iran, Turkey, and Israel, the naming system is much like that in the West, with a given name and a family last name (the father's name, in all cases).

Titles. Western readers used to standard political titles like "president" and "prime minister" may find Middle East titles confusing. Some Middle Eastern and North African countries use the titles "president" or "prime minister," but others use titles that are more traditional. Some Gulf countries use "Emir" (sometimes spelled "Imir"), meaning "commander" (or "prince"), while in Oman the ruler holds the title of "sultan" (the only country in the Middle East using this title for the national ruler). The term "sheik" is also common to the Middle East for a ruler's title (as in the case of the United Arab Emirates); the title does not automatically mean "ruler" but simply connotes respect. A male elder is often referred to as "sheik" even if he has no formal political title, for women it is "sheika." "Imam" literally means "prayer leader," conveys knowledge of Islam, and is informally bestowed.

In some Middle Eastern countries, leaders take on or inherit additional titles. King Fahd and his successor King Abdullah of Saudi Arabia titled themselves "Custodian of the Two Holy Mosques" on assuming the throne to emphasize Saudi Arabia as the birthplace of Islam as commemorated by the Grand Mosque in Mecca (or Makkah) and the Prophet's Mosque in Medina, where the Prophet is buried. King Muhammad VI of Morocco inherited his family title of "Commander of the Faithful" to emphasize his dynasty's claim of descent to the Prophet Muhammad.

Terminology. This book uses terminology partly to reduce confusion. Unfortunately, this is not always possible, so the best solution is to clarify terms here and to indicate the considerable ambiguity that often accompanies them. For example:

The term "Middle East" normally refers a region encompassing a section of Southwest Asia and North Africa, as the map on p. xviii shows. The term "Near East" also remains in use. Some scholars recognize this and commonly refer to the combination of the Middle East and North Africa as MENA, but for simplicity, this book will use the term "Middle East" when referring generically to both areas.

An "Arab" is one whose native language is Arabic.[2] An Arab country is one where Arabic is the majority language, specifically Syria, Jordan, Lebanon, Palestine, Egypt, Morocco, Libya, Tunisia, Algeria, Saudi Arabia, Bahrain, Kuwait, Qatar, Oman, the United Arab Emirates, and Yemen. There are other countries with large minority Arab populations, like Sudan with a 39 percent Arab population and where Arabic is the official language, or Mauritania, or the Republic of Comoros, where 86 percent are Islamic and both French and Arabic are considered the official languages.

The three major non-Arab countries in the Middle East are Iran, Israel, and Turkey. Iranians speak Persian, today known as Farsi, derived from the original name of their country, which became "Iran" only in 1935. Iranians have both linguistic and cultural differences that set them apart from others in the regions, and

Shiite Islam became dominant in Persia after the fifteenth century. Israel is a political newcomer to the Middle East (though not the most recent), established as a state in 1948 with a Hebrew-speaking population, despite the fact that almost 20 percent of Israelis are Arab speakers. Turkey is another major non-Arabic speaking country with a predominately Muslim population and cultural ties to the Arab world through long contact, primarily through the Ottoman Empire, which served as a vehicle to blend traditional Arab and Turkish culture.

The "Persian Gulf" is the body of water and its adjacent countries generally referred to in American media circles as the Persian Gulf. Most Arabs call it the Arabian Gulf, as does the United States Central Command, which has responsibility for US military policy in the region. However almost all media sources (the most common source of world information for the non-specialist) call the Gulf the Persian Gulf, so that more familiar term appears in this book.

Customary dating practices use BC (before Christ) and AD (anno domini: in the year of our Lord) to indicate dates before and after the believed time of the birth of Christ. Later practices use BCE (before the common era) and CE (common era) to reduce the apparent Christian bias. However, the terms mean the same thing as previous practice; BCE is still before year 1 and CE is year 1 and after. The terms BCE and CE are used here, but readers should recognize that they are Christian in origin. Another dating system is used in the Muslim world, and yet another in Israel. In the Muslim calendar, the term AH (anno Hijrah) designates dates after the Christian calendar year 622, which on the Islamic calendar is the year 1. In that year the Prophet Muhammad journeyed from Mecca to Medina (then called Yathrib) at the invitation of some citizens to resolve a dispute, and the Islamic calendar begins at that point. And there is a Jewish calendar that starts at the year Jews believe man first appeared on earth, 3761 BCE. Therefore the Christian year 2000 was the Islamic year 1420 and the Jewish year 5760.

This book relies on a combination of scholarly books, articles, and papers for information, and on both American and international news sources. While recognizing that no information source is completely without bias, an effort was made to avoid sources whose purpose is more propaganda than information. Some international media are translated through a service known as the Open Source Center, but formerly as the Foreign Broadcast Information Service, indicated in endnotes as FBIS. The author collected additional information in Turkey, Israel, Saudi Arabia, Morocco, Tunisia, Egypt, Kuwait, Oman, Syria, Israel, Jordan, the United Arab Emirates, Qatar, Algeria, Yemen, and Bahrain.

Updating Information in This Book.   The Middle East is a dynamic place, and some of the current information in this book may soon become outdated. Therefore, for updates, the following websites are useful:

- CIA World FactBook:
  www.odci.gov/cia/publications/factbook/index.html
- Arab News:
  www.arabnews.com

- Freedom House:
  www.freedomhouse.org
- Middle East Institute:
  www.mideasti.org/
- al-Jazeera:
  http://english.aljazeera.net/HomePage
- *Jerusalem Post:*
  www.jpost.com

Updated maps are available at the Perry-Castaneda Library at the University of Texas, www.lib.utexas.edu/maps/index.html.

This listing does not endorse the contents of these websites, and, like all other information on the region, there is room for error and differing interpretations.

ACKNOWLEDGMENTS

No book stands as an individual effort, and this one is no exception. It started when the Air War College granted me a sabbatical leave, and I am grateful to the Air War College leadership for this support. I also benefited from earlier service on the faculties of Denison University and the Mershon Center at Ohio State University. Numerous colleagues and referees have read all or parts of the manuscript, including W. Andrew Terrill, Louis B. Ware, Susan Waltz, Ronald Edwards, Robert Wendzel, Judith Gentleman, Grant Hammond, Christopher Hemmer, Yahia Zoubir, Stephen Burgess, Ahmed El-Afandi, Christopher M. Jones, John D. Stempel, Peter B. Heller, and Mary Ann Tétreault. John Duke Anthony gave me several opportunities to observe the Middle East as a Malone Fellow, sponsored by the National Council on US-Arab Relations. Thanks also to my editors at Westview Press—Karl Yambert, Meredith Smith, Erica Lawrence, and Chrisona Schmidt—for making this a better product than it was when they first got it. None of these colleagues or organizations, though, are accountable for the remaining shortcomings, which are my responsibility alone. My spouse, Sharon Tyler, supplied editorial work and personal encouragement. She also raised two daughters as I traveled in the Middle East, for which I am most grateful. The views in this book do not necessarily reflect the position of the US Air Force or any other government agency.

GLOSSARY

Abbasid	Islamic dynasty, 750–1258 CE.
Abu Bakr	The first caliph to succeed the Prophet Muhammad.
Alawi (Alevi in Turkish)	Religious sect found largely in Syria, but also in Turkey, claims to be a branch of Shiite Islam.
Ali	The Prophet Muhammad's son-in-law, who became the fourth caliph.
Allah	Arabic name for God.
Arab	A person whose native language is Arabic.
Ashkenazi	Occidental, or "Western" Jews, largely of European origin.
Assassins	A Shiite tribe living in the Zagros Mountains in Persia (modern Iran) during the Umayyad and Abbasid period.
Ataturk, Kemal	Founder of modern Turkey.
Ayatollah	Title of a high-ranking Shiite leader.
Ayyubid	Islamic dynasty founded in Cairo by Salah ad-Din, 1171–1260.
BCE	Before the common era, used to replace BC as designating the years before the birth of Christ.
Baath	In Arabic, "renaissance," political parties organized around Arab nationalism.
Bahai	A religious group founded in Persia in the nineteenth century.
Bedouins	Nomadic peoples.
Bey	Ottoman rank for district governors, right under the rank of pasha.
Bida	Innovation, practices against Islamic tradition.

CE	Common era, the time period corresponding to AD, following the birth of Christ.
Caliph	Title conferred to one who claims succession to the Prophet.
Confessional	A political system divided along religious lines, particularly in Lebanon.
Coptic	A Christian sect, found mostly in Egypt, Sudan, Ethiopia, and Eritrea.
Dar al-harb	The world outside Islam, literally "the abode of war."
Dar al-Islam	The Islamic world, literally "the world of Islam."
Dhimmi	Muslim term for Christians, Jews.
Druze	Derivation of Ismaili Shiite, found mostly in Lebanon, Syria, and Israel.
Emir	Title of ruler, used mostly in the Persian Gulf Arab states.
Fatimid	Shiite dynasty started in North Africa around 911 CE.
Fatwa	A religious advisory opinion.
Fiqh	Islamic jurisprudence.
Fitna	Rebellion, or disorder.
GCC	Gulf Cooperation Council formed in 1961, including Saudi Arabia, Qatar, Kuwait, Bahrain, the United Arab Emirates, and Oman.
GDP	Gross domestic product, a measure of economic performance.
Hadith	Islamic lessons based on sayings or actions of the Prophet Muhammad.
Hajj	Pilgrimage to Mecca, required of all Muslims capable of performing it.
Halal	Activities permissible for Muslims.
Hanafi	Liberal school of Sunni Islamic law.
Hanbali	Conservative school of Sunni Islamic law, prevalent in Saudi Arabia.
Haram	Activities forbidden for Muslims.
Hashemites	Ruling family of the Najd region of Saudi Arabia; became ruling families of Iraq (until 1958) and Jordan.
Hijab	Head covering worn in public by Muslim women.
Hijrah	622 of the common era, the year of Muhammad's journey to Medina, and year 1 of the Islamic calendar.
Hizbollah	(1) Shiite political movement based largely in south

Lebanon, literally "Party of God." (2) Turkish Islamist group, unaffiliated with the Lebanese Hizbollah.

Hussein ibn Ali	Son of Ali, major figure in Shiite religion.
Ibadi	Kharijite-inspired Islamic religious sect, predominately in Oman.
Ibn	Literally "son of" in Arabic.
IDF	Israeli Defense Force.
Ijtihad	In Islam, reasoning independent of Islamic tradition.
Imam	Muslim prayer leader, spiritual leader in Shiite communities.
IMF	International Monetary Fund.
Intifadah	Term for two Palestinian uprisings against Israeli occupation, literally meaning "shaking off" in Arabic.
Islah	"Reform" in Arabic, often the name taken by a party advocating reform.
Istiqlal	Moroccan independence party.
Islam	Religion based on the Quran and the life of Muhammad.
Ismailis ("Seveners")	Shiite followers of the seventh imam, Ismail.
Ithna Asharis ("Twelvers")	Shiite followers of the twelfth imam, born Abu-Qasim Muhammad ibn Hasan, or "Mahdi," the "Hidden Imam."
Jihad	Literally, "struggle" or "striving" in Arabic.
Jizya	Tax paid by non-Muslims (specifically Jews and Christians) who live in Islamic societies.
Kaaba	Black building in the center of the Grand Mosque in Mecca, and the focus of Muslim prayers.
Kafir (Kefir)	In Islam, an unbeliever.
Kharijite	Rebellious movement against Muslim leaders, dating to seventh century.
Kurds	A linguistic minority living in Turkey, Iran, Iraq, and Syria.
Levant	The region of the eastern Mediterranean.
Madrassa	Muslim religious school (literally "school" in Arabic).
Maghreb	The part of North Africa west of Egypt.
Maliki	Sunni school of law emphasizing public welfare.
Mamluk	Term applied to slave soldiers who founded a dynasty of the same name in Cairo, 1260–1517.
Maronite	A Monophysite Christian sect, dating to the time of St.

	Maron. Its members live mostly in Lebanon.
Mecca (Makka)	Birthplace of the Prophet Muhammad, considered the holiest city in Islam, located in modern Saudi Arabia.
Mesopotamia	Historical land now occupied largely by Iraq and parts of Syria.
Miraj	The Arab name for Muhammad's nocturnal journey to Heaven.
Muhammad	The individual believed by Muslims to have received the revelations from God (Allah) that became the Quran.
Muslim	A person believing in Islam.
Mutawwa	Once scholars of religion specializing in religious ritual, now the Committee to Propagate Virtue and Prohibit Vice in Saudi Arabia.
OAPEC	Organization of Arab Petroleum Exporting Countries.
OPEC	Organization of Petroleum Exporting Countries.
Ottoman	Turkish empire, late thirteenth century to the end of World War I.
PA	Palestinian Authority.
Pasha	Ottoman title for provincial rulers, above the title of bey, also an honorary title.
Persian	Language spoken in Iran, also called Farsi.
PLO	Palestine Liberation Organization, later to become the PA, or Palestinian Authority.
PKK	*Partiya Karkeren Kurdistan,* Kurdish separatist group.
Purchasing power parity	Standardized dollar price weights applied to goods and services in a particular national economy, used to compare economic strength.
Qadi	Judge in Islamic jurisprudence.
Quran	Text Muslims believe to be collected revelations from God given to Muhammad (literally "recitation" in Arabic).
Ramadan	Ninth month of the Islamic calendar, requiring fasting and sexual abstinence for Muslims.
Rashidun	"Rightly guided," the Islamic terms for the first four caliphs after the death of the Prophet Muhammad.
Salafiyya	Literally "pious" or "venerated ancestors," a term for those who turn to the earliest Islamic community for current inspiration and guidance.

Sasanian	Ancient empire stretching from Iraq and Iran into Central Asia.
Sephardi	Oriental, or "eastern" Jews, largely of non-European origin.
Shafi	School of Sunni Islamic law, integrates the Hanafi and Maliki schools.
Shah	Persian title for ruler.
Sharia	Islamic law.
Sheik	Title of honor for an elderly man.
Shia	Islamic branch that supported the claim of Muhammad's son-in-law Ali as caliph.
Shura	"Council" in Arabic, often the title of a legislature.
Sufi	Form of Islamic mysticism.
Sultan	Islamic leader title, used in the Arab world only in Oman.
Sunni	Islamic branch that followed from the succession of the first three caliphs, today the majority Islamic branch.
Takfir	In Islam, a declaration of Muslim heresy, or excommunication.
Tawhid	In Islam, the unity, or "oneness," of Allah.
Ulama	Muslim religious scholars.
Umar ibn al-Khattab	Second of the four "rightly guided" caliphs.
Umayyad	The first Sunni dynasty, 681–750 CE.
Umma	Muslim community.
UN	United Nations.
Uthman ibn Affan	Third of the four "rightly guided" caliphs.
Wahhabism	Puritanical form of Islam inspired by Muhammad al-Wahhabi, also called al-Muwahiddun.
Waqf	In Islam, a religious endowment, or those who manage such an endowment.
WMD	Weapons of mass destruction, including nuclear, chemical, and biological.
Zakat	One of the five pillars of Islam, a tax fulfilling the obligation to give to the poor.
Zaydi	A branch of the Shiite faith whose followers recognize Zayd ibn Ali, the fifth imam.

MAP 0.1   THE MIDDLE EAST

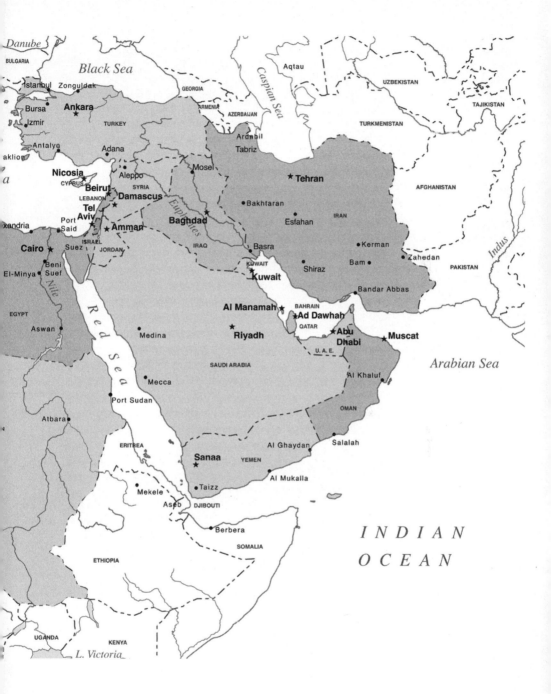

Introduction

THINKING ABOUT
THE MIDDLE EAST

IMACES | *The ticket agent scans the passport, and her face reacts to the visas marked "Jordan" and "Egypt." "Oh," she states with alarm, "you're going to the Middle East; I would never go there!" "But you're driving home tonight," comes the response, met by a blank stare. "You have a greater risk of dying in traffic going home than I do going to the Middle East. It's really quite safe there." "Oh, is that because they behead people there?" she asks. "It's a bit more complicated than that. . . what gate does the flight leave from?"*

To MANY OUTSIDERS, the Middle East seems remote, lying almost halfway around the world from North America and Japan, though they are more familiar to Europeans. Middle Eastern culture and customs seem foreign to Westerners, and few outside the area understand its primary religion, Islam. When reports of the Middle East filter through the American media, they are usually negative, depicting acts of terrorism and anger toward the United States. Literature and other forms of entertainment rarely depict the Middle East in a positive light. Movies tell of an American mother desperately trying to regain a child whose father kidnapped her and took her back to his country or depict the Delta Force combating ruthless terrorists who brutalize passengers on hijacked planes. Most Americans are familiar with "Islamic fundamentalism," and the Middle Eastern leaders most Americans recognize are Saddam Hussein and Muammar Qadhafi. The horrific images of the attacks on September 11, 2001, only reinforced negative associations with the Middle East, as does the continuing calamity in Iraq. Unfortunately there are few positive portrayals of the Middle East.

Yet the Middle East is a vital area for world interests, and for reasons that go far beyond oil, its best-known commodity. Oil is the most significant natural resource in the Middle East, with around three-quarters of the global supply located there, but petroleum is only one factor that makes the Middle East important. World commerce today sustains the livelihood of billions of people, and much of that commerce moves by land, sea, and air through the Middle East. The seaborne trade between Europe and Asia generally passes through the Suez Canal and into the Red Sea, while much of the world's oil transits the narrow Straits of Hormuz at the mouth of the Persian Gulf. Other ocean trade moves through the Mediterranean Sea, north of the coast of Morocco, Tunisia, Algeria, Libya, and Egypt. That makes the stability of those countries important.

Less tangible factors also connect the Middle East to the rest of the world. It is the birthplace of the world's three monotheistic religions—Islam, Judaism, and Christianity. Jerusalem best demonstrates this, a city where one can visit the Church of the Holy Sepulcher, the Western Wall, and the Dome of the Rock in less than an hour.[1] They are, in order, the purported site of Christ's crucifixion, the possible remains of the Hebrew Second Temple (destroyed by the Romans in 70 CE), and the place from which Muslims believe the Prophet Muhammad ascended to heaven after a night journey from Mecca. These places lie within a small section of the old city of Jerusalem, no more than around 5 square kilometers in size. The Western Wall (sometimes called the Wailing Wall) is the holiest site in the world for Jews, who come to pray there and connect to both their faith and their past. Muslims regard the Dome of the Rock as the third holiest place in the world, ranking only behind the Prophet's Mosque in Medina and the Grand Mosque in Mecca. Christians make pilgrimages to the holy places representing the life and crucifixion of Jesus, including the Stations of the Cross and the Church of the Nativity in nearby Bethlehem.

FOUNDATIONS

The Middle Eastern region is the historic site of many of the world's ancient civilizations, and their history alone covers thousands of years of migration, urbanization, invention, bloodshed and conquest, and ultimately decay and disappearance under the desert sands.

The Middle East, along with China, India, and another few scattered places around the world, is one of those few "core areas" where human civilization developed many thousands of years ago. The early inhabitants of the region between the Tigris and Euphrates Rivers who built such ancient civilizations as Sumer and Babylon in the land known as Mesopotamia left footprints thousands of years ago for those who came after them to follow. While it is true that the connection between the early Mesopotamians and those who settled the land after them was broken, the people who live there today still feel links to those ancient cultures. Sometimes modern-day leaders use those links to inspire their followers. For example, former Iraqi ruler Saddam Hussein rebuilt part of the great city of Babylon, and the former shah of Iran celebrated the 5,000th birthday of Persia (now Iran) in the ruined city of Persepolis.

The Currency of History

When Osama bin Laden issued his calls to Muslims to fight against the United States and the West, he consistently characterized his targets as "Crusaders," referring to the Christian occupiers of the Holy Land between the eleventh and thirteenth centuries. Dean Abdullah Hassan Ali Barakat of al-Azhar University in Cairo, speaking in 2006, remarked, "He mentions the Iraq War as proof and, without irony, the fact that medieval churches burned scientists at the stake at a time when the Islamic world emphasized research at places like al-Azhar. He says this as if it were yesterday and as though nothing has changed since."[2] Such imagery is not uncommon. As Mary-Jane Deeb explains, "Arab societies have a very fluid sense of time. For them, events like the Crusades a thousand years ago are as immediate as yesterday. Moreover, they are very, very powerful events in the Arab mind. A lot of Islamic rhetoric revolves around the Crusades."[3] The legends live on as the centuries pass. The impact is often a strong belief that the West (and the most powerful Western country, the United States) is once again plotting against the Arab and Islamic world. President George W. Bush's unfortunate reference to his campaign against al-Qaeda as a "crusade" after the September 11 attacks only fueled such beliefs, even though the White House quickly retracted the statement. When Pope Benedict XVI quoted a fourteenth-century text critical of Islam in September 2006, and a Danish newspaper published unfavorable cartoons of the Prophet Muhammad in the same year, many Muslims recoiled in anger. The reaction came in the face of a long history of humiliation at the hands of Westerners, whose impact over the past century is especially painful for the peoples whose grandparents often recite from memory the sights of British or French soldiers dishonoring Arabs as though they were animals. Only those who have heard such stories can understand the full impact of disgraces like the actions of a few Americans at Iraq's Abu Ghraib prison and the plight of the Palestinian population, half of which continues to live in refugee status decades after their expulsion from Israel.

Jewish history shapes beliefs for the modern inhabitants of Israel. The constant oppression experienced by Jews reinforces the belief today that the paramount role of the state of Israel is to provide physical security for the Jewish people, who, for the first time since the Roman conquest of Jerusalem in 70 CE, have their own state and their own security apparatus. In modern Israel, numerous holidays commemorate disasters that befell the Jewish people in their long history, serving to either remind them of their vulnerability to or burden them with the sense of perpetual victimhood. Persian (and Iranian) history is similar, flush with memories of historical occupations, illustrated by such things as photographs taken around 1912 showing smiling Russian officers posing in front of gallows from which hang the bodies of Persian nationalists.

Most Westerners have little awareness of their cultural and historic connection to the Middle East, largely because those connections date back many centuries and have often been filtered through European culture. However, consider the following:

- Developments in literature, theology, science, philosophy, medicine, mathematics, music, and other such things that make up what is often called "Western civilization" came from, or at least through, the Middle East. Arguably, the first great work of literature was the Mesopotamian tale of Gilgamesh, a Noah-like hero who survived a global flood, written around 2000 BCE. The Babylonians developed sophisticated mathematical skills, including geometry and the computation of exponentials. They also developed the idea of time measurement, dividing a day into twenty-four hours, an hour into sixty minutes, and a minute into sixty seconds, a concept that remains universal after 4,000 years. The ancient Egyptians left records indicating an advanced understanding of diseases and their causes. The concept of a college as a place of higher learning is of Islamic origin, and the world's first university, al-Azhar in Cairo, dates back to the ninth century. The idea of zero, algebra (itself an Arabic word), trigonometry, and discoveries in medicine (including the circulation of blood) came from the Greek and Indus civilizations and were rediscovered and refined in the Arab and Islamic worlds. In the eighth century, al-Uqlidisi discovered the decimal fraction, and a Persian mathematician may have invented the calculating machine.[4] The work of Nasiruddin Tusi on celestial motion in Persia in the thirteenth century was translated into Greek and influenced Copernicus as he developed the heliocentric theory of the solar system.[5] Abu Abdallah Muhammad ibn Jabir al-Harrani, who lived in what is now Iraq (858–929 CE), was probably the first to calculate the solar year and the timing of the seasons. Abu Yousuf Yaqub ibn Ishaq al-Kindi, also born in what is today Iraq, wrote pathbreaking books on a wide range of subjects that would later inform European scientists. Abu al-Qasim Az-Zahrawi, born around 938, known as the father of surgery, performed tracheotomy and lithotomy operations, introduced the use of cotton and catgut, and described extra-uterine pregnancy, breast cancer, and the sex-linked inheritance of hemophilia. Ibn Firnas, who lived in the ninth century, investigated the mechanics of flight. He constructed a pair of wings out of feathers on a wooden frame and made the first attempt at flight, anticipating Leonardo da Vinci by 600 years. Some modern scholars consider the political theories developed by Ibn Khaldun (1332–1405) as superior in thought to the much better-known political theories of Machiavelli.[6] The Arab philosopher al-Farabi (870–950) analyzed Plato's discussion of metaphysics and developed pathbreaking theories on logic.[7] Other Arabs discovered and developed knowledge from cultures they encountered in, for example, the Indus Valley and China. The diaries of the great traveler ibn Battuta, who traversed much of the known Islamic world shortly after Marco Polo's journeys, enhanced greatly the knowledge of geography and the culture of the time.[8] However, none of these great scholars gets much recognition outside of the Islamic world. For example, in December 1999 the American Discovery Channel ran a list of the 100 most influential people of the past millennium. While many of the great Western scientists and thinkers were listed (Copernicus, Galileo, Bacon, Machiavelli, Locke, and Newton, for example), the presentation mentioned none from the Islamic world.

- Spanish-style architecture, so popular in places like California or Texas, is actually Middle Eastern in origin, coming to Spain with the Islamic armies who occupied much of the Iberian Peninsula between 711 and 1492 CE. Arched porticos, red tile roofs, courtyards with fountains, and stucco walls characterized Middle Eastern and North African houses thousands of years ago. When the Muslims crossed into Spain, they took their architecture with them, and it flourished there and elsewhere in Europe. Music and musical instruments also have Middle Eastern origins. The guitar has indirect links to the Spanish lute, which originated as the *oud*, a stringed instrument still popular in the Arab world today. The famous Turkish Janissary bands that were often part of early European courts influenced European composers, as reflected in Mozart's famous piano Sonata 11, the "Turkish March." Soap and daily bathing were habits discovered in the Middle East by the Crusaders and taken back to Europe after the thirteenth century, as were eating utensils such as forks (first used in the Middle East in the seventh century) and knives, unknown to the Crusaders who ate mostly with their hands, heaping their food on stale bread instead of plates. Forks were not widely used in Italy until the sixteenth century. Toilets flushed by running water were used in the Middle East before the common era and may date back to early Mesopotamia, while outdoor privies existed in much of Europe and the United States until the twentieth century. Perfumes distilled from roses came from Persia long before they came from Paris.

- Common foods and beverages originated from or passed through the Middle East to the West. Yogurt was a Mongol dish left with the Arabs after the Mongol defeat in the thirteenth century. Citrus trees arrived in Europe from the Crusades. Coffee has obscure origins, but Sufi mystics in Yemen seem to have first used the drink to stay awake for evening religious services. The Arab word for the drink, *qahwah,* became "coffee" and reached Europe through Turkey. Middle Easterners probably popularized fast food meat sandwiches with shwarma (roast lamb or chicken, sliced into pita bread) long before the first McDonald's opened. The world's first known cookbook appeared in Babylon almost 4,000 years ago and included a recipe for goat kid stewed with onions, garlic, sour milk, and blood.

- The concept of law, used today to regulate almost every society, first appeared (at least in written form) in the Babylon of King Hammurabi, who ruled from 1795 to 1750 BCE. His code, divided into 282 sections, defines rules and penalties for a variety of activities, including business law, civil relations (including marriage and divorce law), and criminal law. Hammurabi's Code also contains the first known statement of the rights of women, including the right to divorce (they got their dowry back if they could prove cruelty, but the man suffered no additional penalty).

- Theological thought and the concept of monotheism came from the Middle East thousands of years ago. The Hebrew Bible, filled with prophets, kings, and events such as the Great Flood, is a history of the ancient Middle East. Some contend that the belief in one god originated in Egypt around 1500 BCE with Pharaoh Akhenaton, who broke with Egyptian polytheism and formed the cult of Amun, the sun god. There were also ancient Mesopotamian beliefs in such things as immaculate conception, the story of Cain and Abel, and a massive flood that serve as precursors to the Old and New Testaments. Places in ancient Middle Eastern history get constant mention in church sermons and hymns: Galilee, Nazareth, Sodom and Gomorrah, the Street Called Straight, the Mount of Olives, Zion, and many others. Islam and Christianity both developed their philosophical orthodoxy through the thought of Aristotle, as rediscovered and distilled by early Islamic scholars like Abul-Walid ibn Rushd, known in the West as Averroes (1126–1198), Abu Ali al-Hussein ibn Abdallah ibn Sina, also known as Avicenna (980–1037), Abu Yusuf Yaqub ibn Ishaq al-Sabbah al-Kindi (801–873) and Abu Bakr Muhammad ibn Zakariya al-Razi, known to Europeans as Rhazes (865–925), and further developed by Christian philosophers during medieval times.[9]
- European languages contain many words from the Middle East, including algebra, admiral, arsenal, alcohol, cane, hazard, soda, tomato, salad, saffron ("yellow" in Arabic), and a host of others. Tennis players swing a racket (from the Arabic *rahat,* or palm of hand) and hit tennis balls named after Tinnis, a town in Egypt from which linen for the balls originated. When Egyptian Sultan Salih built quarters for his troops along the Nile River in 1240 CE, he drew the troops' name, Bahris, from the common name for the Nile, *bahr,* or sea.[10] The term evolved into "barracks" now used worldwide to refer to military quarters. The word "salt" appears to originate from the name of a Jordanian city, al-Salt, near Amman. The "julep" in "mint julep" comes from the Arabic word *julab,* or rosewater. The name of the famous Rock of Gibraltar comes from the Arabic *Jebel Tariq,* or "Mountain of Tariq," named after the Berber general Tariq ibn Zayid who crossed by Gibraltar to conquer Spain in 711. The Latin alphabet originated from the Ugaritic alphabet, dating back to around 1200 BCE. A text from Ugarit (now in modern Syria) containing twenty-six letters is on display at the National Museum in Damascus.

STUDYING THE MIDDLE EAST: ORIENTALISM AND ITS CRITICS

Some critics claim that Western scholars impose a particular frame of reference on the Middle East, following a path set by earlier chroniclers of the region.[11] The late Edward Said labels much of British and French literature on the "Orient" (or "East") as "Orientalism," defined as "a Western Style for dominating, restructuring, and having authority over the Orient."[12] Said concentrated largely on nineteenth-century writers (Ernest Renan, Gustave Flaubert, Mark Twain, and Richard Burton, for example), who describe an Orient of courtesans, pyramids, backwardness, and syphilis.[13] Their reductionism of Eastern people and culture opens the door for a mythology of Western superiority and the need for Western control, often through empire. In his final chapter Said singles out the Middle East Studies Association, US government–funded institutes like the RAND Corporation and the Hudson Institute, and scholars like Raphael Patai (author of *The Arab Mind* and other works), P.J. Vatikiotis, and Bernard Lewis who retain, according to Said, "the traditional Orientalist outlook which had been developed in Europe."[14] One study argues that Orientalism continued to influence American policy toward the region throughout the cold war and after.[15] Lockerman maintains that an Orientalist thread leads to the Bush II administration's policy on Iraq since 2003.[16]

Reaction to Orientalism in the United States has been both negative and defensive. A critique of Middle Eastern studies argued that scholars such as John Esposito, John Voll, Richard Bulliet, and Michael Hudson produce an academic "whitewash" of Islam. They and others, according to Martin Kramer, seek to varnish Islamic politics as inherently democratic and leading to stable political systems. Consequently they failed to explain the resurgence of Islamic violence characterized by September 11, 2001.[17] Kramer paradoxically joins Said as the target of critics who accuse both of malicious persecution without much evidence, possibly influenced too much by their own identities and mind-sets (Said was Palestinian-born and Kramer, although born in Washington, DC, served for years on the faculty of Tel Aviv University in Israel). Others sustain Said's argument, emphasizing the mistaken lessons from history (Lewis's focus on Ottoman reactions to premodern Europe, for example), or the emphasis by Orientalists on the narrative of a static Islam in public and private life, or an Islam marked by systemic violence.[18]

The debate over Orientalism underscores the fragility of Middle Eastern studies. There are certainly disparaging comments about Arabs (notably in Patai's *The Arab Mind*)[19] and continuing charges of "neo-Orientalism" against journalist Robert Kaplan and scholars Daniel Pipes and Samuel Huntington.[20] But if Huntington, for example, cites clear failures of Islamic countries to maintain economic growth rates comparable to those of non-Islamic countries, is that "Orientalist" or is it simply true? In a similar fashion, to suggest that Middle Eastern studies has "failed," as Kramer does, because of an oversensitivity to "Orientalism" ("Said's disciples govern Middle East studies," he claims) begs the question, Failed at what?[21] Kramer fails to demonstrate that the "counter-Orientalists" like John Esposito are wrong; he simply finds them guilty by association (Esposito and Said praise each other's work).[22] Moreover, if Middle Eastern studies "failed" to inform policy or to provide warnings about something like September 11, was it because the discipline "failed" or because US policymakers failed to pay attention to what serious Middle Eastern scholars were writing and saying? Finally, is it the duty of Middle Eastern studies (or any other area studies, for that matter) to construct policy foundations or to inform students and scholars who utilize the fruits of its endeavors to enhance their own understanding of this region?

These debates are noted to remind readers that few disciplines are value-free no matter how neutral they profess to be. The history profession is imbued with debates about what is and is not true because of inherent biases and professed norms that shackle the profession. Consider, for example, the strident debate over Israeli modern history and responsibility for the Palestinian exodus.[23] Narratives about politics and religion are even more laden with charges and countercharges of favoritism or unsupported criticism or one-sidedness. Readers should demand fairness and accuracy and nothing less, but must also understand that critiques in Middle Eastern studies go beyond challenges to veracity to include emotional reactions to perceptions (real or not) of misunderstanding and unfairness. Some parts of this book may be labeled Orientalist because they emphasize things that are sometimes depicted as Western values. However, values such as democratization, equality for minorities and women, and civil liberties are increasingly esteemed around the world if not practiced, and the very fact that most Middle Eastern and North African countries are increasingly putting them into practice suggests that they are well beyond worrying about Orientalism.

A chapter on modern history follows, from World War I to the present, to pave the way for the chapters on themes and individual countries that follow.

Section I

THE HISTORICAL, RELIGIOUS, ECONOMIC, AND POLITICAL FOUNDATIONS OF THE MIDDLE EAST

The four chapters in this section illustrate the complexity of the Middle East, whose multidimensional nature allows many contending voices to claim different conclusions from often contradictory information. They also illustrate the clash of ideas that pushes Middle East politics between a quest for stability and demands for change. These chapters consider the constancy of political history and the range of political and economic experiments that range across the Middle Eastern experience. They also delve into the complex religious foundations that often become the very focus for the Middle East. The laboratories for these foundational ideas are the country chapters that follow.

This section begins with a chapter on modern Middle Eastern history, with "modern" defined as the post–World War I (1914–1918) period. This is an obviously contracted history, since Middle Eastern history runs to over 4,000 years of records, one of the richest in the world. However, since the primary purpose of this book is to facilitate an understanding of the contemporary Middle East, the modern emphasis with its colonial and state-building periods is most appropriate, though I leave out the earlier periods with reluctance.

The second chapter features a discussion of the primary religions of the Middle East, with an emphasis on Islam. The focus on all religions is their *political* import, rather than the rich tapestry of theology evolving from thousands of years of debate. The subsequent chapter covers economic issues in the Middle East, including economic development and the complex interplay between economic and political dynamics. The final chapter in the section covers the Middle East's political matrix, with emphasis on political transitions, religion and politics, civil society, and the challenges involved with gender and politics.

These chapters provide thematic material for the country-specific chapters in Sections II, III, and IV.

1

THE MODERN HISTORY
OF THE MIDDLE EAST

IMAGES

The Cairo diorama clanks slowly around the painted battle scenes, with martial music playing in the background and the announcer's solemn voice intoning the meaning of the slaughter. The paintings show bold Egyptian troops slaying their Israeli foes in the 1973 war, as smoking Israeli jets plummet to the ground. There are no dead Egyptian troops, just as there are no dead Syrian troops in the same type of diorama in Damascus (both gifts of the North Korean government). In Jerusalem, the final room of the Holocaust Memorial (funded partly by the United States) forms the horn of a cornucopia offering a dramatic vista of Jerusalem, as though the Holocaust justified Israel's claim to the city. These historical portrayals in service of the desired messages are extracted from the pages of history to serve the regimes that built them, and perhaps need them to sustain their own legitimacy.

THE HISTORY OF THE MIDDLE EAST

Americans accustomed to a history measured in centuries may find it difficult to contemplate the Middle East's time lines. Great cities with running water, thriving commercial systems, libraries, paved streets, and other "modern" amenities existed more than 5,000 years ago in the Fertile Crescent. Yet in distant times peoples living in what is now called the Middle East developed alphabets, astronomy, theology, architecture, literature, engineering, agronomy, and political systems to govern and organize society. Egyptians living along the Nile River developed a civilization that stood in its time as one of the most advanced in the world, with their massive monuments remaining as mute testaments to their greatness.

History provides a sense of identity, pride, grandeur, shame, or impotence. Lessons from history sustain peoples in successive eras; they explain why things are so and sometimes support government arguments that certain things can or cannot be done. Modern regimes use such "lessons" for legitimacy, to preserve the status quo, to justify brutality, or to support or suppress peace efforts. All countries and all societies have their myths, rooted in history and designed to solidify support for goals that further the country's purpose—or the regime's purpose. They do not have to be true to be believed; they just have to be believable. Consider two contradictory myths about Palestine:

- The Palestinians were actually bedouins and did not own the land of Palestine; consequently it is appropriate for the descendants of the ancient Israelites to take possession of it.[1]
- There is no physical evidence of the First Temple or the Jewish kingdom of Israel, and even if there was a Moses who led Israeli wanderers into Palestine, they took the land from the Canaanites, who were the progenitors of the Palestinians, who are thus entitled to take it back.[2]

It does not matter much which myth is true, for historical truths are often inconclusive, depending on fragments of pottery, carbon dating, or scraps of bone. Even with such evidence, the story often remains incomplete. Archeological evidence frequently points in uncertain directions. Floods, earthquakes, and other natural phenomena mix together fragments from different ages. Scholars still cannot decipher some writings left by ancient civilizations. Much remains to be uncovered, but archeologists often lack the funds to excavate the hills covering many ancient ruins.

The lack of physical evidence does not stop people from making claims with historical bases. Morocco claims the western Sahara on the belief that old trade ties linked western Saharans and Moroccans. For years, Qatar and Bahrain made competing claims to some small islands because the ruling families of both countries once ruled them. Iraqi leader Saddam Hussein claimed Kuwait was historically a part of Iraq when he invaded it in August 1990. Some Israelis believe that the West Bank of the Jordan River is part of historical or Eretz Israel and thus they argue that no leader should ever return it to the Palestinians, since they believe that it is a part of the Promised Land.

THE PAST AS PROLOGUE

Those living in the modern Middle East view their past with a mixture of pride and regret. They point to the accomplishments of the Umayyad (around 691 to 750 CE) and Abbasid (750–1258 CE) periods in comparison to Europe in those times, where most of the population lived in mud huts and used rudimentary tools during a time known as the Dark Ages. Defenders of Islamic civilization note that much of what is now part of European or Western civilization originated in the Islamic world, which might have continued its cultural dominance had it not been for the invaders who derailed this grand civiliztion. The Crusaders came first, looting the region of many of its treasures. The Mongols then swept out of Central Asia to sack Baghdad and thus end the Abbasid period. After the Mongols came the Ottomans and finally the Europeans. France and Britain became regional powers after the defeat of the Ottoman Empire in 1919 and divided the area, with the French getting most of North Africa plus Syria (from which they carved out Lebanon to protect the Christian Maronite majority). The British got protectorates along the Arabian side of the Gulf, and most of the Levant, from which they created Iraq, Palestine, and Trans-Jordan. Britain also gained access to Egypt and to Suez, since they depended on the Suez Canal to reduce transit time from Britain to the Asian domains of the British Empire. Under the impact of European outsiders, much of the old Ottoman Middle East became nation-states after World War I.

Westerners should consider carefully the impact of this history. The idea of independent states in the Middle East is a relatively new one. Those who live in these states are unsurprisingly affected by their modern identity. For example, when Egypt was on the brink of war with Israel in 1967, an American reporter observed, "It is interesting that after hours of conversation and countless cups of Turkish coffee, Mr. Heikal, the editor in chief of *al-Ahram* (Egypt's leading newspaper) and the others close to President Gamal Abdul Nasser talked less about the present crisis than about the past, less about the strategy or diplomacy of the emergency than about the psychology, the humiliation and the dignity of the Arabs."[3] It was the Arab, more than the Egyptian, legacy that troubled the editor, as it does so many Arabs, who are often torn between allegiance to the nation-state and to the broader Arab world that stretches from the Atlantic Ocean to the Persian Gulf. The Turkish- and Persian-speaking peoples had maintained strong ties to nation-states for many centuries, unlike the Arabs and, for that matter, the Israelis, who had to rediscover the idea of a modern state after centuries of existence as an often persecuted Jewish minority in other countries.

IMAGES

A riot of bright colors covers the fields, rare for Syria except in March. Paper-thin red poppies, tiny blue lupine blossoms, and yellow buttercups dot the rolling green hills. The narrow road leads through small villages, some dominated by a white dome marking a tomb. A lone figure emerges by the side of the road to open a gate. This is the site of Ebla, the long-lost city that may be mentioned in Genesis. Only in 1964 did archeologists dig the hills away here, revealing foundations and walls made of stone carefully fitted together. "There is the kitchen," the man said, introducing himself as a staff archeologist who had been excavating this area for several years. There was nothing to tell the untrained observer that this was the kitchen, nor could one tell that the "library" was really a library. However, diggers discovered a treasure trove of clay tablets there, baked into preservation by the fire that destroyed the building thousands of years ago. The tablets revealed much about Ebla, including the affairs of its citizens and its relations with other city-states of the area. The hills surrounding the excavations cover other foundations, but there is neither time nor money to dig, and so what lies under the flowers must remain a mystery for now. Once this was a city possibly ruled

by the great-great-great-great grandfather of Abraham. The sounds of ancient people once rang out; the chisel of the mason, the laughter of children, the call of the merchant, the sentry's shouted warning from the fifty-foot-high city wall alerting the city to the arrival of the Akkadians, who would lay waste to it around 2250 BCE. The fate of the citizens of Ebla is unknown, though the Akkadian leader boasted of other conquests where he slaughtered everyone he found, flaying them and decorating his columns with their skins.

Today the area around Ebla is silent, except for the breeze blowing through the low scrub brush and the distant bleating of goats. The carpet of flowers reseeds itself each year, although there is almost no one left to pick them. It has been this way for forty-five centuries.

THE COLONIAL HISTORY OF THE MIDDLE EAST

After the Crusaders were defeated in 1290 CE, European influence and interest in the Middle East waned. Preoccupied with their own struggles and the opening of the New World, Europeans left the Middle East largely alone for centuries. There were occasional forays into the area, as when Napoleon attacked Egypt and Palestine between 1798 and 1801, or when the combined forces of Europe and the new United States attacked the North African Barbary states whose corsairs pirated commerce in the Mediterranean. In the 1830s, British sailors and diplomats gained control over the Persian Gulf, with British diplomats negotiating with the various sheiks in the Gulf to provide the British access to their ports. However, much of the Middle East had been incorporated in the Turkish Ottoman Empire, which dated to the twelfth century. The Ottomans expanded their domain over the centuries to include most of the Arab world up to Morocco and much of the Balkans, but excluding the great Persian culture from its sway. However, a combination of factors, including internal decay and growing power in western Europe, contributed to the centuries-long decline of the Ottoman Empire.

After the French Revolution, European political ideas began to trickle into the Middle East. European travelers and conquerors engaged in a limited dialog in those societies, sometimes pressing for political reform that would make colonial rule more efficient. This contact inspired a dialog within the Muslim community between conservatives and reformers, where reformers rekindled early arguments over the place for individual reason and science within the Muslim community (see Chapter 4 for a discussion of religious reform). Although the contact turned bitter as Western power spread rapidly, the revolutionary ideas and the means for communicating them (the printing press), remained.[4]

One justification for European intervention in the Middle East was the waning Ottoman Empire. European diplomats believed that if the Ottoman Empire collapsed, European powers and Arab nationalists would try to fill the resulting power vacuum. Consequently Britain supported the Ottomans against France, and later France supported the Ottomans against Russia; both France and Britain assisted

Turkey against Russia in the Crimean War. However, Russia and Britain maintained an interest in Iran, since both had interests adjacent to it. However, Western interest in the Middle East proper would transcend natural resources and access, especially as a consequence of the events leading up to World War I.

Germany became a unified modern country only in 1871, and thus was a new-comer to the colonial race. German power and interests grew, however, as Germany established colonies in East Africa and elsewhere. German activity in the Middle East included a proposal to build a Berlin-to-Baghdad railroad, along with military and political relations with Ottoman Turkey. Britain maintained an interest in the Middle East for two related reasons. First, Britain relied on its far-flung colonial empire for its raw materials and consequently needed a navy and required oil to fuel its ships. The Persian Gulf, for the British, offered more convenient access to the Indian Ocean and the colonies that lay beyond. They got this capacity when French engineer Ferdinand DeLesseps gained a concession from the Egyptian government to build a canal between the Mediterranean Sea and the Red Sea, constructed between 1859 and 1869 (costing the lives of over 125,000 Egyptian workers). Great Britain bought shares in the Suez Canal in 1875 and thus gained a partial interest in it. Britain defended what interests it had in the Middle East and expanded into other areas held by Ottoman Turkey, fearing that her European rivals wanted to limit British power in the area. Britain built ports, cultivated local leaders, and invested in the Middle East, eyeing the decline of the Ottoman Empire and the uncertainty that lay beyond.

European history affected the Middle East in another way when discrimination against Jewish citizens broke out in Russia and Poland. These attacks, known as pogroms (Russian for "devastation"), began in Russia in the late nineteenth century and intensified during the Russo-Japanese War of 1904. Seeking the believed safety of their ancestral home, waves of Jewish immigrants (or *aliyas*) fled to Palestine, from where Rome had exiled them around 70 CE. During the first aliya, over 25,000 Jews arrived in Palestine from Russia between 1882 and 1903. They were joined by 40,000 additional Russian Jews in the second aliya between 1904 and 1914, and a third group of around 25,000, also from Russia, arrived in Palestine immediately after World War I. The final and largest aliya, consisting of 60,000 Polish Jews, landed in Palestine between 1923 and 1926. These Jews bought land from Palestinians in some cases, or expropriated land in other situations, and started the kibbutzim, or rural communes, that sowed the seeds of modern Zionism. Thousands of other Jews would follow the example of these early Jewish settlers in the aftermath of the Nazi Holocaust, setting the stage for one of the Middle East's most intractable problems.

World War I

While World War I was primarily a European war, it extended into the Middle East. Ottoman Turkey joined Germany in 1914 in hopes of offsetting pressure from Russia and Britain, which were allied against Germany. Turkish forces attacked British positions on the Suez Canal in January 1915, but the British drove them off with heavy casualties.5 Britain then launched a countercampaign against Turkey, attacking Turkey directly at the battle of Gallipoli in March 1915 and indirectly against Ottoman-controlled areas in the Arabian Peninsula, Palestine, and Mesopotamia. In early 1915, Britain landed forces in the Shatt al-Arab, the marshy confluence of the Tigris and Euphrates Rivers in southern Mesopotamia, and marched them north against Turkish forces. After a brutal siege of Kut al-Amara in April, British forces captured Baghdad and secured a political hold over Mesopotamia that they hoped would result in oil and easier access to India.

The Palestine Campaign

British forces also struck into Palestine from Egypt and, along with members of the Arab Revolt (see below), secured Aqaba in southern Jordan as a supply port, and achieved control of the northern Arabian Peninsula. British Gen. Edmund Allenby captured Jerusalem in December 1917, with considerable assistance from Faisal's Arab forces. The campaign was difficult against a heavily fortified city during the cold winter rains; the British suffered around 18,000 casualties and the Turks, roughly 25,000. Coordination between the British and Arab forces was the responsibility of British officer T.E. Lawrence, later remembered as Lawrence of Arabia.

The Arab Revolt of 1916

With the outbreak of World War I, Ottoman forces arrested many Arab nationalists, fearing that the British and French might use Arab nationalism as a force against Turkey. Those fears became real as the British encouraged the sharif of Mecca, Hussein ibn Ali, to revolt against Turkish control over the Hijaz. Hussein supported Britain in exchange for an unspecified but large Arab empire.6 Britain offered him the title caliph of the Hijaz (the western region of modern Saudi Arabia) and, after World War I, offered the thrones of Syria and Iraq to his sons Faisal and Abdullah.7 The British even supplied Faisal with troops taken from Arab prisoner of war camps in India. Faisal Hussein commanded the Arab Revolt forces, and later was the chief negotiator whose task was to fulfill Sharif Hussein's dream of an independent Arab kingdom stretching from northern Syria to Yemen. The Arab armies, sometimes led by T.E. Lawrence, cut the railroad linking the Arabian Peninsula to Damascus, preventing the Ottoman troops there from reinforcing Damascus. In the summer of 1918, Allenby advanced on Damascus, again in league with Faisal's Arab forces.

The Sykes-Picot Agreement

After they captured Damascus, the British informed Faisal that France would be the "protecting power" over Syria. At that point, Faisal realized that British representative Mark Sykes and French representative François-Georges Picot had negotiated secret arrangements to divide much of the Ottoman Empire between their two countries after World War I ended. The secret Sykes-Picot Agreement of 1916 thus negated British promises of Arab independence.[8] This agreement divided up areas of interest to France and Britain into four zones: a blue zone covering eastern and northern Syria, as well as southern Turkey, to be directly administered by France; a red zone covering central Mesopotamia and the Persian Gulf, directly controlled by Britain; a B zone in northern Arabia stretching into Jordan, under British influence; and an A zone, including central Syria and northern Mesopotamia, under French influence.[9] The British hoped that the French areas would provide a buffer against a potential Russian expansion into the southern part of Iraq and the Gulf.[10] France wanted a special administration for the Holy Land and, while granting Britain control of the port of Haifa, did not want Britain to control all of Palestine. French interests also concentrated on separating "inner Lebanon" from Syria and gaining control of the Syrian ports of Latakia and Alexandretta so that France, like Britain, would have ports in the eastern Mediterranean. Subsequently in September 1920 France formed the Lebanese Republic from greater Syria, shaping it in a way that ensured a Maronite Christian majority.[11]

France remained in Syria until 1946, although Britain and France disagreed over how much of Syria France would actually occupy. Moreover, Britain worried that a French takeover of Syria would engender violent Arab anti-imperialism that might spread into British-occupied Mesopotamia.[12] The British were right. The French occupiers faced insurrection by Syrian Arab nationalists, sometimes violent, throughout the occupation period. In the late 1930s, fascist Germany and Italy established contacts with Arab and Islamic nationalists in Syria and elsewhere in the Arab world. Some Arab nationalists embraced Nazi Germany's anti-Jewish campaign, while others disassociated themselves from it.[13]

The Balfour Declaration

In November 1917 the British Foreign Office issued the so-called Balfour Declaration, proclaiming that Britain would look "with favor" on a Jewish homeland in Palestine. The actual Balfour Declaration, issued by British Foreign Secretary Arthur James Balfour, was vague on where a Jewish homeland should actually be, and it showed awareness of the consequences of such a homeland for Arab residents.[14] The text read,

> His Majesty's Government view with favour the establishment in Palestine of a national home for the Jewish people, and will use their best endeavours to facilitate the achievement of this object, it being clearly understood that nothing shall be done which may prejudice the civil and religious rights of existing non-Jewish communities in Palestine, or the rights and political status enjoyed by Jews in any other country.[15]

The British tried to clarify their intentions in a white paper issued in June 1922, claiming that the purpose of the Balfour Declaration was not to establish a Jewish state of Palestine.[16] However, by 1939, the British acknowledged that the wording of the Balfour Declaration was one of the causes of hostility between the Jewish and Arab populations in Palestine. They attempted to quench the growing tensions by limiting Jewish immigration to Palestine to no more than 10,000 per year for five years and curtailing all Jewish immigration after those five years unless the Arab population approved a continuance.[17] The Holocaust in Europe had barely begun, and the British had little warning of coming events that would turn a trickle of 10,000 into a tidal wave of immigrants.

After World War I, France solidified its hold on North Africa except for Libya, now an Italian colony. Britain exercised a strong influence in Egypt, ruled now by the descendants of Muhammad Ali. British forces kept order in Iraq and Trans-Jordan, sometime using tools of war developed in World War I. The British stationed seaplanes on the Tigris River, which they used along with land-based bombers to bomb rebellious Arabs into submission. British warships policed the Persian Gulf, even designing flags for the sheikdoms of Bahrain and Qatar in order to distinguish their boats from pirate vessels. Those flags remain the national emblem for both countries today.

Palestine was important to Britain largely for strategic reasons, including control of the eastern approaches to the Suez Canal.[18] Yet control of Palestine brought problems for Britain as well. An influx of Jewish refugees from Europe in the 1930s added to pressure from previous Jewish immigrants to build a Jewish homeland in Palestine and counterpressure from the Arab Palestinian inhabitants to protect their land from the European refugees. The situation deteriorated as Arab extremists murdered Jews, Jewish extremists murdered Arabs, and the cycle of retribution made a peaceful resolution harder. The British accused the grand mufti of Jerusalem, Hajj Amin al-Husseini, of stoking anti-Zionist feelings among Arabs in Palestine that contributed to the riots of 1929 in which 113 Jews and 116 Arabs died.[19] Following similar riots in 1936, the British exiled the grand mufti, but the hostility between Arab and Jew in Palestine grew nevertheless.[20]

In 1937 a British Royal Commission under Lord Robert Peel investigated the situation and determined that the mandate previously granted to Britain by the League of Nations was unworkable. The Peel Commission recommended partitioning Palestine into separate areas, with a coastal strip and the Galilee set aside for the Jewish population and the Negev desert and West Bank of the Jordan River for the Arab population. In November 1938 the Woodhead Commission issued a report discounting the Peel Commission recommendations when the Woodhead members could not agree on a partition plan. In the end they recommended against partition while hoping for some unspecified Jewish-Arab agreement. The British government made one more futile effort at the St. James Conference of 1939, but when the Arab and Jewish delegations refused to talk to each other, the British abandoned any hope of negotiation.

World War II

World War II brought further changes to the Middle East. Germany sought control of the area as a way to sever the British lifeline to her colonies in Asia, and thus German troops came into North Africa, ostensibly to support the Vichy French (the forces led by Marshal Pétain that capitulated to Germany in 1940). Germany also supported several fascist nationalist movements, particularly the regime of Rashid Ali, which took power in Iraq in May 1941.

British and American forces landed at several sites in Morocco, Algeria, and Tunisia to support British efforts to keep German troops out of Egypt. The 1941–1942 campaign taught the British and US forces valuable lessons for later campaigns in Europe. The German forces under Field Marshal Erwin Rommel retreated across North Africa under American and British pressure, denied victory by, among other things, the loss of German supplies in ships sunk by the British and American naval and air forces.

IMAGES

> *The accounts of the fighting at El Alamein on the Egyptian Mediterranean coast tell of its importance historically—one of the several places in the world, like Midway or Stalingrad, where the Allies halted the Axis advance in October 1942. The ferocity of that battle in the Egyptian desert, where the terrain fades into the hazy distance with almost no hills or other terrain to hide troops or tanks or artillery, is highlighted by the long rows of grave markers in the national cemeteries near the battle site. Many gravestones have a name carved on them, but many others do not. "Here lies a British soldier known but to God," reads an inscription, but some hold more. "Here lie 13 British soldiers known but to God"; "Here lie 7 British soldiers known but to God." It is usually an axiom of war that the more unknowns, the fiercer the combat. By those standards, war at El Alamein was an intense and deadly affair. For the few Arabs who live nearby, however, it was mostly the outsider's war, someone else marching, fighting, dying, and then passing on, and they hardly pay the graves any attention.*

Germany hoped to build on anti-British and anti-French nationalism in the Middle East, but nationalism in the Middle East did not need German support to grow. In Egypt, the Wafd Party formed with pro-Nazi sentiments, largely because Germany was Britain's enemy. In Iraq the staunchly anti-British nationalist Rashid Ali al-Gaylani ousted the pro-British regime of Nuri as Said in April 1941, but later that month the British landed troops and in May forced Rashid Ali to flee to Germany. When German forces were defeated in North Africa and their allies, the Vichy French, were also defeated, the Free French regained their status as colonial power after the war.

For the citizens of the Middle East, World War II was largely fought for European aims. The victors maintained their hold on old colonies, and for some years afterward, war-generated scrap metal was a prime source of economic development for North African countries in particular. However, the currents of nationalism fueled in part by World War II continued to grow.

THE RISE OF ARAB NATIONALISM

The appearance of European power in the wake of World War I galvanized Arab nationalism, rekindling movements begun centuries earlier with the arrival of the French and British imperialists. Arabs who studied in Europe often inspired Arab nationalist movements. They included Michel Aflaq, one of the founders of the Baath movement, and Syrian nationalist Sati al-Husri, who studied in Italy and found inspiration in German romantic writers and in the works of Ibn Khaldun to envision a pan-Arab political community. These nationalists, inspired by the ideals of modernity and independence, looked to a post-Ottoman future for the Arab world based on the ideas that elevated Europe to the pinnacle of world power.[21]

As Barnett notes, at least three factors fueled the rise of Arab nationalism. The first was the intrusion of the Europeans, the second was the void in Islamic leadership created by the end of the Ottoman Empire, and the third was the communication technology that allowed the transnational expansion of Arabist ideas.[22] While Arab nationalism produced many divergent ideas in its formative stages, paramount among them was independence and the notion of sovereign Arab states. Whether or not that meant separate Arab states as created largely by the colonial powers or Arab unity with its goal as a single Arab state remained undecided. However, rivalry between Arab elites prevented the reality of pan-Arabism, even as pan-Arabist language survived.[23] The British, more than the French, understood the appeal of Arab nationalism and hoped to use it to limit the influence of both France and the Zionists.[24] In one sense they were correct; Arab nationalism and ultimately independence triumphed in French-ruled Syria and Lebanon in 1946, while the British held on to some of their protectorates in the Persian Gulf until the 1970s. Ultimately the British could not endure the spread of Arab nationalism, in addition to the costs of empire, and the final remnants of the British Empire east of Suez reverted to Arab rule in 1971.

THE POST-WORLD WAR II ERA

The World War II alliance between the Soviet Union and the Western powers fell apart after the war amid mutual recriminations and suspicions, along with real differences over power and control. The Soviet Union, influenced by Stalin's paranoia and a Leninist perspective that the capitalist countries would ultimately surround the one successful socialist country, quickly expanded its territory. Whether that action was intended to create buffer states between the West and the Soviet Union or to expand communism remains a debatable subject today. The United States and Britain viewed such expansion with alarm and acted to support, or in some cases to create, pro-Western governments in the Third World, and the rivalry between East and West for power and influence quickly spread to the Middle East.

Both East and West were compromised in their approaches to the Middle East. The West bore the legacy of colonialism, which played right into the hands of Soviet anti-imperialism rhetoric. The Soviet Union offered support to postcolonial countries, often after Western countries refused, but atheistic communism did not appeal to Islamic societies. The Soviet Union also lacked the financial capacity of the West, and the United States in particular. Moreover, both the West and East were outside powers, and the Middle East had suffered enough from the sweep of invaders who brought both destruction and foreign ideas. However, the opportunities fell more to the Soviet Union, given the number of Arab countries that were once a part of some European empire. Therefore, when nationalist groups successfully deposed the old monarchies that either supported or were created by imperialist regimes, the Soviet Union was quick to recognize them. That happened in 1952 in Egypt, and in 1958 in Iraq. In 1966 the left wing of the Baathist Party took power in Syria, opening a door for Soviet recognition and cooperation. The rise of Ahmad ben Bella in Algeria following the successful drive for independence in 1962 also led to a Soviet connection, as did the 1969 ouster of King Idris by Colonel Muammar Qadhafi in Libya.

In the summer of 1953, Soviet leadership developed a view that the struggle between imperialism and socialism would be waged in the so-called Third World, and that the developing Arab countries were the front lines of that struggle. One vehicle for this struggle was the local communist parties in various Arab countries. However, Arab leaders viewed these Marxist-inspired movements as atheistic challenges by outsiders to the Islamic faith. Thus Arab leaders frequently jailed national Communist Party leaders and followers. Nasser imprisoned members of the Egyptian Communist Party shortly after assuming power (though he would release them just before a visit by a Soviet VIP). In Iraq Gen. Abd al-Karim Qasim did the same thing after bloody confrontations between the Baathist and Iraqi Communist Parties.[25] Arab leaders also resented Soviet curbs on their policy options, as when the Soviet Union severely criticized Syria for its Lebanon policy and counseled Egypt against war in 1970 and 1973.[26] Egyptian President Anwar Sadat ended the relationship in July 1973, right before he launched the attacks that initiated the October 1973 war. The demise of the cold war ended the role of superpower intervention in the Middle East. Soviet aid continued to trickle into Syria and Iraq but at lower levels.

The former Soviet Union also sought to regain influence in Iran, where it had a significant role prior to World War II. In 1946 growing Soviet political and military pressure on Iran's northern border resulted in stronger American support for a noncommunist Iran.[27] Iran, with its oil reserves, seemed to offer the Soviets access to the greater Middle East. This, along with Soviet pressure in Turkey and Greece, brought about the Truman Doctrine of 1946.

STATE AND NATION BUILDING BEGINS

Independence started slowly before World War II, with Egypt in 1922 (though British influence remained) and Saudi Arabia in 1932, and grew as the war made the cost of imperialism too high to bear. The long period of foreign rule and influence ended over several decades for a majority of Middle East countries. The new rulers of these countries were hardly prepared for self-rule, however, and there were few governance models from which to choose. The need to catch up with the industrial world drove many Arab elites to the conclusion that they would have to construct nation-states quickly. Some elites favored strong state-centered systems to accelerate economic development and national identity, hoping to unify tribal identities into single-nation pluralism. Others wanted Arab identity to become the core for political organization, fusing Arabs into a single structure that could both resist recolonization and prevent the establishment of a Zionist state. Others argued that the military, often the most powerful single societal element, should take the reins of power, as happened in many countries (Egypt, Algeria, Syria, and Libya, for examples), while yet others favored the tradition of tribal elder monarchs from traditional powerful families. The most common was the military regime, emerging before World War II in Turkey and after World War II in countries like Egypt and Syria, led by powerful military officers who shed their uniforms and anointed themselves as presidents. They created one-party states with a supporting party cast to mobilize popular support, and resources for new militaries that would often become the centerpiece of state power. The military often remained behind the scenes, serving as shadow guardians of a military image of a secular strong state, as they did in Turkey, Algeria, and Syria. However, the events of 1948 and beyond sorely challenged these militaries.

The Arab-Israeli Wars Begin

In one sense, there has been a continuing war between Israel and select Arab states and peoples since 1948, punctuated by sharp and costly escalations. There were four such escalations, the first in 1948, the second in 1956, the third in 1967, and the fourth in 1973. There was also a protracted series of battles between Israel, Egypt, and Jordan between 1969 and 1970 and the Israeli military operations in Lebanon in 1978, 1982, and 2006.

The 1948 War

This war has several names; Israelis refer to it as the War of Independence, but Arabs generally refer to it as the Palestine War; Palestinians refer to it as al-Nakba, or "the catastrophe."

Jewish immigration into Palestine accelerated as Nazism spread throughout Europe. Some 200,000 Jews arrived in Palestine between 1932 and 1938. By 1939, Jews constituted 30 percent of the population in British Palestine, up from 4 percent in 1882. Another 75,000 came between 1945 and 1948. They joined those from the earlier aliyas noted above. By February 1947, Britain could no longer maintain control in Palestine. The growing tensions between the Arab and Jewish populations and a British treasury strained by years of war and colonialism prompted the British to pull out of Palestine in May 1948. The British withdrawal left a political vacuum that the United Nations tried to fill. In May 1947 the General Assembly voted to charter a Special Committee on Palestine (UNSCOP), and in November 1947 it passed Resolution 181 calling for independent Arab and Jewish states bound by a customs union, and a special status for Jerusalem. The proposal outlined a partition system creating homelands for both Jews and Arabs, with Arabs getting 44 percent of Palestine and Jews 55 percent. One obstacle for the Arabs was that the Jewish area would also contain a 45 percent Arab minority whereas only 1.5 percent of the Jewish population would live in the Arab state. The Arab Palestinians and the Arab members of UNSCOP rejected the partition plan for that reason and argued that it violated the UN Charter provisions for self-determination. The Arab leaders also had their own ambitions about the future of Palestine: Jordan's King Abdullah I hoped to lead the Arab League and possibly bring Palestine into his vision of Greater Syria, while Egyptian and Syrian leaders were preoccupied with governing their own countries.[28] Most importantly, to quote Michael Cohen on the Arab position on UN Resolution 181, "It was unduly optimistic to expect the Arabs to acquiesce eventually to partition. Before long, the Jewish government, faced with an overpopulation problem, and driven by 'ultra-nationalist political parties,' would try to expand its frontiers."[29]

Both Palestinian factions were arming for war, as armed gangs exchanged gunfire, bombs exploded, and the death toll mounted. In November 1947, Arabs murdered thirty-nine Jewish workers in Haifa, and, reinforced by foreign mercenaries, carried out a wave of bombings in both Jerusalem and Haifa.[30] In April 1948 the Jewish Irgun (short for Irgun Zevai Leumi) movement attacked the Arab village of Deir Yasin and massacred between 120 and 250 inhabitants. The news of Deir Yasin accelerated the flight of Arabs out of Palestine. Whether "Arab leaders wished to exploit the incident for propaganda purposes," or whether the news itself drove the Arab exodus is still debated.[31] Haganah, the military arm of the Jewish Agency (the semiofficial Jewish group negotiating with the British), then attacked the port cities of Acre and Haifa as Arabs fled the violence there. As the fighting raged, David Ben Gurion proclaimed the establishment of Israel on May 14, 1948.

IMAGES | *Sunrise on the road between Haifa and Nazareth as the morning fog burns off the green fields. In the middle of the green, the sun barely glints on the skeletons of small houses, once the homes of Palestinians who left everything behind in 1948. The houses, now just stone walls, now swallowed into Israel, are scarcely visible unless one looks hard for them.*

Arab leaders decided on war in Cairo in May 1948. However, the Arab armies formed under inexperienced regimes lacked the training or cohesion of the Jewish militias, including both the official Haganah and the underground groups, including Irgun and Lohame Herut Yisrael or Lehi (known as the Stern Gang by the British). The Arab forces also handicapped themselves by competing for differing objectives. Jordanian King Abdullah, in a move opposed by other Arab leaders, seized Jerusalem and the proposed UN Palestinian lands for himself.[32] The other Arab parties to the war fought largely to sustain their own objectives; Egypt, Syria, and Lebanon opposed the Hashemite bloc led by Iraq and Jordan. The leaders of the non-Hashemite countries feared efforts by King Abdullah of Jordan to build a Hashemite Greater Syria, including Palestine and Iraq.[33] Elite cleavages hampered Palestinian unity, including divisions between local leaders and the British-appointed Grand Mufti Hajj Amin al-Hussein.[34]

Abdullah's army (around 5,000) initiated the war, joined by the Arab Liberation Army, sponsored by the newly founded Arab League and consisting of around 3,800 volunteers and the Jordanian Arab Legion. The armies of Egypt, Syria, Lebanon, and Trans-Jordan linked up with these forces after Britain's final withdrawal on May 15, 1948. Israel reorganized its forces as the Israel Defense Force (IDF) in late May, and the IDF quickly mobilized fighters and weapons. Despite a UN weapons embargo, transport, fighter, and even bomber aircraft arrived, sometimes obtained and flown by sympathetic American or British pilots. Some arms flowed in from Czechoslovakia, raising suspicions in the West of a Soviet effort to dominate an independent Israel, though the motives appear more related to Czech efforts to generate income.[35]

In 1948 Israeli forces, for the first and only time, actually outnumbered their Arab opponents; the Haganah forces mobilized around 30,000 fighters while the combined armies of Trans-Jordan, Egypt, and Syria numbered approximately 21,500.[36] Arab forces took the offensive and attempted to isolate Jewish settlements in Jerusalem from the Israeli-occupied cities on the coast. The Israelis managed to build a second road to allow them to supply Jerusalem, taking heavy losses in doing so. In the meantime the Arab League failed to unite the various Arab military forces. When King Abdullah assumed command, it was in name only. Both the national and irregular Arab forces maintained and fought for their own objectives with little coordination or cooperation, greatly limiting their effectiveness. Other problems such as poor tactical performance and management of combat information also hampered the Arab militaries.[37]

The United Nations brokered a temporary truce on June 11, after the first phase of the war. When it ended on July 6, Israeli forces took the offensive, capturing areas like Lod in the center and Nazareth in the north, all in the area originally designated by the United Nations as Arab territory. Israeli government forces were able to consolidate after the government arrested members of the Lehi and Irgun groups, after both were implicated in the assassination of Folke Bernadotte of Sweden, who was attempting to mediate a UN cease-fire. By October Israeli forces launched a general offensive against select Arab militaries. A thrust south against the Egyptian forces in the Negev desert and south of Tel Aviv and north on the Lebanese border brought more land under Israeli control. Israeli units also struck into the Sinai, but the UN cease-fire of December halted their advance and cleared the way for the armistice negotiations of 1949.

Following the 1948 war, Israel controlled more territory that it would have under the UN partition plan, as the war turned out to be a net loss for the Arabs living in Palestine. Israel added 2,380 square miles to the 5,760 square miles it received under the UN partition, mostly in the Negev desert and western Galilee. Jerusalem, the capital of the ancient Hebrew kingdom, became the capital of modern Israel in the sense that Israelis built government buildings there, but only in new (or west) Jerusalem. Arab troops defeated Haganah forces in the Old City, where the Western Wall, the Church of the Holy Sepulcher, and the Dome of the Rock and Al-Aqsa Mosque are located. That area became a part of Jordan, and Jordanian authorities excluded Jews from prayer at the Western Wall.

During the war, over 700,000 Palestinian Arabs became refugees, though some Palestinians remained, and today constitute around 20 percent of Israel's population. Whether or not the refugees fled because of Arab encouragement or because of Israeli actions remains in dispute. One argument holds that the Jewish high command formulated something called Plan Dalet (Plan D) calling for attacks calculated to drive out the resident Palestinian population and thus free land for Jewish areas.[38] Safran states that "the Arabs wanted to remain in the areas that fell under Israeli control, but most of them were forcibly driven out by the Jews, who sought thereby to secure the advantage of a more homogeneous population."[39] As archival evidence continues to materialize, more evidence of a purposeful Israeli plan to drive out the Palestinian Arab population emerges.[40] It is also likely that many fled, as most refugees do, out of a general fear of uncontrolled warfare raging about them. Whatever the reason, most Palestinians remain refugees, living in squalid camps in Jordan, Syria, Lebanon, Egypt, and other Arab countries more than fifty years later. They helped sow the seeds for future Arab-Israeli conflicts, and they remain a potent source of discontent, with Palestinian refugee camps serving as breeding grounds for terrorism. Jewish immigrants, mostly from Europe but also from other Middle Eastern countries, displaced the Palestinians in Israel. In the first three months some 685,000 immigrants arrived in Palestine (304,000 from Europe), followed by a second wave of 160,000 in 1955 through 1957, and 215,000 more between 1961 and 1964. The Israeli policy of accepting and encouraging these new immigrants reinforced the perception among Palestinians and their supporters that Israel drove them from their homes to make room for Jewish immigrants.

Arab Nationalism and the 1956 War

Egypt and Israel soon fought again, but this time Britain and France joined the conflict. The cold war was not directly responsible for the war, which nonetheless took on serious cold war overtones. The United States and the Soviet Union remained on the sidelines of the fighting but exerted considerable influence on the outcome of the war.

In 1952 Egypt experienced one of the first Arab nationalist revolutions when the Free Officers movement ousted King Farouk, a descendant of Muhammad Ali. A leader of the movement, Gamal Abdul Nasser, eventually assumed the presidency of Egypt. Britain and the United States feared potential Soviet influence in the Middle East, and in late 1954 the two countries engineered a pact between Turkey (also fearful of Soviet expansion), Pakistan, and Iraq (led by the pro-British Nuri as Said) that would become known as the Baghdad Pact. Nasser tried hard to dissuade Nuri from signing the pact, and bitterly denounced him when he did sign. Nasser had been attempting to retain good ties to the West, but when the pact was signed he abruptly moved to seek Soviet military and economic assistance against what he apparently believed was a renewed Western effort to dominate the Middle East.[41]

Nasser sought funding from the United States and Britain for the Aswan high dam, which he needed to expand Egypt's agriculture and electric supply, thus allowing Egypt's economy to grow rapidly. In September 1954 Nasser turned to Czechoslovakia for military assistance, and after US Secretary of State John Foster Dulles found out that Soviet bloc aid was arriving in Egypt, he canceled US funding for the planned Aswan high dam in July 1956. Britain also withdrew its aid offer, and these actions galvanized Nasser to nationalize the Suez Canal, at that time still valued by the British as a sea link to Asia. Britain decided to seize the canal and was joined by France, which was unhappy with Nasser for supporting anti-French rebels in Algeria. Israel also committed forces out of a common antipathy to Nasser, who had supported guerrilla attacks on Israel by Palestinian fighters.[42]

British and French forces joined Israelis in late October 1956 for air assaults against Egyptian air bases.[43] British paratroopers parachuted onto facilities near Port Said and Israeli troops captured Sharm al-Sheik in November, while French paratroopers landed south of Port Said. Egypt sank ships to block the Suez Canal and Syria blocked the oil pipeline from Iraq to the Mediterranean, putting economic pressure on Britain in particular. That in turn allowed the United States to register its growing opposition to the whole endeavor. Soviet Premier Nikita Khrushchev threatened bluntly to "rain rockets" against Britain and France if they continued their war against Egypt. France got less than full assurances from the United States that Americans would respond forcefully to such an attack.[44] American policymakers believed that colonialism was a stimulus for a communist reaction, and British and French actions were too reminiscent of neocolonialism for the United States to support. It decided that the time was right to deescalate the situation and led the fight in the United Nations to halt hostilities. The United Nations created the United Nations Emergency Force (UNEF) to monitor the cease-fire. Subsequently Nasser could announce that he had defeated both Israel and the old European imperialists. This claim, despite dubious accuracy, gained support for both Nasser and Arab nationalism in the Arab world and beyond.

The 1967 War

The 1967 war began after a long buildup of tension between Israel and its immediate neighbors, Syria and Egypt. Egypt moved to seal off the Gulf of Aqaba to ships destined for Israel, cutting off the southern Israeli port of Eilat. Consequently the United States suspended food assistance to Egypt worth around $150 million per year. Egypt was also at war in Yemen (where it had troops since 1962), which kept thousands of Egyptian troops away from the Israeli border. The Israeli national reaffirmation of the Holocaust conditioned by the Eichmann trial of 1960 may also have contributed to the outbreak of war: in Zertal's words, "The 1967 Six Day War elevated the rhetoric of holocaust and power to new heights, and restored to it an additional, central component—the state's—and the land's—borders."[45]

On the Syrian-Israeli border, tension grew between Israeli settlers and Syrian forces, even though, according to Zeev Maoz, Syria did not pose a serious threat to Israel.[46] According to one version, Syrian heavy artillery on the high places in Golan fired on Israeli settlers in the eastern Galilee, prompting Israeli retaliation, with Israel ultimately taking the Golan from Syria.[47] According to another version, Israeli settlers encroached into the Syrian Golan, accompanied by Israeli troops, who counterattacked when fired on by Syrian artillery.[48] General Moshe Dayan supported the first version, claiming that Israelis sent tractors to plow demilitarized zones, hoping that the Syrians would fire on them, thus allowing the Israelis to counter with artillery and attack aircraft.[49]

In May 1967, Egypt received a false warning from the Soviet Union that Israeli troops were massing on the Syrian-Israeli border. Nasser, believing that Israel was preparing a surprise attack against its Arab neighbors, mobilized Egyptian forces, thus heightening the tension.[50] Nasser also ordered the evacuation of UNEF forces that had been stationed on Egyptian territory since the 1956 war.

Israel had to contend with an unfavorable balance of force against the potential Arab armies, which exceeded the Israel military by considerable margins.[51] However, Israeli training, tactics, and equipment largely determined the outcome. On the morning of June 5, Israeli military aircraft streaked out of the rising sun to strike Egyptian aircraft as their pilots were leaving the cockpits for breakfast, destroying most of the Egyptian air force in minutes. The day after the attack Israel reported destroying some 374 Egyptian, Syrian, and Jordanian warplanes. Egypt lost 309 of the 340 combat aircraft in its inventory. Israeli forces crossed the Sinai and attacked Gaza, adjoining the Sinai, while the government claimed that its goals "did not include the conquest of Arab territory."[52]

The losses temporarily united the Arab world, with calls of support coming from Algeria, Tunisia, Kuwait, and Libya, and threats to cut off oil exports to the United States.[53] Other Arab countries came in more directly; Jordanian artillery opened fire on Israeli positions in Jerusalem on June 6, while Israeli troops captured towns on the Jordanian border. The United States limited its activities to monitoring events. Nonetheless, thirty-four US sailors were killed when Israeli aircraft attacked the surveillance ship USS *Liberty,* which was operating in the eastern Mediterranean.[54]

After thirty-six hours of fighting against Jordanian units, Israeli forces took East Jerusalem after King Hussein decided to quit the fight rather than risk destruction of the holy places there.[55] Later he would claim that it was the hardest decision of his life. On June 7, the Soviet Union introduced a resolution calling for a cease-fire, which unanimously passed the Security Council, but all the Arab participants except Jordan initially rejected it. However, Israeli forces captured Sharm al-Sheik in the southern Sinai, and broke the blockade of Eilat. Israeli paratroopers took Jericho on the West Bank, and the culmination of Israeli battlefield successes made it clear to the most hardline Arab defenders that their armies had lost the struggle.

Their militaries suffered from poor tactical performance and their leaders did not react quickly when the military commanders withheld news about how bad things were on the battlefields.[56] The war became particularly dangerous for Syria when Israeli tanks got within thirty miles of Damascus. Consequently, both Egypt and Syria accepted a cease-fire on June 9. The next day Egypt's President Nasser submitted his resignation but the National Assembly rejected it. Although Nasser stayed on as president, the bitter defeat tarnished the mantle of Arab nationalism, espoused by Nasser as a solution to both economic development and the existence of Israel. Peace, however, did not mark the aftermath of the war.

The 1967 war almost doubled the size of the territory Israel controlled and fertilized the seeds of future Israeli-Palestinian conflict because Palestinian demands for a territorial state focused on land seized by Israel in 1967: Gaza and the West Bank. The Palestinian refugee problem grew, according to some estimates, by over half a million. The Palestinians' plight seemed hopeless despite al-Fatah (or "the Conquest"), founded by Palestinian nationalist Yasir Arafat in October 1959. Fatah would later become the core of a new organization, the Palestinian Liberation Organization (PLO), founded by the Arab League in May 1964 and headed by Arafat after 1968.

The War of Attrition

After the cease-fire, Egypt sank the Israeli destroyer *Eilat* with a Soviet-made Styx missile, claiming that the ship intruded into Egyptian waters. That action set off an Israeli retaliation against Egyptian oil refineries near Port Said, almost resulting in a renewed outbreak of the 1967 war. Instead, the event would be the first in a series of attacks that avoided all-out war, but the period could hardly be called "peaceful." Nasser believed that a political settlement from the 1967 war would flow only from successful military actions. Apparently believing that Egypt had gained military superiority over Israel by late 1968, Nasser decided to launch a limited war to push Israel into negotiating the return of the Sinai.[57] Israel's strategic objectives involved preserving the post-1967 status quo and preventing escalation to major war, something seen as likely in Israel given the heavy Soviet presence in Egypt.[58] But as Israeli casualties mounted from Egyptian artillery fired across the canal, Israel took the offensive. Israeli planes bombed Egyptian positions on the canal, and Israeli commando raids penetrated into Egypt.

As the violence escalated, the United States and Soviet Union again attempted to arrange a peace accord, producing the so-called Rogers Plan (named after Secretary of State William Rogers), but Israel, Egypt, and the Soviet Union ultimately rejected the proposal. Diplomatic efforts went nowhere, and another war appeared even more likely. Nasser agreed to mediate his dispute with Saudi Arabia over Yemen and drew closer to the oil-rich Gulf states, hoping for revenues as well as possible closer contacts with the West. However, Syria, backed by Algeria and Iraq, refused to discuss peace proposals.

Nasser died in September 1970, and Vice President Anwar Sadat assumed the presidency. Sadat changed Egypt's international course almost immediately. He did not trust the Soviets, who had ceased their resupply of the Egyptian military after the 1967 debacle, and Sadat increasingly resented their behavior. However, the transfer of American military equipment to Israel rose, even though Israel lost proportionately less than their Arab foes in the 1967 war. Sadat had reason to believe that if he did not initiate another war the balance might fatally tip against the Arabs.

Many Palestinians acquired a new determination to go it alone as doubts grew that Arab countries could gain back their old homelands. Shortly after the 1967 war, Palestinian leader George Habash formed the Popular Front for the Liberation of Palestine (PFLP) and claimed that revolutionary violence "was the only weapon left in the hands of the people."[59] That started a string of violent actions (including aircraft hijackings) that increased regional tension. Israeli counteraction limited the threat of a Palestinian guerrilla war in the occupied territories, but the tension remained. When the Fatah wing of the Palestine Liberation Organization (PLO) launched attacks against Israel from Jordan, Israel retaliated against Jordanian targets.[60] As both PLO and PFLP attacks escalated, civil war broke out in September 1970 (known as Black September) between Jordanian troops and Palestinian guerrillas. When Syrian tanks threatened to intervene to support Palestinian fighters, both the United States and Israel threatened to intervene. Many fled Jordan for Lebanon, where they would help sow the seeds of the tragic and brutal Lebanese civil war (1975–1990).

IMAGES

Jordan, like most Middle Eastern countries, has a military museum commemorating victories large and small; this is the Martyr's Museum in Amman. The almost obligatory tanks and artillery pieces are outside, but the items inside are more stark and meaningful. The one that best demonstrates the ferocity of war is in a small display case—the pistol worn by an Israeli pilot who went down with his aircraft after Jordanian forces shot it out of the sky. The force of the impact bent the heavy steel .45 caliber pistol in half. One warrior, one violent death, one of hundreds of thousands remembered in such museums. Later a Jordanian officer, discussing the peace process with Israel, asks the visitor if he has been to the Martyr's Museum. "Then you will understand that the point of the peace process is so that we don't have to build any more Martyrs' Museums."

Israeli Settlements Begin

After the June war, the Israeli government extended Israeli law to the territories taken from Egypt and Jordan, and declared Jerusalem the eternal capital of Israel. The Israeli government also began seizing Palestinian land (1,000 acres in 1968, and another 3,000 acres in 1970) to settle Israeli citizens.[61]

The 1973 War

The seeds of the 1973 Yom Kippur War (also known as the October War) were sown by the outcome of the 1967 war and, for some analysts, the failure to resolve the 1967 issues by diplomacy: "Israel bears the major burden for this diplomatic failure."[62] As soon as the war began on October 6 with a surprise attack by Egypt and Syria, charges and countercharges flew over which side initiated the conflict. The Egyptian foreign minister claimed that Israeli aggression (particularly against Syria in September 1973) caused the war, while the Israelis charged that the Arab coalition launched the campaign. The Israelis seemed surprised by the attack, though some analysts hold that they had known about the preparations for the attack but withheld their forces due to the calculated negative political price they would have paid for striking first.[63] The other view is that despite warnings of a potential Arab attack, the Israeli leadership found ways to deny the possibility. The withdrawal of Soviet advisers, the beginnings of Soviet-American détente, and the Israeli-Arab balance of power favoring the Israelis combined to cause Israeli leaders to downgrade warnings of an Arab surprise attack.[64] Arab leaders told almost no one outside the top military officers about the attack plans and thus prevented the intelligence leaks that had plagued them in the past. Egypt also contributed to the surprise by erecting huge sand berms on their side of the canal. Israeli intelligence, suspecting an attempt to mask a surprise attack, looked over the berms every day, only to see the Egyptians constantly practicing to cross the canal. After some months, the Israelis stopped watching, just as the Egyptians knew they would. The head of Mossad, the Israeli intelligence service, met with a double agent on October 4 in London who warned of an imminent Arab attack, but the Israelis did not respond.[65] On October 6, the Arab practice maneuvers became real.

The attack opened before dawn with an Egyptian barrage of 10,500 artillery shells in the first minute, fired across the canal to weaken the Israeli berms on the other side. Egyptian soldiers streamed across the canal on rubber boats, while the Israeli defenders tried to open pipes to flood the canal with flaming gasoline. They would not open, since Egyptian swimmers had sealed them the previous night. The first Egyptian soldiers to cross carried fire hoses that washed away the sand berms on the Israeli side, permitting tanks to penetrate. In fifteen minutes, over 8,000 troops crossed to land on the Israeli side and constructed eleven bridges to carry heavy equipment. By the time the sun had set, some 80,000 Egyptian troops were in the Sinai. The Israeli forces suffered casualties greater in proportion than the American casualties on the first day of the Normandy invasion in World War II.

Syria too had been preparing for a surprise attack, and Syrian forces on the Golan penetrated Israeli lines in three places at the same time as the Egyptian forces crossed the Suez Canal. They struck Israeli armored units, but the combination of Israeli preparations and poor Syrian tactics allowed Israel to stop the Syrian advance into their positions. Syrian armor moving south of the provincial capital of Qunaytirah had more success against the Israelis, particularly after dark when the Syrian advantage in night vision equipment worked in their favor. Syrian forces annihilated an Israeli observation post on Mount Hermon, denying Israel critical military intelligence. Syrian air defense inflicted serious losses on the Israeli aircraft in the area, using the same kind of Soviet-supplied antiaircraft missiles as used by Egypt. The Israelis launched a counteroffensive, with Israeli aircraft attacking numerous military targets. On the ground Israeli forces stopped the Syrian and Egyptian forces after about thirty hours of fighting and then prepared a counterattack. Iraqi forces joined Syrian forces on the ground, but their armored division drove right into an Israeli ambush, and the Iraqis lost eighty tanks in a matter of minutes. In all, Iraq committed some 18,000 troops and 100 tanks to the war. They fought poorly and took heavy losses, in the end doing little to change the situation. Other Arab militaries proved more capable, particularly the Jordanian, Moroccan, Saudi Arabian, and Kuwaiti units, which, along with Jordanian tanks and infantry, helped stem an Israeli advance. Moroccan units held the Israelis until a dispute with Syrian forces occurred.

As the Israeli counterattack gained momentum and superpower pressure to stop the war mounted, Sadat proposed a cease-fire on October 6. Soviet Foreign Minister Andrei Kosygin and American Secretary of State Henry Kissinger met to further the cease-fire discussion. However, Syrian President Hafiz al-Asad refused to discuss a cease-fire agreement, and the Israeli army trapped a large Egyptian military unit in the Sinai. The Soviet Union, apparently fearing the annihilation of Egyptian forces, pressed the United States to stop the Israelis, and then threatened to intervene unilaterally if the Israeli siege of the Egyptian Third Army was not broken. When it detected what appeared to be Soviets loading transport aircraft in the Soviet Union, the United States briefly raised its defense condition alert status on October 25. Further discussions ensued under the specter of a superpower conflict, helping to achieve a final cease-fire.

Overall, the combined Arab militaries fought much better than they had in 1967 but showed many of the same weaknesses, including unimaginative tactical operations, misleading information from the front, and disappointing air combat performance. The Arab militaries fought with remarkable bravery, the Arab strategy was appropriate to the situation, and the outcome might have been different had the tactics succeeded.[66]

Events After the 1973 War

The combined impact of the 1967 war, the war of attrition, and the 1973 war finally galvanized efforts to achieve a diplomatic solution. In January 1974, Egypt and Israel signed an agreement to disengage their forces. That, according to Egyptian President Anwar Sadat, was the real objective of the 1973 war, to provoke Israel into discussing what the United Nations mandated after the 1967 war—land for peace. That would be a long time coming, but the process at least started after 1973.

Secretary of State Henry Kissinger engaged in "shuttle diplomacy," traveling from capital to capital in search of a diplomatic settlement to Middle East disagreements on both the Egyptian and Syrian fronts. Those efforts resulted in a disengagement pact between Israel and Syria in the Golan, with Israeli forces pulling back from the Syrian border, creating a buffer zone policed by the United Nations

Disengagement and Observer Force (UNFOR). That force remains in place today, one of the oldest and most successful peace efforts.

Part of the Kissinger-brokered agreement was a new line separating Israeli and Syrian forces on the Golan. The Israelis withdrew to the other side of the provincial capital of Quaytirah, but when the Syrians moved in to reclaim the city, they found it leveled. Israel claimed that the city had been destroyed by heavy fighting, while Syria argued that withdrawing Israeli troops had systematically destroyed it, partially to keep Syrians some distance from the new border.[67]

President Jimmy Carter quickly involved himself in Middle East politics, initiating talks with regional leaders to explore the possibility of a inclusive Arab-Israeli peace process. However, after efforts at a comprehensive peace conference of all the principals failed, President Sadat took the first step on his own by flying to Jerusalem in November 1977 and speaking in the Israeli parliament. Sadat hoped to build a peace process to include the Palestinian issues with Israel. When strains developed between Sadat and Israeli Prime Minister Menachem Begin, Carter invited both to the presidential retreat at Camp David, Maryland, for an effort to build a lasting peace in the region. After many tense days, the outline of a treaty emerged, which became final after months of subsequent negotiations. Diplomats finalized the document in March 1979 and the leaders of Israel, Egypt, and the United States signed it on the White House lawn. Because of Camp David, Israel withdrew its forces and settlers from the Sinai, and both countries normalized relations.[68] The United States committed a considerable foreign assistance package to both parties to support the agreement, and for years afterward, Egypt and Israel alone accounted for half of total American foreign assistance.

The United States moved to improve relations with the Arab world as Soviet influence declined. It reestablished diplomatic relations with Damascus in 1986, though Syria remained several rungs down from full State Department approval because of allegations that the Syrian government supported terrorist groups. The US also worked to settle the issues remaining from the 1967 and 1973 wars, including the implementation of UN Resolutions 242 and 338. Resolution 242, passed by the Security Council in November 1967, called for the withdrawal of Israeli forces from the occupied territories and the cessation of belligerency by Arab states against Israel. Resolution 338, adopted in October 1973, required all parties to implement the provisions of 242. American diplomats also continued to seek a political solution to the tragic situation in Lebanon (see Chapter 13), where factions loyal to Syria and Israel joined a violent civil war. The US briefly threatened Israel with the suspension of arms deliveries after Israeli pilots flew American-built fighters in July 1981 to bomb an Iraqi nuclear reactor that Israelis believed was capable of producing nuclear weapons. The attack obliterated the reactor, built by French engineers, and the Israeli attack drew strong protest from France, which claimed that the reactor was designed to generate electricity.

Israel Moves into Lebanon

The border between Israel and Lebanon remained tense as Palestinian guerrillas took advantage of Lebanon's inability to police its southern area. They fired rockets into Israeli villages and towns in the northern Galilee, slipped through border defenses to shoot settlers, and, in one bold move, tried to infiltrate silently at night in a hang glider. In London, an assassination plot reportedly carried out by Palestinian activists targeted the Israeli ambassador.[69] Still, for Maoz, the PLO was exercising restraint on the Lebanonese-Israeli border, and the Israeli operations into Lebanon came at the behest of Defense Minister Ariel Sharon and Prime Minister Menachem Begin.[70] In early June 1982 Israeli forces streamed across the Lebanese border and drove north toward Beirut, even after President Ronald Reagan pleaded with Begin to limit the conflict. Israel stated that its goal was to clear a security zone to put Israeli settlements out of the range of Palestinian artillery. Both Syria and Israel attempted to avoid military contact in Lebanon, given the bloody conflicts of the past. Syria kept its forces in northern Lebanon, but the Israeli forces rapidly moved north. Syria began to move forces south, and the United States demanded an immediate cease-fire. However, US officials claimed to have limited leverage to pressure Israel. The UN peacekeeping force in southern Lebanon could not block the Israeli move northward. Israeli and Syrian pilots clashed the next day in an air battle that would see the Israelis shoot down eighty-two Syrian aircraft with no losses to their own forces. That prompted Hafiz al-Asad to ask for Soviet assistance in evicting the Israelis from Lebanon, and Soviet leader Leonid Brezhnev in turn contacted President Reagan to demand that the United States do everything in its power to stop the Israeli operation. In July, Israeli forces entered the suburbs of Beirut and destroyed much of the western part of the city with both air and artillery attacks. In August the parties achieved a cease-fire, and PLO units evacuated from the city.

Partially out of concern over greater Soviet involvement in the defense of Syria, the United States and France sent in peacekeeping forces. They were withdrawn after a brief period with assurances that the Israelis too would withdraw. President Reagan increased pressure on Israelis to withdraw from the outskirts of Beirut, which they gradually began to do. However, after a bomb killed newly elected President Bashar Gemayel in September, the Israelis returned.[71] Supporters of Gemayel apparently believed that the Palestinians were responsible for killing him, and they massacred civilian Palestinian refugees in two camps, Shatilla and Sabra. The attack triggered a horrified response in both the United States and France, and peacekeeping forces returned to Lebanon, having departed after the PLO evacuation from Beirut. Small contingent British and Italian forces joined them. The United States established its base around the Beirut airport, and Marines engaged in limited patrols around the perimeter, sometimes exchanging fire with Shiite militia members, while a U.S. battleship lobbed shells into the Lebanese hills. However, danger was never far away. In April, a bomb destroyed much of the US embassy, killing sixty-three people, including seventeen Americans. On October 23, a truck bomb with around 2,000 pounds of explosives rammed the Marine barracks, killing 241 troops. At almost the same moment, another bomber attacked the French headquarters, and fifty-nine French soldiers died in the rubble. In November Israeli troops were also bombed, with a loss of thirty. Those attacks paved the way for a complete withdrawal of French and American peacekeepers, and Israeli withdrawal to the so-called and self-proclaimed Security Zone in south Lebanon, where they re-mained until June 2000, when Prime Minister Ehud Barak withdrew them.

The civil war in Lebanon resisted several efforts at negotiation until Saudi Arabia brought the parties to the Saudi city of Taif and brokered an agreement on October 22, 1989. The agreement reconfigured the Lebanese political system to give Muslims and Christians parity in the government, disarmed many of the militia groups, and created a formula for Syria to withdraw, though that withdrawal occurred only in 2005 after the assassination of former Lebanese Prime Minister Rafiq Hariri.[72]

Iran and Iraq Go to War

Iran and Iraq had long disputed the border between them along the Shatt al-Arab waterway. But in Algiers in 1975 the two countries signed an agreement that established a boundary down the center of the waterway.[73] The situation changed with the Islamic Revolution in Iran; among other differences between Iran and Iraq, Saddam Hussein had exiled Iranian dissident Ayatollah Ruhollah Khomeini from his haven in Iraq in a deal with the shah of Iran, and the Ayatollah wanted revenge. Khomeini denounced Iraqi president Saddam Hussein as an atheist and demanded the overthrow of his regime; Saddam denounced Khomeini in turn and called for an uprising by the Arab minority in Iran. Iraqi soldiers also suppressed Shiite uprisings in southern Iraq. The borders of the Shatt al-Arab, the confluence of the Tigris and Euphrates Rivers which formed a border between the two countries, was also in dispute. The stage was set for one of the bloodiest and most pointless of Middle Eastern wars.

Iraq attacked in September 1980, in the mistaken belief that the Iranian revolution of 1979 had so weakened the Iranian military that the country was ripe for defeat. Reports held that some 60 percent of Iran's 171,000-strong army had deserted, and that the Islamist rulers had purged, tried, or executed over 12,000 officers, and removed between 30 and 50 percent of midgrade officers (majors and colonels) by autumn 1980. But instead of a quick victory for Iraq, the war began to take on the characteristics of World War I, with both sides digging in and launching indecisive attacks and producing horrific casualties. Iranian forces used religious zeal and mass attack tactics as a substitute for modern weapons and supplies. The war escalated to include missile attacks against cities in both countries, the use of poison gas by Iraq, and attacks on oil tankers in the Gulf.

During the Iran-Iraq war, the United States tilted politically toward Iraq, partly because of the old adage that the enemy of my enemy is my friend. The United States provided Iraq with equipment that could be used in Iraq's weapons of mass destruction programs. Although the Defense Department objected to these sales, which totaled $1.5 billion between 1985 and 1990, the State and Commerce Departments approved them, and the Defense Department did not appeal the decision.

Despite aid from others, Iraq was not able to capitalize. Iran fought a largely defensive war until February 1986, when their forces captured the strategic Fao peninsula in southern Iraq. But Iran could not gain more territory, and with treasure and blood wasting away, Ayatollah Khomeini agreed to peace talks. The war ended in 1988 with Iraq gaining small pieces of Iranian territory, which Iraq gave back to Iran several years later to keep Iran out of Saddam's next war. The casualties from the conflict were staggering; Iraq suffered more than 400,000, including 120,000 dead, while Iranian casualties were around 750,000, with more than 300,000 dead.

Iraq Invades Kuwait

After the conclusion of the war with Iran, Iraq found itself in a dispute over oil rights and debt with Kuwait, a small Gulf kingdom. Kuwait had loaned Iraq billions of dollars to fend off what Iraq claimed was a militant Islamic threat to the Arab Gulf countries. Iraq and Kuwait also shared a large oil deposit, the Rumallia field. Iraq charged that Kuwait was slant drilling (drilling at a 45 degree angle) into the Iraqi side of the field to enrich its own coffers. Iraq demanded an end to the practice and insisted that Kuwait pay $2.4 billion in compensation.

The United States had showed tacit support for Iraq during its eight-year war with Iran. However, Washington also courted Kuwaiti support, as evidenced by the decision to reflag Kuwaiti tankers during the Iran-Iraq war. Fearing that Iraqi-Kuwaiti differences might flare into open conflict, the Bush administration asked US ambassador to Iraq April Glaspie to meet with Saddam Hussein. According to reports, Saddam assured Glaspie that Iraq would not resort to military force, and Glaspie in turn stated that the United States "took no position" with regard to Iraqi-Kuwaiti relations. This remark, later criticized widely as lending encouragement to Saddam's decision to invade, was reportedly tempered with Glaspie's warning to Saddam not to take "rash action" against Kuwait. Nevertheless, on August 2, 1990, Iraqi forces launched a massive attack on Kuwait. Their forces quickly swept away the small Kuwaiti military, although many Kuwaitis fought to defend the country. The royal family fled Kuwait just hours before Iraqi troops marched into Kuwait City. Within days, Iraq was in control of Kuwait.

President George H. W. Bush initially sought a political solution to the situation, but at the same time began building diplomatic support for a military response. Days after the initial invasion American Secretary of Defense Richard Cheney flew to Saudi Arabia with intelligence photographs purporting to show Iraqi forces on the border with Saudi Arabia. That evidence helped persuade Saudi Arabia to permit the stationing of American and other foreign forces on Saudi soil. A massive buildup of military supplies and personnel flowed into Saudi Arabia and elsewhere in the Middle East in preparation for a military campaign to oust Iraqi forces from Kuwait. The United Nations gave sanction to the use of military force if necessary.

Saddam apparently believed that he could count on the support of much of the Arab world and offered a full peace accord with his enemy Iran, hoping to keep them out of any pending war. He justified his invasion with the claim that Kuwait was not an independent country but rather a part of Iraq. Reviving old claims by Iraq against Kuwait, Saddam claimed that he was "liberating" Kuwait from its "corrupt" leaders in line with the wishes of the Kuwaiti people.[74] Many Kuwaitis became victims of Iraqi brutality, with many hundreds killed, tortured, imprisoned, or raped.

President Bush also lobbied hard to gain UN Security Council backing for the use of military force to require Iraqi compliance with the embargo imposed after the Kuwait invasion. As 1991 approached, Bush warned that Allied military air operations would commence if Iraq refused to quit Kuwaiti territory. The United States and other countries took advantage of Iraq's decision not to invade Saudi Arabia to build a substantial force based there. The administration also worked to gain the support of Arab coalition members. In November 1990, the United States forgave some $7 billion in Egyptian debt for past weapons purchases. American diplomacy also worked to try to convince Israel to remain out of the fight, fearing that Saddam Hussein would attack Israel to draw it in, thus driving Arab forces out of the conflict. That effort became even more difficult when Israeli forces killed seventeen Palestinians and wounded hundreds more on Jerusalem's Haram al-Sharif (Temple Mount) in October 1990. Fearing that the crisis in Jerusalem would weaken the coalition, the United States stepped up the escalation.[75]

Saudi Arabian diplomacy was equally important in building and maintaining the Allied coalition. The Arab members would not agree to be under an American command, so Saudi Prince Khalid ibn Sultan al-Saud, the son of Deputy Prime Minister Sultan ibn Abdul Aziz al-Saud, took command of the Arab members of the coalition. His skillful efforts with Syria and Egypt kept the Arab coalition largely intact during the war.[76] The United States, meanwhile, began to believe that Iraq would not give in to sanctions, and that Iraqi forces would destroy Kuwait rather than surrender it. The United States continued efforts to build a coalition that would specifically include Arab countries to avoid the image of US intentions to predominate in the Persian Gulf region.[77]

In mid-January, the US Congress voted to authorize war in the Gulf, although by a very narrow margin. Military operations began with a crescendo of bombing attacks that destroyed Iraqi air defenses and the Iraqi air force in a matter of days. Having established air superiority over Iraq, Allied aircraft struck Iraqi military targets in Iraq and Kuwait. More countries joined the effort, with twenty-eight countries playing a military role. Saddam Hussein hoped to disrupt the Arab component of the coalition by attacking Israel and thus driving Israel to attack Iraq. Consequently, Iraq began to attack targets in Israel using Scud missiles fired from Western Iraq, killing a small number of Israelis.

The ground war actually began with an Iraqi foray into the Saudi border town of Khafji, repulsed by a coalition effort of Saudi, Qatari, and US troops. On February 25, Allied ground forces crossed into Kuwait, encountering thousands of surrendering Iraqi soldiers in the first hours of the war. Retreating Iraqi troops torched oil wells in Kuwait, leaving behind a deadly pall of black smoke. Allied forces drove Iraqi forces from Kuwait and destroyed much of the Iraqi military, including 3,008 of Iraq's original 4,230 tanks. They also killed, wounded, or captured an estimated 300,000 Iraqi soldiers.

The resulting agreement that ended the war drew in the United Nations as a supervisory body, a role that grew from UN resolutions on the outcome of the war.

The pact required Iraq to withdraw from Kuwait, pay reparations for war damages, and cease the production of weapons of mass destruction. This latter proviso was to cause more controversy than other parts of the agreement, which would last much longer than expected at the time of signing.

Saddam Hussein remained in power and resumed attacks on Iraqi Shiites and Kurds. Subsequently the United States and Britain patrolled the skies over Iraq to limit Iraqi aircraft attacks against those populations. However, Operation Deny Flight, as the program was called, only partially restricted Iraqi efforts to curb the activities of the Shiites in the south and the Kurds in the north. Iraqi engineers tried to deny the Shiites hiding places by draining the vast marshes in southern Iraq where large numbers of them lived. In the northern part of Iraq, Kurdish groups continued to fight among themselves, occasionally interrupted by Turkish invasions into Iraq to prevent Iraqi Kurds from collaborating with Turkish Kurds who were in revolt against the Turkish government.

Reengaging the Israel-Palestinian Conflict

In 1987 the Palestinian uprising known as the intifadah began (see Chapter 11 for details). The Palestinians rose in an effort to "shake off" (the Arabic meaning of "intifadah") Israeli occupation, and as the movement continued, it spawned new Palestinian groups like Hamas, founded in December 1987 (Hamas means "enthusiasm" or "zeal" in Arabic). Hamas was a radical Palestinian Islamic organization that challenged the PLO for Palestinian leadership. As Yasir Arafat and his increasingly isolated PLO appeared to lose influence among Palestinians, he shifted tactics. In 1989 he offered publicly to end violence and recognize Israel in exchange for a limited Palestinian state, thus paving the way for peace talks with Israel. In late 1992 Norway initiated contacts with both PLO and Israeli officials in Oslo in an effort to build on the gradual efforts at peace begun in 1988 when the PLO recognized UN Resolution 242, and thus implicitly Israel. Tensions flared both between and within the Palestinian and Israeli negotiating teams, but the Norwegians' diplomatic skill and the tenacity of Israeli Prime Minister Yitzhak Rabin and PLO leader Arafat led to the Declaration of Principles (DOP) that fused the Palestinian-Israeli peace accords, now known as the Oslo Accords.

The United States began low-level talks with the PLO in 1989, assisted by Egypt. As American-Israeli relations deteriorated under Prime Minister Yitzhak Shamir, the Bush administration began to criticize Israel's settlement policy on the West Bank and in Jerusalem. The Gulf War of 1990–1991 interrupted the discussions, but after that conflict ended Bush reengaged Arab-Israeli peacemaking, driven partly by fears of another Arab-Israeli war.[78] In October Bush and Soviet president Mikhail Gorbachev opened a peace conference in Madrid, Spain, with Israel, Syria, Lebanon, and a joint Palestinian-Jordanian delegation in attendance. More meetings followed that conference, as Israelis and Palestinians negotiated with each other for the first time. Israeli elections held the following June saw a significant defeat for Shamir, and Yitzhak Rabin became prime minister. George Bush was defeated in the November presidential elections, and it fell to his successor, Bill

Clinton, to construct and implement the Declaration of Principles in September 1993. The May 1994 Cairo Agreement followed, along with the so-called Oslo II Agreement signed with great fanfare on the White House lawn in September 1995.

By mid-1996, negotiations broke down over implementation of the Oslo Accords. Binyamin Netanyahu won a close election in Israel against Shimon Peres, who filled in for Rabin, assassinated by a right-wing Israeli law student in November 1995. The Declaration of Principles on Interim Self-Government Arrangements signed in September 1993 called for the withdrawal of Israeli forces from certain parts of the West Bank and Gaza. In September 1998, Clinton hosted Netanyahu and Arafat in Washington and despite posed pictures (with no smiles) no progress resulted. In October Clinton invited both to the Wye Plantation in Maryland, and, despite some last-minute snags, an accord was signed in the White House on October 23.

Reengaging Saddam Hussein

By November 1998, the Clinton administration faced an Iraqi refusal to cooperate with UN weapons inspectors and built up a considerable force in the Persian Gulf to once again threaten Saddam Hussein should he fail to agree to weapons inspection. The alternatives available to the administration appeared to be running out; both diplomatic and economic pressures failed to break Saddam's defiant behavior, and yet military force carried its own uncertain outcomes. However, by November 15, 1998, Iraq signaled a willingness to readmit the UN inspectors. Later Iraq reneged on its agreements. American and British officials warned the UN inspectors to leave the country so they would be protected from an aerial bombing campaign that was supposed to target Iraqi military targets (though a misfired cruise missile hit the al-Rashid Hotel in Baghdad and killed one of Iraq's most popular singers).

Reengaging the Israeli-Palestinian Situation

With potential crises brewing in the Balkans, Iraq, and the Palestinian-Israeli theater, President Clinton needed to reduce tension somewhere and hoped that the election of Ehud Barak as Israeli prime minister and Arafat's stated willingness to negotiate would open the door to settling at least one potentially dangerous situation. In June 2000 Clinton summoned Arafat and Barak to Camp David. However, the talks broke down over control of parts of Jerusalem, with both sides wanting possession of the Temple Mount (for the Israelis) or the Haram al-Sharif (for the Muslim Palestinians).

Shortly after that, in a defiant gesture, Israeli opposition leader Ariel Sharon visited the Haram al-Sharif/Temple Mount in September 2000, and Palestinian riots followed. Peace seemed more elusive than ever, as Israeli voters selected Sharon as prime minister in March 2001. Sharon responded to growing Palestinian violence by sending Israeli troops into the territories to reoccupy them. Sharon won an even larger reelection in January 2003, and the violence between Israelis and Palestinians escalated. Sharon marginalized Arafat, and the Palestinian leadership appeared hopelessly weak.

Post–September 11, 2001

In 2000 incoming President George W. Bush paid little attention to the Middle East, but that changed dramatically with September 11. Bush successfully targeted the Taliban regime in Afghanistan, which hosted al-Qaeda training camps and leaders, and then turned his attention to Saddam Hussein. His State of the Union speech in January 2002 listed Iraq, Iran, and North Korea as members of an "axis of evil." After an effort to restart the UN weapons inspection process in late 2002, Bush mobilized US military forces in March 2003. American troops, joined by British and Australian forces, swept into Iraq almost unopposed by regular military force. By April 2003, they occupied Baghdad, and Saddam Hussein and most of his government fled. Saddam apparently refused to believe that the United States would invade, and if it did, somehow French and Russian diplomacy would rescue him. His military did not have any coordinated plans for defending the country and, according to one general, they had no plans to use chemical weapons as a final defense (not surprising, since Iraq did not have any chemical weapons to use).[79]

In May 2003, Bush announced the end to conflict, but in reality US soldiers and Iraqis continued to die as the country plunged into political and social chaos. By the fall of 2003, more Americans had died after the "end of the conflict" than had died during it. It appeared that US forces might be there for a long time, as they were in Afghanistan, adding to the overall US defense burden worldwide. However, President Bush would continue to threaten both Syria and Iran for continuing both WMD programs and for alleged support for terrorism.

Shortly after the ouster of Saddam Hussein, President George W. Bush tried to reenergize the Israeli-Palestinian peace process. He insisted on a change in Palestinian leadership, and Yasir Arafat reluctantly agreed to appoint Mahmoud Abbas, his long-term deputy, as Palestinian prime minister. With a fresh face at the table, Bush then urged Sharon to begin a peace dialog with Abbas, and an uneasy discussion began in the summer of 2003. It lasted only weeks before Abbas resigned, leaving the process in more turmoil than ever. The tragedy seemed even more profound since no one appeared on the scene to enable significant political progress. In November 2004 the Palestinians lost one of the most significant symbols of their struggle when Arafat died. Israeli-Palestinian peace talks ended, and by 2006 Israel was completing a security barrier that symbolically reflected the failure of those talks.

CONCLUSION

Foreigners rarely understand or appreciate the impact that Middle Eastern history has on the people who live there. Almost all Middle Eastern children get lessons on this history in school, which are reinforced frequently by events in the present. This history also exerts a powerful impact on modern Middle Eastern politics, motivating some to join violent leaders who use the language of history to cultivate their cause. When Osama bin Laden referred to the post-Ottoman period as "80 years of disgrace" and warned about repeating the "tragedy of al-Andalus" (the fall of Islamic

Spain to Christians in the fifteenth century), he appealed to many in the Arab world, even to those who otherwise eschew his violent tactics.[80] Yet this history contains positive lessons as well, including the record of peoples of different faiths and ethnicity who have lived together for centuries in the Middle East. It is not beyond the realm of possibility to imagine that they will do so again.

SUGGESTED READINGS

General History

Burke, Edmund, III. *Struggle and Survival in the Modern Middle East.* Berkeley: University of California Press, 1994.

Cleveland, William L. *A History of the Modern Middle East.* 2nd ed. Boulder, CO: Westview, 2000.

Cline, Eric H. *Jerusalem Besieged: From Ancient Canaan to Modern Israel.* Ann Arbor: University of Michigan Press, 2004.

Dawisha, A. I. *Arab Nationalism in the Twentieth Century: From Triumph to Despair.* Princeton, NJ: Princeton University Press, 2003.

Hourani, Albert. *A History of the Arab Peoples.* Cambridge, MA: Harvard University Press, Belknap Press, 2002.

Karsh, Efraim. *Islamic Imperialism: A History.* New Haven, CT: Yale University Press, 2006.

Lewis, Bernard. *The Middle East: A Brief History of the Last 2,000 Years.* New York: Scribner's, 1995.

_____. *What Went Wrong? Western Impact and Middle Eastern Response.* New York: Oxford University Press, 2002.

Makdisi, Ussama, and Paul A. Sliverstein. *Memory and Violence in the Middle East.* Bloomington: Indiana University Press, 2006.

Pre-World War II

Fromkin, David. *A Peace to End All Peace: The Fall of the Ottoman Empire and the Creation of the Modern Middle East.* New York: Avon, 1989.

Gomaa, Ahmed M. *The Foundations of the League of Arab States.* London: Longman's, 1977.

Karsh, Efraim. *Empires of the Sand: The Struggle for Mastery of the Middle East, 1789–1923.* Cambridge, MA: Harvard University Press, 2001.

The Post-World War II Era

Bickerton, Ian J., and Carla L. Klausner. *A Concise History of the Arab-Israeli Conflict.* 3rd ed. Upper Saddle River, NJ: Prentice-Hall, 1998.

Cohen, Michael J. *Palestine and the Great Powers, 1945–1948.* Princeton, NJ: Princeton University Press, 1982.

Fischback, Michael. *Records of Dispossession: Palestinian Refugee Property and the Arab-Israeli Conflict.* New York: Columbia University Press, 2003.

_____. *The Origins and Evolution of the Arab-Zionist Conflict*. Berkeley: University of California Press, 1987.

Lesch, David W., ed. *The Middle East and the United States: A Historical and Political Reassessment*. Boulder, CO: Westview, 1996.

Louis, William Roger, and Roger Owen, eds. *Suez, 1956: The Crisis and Its Consequence*. Oxford: Clarendon, 1989.

Murray, Williamson, and Robert H. Scales Jr. *The Iraq War: A Military History*. Cambridge, MA: Harvard University Press, 2003.

Pappé, Ilan. *The Making of the Arab-Israeli Conflict, 1947–51*. London: Tauris, 1992.

_____. *A History of Modern Palestine: One Land, Two Peoples*. Cambridge: Cambridge University Press, 2004.

Pollack, Kenneth M. *Arabs at War: Military Effectiveness, 1948–1991*. Lincoln: University of Nebraska Press, 2002.

Quandt, William B. *Peace Process: American Diplomacy and the Arab-Israeli Conflict Since 1967*. Washington, DC: Brookings Institution; Berkeley: University of California Press, 2001.

Rogin, Eugene, and Avi Shlaim, eds. *The War for Palestine: Rewriting the History of 1948*. Cambridge: Cambridge University Press, 2001.

Rubinstein, Alvin Z. *Red Star on the Nile*. Princeton, NJ: Princeton University Press, 1977.

Safran, Nadav. *Israel: The Embattled Ally*. Cambridge, MA: Harvard University Press, Belknap Press, 1978.

Shlaim, Avi, and Yezid Sayigh. *The Cold War and the Middle East*. Oxford: Oxford University Press, 1997.

Smolansky, Oles M., with Bettie M. Smolansky. *The USSR and Iraq: The Soviet Quest for Influence*. Durham, NC: Duke University Press, 1991.

2

RELIGION IN
THE MIDDLE EAST

It is called the Dome of the Rock in reference to where it stands: the shimmering dome rises above an octagonal building sheathed in decorative tiles, built on a rocky outcrop where Jews and Christians believe Abraham offered Isaac for sacrifice, and Muslims believe the Prophet Muhammad ascended to heaven to receive the last of God's messages to his Muslim community. The Dome towers over the Western Wall, the remnant of what Jews believe was the Second Temple, and is but a short distance from the Church of the Holy Sepulcher, the believed site of the death and resurrection of Jesus Christ. To visit these sites is to step from one set of religious beliefs to another to another, culling the remarkable similarities of belief that the embrace of politics has obscured if not obliterated.

RELIGION IS A KEY to understanding politics in the Middle East, as it is elsewhere in the world. No one can truly understand European politics, for example, without understanding the history and role of Catholic and Protestant faith in Europe, or understand Indian politics without understanding Hinduism. In the Middle East, religion has a pronounced impact on society and politics. As George Sfeir describes it, "In Arab Muslim societies, where tradition is closely identified with religion, the constitutional declarations of basic freedoms, themselves a product of the modern liberal state, are more often than not frustrated, not so much by the actions of oppressive governments (although that cannot be completely dismissed), as by the contradictions in the legal culture between traditional religious values and the newly adopted attributes of the modern state."[1] Barakat notes that "rulers throughout Arab history have used religion to discourage rebellion *(fitna)* on behalf of unity of the community, or *umma,* and the need to safeguard it against internal and external threats. Political actors use religion to undermine liberal and radical opposition and to justify repressive policies. Traditional governments and authoritarian rulers have attempted to establish their legitimacy and authority by the strict application of the Sharia in alliance with religious movements."[2] Religion shapes not only Muslim Middle Eastern countries but also predominately Jewish Israel. As Ira Sharkansky observes, "Perhaps the most fundamental reason for there being a thick mixture of politics and religion in Israel is that there is a great similarity in the underlying characteristics of religion and politics."[3]

The vast majority of the people who live in the Middle East belong to one of the three monotheistic religions: Islam, Judaism, or Christianity. Islam has by far the largest number of adherents, with all countries in the Middle East except Israel having Muslim majorities. Lebanon is the only other Middle Eastern country with a significant non-Muslim population; around 30 percent of Lebanese are Christians. In the rest of the Middle East, Christians are a small minority. In Israel, where Christianity originated, only 3 percent of the present population is Christian; in Egypt, Christians probably constitute around 5–9 percent of the population.

RELIGION AS A SOURCE OF POLITICAL BELIEF

Religious beliefs and practices have a profound impact on both political philosophy and the formation of political institutions. Practically every national government in the world borrows from religious teachings. Some regimes link politics and religion because of a conviction that religion demands such ties. Other regimes use religion to bolster claims of political legitimacy. Religion provides powerful symbols ("In God We Trust," or "There is no God but God, and Muhammad is his Messenger") to support the image that divinity supports and protects the political system and its rulers. Some symbols support democracy—Vox populi, vox dei ("The voice of the people is the voice of God")—while others support dictatorship and repression (Spanish dictator Francisco Franco pointed to Pope Pius XI's positive comparison between Spanish Nationalists and the Crusaders).

In many societies, political beliefs become the source of law. Almost all law existing in Middle Eastern countries stems at least partially from religious belief. In some countries religious law is the law, as in Saudi Arabia, where the Sharia informs jurisprudence. In other Middle Eastern countries, religious groups pressure their governments to adopt religious law, leading to compromises where at least some of the legal code derives from religious belief. Thus in many Arab countries and in Israel, religious codes form the basis of family law.

RELIGION AS A SOURCE OF CONFLICT

Some portray religion as a source of war and internal conflict in the Middle East. Religion may contribute to the passions that ignite war, and it may inspire warriors to fight. Egyptian soldiers shouted "God is great" as they crossed the Suez Canal to fight the Israelis on the other side in 1973. However, wars are mostly fought for power, in response to fear, or for wealth or the glory that victory can bring. These factors have all contributed to war in the Middle East. That the participants belong to different religions may give the appearance that they are fighting over those beliefs. But that is no more the case than the US-Japanese war between 1941 and 1945 was a struggle between Christianity and Shinto.

All three monotheistic religions exist in the Middle East, although Islam is by far the majority religion. However, it is much less well understood in the West than are the other two faiths.

ISLAM

Islam is the recognized title of the religion whose adherents believe that God revealed testimony to the Prophet Muhammad during his lifetime. Those messages, recorded as the Holy Quran, along with lessons from the life of the Prophet, make up the core beliefs of Islam. The term Islam in Arabic translates as "to submit," meaning that devotees of Islam submit to the will of God, in Arabic, Allah.[4] A Muslim is one who believes in and adheres to the basic tenants of Islam. A majority of the world's Muslims are not Arabs (Arabs constitute around 20 percent of the total Muslim population); considerable numbers of Muslims live in Pakistan, Southeast Asia (Indonesia is the world's largest Muslim country), Turkey, China, and the former republics of the Soviet Union. Altogether, there are around 1 billion Muslims in the world. However, no matter where they are, they acknowledge the importance of the Arab roots of the religion by facing Mecca when they pray, and almost all of them will travel to that city sometime in their lifetime.

Large majorities of the world's Muslims follow five fundamental practices:

- The *shahadah*, or testament of faith (literally, "there is no God but God, and Muhammad is his Messenger.")
- Prayer, or *salat*, five times a day at prescribed times
- Observance, or *siyam*, of the holy month of Ramadan, during which time Muslims must not eat, drink, smoke, or engage in sex during daylight hours
- Performance of the *hajj*, the religious journey to the city of Mecca at least once during one's lifetime[5]
- *Zakat*, or alms giving, sharing personal wealth with those less fortunate[6]

There are other beliefs and practices in Islam, though not all Muslims universally accept them. They include:

- A taboo against eating pork, which is widely followed by Muslims (and Jews as well).
- A taboo against the consumption of alcohol, followed selectively in the Muslim world. In some Muslim countries, laws prohibit the production, sale, or consumption of alcohol. This is the case in some Gulf countries like Saudi Arabia and Kuwait, although neighboring Bahrain and the United Arab Emirates allow alcohol.[7] Most Islamic countries allow for the production and sale

of wine, beer, and in the eastern Mediterranean, a distilled beverage called *arak* (or *raki* in Turkish), though in many of those countries, there is Islamist pressure to curtail alcohol consumption.

- Sabbath observed on Friday.
- Abandoning Islam once one is a Muslim—apostasy—is equivalent to treason.[8]
- A prohibition on charging interest on money loaned, which some Muslims consider as exploitative and unfair risk sharing. In some Islamic countries, banks must find other ways to be profitable, including imposing service charges or to pay returns from profit/loss returns.[9] Other Islamic countries allow the charging of interest on loans (see Chapter 3 for more on Islamic banking).
- A prohibition on portraying Allah or the Prophet, often taken from the Quran Suras 41 to 52. The angry reaction in many Muslim countries to cartoons in a Danish newspaper in 2006 unfavorably depicting Muhammad was an expression of this belief.[10]
- A belief that Muhammad was the final messenger from God.
- A belief that the Quran is the last word from Allah revealed to Muhammad in Arabia because the community of Arabs there had become ignorant of God's earlier messages to Adam, Abraham, Moses, and Jesus. They view these earlier figures as messengers. Jesus is controversial. Muslims hold that if one accepts the phrase "there is no God but God," then by definition God cannot have progeny. They hold that Jesus was human and was chosen by God to reveal earlier messages to humankind. They also believe that God would not let a messenger die by crucifixion.

SOURCES OF ISLAMIC FAITH

There are two prime sources of Islamic belief—the Quran and the Hadith, or sayings of the Prophet.

The Quran

The holy book for Muslims is the Quran, the written collection of the revelations given by Allah to Muhammad. The Quran has never been revised, for to do so would be to alter the unalterable word of Allah. It contains 114 chapters, or suras, arranged in order of the length of each sura, with the longer chapters coming first. Muslims believe that the true Quran exists only in the Arabic language. They claim that God sought an Arabic speaker to reveal messages that Arabs later wrote in Arabic script. Thus many non-Arabs learn written Arabic so that they can read the Quran in its purest language. Some Muslims regard Arabic itself as sacred script, and to ensure that human feet cannot trample a piece of Arab writing, carefully discard old Arabic newspapers so that they do not wind up on the street.

There is discussion about the authority of the Quran, as there is about other holy texts. Some argue that its interpretation should be literary rather than literal. The

Quranic texts contain contradictions, as for example between the earlier and later revelations. Thus the Quran may be understood to have different meanings, as opposed to absolute law, a single meaning in its suras. Such a view, known as *Mutazilism,* argues that while God created the universe, that act did not predispose human actions, and thus Mutazilism accepts human determination of self-conduct. The opposing view, known as Asharism, argues that people acquire actions from God, though God is not responsible for the outcome of evil actions, which are the responsibility of humans alone, thus negating self-will.[11] Asharism as a doctrine prevailed in discussions on Islamic theology after the twelfth century, though its rationalist views became more prevalent in the Shiite community.[12]

The Hadith

The other sources of Islamic belief are the Hadith, or traditions from the life of the Prophet. Muslims emulate such traditions where they can, believing that Muhammad was "the perfect man" since Allah chose him to receive the Quran; thus early followers collected these sayings and actions. Muslims believe that the life of the Prophet holds lessons for them, since it was Muhammad whom Allah chose to receive the messages recorded in the Quran. The lessons extracted from that life became the Sunna, or "way" of the Prophet.

As in all recorded oral tradition, disputes arise among Muslim scholars about the meaning of particular hadith, particularly where they appear to contradict the Quran. Since others recorded the hadiths, their veracity depends on the interpreter, and the degree that a particular hadith may be traced directly to the Prophet.[13] In cases where a hadith does contradict the Quran, the Quran takes precedence, as it is believed to be the direct word of God.

Muhammad was born in the trading city of Mecca in 570 CE. A merchant uncle adopted him after Muhammad's parents died at an early age. When he reached adulthood, he became a merchant and a notable citizen in Mecca. He married a widow, Khadija, and had two daughters, one of whom, Fatima, would marry his cousin Ali. After Khadija's death, Muhammad married again, and at one time had eleven wives, partly to cement ties to local tribes.

Muhammad was a contemplative man who sometimes left the bustle of the city to meditate in a cave south of Mecca. There, according to tradition, around 610 CE, the Angel Gabriel visited him and told that he had been chosen to receive God's word. For the next twenty years, he continued to receive messages that he initially revealed only to a small group of followers. Those followers of Muhammad would later record these messages as the Quran in the time of Caliph Umar. Part of the message was to disseminate the messages to community members and bring them into the flock. However, many citizens in Mecca resisted Muhammad's teaching, and he had to fight to preserve his small flock.

Islamic tradition holds that in his later years, Muhammad journeyed by night on a mythical animal to Jerusalem, where he ascended to heaven to receive the final revelations. The Dome of the Rock now marks the site where Muslims believe he started his ascension, known as the *miraj*. They consider it the third holiest place in Islam, after the mosques in Mecca and Medina. Control over this place, which now contains both the Dome of the Rock and Al-Aqsa Mosque, is a bitter issue between Israel and the Palestinians. The Palestinians, who are predominately Muslim, argue that as Muslims they should have sovereign control over the mosques and the land on which they stand (see Chapters 11 and 14 for more on this issue).

Sunni and Shiite: Branches of Islam

Like Christianity and Judaism, Islam's followers are divided into sects, the most important of which are Sunni and Shiite. A majority of Muslims are Sunni, but around 10 to 15 percent of the world's Muslims are Shiite. They constitute a large majority of Muslims in Iran, and are in the majority in Bahrain and Iraq.

The Origins of Sunni-Shiite Differences

At the time of the Prophet's death in 632 CE, there was no human successor to lead the small band of Muslim followers. The Muslim community (or *umma*) thus selected the Prophet's closest companion and father-in-law Abu Bakr (the father of Aisha, Muhammad's last wife) as his successor, or caliph. While some cite evidence that the Prophet expected Ali to succeed him, factors like clan rivalry led to the choice of Abu Bakr.[14] But he died after only two years, when the *umma* chose the second caliph, Umar ibn al-Khattab. He ruled for ten years and led the conquest of Jerusalem.[15] When Umar died in 644 CE (killed by a Persian prisoner of war), the third caliph, Uthman ibn Affan, a member of the Umayya clan, served until 656, when he was murdered by an Egyptian soldier who may have been the son of Abu Bakr.[16]

Finally a relative of the Prophet, Ali ibn abi Talib, the husband of Muhammad's daughter Fatima by Khadija and Muhammad's cousin, was chosen as the successor. A rival from the Umayyad clan, Muawiya, a cousin of Caliph Uthman, challenged the selection. Muawiya had moved to Damascus with another group of Muslims, including Aisha, who had a dispute with Ali.[17] Mu'awiya believed that those who murdered Uthman supported the succession of Ali. After initially defeating the rebels at the battle of the Camel at Basra in 656, Ali agreed to discuss the succession decision after his forces and those of Muawiya met at the battle of Siffin in 657. Ali's soldiers showed little will to fight after Muawiya's troops posted Qurans on their spears, and thus negotiations began between the parties that would last a year. This enraged one of Ali's followers, who murdered him in 661 CE. The succession first passed to Ali's eldest son, Hasan, but he declined the title and moved to Mecca. Ali's second son, Hussein ibn Ali, then took up his father's cause and moved to the city of Karbala (or Kerbala), now in southern Iraq. Muawiya died in 680 and his son Yazid succeeded him. Hussein ibn Ali refused to recognize Yazid as caliph and decided to eliminate him as a rival. He sent an army to Karbala, and in 680 CE Yazid's forces defeated the small group under Hussein ibn Ali and beheaded its leader. The survivors, now calling themselves the Partisans of Ali, or Shia Ali (later shortened to Shia), never again challenged the dominant role of the Sunni until the modern era, thus indicating the significance of the 2005 elections in Iraq.

This may seem like a small incident in the scope of human history. However, as Ajami notes, "Kerbala cast a long shadow; for the faithful it annulled time and distance. Succeeding generations had told and embellished the tale, giving it their sense of separateness and political dispossession."[18] It also contributes to a sense among the Shiites that their role is to continue the tradition of suffering and martyrdom epitomized by Ali and his son.

The Shiites

Both Sunnis and Shiites practice the fundamentals of Islam, though they may differ in details. For both, the Quran is their holy book, and the hadiths guide them. Yet there are differences that date back to the question of succession after the death of the Prophet in 632 CE. They remain divided on the selection of the early caliphs, even though the caliphate disappeared, either in 1517 with the Mamluk defeat by the Ottomans, or in 1924 when Turkey's new leader Mustafa Kemal formally abolished the post. The Sunni followed the first three caliphs and ultimately rejected the selection of Ali as the fourth "rightly guided caliph." They take their name from the phrase *ahl al–Sunna wa-l-jammaah,* which in Arabic means "peoples of custom and community." They believe in the election of the caliph by members of that community, while the Shiites believe that the caliph, whom they refer to as the "imamship" is nonelective and should remain within the family of the Prophet. That distinction has blurred over the centuries, but it has also led to another distinction between Sunnis and Shiites. The Shiites have a formal leadership structure while the Sunnis do not. In Sunni practice, an *imam* or prayer leader leads the prayers in the mosque, but that person can be chosen from among the community. In Shiite tradition the imam (coming from the term "righteous individual," or *al-imama*) is more than a prayer leader. He (only males can become imams) is also considered a jurist, particularly for members of the Twelver Shiite community (see below). However, all Shiites hold that the role of Imam as a jurist *(qadi),* and thus a political leader, is important. The jurist must understand the Quran in all its manifestations (including the "five pairings" of verses), and the various forms of hadith.[19]

The formal clerical structure normally found in Shiite Islam is:

- Grand Ayatollah (Ayatollah uzma) or "Great Sign of God"
- Ayatollah (Sign of God)
- Hojat al-Islam (Authority on Islam)
- Mubellegh a-Risala (Carrier of the Message)
- Mujtahid (a graduate of a religious seminary)
- Talib ilm (a religious student)[20]

The Shiites are further divided into subsects, usually based on which imam they follow:

- The Zaydi, found largely in Yemen, believe that the true line of succession ended with Zayd ibn Ali, the fifth imam and grandson of al-Hussein. The Zaydi have no tradition of a hidden imam and instead hold that the imamate can continue, even though the Zaydis in Yemen (the majority there) are currently without a religious leader.

A majority of Shiites disagree, believing instead that succession passed to the sixth imam, Jafar al-Sadiq, the son of the fifth imam Muhammad al-Baqir, who had a pronounced influence on the development of Shiite law. The Shiites disagree, though, on the next path to succession, with one group holding that Jafar's son Ismail is the rightful successor, while the larger majority believe that the true successor is the twelfth imam. Consequently there are two other Shiite groups.

- The Ismaili, or "Seveners," who believe that the seventh Imam, Ismail, was the last true Shiite descendant of the Prophet. Their early leader Ubayd Allah attempted unsuccessfully to conquer Syria and then fled to Tunisia, which he did conquer in 909, declaring himself the Mahdi. He named his dynasty the Fatimid (after the Prophet's daughter Fatima, to whom he claimed kinship). The Fatimids conquered Egypt in 969 and ruled there until Salah al-Din defeated them in 1171.[21] Most Ismaili now live in India, with few left in the Middle East.

- The Imamiyya, or "Twelvers," believe that the correct line of succession runs through the ninth, tenth, and eleventh imams (Muhammad al-Jawad, who died in 818, Ali al-Hadi, who died in 868, and Hassan al-Askari, who died in 874),[22] to al-Askari's son, the twelfth imam, Muhammad al-Mahdi (born Abu-Qasim Muhammad ibn Hasan), who "disappeared" or "was hidden" (or went into "occultation") in 874, at around age eight, near Samarra in modern Iraq, but will someday return to establish a perfect Islamic society on earth. The reason for occultation involves the danger to imams and occultation continues because of the threat. Occultation became a tradition largely in the tenth century when the reality of a living imam would have attracted messianic attention away from the Twelver leaders, who thus claimed that their imam was alive but "hidden."[23] They are the largest Shiite group. They include in their traditions the practice of *kalam*, or free will developed by Muhammad ibn Muhammad al-Harithi which carries forward to this day. According to Heinz Halm, "The success of the Iranian Shi'a today cannot be understood without taking this into account."[24]

The Sunni

The Sunni branch of Islam is the largest Muslim group, constituting around 85 percent of the world's total Islamic population. Common to the Sunnis is a belief that the "rightly guided" caliphs were successors but not spiritual leaders. Thus the Sunnis expected their leaders to be responsive to the guidance of those schooled in Islam but not to be clerics. Like the Shiites, Sunnis differ among themselves. One distinction lies in the different schools of Sunni Islamic law, or jurisprudence. The distinction helps explain certain regional differences in Sunni behavior, for example, the more conservative attitude in Saudi Arabia versus the more liberal mores in Morocco.

Schools of Sunni Jurisprudence

Islamic law, designed to regulate the behavior of both individual Muslims and the Muslim community, has many sources. The most basic is the Quran itself, and the hadith and the sunna. Juridical renderings also come from religious scholars *(ijamaa)* through analogy *(qeyas)* and reasoning *(ijtihad)*. However, confusion arose in the Umayyad period when *qadis,* or religious judges, had considerable leeway to interpret the law. By the eighth century, legal scholars attempted to provide legal guidance, and those efforts resulted in four Sunni schools of law.[25]

The *Hanafi* school, named after its founder, Abu Hanifa (d. 767 CE), has spread throughout the Middle East,[26] except the Arabian Peninsula and Iran, and is the most liberal of the schools, except in areas regarding women and personal status.[27] It emphasizes the role of reason and independent judgment, or *ijtihad.* Abu Hanifa was once a student of Jafar al-Sadiq, the Sixth Imam in the Shiite imamate line, suggesting possible Shiite influence in the Hanafi school.

The *Maliki* school came from the teachings of Malik ibn Abnas (d. 796 CE), who emphasized the importance of public welfare and the public interest. The Maliki school is most commonly found in the Maghreb and sub-Saharan Africa.

The *Shafii* school follows Muhammad al-Shafi (d. 819 CE) and his emphasis on the importance of legal doctrine, and upon methodology for determining the authenticity of the Prophet's reports (sayings and practices).[28] Shafii adherents also hold that it is important to avoid deviation through reason from those sayings and practices deemed authentic.[29] Adherents of the Shafii school are found in Egypt, Yemen, East Africa, and Southeast Asia, and a majority of Kurds (a linguistic group discussed later in this chapter) are followers of the Shafii school.

The *Hanbali* school is the most conservative of the four, originating in the teachings of Ahmad ibn Hanbal (d. 855 CE). It is most influential in Saudi Arabia and Qatar. The teachings of ibn Hanbal emphasize the oneness of God *(tawhid)* and particularly the banning of unacceptable innovations *(bida).*[30] The Hanbali school, like the Hanafi, does allow for *ijtihad* in matters not covered by religious text.[31] It also emphasized the body of a woman as "sexually provocative and private," thus leading to the requirement for full body and face covering for women in conservative Hanbali-influenced countries like Saudi Arabia.[32]

The Schism Between Sunni and Shiite

Despite such theological and differences of praxis, Keddie notes that before the Persian Safavid dynasty (1501–1722 CE), the Shiite and Sunni communities coexisted in relative harmony. But after forcible Shiite conversions of Persian Sunnis and persecution of the Shiites by the Ottomans, the fissures between the two communities widened greatly.[33] The Sunni realm gained power over the Shiite dynasties by the middle of the eleventh century, particularly after the Seljuq Turks occupied Baghdad around 1055, replacing the Twelver Shiite leaders who considered Baghdad their intellectual center.

Is there still a schism between the followers of Shiite and Sunni Islam? Despite efforts to cement ties between the two interpretations (like the 1959 *fatwa,* or religious instruction, by the Sunni Al-Azhar University in Cairo declaring Shia the fifth school of Sunni Islamic jurisprudence), problems continue. They occur mostly in Islamic countries where Shiites are a significant minority or majority of the population. They remain targets of oppression and discrimination in some majority Sunni Middle Eastern countries, forcing some to engage in the practice of *taqiyya,* or hiding one's true beliefs. In Saudi Arabia, for example, where Shiites may be 8 percent of the total population, intolerance from the majority al-Muwahiddun (Wahhabi in the West) regime remains a problem.[34] The problem is more serious in Iraq, where the minority Sunni regime of Saddam Hussein waged open warfare on the Shiites in the south until its elimination in 2003. The long-standing resentment by Iraqi Shiites against the Sunnis remains. After the 2003 ouster of Saddam Hussein and American-led efforts to install a majoritarian government, Shiite and Sunni militias formed and attacked each other's populations, with Sunnis fearing a loss of traditional dominance and Shiites trying to gain and hold what they believed was their rightful place in Iraq after centuries of Sunni domination. In some Sunni neighborhoods, citizens adapted the Shiite practice of *taqiyya,* dressing like Shiites and putting pictures of Hussein and Ali in their houses in an effort to escape the Shiite militias.

Other Islamic Sects

Not all sects claiming Muslim identity abide by the practices noted above; the Sufi, Druze, and Alawi are exceptions.

The Sufi

Most religions have elements of mysticism within their corpus, and Islam is no exception. The most notable mystics in Islam are the Sufi, who date back to the teachings of Hasan al-Basri (643–728) and Rabia al-Adawiyya (d. 801), the latter attracting a circle of followers because of her asceticism. Sometimes described as an esoteric version of Shia,[35] the Sufi work to achieve a spiritual sense of the meaning of God, often resorting to repeated prayer, music, dance (including the dance of the so-called whirling dervishes symbolizing the order of the universe), and the teachings of Sufi masters.[36] Such masters reflect a Sufi belief in the requirement for the "perfect man" (or *qutb*) to serve as an intermediary between God and humans, reflecting a similarity to the concept of the Shi'a imams. These masters often head Sufi orders, where disciples learn Sufi practices of religious self-discovery, including how to sweep aside worldly concerns and practices to truly know the meaning of God's will.[37] Some masters (or *pir*) became missionaries and were responsible for the spread of Islam into Africa and Southeast Asia, far more so than the Arab merchants who traded there.[38] In modern times, some Sufi have risen to political prominence—Recep Tayyip Erdoğan, the prime minister of Turkey, is Sufi.

The Sufi may be either Sunni or Shiite, but most Sufi live in Sunni areas.[39] However, whatever the preference, some Sufi practices go beyond the normal practice of both streams of Islam. A common Sufi practice involves the construction of shrines at the tombs of saints, a custom heterodox Muslims eschew. Some Sufi believe that a pilgrimage to such a shrine can substitute for the *hajj*, a view also at odds with traditional Muslim practice.[40] The Sufi have no formal structure and rarely have structured ties to regimes. Consequently the Sufi may benefit when regimes relax or cut ties to religious leaders, as happened in Turkey under and after Kemal Ataturk, whose secularation of Turkish social and political space allowed certain Sufi groups to develop strong networks in business, politics, the media, and welfare services.[41]

The Druze

The Druze live mostly in Lebanon and Syria, with a smaller number in Israel. They do not perform the *hajj* or observe Ramadan, and thus many Muslims do not regard them as true Muslims. They refer to themselves as al-Mowahideen (roughly "monotheist"). The name "Druze" came from the westernized name of a Druze preacher named Nashtakin al-Darzis, though contemporary Druze consider his teachings blasphemous.

The Druze date back to the ninth century CE, when Darzis and Hamza ibn Ali ibn Ahmad proclaimed that God had become human and taken the form of man, al-Hakim bi-amr Allah, between 996 and 1021 CE in Fatimid Cairo.[42] They further believe that Hamza ibn Ali was a reincarnation of many prophets, including Christ, Plato, Aristotle, and Adam, and revealed the truth to all Mowahideen who took an oath to accept and advance those truths. After the death of Druze leader Baha al-Din in 1031, the Druze decided not to accept converts, and thus Druze may marry only other Druze. Their beliefs include a single god (thus no Holy Trinity), the truth in a book known as Kitab al-Hikma, which contains not only Quranic verses but other beliefs as well, including reincarnation (the concept of heaven and hell are believed to be spiritual and not virtual).[43]

Israeli policy treats the Israeli Druze differently from Israeli Muslims in that the Druze are eligible for military service while Muslims are not. Some argue that because the Druze keep their religious practices secret, they are not real Muslims but are practicing *taqiyya*. This interpretation, as Parsons notes, means that while the Druze "may seem to be participating in Muslim Arab culture, they are in fact just pretending. They are practicing taqiyya."[44]

IMGES | *Fog and sleet fill the valley, making the platforms on each side difficult to see. The dim figures of several people appear on the Syrian side of the valley, while off in the distance a wagon draws slowly down the narrow road from the Golani Druze village on the occupied Israeli side. Figures emerge from the wagon and shouting begins from one of the platforms.*

One figure calls out the attributes of his son or daughter (it is too misty to tell) over the fierce wind to the other side, from which someone in turn shouts the qualities of his offspring. This is the only place where Druze families in Golan can arrange a marriage between their progeny and the offspring of Druze parents in Syria. It is called the "shouting place," and it represents the only avenue out of occupied Golan for the 18,000 or so Druze who still live there, for only marriage to a Syrian Druze allows one to leave. The outcome of this particular shout was uncertain, but it was clear from the effort on that bone-chilling day that the stakes for both families were very high.

The Alawi

The Alawi (Alawiyun, anglicized to Alawi Nusayriyah, or Alawi, or Alawite; Alevi in Turkish) date to at least the teachings of Hussein ibn Hamadan al-Khasibi, a Twelver Shiite who died around 957. The Alawi are found mostly in Syria and Turkey, and hold secret religious observances that cause other Muslims to regard them largely as pagan.[45] The problem was especially keen for Syrian President Hafiz al-Asad, and later his son Bashar, who came from the Syrian Alawi community. Hafiz al-Asad asked a Shiite cleric in Lebanon, Musa al-Sadr, for a religious ruling *(fatwa)* declaring that the Alawi were actually Shiite Muslims. The term "Alawi" roughly means a follower of Ali ibn Abi Talib, the son-in-law of the Prophet, so the Shiite tie is clearly implied, if not evident to other Shiites. The Alawi belong to a Shiite group known as the Ghulat, or exaggerators, who consider Ali beyond veneration as the son-in-law of the Prophet, a manifestation of the deity. They did not consider themselves descendants of the family of Ali, but rather gatekeepers. The office of *bab*, or "gate," is still significant in the Alawi faith.[46] After the arrival of the Crusaders in the eleventh century, certain Christian ideas seem to have permeated the Alawi. They adopted the concept of a Trinity (not a part of Islam), with Ali as the meaning and essence *(mana)*, Muhammad as the outward exoteric name *(ism)*, and Salman al-Farsi as the gate to Ali's esoteric essence *(bab)*.[47] They also celebrate Christian feast days such as Christmas, Epiphany, and Pentecost. The Alawi hold mass-type ceremonies during which the congregation chants hymns, also not an Islamic practice. Finally, most Alawi believe in reincarnation, although it is more restricted than in Hindu belief.

The attacks on the Alawi began with Ahmad ibn Taymiyya (d. 1328), an early critic of Islamist laxity, who claimed that the Alawi drank wine, believed in reincarnation, and considered Ali ibn Abi Talib as a god. The Hanbali school banned Sunni marriage with the Alawi. However the Alawi benefited when the Ottoman governor of Syria created a separate administration for them in the nineteenth century, and the French built a unique armed force from Alawi soldiers in former Ottoman territories, giving them the special military status that carried over into modern Syria. Today an Alawi elite rules Syria, though this elite also includes members of other branches of Islam as well as some Christians (see Chapter 12).

The Bahai

The Bahai sect is more recent, dating to the 1860s in Persia.[48] The Bahai are inspired by the teachings of Mirza Hussein Ali, who took the name Bahaullah, and taught that God has manifested himself in the forms of Abraham, Moses, Jesus Christ, Buddha, Muhammad, and in Bahaullah himself. These teachings include the unity of God across all religions, equality of the world's people (including the equality of men and women), eradication of poverty, avoidance of politics, and abstinence from drugs and alcohol. The Bahai claim to be Muslim because they recognize the Quran as the word of God revealed to Muhammad. However, they recognize other messengers, and they do not perform the Five Pillars of Islam. The faith attracted Iranian Jews, Zoroastrians, and Shiites seeking a more modern faith. However, Bahai beliefs and practices came under attack in Iran after the 1979 revolution (and before that in other countries like Egypt and Morocco), and followers there faced widespread persecution. According to Bahai officials, the Iranian government has killed over 200 of their faithful.[49] Many have fled Iran, and now their main temple is in Haifa, Israel.[50]

Islam and Politics

Early Muslim thinking on politics consisted largely of a code of good conduct for rulers based on norms developed from the early ideas on Islamic communities. Emphasis was on obedience to authority, and, as Brown notes, "the weight of Muslim tradition was on the side of political submission."[51] During the caliphate periods, Islamic political theory concentrated largely on the leadership qualifications for rulers, and contained little guidance on such matters as state administration, and almost no mention of individual rights.[52] Islamic politics evolved through the caliphate periods into modernity and confrontation with European colonialism. What Tibbi calls Islamic modernism began in the nineteenth century, seeking fusion with Western ideas to resist colonialism, and developed in parallel with other movements, like the Wahhabist elements from Muhammad al-Wahab seeking to purify Islam, the idea of a relatively secular Muslim state. All these movements ultimately affected political Islam.[53]

During the times of Caliphs Uthman and Ali, a group calling itself the Kharijites or Khariji revolted against Ali when he agreed to mediate a challenge to the legitimacy of his succession, and they continued to revolt against the Umayyad and Abbasid caliphates. They emphasized a strict literal interpretation of the Quran as well as an egalitarian society.[54] Kharijite doctrine also emphasized jihad, or holy war, as the Sixth Pillar of Islam. The Khariji later split into factions (divided over, among other issues, the legitimacy of violence against sinners), and one faction under the guidance of Abd Allah ibn Ibad of Basra became the Ibadi around 680. These Ibadis (taking the name of ibn Ibad), eschewed violence, believed in redemption, and agreed to live with other Muslims who differed from their strict moral code. Some Ibadis left Iraq and settled in Oman, where they remain today as the majority religion (See Chapter 6). Others live in remote parts of Algeria, Libya, and Tunisia.

Contemporary Islamist Ideas

Islam as a political resistance movement dates to the early caliphs. It waned but later revived, largely in response to European incursions.[55] Twentieth-century Islamist thinkers built on earlier traditions, with particularly important links to Taqi al-Din Ahmad ibn Taymiyya who wrote after the Mongols sacked Baghdad in 1258, calling for a return to the fundamentals of Islam in the face of outside threats and an emphasis on the importance of revelation over reason. Ibn Taymiyya also rejected the Shiite importance of imams, claiming they had no more authority than any other Muslim to interpret religious tradition.[56] One prominent scholar who followed ibn Taymiyya in the twentieth century was Said Qutb, an important figure in the Egyptian Muslim Brotherhood. Qutb, writing in the early 1950s, argued that Muslims lived in a period of ignorance *(jahiliyya)* of Islam, similar to pre-Islamic times, and he called on a new "Quranic generation" to build a modern Islamic community on the remains of nationalism as the Prophet built his community on the remains of paganism.[57] Noted Qutb, "The basis of our economic life is usury, our laws permit rather than punish oppression, the *zakat* is not obligatory, and is not spent in the requisite ways. We permit the extravagance and the luxury that Islam prohibits."[58] For Qutb, *tawhid* should be the basis of Islamic society, to include its laws and a refusal to submit to un-Islamic authorities or nontextual laws, though Qutb accepts the possibility of contemporary understandings of religious text,[59] which separates Qutb from some of the more fundamental Salafiyyists (see below).[60] Hassan al-Banna, born in Egypt in the same year as Said Qutb, founded Egypt's Muslim Brothers in 1928 with a vision similar to that of Qutb. Al-Banna's anti-British sentiments pushed him to admire Hitler and Mussolini, but his primary message to Egypt's Muslims was not that they needed to resist alien domination, but that they needed to turn back from the brink of *jahiliyya*, the period of pre-Islamic existence or ignorance, that many Salifiyyists argued would return without a continual and emphatic Islamic purification by its adherents.

Ruhollah Khomeini, who became the supreme ruler of Iran in 1979, held similar views on secular government, writing scathing criticism of the ruling Pahlavi family's claim to nationalism based on the modernist nationalism views of Turkish Republic founder Kemal Ataturk. These and other Islamist theorists also rejected the quasi-Marxist politics embraced by many Arab nationalists. Khomeini called for rule by the experts in Islamic jurisprudence, *the vilayat-i faqih,* who can carry out the same functions as would the Imam, even though the *vilayat-i faqih* would not have the Imam's status.[61] As Nasr points out, Khomeini studied, among other texts, Plato's philosopher-king template of governance and applied it accordingly.[62]

Political Islamists have varying objectives, depending partially on their orientation. As noted above, most Shiite Islamists believe that the supreme leader of a country should be an Islamic figure (an ayatollah, for example), that the Sharia, or religious law, be the law of the state, and that a literal interpretation of the Quran be followed by society. Sunni Islamists tend to enforce Sharia but rarely have religious heads of state. One Sunni sheik in Egypt, when asked if he sought the elimination of Egypt's secular state, responded, "No, Islam is not a style of ruling. We don't want the president of the republic to be a sheik, only to have the Sharia as the law of the land."[63] Still, Sharia requires interpretation from doctrine to particular circumstances. Is it to be viewed as immutable and unchanging, a reflection of its origins, or can it accommodate change? The duty of interpretation of the Sharia itself through *usul al-fiqh* or "method of study" by scholars to link specific events and facts to the Sharia, and to determine if the outcome stems from the Sharia itself or through reason, or *ijtihad*. However, as Masmoudi comments, *ijtihad*, or reasoning between a strict interpretation of Sharia and other principles (like mercy or justice) was common in the fifth century, but recent attempts to revive it have been "modest and not very successful."[64] Thus Sharia construal may reflect a literal view of Islamic law in many Middle Eastern societies since, as Tibi notes, "the Islamic cultural system does not admit a category of 'change.'"[65] Consequently political Islamists demand that the secular state should abide by their traditionalist views of Islam: formulate and enforce state laws that forbid the consumption or possession of alcohol and require women to dress modestly (often with head covered and veiled), for example, to further their view of Islam as a purifying force to drive out corrupt ideas and practices.

In many ways, political Islam becomes a replacement or an adjunct to the state, where the state is either weak or narrowly focused. Islamist movements supply education, food, and public protection where the state cannot or will not provide such things in adequate quantity. In Cairo, people living in sections devasted by an earthquake in 1992 waited for over two weeks for the government to respond, but the mosques showed up immediately with food, shelter, and medical care. In Lebanon's Shiite areas, the Islamist group Hizbollah supplies much of the daily needs for the poor. In Turkey, the Islamist-oriented AKP Party supplements the state: "In practices that would be familiar to Shiite Muslims in Lebanon or Palestinians in Gaza, women's groups go door to door offering aid, community centers offer women's literacy classes, and sports centers give free physical therapy to handicapped children."[66]

The Salafiyya

Some Islamist movements set as their vision the life and times of the Prophet and the first three generations of the Islamic community, which serves as a guide for proper Islamic society. Such movements are known as the Salafiyya, or "pious ancestors." The Salafiyya are commonly associated with a return to a puritanical and conservative vision of Islam, but because early Islamic times saw a ferment of ideas and theological interpretations, the Salafiyyist tradition also included discussions of modernity. Such Salafiyyists as Jamal al-Din al-Afghani, Muhammad Abduh, and Rashid Rida, writing mostly between 1880 and 1935, argued in favor of *ijtihad* and a limited dialog with the West, particularly in areas where Islam did not provide adequate guidance; some modernists find early Quranic justifications for parliaments and constitutions.[67] Yet other Salafiyyists drew inspiration from Ahmad ibn Taymiyya, noted above.[68] They emphasize the original purity of Islam by focusing on the impurity and temptation offered by the West (and the United States in particular), and by the Islamic regimes supported by the West that, in the Salafi view, only pretend to be Islamic. There is a particular emphasis against *shirk*, or the attribution of powers reserved only for God. Thus Salafiyyists attacked shrines to saints and assaulted the mosque erected to commemorate Hussein Ali (see above) because they regard the Shiites as apostates. The Salafiyyi also reject *ijtihad* because the practice might refute the original sources of Islamic belief, the Quran and the life and sayings of Muhammad.

These are the Islamist roots of the Egyptian Islamic Jihad and Osama bin Laden's al-Qaeda. In his application of Salafi thinking to both the Egyptian Islamic Jihad and al-Qaeda, Doran states that "the magnitude of the attacks on New York and Washington indicates that al-Qaeda does indeed believe itself to be fighting a war to save the umma from Satan, represented by secular Western culture."[69] However, the Salafi do not limit their quest to circumscribing the impact of Western culture on Muslims, but also campaign against "un-Islamic" practices in their own societies. Thus unveiled women or men who consume alcohol may become the victims of a Salafi attack, as happened in Morocco in 2003 when half a dozen people died at the hands of Salafiyya Jihadia, some with their throats slit.[70]

Besides al-Qaeda, the best-known form of Salafiyya is the Wahhabi or, properly, the Muwahiddun or "Unitarian" interpretation of Sunni Islam, which differs from mainstream Salafiyyism in that it is far less tolerant of religious diversity.[71] This stems from the influence of *tawhid* and its stress on the unity of God and the destruction of all that challenges that unity. The origins of this offshoot of Sunni Islam are in its name, from Muhammad ibn Abd al-Wahhab, a scholar whose puritanical teachings and interpretations of the Hanbali school influenced the al-Saud family of Saudi Arabia, and today form the basis of Saudi Arabian Islam (see Chapter 5).[72] However, since many Muslims object to taking the name of a person for an Islamic sect, the formal name for its adherents is Muwahiddun. While Saudi Arabia is the most noteworthy example of Muwahiddun influence, it is also spreading into Central Asia and other parts of the Islamic world. It is the chosen Islamic interpretation of Osama bin Laden, the Saudi Arabian–born leader of al-Qaeda, who uses its strong opposition to *bida* (see above) to motive followers into extreme deeds.[73] It would be mistaken, however, to regard the Muwahiddun, al-Qaeda, and other Salafiyya groups as in agreement on theology or politics. The Saudi Arabian regime is itself under attack by al-Qaeda and other Salafiyyist groups have tried to discredit beliefs and practices of the Muwahiddun.[74] Others attack it because they believe that it rests on false premises. One Saudi Arabian theologian, whose views have drawn the ire of the Saudi government, argues that the authoritarian tradition in Saudi Arabia (and presumably other authoritarian countries) comes from the Umayyad rulers. Says Hassan al-Maleky, "The salafis blindly defend the Umayyads despite their many injustices."[75] The Muwahiddun also believe that only the ruler may declare the permissibility of jihad whereas al-Qaeda argues that rulers may become apostate, and thus al-Qaeda members may declare jihad, even against rulers regarded as apostates.[76]

While the roots of Muwahiddun belief lie in the Hanbali school, there are additional components to the sect. Its contempt for Shiites is greater than in other Salafiyyist groups. From its origins it attacked Shiite communities in eastern Arabia (in 1788–1792) and between 1801 and 1811 repeatedly attacked and destroyed Shiite shrines at Karbala and Najaf, as well as the Shiite communities in Bahrain, until Ottoman Governor Midhat Pasha annexed the island in 1871.

Hizb ut-Tahrir and the Caliphate Movement

Efforts to restore the Islamic caliphate date back to Arab efforts to restore the Mamluk caliphate after its defeat in the early sixteenth century. In 1953 a Palestinian judge, Taqiuddin al-Nabhani, founded Hizb ut-Tahrir, or Party of Liberation, as he believed that the Muslim Brotherhood was not radical enough to cope with growing Western and Israeli power in the region. According to Palestinian intellectual Abdullah Azzam, "If the enemy has entered Muslim lands, the jihad becomes an individual obligation," linking jihad (see below) as a means to restore lost Muslim lands.[77]

Hizb ut-Tahrir beliefs emphasize that the problems of the Muslim *umma* date to the loss of both the Mamluk and Ottoman caliphate (the latter in 1924), and thus project a strategy to convert Muslims to the concept of a caliphate that would unite them in the face of threats from the world outside Islam.[78] Hizb ut-Tahrir is more active in Central Asia than in the Middle East, and numerous Arab governments and Turkey have banned the movement. While its message has been used by others (including al-Qaeda), other Islamists widely reject it, preferring to focus attention on more modern problems.

Islam as a Reactive Force

The reaction to the Islamic revolution in Iran surprised observers in the West (and elsewhere), and particularly in the academic world. Academic models of revolution stressed leadership by the "modernizers" like Nasser or Kwame Nkrumah of Ghana, who offered their own vision of a postcolonial society. However, as Benard and Khalilzad note, such models were too simplistic, failing to understand the political attractiveness of a religion that emphasizes opposition to illegitimate authority.[79] Islam emphasizes a purity of rule as well as spirit, and Islamic reformers find a powerful message in its humility and its calls to not only Islamic leaders but also the Islamic faithful in general to take responsibility for combating evil. The world outside the Islamic community became a world of temptation, filled with alcohol, sexuality, and an obsession with the material over the spiritual. For its protectors who see the world this way, the purpose of Islam is not to spread the faith to those who do not have it (because only God can determine who should be a Muslim), but rather to protect the Islamic community from inducements from outside the *umma*. For reactive Islam, though, members of the *umma* do have a responsibility for policing conformity with what they believe is proper Islamic conduct, thus they believe in the right of *takfir*, the obligation to excommunicate Muslims from the *umma* for behaviors and beliefs that counter what the reactivists hold proper.

The difficulty of any reactive movement is that it rarely has anything positive to offer in place of what it opposes. Islamists are able to organize opposition but few alternatives. Doran notes that "apart from insisting on the implementation of the Sharia, demanding social justice, and turning the umma into the only legitimate political community, radical Salafis have precious little to offer in response to the mundane problems that people and governments face in the modern world."[80]

The Perception of External Threat

Islam is the newest of the three monotheistic religions (although it is over 1,400 years old), and Muslims feel a challenge from the other established religions, particularly Christianity and Judaism. Early Muslims believed that the established religions would not tolerate a competitor for the faithful. This was one reason why Muslim armies spread into areas where Christians, Jews, pagans, and Persian Sassanians held sway. That campaign began in 632 CE and lasted for a century, bringing much of the known world under Islamic control. That drive, and others that followed (the Ottoman campaigns into central Europe in the sixteenth and seventeen centuries, for example), raised the specter that the Islamic community was bent on spreading Islam by force into the non-Islamic world, a concern that remains today. Bernard Lewis, in commenting on the Ayatollah Khomeini's denunciation of the United States as the Great Satan, said, "America was by then perceived—rightly— as the leader of what we like to call 'the free world.' Then, as in the past, this world of unbelievers was seen as the only serious force rivaling and preventing the divinely ordained spread and triumph of Islam."[81] In the modern era, many Muslims still express fear that the Islamic world remains under siege from the outside world, especially the so-called Christian world. That assault is not simply physical and political but also cultural. It is the things that corrupt a conservative belief system—alcohol, unveiled women, slot machines, and the emphasis of the material over the spiritual. Muslims view the West as the source of not only the temptations themselves, but also the political and economic power to spread them through the Muslim world.

The Nature of Jihad

The jihad aspect of Islam is one of its more controversial characteristics. The question is about the purpose and essence of jihad: is it to spread Islam to nonbelievers, eliminate all unbelievers, or defend Islam from its enemies? Is it against apostasy, or is it primarily concerned with the internal human struggle against evil? The answer is all of these, though scholars disagree about the validity of the latter goal. The Quran calls for a literal struggle by Muslims against nonbelievers, and certain hadiths call for the propagation of Islam through combat.[82] It can also mean striving for excellence,[83] and in one Arab-English dictionary, it translates to "fight, battle, holy war (against the infidels) as a religious duty."[84] The earliest calls for jihad came after the death of the Prophet, when some Muslim converts left the faith to return to paganism, and the Muslim armies under Abu Bakr swept into these apostates' homelands. John Esposito casts the word contextually, "Muslims are enjoined to struggle (jihad) to implement their belief, to lead a good life, to defend religion, to contribute to the development of a just Islamic society throughout the world."[85] "To lead the good life" is sometimes referred to as the "greater jihad" and means that the most important jihad for Muslims is the resistance of personal temptation. David Cook argues, though, that this definition is bereft of support in Islamic thought except in some Sufi traditions, and that jihad is warfare against the enemies of Islam, authorized by a Muslim who had the legitimate right to authorize jihad.[86]

The defensive nature of jihad has its origins in the Quran, which states, "Fight in the cause of Allah those who fight you. . . and fight them on until there is no more tumult or oppression."[87] However, does this passage (and others like it) call for a defensive struggle against the enemies of Islam? Are the enemies of Islam those who actually attack the Islamic community, or those who might attack it? Some suggest that it sanctifies an aggressive holy war to spread Islam, and that the Prophet and his followers started such wars to spread Islam across much of the known world by the early eighth century.[88] The Quran provides a different context. In Sura 8:39 it calls for Muslims to "fight. . . till there is no fitna and the religion is God's entirely," where *fitna* describes either infidelity or polytheism but not other religions.[89] However, the Arab Muslim militaries that swept into the Byzantine world in the seventh century did not force conversions of Christians and Jews once they came under Islamic rule. Both goals may lie at the root of early Islamic expansion. The conquest of Syria included the religious goal of conquering Jerusalem and Hebron, which is location of the tomb of Abraham (Ibrahim). However, early Muslim leaders also understood the commercial value of Syria with its trade routes.[90] These leaders also wanted to convert the nomadic tribes in Syria to Islam before the Christian Byzantines could recruit them to build a coalition of tribes against the Muslims to the south.[91] Later, when the Muslim armies swept across the Straits of Gibraltar into Spain and then across the Pyrenees into central France, the objective was again believed by Europeans of the time (and since) to have been an effort to spread Islam into Europe by force. However, as Cardini notes, "The Muslim commander Abd ar-Rahmen wanted. . . to plunder Saint-Martin, the national sanctuary of the Franks. It was probably never his intention to proceed any further, and he did not have the military might to do so."[92] Should it be surprising that Muslims might have the same objective for conquest as any other conqueror: plunder? Plunder, after all, in the days before income taxes, was a major source of income to maintain the empire. Muslims could be as crassly materialistic as other leaders of the time, even as they might use religious passion as a cover.

The question also arises as to who may call for jihad. Was it legitimate for a respected Islamic jurist or warrior to call for jihad, for example? Could someone like Osama bin Laden demand jihad from all Muslims against Americans, as he did prior to the terrorist attack against the United States on September 11, 2001? Saudi

Arabian scholar Muhammad al-Salem says not. "This is not about jihad," he states, referring to bin Laden's declaration. "Nobody has the right to declare war. It is done through the leadership."[93] Hizbollah leader Sheik Muhammad Hussein Fadlallah echoes that sentiment, claiming that the September 11 attacks were against Sharia law, and that the attackers were not martyrs as bin Laden claimed, but "merely suicides" because they killed innocent civilians. He accused bin Laden of relying on "personal psychological needs" rather than on Quranic texts.[94] Other Islamist critics of the global (or "far") jihad of bin Laden include ranking members of al-Jama al-Islamiyya, like Karam Zuhdi and Mohammed Essam Derbala, who criticize the September 11 attacks as violating Islamic prohibitions on killing civilians as well as strengthening the hand of the United States and other Western powers as they increased their presence in the Islamic world after the al-Qaeda attacks.[95]

Martyrdom

Martyrdom *(shahid)* status in Islam is normally accorded to those who die in the defense of Islam, in battle, or through individual actions. Martyrdom brings the reward of an immediate journey to Paradise and, in some Islamic traditions, marriage to maidens, though, as Bonner notes, such a privilege is accorded to all righteous Muslims and not just those who die in battle or take their lives in defense of Islam.[96] The martyrdom tradition is particularly significant for the Shiites, who venerate Ali and his son Hussein who died in defense of the Shiite claim to succeed the Prophet.

Some Islamists link Islam to the concept of martyrdom, or choosing actions likely to take the life of the martyr in the name of defending Islam from its enemies. Those who choose martyrdom through acts likely or certain to cause their death believe that Allah actually made the choice, and that the result of martyrdom is immediate passage to Paradise without judgment. Some Islamists argue that martyrdom is not suicide, since Islam prohibits the act, but rather consider it a weapon against a stronger opponent.[97] Others argue that Muhammad used the term *shahid* in a way closer to the Christian concept of "confessor," and that it was later Islamic interpreters who provided the contextual identity of death by choice in battle.[98] There are few Quranic references to martyrdom, but some that are used include, "And some people sell themselves for the sake of Allah's favor," or "Indeed you will find them (evil-doers) of all people the most attached to life," both from Sura 2 but nowhere in the Quran are Muslims directed to kill themselves to defend Islam.[99]

Islamic Reformation

Islamic reformation emphasizes moderation, toleration, and adaptation to modernity.[100] For example, Muhammad Shahrur argues that for too long conservative religious jurists have shackled the development of Islam, and that Islam must grow beyond adherence to the old ways and practices.[101] Reform, or "liberal," Islam emphasizes limited government and individual rights, resembling in many ways classical

European liberalism.[102] Its roots took hold in Egypt, where scholars and writers like Muhammad al-Ghazzaly, Fahmy Huwaidy, and Kamal Abul Madg critiqued the ideas of the militant Islamists. They noted that their embrace of hadiths was inconsistent with the more tolerant passages in the Quran, thus permitting wrongful interpretation by militant opportunists. Instead, the "new Islamists embrace the importance of *ijtihad* and the equality of peoples, criticizing the unequal treatment of women (and Shi'a by some radical Salafiyyists)."[103] Iranian thinker Abdol Karim Soroush criticizes the *ulama* for developing ideological positions outside of the Quran to justify their power.[104] Tunisian leader Habib Bourguiba represented reformist Islam, and his emphasis on *ijtihad* allowed him to interpret Islam as favorable to Tunisian modernity.[105] This "reformation" may grow as more Muslims move up the education ladder, and the ability of local Islamic leaders to control information wanes in the face of the information age. However, Muslims who discuss Islamic reformation run the risk of being labeled apostates for suggesting an alteration of standard interpretations of the Quran and the life of the Prophet by their more conservative peers.

For some scholars, democratization offers the prospect that open political systems will attempt to accommodate religious-based politics with secular movements, often as a part of common interest coalition building. The expectation is that religious movements will moderate their positions when sharing political space with actors whose agendas differ from their own. The calculus is that leaders and followers of religious movements would rather be in the political tent, even if the payments for such inclusion are smaller because of compromise and minority position, than to be outside and excluded altogether. The evidence does not entirely support inclusion expectations in the Middle East, however. Clark found that the Jordanian Islamist Action Front (IAF) refused to compromise in its coalition with the Higher Committee for the Coordination of National Opposition Parties on issues involving women that the IAF claimed were against religious rulings.[106] Schwedler finds that the IAF did moderate on a broader set of issues, while the Yemeni Islamist Islah Party retained it positions without much moderation, though this may have reflected the personal position of its leaders as much as it did Islah followers.[107] Given that Islah did poorly in the 2006 Yemeni elections when the ruling General People's Congress coopted some Islah issues, Islah's future may not include further participation in electoral politics.[108] By contrast, the moderate Islamist Adalet ve Kalkynma Partisi (Justice and Development, or AKP) has moderated its stance as the dominant party in Turkish politics, following in part on the lessons of the Refah Partisi (Welfare Party), which the military outlawed in 1998 because it did not moderate enough for its political tastes. Turkey also has a tradition of political compromise, which several military coups have enhanced.

Islam and Democracy

Islam, as the major religion in the Middle East, clearly affects political practice there. Some argue that Islamic practices and beliefs sanction democracy, while others claim that Islam is fundamentally antidemocratic.

Democracy emphasizes collective decisionmaking, the rule of law, and the accountability of leaders to the polity. The earliest versions of Islamic practice emphasized consultation *(shura)* within the *umma* for significant decisions like choice of leadership. The Quran contains numerous references to the desirability of democracy and participation by the *umma*.[109]

There is evidence of early democratic practices within Islam. Within the centralized rule of the tribe, consultation with elders was a part of tribal routine. The elders would meet and discuss a variety of issues in an effort to reach consensus over how to address them. As urbanization grew in the Arab world, the practice, known as the *majlis* or *shura* tradition, continued. Today the *majlis* continues, particularly in the Persian Gulf, as a way to connect ruler and ruled. Provincial governors in Saudi Arabia, city mayors, and national government ministers all hold *majlis* on a regular basis, and citizens come to petition them for favors or redress of a grievance. In some Arab countries, the *majlis* tradition forms a kind of democracy that connects citizens to their rulers more directly than might be the case in a parliamentary democracy. However, not all agree that the *majlis* or *shura* tradition means that Islam is inherently democratic. The Islamic modernist scholar Mohamed Talbi claims that the *shura* tradition is pre-Islamic, and that certain ethical principles that are both Islamic and universal are what actually connect Islam to democracy.[110]

Tunisian Islamist thinker Rachid Ghannouchi argues that the roots of democracy lie in medieval Europe, which in turn got its influence from earlier Islamic civilizations. Ghannouchi also argues that suspending democracy in Islamic societies would only give rise to radical and ultimately unstable politics.[111] Turkish Islamist leader Recep Erdoğan, who became Turkey's prime minister in 2002, stated that Islam is not an obstacle for democracy. Democracy includes Turks who are devout and those who are not.[112] Finally, a comparison of Christian and Muslim populations on the World Values survey suggested that both Christians and Muslims hold democracy to be highly desirable as a political system, though they differ on social values such as abortion, gender equality, and gay rights.[113]

One interpretation of Islam is that it is inherently undemocratic because the source of laws is the Quran, and the duty of good Muslims is to obey them rather than to debate them. The ruler in a classic Islamic polity is obligated to demonstrate fidelity to God's wishes as revealed in the Quran and to uphold the Sharia, or religious law. Such commitments constitute authority to rule rather than popular sovereignty.[114] As a liberal member of the Kuwaiti parliament asked as his legislature debated a motion to adopt the Sharia as Kuwait's legal code, "How can you be a democrat and follow a fatwa?"[115] Algerian Islamist Ali Belhaj views democracy as a contrived instrument placing popular will above the cohesion of the *ulama*.[116] There is also the weight of tradition in many Muslim countries, where during the Islamic empires the *ulama* generally supported authoritarian rule, thus placing the religious establishment in the position of defenders of authoritarian rule.[117] Islam does not recognize the principle of separation of church and state, which some argue is almost mandatory to prevent the hijacking of democratic processes by religious leaders who argue that the ultimate source of political authority is God, not the people.

However, as Stepan observes, half of the world's Muslims live in partial or complete democracies, in such places as Pakistan, Turkey, and Indonesia, but "there are no democracies in the Islamic countries of the Arab world."[118] Thus the real barrier to democracy may be Arab culture rather than Islam. In the Arab world, tribal traditions emphasize the role of chiefs and other elders as leaders who rule through experience and wisdom, rather than being elected by the tribe. Such roles in some cases remain necessary because of the harsh challenges of the desert environment and the need to draw on the wisdom of elders without question.

The *majlis* heritage may explain the limits to democracy in the Gulf states, but it does not necessarily extend to the rest of the Arab world. Here traditional thinking about Islam and leadership may also play a role in reinforcing current beliefs in the value of authoritarian rule. As Charles Butterworth notes, most students in Arab countries from elementary schools to universities study formal principles of the state that take their meaning from the Quran. Students of politics read the works of Alfarabi or Averroes (ibn Rushd), or Nizam al-Mulk, who, in contrast to some Western thinkers like Rousseau or Locke, espouse a belief that few citizens are capable of good governance, and that the universe of God must be understood and not simply overcome.[119] Bernard Lewis reinforces the "reluctance to democratize" argument by noting that the few Islamic rulers to attempt some type of constitutional government did so in "not so much imitation as propitiation, not of their own subjects but of the European powers whose political pressure they feared and whose financial support they wanted."[120] However, to suggest that this adoption of democratic standards was blind imitation imposed by fear is to downplay the reality that some of these same European powers failed to create the prerequisites for democracy in the Middle East in the first place.

Islam and Pluralism

Islamic tradition often limits political participation in predominately Islamic countries to Muslims. That tradition places great importance on the notion of the *umma* as a distinct and special entity. The *umma* received preferential treatment by Islamic leaders, usually at the expense of other religious communities.[121] Yet there is evidence of tolerance and even a desire for the well-being of other religious groups by Muslims. Abdulaziz Sachedina argues that the Quran refers to the need for a pluralist society, to include believers and nonbelievers alike. The problem, he argues, is that Muslim jurists regarded pluralism as a source of instability to the Islamic order, despite the teachings of the Quran.[122] The Fatimid Caliph al-Hafiz wrote in 1136, "We believe that we should spread wide the mantle of justice and benevolence and embrace the different religious communities with mercy and compassion. Measure to improve conditions should include Muslims and non-Muslims alike, who should be provided everything they might hope for in the way of peace and security."[123] Centuries later, Abdou Filali-Ansary argued for a liberal pluralist vision of Islam, stating, "Islam, properly understood, is not a system of social and political regulation [that] frees up space for cultures and nations in the modern sense of these words to lay the foundations of collective identity. . . and opens the way to a full respect for civic spheres in which Muslims can coexist as equal citizens with non-Muslims."[124] Mahdi, interpreting the work of Islamic philosopher al-Farabi, claims that "democracy is a composite regime: various groups, aiming at the ends characterizing the other regimes, exist side by side and pursue different ways of life. . . and they are free to fulfill their distinct aims independently or in cooperation with others."[125] Not all Muslim scholars hold such views. Ibn Hazm has a much more restricted position that non-Muslim *dhimmi* (meaning roughly "protected status") could have such status only if they recognized the status of the Prophet for the Arabs and honored him, while other writers emphasize the secondary status of the *dhimmi* and, for example, prohibit Muslims from consuming meat slaughtered by *dhimmi*.[126]

Jews living in predominately Islamic areas were traditionally subject to certain restrictions, such as paying a tax (or *jizya*) to the Muslim community, or in their dress or in the buildings they constructed. Some Islamic dynasties, such as the Almohads in Morocco or the Safavids in Persia, were particularly harsh in their treatment of Jews. However, it is also true that Jews were often integrated into Islamic communities, even serving as court physicians and advisers to Islamic courts.[127]

Islam is the majority religion in the Middle East, but it is not the only one. Israel is around 80 percent Jewish, and Lebanon has a large number of Christians. Around 12 percent of Syria's population is Christian. Iran has a small population of Zoroastrianians, whose beliefs predate Islam.

JUDAISM IN THE MIDDLE EAST

Of the world's three monotheistic religions, Judaism is the oldest. It dates to the time when tradition holds that Abraham left the city of Ur in modern Iraq at God's command for the Promised Land, which was to be the home of the Jewish people. However, famine drove them to Egypt, where they multiplied until driven out. That same tradition holds that the Jews, led by Moses, received the Ten Commandments on their journey of return to the Promised Land, and entered it after the death of Moses. Under Joshua, they drove out the Canaanites in retaliation for Canaanite attacks against the Jews as they tried earlier to enter Israel. Israel thus became a theocracy as well as a home for the Jews, and the tradition of political Judaism grew from that time.

As in Islam, the Jewish religion has a few core beliefs, and numerous differing interpretations of faith. The Thirteen Articles of Faith capture the essence of Jewish belief, which include the following beliefs: there is only one God; God has no physical shape or form; there have been no other gods before God; humankind must worship God directly; the prophets were sent by God; God gave the Law of Moses to the Jewish people; good is rewarded and evil is punished; God is supreme ruler of the world; there will be a Messiah and one must never cease to believe in his eventual coming; the coming of the Messiah will bring about a resurrection of the dead.[128]

Jewish Law

Jewish law, or Halacha, stems from the five books of Moses, which became the Torah, and the Talmud, which is an interpretation of Jewish history by early rabbis (collected around 200 CE). The nature of the Torah in particular divides Orthodox from Reform Judaism, as noted below.

As in Islam, a large majority of Jews follow ritualistic practices, including observation of the Sabbath (which starts on Friday at sundown and continues to sundown on Saturday), and other religious holy days (including Passover and Rosh Hashanah, the most important). Other practices include male circumcision, a prohibition against eating certain foods (pork, for one, as in Islam), and taboos regarding such things as death, menstruation, sex, and childbirth.[129] In modern times, Jews differ considerably on actual practice, which are more common among Conservative Jews than Reform (see below).

Jewish Sects

Before around 1700 CE, there were few differences in the beliefs and practices of Judaism, and local customs and cultures often shaped such practices. However, when exposed to the currents of change in eighteenth-century Europe, Jews there began to separate into divisions. There are three such divisions common to Judaism: Orthodox, Conservative, and Reform.

Orthodoxy is distinguished by its emphasis on orthopraxy, or faithful adherence to the belief that both the Torah and the oral law (or Mishnah) are divinely inspired and fully authoritative.[130] Orthodoxy also requires adherence to the code of Shulhan Arukh, demanding daily religious observance. Those who hold Orthodox views see themselves as the only true followers of the Jewish faith and traditions. They believe that God issued the Torah, and that it must thus be accepted literally.

Within the Orthodox tradition, there are several subdivisions. The Modern Orthodox largely adopt the position that they can coexist with others who are not like-minded while at the same time maintaining observance of Jewish law in their daily lives. In Israel, they are often referred to as observant Jews, to distinguish them from the ultra-Orthodox, who believe that the Orthodox community must live separately from those not of their faith. They have built settlements in the Occupied Territories, or live in separate neighborhoods in Israel proper, such as Mea Shearim in Jerusalem. The ultra-Orthodox themselves are subdivided into several groups, with most identifying with the Hasidism.

The Hasidim draw from the teachings of the Ukrainian folk preacher Israel ben-Eliezer Baal Shem Tov, known often by his acronym Besht, who gathered a flock of followers around 1735 CE. The Hasidic ideal, for who follow it, was panentheism: God is the ultimate and only reality; the world is illusory.[131] Fundamental to Hasidic practice is the doctrine of the *tsaddik*, a channel through which all godly grace flows, leading to a permanent and uninterrupted thought of God in all that one does. Such an accomplishment is approachable by the close study of a rebbe, or communal leader. Some of these leaders came close to associating Hasidism with mysticism and miracles, though other Hasidic leaders and non-Hasidic Jews denounced such teachings. Hasidic Jews set aside much time for religious study, and consequently the Hasidim have gained an exemption from working and from the military draft.[132] For some Hasidic interpreters, religious study is an essential ingredient for political leadership. As Rabbi Yehoshua Shapira put it in a speech denouncing Ariel Sharon's planned Gaza disengagement (see Chapter 14), "I do not believe in a leader who does not come from the *beit midrash* (religious study house). The spirit can come only from the beit midrash."[133]

In Hasidic practice, the Yiddish language is widely spoken, and even the dress is distinctive. Hasidic men wear the wide-brimmed fur hat (with 13 sable tails representing the 13 qualities of Divine Mercy), while letting their hair drop into side locks in the old Polish style. Hasidic women dress in traditional modest clothing. The Hasidim believe in the importance of living in one's own community, and thus reserve neighborhoods in towns and cities that are exclusive to them. Signs posted at the entrance to such neighborhoods warn immodestly dressed visitors not to enter, and caution against driving vehicles there on the Sabbath.

Jewish Mysticism

As in Islam, there is a Jewish mystical tradition, often epitomized by the Kabbalah school, which Rabbi Yitzhak Kadouri led until his death in January 2006. His visions reportedly paved the way for the choice of Moshe Katsav as Israeli president in 2000 as well as Israeli rejection of a deal with Syria to return the Golan (see Chapter 14). Kabbalah emphasizes the importance of revelation to particular individuals of the specific meanings of ancient Jewish texts, giving rise to the importance of such figures as Kadouri.

Judaism and Politics

Like all other religions, Judaism provides political lessons from its recorded writs. Judaism was the early basis for Israeli statehood, though the role of Judaism in modern Israel remains a subject of intense debate. Two Jewish religious traditions, liberty and equality, have roots in the Torah and in prophets such as Amos, Micah, and Isaiah.[134] Other lessons flow from the history of Judaism and particularly from its early history.

Sicherman argues that Judaism is the covenant between God and the people of Israel, where the Israelis are promised security and prosperity in exchange for fidelity to the commandments of God.[135] This belief is the major tenet behind the Zionist commitment to the Promised Land (see Chapter 14) and to Jerusalem in particular, which still inspires arguments about its place in the founding of Judaism.[136] However, God not only bestows title to land but can also take it away for immoral behavior, as in the case of the Canaanites, who lost title to the land that became Israel, according to Jewish interpretation, when they polluted it with idolatry.[137] Moreover, the Torah eschews pacifism and instead commands preemptive action against and death for those who kill a member of the Jewish faith.[138] For Jews who believe in a literal interpretation of the Torah, compromise with anyone outside the community of the Chosen People is difficult to accept. Some conservative strains, particularly those influenced by the ideas of Rabbi Avraham Yitzhak Kook and his son Zvi Yehuda Kook, claim that any compromise over land occupied by Jews is violation of Jewish sacred writ. Followers of the Kook interpretations were in the vanguard of protests against the evacuation of Gaza in 2005.[139] For others, though, relations with neighbors are to be respectful, and violating a treaty is tantamount to profaning God's name.[140]

Prime Minister David Ben Gurion understood that interreligious strife could weaken Israel, and thus in June 1947 he wrote a letter outlining the policy that Israel follows today with respect to Jewish religious observance. It includes the following provisions: The Jewish Sabbath, Saturday, is the official day of rest. No national public transportation is run on the Sabbath. The religious school system is funded by the state. Rabbinical courts apply the Halacha (religious law) to personal matters, such as marriage and divorce.

The Law of Return, passed by the Knesset in 1950, was supplanted by a new law allowing any person claiming to be a Jew to immigrate to Israel and become a citizen on the basis or his or her Jewishness. So while Israeli nationality could be granted to non-Jews (as a result of the Nationality Law of 1952 which granted Israeli citizenship to those living in Israel in 1948, including Muslims and Christians), only Jews could become new citizens of Israel. However, a sharp debate developed inside Israel over Jewish identity, particularly over sects that do not accept rabbinical law, or groups like the Ethiopian and Somalian Falasha Jews, whose practice of Judaism differs from mainstream customs. It continues to be an issue for the Orthodox in particular, who invalidate any conversion to Judaism by Reform or Conservative congregations because they do not use Jewish law as the sole means of conversion.

CHRISTIANITY IN THE MIDDLE EAST

The events in the life of Christ took place by tradition in the Middle East, but Christian thinkers and leaders shaped Christian thought, practice, and authority largely in Europe, with the exception of the Orthodox Church in Asia Minor. This is one of the reasons why Christians who live in the present Middle East remain largely outside of mainstream Christianity. The three main branches of Christianity worldwide—Catholic, Eastern Orthodox, and Protestant—have relatively few adherents in the Middle East, and Christianity itself is a minority religion there. The largest Christian sects in the Middle East include the Copts of Egypt, the Maronites, the Nestorians, and the Chaldeans.

The Coptic Faith

The Coptic Church dates back to the teachings of St. Mark in the first century CE.[141] St. Mark arrived in Alexandria, Egypt, where he preached and wrote until 68 CE, when the Romans crucified him for his beliefs. The Copts have contributed much to Christianity, including the Nicene Creed (authored by Coptic Pope Athanasius), the oldest catechetical school in the world (in Alexandria), and monasticism (first practiced by Copts). However, other Christian sects accused the Copts (wrongfully, it turned out) of believing in monophysitism.[142] This view, in contrast to the belief in the dual nature of Christ (equally human and equally divine) was the focus of discussion at the Council of Chalcedon, held in 451 near Constantinople. At Chalcedon, the accusations of monophysitic belief against the Copts engendered a break from both the Catholic and Orthodox Churches that exists to this day. The Copts disdain the charge of monophysitism, claiming that either their Pope Dioscurus failed to convince the Council, or that the Council wanted to punish the Copts for believing in the separation of church and state. Perhaps confusion arose from their claim that while the perfection of Christ's humanity and the perfection of his divinity were separate, both are united in what Copts refer to as "the nature of the incarnate word," as preached by St. Cyril of Alexandria.

The Copts suffered persecution in Egypt after Chalcedon by Christians until Islamic conquerors arrived in 641 CE. After that, they found themselves coexisting with their Islamic rulers, sometimes under an uneasy but peaceful truce, and sometimes under attack. Chapter 10 covers their history in Egypt.

The Maronite Faith

Around 410 CE a group in Syria formed a Christian religious order consecrating the memory of St. Maron (or Maro), a hermit monk known for his life of prayer. Forced to accept monophysitism under Byzantine Emperor Heraclius in an effort to unite all Middle Eastern Christians against the Islamic invaders, the Maronite leaders claimed at the Council of Chalcedon that their doctrine actually rejected monophysitism.

After Islam came to the eastern Mediterranean in 636, the Maronites began to leave Syria for the mountainous area of Lebanon, and the first Maronite church began there in 749. The mountains of Lebanon provided sanctuary for the Maronites until the coming of the Crusaders, whom the Maronites eagerly welcomed. That contact with the Catholic Crusaders began to link the Maronites to the Church, and in 1215, the Maronite patriarch visited Rome and participated in an Ecumenical Council. In 1584 Pope Gregory XIII founded the Maronite College in Rome, further strengthening ties to Catholicism. While the Ottomans restricted contact between the Maronites in Lebanon and Catholic Rome, France made Lebanon a protectorate under the guise of assisting fellow Catholics. Despite such ties, Maronites do have some independent traditions, such as selecting their own patriarch, allowing some clergy to marry, and conducting the liturgy in the Syriac language.

Other Christian Denominations in the Middle East

There are small groups of Nestorian Christians in the Arab world and in Iran. They were inspired by Nestorius, once the patriarch of Constantinople, then banished to the Libyan desert after the Council of Ephesus in 431. Iraq has a small population of Chaldeans (a group once affiliated with the Nestorians but separated in the sixteenth century, when Catholic Pope Eugene II declared their affiliation with Catholicism).

Christianity and Politics in the Middle East

Some charismatic Christians have attempted to gain converts from Israel's Jewish population, and the Israeli government has deported several Christian ministers found to be engaged in active conversions. However, other evangelical Christians outside of Israel have become strong supporters of Israel, particularly since the 1967 conquest of the holy sites in Jerusalem. Some believe that the temple must be rebuilt on its purported original site on the Temple Mount (Haram al-Sharif) in order to initiate the final battle of Armageddon and the thousand-year reign of Christ on earth.[143] If such beliefs inspire an effort to rebuild the ancient Jewish temple, the reaction in the Islamic world will be fierce, since the old Temple stood on ground now occupied by the Dome of the Rock and Al-Aqsa Mosque.

ZOROASTRIANISM

This is an ancient religion whose origins are uncertain. The name comes from its founder, Zarathushtra, or Zoroaster, who lived sometime between 1000 and 600 BCE, possibly in India. The sacred text of Zoroastrianism, the Avesta, refers to one god and a concept of dualism that describes two universes, one good and one evil. The religion took root in Persia, and its followers managed to coexist with the Muslims when they arrived, since Muslims first considered Zoroastrianism a monotheistic religion. Later Zoroastrian practices, however, shifted to polytheistic traditions. Its followers remain in Iran, but they have faced persecution for centuries, and now make up less than 1 percent of the Iranian population.

YAZIDISM

This is a small religion with perhaps not more than 100,000 followers scattered in rural parts of Iraq (where the majority live), Syria, and Iran. Most Yazidi are ethnic Kurds. The Yazidi faith appears to draw from Islam, Judaism, Nestorian Christianity, and Zoroastrianism for its doctrine, though the Yazidi understanding of God is considerably different from those religions. The Yazidi worship Malak Taus, who is believed to rule the universe in the form of a peacock angel, and pay homage to Sheikh Adi, a twelfth-century mystic. Because the Yazidi do not believe in sin and argue that the devil was forgiven and has repented, they are sometimes accused erroneously of devil worship. Followers of the 4,000-year-old religion tend to live in isolated villages, partly to avoid clashes with Muslims who regard them as infidels. In August 2007, over 250 Yazidis died in the Iraqi town of Qahataniya at the hands of suspected al-Qaeda suicide bombers.

Religion plays a significant role in Middle Eastern and North African politics, but its impact must be understood in conjunction with other sources of influence.

Along with the legacy of history, religion combines with economic factors to shape political beliefs, practices, and preferences. The next chapter covers the connection between Middle Eastern politics and the economics of the region.

SUGGESTED READINGS

Ajami, Fouad. *The Vanished Imam: Musa Sadr and the Shiia of Lebanon.* Ithaca, NY: Cornell University Press, 1986.

Appleby, R. Scott, ed. *Spokesman for the Despised: Fundamentalist Leaders of the Middle East.* Chicago: University of Chicago Press, 1997.

Baker, Raymond William. *Sadat and After: Struggles for Egypt's Political Soul.* Cambridge, MA: Harvard University Press, 1990.

_____. *Islam Without Fear.* Cambridge, MA: Harvard University Press, 2003.

Betts, Robert Brenton. *The Druze.* New Haven, CT: Yale University Press, 1988.

Binder, Leonard. *Islamic Liberalism: A Critique of Development Ideas.* Chicago: University of Chicago Press, 1988.

Black, Antony. *The History of Islamic Political Thought.* New York: Routledge, 2001.

Bonner, Michael. *Jihad in Islamic History: Doctrines and Practice.* Princeton, NJ: Princeton University Press, 2006.

Brown, L. Carl. *Religion and the State: The Muslim Approach to Politics.* New York: Columbia University Press, 2000.

Bulliet, Richard W. *Islam: The View from the Edge.* New York: Columbia University Press, 1994.

Cook, David. *Understanding Jihad.* Berkeley: University of California Press, 2005.

Crone, Patricia. *God's Rule: Government and Islam.* New York: Columbia University Press, 2004.

Esposito, John L. *Islam: The Straight Path.* 3rd ed. New York: Oxford University Press, 2005.

_____. *The Islamic Threat: Myth or Reality?* New York: Oxford University Press, 1995.

Esposito, John L., and John O. Voll. *Makers of Contemporary Islam.* New York: Oxford University Press, 2001.

Gerges, Fawaz A. *The Far Enemy: Why Jihad Went Global.* Cambridge: Cambridge University Press, 2005.

Halm, Heinz. *Shi'ism.* 2nd ed. New York: Columbia University Press, 2004.

Hefner, Robert W., ed. *Remaking Muslim Politics: Pluralism, Constestation, Democratization.* Princeton, NJ: Princeton University Press, 2005.

Karsh, Efraim. *Islamic Imperialism: A History.* New Haven, CT: Yale University Press, 2006.

Kepel, Gilles. *Muslim Extremism in Egypt: The Prophet and the Pharaoh.* Berkeley: University of California Press, 1986.

_____. *Jihad: The Trail of Political Islam.* Cambridge, MA: Belknap, 2002.

_____. *The War for Muslim Minds.* Cambridge, MA: Belknap, 2004.

Lapidus, Ira M. *A History of Islamic Societies.* Cambridge: Cambridge University Press, 1988.

Lewis, Bernard. *The Jews of Islam.* Princeton, NJ: Princeton University Press, 1984.

_____. *What Went Wrong? Western Impact and Middle Eastern Response.* New York: Oxford University Press, 2003.

_____. *The Crisis of Islam: Holy War and Unholy Terror.* New York: Modern Library, 2003.

Majid, Anouar. *Freedom and Orthodoxy: Islam and Difference in the Post-Andalusian Age.* Stanford, CA: Stanford University Press, 2004.

Mayer, Ann Elizabeth. *Islam and Human Rights: Tradition and Politics.* Boulder, CO: Westview, 1991.

Momen, Moojan. *An Introduction to Shi'a Islam.* New Haven, CT: Yale University Press, 1985.

Munson, Henry. *Islam and Revolution in the Middle East.* New Haven, CT: Yale University Press, 1988.

Nasr, Vali. *The Shia Revival: How Conflicts Within Islam Will Shape the Future.* New York: Norton, 2006.

Norton, Augustus Richard. *Hezbollah: A Short History.* Princeton, NJ: Princeton University Press, 2007.

Piscatori, James P., ed. *Islamic Fundamentalism and the Gulf Crisis.* Chicago: University of Chicago Press, 1991.

Reuter, Christopher. *My Life as a Weapon: A Modern History of Suicide Bombing.* Princeton, NJ: Princeton University Press, 2004.

Roy, Olivier. *The Failure of Political Islam.* Cambridge, MA: Harvard University Press, 1994.

————. *Globalized Islam: The Search for a New Ummah.* New York: Columbia University Press, 2004.

Schwedler, Jillian. *Faith in Moderation: Islamist Parties in Jordan and Yemen.* Cambridge: Cambridge University Press, 2006.

Tibi, Bassam. *Islam Between Culture and Politics.* New York: Palgrave, 2001.

Tsafrir, Nurit. *The History of an Islamic School of Law: The Early Spread of Hanafism.* Cambridge, MA: Harvard University Press, 2004.

Voll, John O. *Islam: Continuity and Change in the Modern World.* 2nd ed. Syracuse, NY: Syracuse University Press, 1994.

Watt, William Montgomery. *Islamic Political Thought.* New York: Columbia University Press, 1998.

3

THE POLITICAL ECONOMY
OF THE MIDDLE EAST

IMAGES

They are sometimes called bazaars, but the Arabic term is "souq." The word means marketplace, but souqs are much more than marketplaces. They are the heart of the city and a magnet for settlers in rural areas. They also say a lot about economic and social health.

Sometimes souqs appear in the desert, with tables covered with goods tended by wizened old men or women—the shrewdest bargainers in the Arab world. The cold January wind whistles through the tents and across the tables, but the blowing sand seems to invigorate the bedouins as they wrap their burnooses tight around their faces. Tables are dotted with the things of the desert: brass coffee pots, shovels, tent rope. Potential buyers carefully inspect camels as they lie patiently in their hobbles. Buyer and seller strike deals only after numerous tiny cups of aromatic cardamom coffee are poured and drained. The pace is slow, the customers few, and the rewards slight. But the importance of the desert souq is that it allows customers and merchants to avoid what they would otherwise have to do: shop and sell in the cities, which are anathema to the bedouin.

Souqs are also found in city centers, usually in the oldest parts. In Damascus, the Hamediyya souq snakes through narrow lanes running off the main street. Goods are divided into categories; clothing, shoes, jewelry, spices, and meat so shoppers can quickly compare prices and quality. The intoxicating scent of spices—cumin, cinnamon, allspice, sumac—draws potential buyers from blocks away in the adjacent Mindat Pasha souq. One shop near Bab al-Chark holds an ancient sword crafted from Damascus steel, whose price escalates by thousands of dollars every few years. "It has cut off many heads," says the shop owner proudly. In Cairo, the Khan al-Khalili is a warren of alleys next to the old Hussein mosque, with thousands of tiny shops catering to tourists and natives alike. At Marrakech, much of the souq is outdoors in a huge plaza, where shoppers are entertained by dancing monkeys, snake charmers, and flute players from the nearby Atlas Mountains. A trek through the antique souq in Riyadh can lead through dusty lanes until it ends in a dark room filled with hundred-year-old muskets, decorated for desert warfare generations ago. Torched by the Iraqi invaders, the souq in Kuwait City lay in charred ruins, but the enterprising merchants still set up their displays each morning in front of their gutted shops. In Jerusalem's Arab Quarter, the souq was once a bustling place with meat hanging on hooks over the sidewalk, the call of vendors echoing through the narrow lanes, the heady aroma of grilled lamb, and dust blowing over the pushcarts heaped with green almonds fresh from the fields. Now it is clean and orderly, with the mounds of spices behind glass windows instead of in neat piles on the stone streets. Something has been lost in the process.

SOUQS ARE MORE THAN just places to sell things or magnets for tourists seeking something from the mysterious Orient. They are barometers that tell much about the economic—and thus the social and political—health of a country. When one merchant physically attacks another for luring a prospective customer out of his shop (as the author witnessed in Riyadh) or when merchants refuse to bargain because of existing heavy losses, it may be a sign that times are bad. When the governments sometimes took over foreign and wholesale trade, the merchants in the souqs suffered, and the economy grew more inefficient until the regime restored some autonomy to the souq shopkeepers. In Iran merchants lost hope in the shah's economic reforms, turned to Ayatollah Khomeini, lost hope in him too, and then turned to reformer and President Muhammad Khatami. The bazaar's ability to tilt the political balance was crucial to regime change in both cases.

Perhaps there are few places outside of the souq to understand better the Middle Eastern way of negotiating, of dealing with people. Arrangements between buyer and seller become cacophonous, with vigorous arm waving and passionate vocal inflections. The merchant offers another cup of coffee or tea, then more discussion, and after another hour, the deal is consummated. Both parties have moved only inches from their initial position. Americans, used to the quick trade or the purchase with no haggling, are amused and perhaps mystified by such interpersonal relations. However, they neglect to see it in political negotiations, where again time passes in negotiations that in the end produce a small compromise. Acquaintances strengthen and trust slowly builds. The logic of the souq is basic to Arab culture, and there are many things that outsiders (including Americans) can learn from it.

Political and economic issues are deeply interwoven in the Middle East, as they are elsewhere in the world. Political stability is partly a function of economic prosperity, or at least of rising economic expectations. Political democracies appear to develop best when integrated with market economies. By contrast, autocratic leaders often manipulate the resource distribution process to remain in power, and thus autocracies tend to feature corporatist or socialist ownership. The least accountable political systems often run the most inefficient economies (Cuba and North Korea, for example), and the leadership of such systems prefer to suppress public discontent over economic failure with often huge state security bureaucracies that in themselves cost the society resources that might otherwise be used to improve economic conditions.

Economic development issues are especially prevalent in the Middle East. The region lacks many of the resources necessary to build viable economic prosperity (adequate land, water, power, and mass education, to name only a few) and thus political systems face daunting challenges. There is evidence that resource scarcity created by growing population pressures is one source of political violence, and the Middle East is clearly one area where resource paucity is becoming worse.[1] The problem is compounded by many factors, including a colonial legacy that continues to shape the political economy of many Middle Eastern countries, high population growth, resource scarcity, and the oil economies of so-called rentier states that use the rent from resource transfer to inhibit political opposition and democratization.

THE ECONOMIC LEGACY

As noted in Chapter 1, most of the Middle East was once part of an empire or had the status of a European protectorate. In some cases, the colonial or protecting power used its favored Middle Eastern area to supply the mother country with raw material. In Egypt, the British built on Muhammad Ali's development of a cotton-based economy to export cotton to the looms of England. France used its North African colonies to supply it with food and fiber. Both the United States and Great Britain concentrated on the oil-rich Persian Gulf after World War II, supporting leaders who could deliver crude petroleum to large Western oil companies.

One consequence of European colonial economic policy was to thwart transition in Middle Eastern countries from producer to industrial and service economies, and delaying nation building because the colonial power (e.g., Britain) supplied both law and order, plus basic services. Moreover, local economic elites could not compete with foreign capital, so they either engaged in unproductive activities, such as land purchasing or usury, or entered the import-export business.[2] Once established, such patterns continued as family businesses were passed on over generations without much change. The European penetration of Middle Eastern economies reduced the power of the state (prevalent before the nineteenth century) and substituted an economic class structure, much of which remains today.[3] It was also the case that colonial and mandatory powers developed regions in the Middle East to support their own rather than local economies, often pushing the development of agriculture for European markets rather than establishing the groundwork for industrialization. Europeans frequently employed financial polices that left the newly independent Arab states bankrupt. As Gelvin argues in his study of Syria, "Decisions made by Britain and France pushed the Arab governments to the brink of insolvency and reduced its capacity to provide basic services. . . the already ailing economy of Faisali went into a slide from which it never recovered."[4]

There are other reasons as well why the Middle East did not move toward economic modernity. The region does not have many of the resources found in places like Western Europe, North America, or Japan, which industrialized rapidly in the nineteenth and twentieth centuries. It lacks coal, abundant wood, iron ore, adequate water supplies, and a mechanized agricultural sector that can spare labor for industrialization. Most Middle Eastern countries must struggle to mobilize water resources, with large collective waterworks required for even limited agriculture, making agriculture both expensive and relatively inefficient compared to countries where adequate rainfall waters fields without such effort.

Other factors also influence Middle Eastern economic development, though there is considerable debate about causal linkages. One is religion. David Landes argues that Islam is to blame for some of the Middle East's economic misfortunes because Muslims rejected the printing press (among other things) because it was a potential source of heresy. Thus, he states, the Islamic Middle East fell behind the Europeans because knowledge about things like technology could not be diffused.[5] Landes claims that culture in the Islamic Middle East "(1) does not generate an informed and capable workforce; (2) continues to mistrust or reject new techniques and ideas that come from the alien West (Christendom); and (3) does not respect such knowledge as members do manage to achieve."[6] He also argues that the systematic exclusion of women from workplaces and positions of responsibility in many Arab Muslim countries deprives those countries of a vital source of wealth.[7] Bernard Lewis makes similar arguments, noting the avoidance of such things as European language study or European scientific achievements in the early Islamic world.[8] Timur Kuran notes that "the relative openness of the West's public discourse created an engine of growth that the Islamic world, because of its expressive constraints, failed to develop."[9]

Such arguments suggest cause and effect without exploring alternative explanations or exceptions. To imply a lack of interest by Muslims in either Europe or the rest of the world ignores the reality that Muslims did travel and study other cultures during their long historical sweep. The great traveler ibn Battuta explored much of Asia in the early part of the fourteenth century, as did numerous Arab seafarers.[10] Considerable knowledge passed back and forth between Islamic Spain and the Christian part of Europe, though contact was also limited by centuries of conflict between Christians and Muslims in the Mediterranean and beyond.[11] During the nineteenth century, as Barakat observes, Arab and European economies integrated, and one consequence was "the gradual emergence of new classes, particularly a local bourgeoisie directly linked to the West and serving as the mediator between the local consumer and the European producers."[12] The evidence suggests that Islam was not nearly as much of a factor in limiting Middle Eastern economic growth as was the economic interests and power of European colonialism.

THE PROBLEMS OF
ECONOMIC GROWTH AND DEVELOPMENT

One of the most fundamental political goals of any society is economic prosperity for its citizens. Perhaps more fundamentally, societies minimally expect that economic conditions will not worsen and will grow to at least match the population growth rate, and hopefully improve over time.[13]

Not all countries in the Middle East count as developing countries, as some (the Gulf Arab countries, Turkey, and Israel) are developed in every sense of the term. However, a majority of Middle Eastern countries count as developing or less developed. Part of the difficulty is that, according to the United Nations, "there is no established convention for the designation of 'developed' and 'developing' countries or areas in the United Nations system. In common practice, Japan in Asia, Canada and the United States in northern America, Australia and New Zealand in Oceania and Europe are considered 'developed' regions or areas. In international trade statistics, the Southern African Customs Union is also treated as a developed region and Israel as a developed country; countries emerging from the former Yugoslavia are treated as developing countries; and countries of Eastern Europe and the former USSR countries in Europe are not included under either developed or developing regions."[14] Under this definition, only Israel qualifies as a developed nation, though the Gulf Cooperation Council (GCC) countries might also be developed. In general, though, most of the Middle East must be regarded as developing.

The economic structure of developing countries is often different from that in developed countries and some argue that it must change if developing countries are to enjoy positive sustainable growth.[15] However, the cost and time involved in constructing a development structure allowing a chance to compete with more developed regions is often beyond the means of developing countries. This makes it difficult for them to compete with the advanced countries, even in their own home markets. Consequently some developing countries adopt structuralist approaches, including import-substitution industrialization (ISI), to increase their own capability. The purpose is to invest rapidly in industrial capacity to free these developing countries from costly imports of manufactured goods. In Latin America, for example, ISI was replaced with export-led growth efforts and opening to international markets.[16]

The Burden of Low Income

The Middle East represents extremes of wealth and poverty, as measured in per capita income. The GDP per capita income for the United Arab Emirates in 2006 was $45,200; for Yemen it was $900. By comparison, the GDP per capita for the United States in the same year was $41,600. For a majority of Arab Middle Eastern countries, the GDP per capita lies between $2,000 and $4,000, with Israel at $25,000. The average annual income in Muslim countries was only half the world average, and some developing countries in other parts of the world (Singapore, Taiwan, and South Korea, for example) have advanced more rapidly than have the Arab and Persian countries in the Middle East. So have the wealthy members of the Organization for Economic Cooperation and Development (OECD). The average Arab per capita income was 21.3 percent of the average OECD citizen in 1975, and that percentage fell to 13.9 percent by 1998. Only Egypt, Jordan, and Tunisia moved slightly closer to the OECD average, while all other Arab countries moved farther away from it.[17] Most telling of all is the fact that the sum total of all Arab countries stood at $531.2 billion in 1999, less than that of a single European country—Spain—at $595.5 billion.[18] By 2007 Arab world GDP was $1.6 trillion, which exceeded Spain but fell below Italy ($1.67 trillion).

Civil Wars and Development

One of the most debilitating conditions for any nation is civil war, which can destroy decades if not centuries of economic progress. Civil wars, when they become widespread, cause a regime under internal challenge to mobilize considerable resources to stay in power, thus depriving its citizens of growth potential. Civil wars also wreak havoc within poor countrys, which, as Collier indicates, are much more likely to have civil wars than rich countries, further compounding their misery.[19] A number of Middle Eastern countries have suffered from civil war, including Yemen and Lebanon. There appears to be a growing civil war in Palestine between Hamas and Fatah (see Chapter 16), and Iraq is deep in the throes of a civil war that has contributed to its status as one of the most economically devastated countries in the Middle East.

The Population Challenge

One obvious reason for economic development challenges in the region is high population growth rates. Until recently the Middle East had one of the highest population growth rates in the world. The world average population growth rate is 1.1 percent; in Japan, it is 0.11 percent, in Austria 0.22 percent, and in the United States, 0.92 percent. Some Middle Eastern countries have population growth rates that top those of China or India, at 0.6 and 1.47 percent.[20] Saudi Arabia, by contrast, has a population growth rate of 2.18 percent.[21] The problem becomes more acute when the percentage of the population under fourteen years of age is considered. In Jordan, the percentage is 35 percent, in Syria 37 percent, in Iran 27 percent, and in Yemen 47 percent. By comparison, in China the population fourteen and under is 25 percent, in the United Kingdom, 19 percent, and in the United States, 21 percent. At issue are the resources necessary to educate these young people and find jobs for them. Children require schools, day care, food, medical care, and all the other necessities of life. If the poorer countries cannot find jobs for this ballooning number of young people, then the gap between the wealthy and poor Middle Eastern countries can only increase. Also at issue is the question of their own reproduction rates when they reach adulthood. Should this population have the same birth rate as their parents, the resulting population growth will strain resources even more in a region where resources are already in short supply. There is evidence, though, that this may be changing. Phillip Longman states that "fertility rates are falling faster in the Middle East than anywhere else on earth," noting that Algeria will see its median age rise from 21.7 to 40 by midcentury, and

Iran will have more senior citizens than children by 2050.[22] Still, it will take a decade or so for this decrease to start offsetting the large number of children now reaching school age.

A significant migration from rural to urban areas is one consequence of high population growth, since rural areas tend to have higher birth rates and fewer jobs than cities. Cairo is now a teeming metropolis of almost 20 million people. The population growth has overwhelmed the city's infrastructure and thus many neighborhoods, especially slums, lack running water, police and fire protection, and other services. Sewage often seeps into the streets from leaking sewer pipes and garbage sits uncollected for days. The city streets are so crowded that visitors are cautioned against waiting for an ambulance in case of medical emergency, since the average emergency response time through Cairo's choked streets is around forty-five minutes. Cairo residents work in shifts, so that rush hour is staggered. The traffic jams start at around 7:00 AM, and the first shift heads home at around 3:00 PM, clogging streets with a horn-honking bedlam that rattles even the natives. The second rush hour starts around an hour later and resumes around 7:00–8:00 in the evening. The streets become relatively safe for pedestrians to cross around 10:00 PM, but caution is required since many drivers drive at night without lights to save their car batteries.

The Foreign Debt Challenge

During the past several decades, many developing countries have accumulated large foreign debts that they are unable to service. As their economies slow because of factors like rising fuel prices or lower commodity prices, the debt becomes larger relative to their gross domestic product (see, for example, Chapter 13 on Lebanon), and they must turn to international financial institutions like the International Monetary Fund (IMF) to bail them out. The IMF examines the economies of indebted countries and concludes that they need to reform regimes designed to produce political stability at the expense of economic efficiency. Thus many Middle Eastern governments have had to make painful choices to end price subsidies (on items like bread in particular), to cut inflation (which often means cutting employment), and to privatize their economies. Sometimes IMF demands contribute to instability rather than harmony. In Tunisia IMF-mandated suspension of bread and flour subsidies doubled the price of these goods and led to riots and thousands of casualties in 1983.[23] Similar riots broke out in Egypt in 1977 and Algeria in 1988 for the same reason.

State Ownership and Privatization

Like many other developing areas, the Middle East worked to catch up with the industrial West and the socialist countries of Europe through state planning and public ownership of the facilities of production. Such endeavors mobilized often scarce resources and allowed for rapid assimilation of labor. Since high levels of unemployment threatened embryonic governments, political leadership emphasized jobs over enterprise efficiency. Newly independent regimes also wanted to gain independence from both the East and West, and thus import substitution became a major priority. So things like steel mills, shipyards, cement factories, along with the planning ministries to run them, became fixtures in many Middle Eastern countries. State-run airlines that were symbols of national pride and independence more than models of economic efficiency sprang up in most Middle East countries. State-run oil companies controlled the facilities of newly nationalized international oil companies. National banks served to distribute political patronage to favored clients in an effort to sequester potential opposition. Bureaucracies served to channel resources to clients approved by political leaders, and bureaucracies themselves became favored sources of employment because the spoils of corruption could easily supplement low wages. Bureaucracies soak up valuable resources that might otherwise go to more productive activities, but they are difficult to trim because of the unemployment consequences. In the Middle East, central government wages averaged around 11 percent of GDP in the late 1990s, almost twice the rate of developing countries overall.[24] State-owned facilities have no real incentive to modernize and reform production practices since there is no profit incentive, but the consequence is production rates that fall well below world averages. For example, Egypt's state-owned cotton mill efficiency is less than 60 percent, well below the 85–90 percent world average.[25] In other cases, large revenue sources from commodities like petroleum mean that wealthy countries like the Gulf energy-producing emirates may provide very low charges on things like electric rates because of the heavy state subsidies involved. The electric rates in countries like Kuwait and Saudi Arabia are among the lowest in the world, but they would be much higher under private ownership.[26] Pharmaceuticals are also widely subsidized. However, such subsidies are often inefficient means to purchase political stability in otherwise politically unaccountable regimes.

The preferred solution by many reformers is privatization, dismantling the state planning apparatus and converting state-run enterprises to private ownership. However, privatization brings its own costs, including the loss of jobs in ministries and state-run enterprises and the creation of a new economic elite of private entrepreneurs to replace government cadres. High tariffs protecting national firms from foreign competition are often repealed (under pressure from international financial institutions like the International Monetary Fund), but then the regime may have to hike personal taxes to replace lost tariff revenue, as in the Iraqi case when American administrators imposed a 15 percent flat tax on all incomes.[27] Privatization is also difficult to accomplish in many Middle Eastern countries because the power of those benefiting. However, privatization can also create opportunities for positive economic growth and some Middle Eastern countries have experienced benefits. Turkish Airlines, for example, ended the year 2001 with a profit, one of a few world airlines in black ink, due partially to privatization and the resulting cost-cutting measures and modernization that state ownership often prevents.[28]

The reform requirements levied by international financial institutions like the IMF and the World Bank have other costs associated with them. Despite their efforts to improve social welfare in the Middle East, "not only did unemployment and poverty increase, inequality of income also worsened in all of them except Tunisia."[29] One consequence was that shortfalls in economic performance empowered the alternative Islamist sectors, as El-Said and Harrigan observe. "There is already a growing body of evidence that economic liberalization and other forms of globalization have opened up a space which is rapidly being occupied by religious groups in the Arab region, some of which are politically motivated."[30]

Economic Development and Democracy

Economic development is also a factor in political participation, and the level of development may affect participation levels in the Middle East. The traditional liberal model of development and democracy holds that socioeconomic development leads to societal stability and thus facilitates democratic development.[31] The process is hardly automatic, though. Bueno de Mesquita and Downs argue that autocrats can delay democratic development as economies grow by blocking "coordination goods," resources that facilitate communication and coordination between political reformers, such as the Internet and higher education, while taking credit for high growth rates.[32] As Luciani notes, "There is, of course, no assurance that political liberalization will yield a government willing and capable of engaging in economic reform." Under democratic conditions public discourse can direct policy in the direction of religious or international alignment rather than economic reform measures.[33] That may be true, but there is powerful evidence that democracies outperform autocracies economically. Even poor democracies outperform authoritarian countries because, according to Siegle, Weinstein, and Halperin, "their institutions enable power to be shared and because they encourage openness and adaptability. . . Democratic leaders have incentives to respond to the needs of common citizens. Otherwise they find themselves out of office."[34]

The Lack of Trade and Investment

Capital investment is critical to economic progress. International investors move billions of dollars every day to markets around the world, lured by the promise of high returns. During the 1990s, much of that investment flowed into East and Southeast Asia, as countries there engaged in a spate of almost unrestricted state-managed capitalism. Investment also flowed into and around the European Union and North America (with the North American Free Trade Area) as trade barriers and other restrictions fell. However, foreign investment did not flow into other regions at similar rates, including the Middle East. Even the wealthy Gulf Cooperation Council states found that more investment was leaving than coming in. While the Gulf area generates great wealth, much of it is leaving the Gulf to be invested in other places. Many wealthy Arabs prefer to invest in real estate rather than industrial development because they realize that their own people cannot purchase industrial goods at profitable rates because of their low incomes, and that industrial goods produced in the Middle East, given high production factor costs, cannot compete successfully outside the region.[35] The lack of peace between Israel and its neighbors and the overall fears of political violence also contribute to the lack of foreign investment. During the heady days in the 1990s when peace seemed a real possibility, Israeli Prime Minister Shimon Peres dreamed a region united by Israeli expertise, American influence, Arab Gulf oil wealth, and cheap Arab labor transforming the Middle East into another economic "tiger" like those of Southeast Asia.[36]

Foreign investment is critical to the Middle East, but investors are hesitant. For example, in 1998, the United States invested $149 billion in Europe, $48 billion in Latin America, $47 billion in Asia and the Pacific, but only $2.3 billion in the Middle East, with $2.1 billion going to Israel.[37] The Arab world's share of world total direct foreign investment shrank from 2.6 percent in 1975–1980, to 1.3 percent in 1980–1990, to 0.7 percent in 1990–1998.[38] Of the total FDI to developing countries, the Arab world fell from 11.4 percent in 1990 to 4.5 percent in 1999.[39] In dollar amounts foreign direct investment shrank in 2003 to $4.6 billion from $5.8 in 2002. According to the United Nations Development Program, Arab countries drew less than 1 percent of total direct investment in the world over the past two decades, largely because of the political violence there.[40]

Many Middle Eastern and North African countries remain largely excluded from world trade patterns, partly because high tariff structures remain in most of the region's countries outside of the primary oil producers. One reason is that many Middle Eastern and North African countries rely heavily on tariff duties for state income. Almost one-third of Tunisian taxes result from tariff revenues, and Lebanon's are almost as high. Thus when these countries reduce trade barriers, they must either raise other taxes or reduce services.[41] Without trade liberalization, many Middle Eastern and North African countries protect local producers who are not forced to compete with more efficient foreign producers. They also find themselves falling behind other developing countries that have liberalized their trade policies, particularly in East Asia.[42]

Rentier States

Rentier states depend on foreign revenues for most of their income, with the rent accruing to governments. Only a few people are involved in the production of rentier wealth (very few are needed to pump and move oil in the Middle East, compared to the large number of workers involved in, for example, automobile manufacturing). Moreover, in rentier states, as the *Arab Human Development Report* for 2003 noted, "Economic returns do not necessarily accrue from hard work and high productivity, particularly in political systems that constrain freedom and do not encourage people to be industrious."[43]

The oil-producing countries in the Middle East qualify as rentier states, a situation with important political implications. So do states that derive a considerable portion of their national income from other rentier states. Jordan is poor in natural resources but is favored by oil-rich Gulf states with large subsidies as well as jobs for Jordanians (often of Palestinian extraction), who then send their wages home.[44]

Libya is another example, with funds from oil flowing directly into the five most powerful ministries, which then distribute over 80 percent of the total state budget.[45]

Some authorities argue that the rentier wealth allows governments to placate political opposition by controlling its distribution. Moreover, as Birdsall and Subramanian argue, rentier states do not normally tax their citizens because the regime already has wealth; thus there are no taxes and citizens do not feel an obligation to hold rentier regimes accountable for, among other things, misuse of tax revenues.[46] Classical rentier states may stall the privatization of state facilities, since state operation of such facilities is a means of distributing rentier wealth. Thus authoritarian rentier states may defer political reform efforts by exchanging economic rewards from the state at the expense of political participation and reform. Bahgat observes that the classical rentier states in the Persian Gulf have experienced low levels of internal violence due to their high oil wealth. This is partly because rentier states have tremendous potential to distribute goods and services free of charge to citizens but do not have to tax their subjects, as noted above.[47] However, as Okruhlik notes, the heightened expectation of the supposedly pacified population may produce a sharp rise in dissent if an economic downturn stops the flow of rewards.[48] Thus rentier states only buy temporary peace through their policies before opposition rekindles. Rentier states may also suffer from resource mismanagement or the personal greed of a few spendthrifts at the top, especially if the governing body is a royal family, with few if any political constraints to control spending.[49]

Do rentier states retard the development of democracy? In the Middle East, the primary rentier states—Saudi Arabia, Bahrain, the United Arab Emirates, Kuwait, Qatar, Oman, and Libya—are all countries with limited legislative powers (if a legislature exists at all), and all feature nonelected leaders. While other factors play a role in this type of government (see Chapter 2), a broader study of rentier states both in- and outside the Middle East finds some support for the argument that oil-exporting rentier states use both low tax rates and public spending to ward off pressures for democracy.[50] A more recent study, however, tempers this conclusion, finding that rentierism harms the prospects for democracy less than do other factors such as total state income and the Muslim share of the population.[51]

Governmental responsiveness to the demands of those affected by economic downturn may also be necessary, as in the case of Libya. Libya's President Qadhafi responded to high dissatisfaction to the loss of rentier distributions by engaging in limited reform, an action that "goes against the argument that rentier states are autonomous in relation to their societies."[52] However, Qadhafi's "reforms" were largely in the economic and foreign affairs realms, with no effort at internal political reform.

THE BLESSINGS AND CURSE OF PETROLEUM

Around 75 percent of the world's proved petroleum reserves are found in the Middle East, one of the region's few marketable natural resources. Most of it lies in the

Persian region. Saudi Arabia leads the region and the world with around 261 billion barrels, followed by Iraq with 113 billion barrels, the UAE at 98 billion barrels, Kuwait at 97, Iran holding around 90 billion barrels (some estimates exceed 100 billion barrels), and, in North Africa, Libya with 30 billion barrels.

The size of the reserves is just one of several factors that make the Middle East the center of world petroleum activity. The oil is so abundant that little effort is required to lift it to the surface because associated natural gas pressurizes the oil deposits. Thus oil wells in the Persian Gulf are mostly pipes from underground that direct the free-flowing oil to nearby tanks. The oil fields are located close to water in most cases, reducing the cost of a pipeline network. The cost of production is thus considerably lower than in many comparable regions where there is less oil and thus less pressure. Middle Eastern oil also has a relatively low sulfur content, known in the oil trade as "sweet" oil. Some oil found in China or Indonesia, for example, has a high sulfur content, making it more expensive to refine since the sulfur must be removed during the process. Finally, oil workers in most Middle Eastern oil-producing countries come from very poor third world countries and are willing to work for very low wages compared to oil workers from industrial countries like the United States. Thus Middle Eastern oil producers enjoy lower production costs by comparison.

The Demand for Oil Grows

As their oil exports increased, some leaders in the oil-rich Middle East countries began to recognize that their abundant resource was being sold in the industrialized states for much higher prices after refining. They also recognized that outsiders (the Europeans and Americans, as well as industrial Asian countries like Japan) viewed the oil-rich areas of the Middle East as essential to their security, and access to its relatively inexpensive oil was a part of that security.[53] However, they also understood that their power as individual countries was limited relative to the large oil companies that controlled most of the world oil production. That control dated back to the pre–World War II period, when large American, British, and French petroleum companies obtained drilling rights in a number of Middle Eastern countries.[54] American oil firms began to explore for oil in the Middle East in the 1930s. Standard Oil of New Jersey and Standard Oil of New York bought into the Iraqi Petroleum Company in 1928, and Gulf bought 50 percent of Kuwait Oil, while Texaco and Standard Oil of California established the Bahrain Petroleum Company. In 1933 Standard Oil of California and Texaco (joining in 1936) gained control of Saudi Arabian oil, forming the Arabian American Oil Company (Aramco) in 1946.[55]

OPEC and OAPEC

By the mid-1950s Middle Eastern oil-producing countries began to collaborate. Following a series of oil price cuts by the major oil companies in the late 1950s, representatives from Iraq, Iran, Saudi Arabia, and Venezuela met in Baghdad in September 1960 to form the Organization of Petroleum Exporting Countries (OPEC).[56] The founding members of OPEC realized that their efforts to control the price of oil would be more successful if OPEC included other developing countries with oil, so both Middle Eastern and non–Middle Eastern countries with oil reserves were encouraged to join. Qatar joined in 1961, followed by Indonesia and Libya in 1962. The UAE joined in 1967, followed by Algeria in 1969 and Nigeria in 1971. Significantly, a number of oil-producing countries do not belong to OPEC: China, Angola, Brunei, Bahrain, Colombia, Egypt, Mexico, Canada, Russia, Kazakhstan, the United Kingdom, Oman, Norway, the United States, and Yemen.

Inaction marked OPEC's early years, but events in 1970 revealed to OPEC how vulnerable the oil companies were when challenged by an oil-producing country. After Muammar Qadhafi ousted King Idris in Libya in 1969, he nationalized half the holdings of Occidental Petroleum, Libya's largest producer. OPEC members watching this takeover expected the other oil companies to come to Occidental's rescue, supplying it with crude so it would not have to use the wells Qadhafi nationalized. But the oil companies remained on the sidelines, and Occidental capitulated.[57] Perhaps encouraged by this lack of support, OPEC began a program of nationalizing foreign oil holdings in their countries. Aramco, once owned jointly by Saudi Arabian and American interests, became a sole Saudi Arabian company as the Americans partners were bought out.

In January 1968, Libya, Kuwait, and Saudi Arabia met in Beirut to form OAPEC, the Organization of Arab Petroleum Exporters, and by 1982, eleven Arab oil-producing countries had joined. OAPEC collaborated on the oil embargo to some of Israel's supporters after the start of the 1973 Arab-Israeli war. After a brief general withholding, the embargo focused on two countries that had provided more support than most, the United States and the Netherlands.

OAPEC intended to punish countries that supported the Jewish state. Says Licklider, "they had explicit political motives—to force Israel to return territories captured in the 1967 war, obtain 'legitimate rights' for the Palestinians. . . and alter the status of Jerusalem."[58] The most direct impact of the OAPEC embargo was to bring about a change of posture in the United States from outright support of Israel to a more evenhanded posture. President Nixon responded to Egyptian overtures, setting a more conducive climate for President Carter to initiate the Camp David peace talks of 1979.

The OAPEC oil embargo was followed in 1979 by the second oil shock when the shah of Iran was overthrown and replaced by the Ayatollah Khomeini. Iran then withheld its oil from the market in an effort to punish countries that supported the shah, and again the target was the United States. Oil prices rose again immediately, but the United States did not capitulate to Iranian demands to return the shah to stand trial in Iran.

The long-term impact of the oil embargos for the oil-producing countries, however, was ultimately negative. Most of them adopted measures to conserve oil and thus reduce demand relative to supply. Tax credits for increased energy efficiency for home and industry use, rules restricting motoring speed, and efforts to find alternative sources of energy were just a few of the ways oil consumers reacted to price hikes.

Middle Eastern Oil Pipelines

Middle Eastern oil must be transported from the fields to transportation hubs, often seaports. Oil pipelines crisscross much of the Middle East as oil moves across borders to tanker loading facilities. This fact has political as well as economic implications, since countries with pipeline routes have considerable leverage over their neighbors. For example, some Iraqi oil moved across Syria during Saddam Hussein's rule in an apparent effort by Iraq to keep Syrian support for the Saddam regime. Sabotage along a pipeline from Iraq through Turkey, capable of moving over 800,000 barrels daily, means that US officials running Iraq's oil industry must pump 300,000 Iraqi barrels back into the ground, depriving the post-Saddam regime of badly needed money.[59] Another interesting sideline was the possibility of Israel opening a long-closed pipeline from Mosul through the Israeli port of Haifa, thus providing Israel, with no oil of its own, with a potentially large supply.[60] Turkish pipeline politics also represent a strong Turkish national interest in reaching out politically to Central Asian areas of the former Soviet Union. One way Turkey is cementing those ties is through a new pipeline bringing in oil from Baku in Azerbaijan to the port of Ceyhan in southern Turkey. The 1,100 mile, $3 billion project also gives Turkey access to oil from a source outside of Iraq. Turkey has a large network of pipes that can transport either gas or liquid petroleum from the Caspian Sea and other producing areas to Europe. This strengthens Turkish-European relations and consequently may assist Turkey's long-standing application to join the European Union.[61] Pipelines can help two states improve political ties, as is the case with Egypt and Libya. As relations warmed between them (see Chapters 10 and 18), Cairo and Tripoli agreed to establish twin pipelines connecting the two countries to move Libyan crude oil to Alexandria and Egyptian gas to Libya.[62]

The Future of Oil

Although the technical means of forecasting oil reserves have improved dramatically, uncertainty still marks estimated future oil reserves. Campbell and Leherrère conclude that future supplies (from 2000) are around 1 trillion barrels, with maximum production reached in fifteen years.[63] Moreover, they predict that Persian Gulf production will again rise as a percentage of total oil pumped, hitting 50 percent by 2010.[64] The International Energy Agency agrees, forecasting that Middle Eastern OPEC production will double from 20 mb/d to 40 mb/d by 2010.[65] On the other hand, Jaffe and Manning argue that the world's oil reserves are 2.3 billion barrels, possibly closer to 4 billion barrels if shale and tar sand oil is counted. They claim that instead of oil scarcity, an oil glut will depress prices and possibly lead to social and political turmoil in oil-producing states.[66] However, oil demand may also drive prices up, particularly if producers do not increase drilling or refining capacity. While energy demand forecasts suggest that world energy demand may double by 2030 and quadruple by 2100, energy investment remains low due to concerns about unstable energy prices.[67] Consequently new petroleum rivals, particularly Russia, may try to replace Saudi Arabia as a future major oil supplier.

Natural Gas

Around 33 percent of the world's total estimated supply of natural gas is located in the Middle East.[68] Deposits lie not only in the oil-rich Persian Gulf but also in Egypt, off the coast shared by Israel and the Palestinian Authority, and in Algeria. While the demand and price for natural gas make it less attractive than oil, and it is difficult to transport across broad oceans, its relatively clean burning qualities make it attractive for the future. There is a downside for OPEC oil producers in that natural gas production (particularly liquefied natural gas) is cutting into the oil market and may reduce revenues to OPEC oil-producing countries by as much as $30 billion annually.[69]

The Middle East leads the world in natural gas deposits with 2,346 trillion cubic feet (tcf). Iran and its estimated 944 tcf has the largest reserves of any country in the Middle East and the second largest in the world. Almost 62 percent of those deposits have not been tapped, giving Iran considerable potential for future economic growth. Qatar ranks third in the world with around 509 tcf.[70] Algeria also has significant quantities that it pipes to Europe through Morocco into Spain.

Difficulties in Securing Alternative Economic Resources

Countries with significant deposits of oil and gas understand that they will not last forever, and the revenues from petroleum may rise and fall precipitously in relationship to supply and demand functions plus factors related to regional stability. Moreover, as noted above, a majority of Middle Eastern countries do not have significant petroleum reserves. Few Middle Eastern or North African countries have other natural products that they can extract and process at commercially viable rates (even much of the sand in many Middle Eastern countries is unsuitable for cement or glass production). Tourism is a factor for many countries in the region that have attractive beaches or mountains, or notable historical sites like the pyramids or Petra in Jordan. The Gulf Emirates are using their petroleum wealth to attract visitors to their beaches, and new hotels spring up almost weekly to house the expected tourists. A number of Middle Eastern and North African countries saw considerable increases in tourism, with Egypt and the UAE up 12.6 and 31.7 percent respectively in 2001. Political violence is always a risk, as figures for Morocco and Tunisia show. When both countries saw bombings by groups linked to al-Qaeda, Morocco's tourist numbers dropped by 0.7 percent while Tunisia's fell by 6 percent.[71]

WATER

For centuries, water has determined the shape of civilization in the Middle East, and in modern times, water distribution is increasingly shaped by political considerations. That will become even more important in the near future as population pressures make water even more scarce and expensive, and countries become even more determined to control the water they have and, in some cases, to get more from their neighbors.

IMAGES

The tether on the ox means that the animal must walk around in a circle to graze on the grass in front of it. As it turns this slow circle, the yoke attached to its shoulders drives a primitive wooden pump. A slow trickle of water flows from the pump and runs into the adjacent fields in little rivulets. These small plots of rich soil are just starting to sprout green shoots in the warm March sun. A few miles away, the timeless Nile River flows by. Human efforts lift its water by using a wooden wheel fixed with buckets and propelled by a young boy turning pedals on a shaft attached to the wheel. The buckets scoop up muddy water and dump it into a pond, from which the canals run into smaller ponds, where oxen (or sometimes people when the oxen get full of grass and stop) drive the ancient pumps that give life to the fields. The light-brown water runs down carefully carved troughs only a foot wide, as it has for thousands of years. In the dusty little villages along the Nile, nothing seems to get more careful stewardship by the villagers than water. A blunt reminder of how precious it is lies a few miles away from their simple mud and straw huts. A person standing on the bluffs overlooking the Nile on its western side can see the narrow ribbon of life running along either side of it, but turn around, and there is nothing but lifeless desert stretching for over 2,000 miles. The only difference between the empty desert beyond and the teeming life in that green ribbon of Nile Valley is water.

The origin and distribution of Middle Eastern water is the source for real and potential conflict, as was the case when Iran and Iraq fought a bitter war that was partially a function of the long-disputed border of the Shatt al-Arab waterway that divides the two countries. The potential for water to become a source of conflict is, like most issues, a matter of debate. Jan Selby argues that historically it has not been the subject of conflict (not even in the 1967 war), and, moreover, dependence on water is declining, as agriculture plays a diminishing role in the national economies of the region.[72]

The outlook for much of the world's water availability is grim, and that is especially true in the Middle East. According to the World Bank, while the Middle East has 5 percent of the world's population, the region has only 1 percent of the world's available fresh water.[73] The International Water Management Institute reports that one-third of the world's population will experience severe water shortages within the next twenty-five years, and seventeen countries are expected to face "absolute water scarcity" (not enough water in 2025 to maintain 1990 food production levels despite larger populations): Afghanistan, Egypt, Saudi Arabia, Pakistan, Israel, Jordan, Iran, Iraq, Kuwait, Syria, Tunisia, the United Arab Emirates, Yemen, Singapore, South Africa, Oman, Libya, and parts of India and China.[74] Another measure of water scarcity is the cubic meter availability per capita. Should this fall below 500 cubic meters, the country becomes subject to "absolute water scarcity," and in the 1990s, eight countries were in this category: Kuwait (75), Qatar (117), Bahrain (179), Saudi Arabia (306), UAE (308), Jordan (327), Yemen (445), and Israel (461).[75] While this category does not necessarily mean imminent collapse, it does make a country more vulnerable to water supply reduction, and it contributes to potential tensions between countries competing for the same water resource.

Rivers

Most water in the Middle East comes from a few large rivers that transit the territory of several countries. These include the Tigris and Euphrates, the Nile, and the Orantes. Aquifers are a second source of water—underground reservoirs of water stored in porous rock, and replenished by rainfall or river runoff. Some aquifers are continuously replenished by rainfall and snowmelt, but others contain "fossil water," stored thousands or millions of years ago in limestone but not currently replenished. A third potential source of water is the sea; fresh water can be extracted by desalinization—heating water in large plants to boil off the water from the salt.

The Nile River runs from Uganda and Ethiopia through Sudan into Egypt, which uses a majority of its water but contributes nothing to its flow. The Tigris and Euphrates Rivers both originate in mountain snows in Turkey, and then run into Syria and Iraq. Neither Syria nor Iraq contributes much water to the flow, but both countries rely on these rivers—Syria on the Euphrates and Iraq on the Tigris and Euphrates—while Turkey captures an increasing amount from both rivers before it reaches the two downstream countries. Turkey is trying to develop its central and southern parts by providing water for electricity and irrigation, and this involves building a series of dams and reservoirs that threaten to block the flow of both rivers to their downstream users (see below). Snowmelt from the Lebanese mountain ranges feeds the Jordan River, which then flows into Israel and Jordan. Studies show that the Jordan River has dropped 90 percent from its 1.3 billion cubic meters of water in the 1960s to 100 million cubic meters (MCM) in 2005. Said Munqeth Mehyar, chair of Friends of the Earth Middle East (FOEME), an Israeli-Jordanian-Palestinian group, "The Jordan River will disappear if nothing is done soon. More than half of it is raw sewage and runoff water from agriculture. What keeps the river flowing today is sewage."[76] Gidon Bromberg, FOEME's Israeli director, noted that "the story of the demise of the

River Jordan is the competition between Israel, Jordan and Syria for water. It is about grabbing as much water as they possibly can."[77]

The 1994 treaty committed Israel to provide 200 mcm (million cubic meters) annually to Jordan, most of it drawn from the Yarmouk River. However, half of this water depends on Israel building new dams on the river, which Israel has not started. Therefore, in 1997, for example, Israel supplied only 50 mcm to Jordan.[78] Israel had already effectively established control over the waters of the Sea of Galilee/Lake Tiberias/Lake Kinneret when it dammed the southern outlet without international agreement and extended the National Water Carrier system to the south.[79] It now reaches the Negev desert, about 130 miles away.

Aquifers

A second source for water in the Middle East is underground aquifers. Water accumulation creates these aquifers when rainwater soaks into porous rock, often in front of mountain ranges. The water may accumulate over thousands or millions of years, and sometimes, depending on the rock time, may become heavily saline over time. Some of these aquifers are renewable, but others are "fossil water," locked in the ground for millions of years and no longer replenished by natural sources. In the Middle East in 1996, for example, extensive water use removed some 28.3 billion cubic meters of water from aquifers, but only 18.5 cubic meters would be replenished.[80]

The Arabian Peninsula features a large underground aquifer that may hold more water than does the Red Sea. Saudi Arabia taps this water through artesian wells that connect to what is called pivot irrigation, a long pipe that pivots around the wellhead with a wheel at the end and spray nozzles along the pipe to distribute the water. The results can be observed from the air as a series of green circles in an otherwise tawny desert. Here Saudis grow wheat, barley, and alfalfa, using the latter to feed cattle for dairy production.

Other aquifers underlie the West Bank and are shared by Israelis and Palestinians. The bulk of the water goes to Israel, which uses around 747 cubic meters per year, compared to 121 for the Palestinians. The Yarqon-Tanninim aquifer is located closest to Israel proper and supplies water for urban use to Tel Aviv, Jerusalem, and Beersheva. The Nablus-Gilboa aquifer supplies water mostly for agricultural use, as does the Eastern aquifer. The Yarqon-Tanninim aquifer is clearly the most important to Israel, and control over its use in the future will obviously be the subject of difficult negotiations between Israel and the Palestinians.

Israel is already consuming more water than it can replenish annually. The annual freshwater supply is around 1,950 mcm, but current demand (including in the Occupied Territories) is around 2,150 mcm.[81] Consequently Israel is tapping heavily into underground aquifers. A coastal aquifer was drained of fresh water during the 1970s and 1980s, and Israel is now tapping the mountain aquifers that lie partially or wholly in the Occupied Territories. The problem can only worsen as Israel's projected water use by 2020 rises to 2,600 mcm. Israel's shortcomings with waste management also contaminate the aquifers, as one is in danger of becoming unusable because of levels of sewage, arsenic, chrome, and chemical fertilizers, resulting in the closure of over 160 wells in the past decade.[82]

Overconsumption

Water consumption may become a critical problem when it exceeds renewable supplies, as it does in Egypt, Oman, Saudi Arabia (which has the highest withdrawal rates in the world), Bahrain, the UAE, Qatar, and Kuwait.[83] For the latter countries, water desalinization has supplied a margin of safety, but in some Gulf countries, water consumption still draws down aquifers. The UAE has the highest water consumption rates in the world (500 liters per day, compared to Britain at 330 and Jordan at 150), and aquifer levels are dropping at around 1 meter per year, meaning that up to 79 percent of the aquifer resources are not refreshed by rainfall.[84] Jordan also runs high water deficits, around 500 million cubic meters annually, which are some of the highest in the world.[85]

Israel provides examples of both water problems and water solutions in the Middle East. Israeli usage stands at 350 cubic meters per capita, compared to the United States, at 35,000 cm/c. In the Levant, only Jordan stands lower.[86] Israelis, moreover, use considerably more water per capita than do the neighboring Palestinians; between 65 to 75 gallons per day, compared to around 13 gallons per day by Palestinians.[87]

Some 70 percent of water use in Israel is for agriculture, partly reflecting an increase in cultivated acreage from 408,000 acres in 1948 to 1.1 million in 1998.[88] Moreover, much of this agriculture lies over the coastal aquifer, resulting in contamination from agricultural chemicals and increased salinity from fresh water pumping. Over the past two decades, the nitrate concentration in the aquifers has doubled.[89]

Turkey faces a population growth problem, and has difficulty supplying electricity to its towns and cities. Consequently, Turkey planned the Guney Doğu Projesi (GAP) project to gather water from the Tigris and Euphrates Rivers. The project consists of twenty-two dams of varying size to store water to irrigate over 1.7 million hectares of land. Some nineteen hydroelectric installations are expected to generate over 27 billion kilowatt hours of electricity when the project is completed, which will represent over 40 percent of Turkey's total electrical output. That system threatens to greatly deplete downstream water to Syria and Iraq, which came close to war in 1974–1975, when Syria's construction of a dam on the Euphrates creating Lake Asad seriously constricted the Iraqi share of Euphrates water. Syria closed its airspace to Iraqi aircraft and moved troops to the Iraqi border, while Iraq threatened to bomb the dam at al-Tabqa. The conflict dimmed only after Soviet and Saudi Arabian mediation.[90] More recently, Syria and Iraq have drawn together as they both face the Turkish water threat, though the future of water sharing between Iraq and Syria without Saddam Hussein in power remains to be seen.[91]

Part of the Middle Eastern water problem lies in inefficient agricultural applications; flooding fields, for example, allows much of the water to evaporate before it penetrates the soil, leaving a saline residue behind. In Iraq, this practice turned once fertile fields into hard saltpans. Partly because water is often not priced, investment in new water delivery systems lags in many Middle Eastern and North African countries. Water continuously seeps up through the streets of Cairo from leaking water mains and then mixes with sewage from leaking sewer mains. In Jordan, the government estimates that around half of the water pumped to Jordanians either leaks from old pipes or is stolen by people who knock holes in delivery pipes and help themselves to free water.[92]

Water is a renewable resource, unlike oil. It can be recovered after initial use, cleaned, and reused. Seawater can be converted into fresh water by desalination, although the process is expensive due to the structural and energy requirements. But only a few countries in the Middle East make use of these nonconventional water sources. In Saudi Arabia, nonconventional water makes up only 5.48 percent of total water use, in Syria 2.6 percent, while in Egypt it is less than 0.5 percent. Only Kuwait with 23 percent and the UAE with 53 percent rank as countries with significant water recovery as a percentage of total use.[93]

The seriousness of the water crisis in the Middle East becomes even starker in the face of a World Bank report noting that between 1960 and 2025 stored renewable water per capita annually dropped from 3,430 cm to 667 cm. Even a partial remedy for the situation will require at least $35 million of investment in water projects throughout the region just for the Arab states.[94] When the continuing population growth in most of the region is factored in, as well as the uncertainties inherent in global warming and continuing government reluctance to invest in new water storage and distribution facilities (Egypt is a notable exception), it becomes even more apparent that water, not oil, is the region's most serious liquid crisis.

This chapter introduced some of the social and political issues that will reemerge in the chapters that follow. The next section covers the Persian Gulf countries, a region that has contributed richly to the Arab and Islamic world in the modern era.

SUGGESTED READINGS

Economic Development

Azzam, Henry T. *The Arab World Facing the Challenge of the New Millennium*. London: Tauris, 2002.

Glain, Stephen. *Mullahs, Merchants, and Militants: The Economic Collapse of the Arab World*. New York: St. Martin's, 2004.

Gulf Security in the Twentieth Century. Abu Dhabi, UAE: Emirates Center for Strategic Studies and Research, 1997.

Henry, Clement M., and Robert Springborg. *Globalization and the Politics of Development in the Middle East*. Cambridge: Cambridge University Press, 2001.

Kuran, Timur. *Islam and Mammon: The Economic Predicaments of Islamism*. Princeton, NJ: Princeton University Press, 2004.

Richards, Alan, and John Waterbury. *A Political Economy of the Middle East: State, Class, and Economic Development*. Boulder, CO: Westview, 1990.

Warde, Ibrahim. *Islamic Finance in the Global Economy.* New York: Columbia University Press, 2000.

Oil

Bialer, Uri. *Oil and the Arab-Israeli Conflict.* New York: St. Martin's, 1998.

Gillespie, Kate, and Clement M. Henry, eds. *Oil in the New World Order.* Gainesville: University Press of Florida, 1995.

Gulf Energy and the World. Abu Dhabi, UAE: Emirates Center for Strategic Studies and Research, 1997.

Yetiv, Steve A. *Crude Awakenings: Global Oil Security and American Foreign Policy.* Ithaca, NY: Cornell University Press, 2004.

Water

Allan, J. A., and Chibli Mallat, eds. *Water in the Middle East: Legal, Political, and Commercial Implications.* New York: Tauris, 1995.

Hambright, K. David, F. Jamil Ragep, and Joseph Ginat, eds. *Water in the Middle East: Cooperation and Technological Solutions in the Jordan Valley.* Norman: University of Oklahoma Press, 2006.

Hillell, Daniel. *Rivers of Eden.* New York: Oxford University Press, 1995.

Shapland, Greg. *Rivers of Discord.* New York: St. Martin's, 1997.

Sherman, Martin. *The Politics of Water in the Middle East.* New York: St. Martin's, 1999.

Soffer, Arnon. *Rivers of Fire: The Conflict over Water in the Middle East.* Lanham, MD: Rowman & Littlefield, 1998.

4

POLITICS IN
THE MIDDLE EAST

IMAGES *The legislators stand outside the parliament building during a break in a rare evening session. As the smoke from their Galois cigarettes drifts up into the jacaranda trees in the humid night air, they joke quietly among themselves. "What are you voting on?" queries a passerby. "We're not sure," comes the reply from one of the parliamentarians. "Then how do you know how to vote?" the passerby asks. "Simple, we just do what the president wants," answers the legislator.*

MIDDLE EASTERN COUNTRIES have their own unique political identities, deeply rooted in their own histories and cultures. As Lapidus explains, Middle Eastern identity started with families and tribes, evolving gradually into religious associations and then slowly into states and empires.[1] Yet family, tribal, and religious identification remains part of the political landscape in the modern Middle East, and loyalties in the area often divide between family, faith, and nationalism. Barakat notes that tribalism undermines both Islamic and nationalist identity, and that nationalist leaders in particular have combated tribal identity, seeing it as a barrier to their own state aspirations.[2] As Khoury and Kostiner observe, new state formation in the Middle East was often incomplete, and thus "the new states still reflected certain tribal habits and had to accommodate a certain measure of tribal power."[3] In stressed nation-states, tribal identity is particularly important, as in post-2003 Iraq, where ungoverned provinces like al-Anbar are the closest thing to a regime, and the central government has attempted to mobilize tribal councils to combat violent militants, whose identity is also often tribal.[4] Language is also important as an identifier. The Kurdish people, whose identity is embedded in their language and their history, have little loyalty to the Iraqi, Turkish, and Iranian regimes that too frequently have subjugated their lives. Many Middle Easterners may switch fealty from tribe to country to religious faith. Some Jews in Israel reject Zionism, a form of Jewish nationalism, and instead await what they believe will be the coming of the true

Messiah and, only then, the emergence of a truly legitimate Jewish state. Some poor peasants along the Nile or in the slums of Casablanca or in other places of poverty turn to Islamist movements after they lose faith in the ability of their governments to provide a better future for them.

The idea of globalization suggests that political issues and institutions are increasingly universal, to include such things as human rights, democracy, civil liberties, and other concepts common to most liberal democracies. However, in some parts of the world, such practices are not as common. The countries of the Middle East display a wide divergence on institutions like liberal democracy. This is partly because the Middle East has a unique set of political cultures and practices. Consequently, a political understanding of the region must blend in its unique background when considering its adaptability to modern political institutions common to Western experience.

An examination of the following themes helps to facilitate understanding of the Middle East. This list is not all-inclusive, but it includes some of the more significant issues that help to explain the complex political interactions of the region. The themes covered in this chapter are (1) types of governance, (2) law and politics, (3) elite rule, (4) civil society, (5) human rights, (6) minority groups in the Middle East, (7) women in the Middle East, (8) political succession, and (9) foreign affairs. Subsequent chapters cover Middle Eastern political economy, and religion and politics in the Middle East.

SHAPING THE MIDDLE EASTERN POLITICAL LANDSCAPE

As the postcolonial period dawned in the Middle East, mostly after World War II, numerous actors, ideas, and social forces interacted to shape governance and polity in the modern Middle East. Players in the process included the often well-positioned military and tribal elites, religious figures, and old ruling families who had dominated their regions for centuries. Competing ideas included nationalism, religious rule, European-style socialism, and liberal pluralism. Some contenders for power sought to encapsulate the past, while others saw their political compasses pointing to Europe or America. Those who sought modernity (Turkey's Kemal Ataturk or Iran's Pahlavi family) contrasted with the al-Saud family and its return to eighteen-century Islamic ideals, and the military elite of Egypt and Syria, whose image of their countries rested on national unity around the Arab voice and its dispossessed millions. Thus the process of nation building took on different casts depending on the prevailing political forces and their ability to shape nations in their chosen images.

Political culture formed one nexus of postcolonial development in the region, though authorities disagree on its content and form. Some argue that the desert environment which covers around 80–90 percent of the Middle East and the culture which stems from its harsh demands undergirds the authoritarian nature of Middle Eastern politics. They might note that countries with a mountainous topography

(Turkey, Lebanon) have advanced farther on the road to democracy than, for example, Saudi Arabia, which is almost all desert or semidesert. Survival in the desert necessitates communitarian living rather than the fabled rugged individualism of the American experience. Others cite modified hydraulically determined societies in the spirit of Wittfogel, who decades ago argued that "oriental despotism" sprang from the need to mobilize river water resources that gave birth to traditional authoritarian systems, which thus became part of Middle East political culture.[5] Others argue that the foundations of Middle Eastern politics lie in Islam and its traditions, which range from starkly authoritarian rule to liberating democracy (as discussed below); yet another source of political tradition is the tribal structure of many Middle Eastern countries, which remains influential despite the growth of state-focused political identity.

Family structure is also significant in Middle Eastern politics, ranging from long-standing ruling families in the Gulf Arab states (the al-Saud in Saudi Arabia, the al-Sabah in Kuwait, the al-Thani in Qatar, and numerous others). In these small states the ruling families control not only access to the head of state but also to the key ministries and other critical sectors (head of the leading telecommunications outlets and newspapers, for example). In other Middle Eastern countries family control is more restricted, but family access to top positions is evident in Lebanon, where clans like the Jumblatt (Druze) or Chamoun, Gemayel, and Franjeih (Christian) have dominated Lebanese politics for centuries; in Syria, where the al-Asad family has reigned at the top since 1971, and possibly in Egypt and Libya, where the rulers of both countries are reportedly grooming sons to succeed them.

Other socializing factors shape political currents in the Middle East. With limits on formal political discourse in many countries, the Gulf has the tradition of the social meeting called the *diwaniyya*, the exchanges at the souq, where political rumors are consumed along with the goods for sale, and the ever-present *qawa*, the coffee café, where intellectuals gather to discuss the latest political news. All cities have them, and some are famous, such as the one in Cairo south of Tahrir Square where Naguib Mafouz, Egypt's Nobel Prize laureate, would sometimes hold forth, or the Haydarkana or Maqha al-Zahawi in Baghdad, where the illiterate could hear newspapers read aloud, all in the name of keeping national memory alive.[6]

IMAGES

> *The apple-scented smoke fills the small room as patrons pull on the stems of their narguila, the classic water pipe of the Middle East. Waiters move easily through the crowd filling the small cups of Arab coffee, anxious to complete their tasks before the storyteller begins. Tonight in this ancient qawa next to the Umayyad mosque in Damascus, the tales are of Salah al-Din, whose tomb is just around the corner. The storyteller, his eyes flashing and his arms moving rhythmically, gives the great Muslim liberator almost mythic powers as he slays the Crusaders and returns the land to Islam. His audience knows the tales well, having heard them since childhood. They join in, cheering and laughing as the Crusaders perish in the dust, perhaps knowing that such victories have been rare*

*for Syrians in the past few centuries. But they live on, perhaps under-
pinning the regime's autocratic hold over the country. After all, the new
invaders must be driven from the land, even if it takes centuries, and all
must join in the fight for the umma, perhaps to be mobilized by orders
from the remote palace on the hills behind Damascus from which the al-
Asad family rules.*

TYPES OF GOVERNANCE

Middle Eastern political systems range between authoritarian and democratic
rule, with most regimes somewhere between the extremes of despotic rule and full
democracy.

Authoritarian Regimes

Authoritarian regimes still exist worldwide despite the global trend toward democratization. Their characteristics include rule by a single leader with almost unbridled power, often within a single political party. They often base their ruling
authority on some ideology; in the Middle East Baathist socialism remains the governing ideology in Syria and was the dominant force in Iraq before the spring of
2003. Such regimes often confer hero status on the ruler, based on some exploit
(wartime service or imprisonment by a previous regime, for example), and such status sometimes stands in for legitimacy conferred by popular choice.[7] They usually
construct their own narrative to support regime mythology, sometimes reaching
into the distant past where memory reconstruction becomes more difficult to challenge—the shah of Iran wrapped in the mantle of ancient Persia and Saddam Hussein's purported mythical lineage to the powerful Hammurabi, king of Babylon
between 1795 and 1750 BCE, or King Nebuchadnezzar, who faced Persians (modern Iranians) and Jews, just as Saddam claimed he faced.[8]

While the fundamental premise of democratic regimes is legitimacy based on
popular consent, many authoritarian regimes base their authority claims on nationalism or ideology, while others seek religious legitimacy as a foundation. Several authoritarian regimes in the Middle East draw their claimed authenticity from Islam,
Saudi Arabia and Iran being only two examples.

Authoritarian regimes are systems with total rule by a single individual or small
group, with only symbolic opposition. They may have parliaments, but the ruling
party appoints the legislators; they may have a court system, but their function is to
uphold the dictates of the ruler rather than to dispense objective justice; there may
be a news media, but the ruling party owns it. Opposition is illegal in autocracies,
so political opposition is usually underground or out of the country. Open public
discourse is strictly limited, and criticism against the regime or its policies can bring
swift retribution by security forces. Since the rulers in authoritarian regimes may
lack political legitimacy, they generally try to create it through actions (invading a
neighboring country, for example). Others claim a religious mandate for the right
to rule. Constitutions may exist, but there is no means of enforcing their provisions.

Democratic Regimes

The political phenomenon of the 1990s was the spread of representative democracy to areas previously dominated by authoritarian governments. Democracy swept through such traditionally autocratic regions as Latin America, Southeast and East Asia, Africa, and Eastern and Central Europe.[9] The reasons why this wave of democratization happened in this decade are instructive for lessons about democratization prospects for the Middle East.

"Democracy" is a loose term encompassing a variety of institutions, expectations, and behaviors but emphasizes government accountability to the public. In a democracy, regimes serve at the behest of citizens who have the power to hold them responsible for meeting public needs and expectations, and who may remove the elected rulers peacefully should they fail public hopes. The rule of law is also paramount for democracies, and thus they normally require a constitution to serve as a legal contract between the governed and the governors. Mechanisms allowing for accountability include regularly scheduled elections, legislatures that are at least partly independent of the executive branch, legalized political parties independent of the state, and a free press to inform the public of government actions. Elections should offer real choices, be fair, and be decisive: the leadership must leave power if it loses the vote.[10] Democracy also emphasizes majority rule, although it carries the risk of minority repression by the majority. This is one reason that constitutional provisions for equal protection often are included in majority rule systems. Democracy also makes assumptions about equality of persons, at least with respect to the equality of political participation. Sometimes democratic goals expand beyond equal participation in politics to attempt a more equitable distribution of resources to avoid the classic democratic problem of the power of the small but privileged few who can use their wealth to tilt a democratic system in their favor.

The presence of these democratic characteristics does not guarantee democratic practice, nor must they be present to ensure democracy. Israel, for example, does not have a constitution; its Basic Law serves as a substitute, but Israel is widely regarded as the most democratic country in the Middle East. Other countries have constitutions promising a variety of "rights," but they are rarely available to the populace in practice.

While political freedom and democracy are not the same, they are clearly related. It is not enough to put democratic mechanisms in place; citizens must be free to use them. This is the essence of liberal democracy, which implies that a basic grant of rights comes from a charter between the majority (which the government claims to represent) and citizens. Many polities may elucidate such rights in a constitution, but the process involving adjudication and protection is the real test of a truly liberal democracy. Here an independent judiciary, answerable only to the constitution, is essential to prevent a declaration of individual and group rights from becoming window dressing for autocratic regimes.

Israel and Turkey are the only countries in the Middle East that come close to the definition of full democracy. However, both Israel and Turkey receive criticism for undemocratic practices carried out in the name of security. Israel's Arab population does not share rights equally with Israel's Jewish citizens, and Turkish Kurds still have unofficial limits on free expression.

Democratic Transformation

Autocratic states may transform for many reasons, among them the loss of legitimacy of the regime, revolution, the impact of successful democratization elsewhere, or the effort of a ruling regime to try to stave off opposition by coopting it through democratic processes. The offer of a handful of seats in a parliament otherwise controlled by the ruling party or membership on an advisory council may be enough to quell a violent opposition movement.

The first case seems to typify the emergence of democracy in former communist states. After decades of broken promises and unfulfilled expectations, Marxist regimes throughout the world simply collapsed under the weight of poverty and inequity in the 1980s and 1990s. As their citizens became increasingly aware of how much better life was in neighboring democracies, they simply refused to back the communist oligarchies and turned instead to political competitors. Another example is Indonesia, where President Suharto resigned in the aftermath of 1998 riots brought on by decades of alleged corruption and economic mismanagement under his rule. The national elections in July 2001 represented a genuine expansion of Indonesian democracy.

In other cases, autocratic leaders engineered a transformation to democracy because the alternative was violent upheaval that threatened to destroy everything built up under one-party rule. A case in point is South Africa, which extended political franchise to nonwhites in 1994 partly out of recognition that the small white minority faced increasing violence as it tried to hang on to control of the country.

Numerous factors affect democratic transformation. One is the degree of economic development. Countries that have successfully transformed from rural to urban-based economies are more likely to be democratic than countries with a large percentage of the population engaged in agriculture.[11] Other factors include the efforts of outside actors to leverage democratic transformation. The national security strategy of the United States for the past several administrations has articulated the desirability for political change, particularly in the Middle East, grounded in the belief that democratic regimes there would be less likely to harbor religious militants and more willing to keep the peace with their neighbors. However, efforts to push for such transformation have not produced demonstrable results, and may actually impede reform. A recent summit of the Arab League collapsed in acrimony when a US proposal for democratization in the Arab world was leaked, leaving the impression that the United States exercised too much control over the Arab political agenda.[12]

Democratization in the Middle East

The United States is hardly the only source for democratization in the Middle East; indeed American foreign policy aligns with numerous nondemocratic polities in the region. It is rather the citizens of the region who have held democracy in high value, as noted below. The roots of democracy are deep in the Middle East, and certainly in the Arab Middle East. Sadiki's majestic work shows the impact of Islam (a liberating movement against the minority Meccan elite), the democratic reaction to Napoleon's invasion of Ottoman lands (noted below), and the power of Greek-inspired democratic ideals distilled by Muslim philosophers like al-Farabi (870–950).[13]

Despite such foundations and popular support, democracy remains a rarity in the Middle East. The New York–based Freedom House carries out an annual survey, rating countries as free, partially free, or not free.[14] In its 2006 survey, Freedom House gave the following designation to Middle Eastern countries:

FREEDOM HOUSE 2006 POLITICAL RANKINGS

Country	Free	Partially Free	Not Free
Algeria			•
Bahrain		•	
Egypt			•
Iran			•
Iraq			•
Israel	•		
Jordan		•	
Kuwait		•	
Lebanon		•	
Libya			•
Morocco		•	
Oman			•
Qatar			•
Saudi Arabia			•
Syria			•
Turkey		•	
Tunisia			•
UAE			•
Yemen		•	

The Freedom House rankings themselves have been questioned. For example, when Algeria held relatively free elections (by the accounts of outside observers) in 2004, its Freedom House ranking remained "not free," as was the case with Iraq, where several elections took place after 2003. Iliya Harik notes that relatively undemocratic Kuwait and relatively democratic Turkey hold the same score ("partly free"), and that some sub-Saharan African nations with severe democratic challenges rank higher than do most Arab countries.[15] "The argument here is not that Arab countries have a stellar record of democratization, as indeed they do not. It is a matter of whether FH's quantitative measurement of democratization across the board is reliable at all."[16]

The United Nations Arab Human Development Project notes the lack of democracy in the Arab world. The report examines a key component of democracy, "voice and accountability," with a cluster of measures (including independent media, civil liberties, and political rights), and found that only Jordan and Kuwait were equal or above the world average score on this variable, while all other nineteen Arab countries lie below the average.[17]

Why is it that so many Arab countries, along with Iran, have not achieved levels of democratization comparable to other developing areas of the world? According to Mustafa Hamarneh, a committee member and director of the Center for Strategic Studies in Jordan, "For some reason, the system seems to cave in to the first signs of resistance, then it follows with policies of appeasement, and the reformers are abandoned. The national agenda was going to be a road map to reform in the country, but it suddenly disappeared off the radar screen. It is no longer part of the official discourse."[18] Several explanations are made, ranging from the impact of Islam to the persistence of traditions linked to the history and environmental factors common to the Middle East.

Islam as a Barrier to Democracy?

Islam is the predominant religion in every Middle Eastern country except Israel, but does Islam account for the lack of democracy, or are there other cultural reasons behind the slow pace of political accountability in the Middle East? Stepan and Robertson note that non-Arab Muslim countries have outperformed Arab Muslim countries on all measures of democratic performance, including longevity of the practice of democracy. Examples of such Muslim democracies include Turkey (listed as "partially free" above), Indonesia, and Malaysia. Stepan and Robertson also argue that the Arab Muslim countries are less likely to have transitioned to democracy, noting that some Arab countries have actually regressed from democratic reform (for example, Jordan and Yemen).[19] That may be more a function of "Arabness" than Islam, and even then relative commitment to and accomplishment of democratic identity varies considerably across Arab countries.

It is more difficult to argue that Islam as a theology (as opposed to a political system) should impede democracy, and some claim that it should actually accelerate authoritarian challenge in the name of popular rule. Says Moussalli, "If the Qur'an and sunna are the source materials for a comprehensive Islamic revival, then removal of the elites is a Qur'anically legitimate matter. . . the quest for an Islamic state should be seen as a quest for liberation from the authoritarian states. . . that have dominated the Islamic arena for a long time."[20] Moreover, Islamists have embraced democracy in certain political environments in the Middle East.[21] Turkey's Justice and Development Party, modestly Islamist in tone, holds an outright majority in the Turkish parliament, and the Islamist Hamas holds a majority of seats in the Palestinian parliament. Some Islamist parties, like Egypt's Muslim Brotherhood, compete in elections, run women candidates, and form alliances with Christian groups. Whether or not such an embrace of democracy results in Islamist moderation, or whether it would mean more radicalization once such groups attained power remain debatable. Says Emad Gad, "I'm sure the Brothers still want to apply an old-fashioned version of Shari'a, treat Coptic Christians as second-class citizens and stay in power forever when they form the government. They are coming up with all these moderate slogans so as not to frighten anyone, especially the West." Another Egyptian scholar, however, argues, "Forget about the Islamic state, the caliphate and so on. The more the Brothers get dragged into the political arena, the more they are integrated, and the more they try to operate according to the rules of the arena."[22]

Public Preferences as a Barrier to Democracy?

It might be argued that populations long used to autocratic rule come to prefer it over the disorder of democracy, and that the long tradition of nondemocratic rule in the Middle East has reinforced those preferences. However, values surveys of the region do not support such a position. They find that support for democracy in the Middle East is very strong, as indicated by results of the World Values Survey, showing that the percentage agreeing with the statement "democracy is the best form of government" tops all other regions in the world.[23] Citizens in some Arab countries (Egypt, Morocco, Jordan, and Algeria) actually exceeded agreement indicated by citizens in the United States and other Western European countries. As Singh argues, "Wherever Arabs have had a free vote, they have used elections not simply to improve governance, but to strengthen their hand against authoritarian and corrupt regimes and/or foreign occupations that control their lives."[24]

The Staying Power of Autocracy as a Barrier to Democracy?

Historically, autocratic rule colored the political mosaic of the Middle East, varying mostly by the name of the institution (sultanate, emirate, caliphate, and so on), but, unlike much of the rest of the world, autocracy persisted. There are explanations as to why the Middle East traditionally featured highly centralized political systems. Arguably, the political foundations for democratization in the Middle East are not strong. From the early twentieth century on, Middle Eastern elites placed more emphasis on nation building, independence, and economic development than on democratization. They were keenly aware of their weakness relative to the European powers in particular, and recognized that authoritarian regimes had greater potential to develop quickly than would democratic governments.[25] Moreover, as Talbi judiciously notes, many autocrats in the Middle East (and elsewhere) can reap fantastic fortunes; of the ten wealthiest rulers in 1999, seven were from the Middle East, including four with fortunes exceeding $10 billion.[26] They were, without exception, autocrats.

Many countries have the requisite institutions for the construction of democracy, but, as Dorr notes, "many Middle Eastern states have multiparty political systems. They are often manipulated by the regime in power, or dominated by a single party."[27] Regimes may allow small parties to exist only if they do not pose a significant challenge to established authority.

The Long Shadow of Colonialism

Another barrier to democracy in the Middle East is the legacy of the colonial powers and, following that era, the superpower competition of the cold war. To enhance their legitimacy, the colonizers tried limited democratic experiments, and consequently democracy itself became tarred with the charge that it was only a facade for illegitimate rule.[28] In other cases, Europeans thwarted efforts at democratization. In Tunisia, for example, European settlers objected to the declarations of equality in efforts to establish constitutional law in 1861.[29] Ibrahim notes that as France was crushing democratic reform in Tunisia, Britain throttled democratic efforts in Egypt under Ismail Pasha (ruled between 1863 and 1879) and in Iraq under Dawood Pasha (1830–1869).[30] Milani claims that both Britain and the Soviet Union openly intervened in Iranian elections to ensure that those chosen supported the agenda of the outside powers.[31] Therefore, William Quandt argues, "It is certainly understandable if Middle Easterners are skeptical about importing some Western models of government. After all, the colonial powers that ruled them professed to be democratic and respectful of human rights. Disillusioned by the hypocrisy of the West, Middle Easterners seek indigenous traditions upon which to build more responsive, humane, and stable political systems."[32] Moreover, early efforts to create multiparty political systems (in Egypt, Iraq, Iran, Jordan, and Syria, for example) failed because challenging parties typically threatened the interests of the dominant elite, which the colonial power created to take the reins of power after independence.[33] Additionally, after the colonial period the cold war powers intervened to protect autocracies so long as they served the superpower's purpose. As Richards notes, "An authoritarian military regime could always count on support from one superpower, provided that such an Arab regime made suitable political moves against the other superpower. In short, the fact that the often violent struggle for independence was followed by a half-century of conflict with Israel, in a context of global Cold War, greatly strengthened authoritarianism."[34] Once entrenched, those authoritarian regimes managed to prevent democratic transition because they could afford to fund effective security forces, reward political loyalty though appointments, promotions, and the like, unchallenged by a general public reluctant to confront authoritarian regimes, partly due to the power of the security forces.[35]

Paths to Democracy in the Middle East

None of this should imply that there are no democratic foundations in the Middle East, or that there has been no significant change away from absolute regime structures. Baaklini, Denoeux, and Springborg view Arab democratic transitions as a three-stage model. The process begins at stage one, *al-mithaq*, with the incumbent elite responding to civil dissatisfaction through political liberalization and an agreement to enter a dialog with the opposition. That leads to stage two, *al-hiwar al-qawmi* (the national dialog), where trade-offs may include a role for the opposition in shaping public policy in exchange for opposition recognition of regime legitimacy. Stage three occurs when a vehicle for the opposition, usually a legislature, becomes more independent from the executive and capable of sustaining meaning-ful challenges to executive authority.[36]

A number of Middle Eastern and North African countries have democratic structures in place. Elected legislative bodies exist in several countries, although their power varies. Egypt has a well-established National Assembly, although the electoral system almost guarantees that the National Democratic Party will hold a large majority of the seats, though independents made large gains in the 2006 elec-tion. Jordan too has a parliament, and several years ago the Islamist Party gained a plurality of seats before surrendering them in a 1997 electoral boycott. Kuwait also has a National Assembly that the regime closed before the Gulf War of 1990–1991. It was reopened after the war in response to pressure from the United States.

Informal Democracy

Democracy does not have to mean formal institutions and elections. Under some interpretations, democracy is a contract between ruled and rulers that ensures, among other things, that the ruled will have a chance to gain access to goods and services that rulers provide. They want some input into decisions that affect them. Under tribal rule, such input came informally through consultation between tribal leaders and the males in the tribe. Bedouin tradition demanded that under the harsh conditions of the desert, such consultation was almost mandatory.

Those traditions carry over to some Persian Gulf states where formal legislatures do not exist. Leaders do have an obligation to hold a *majlis*, or *shura*, to allow their followers to meet with them to request assistance, criticize someone, air general grievances, or present gifts.[37] Often a provincial ruler will hold a *majlis* in a court-yard of the capitol building, receiving each subject personally. As Al Rasheed notes, however, the *majlis* is also a vehicle through which men of authority can demon-strate both their power and their wealth. Although they were traditionally open to all men, only those with business to discuss could actually attend.[38] Moreover, there is no public record of the proceedings of a *majlis*, as there would in a formal parlia-ment, thus limiting the accountability of the system.[39] Still, the process allows ac-cess, and direct access at that, to a ruler who has the power to grant favors or listen to grievances. It does not have the power to recall inefficient, corrupt, or indulgent leaders, for that would go against the tribal tradition of having leadership choices made only by a small circle of elder males. However, it does link leaders and subjects together, which is one thing expected of democracy.

What Democracy Can and Cannot Do in the Middle East

Evolving democracy movements can empower popular belief in the value of partici-pation, channeling frustration stemming from exclusion into peaceful political ac-tivity. Democratic polities can challenge inherent impulses of government secrecy, removing veils that cover corruption, cronyism, and other state malpractices, often paving the way for more robust economic development in the process. Democracy, when it functions and, more importantly, is *seen* to function by the population, can take the fire out of antiregime demogogery and bring a certain equilibrium to the political stage.

However, democracy cannot always reduce the power of entrenched elites (see below), whose available resource base often allows them to manipulate elections for their own benefit. Democracies often increase the power of factions at the expense of the whole, and one consequence is that the formation of policy emerges very slowly through a multitude of compromises resulting in almost no change to existing policies. Moreover, democracies do not automatically guarantee the protection of minority rights.

Democracy is not an antidote to terrorism, confounding the hopes of Western leaders such as President George W. Bush, whose foreign policy has selectively pushed democratization in the Middle East based on such expectations. Gause, though, notes that there have been terrorist incidents in democratic countries, often carried out by citizens (London in 2005 and Turkey in 2006, for example). Thus the Bush administration, according to Gause, is mistaken to hope that its push for Arab democracy will result in fewer terrorist incidents. He notes that the administration may not like the results of the democracy that it does get in the Arab world, a prophecy borne out by recent elections in Palestine, Egypt, and elsewhere.[40] Audrey Kurth Cronin states that "there is no evidence that democratization correlates with a reduction in terrorism; in fact, available historical data suggests the opposite. . . Moreover, democracy in the absence of strong political institutions and civil society could very well bring about radical Islamist governments over which the West would have little influence."[41] Nor are democracies necessarily pacifistic, despite the theorists who argue that democracies rarely if ever go to war by public choice, particularly against other democracies. Mansfield and Snyder claim that emerging democracies are more prone to war than developed democracies and that the slow process of democratic institution building may actually encourage war making.[42]

LAW AND POLITICS

The judicial systems in most Middle Eastern countries support a mix of civil and religious law. European powers passed on their judicial codes to the countries they colonized or protected during the nineteenth and early twentieth centuries. It took a while for many Muslim countries in the Middle East to replace religious courts with a civil law system (Egypt transformed only in 1956). Most countries have a combination of religious and civil courts, with so-called personal status matters generally heard in religious courts. In Israel rabbinical courts still decide family matters (divorce and child custody cases, for example), and many Muslim countries retain religious courts for the same purpose. In predominately Sunni countries, different schools of Sunni jurisprudence influence the thinking that religious courts bring to their deliberations and decisions (see Chapter 3 for a discussion of these schools of thought). The conservative Hanbali school predominates in Saudi

Arabia, influencing decisions on public morality, for example, while the more legalistic Shafii school influences Egypt's judicial emphasis on court procedure and process.

In many Middle Eastern countries, the judicial branch is independent of other branches of government, but in some cases, the executive branch also has judicial discretion. In Kuwait, for example, the Ministry of Religious Affairs has the authority to issue judicial suspensions against clerics who criticize the regime. Lebanon has a Court of Audit attached to the prime minister's office with powers to investigate spending by public officials.

ELITE RULE

In some political systems, irrespective of type, members of society participate in most decisions, but such systems are rare. The more common political system restricts political participation to influential groups known as elites. They may be religious elites, seen in the small clerical circle in Iran that has almost absolute power over that country, business elites, or military elites who may steer their countries first to independence and then to military rule or exert a strong military influence in politics.

The term "elite" refers to a small subsection of political society that holds disproportionate power and influence. Elites usually have high social status, group cohesion, a consensus on values and beliefs, and a lack of accountability to the majority of society.[43] Elites usually form their consensus through shared experiences, for example, by attending the same military schools and maintaining the bonds established during their careers.[44] Elites may be graduates of the country's most prestigious university, or attain university education in Europe or North America. In traditional societies, elites may come from the same dominant tribe or clan. Elites usually hold a disproportionate share of society's wealth because of their positioning and access to power. Elites often dominate the professional military or control access to the military. In many developing societies, the military is the dominant elite, often because of its heroic status as liberator and defender of the nation, and because of its unique position to control politics from the barrel of a gun. Yet in other cases, the military emerges as an "antielite," with many officers coming from humble origins (Saddam Hussein or Hafiz al-Asad, for example) and seizing power by ousting the established business or family elites. However established, the military is often a source of patronage, doling out favors because it controls a considerable portion of societal resources. Officers may either rule directly or, more commonly, become the power behind a facade of civilian rule, installing and removing rulers in line with military interests.

Elites exist in all types of political systems. Some students of democratic systems argue that while a democratic system may theoretically be open to all or most, elites have much more influence in those systems than do nonelites.[45] Thus democratization may not eliminate elites but give them more legitimacy should they come to power through democratic means. Crises may also enhance elite legitimacy, particularly if elites use a crisis to bring about popular changes or stability.[46]

Elites in the Middle East

Elite-dominated political systems are typical in many Middle Eastern countries. Leaders come from either royal families or wealthy families that allow them access to power. Others come from dominant tribes or from the military, where the elites usually dominate the officer ranks, as is the case in Baathist Syria (see Chapter 12).

Military elites form one of the strongest political bases in the Middle East. In many countries the military became an agent for change, as many officers saw themselves as nation builders, rescuing their societies from what they argued were feudal, corrupt regimes in the service of colonialists. Militaries often lead their countries' liberation movements (in Algeria, Syria, and Egypt, for example) and then march into the presidential palace to take over the reins of government, arguing that their role in independence gives them the right—and the mandate—to rule.[47] Often they represent a diametrical mix of conservative and modernist views on society and politics: upholding the status quo against leftist political currents while guarding against religious rule. Middle Eastern militaries tend to prefer secular governance, often modeled after Kemal Ataturk's secular Turkey, though few Arab militaries have restricted the practices and expressions of faith as much as Ataturk and his successors have done. In many Middle Eastern countries, the military holds considerable economic influence, not only from large defense budgets, but also because of their involvement in industrial and agricultural sectors that originally supported the armed forces, but grew beyond to become major sources of income and employment.[48] In numerous Middle East countries, the military has provided rulers, as in Egypt, Turkey, Algeria, and Israel, including prime ministers Yitzhak Rabin, Ehud Barak, and Ariel Sharon, which is partly a reflection of the high status the Israel Defense Forces enjoy. In other cases, the military is the power behind the throne, supporting leaders who focus on military objectives and withdrawing that support when their leaders disappoint them.[49]

Elite-dominated countries may be democratic or semidemocratic. Some argue that elites play a positive role in democratization, such that elite consensus, supported by viable political institutions, is essential for stable democracy, as in Lebanon.[50] Elites may also push for political liberalization, as they did in Jordan.[51] The move toward democratization in Iran pitted two elites, the technocratic and the religious, against each other, with the former able to gain enough power to set the stage for the election of moderate political leaders.[52] However, the religious elite took advantage of its position to nullify the small gains of the technological elite after the 2005 election.

Islamist movements may be a popular reaction to dominance by secular elites, partly because Islamist leaders charge that these elites substitute material goals over spiritual ends and engage in coziness with the West. However, some Islamist movements may be just one more manifestation of elite power in contention with secular elites. Many Islamist leaders enjoy their own privileges and live lives removed from the impoverished communities they serve. Gaffney notes that the "rural peasants and urban masses who continue to regard Islam as the primary basis for their identity have not responded positively to the summons of the current (Islamic) revival," possibly because the Islamic revival cannot always paper over the old cleavages between the top and bottom rungs of society.[53]

CIVIL SOCIETY

Political discourse about political power and influence normally focuses on the relationship between state and society. However, this relationship downplays the role of informal organizations outside the state. As it became more apparent that such organizations contributed to the downfall of numerous authoritarian regimes in the 1980s and 1990s, the focus on civil society grew. "Civil society" refers here either to organizations and societies that exist as alternatives to the state or in coexistence with it.[54] Diamond describes such organizations as "voluntary, self-generating, largely self-supporting, and bound by a legal order or set of shared values," and include professional, educational, and religious organizations, alternative political movements, and even institutionalized private meetings.[55] Civil societies serve as an alternative provider of goods and services, and as a means to resolve disputes.[56] They may be particularly strong in countries with weakly developed central governments.

Some observers of civil society in countries transformed from authoritarian regimes to democracies speculate that a vibrant civil society may have contributed to the transition, enabling pluralistic democracy by preventing the domination of elected bodies by traditional and powerful elites. The post–cold war transformation of Eastern and Central Europe become classic cases of this argument. Civil society may either be a prelude to democratization or may serve as a substitute for it. If a critical element of a country's population loses faith in both its current regime and the potential for greater rewards through democratization, it may simply institutionalize civil society organizations in response.

Civil Society in the Middle East

Tribes (organizations based loosely on kinship and common ancestry) in the Middle East were the primary form of social network before the coming of the modern state, and their influence persists. Because one central tenet of tribes is autonomy, they resisted the encroachment of centralized state power. In many Middle Eastern countries they provide alternatives to what the state offers to provide to the populace.[57] So civil society may represent either old tribal support structures or new institutions like women's advocacy groups.[58] Civil society in the Middle East also grew in the past century, in a period Ibrahim calls "the first Arab liberal age," with more than sixty-four civil society organizations established at the end of the nineteenth century, 300 by 1925, and more than 3,000 by 1950. These organizations provided the incubators in many cases for the post–World War II independence movements that came to power in the postcolonial era.[59]

There are numerous civil societies in the modern Middle East today. Al-Said would include "political parties, professional associations, business groups, trade unions, private societies—*jamiyyat,* that is, social clubs, literary and scientific societies—all are accepted as part of civil society."[60] Some existed long before the creation of the central state, while others are new. The practice of the *diwaniyya* in the Gulf countries and Iran is an example of the former, where semiformal gatherings occur in private homes and participants exchange what many regimes try to control—information.[61] In other cases, civil society includes women's groups, Islamic study groups, and charitable organizations, known also as nongovernmental organizations, or NGOs. NGOs often do what regimes fail to do, care for the least well off. Other civil societies promote human rights and press freedom and are potential vehicles to promote democratization. As al-Khafaji suggests, the absence of parliamentary democracy in Iraq (and elsewhere) "was not mainly the produce of the malevolent will of the ancient régime nor of imperialism, as many Arab writings imply, but has to do with the virtual absence of civil society, whis is the necessary condition for the rise of a pluralist democracy."[62] However, civil societies in general have not weakened Arab authoritarianism where it exists, partly because regimes can easily repress critical civil societies and because Arab social and political life still revolves around tribe and clan, rather than voluntary organizations outside traditional ties, and thus membership and activism in Arab civil society is quite low.[63]

THE NEWS MEDIA AND POLITICS

Part of the reason for the popularity of informal exchanges that Middle East civil society practices is related to the control over information practiced by many Middle Eastern governments. Most censor the press and control other avenues of information from outside the region. Some news outlets are directly run by the state (in Syria, Saudi Arabia, Iran, for example), but numerous independent daily news papers exist in many parts of the Middle East, often representing a wide spectrum of political views. Internet and satellite television is growing rapidly throughout the Middle East, making it much more difficult for restrictive governments to control public information. Some governments place clamps over Internet access, for example, blocking sites and monitoring e-mail. Some argue that civil society loses its effectiveness without open communication, while government censors argue that they are simply blocking or monitoring sites that advocate political violence.[64]

Middle Eastern media growth has accompanied political liberalization and, in some cases, may have helped further it, as in the case of Algeria in the late 1980s.[65] By the late 1990s satellite television had spread through the region, initiated in 1996 by the introduction of al-Jazeera in Qatar. Drawing from experienced television journalists and producers, al-Jazeera quickly established a wide following for its broadcasts. Normally taboo topics like polygamy, human rights, Islamic debates, and interviews with Israeli officials got airtime on al-Jazeera. Soon other Arab satellite televisions stations took to the air, and Arab Radio and Television, al-Arabiyya, and NileSat joined al-Jazeera as satellite dishes proliferated in the Middle East.[66] In the United Arab Emirates, Media City has sprung up in Dubai, bringing together technology and training in new broadcasting techniques that offer even more open communications in the Middle East and beyond. These venues, as Eickelman notes, open doors of political discourse to new publics outside of the traditional elites, including women and minorities. Moreover, the often lively and candid political talk shows offer differing points of view, rather than the often one-sided views from traditional media, and perhaps paving a way for a fundamental core of democracy.[67] What remains to be seen is whether this new emphasis on open discussion of controversial topics will bring about a more robust role for civil society and a demand for more accountable governance.

HUMAN RIGHTS

In the past several decades, there has been concern about violations of human rights in many Middle East countries. Since much of that concern comes from Western countries, it may create the impression that human rights is a bundle of issues of primary concern to Westerners. In reality, however, the growing awareness that governments have obligations to abide by an increasingly universal list of human rights is global. States and groups all around the world now participate in efforts to both codify and enforce human rights.

The problem is that there is no agreed-on definition of human rights. The closest thing is the Universal Declaration of Human Rights adopted by the United Nations in 1948. Its provisions emphasize human equality, prohibition of slavery, torture, or other degrading treatment, equality before the law, right of privacy, freedom of movement, freedom of conscience, religion, and thought, presumption of innocence until proven guilty, and others.[68]

While these rights sound fundamental and basic, they may conflict with state security requirements. States may restrict human rights by claiming that the exercise of such rights is a pretext for antistate elements to challenge the existing power structure. Human rights violations are more likely to occur when social conflict becomes violent, or when alternative societal groups challenge a ruling elite in ways that threaten to weaken or topple it. Under such circumstances, social organizations as well as states often escalate violations of human rights, as in the case of Israel and the Palestinians, or the Lebanese civil wars during the 1970s and 1980s.[69]

In Islamic societies, the concept of human rights may differ from that in secular Western thought and practice. Monshipouri states, "According to Islam, rights are wholly owned by God. Individuals (as vice-regents of God) can enjoy human rights in their relationship with God insofar as they fulfill obligations to God. Moral obligations to other persons and peoples take precedence over individual human rights."[70] In the Middle East, limits on individual human rights are often more a function of regime restrictions than of religion. Some regimes allow opposition groups to publish newspapers critical of the government, but at the same time, regimes can make the papers disappear and arrest their editors if the criticism is too trenchant. Opposition groups may call for rallies and demonstrations, but police often monitor such events, often photographing participants for later arrest. Other cases of alleged violations of human rights include imprisonment for long periods without charges or trial, and sometimes under conditions of mental or physical torture. Several organizations document cases of alleged human rights abuse, including the US Department of State and the international organization Amnesty International.[71]

MINORITY GROUPS IN THE MIDDLE EAST

Almost all Middle East countries have minority groups. Some are religious minorities, while others are linguistic minorities. Some are both. The issues raised by minorities in the Middle East involve their rights to the same things that majorities have, their assimilation into the greater society, and their aspirations for a separate community. Some of the more important minorities in the Middle East have wanted a separate national home, while others are satisfied with grants of equal rights within a country. Other minorities may be represented in the presidential palace, and they may simply desire to preserve the status quo.

The Kurds

One of the larger minority groups in the Middle East is the Kurds, distinguished by their Kurdish language. There are somewhere between 25 and 30 million Kurds, making them the largest linguistic group in the Middle East without its own nation-state. The largest Kurdish population is in Turkey, where about 10–12 million live. Iran has some 5–6 million Kurds; Iraq has 3.5 million, and Syria 1 million. These countries all agree on one thing despite other differences: there will be no sovereign nation-state named Kurdistan.

The Kurds trace their written language back for thousands of years; it probably originated somewhere on the Asian subcontinent. Around 2,000 years ago, they migrated to the mountainous regions where most of them live today. Some rose to high positions (Salah al-Din, the Muslim leader who fought the Crusaders, for example), but most remained in isolation. While Kurds maintain their distinctive language, most adopted Islam over the years, though a few practice Christianity or Judaism. Their remoteness tended to keep them out of the sweep of events in the Middle East, and the Ottoman Empire incorporated most Kurds after Ottoman forces defeated Persia in 1514. The Ottomans initially granted the Kurds semisovereignty, but during the nineteenth century, Kurdish-Ottoman relations were marked with a series of bloody revolts, leading to increased demands for an independent Kurdistan.

Other Minorities

Other linguistic minorities in the Middle East include the Armenians (who live in Iran and Egypt, among other places), Aramaic speakers (an ancient language now spoken in a few Syrian mountain villages), and the Berbers (or Amazigh) who live mostly in North Africa. Religious minorities also live in the Middle East. A number of Arab countries (Syria, Morocco, Iraq) and a Persian country, Iran, have small Jewish minorities.[72] Iran has populations of the Bahai and Zoroastrians, regarded by many Muslims as nonbelievers. Egypt has a small population of Coptic Christians. Non-Muslim religious minorities in majority Muslim states face a particular challenge in that some Muslims argue that non-Muslims cannot hold government posts in Muslim regimes, and in practice, very few non-Muslims actually hold such positions.[73] Each linguistic and religious minority has had its own struggles with the majority population, chronicled in more detail in the country chapters that follow.

WOMEN AND MIDDLE EASTERN SOCIETY

Until the twentieth century, women in almost every part of the world found themselves largely subjugated to the will of men. Women were frozen out of society by rules largely made by men, and thus restricted to a very few opportunities outside the traditional household. While scattered feminist political movements began in some parts of the world before the twentieth century, change in the status of women was glacial until their efforts to gain access to the vote finally succeeded in some countries in the early 1900s. In many parts of the industrialized world today, women have gained entry to the business, social, athletic, and political worlds, although much remains to be done before women hold equal status and opportunity. However, progress must be understood in regional terms. In some parts of the Middle East, women have won rights that made a significant difference in their lives, but in other areas, there has been almost no progress at all, as noted in the following chapters focused on individual countries.

The history of women in the Middle East compares with that of other societies. Women rarely make the pages of the history books as great leaders, warriors, scholars, or athletes because rules or tradition excluded them from such realms (pharonic Egypt was an exception). They made their contributions in areas where they could, as in the arts and literature. Women also did much of the manual labor.

In ancient Egypt, women appear to have shared relatively equal status with men, with several, including Ahhotep and Hatshepsut, rising to rule as pharaoh or regent.[74] Women had similar property rights as did men, and temple depictions show them mixing easily with the opposite gender. In other ancient societies, women rulers are extremely rare; an exception is Syria, where Queen Zenobia ruled over Palmyra from 270 to 274 CE before the city fell to the Roman general Aurelian. Aurelian dragged Queen Zenobia to Rome in chains when she refused to submit to his terms. In later times, Shajarat al-Durr took the title of sultan in Mamluk Egypt after her husband died and rallied her troops to defeat the Crusaders at Damietta in 1249. Yet these cases are exceptions. In the Middle East, as was the case elsewhere in the world, male-dominated society generally relegated women to secondary economic roles, with no possibility of upward mobility or change in status.

Both religion and tradition shape status and role for women in the Middle East. For Muslims, the Quran in Sura 2:228 holds that "women shall have rights similar to the rights against them, according to what is equitable; but men have a degree of advantage over them." This follows from Sura 4:34, "Men are the maintainers of women because Allah has made some of them to excel others and because they spend out of their property; the good women are therefore obedient, guarding the unseen as Allah has guarded; and (as to) those on whose part you fear desertion, admonish them, and leave them alone in the sleeping-places and beat them; then if they obey you, do not seek a way against them; surely Allah is High, Great." There is a tradition, lost until recently, of Muslim women occupying significant places in the corpus of Islamic thought, including an observation that perhaps 15 percent of hadith scholars in medieval times were women.[75] Orthodox Jewish tradition holds that during menstruation, women are unclean and must be restricted. Traditional Christianity also limited the rights of women, and many current legal statutes in Lebanon, the Middle Eastern country with the largest Christian population, reflect that fact (see Chapter 13).

The role of women in Middle Eastern society varies from country to country. Rules in some countries exclude women from public life to prevent them from coming into contact from men, or so the rationale goes. In other countries (Jordan, Israel, Morocco, Turkey, and Tunisia, for example) women can participate in most societal functions, serving in the military and standing for election. Educational opportunities for women differ considerably from country to country. Only 44 percent of girls attend primary school in Yemen, but more girls than boys attend primary school in Bahrain, Qatar, and the UAE, while larger numbers of girls than boys attend secondary school in numerous Arab countries.[76] However, while legal barriers have fallen in many Middle Eastern and North African states, less tangible but no less real hurdles remain. Traditional beliefs and practices, particularly in rural and poor urban areas, restrict women to achieving status only through marriage and childbirth.

Women in some Middle East countries do not have access to high-status employment and are not permitted to move up the promotion ladder on a pace with men. Women's access to politics is also restricted, since women cannot vote or run for office in some Middle East countries. While women have been heads of state or significant leaders in Muslim countries (Pakistan, Indonesia, Bangladesh, and Turkey) and in Israel (Prime Minister Golda Meir), no woman has served as head of state in an Arab country or Iran. Women have the right to vote in Iran, Israel, and Turkey, and in the Arab countries of Algeria, Bahrain, Egypt, the Palestinian Territories, Morocco, Qatar, Yemen, Syria, Tunisia, Jordan, and Lebanon.[77]

In some Gulf countries, men may take up to four wives if they can support them equally, a practice that dates back to Muhammad. While the Quran, in Sura 4.1 allows up to four wives, it cautions about the need to treat them equally, "then marry such women as seem good to you, two and three and four; but if you fear that you will not do justice (between them), then (marry) only one or what your right hands possess; this is more proper," and "No matter how you try, you will never be able to treat your wives equally," which some regard as an endorsement of monogamy. The Prophet married multiple wives to cement ties to allies and potential foes. Opponents of polygamy note that only men may take multiple marriage partners, while its defenders claim that it protects older women from divorce and allows women motherhood opportunities should large numbers of men die in war.[78]

Marriage in many Islamic countries may end through *talaq*, or divorce by decree. Shiite divorce law is stricter than Sunni law, requiring witnesses and waiting between the testament of divorce.[79] In both branches, the male spouse initiates the divorce without need for cause, and women do not always have recourse through the law on matters of alimony or child custody, depending on the country. Divorce often favors men in child custody decisions, particularly when religious courts decide them. In many Islamic countries, divorce reformers push for changes in national laws that would put family cases in civil rather than religious courts.[80] Israeli women face the same problem, as divorces in Israel fall to rabbinical courts rather than civil courts, which are often unwilling to grant a divorce to a woman.

Access to education and employment remains an issue for women in the Middle East. This is a particular problem in some of the Gulf monarchies. While women and men have almost equal literacy rates in Qatar and the UAE, there is considerable difference in Bahrain, Kuwait, and Saudi Arabia. In Kuwait, for example, almost one-fourth of the women are illiterate while only 8 percent of men cannot read. The United Nations estimates the overall illiteracy rate for Arab women at 55 percent.[81] In Yemen, it is 30 percent for women. In an interview with a Jordanian newspaper, the editor of Egypt's *al-Ahram* newspaper noted that women in some Arab countries have illiteracy rates of 80 to 90 percent, limiting their ability to vote and serve in parliament.[82]

Women's access to employment in the Arab world is also limited. The 2005 *Arab Human Development Report* indicates that Arab women's economic activity rate (the rate at which women fifteen years old and above supply labor) is 33 percent, the lowest in the world, compared to a world average of 56 percent.[83] Moreover, current attitudes in the Middle East may make the achievement of employment gender equality difficult, since, according to the World Values Survey, support for gender equality in the workplace is the lowest of all regions of the world.[84] However, women in many Middle Eastern countries are filling both home and workplace vacuums caused by absent males, who leave their native country for long periods to work abroad. According to Fernea, male absences create new opportunities for women to work outside of the home, and to advance up the economic ladder.[85] Women have also, perhaps paradoxically, advanced in at least two Islamist parties, taking active roles in both Yemen's Islah Party and in Jordan's Islamic Action Front (see Chapters 7 and 15).[86]

Women face other situations in traditional rural areas. Male family members sometimes accuse an unmarried woman seen with a man outside her family of bringing shame to the male members of her family. Sometimes a father or a brother takes responsibility for killing her, a practice known as honor killing. In the 1990s, around one-third of murders in Jordan were honor killings, as were 70 percent of murders in the West Bank and Gaza and between 25 and 30 percent in Lebanon.[87] In some rural areas, female genital mutilation still occurs (in Egypt, for example), though it is illegal in most Arab countries. The practice, sometimes called female circumcision, is technically known as clitoridectomy. The words "genital mutilation" connote the fact that it is usually done on unwilling women at a young age, purportedly to keep them faithful to their husbands. These procedures are often performed in rural areas under unsanitary conditions, and frequently result in infection, sterilization, and sometimes death from complications. The practice is discussed again in the chapters covering the individual nations where it occurs.

Some Islamic countries in the Middle East impose restrictive clothing on women by law (Saudi Arabia and Iran, for example), and in other countries there is considerable social pressure for women to adopt covering garments in public. Such coverings, known collectively as *hijab*, symbolize the early teachings of Islam holding that women tempt men, and thus society must protect men from their sexuality. Defenders of *hijab* argue that the custom protects women from predatory sexual behavior by men.[88] Barlas argues that such practices are rooted more in the hadith than they are in the Quran, which changed meaning through improper translation and through the insertion of patriarchal values following the Abbasid period. She notes that *hijab* traditionally applied only to slave women, and that the practice later applied to Muslim women as conservative tradition overcame the egalitarian messages found in the Quran.[89]

In many countries, women have organized to advance their status in society. Their most common vehicle is civil society groups, which many women prefer to existing organizations such as labor unions that are dominated by men and pursue a traditional agenda that pushes newer issues aside. One such group is the Jordanian National Committee for Women, founded by Princess Basma Bint Talal Hussein (the sister of the late King Hussein), which has produced studies that resulted in policy changes in areas such as education and legislative representation (see Chapter 15). Of course, not all countries have a prominent woman from the royal family who supports women's issues. Still, women's groups have been engaged in struggles that have produced changes in Egypt, Tunisia, and other Middle Eastern countries.

Scholars and activists outside of the region influence much of the discussion about women and society in the Middle East. Some women from the region urge caution by outsiders regarding the conditions faced by women and the appropriate responses. Nouha al-Hegelan implies that Westerners stereotype Arab women and fail to recognize that the coming of Islam gave women in traditional societies rights that did not previously exist.[90] Moreover, Islamist parties in Yemen and Jordan have actively recruited women and given them significant positions in those organizations (see Chapters 7 and 15). And while it may strike some as a paradox, according to White, "many Islamist women want to use Islam to liberate themselves from conventional patterns of life and patriarchal constraints. . . they believe that Islamic doctrine also supports women's becoming educated, working, and being politically active."[91]

IMAGES

Two young women dressed in fireproof racing suits stride confidently toward their modified rally car, proud of the fact that they are the first Bahraini women to compete in the Bahrain road rally. They exchange high-fives with some of their male competitors and then their car roars off the starting podium and disappears into the desert, trailing a rooster tail of dust. The crowd seems to give them extra applause. They do not win, but their presence in a male-dominated sport and the crowd's acceptance indicate how far women have come in the relatively conservative Gulf.

FOREIGN AFFAIRS

Like most other regions of the world, the Middle East has long been marked by violent conflict. Wars between tribes, religious groups, nation-states, and empires are age-old, and while many of the root causes are long gone, conflict remains a feature here. War as an instrument of power has diminished and there has not been a major war between two internal countries since Iraq invaded Kuwait in 1990. The most recent war involved the United States and a small number of outside countries against the Iraqi regime of Saddam Hussein in 2003.

A number of potential conflicts still brew in the Middle East, although the potential for serious interstate conflict is lower in the twenty-first century. Morocco and Algeria have tense relations over their border, and Morocco remains embroiled in a dispute over the status of the western Sahara. The Israel-Palestinian conflict remains tense. It is partially conditioned on the results of the three major wars fought between the Israelis and their Arab neighbors, although there are clearly other causes as well. The peace process, under way in some form since 1948, has focused largely (though not exclusively) on resolving the outstanding issues left from the 1948 and 1967 wars.

Peace in the Middle East

Periods of major war in the Middle East appear to have ended for now, but the ongoing violence between the state of Israel and the Palestinian population in the occupied territories remains a serious problem, as does the continuing sectarian violence in post–Saddam Hussein Iraq.

Following the 1967 war, the United Nations created what its members hoped would be the roots of peace in the Middle East, Resolutions 242 and 338. United Nations Resolution 242 passed the Security Council in November 1967 and Resolution 338 in 1973. Resolution 242 set forth several principles, including the withdrawal of Israeli forces from territories seized in 1967 in exchange for the "respect for and acknowledgement of sovereignty, territorial integrity, and political independence of every state in the region." The resolution also called for freedom of navigation in international waters, a "just settlement" for the refugee problem, and measures to establish demilitarized zones to help insure security of borders. UN Resolution 338 followed 242, passed again by the Security Council in the wake of a war, this time the 1973 war. The resolution approved in October 1973 called for the immediate implementation of 242 and for a cease-fire and the beginning of peace talks. However, almost eighteen years would pass before this happened. Neither side hurried to the peace table. The leadership of most Arab countries appeared to fear inflaming their own publics through negotiations with Israel. As Rabinovich notes, Israel seemed to regard negotiations with the Palestinians as a zero-sum game, "that Palestinian demands and expectations can be met only by intolerable terms," preferring instead to negotiate with Egypt, Syria, or Jordan over tangible terms like water and borders.[92]

In the aftermath of the 1973 war, Egypt's President Anwar Sadat launched a peace effort. Following his sudden trip to Israel in 1977, Sadat and Israeli Prime Minister Menachem Begin traveled to Camp David, Maryland, in 1978 at the invitation of American President Jimmy Carter. Carter assisted the two leaders in negotiations that ultimately led to the pioneering Israeli-Egyptian peace accord of 1979, signed in a ceremony in Washington that year (see Chapter 1).

Many hoped that the Camp David accords would be the first step in achieving a broader peace between Israel and her neighbors. Instead, most Arab leaders castigated President Sadat, and many Arab nations broke ties with Egypt, because of the widespread belief in the Arab world that peace is not divisible and must involve all Arab countries losing territory to Israel. The Arab League expelled Egypt and moved its headquarters from Cairo to Tunis. Sadat himself would fall under the bullets of assassins in 1981. The prospects for peace appeared dim.

However, events following the Camp David accord would ultimately drive both Israel and its neighbors towards the peace table. Israel fought a bloody and relatively indecisive war in Lebanon in 1982, and the first Palestinian uprising, or intifadah, began in December 1987. Both Israelis and Palestinians recognized that the situation of "no war, no peace" could last indefinitely, and Lebanon's fragile political structure was almost destroyed by the Israeli invasion and the violent civil war that had raged there between 1975 and 1989. Jordan, a small nation that risked entanglement in the conflict due to its proximity to Israel and its large Palestinian refugee population, also recognized the need to start a process leading to peace.

On October 31, 1991, the United States and the Soviet Union invited the leaders of Syria, Jordan, Lebanon, Israel, and the Palestinians to attend a peace conference in Madrid, following the successful ouster of Iraqi forces from Kuwait. The letter of invitation specified that the process would hinge on two United Nations Resolutions, 242 and 338, as the basis for a lasting settlement. The Madrid Conference lasted for three days and proceeded along two paths, a bilateral track to include discussions between Israel and Jordan, the Palestinians, Syria, and Lebanon, and a multilateral track focusing on issues of common concern. In the end, Israel signed agreements with Jordan and with the Palestinians (who joined Jordan as a joint delegation). However, negotiations hit a dead end with both Lebanon and Syria.

In an effort to restart the peace process, secret talks began in Oslo, Norway, in January 1993, hosted by Norwegian Foreign Minister Jøhan Jurgen Holst. Representatives from the Palestinian Liberation Organization and the Israeli government reached agreement on a set of principles, which was signed in a dramatic ceremony in the White House Rose Garden by Rabin and Arafat, with a beaming President Bill Clinton maneuvering both men into an uneasy handshake in September of that year. What they signed was an interim five-year agreement allowing for a Palestinian Authority political system, the withdrawal of Israeli forces from parts of the Gaza and West Bank, and other measures designed to allow for the transition into a final settlement. That would not happen, as noted in Chapter 1. What followed was a flurry of activity encouraged by Clinton to bring peace between Israel, Syria, and the Palestinians in 2000. The negotiations between Syria and Israel at Shepards-town, West Virginia, in January 2000 never achieved even a draft accord and Clinton's efforts later that year to rekindle the Syrian-Israeli peace process also failed. However, Syrian-Israeli relations remained at a tense but peaceful standoff since the interim agreement in 1974, so the peace process between the two countries was less important by comparison to the Israeli-Palestinian process.

The United States, Israel, and the Palestinian Authority attempted to build a permanent peace accord in a series of preliminary meetings leading up to a summit between Clinton, Barak, and Arafat at Camp David, Maryland, in July 2000. Clinton offered not only his "good offices," but also an aid package of $35 billion to both sides. Those meetings ended without agreement, and subsequent efforts in Washington and at Taba, Egypt, also failed to bring accord.

Some analysts concluded that the primary cause of the failure was the lack of leadership. Pundak faults both Barak and Arafat for the collapse of the Camp David summit and, in part, for the rapid slide into violence that followed. For Pundak, Barak failed to build presummit goodwill by failing to implement previous agreements, and failed to provide a clear negotiating position to the Palestinians.[93] Arafat tried to have it both ways, by calling for peace with Israel on the one hand and either encouraging or failing to stop Palestinian violence against Israel on the other hand.[94] Clearly neither the Israelis nor the Palestinians can reach a meaningful peace accord without strong leaders. Moreover, as Lasensky notes, while American aid sustained the peace process between 1993 and 2001, aid and the promise of more aid did not help to bring about a peace agreement.[95]

The issue of Jerusalem seemed particularly difficult. It is a sacred city to all three religions, and the right of access to holy places is paramount to their followers. The Israeli public demanded access to the Jewish holy places (including, but not necessarily limited to, the Western Wall of the Second Temple), since the site had been off limits to them between 1947 and 1967. However, that did not necessarily mean that a majority of Israelis might not approve of some part of Jerusalem as a Palestinian capital. The city has been historically divided two ways, the new city, and what is simply called "the old city." The new city is the modern bustling part of the Israeli capital, while the old city is the part surrounded by the sixteenth century wall built by the Ottomans and containing the Church of the Holy Sepulcher, the Dome of the Rock and Al-Aqsa Mosque, and the Western Wall. The old city was historically divided into the Arab Quarter, the Christian Quarter, the Armenian Quarter, and the Jewish Quarter. A vast majority of Israelis opposes making Jerusalem the capital of Palestine, even as the vast majority of Palestinians want Jerusalem as their capital. However, the vast majority of Palestinians believe that parts of the old city sector should be the basis for a Palestinian capital, a case that John Quigley finds to be consistent with principles of international law.[96] That prospect is increasingly hampered by Israeli settlement policy that rings Jerusalem with settlements that will block off the city from the Palestinian territories when completed, as well as the "security obstacle" erected through parts of the city by Israeli authorities to combat armed incursions into Israel. There are also unconfirmed reports that Israel plans to partition Jerusalem into Arab and Jewish portions between 2008 and 2010.[97]

Whether or not the peace process can be sustained between Israel and the bordering Arab states is problematic at best. The initial peace process between Israel, Jordan, and Egypt has produced some positive achievements, including people-to-people contacts at high levels that can build understanding. Yet they have also produced bitter disappointment in the Arab nations, implying that Arabs remain relatively powerless in dealing with both Israel and the West.[98] The 2000–2008 violence between Israel and the Palestinians and the absence of strong American participation in trying to end it shook faith in two fundamental assumptions of the overall Middle East peace process. "One is that Arabs and Jews had reached a broad consensus that guns, bombs and bloodshed could never resolve the Israeli-Palestinian conflict. The other is that the United States, driven by its deep interest in regional stability, would never stand idly by as the Middle East plunged towards another war."[99] Yet as of this writing, the horrific Arab-Israeli wars of the past have not recurred, and the United States removed the Saddam Hussein regime in Iraq that had twice invaded a neighbor. The George W. Bush administration tried to take advantage of the post–Saddam Hussein climate by announcing support for a "road map to peace" following the selection of Mahmoud Abbas as the Palestinian prime minister. Bush appealed to both Ariel Sharon and Abbas to move their sides toward a peace agreement, and for a few months in the summer of 2003 progress was slow but seemed steady. However, Israeli attacks against Hamas leaders and Palestinian suicide bombings against Israelis suddenly dampened peace prospects. Said Yossi Beilin, an Israeli negotiator, "The Israelis did not dismantle outposts, the Palestinians did no visible acts to fight terrorism," and the American monitoring of the process "was a big failure."[100] The Bush administration, according to some critics, gave insufficient attention to the road map, the Israelis gave too few concessions, and the Palestinian Authority could not stop the continuing attacks against Israelis. By mid-2007 the road map appeared to be dead.[101]

SUGGESTED READINGS

General Politics in the Middle East

Andersen, Roy. *Politics and Change in the Middle East: Sources of Conflict and Change.* 7th ed. Upper Saddle River, NJ: Prentice-Hall, 2003.

Milton-Edwards, Beverley. *Contemporary Politics in the Middle East.* Cambridge: Blackwell, 2000.

Owen, Roger. *State, Power, and Politics in the Making of the Modern Middle East.* London: Routledge, 2000.

Democratization in the Middle East

Baaklini, Abdo, Guilain Denoeux, and Robert Springborg. *Legislative Politics in the Arab World: The Resurgence of Democratic Institutions*. Boulder, CO: Lynne Rienner, 1999.

Bahgat, Korany, Paul Noble, and Rex Brynen, eds. *Political Liberalization and Democratization in the Arab World*. Vol. 1, *Theoretical Perspectives*. Vol. 2, *Case Studies*. Boulder, CO: Lynne Rienner, 1995.

Diamond, Larry J., Mark F. Plattner, and Daniel Brumberg, eds. *Islam and Democracy in the Middle East*. Baltimore, MD: Johns Hopkins University Press, 2003.

Kamrava, Mehran. *Democracy in the Balance: Culture and Society in the Middle East*. New York: Chatham House, 1998.

Sadiki, Larbi. *The Search for Arab Democracy*. New York: Columbia University Press, 2004.

Human Rights

Dwyer, Kevin. *Arab Voices: The Human Rights Debate in the Middle East*. Berkeley: University of California Press, 1991.

Monshipouri, Mahmood. *Islamism, Secularism, and Human Rights in the Middle East*. Boulder, CO: Lynne Rienner, 1998.

Waltz, Susan E. *Human Rights and Reform*. Berkeley: University of California Press, 1995.

Women and Society in the Middle East

Afshar, Haleh. *Islam and Feminism: An Iranian Case Study*. New York: St. Martin's, 1998.

Barlas, Asma. *"Believing Women" in Islam: Unreading Patriarchal Interpretations of the Quran*. Austin: University of Texas Press, 2002.

Bothman, Selma. *Engendering Citizenship in Egypt*. New York: Columbia University Press, 1999.

Brand, Laurie A. *Women, the State, and Political Liberalization: Middle Eastern and North African Experiences*. New York: Columbia University Press, 1998.

Charrad, Mounira M. *States and Women's Rights: The Making of Post-Colonial Tunisia, Algeria, and Morocco*. Berkeley: University of California Press, 2001.

Jawad, Haifaa A. *The Rights of Women in Islam*. New York: St. Martin's, 1998.

Kapchan, Deborah. *Gender on the Market: Moroccan Women and the Revoicing of Tradition*. Philadelphia: University of Pennsylvania Press, 1996.

Keddie, Nikki R. *Women in the Middle East: Past and Present*. Princeton, NJ: Princeton University Press, 2007.

Khoury, Nabil, and Valentine Moghadam, eds. *Gender and Development in the Arab World*. Atlantic Highlands, NJ: Zed, 1995.

Kimball, Michelle, and Barbara R. von Schlegell. *Muslim Women Throughout the World: A Bibliography*. Boulder, CO: Lynne Rienner, 1997.

Moghadam, Valentine M. *Women, Work, and Economic Reform in the Middle East*. Boulder, CO: Lynne Rienner, 1997.

Obermeyer, Carla Makhlouf, ed. *Family, Gender, and Population in the Middle East: Politics in Context.* Cairo: American University in Cairo Press, 1995.

Roded, Ruth, ed. *Women in Islam and the Middle East.* New York: St. Martin's, 1998.

Stowasser, Barbara Freyer. *Women in the Quran: Traditions and Interpretation.* New York: Oxford University Press, 1994.

Tucker, Judith E., ed. *Arab Women: Old Boundaries, New Frontiers.* Bloomington: Indiana University Press, 1993.

Foreign Affairs

Agha, Hussein, Shai Feldman, Ahmad Halide, and Zeev Schiff. *Track II Diplomacy: Lessons from the Middle East.* Cambridge, MA: MIT Press, 2004.

Barnett, Michael N. *Dialogs in Arab Politics: Negotiations in Regional Order.* New York: Columbia University Press, 1998.

Feldman, Shai, and Abdullah Toukan. *Bridging the Gap: A Future Security Architecture for the Middle East.* Lanham, MD: Rowman & Littlefield, 1997.

Kaye, Dalia Dassa. *Beyond the Handshake: Multilateral Cooperation in the Arab-Israeli Peace Process, 1991–1996.* New York: Columbia University Press, 2001.

Rabinovich, Itamar. *Waging Peace: Israel and the Arabs, 1948–2003.* Princeton, NJ: Princeton University Press, 2004.

Savir, Uri. *The Process: 1,100 Days That Changed the Middle East.* New York: Random House, 1998.

Sher, Gilead. *The Israeli-Palestinian Peace Negotiations, 1999–2004: Within Reach.* New York: Routledge, 2006.

Telhami, Shibley, and Michael Barnett, eds. *Identity and Foreign Policy in the Middle East.* Ithaca, NY: Cornell University Press, 2002.

Tibi, Bassam. *Conflict and War in the Middle East.* New York: St. Martin's, 1998.

Section II

THE COUNTRIES OF THE ARABIAN PENINSULA AND ARABIAN GULF AREA

Two Saudia Airlines 747s, two experiences. The first is on a Saudia 747 flying to New York from Jeddah, with ten Americans fresh from a month in Saudi Arabia. They express dismay at some of the things they have seen and heard about; the segregation of women from men, public executions, a controlled press, conspicuous consumption (including a full-size marble replica of the American White House in Riyadh), and even the unavailability of alcohol on New Year's Eve.

The second Saudia 747 flies from New York to Jeddah, filled mostly with Saudi Arabians returning from the United States. They express dismay at some of the things they have seen and heard about; the homeless on the streets, spouse and child abuse, drug wars, pornography, and the death rate from drunken drivers. They wonder aloud how anyone could put their aging parents in a nursing home instead of caring for them in the home.

These two worlds are worlds apart in some ways. Saudi Arabia is the epitome of life in the desert, with harsh rules to fit a harsh environment. Its uscent into modernity has been swift, and the old rules and habits of the desert remain. The United States is the epitome of the Enlightenment, the age of reason, the reign of freedom. Tolerance is practiced, even at a high price. However, when two different cultures like these contact each other, misunderstandings and negative judgments are sure to follow. The reality is that the dividing line between both lies a long way from either.

Prior to the twentieth century, the vast Arabian Peninsula was a mystery to outsiders—the land of frankincense, Sinbad the sailor, and the queen of Sheba. The vastness of the desert made exploration uninviting, and thus most outside contact was made by sea. However, there was little to ship from the peninsula's ports except pearls and animal hides, so they remained largely small mud villages until the twentieth century.

The Arabian Peninsula lies between the Persian Gulf and the Red Sea, jutting down from the Levant. It is one of the few major geographical regions of the world without a significant river. Rainfall is sparse because there is no adjacent body of water large enough to provide moisture for rain. The hot winds that sweep across the Sahara Desert bring almost no precipitation, and the Arabian Peninsula has almost no mountains to trigger rain from the air. The exception is in the southern part of the peninsula, where a mountain range provides a wetter climate and slightly cooler temperatures. This is a relief from the midsummer temperatures of over 120 degrees Fahrenheit that drive those who can afford it to leave for cooler climates. While winter temperatures may approach the freezing mark, they become almost unbearable by summer. Extreme temperatures and the lack of water give the Arabian Peninsula a population density among the lowest in the world. This is especially true in the southern part of the area, known as the Rub al-Khali, or Empty Quarter. A plane trip over Rub al-Khali reveals few signs of human habitation below, in the sand dunes and rocky outcroppings. Military pilots are cautioned not to fly over it since the distances from inhabited areas are too great for rescue forces to reach a pilot should the plane go down. Yet spread out thinly across the vivid desert patterns of ochre, russet, tan, and obsidian black are thin trails made by people. They wander the desert as their ancestors did, finding sustenance from the rare springs and oases that allow life to continue in the barren wilderness that makes up most of Saudi Arabia.

While the history of human settlement on the peninsula dates back for thousands of years, early people did not build cities or organize huge empires from there, as did the inhabitants of the Fertile Crescent. There were no obvious places to build cities except near the few rare oases. The sparse grass meant grazing herds had to keep on the move, so people banded together into nomadic tribes, grazing their flocks until the vegetation was depleted and then moving on. Those who lived along the coast turned to fishing, pearl diving, and trading. Even then, the villages along the Red Sea and Persian Gulf were small even in the early twentieth century. Change was slow to come, and the Bedouin lifestyle remained relatively undisturbed by progress until the

1930s, with the discovery of vast amounts of oil under the waters of the Gulf and beneath the sands.

The Persian Gulf area is home to another culture across its narrow span. If anything, the Persian culture is more ancient than is the Arab culture of the Arabian Peninsula. It includes the great empires of Xerxes and Darius, and the great capital city of Persepolis. Several significant religions and the Persian language developed there. The Shiite culture historically was separate from Arab culture and Sunni culture. The gap between these worlds is old and deep, and continues to influence modern Gulf politics. This is reflected in the generally tense relationship between modern Iran and the Arab countries opposite it.

5

SAUDI ARABIA

*The massive, modern-style terminal building at the international air-
port in Jeddah prepares visitors to Saudi Arabia for what follows:
broad highways with mercury vapor lights leading into cities where
buildings look like they were built yesterday. The steel, aluminum, and
concrete extend for miles through downtown into the suburbs, broken
only by palm trees and oleander bushes set in huge urns along the
roadways. Ornate houses stretch into the horizon, each surrounded by
a wall. Inside the office buildings, polished marble floors reflect the
flicker of computer screens. Oriental carpets the size of soccer fields
cover floors in meeting rooms. A full-size replica of the White House
stands in Riyadh, except that it is made of white marble and there are
no landscaped grounds.*

*This is Saudi Arabia, once barren but now transformed by oil wealth,
and opulent even in the face of a decade-long downturn in oil prices. Yet
the transformation is hardly complete. The men (except for the foreign
workers) all wear traditional robes and headgear, and the women (again,
except for foreigners) are completely veiled and robed in public. The call
to prayer five times a day is vigorously enforced, and diners hiding in
darkened restaurants during evening prayer risk a beating from the self-
appointed religious police, or* mutawwa. *The desert that played such a
role in forming the present culture lies at the edge of each city, stretching
on for hundreds of kilometers, often trackless and barren. It is a country
cloaked in paradox, with one foot in the twenty-first century and one in
the seventh century.*

SAUDI ARABIA IS THE LARGEST COUNTRY on the Arabian Peninsula, and the only
country in the world named after its modern founder, Abdul Aziz ibn Abdul-
Rahman al-Saud, known colloquially as "ibn Saud." (Map 5.1 on page 129 shows
Saudi Arabia.)

THE MODERN HISTORY OF SAUDI ARABIA

Somewhere around 1450, the al-Saud family left the small village of al-Qatif on the Persian Gulf and moved to an oasis in the Najd, the central part of the Arabian Peninsula, founding the village of al-Diriyah. In 1744 the leading member of the family, Muhammad ibn Saud forged a friendship with Muhammad ibn Abd al-Wahab, associated with the Wahhabist form of Hanbali Islam (see Chapter 3). Together, Muhammad ibn Saud and Muhammad ibn Abd al-Wahab pledged to unify Arabia under a puritanical banner known as the al-Muwahiddun or "Unitarians," though often called Wahhabists.

The growing power of the Muwahiddun alarmed the Ottomans, who besieged and destroyed Diriyah in 1819; by 1871 the Ottomans controlled much of the Najd.[1] The disunity of the al-Saud family over succession helped advance Ottoman influence in Arabia. The rival al-Rashidi family, backed by the Ottomans, took over most of the Arabian Peninsula, forcing the al-Saud into exile in Kuwait, where the Emir Mubarak al-Sabah gave them protection.[2] Abdul Aziz ibn Abdul Rahman al-Saud (known as ibn Saud) left Kuwait with a band of followers and conquered Riyadh in 1902. Using the city as a base, ibn Saud then began a campaign to unite the entire peninsula under family rule. His first opponent was the al-Rashid family and its allies, whose stronghold was the northern Najd city of Hail.

The Turks, fearing the growth of al-Saud power, joined the al-Rashidis, while ibn Saud recruited help from the Ikhwan ("Brotherhood" in Arabic), a group of Bedouin who practiced a highly abstemious version of Islam. They joined with ibn Saud and fought ruthlessly for his cause.[3] By 1908, ibn Saud's alliance won control over the Najd, but his ambition to control the Hijaz, or western region of the Arabian Peninsula, gained him a new opponent, the sharif of Mecca, Hussein ibn Ali al-Hashem who claimed to be a descendant of the Prophet Muhammad. The Ottoman Empire sided with the Germans during that war, thus becoming an enemy of the British. Therefore, when the Ottoman Turks tried to support the al-Rashidi clan, ibn Saud's old enemy, he reluctantly turned to the British for assistance. The British offered support to both ibn Saud and Sharif Hussein, encouraging ibn Saud to attack the al-Rashidis while offering the sharif positions of importance for his sons (the thrones of Iraq and Trans-Jordan) in exchange for his willingness to evacuate Mecca.

Ibn Saud then launched his campaign to consolidate the rest of the Najd and the Hijaz. Between 1913 and 1926, his Ikhwan allies helped him gain control over much of the peninsula, but the Ikhwan proved to be undisciplined troops who raided British-controlled Trans-Jordan in 1921. The Ikhwan, along with other tribes, began to oppose Ibn Saud because they feared that a Saudi state would curb tribal autonomy in the Najd.[4] Ibn Saud also faced potential opposition from the *mutawwa*, a group of men educated in religious studies and rituals.[5] The *mutawwa* were predominate in the Najd region and granted Ibn Saud, as al-Rasheed notes, "legitimacy as long as he championed the cause of the religious specialists, becoming the guardian of ritualistic Islam."[6] This began a significant pattern of tacit coop-

MAP 5.1   SAUDI ARABIA

eration between the ruling al-Saud and the religious factions that remains vital in Saudi Arabia to this day.

After defeating the Ikhwan in 1930, Ibn Saud succeeded in bringing the Arabian Peninsula under his control, and by 1932 he named the new country Saudi Arabia after his family.

The Saud Years

Ibn Saud's eldest surviving son, Saud, took the throne when Ibn Saud died in 1953. However, Saud proved to be an inept ruler who squandered millions on luxury living and in 1958 was forced to turn financial management of the kingdom to his brother Faisal. After a series of foreign policy disasters (including involvement in the Yemeni civil war), Saud turned over foreign relations to Faisal as well. Finally, leading members of the royal family joined with key members of the religious elite, who issued a *fatwa* in November 1964 ousting Saud.

Faisal Takes Over

Faisal contrasted sharply with Saud. Deeply pious and spartan in his living habits, Faisal set about undoing the damage that Saud left behind. He chose his brother Khalid to succeed him, and at the same time designated Fahd to succeed Khalid.

Faisal invested in infrastructure to promote economic growth and strengthened Saudi Arabia's position within OPEC, enabling him to lead a boycott of some OPEC countries against the United States in response to the 1973 Arab-Israeli war. His reign was not without internal strife, however, and Faisal repressed rising opposition from the left and from conservative circles concerned about his modernization efforts. A 1969 coup attempt only stiffened his repression and thousands of opponents either fled the country or were arrested.[7] In March 1975 a nephew of one such opponent assassinated Faisal, and Khalid succeeded him.

The Brief Reign of Khalid

Khalid ibn Abdul Aziz al-Saud preferred to leave affairs of state to others and shifted considerable responsibility to Crown Prince Fahd.

Khalid faced a severe challenge when a group of religious zealots took over the Grand Mosque in Mecca in November 1979 and held it for days, allegedly to protest the royal family's lax moral standards. While the siege was finally broken, a shaken regime had to turn to its own *ulama* to reify its right to rule under Islam.[8] Khalid's response to this development (and to the 1979 revolution in Iran) was to intensify the kingdom's attachment to strict Islam in an effort to politically outflank the radical challenge coming from his own people and from across the Gulf.

Khalid died of heart failure in June 1982, and Fahd succeeded him in an orderly transition. Fahd named his half-brother Abdullah as the crown prince and first deputy prime minister, and his full brother Sultan as second deputy prime minister and minister of defense and aviation.

Fahd

King Fahd (who took the title Custodian of the Two Holy Mosques) found his first challenge in a severe drop in world oil prices. The sharp increases in oil price that occurred in 1973 and following the 1979 revolution in Iran provoked conservation measures in oil-consuming countries. Moreover, the rapid rise in oil prices stimulated more oil production, and by the early 1980s, the world began to see an oil glut and thus a sharp drop in oil prices.

The decline in oil revenues was difficult to absorb in a country whose population had become used to a high standard of living. For most Saudi Arabians, education and health care were free. After marriage, every Saudi Arabian couple was entitled to a no-interest loan to build a house. Most other things were heavily subsidized, and while there were some taxes, few paid them. So one of the most significant challenges to the Saudi Arabian political system was how do deal with declining expectations.

The 1990–1991 Persian Gulf War (see Chapter 1) cost Saudi Arabia considerable sums of money as the country contributed funds to support the coalition, coming on the heels of oil price declines. Consequently Saudi Arabians had to curtail economic expectations. Saudi Arabia also faced growing criticism for allowing

American forces to be stationed on Saudi Arabian soil, particularly opponents like Osama bin Laden, the dissident millionaire who organized terrorist attacks both in and outside of Saudi Arabia. Fahd responded to criticism by launching a series of reforms in 1992, including the Law of Government specifying the al-Saud right to rule under Islam, the Law of Consultative Council, and the Law of the Provinces, which attempted to reform local government.[9]

In 1995 King Fahd suffered a stroke, and Crown Prince Abdullah assumed responsibility for running the government. He moderated his brother's policies, tolerating modest criticism of the government and opening the country to some foreign investment.[10] That would change after September 11, 2001, because fifteen of the nineteen hijackers were Saudi Arabian citizens. In May 2003 Saudi Arabia itself became a victim of a terrorist bombing in Riyadh that killed thirty-five people, followed by more bombs in Riyadh in November. The Riyadh bombing prompted the government to clamp down on homegrown terrorism and return to Saudi Arabia those Saudi citizens who had left the country to join radical groups.[11] It also seemed to signal a growing impatience with the slow pace of political reform.[12]

Abdullah

When King Fahd died in July 2005, Abdullah became king and Sultan became crown prince.[13] One of Abdullah's first acts was to pardon a cleric jailed for allegedly supporting Osama bin Laden and two constitutional reform advocates, indicating that he would try to continue the delicate balancing act between constitutional change and Islamic correctness.[14] Abdullah appears to be continuing Fahd's emphasis on improving Saudi Arabian–Iranian relations despite the harsh rhetoric of Iranian President Mahmoud Ahmadinejad, meeting with him in Saudi Arabia in March 2007.

The question of who will succeed Abdullah as king is vexing. Ibn Saud had an estimated 44 sons and 145 grandsons; thus most are half brothers who tend to identify with their mother's line. The most notable are the sons of Hassa bint al-Sudayri (see below), Fahd, Sultan, Abdul Rahman, Nayif, Turki, Salman, and Ahmad. Sultan, the next full brother to Fahd and current defense minister, is expected to become king after Abdullah, and the others will likely get or keep significant positions.[15] Nayif held the post of interior minister in charge of internal security, while Ahmad served as his deputy. Salman served as the politically powerful governor of Riyadh.

THE SAUDI ARABIAN POLITICAL SYSTEM

Deep tradition informs Saudi Arabian political and social discourse. The conservative foundations of the Najd and Riyadh set the political temperature for the rest of the country, along with the even more traditional Asir. Those traditions are steeped in desert culture, which nurtured and sustained the mantle of authoritarian rule, which carried over and still dominates Saudi culture even though few of the kingdom's citizens live in the desert. The Wahhabist vision permeates all social and political space in Saudi Arabia, dominating discourse in ways not seen in other countries in the Gulf.

Since its founding, the al-Saud family has ruled the country in almost absolute terms, which is why Freedom House lists Saudi Arabia as "not free." For decades the only check on the king's power was disagreement in his family, and particularly among his brothers. Saudi Arabian princes control many of the important ministries, including the Ministry of Defense and Aviation, the Foreign Ministry, the Interior Ministry, and Public Works and Housing. The sharing of ministries allows for the sharing of power between Ibn Saud's sons from his twenty wives, who are rumored to engage in rivalry for power. Most are half brothers, and there are widespread reports of conflict between brothers based on which mother they have. The sons of Hassa bint Ahmad Sudayri, by some accounts Ibn Saud's favorite wife, include Fahd, Sultan (current crown prince), Abdul Rahman, Nayef, Salman, Ahmad, and Turki (known as the Sudayri Seven), and the survivors occupy powerful positions. Crown Prince Abdullah is the son of Fahda bint Asi bin Shurayim Shammar, a member of the al-Rashidi family, and he has no full brothers, leaving him with fewer allies but also allowing him to distance himself from the sometimes unpopular positions and charges of corruption that sometimes follow the Sudayri Six.[16] Fahd installed two of his sons in important positions, placing them in potential conflict with other Sudayri members for influence after Fahd's death.[17] That contest has great potential to influence the future course of Saudi Arabia, given the political identity of Abdullah and his powerful half brother, Nayef. While Abdullah has been a proponent of gradual political and economic reform, Nayef embraces a much more conservative religious position (though reportedly not very pious himself) that is close to al-Qaeda in some respects.[18] Nayef's attachment to the principles of *tawhid* (see Chapter 3), and its definition of Shiites as apostates, conflicts starkly with Abdullah's positions, which are closer to the doctrine of *taqarub*, or Muslim acceptance of peaceful relations with nonbelievers.[19] Nayef has reportedly provided tacit support for al-Qaeda, and his faction's rise to power could signal not only a severing of Saudi Arabian relations with the West but also internal disorder should other followers of *tawhid* declare war on Saudi Shiites. Other princes have advocated a faster pace for reform, however, with Prince Talal (a half brother to King Abdullah) calling for increased rights for women, and his son, Prince Walid bin Talal, supporting the right of women to vote.[20] Limits exist on the impact of these cleavages, though, as Glosemeyer notes, "competition is limited by the rule that it must not endanger the political survival of the (royal) family."[21]

There are no elections, and the king selects the members of the Supreme Council of Ulama, and the Majlis al-Shura, although neither body challenges the policy wishes of the monarch. The Supreme Council of Ulama consists of senior Islamic scholars, and they often issue religious rulings *(fatwa)* dealing with religious or social issues. They, according to Raphaeli, are also a significant barrier to reform, partly because they control the powerful religious police.[22] The Majlis al-Shura, as noted below, is an advisory body to the king.

The Executive Branch

The king is Abdullah ibn Abdul Aziz al-Saud, who also serves as prime minister. The crown prince and first deputy prime minister is his younger half brother Sultan ibn Abdul Aziz al-Saud. The Council of Ministers serves as the cabinet and includes many members of the royal family, with the king as head. The monarch appoints all members and may dissolve the body, according to Article 57 of the constitution. There are twenty-two functional ministries represented on the Council of Ministers.

The Legislative Branch

Saudi Arabia does not have a democratically elected legislature. The closest thing to such an institution is the Majlis al-Shura, or consultative council. While consultative councils have long been an informal part of the Saudi regime, King Fahd institutionalized the branch in 1993. The 1993 Majlis was set at sixty members, chosen by the king and consisting largely of scholars and government officials. In July 1997, King Fahd expanded the Majlis to ninety members, who, as in the previous body, serve four-year terms. The Majlis also mediates between the people and the state, taking petitions, complaints, and suggestions through its Committee of Petitions.[23] The Majlis held some 143 meetings between 1993 and 1997 and took decisions on 133 issues during that time.[24] In May 2001, then–Crown Prince Abdullah expanded the Majlis to 120 members and called on it to give alternatives to policy rather than just endorse it, though it is difficult to tell if the Majlis actually followed this new guidance.[25]

The Judicial Branch

The Supreme Council of Justice is at the head of the judicial branch, which King ibn Saud unified in 1927. Under the Supreme Council are the expeditious courts, Sharia courts, and the Commission on Judicial Supervision, which oversees the judicial function. Islamic law forms the basis of the Saudi Arabian judicial system, but several secular codes are also in force, along with some commercial codes. According to Article 46 of the constitution, the judiciary is an independent authority and only the Sharia can control its decisions. The only training judges receive in Saudi Arabia is in Sharia. Three of the four schools of Islamic jurisprudence, the Hanafi, the Shafii, and the Hanbali, were influential in early Saudi Arabia, but the Hanbali is now the most influential in the entire country (See Chapter 3 for a description of the Sunni legal schools).

In Saudi Arabia, some complain that overworked jurists (only 700 in a country of 23 million) issue rulings that are ignorant of the modern world, and increasingly reflect a puritanical view of Islam. Some judges, for example, have issued edicts banning the children's game Pokemon, telephones that play recorded music while on hold, and flowers sent to hospital patients.[26]

CIVIL SOCIETY IN SAUDI ARABIA

As Okruhlik notes, "The prospects for a vibrant civil society in Saudi Arabia are quite good, although it is not likely to 'fit' the standard definition."[27] There are chambers of commerce in most large cities where a considerable amount of business is conducted below the government level.[28] There are also women's societies, physicians' groups, and human rights associations that have sometimes petitioned the ruling family for change. In 2003, for example, prominent members of many of these groups petitioned Crown Prince Abdullah for political reforms, and there is some evidence that he responded with modest changes, particularly in regard to the issue of women's status. Reform thus far draws mixed reviews, however. One position is that reform has stalled, partly because of a more aggressive foreign policy and the oil-driven economic boom. "The curse of the oil money is that it has stopped all reforms," laments Abdullah al-Otaibi, an advocate of political change. "The more money you have, the more arrogant you become, because you think you can implement anything your way."[29] A competing view is that reforms continue in a less visible way, partly to avoid friction in the royal family but inspired by the realization that up to 20 percent of the Saudi Arabian population supports al-Qaeda.[30]

Other Sources of Political Influence

Despite the dominant position of the al-Saud family, it does not have a monopoly on political influence in Saudi Arabia. Bureaucratic and business elites, the foreign national communities, religious opposition, and a small but growing number of reform advocates also try to shape Saudi Arabia's political agenda.

As oil wealth grew, the ruling al-Saud family created huge bureaucracies to manage and distribute the largesse. They recruited heavily from the Najd area of central Saudi Arabia, and many Najdis now form a business and bureaucratic elite that owes more loyalty to each other than to the ruling family or the state. They have considerable influence on establishing the rules for businesses, wealth distribution, and state functions like education and financial management.[31] Many have developed both technical expertise and connections that the al-Saud must take into account at the national-level decisionmaking process.

Saudi Arabia's Islamic community is another source of political influence. The official *ulama* is a shadowy group whose members are not generally known to the public, but they are apparently selected for their religious knowledge and possibly their tribal origins.[32] Despite the dominance of Sunni Wahhabist Islam, there are also other Islamic communities in Saudi Arabia, including advocates of the other Sunni schools of jurisprudence, the Maliki, Hanafi, and Shafii, along with large Shiite and Sufi communities. Roughly 8 percent of the Saudi Arabian population is Shiite, and in the oil-rich Eastern Province, or Ash Sharqiyah, it may be closer to 33 percent. This group also is a source of opposition. The Mowahideen interpretation of Sunni Islam rejects the legitimacy of Shiite belief and practices, which have been forbidden in Saudi Arabia since 1927.[33]

Saudi Arabian Shiites have a lower standard of living than the Sunni, and this is particularly noticeable in the Eastern Province cities of al-Qatif, Damman, and Hofuf.[34] For some years, and particularly after the 1979 Islamic revolution in Iran, Saudi Arabian Shiites called for an Islamic revolution in their country. However, since the Gulf War of 1990–1991, the Shiite leadership has tried to separate itself from religious extremism and steer toward moderation.[35] The Saudi Arabian regime has responded to this change with changes of its own, shifting from oppressive tactics to dialog.[36] Younger Sunni reformers who coauthored with Shiites a manifesto calling for equal rights, an elected national assembly, and freedom of speech, have joined this dialog. They presented this document to Crown Prince Abdullah in the summer of 2003, and though Abdullah met with some of the authors, it was not apparent that he had the authority to begin implementing some of the suggested political changes.[37] Fears that Saudi Arabian Shiites might provide a foothold for Iranian influence brought a few concessions from the regime after a violent crackdown on celebrations of Ashura in 1979.[38]

These other groups have largely lost out to the dominant Muwahiddun in matters of power.[39] The opposition also divides into those who chose a Salafi/Jihadist path and those who take a middle road between the "official" *ulama* and the Salafi, and who call for reform along the lines of what Lacroix calls "Islamo-democratic" activism (see below).[40]

Much of the opposition comes from Salafi Islamists who accuse the al-Saud family of failing to abide by a strict interpretation of the Sunni faith. In November 1979, opposition turned violent as a group of Ikhwan led by Juhayman al-Utaybi took over the Great Mosque, as noted above, and held it for what some reported was several months. Saudi Arabia reportedly had to rely on foreign forces to extricate the Ikhwan after the fighting did considerable damage to the building. Because of this incident, the regime promised to launch reforms in March 1980, but none were forthcoming.

In May 1991, political reformers requested twelve reforms, including an independent consultative council *(majlis al-shura),* a strict accountability of public officials, "justice in the distribution of national wealth," and improvement of the country's religious institutions.[41] In September, Sheik Abd al-Aziz ibn Baz, then head of the Council of Higher Ulama and one of the most prominent religious figures in the country, countered by criticizing the reformers for disrespect to the king, but the effort did not end the Islamist campaign.[42] In 1993, Saudi Arabians demanding less corruption and a more "Islamic" society formed the Committee for Defense of Legitimate Rights (CDLR).

By 2001, much of the opposition against the regime had divided over internal issues, fled the country, or dissipated altogether. Political stability increased, and the regime released Salman al-Audah and Safar al-Hawali, apparently no longer fearful of their ability to provoke opposition. Some of the restored calm is attributed to King Abdullah, who is perceived as pious enough to placate the conservative opposition and flexible enough to bring about needed economic reform.[43] Attacks did continue, though, with bombings in Riyadh, and a brazen assault in al-Khobar that left at least twenty-three dead in May 2004, coming a month after the regime vowed to "strike with an iron fist" its violent Islamist militants.

Opposition to the Saudi Arabian monarchy also comes from outside the country, where opponents from different political preferences have issued proclamations calling for either reform or overthrow of the al-Saud family. Those based in London tend to prefer a relaxation of the regime's strict adherence to Islam, while the Islamists call for an end to the corruption and deviancy from Islam. One of the more notable Islamist critics today is Osama bin Laden, who renounced his family's wealth and left the country, first to fight against Soviet forces in Afghanistan and later to rail against the Saudi regime from his new base in Sudan. He then fled to Afghanistan, where he established training camps for terrorism and directed attacks against both Saudi Arabia and the United States on September 11, 2001. His actions deeply embarrassed Saudi Arabia, since he was a Saudi citizen (though of Yemeni origin), as were some of the essential players in the September 11 attacks. Saudi Arabia's overall response to both bin Laden (whom they exiled in 1992) and the September 11 attack was mixed. They denounced terrorism and bin Laden on the one hand, but expressed doubt as to whether bin Laden was responsible for the September 11 attacks.[44] The attacks sharpened the focus on the remaining religious conservatives in Saudi Arabia and reinvigorated the government's position that extremism in religion must be avoided. They also counseled tolerance of other religions, with Prince Turki ibn Faisal al-Saud claiming, "We are living in a world where there are several other religions. Instead of thinking about bloody confrontations, we should prepare ourselves for coexistence and the exchange of ideas."[45] Still, the pace of reform appeared to be slow at best. In April 2003, then–Crown Prince Abdullah suggested that a planned departure of American forces would be followed by elections for provincial assemblies and an elected national assembly in six years.[46] Still, the voices of liberalism within the country remained viable, and in January 2003 a group of 104 Saudi Arabian professionals sent Crown Prince Abdullah a manifesto, "Strategic Vision for the Present and Future," calling for the institutionalization to guarantee rights to equality, justice, and meaningful participation.[47] Abdullah received forty of the signatories and promised a serious reading of their petition, and even though their strategic vision went beyond Abdullah's modest reform ideas. In April 2003 Prince Nayif announced that he was forming two human rights groups that may ultimately advance that issue to the status of official policy.[48] In November 2003, a royal decree supposedly made it easier for Shura members to propose new laws, but critics argue that the changes were meaningless since the king had the power to dismiss any Shura member who defied the royal will.[49] Thus a new petition went forward in December of that year, signed by academics, Islamic judges, and former ministers calling again for an elected parliament, an independent judiciary, and equal rights for women.[50]

The harsh measures taken against political dissidents generally keep internal disorder underground. Opponents of the regime can be imprisoned without trial or charges, and there are reports of prisoners being tortured for information. The regime also deals harshly with social disorder, publicly beheading murderers and drug dealers; thieves can lose their hand for a second offense. Stoning remains a punishment for adultery, although the practice is very rare now. Homosexual behavior is also a capital offense, as evidenced by the beheading of three men accused of "sodomy and marrying each other" in Asir on January 1, 2001.[51] Even Valentine's Day drew a warning from the semiofficial Authority for Enjoining Good and Preventing Evil (the Mutawwa) as it banned shops from selling red roses or Valentine's Day cards, and warned hotels against Valentine celebrations and drivers against displaying red hearts on their cars.[52]

Other forms of social control seem harsh to outsiders. There are no movie theaters and no bars (alcohol is forbidden, though it is sometimes smuggled in or manufactured illicitly). Homosexuality is banned, the *mutawwa* enforce prayer times, the sale or use of illegal narcotics is punishable by death or life in prison (where families are responsible for providing food and other essentials), and news is censored when it involves allegations of corruption or criticism of the royal family.

In Saudi Arabia it is also true that the crime rate, the drunken driving fatality rate, the drug use rate, the murder rate, and the AIDS infection rate are all very low. The streets in any Saudi Arabian city are safe to walk at night. There are no skid rows in Saudi Arabia, no adult video stores, no liquor outlets, and no homeless people sleeping under sheets of cardboard in city parks. Child abuse is unheard of, and even longtime foreign residents of the country cannot recall a time when they saw a parent physically strike a child. There are no nursing homes to speak of, and no orphanages. Families take care of their own. There appears to be strong public support for the harsh criminal system, particularly among Saudi Arabians who have traveled to other cities in the world where the crime rate is considerably higher.[53]

THE STATUS OF WOMEN IN SAUDI ARABIA

Women are more segregated in Saudi Arabia than in any other Arab country. They cannot check into a hotel alone, drive a vehicle, or work anywhere in the presence of men. They must not appear in public unless fully veiled and gowned. Women may attend school, but only in segregated conditions. Fathers may not visit their children's teachers if they are women. These measures are defended in Saudi Arabia because women are segregated from men for their own protection, since men are by nature lustful and thus likely to attempt sexual harassment if in the company of women. Saudi Arabian courts have acted to punish men in sexual assault cases, though, in one case sentencing a father to ten years in prison for raping his daughters.[54] Both sexes appear to accept and even embrace traditional cultural values, and some women object to the belief in the West that such things as a prohibition on driving and the requirement to wear the *abaya* are forms of discrimination. Said one woman physician to a visiting American delegation, "I don't want to drive a car. I worked hard for my medical degree. Why do I need a driver's license?" Another noted, "I love my *abaya*. It's convenient and it can be very fashionable."[55]

Some venues are open to women. They can own their own businesses and those with means may travel outside of Saudi Arabia to get an education or develop professional contacts. Some areas traditionally closed to women are now open, such as broadcasting, advertising, and architecture.[56] However, the religious *ulama* are, if anything, becoming even more conservative on the issue of women working with men, driving, or abandoning their restrictive public clothing requirements.[57] The issue was highlighted when fifteen schoolgirls died in a fire in Mecca in 2002 because the *mutawwa* prevented firefighters and police from rescuing them since the girls were not wearing proper covering attire. Partly spurred by a reaction to that tragedy, Crown Prince Abdullah has promised an open mind about reforming the situation. The need to continue "Saudization" of the Saudi Arabian economy may mean the necessity to open more employment areas to women, though the trend now is to continue to import foreign workers.[58] Women are also working to circumvent the barrier system by using stipulations to marriage contracts to protect themselves, and computers and women's sections of chambers of commerce to network among themselves.[59] However, obstacles to advancement remain. Only about 50 percent of women can read, compared to around 70 percent of men, making access to higher paying jobs difficult at best. Moreover, as Richards notes, "repeated attempts to force private firms to hire more locals have foundered on the greater energy and lower wage expectations of expatriate labor at lower skill levels, while the difficulties of educational systems. . . make it hard to replace highly skilled expatriates with local workers."[60] Partly to address this problem, the regime announced that certain parts of cities would be set apart for women to pursue various economic activities.[61] Nevertheless, the fact that women cannot drive means that they must hire drivers to get to work, and the additional cost of a driver and car can deter women from working outside the home.[62]

The religious establishment may continue to resist change, but, on the other hand, articles with mild criticism of the treatment of women have appeared in even conservative, religiously oriented Saudi Arabian newspapers.[63] Still, the progression of women into such realms as politics remains nonexistent. In January 2002, Sheik Muhammad bin Jubier, the chair of the Shura (see above), ruled out appointing women to that body, stating that Saudi women actually contribute to the decision-making in the Shura without taking part.[64] The sheik did not indicate how this was done. The daughter of the late King Faisal, Princess Lolwah bint Faisal al-Saud, publicly stated in January 2006 that Saudi Arabian women should be allowed to drive, the first time a high-ranking royal family member advocated such a departure from tradition.

THE STRUCTURE AND PERFORMANCE
OF THE SAUDI ARABIAN ECONOMY

Saudi Arabia remains one of the world's wealthiest countries despite setbacks since 1991. Among a population of almost 27 million, each Saudi citizen had a purchasing parity of $13,100.[65] GDP growth stood at 6.5 percent, spurred partly by rising oil prices. The official unemployment rate stood at 13 percent for males (the only statistic provided), and the public debt was almost 45 percent of GDP. After a disastrous drop in economic growth of over 10 percent in 1999, Saudi Arabia's economy recovered to record growth rates in 2006, sparked largely by a hike in OPEC oil prices. The inflation rate of less than 1 percent is quite manageable, and the country enjoys a positive trade surplus.

As a classic case of a rentier state (see Chapter 4), Saudi Arabia is burdened with a state structure dedicated mostly to the distribution of oil wealth. The bureaucratic mechanisms exist to pass out resources rather than collect taxes and other revenues. Moreover, the *asabiyya* system of crony capitalism has left a network of business elites (disproportionately Najdi) who grow wealthy on the brokerage of contracts based on political connections rather than on economic principles.[66] Corruption is reportedly pervasive, with favors extended to banks managed by the right families, defense contracts, and other government projects.[67]

The Importance of Oil

The Saudi Arabian economy has relied on oil revenues since the 1940s, and that importance continues today. Some estimate Saudi Arabian oil reserves at 260 billion barrels, by far the highest in the world, and more than twice the next highest, Iraq, at around 100 billion barrels. However, an unofficial recent estimate placed the true size of the Saudi Arabian reserve at over 716 billion barrels, and, according to a Saudi Aramco official, might reach 1 trillion barrels with advanced detection and oil field recovery sytems.[68] Saudi Arabia also has an estimated 6.5 trillion cubic meters of natural gas, the fifth largest reserves in the world. In the 1980s, oil revenues accounted for around 75 percent of GDP, but that percentage has slipped to around 35 percent as other sectors are now growing in importance.[69] Oil remains the largest export earner, accounting for about 90 percent of Saudi foreign earnings. However, nonoil exports rose ninefold between 1984 and 1992, amounting to some $2.74 billion.[70] Declining oil prices in the 1990s took their toll, though; actual oil revenues for the 1990–1994 period were 58 percent of what they had been in the 1980–1984 period.[71] Saudi Arabia now attempts to both diversify its own economy and invest in the economy of other growing countries. Saudi Arabian investments in the United States and Europe may total more than $1 trillion, according to some estimates.[72] However, the continuing public spending for both domestic and military expenditures dramatically increased budget deficits (Saudi Arabia spends around 12 percent of its GDP on defense, whereas the United States spends just 3.3 percent). The deficit for 1998 was almost 11 percent of GDP but mushroomed to almost $133 billion in 2000, more than 100 percent of GDP.[73] By 2003, it climbed to $176 billion, which averaged around $7,200 per person, and interest on this debt alone constitutes around 13 percent of the total government budget.[74]

Saudi Aramco, once a joint venture between American oil companies and the Saudi Arabian government, became wholly owned by the Saudi Arabian government in 1988. Its downstream (postpumping) operations include tankers and refineries, and the operation of thousands of gasoline stations in both the United States and South Korea. Refinery deals with both China and India are under way.

Modernizing the Economy

Saudi Arabia benefited from several development plans to modernize the country's economy, starting with infrastructure in the 1970s. The government developed seaports, increased the electrical power capacity by a factor of twenty-eight, and tripled the length of paved highways. A third stage of the plan (1980–1985) saw spending increases for education, social services, and health care, while the fourth plan of 1985–1990 saw the regime expand the role of private enterprise and joint ventures with the state sectors. The fifth plan, encouraged by the Iraqi invasion of Kuwait, emphasized the improvement of national defense. The sixth plan anticipated economic growth at 3.6 percent per year, while the seventh plan (2000–2007) continues to emphasize privatization and diversification away from a petroleum-based economy. Between 1997 and 2002, Saudi Arabia almost doubled its exports of nonoil products.[75]

What these figures do not show is the reduction in public spending that the regime has embarked on since the end of the Gulf War of 1990–1991. Before that conflict, the oil coffers allowed free public education, free health care, heavily subsidized housing, and remarkably low prices on a variety of goods. There was no income tax, no sales taxes, and no corporate tax. Loans were interest free, and all Saudi Arabians who married got one to build a house. Construction projects often were designed more to employ people than to construct something useful. For example, in the late 1980s Shiite discontent in the Eastern Province lead to massive building projects to employ them, even though most of the houses that resulted from this effort stood empty because there were no buyers for them.

Saudi Arabia has also invested heavily in efforts to achieve economic self-sufficiency. The country was once the world's sixth largest wheat exporter, but that crop, which required irrigation from aquifer water drawn from deep underground wells at great expense, cost Saudi Arabia almost ten times what a bushel of wheat from Kansas costs to produce. Saudi Arabia also has the world's largest dairy farm, with 20,000 cows. The cows graze on alfalfa grown with aquifer water, and although that one farm produced 25 percent of all Saudi Arabian milk products, it is a very expensive investment. It would cost even more if the labor costs, almost solely provided by foreign workers, were not so low. Saudi Arabia also invests in such unlikely things as flowers, which are exported to the Netherlands, among other places.

These projects depend heavily on state-provided subsidies, and those subsidies in turn receive support from powerful political interests. However, the regime began to curtail them in the early 1990s, and as a result, wheat production began to decline, dropping from 3.4 million tons in 1993 to 1.2 million tons in 1996.[76] By 2000, it had risen to 1.7 million tons but started to decline as the kingdom reduced water and fertilizer subsidies.[77]

Another effort at both economic development and economic self-sufficiency are the two planned industrial cities of Jubail and Yanbu. Both are strategically located on the coast (Jubail on the Persian Gulf and Yanbu on the Red Sea), so that raw materials as well as finished goods can be moved by sea. Both are the terminuses of oil pipelines that provide the raw feedstock to support petrochemical industries and other petroleum requirements. Jubail now produces aluminum, which seems perhaps unusual for a country that has no bauxite, the raw material for aluminum. However, Saudi Arabia finds it cheaper to import bauxite to Jubail than to export the energy to places where bauxite exists.

As the new industrial cities began to produce, the government effort, led by the Saudi Basic Industries Corporation (SABIC), was to export the products, particularly to growing markets like Asia. However, in 1998 the Asian economies began to decline, causing a drop of 10 percent in SABIC production and 7 percent of world sales.[78] SABIC bounced back and by 2003 sold close to $1 billion of goods, an increase of 224 percent over the previous year.[79]

The Saudi Arabian government led these diversification efforts, creating government commissions to own and manage them. This simply repeated the earlier Saudi Arabian experience, since much of the economic activity comes from enterprises owned by the state. However, there is pressure to privatize many of these firms, and some firms appear to be headed in that direction. Saudi Telecommunication Company is to replace the state-run Ministry of Posts, Telegraphs, and Telephones (PTT) in early 2000, with a capitalization of over $3 billion. Under the PTT, Saudi Arabia lagged way behind other Gulf countries to the point where lampooning PTT became a national sport.[80] Saudi Arabian Airlines is also under consideration for privatization.[81] The airline now deeply subsidizes its domestic routes and offers low-cost fares from all over the world to *hajj* travelers; consequently privatization would conflict with the political goals of the regime.[82] The privatization of these enterprises results in both higher prices for consumers and less political control for the Saudi Arabian government.[83] However, privatization remains on course, and, according to one Saudi Arabian economist, the sharp drop in oil prices following the September 11 attacks against the United States will only increase its pace.[84] In 2004 candidates for privatization included Saudi Arabia's largest bank, insurance and petrochemical companies, and some of the kingdom's largest food and dairy firms.[85]

Since much of the economy remains in state hands and many Saudi Arabians depend on state subsidies, budget cuts bring real hardship. For 1999, Saudi Arabian state spending fell by 16 percent, one of the largest drops in its history.[86] With little prospect of rising oil prices, the economic outlook appeared grim for lower-income groups. Saudi Arabian economists claim that the country must sustain an annual growth rate of 6 percent just to keep unemployment under control, a challenge since the annual average growth rate since 1980 was only 1.5 percent.[87] That has resulted in an official unemployment figure of 9.6 percent, though unofficial estimates place it as high as 20 percent.[88]

The Guest Worker Programs

Saudi Arabia practices an economic policy of self-reliance, but in at least one area remains dependent on an outside source. That area is labor, and in particular manual labor, which, even at the skilled and semiskilled level, is almost entirely done by what Saudi Arabians refer to as third country nationals (TCNs). They come mostly from Asia, and South and Southeast Asia in particular. Nationals from Thailand, the Philippines, Pakistan, Bangladesh, and China work in the streets as servants and cooks in homes and restaurants, as farm hands, as factory workers in the new industrial cities of Jubail and Yanbu—almost everywhere where there is labor to be performed. Workers from Islamic countries are preferred, but workers from almost any country (especially poor countries) are generally welcomed (Palestinians are not welcome due to fears that they will be a source of instability). The government brought in workers from South Korea under contract, but when problems developed, Saudi Arabian contractors replaced them with Chinese workers.[89] In the more technical fields Europeans, Canadians, and Americans provide labor, as in laboratories and hospitals. Americans and British do the maintenance on Saudi Arabian military equipment. Many Egyptians teach in Saudi Arabian universities.

There is real concern about the dependence on TCNs in Saudi Arabia. The government has opened additional universities to educate more Saudi Arabians in fields of science and technology. There are now seven large, well-equipped universities. However, some criticize the Saudi Arabian university system for encouraging rote learning of patriotic and religious subjects, discouraging intellectual curiosity in the process. That may be one reason why the 120,000 students graduating from Saudi Arabian universities between 1995 and 1999 constituted only 2 percent of the total number of Saudi Arabians entering the job market in those years.[90] That may be due partially to cultural factors. A 2004 survey revealed that some 35 percent of Saudi Arabians did not want to enter technical fields or work in areas requiring fieldwork, leading the author, who compared Saudi attitudes toward work to those of industrious Eastern Europeans and Asians, to ask, "Are we going to be a nation of clerks?"[91]

Some Saudi Arabian firms are also trying to address the TCN problem. For example, the Advanced Electronics Corporation located near the airport in Riyadh now employs a workforce that is 68 percent Saudi Arabian and produces products that meet strict US military standards.[92] However, that firm remains an exception. The Saudi Arabian regime is trying to encourage more "Saudization," through a number of measures, including making the importation of non-Saudi workers more difficult. There is also an ongoing effort to further the education of Saudi Arabians in fields of work now commonly done by TCNs, particularly in engineering, medicine, and other technical fields. One problem with Saudization, though, is that it would require Saudi Arabian firms to pay more for Saudi labor and thus reduce their international competitiveness.[93]

SAUDI ARABIAN FOREIGN POLICY

Saudi Arabia is the largest Gulf Arab country, and this position translates to a leading role for the country in Gulf foreign policy. Saudi Arabia does cooperate with the other Gulf Arab countries (including Iraq during the Iran-Iraq war), but at the same time positions itself to take a lead voice in such cooperation.

Saudi Arabia plays a significant foreign and security role in the Middle East because it has the wealth to do so. However, wealth cannot buy power alone. Diplomatic skill and respect are also ingredients for successful foreign policy, and in this sense, Saudi Arabia has done quite well. For example, Saudi Arabia played an important role in attempting to end a number of conflicts simmering in the 1970s and 1980s, including the Soviet occupation of Afghanistan, the Iran-Iraq war, the peace efforts between the Israelis and the PLO, and the Lebanese civil war, which ended after intensive diplomatic efforts managed by Saudi Arabian diplomats in the mountain city of Taif.

Saudi Arabia is a founding member of the Gulf Cooperation Council (GCC) and uses the GCC as a way to reduce trade barriers, increase economic and cultural ties, and build an organization for mutual defense with its small Gulf neighbors. Saudi Arabian–Iranian relations, which cooled after the 1979 Iranian revolution, improved after both sides took measures to decrease the chances of war. Saudi Arabia also exercises foreign policy influence by funding various Islamist groups that share its particular Islamist vision, in the early 1960s as a counter to rising Arab nationalism campaigns led by Egypt's Nasser, and later in reaction to revolutionary Iran. Saudi Arabian funds spread the writings of various Salafiyyist leaders like Hassan al-Banna and others. Saudi Arabia funded the construction of religious schools, and later the Afghanistan Taliban movement sprang up partially through their attendance in Saudi-funded madrassas in Pakistan.[94] After the September 11, 2001, attacks against the World Trade Center, the American government put pressure on Saudi Arabia to cease funding some Islamist groups linked to terrorism, but some critics claimed that the Bush administration was not stringent enough in demanding that Saudi Arabia curtail such aid.[95]

US-Saudi Arabian Relations

Relations between Saudi Arabia and the United States have proceeded with a mixture of cooperation and tension. American support for Israel during the 1973 war provoked a Saudi Arabian–led oil boycott by OAPEC (see Chapter 1). The action prompted the United States to improve its ties to Saudi Arabia, and relations did warm considerably. Saudi Arabia funneled billions of oil dollars into the United States already during the Nixon administration. Saudi Arabian money bought US Treasury Bills, paying down the US budget deficit in the process, and into a variety of programs against drug use and illiteracy, and for veterans. Saudi Arabia also spent over $100 billion on American-built weapons, while the United States built much of the extensive infrastructure that is now modern Saudi Arabia.[96] In 2007, Saudi Arabia spent close to $50 billion on fighters, tank upgrades, missile defense, and a slew of other military equipment.[97] After 9/11, Saudi Arabia rushed some 500,000 barrels a day to the United States, contributing to a crude oil price drop from $28 a barrel in August to $20 a few weeks later. The United States did not express thanks, but political figures and the media launched a wave of criticism of Saudi Arabia, expressing anger that fifteen of the nineteen terrorists involved in the attack were

Saudi Arabian citizens.[98] One reaction was a Saudi Arabian decision to buy European-made Typhoon fighters instead of American-built planes, as Saudi Arabia had done previously.

However, cooperation has its limits, and Saudi Arabian leadership is well aware of them. The apparent dependency on American forces and American power makes Saudi Arabia vulnerable to charges of allowing outsiders to secure the country that was the birthplace of the Prophet Muhammad. Therefore, Saudi Arabia has responded by both word and deed. For example, the commander of Saudi Arabian forces, Prince Khalid bin Sultan bin Abd al-Aziz, stated that the 1998 American and British force build-up in the Persian Gulf against Iraq was "meant to protect the Iraqi people against the mistakes of their leadership, and against the ordeal they have endured since the early eighties. . . and by a desire to avoid the destruction of a military force that should have been on the Arab side in the uneven military balance of power in the Middle East."[99] In December 1998, Saudi Arabia permitted the basing of American and British planes for Operation Desert Fox, the 2001 bombing campaign against Iraq for its refusal to comply with UN inspections. That support, however, was limited. The American planes flying out of Saudi Arabia could patrol over Iraq, but if fired upon by Iraqi forces, needed to summon US planes from outside Saudi Arabian bases to strike back. As King Fahd's health deteriorated and Crown Prince Abdullah became more influential, Saudi Arabia imposed even more restrictions on US forces based there. By early 2002, Abdullah took the lead in the royal family faction arguing that the United States should withdraw its forces.[100] His position highlighted not only Saudi Arabian sensitivity about foreign forces on Saudi soil, but also growing differences in threat assessment. While the United States continued hostile relations with both Iran and Iraq, Saudi Arabia built a détente with Iran, and senior Saudi Arabian officials downplayed the Iraqi danger to their country.[101] When Operation Iraqi Freedom got under way in April 2003, Saudi Arabia did not allow the United States to use Saudi bases, and American aircraft had to use other Gulf bases instead. After that action, American charges of Saudi Arabian funding of terrorism further strained US–Saudi Arabian relations. The Bush administration charged that Saudi Arabian charities funneled at least $10 million to Hamas, the Palestinian group listed as a terrorist organization by the United States. Saudi Arabian officials vehemently denied the charges, claiming that it gave aid only to the Palestinian Authority.[102]

As Saudi Arabia's neighbors, including Israel, Iran, and Iraq, acquired or developed weapons of mass destruction, Saudi Arabia stood increasingly vulnerable to the possible consequences. If Saudi Arabia would decide to acquire nuclear weapons for itself, the kingdom might turn to Pakistan for nuclear warheads to fit on its existing force of Chinese-made intermediate-range ballistic missiles.[103] Saudi Arabian nuclear capability would pose considerable problems for its neighbors, as well as for the United States, which invests considerable effort in opposing nuclear weapons development in Iran and Iraq. The United States would thus find it difficult to sit by quietly should Saudi Arabia go nuclear.

Saudi Arabia shares the Arabian Peninsula with smaller countries, including Yemen on its southern border and the small but important Persian Gulf countries on its eastern border. The next section examines these countries.

SUGGESTED READINGS

Al-Rasheed, Madawi. *A History of Saudi Arabia*. Cambridge: Cambridge University Press, 2002.

Arts, Paul, and Gerd Nonneman, eds. *Saudi Arabia in the Balance: Political Economy, Society, Foreign Affairs*. New York: New York University Press, 2005.

Bronson, Rachel. *Thicker Than Oil: America's Uneasy Partnership with Saudi Arabia*. Oxford: Oxford University Press, 2006.

Champion, Daryl. *The Paradoxical Kingdom: Saudi Arabia and the Momentum of Reform*. New York: Columbia University Press, 2003.

Commins, David. *The Wahhabi Mission and Saudi Arabia*. London: Tauris, 2006.

Fandy, Mamoun. *Saudi Arabia and the Politics of Dissent*. New York: St. Martin's, 1999.

Jerichow, Anders. *The Saudi File*. New York: St. Martin's, 1998.

Kechichan, Joseph A. *Succession in Saudi Arabia*. New York: Palgrave, 2001.

Simons, Geoff. *Saudi Arabia: The Shape of a Client Feudalism*. New York: St. Martin's, 1998.

Vasil'ev, A. M. *The History of Saudi Arabia*. London: Saqi, 1998.

Wilson, Peter W., and Douglas F. Graham. *Saudi Arabia: The Coming Storm*. Armonk, NY: Sharpe, 1994.

Wilson, Rodney. *Economic Development in Saudi Arabia*. London: Routledge Curzon, 2004.

6

THE PERSIAN GULF EMIRATES

IMAGES

Evening on the beach as the sun disappears over the desert. A breeze flows off the water, blending the odor of sulfur with the faint fragrance of flavored water pipe tobacco and mint tea. The Gulf waters change from aqua to azure to scarlet; the setting sun reflects off the water, illuminating the old and the new together. The flickering lights of oil rigs, the wisps of gas flames, and the smell of sulfur are the present and future. The old trading dhows anchored nearby are the past. Their crews, relaxing with glasses of tea and water pipes (called shishas in this part of the Arab world) talk of the same seaports as their ancestors did centuries ago. Oil may be the most valuable commodity now coming from the Gulf waters, but the old links are to the other Gulf commodities: fish, shrimp, and pearls. The marine life and the cargoes carried by the dhows were why people came to these lands and stayed for centuries. Oil may be a temporary interruption of a life rich in tradition and slow in pace, which continued for thousands of years.

KUWAIT

Kuwait lies at the top of the Persian Gulf, a small emirate of around 2 million people. It achieved independence in 1961, and, like many new countries, struggles with its identity. Its considerable oil wealth, coupled with its desert tradition, produces a split political set of goals: an effort at modern democracy and a traditional tribal autocracy.

Kuwait's existence as a country was formed over many centuries, although precious little of historic Kuwait remains today. (Map 6.1 on page 148 shows Kuwait.)

The Modern History of Kuwait

The British began exploring for oil in Kuwait in the 1920s, carving out two neutral zones south of Kuwait where they suspected oil was located and costing Kuwait territory in the process.[1] In the 1930s, Iraq made its first effort to claim Kuwait, inspired partly by these oil claims. Many of Kuwait's merchants supported Iraq's claims, partly because their growing Arab nationalism distanced them from British influence in Kuwait.[2] In 1938, many of these same merchants supported the Majlis movement in an effort to curb the ruler's ties to the British, initiating the political split between the monarch's preference for Western ties and the traditionalist preference for Kuwaiti autonomy.

Kuwait gained its independence from Britain in 1961. Shortly after that Iraqi leader Abd al-Karim Qasim threatened to invade Kuwait, reasserting an old Iraqi claim to the country. Since Kuwaiti oil provided around 40 percent of British petroleum requirements at that time, Britain sent 7,000 troops to protect Kuwait from Iraqi.[3] That would not be the last time Iraq impinged on Kuwait sovereignty. On August 3, 1990, Iraqi leader Saddam Hussein invaded Kuwait, taking the world as well as Kuwait by surprise. The royal family barely had time to flee to Saudi Arabia. Iraqi troops swept over Kuwait's small defense forces as many Kuwaiti military personnel fought bravely against impossible odds (see Chapter 1 for details).

Iraq initially claimed that the purpose of the invasion was to sweep away an unpopular regime, but several days later Iraq reasserted its old claim that Kuwait was a part of Iraq. What followed was a horrific orgy of looting and killing, for no purpose at all.[4] Rapes by Iraqi troops impregnated so many Kuwaiti women that Kuwaiti leaders decided to legalize abortion for those cases, even though the practice violates Islamic custom and law.[5] Much of the property destruction appeared pointless. Iraqi troops burned down the national museum with most of its treasures and torched the planetarium in Kuwait City and smashed its valuable equipment, after first looting its cheap plastic seats.

Kuwait spent a considerable amount of its wealth cleaning up and rebuilding after the invasion. It also moved closer to its Gulf neighbors and the United States. Kuwait was one of the very few countries that vocally supported the spring 2003 American and Allied campaign to oust the Saddam Hussein regime, and Kuwaitis celebrated when American forces captured Saddam in December of that year.

The Kuwaiti Political System

Kuwait is a hereditary monarchy, and the emir and most of the top officials are from the al-Sabah family, which has ruled the area since the late eighteenth century. Kuwait's citizenship law, passed after independence in 1961, designated Kuwaitis as citizens based on whether they had ancestors in Kuwait before 1920.[6] Political identity was based on tribal membership, so those who belonged to a particular tribe on the ancestral list technically could vote. Another group of immigrants, called beduns, migrated without identification papers and thus Kuwait denied them citizenship and the right to vote.

Kuwait's political system stems partially from the constitution of 1962, which emphasized such traditional democratic principles as separation of powers, the rule of law, and individual rights. It also granted considerable freedom of the press and

MAP 6.1   KUWAIT

freedom to criticize the regime, which reflects a tradition of openness in Kuwaiti society.[7] There are limits, though, on the role of women and on the political role of Kuwait's Shiite population, which is almost a third of the 950,000 Kuwaiti citizens. Freedom House ranks Kuwait as "partially free."

The Kuwaiti Executive

The Head of State is Emir Sabah al-Ahmad al-Jabir al-Sabah (since January 29, 2006), and the crown prince is Nawaf al-Ahmad al-Sabah. The head of government is Prime Minister Nasir al-Muhammad al-Ahmad al-Sabah (appointed in February 2006); First Deputy Prime Minister Jabir Mubarak al-Hamad al-Sabah (also named in February 2006); Deputy Prime Ministers Muhammad al-Sabah al-Salim al-Sabah and Muhammad Dhayfallah Sharar, who has held the post since 2003. All come from the Mubarak line of the Sabah family. The Kuwaiti constitution in Article 4 specifies that the emir nominate at least three descendants of the late Mubarak al-Sabah, with the National Assembly choosing one as heir.

Prime Minister Nasir enunciated his aspirations for change in Kuwaiti politics, saying that the "march of reform, modernisation and development. . . does not go without difficulties and obstacles," but critics suggested that his cabinet had corrupt elements and that he would fail to meet reform goals, despite the rhetoric.[8]

A council of ministers appointed by the prime minister and approved by the emir contains the heads of the various government ministers, sixteen in all (with only one Shiite member although Shiites are 30 percent of Kuwait's population). Below the council of ministers is what Crystal describes as one of the largest per capita governmental machines in the world.[9] Funded largely by oil revenues, the bureaucracy administers a vast network of social services, investments, and foreign assistance projects.

The Kuwaiti Legislature

Kuwait had one of the first legislative bodies in the Gulf, with its roots in the re-forms of Abdullah Salim, whose Kuwaiti rule began in 1950s. As the result of a pre-vious family feud over succession, Abdullah backed the merchants and supporters of parliamentary politics, and when he came to power in January 1950, he was in-strumental in opening the National Assembly in 1963.[10]

The National Assembly, or Majlis al-Umma, consists of fifty seats, with members elected in popular elections for four-year terms. There are only five Shiite members despite the fact that Shiites constitute almost one-third of Kuwait's population.[11] Is-lamist parties hold twenty-one seats, government supporters have fourteen seats, liberals with three, and independents hold the remaining twelve seats.

Legislative independence from the executive is limited, since the emir can sus-pend the legislature at any time. However, parliament, by a two-thirds vote, can de-clare the ruling emir unfit and can replace him should he fail to meet the conditions for governing, or for health reasons. Sometimes the National Assembly has pressured the emir to make changes, as it did in 1963, when criticism from the National Bloc caused the emir to dissolve his cabinet. The 1975 elections brought even more critics into the body, and the emir dissolved it the next year. That happened again in 1986, and the legislature remained in suspension until after the 1991 Gulf War, when pres-sure from the United States helped to get it restarted. However, the legislature and executive evolved into an adversarial relationship that often paralyzed government business. In 1999, the information minister was forced by parliament to resign and the legislature was apparently about to sack a second one (Justice and Islamic Affairs) for reportedly allowing incomplete Qurans to circulate) when the emir abruptly sus-pended the body.[12] The emir did allow new elections within the prescribed sixty days, and the 1999 election brought a change to parliament. The body became more liberal, but the traditional forces continued their influence, as was shown when it re-fused to accede to women's suffrage or privatization of the oil industry.[13] In 2000, the legislature passed a law segregating new private universities by gender, and de-bated a bill restricting the travel of Kuwaiti women studying abroad.[14] In 2005, it barely passed legislation granting Kuwaiti women the right to vote.

Some of the limitations of the Kuwaiti legislature might diminish if the parlia-ment could form the government instead of just reacting to it, as Michael Herb ar-gues. However, since this requires that the prime minister be selected from outside the ruling family, it probably will not happen.[15]

The Kuwaiti Judiciary

The judiciary consists of a High Court of Appeal. Kuwaiti Shiites have their own lower court system to rule on personal status matters like divorce and marriage. Ministries also have judicial power to punish or suspend individuals for reported violations of either law or policy. For example, the Ministry of Religious Endowment and Islamic Affairs suspended eight mosque preachers for unspecified criticisms in sermons of government policy on elections in general and on the government's decision to allow women the right to vote specifically.[16]

The Status of Women in Kuwait

The status of women in Kuwait differs considerably from that in neighboring Saudi Arabia. Education for girls in Kuwait began in 1937, and facilities at Kuwait University are coeducational.[17] Women are not required to wear veils, and workplaces are not segregated by gender. In mid-2005, the legislature granted women the right to vote and to run for office, and they voted for the first time in April 2006.

On personal status issues, Kuwaiti law forbids Kuwaiti women citizens to marry non-Kuwaitis, something not forbidden for Kuwait male nationals. Should they marry non-Kuwaitis, Kuwaiti women lose their rights to both government housing and government housing loans.[18] Divorced women find it difficult to collect alimony from former spouses, although the law requires its payment.[19]

Other issues also affect women's lives in Kuwait. There is a debate, for example, over a decision by the Public Institution for Social Security to specify a retirement age of forty-five for women. In reacting to the law, one Kuwaiti man demanded that "we require all the women experts for who we have spent so much money to train in different fields of endeavor, to help boost the socio-economic activities of the nation," while another argued that "women must be involved in their traditional role of caring for the children, no more, no less."[20] The split reflects a deeper conflict. As Tétreault argues, "The dueling trends of modernization and Islamization also shape Kuwaiti state culture. One the one hand, Kuwaiti society is arguably the most modern in the Gulf region. . . . On the other hand, the importation of tribal populations into the heart of the polity, coupled with a policy of (re)tribalization by the regime, validates the counter-culture that seeks to impose, via the 'tyranny of the majority,' its own version of the re-traditionalization of Kuwaiti culture as synonymous with the repression of women and minorities and the rejection of democratic principles."[21]

The Structure and Performance of the Kuwaiti Economy

Before the discovery of oil, Kuwaitis garnered their livelihoods either from nomadic herding or from the waters of the Gulf. Pearl diving was a lucrative source of income, and many Kuwaitis thrived from the profitable yet dangerous job of diving in search of pearl-bearing oysters. When the cultured pearl from Japan broke into the market in the 1930s, Kuwait's pearl industry disappeared almost overnight. Fortunately for that small sheikdom, oil in substantial quantities replaced pearling and made Kuwait one of the world's wealthiest countries.

Kuwait's population is around 2.4 million, though around half are nonnationals. Partly because its population is so small, Kuwait has a high per capita GDP of $20,300, with the economy growing at 8.3 percent in 2006. Unemployment and inflation are both low.

Declining oil prices in the late 1990s had a severe impact on Kuwait's economy, but price increases in 2000 and again in 2006 contributed to healthy 6 and 8.6 percent growth rates, respectively. However, regime commitments to large-scale social spending resulted in a public debt that was over 12 percent of GDP. Kuwait, like other Gulf Arab countries, provides lavish subsidies that guarantee a free education through university and free health care to all Kuwaiti citizens.

Kuwait's wealth stems almost exclusively from its oil production. With proven oil reserves of around 97 billion barrels (almost 10 percent of the world's total reserves), Kuwait could afford to pay for a luxurious lifestyle for its citizens before the 1991 Iraq invasion. That invasion devastated much of Kuwait, and the cost of rebuilding everything from the oil infrastructure to schools to the international airport ran into billions of dollars. The Kuwaiti economy began to show a return to previous performance in 1994–1995, but much of that growth came from developments in industry and finance.

Kuwaitis know that the oil revenues cannot last forever. Research in Kuwait today focuses on potential alternatives, including a return to using Gulf resources more fully. The Kuwait Scientific Foundation runs experimental fish and crustacean farms in an effort to breed a larger harvest. Efforts are being made to explore ways of increasing potable water to expand agriculture (now less than 1 percent of the economy) and thus lessen Kuwait's dependence on food imports.

One barrier to further growth in the Kuwaiti economy is the continued involvement of the state sector in the economy. The state sector can run at a loss, and thus there are few incentives to reduce inefficiencies. Moreover, state sectors can lose money and still provide services to Kuwaitis at subsidized prices to help maintain loyalty to the regime. However, in 1998 a bill was proposed in the National Assembly that would start privatization of some large state firms, including telecommunications, power, and water.[22] The new bill would add to the twenty-five firms turned over to private ownership since 1994, though the state-run oil firms were not included in the total for further state divestiture. However, by 2002 the government sector remained strong, partially because of the political pressure from those it employs. Of the 200,000 native Kuwaitis, the government employs over 93 percent who work, while 98 percent of the 900,000 foreign workers work in the private sector.[23] Still, some progress in privatization came in 2005, as Kuwait became the first Gulf emirate to launch a private airline, Jazeera Airways, to compete directly with the state-owned Kuwait Airways.[24]

Kuwait's economy is linked to Kuwaiti foreign policy objectives through the internationalization of its oil industry. As early as 1956, Kuwait began to move its oil industry "downstream," expanding from pumping crude oil to refining, moving, and marketing petroleum products. In 1980, Kuwait's oil holdings merged into the Kuwait Petroleum Corporation (KPC), and downstream activities increased, to include KPC purchases of exploration and drilling firms in the United States.[25] KPC did the same thing in much of western Europe, and for much the same reason. The expansion of KPC tied the economies of countries hosting KPC investments to the overall well-being of Kuwait, and thus maximized the chances that other countries would commit resources to preserve Kuwaiti sovereignty.[26] While such interdependence was not the sole reason for the allied response to the Iraqi invasion of Kuwait, it clearly helped the Kuwaiti cause.

Kuwaiti Foreign Policy

The events of 1990–1991 serve as a reminder that Kuwait is a vulnerable country that must rely on others for influence and security. The primary threat Kuwait faced prior to 2003 was Iraq, but Iran is also a concern.

Kuwait's dependency on other countries for its security, particularly the United States, now provokes some concern about the real purpose of the US-Kuwaiti relationship. Some Kuwaitis believe that the United States views Kuwait more as a market for military weapons than as an ally against Iraq.[27] Still, Kuwait was willing to host American military forces during the 2003 invasion to topple Saddam Hussein's regime, indicating that whatever suspicions Kuwaitis have about the United States, the country still is vulnerable without its large protector.

OMAN

Oman, the second largest country on the Arabian Peninsula, lies at the southeastern tip of that landmass. With the exception of the Musandam peninsula, it is not a Gulf country but rather an Indian Ocean country. Sparsely populated, the land consists of stark desert, white beaches, and sharp mountain ranges with remote settlements nestled in valleys. The northern part of the country stretches into the vast Rub al-Khali, or Empty Quarter, which is for all purposes uninhabited due to its harsh desert environment. For centuries, Omanis took advantage of their strategic location straddling the major trade routes connecting Europe and Asia, and they built ports to shelter the ships that plied those routes and built ships themselves to join in the trade. The legend of Sinbad the Sailor is Omani in origin. (Map 6.2 on page 153 shows Oman and its location at the mouth of the Persian Gulf.)

The Modern History of Oman

Early Oman became a site for Islamic minorities fleeing persecution. One such group to arrive in Oman after the beginning of Islam were the Qarmatians, a branch of the Ismaili Shiites, who moved to the Gulf to escape Sunni persecution in Baghdad. Another minority religious group, the Ibadi, moved from modern Iraq to

MAP 6.2 OMAN

modern Saudi Arabia in the late seventh century, but the Umayyads drove them into Oman. The Ibadi are the descendants of the Khariji, the group that rebelled against both the Umayyad and Abbasid rulers (see Chapter 3 for a discussion of the Kharijite movement). Except for a small enclave in Tunisia, Ibadi are now found only in Oman, where they are the majority of the population.

Most Omanis lived in tribal areas until the unification of Oman under Imam Ahmad ibn Said in the eighteenth century. His ancestor Said Said ibn Sultan expanded Omani power during his reign from 1832 to 1856, but the British curtailed Omani influence in the trades by making the area a British protectorate. The British established Royal Navy bases and Oman became an important station that the British used to control what they called "east of Suez," the area that gave them access to their Asian colonial wealth. The 1920 Treaty of Sib recognized the rule of al-bu Said Sultan of Muscat over the interior of the country.

After World War II, the British began to dismantle their vast empire, and Oman lost importance. In 1951, they turned the country over to the rule of Sultan Said bin Taymur, who had become the titular head of Oman in 1932. The British protected Oman when Saudi Arabian forces took the Buraymi oasis in 1950. Saudi Arabia, the UAE, and Oman contested this strategic location (one of the few sources of water in the southern part of the Empty Quarter), but British forces took it from Saudi Arabia and returned it to Oman in 1955.[28]

The reign of Sultan Said ibn Taymur, which lasted almost forty years, was marked by political and economic stagnation in Oman. The country's economy lapsed as the sultan spent much of his time in his royal palace in Muscat observing his subjects to ensure their modesty in dress. He forbade the construction of schools, roads, and other amenities that might have helped Oman transition into a modern country. In the sparsely populated region of Dhofar (annexed by Oman in 1879), a rebellion against his rule broke out, with assistance from the rulers of the Marxist-oriented People's Democratic Republic of Yemen.

In 1970, Sultan Said's son, the Western-educated Qaboos ibn Said al-Said, seized power in a coup. Qaboos acted quickly to suppress the revolt in Dhofar, asking Jordan, Iran, and Britain to supply military assistance. Sultan Qaboos's forces finally crushed the revolt, and Qaboos was able to concentrate his efforts on modernizing Oman's economy, raising it from fifteenth-century status to a modern system in the span of twenty years.[29]

The Omani Political System

Oman is a traditional Arab monarchy, headed by Qaboos bin Said al-Said since 1970. There are no political parties and no organized opposition to Qaboos's rule, and no rival governmental structures to restrict his power, though there is an elected legislature with very limited powers. Freedom House rates Oman as "not free." Qaboos is an Ibadi, though not an imam, and thus not considered the head of the faith.

Oman has two deeply rooted traditions that shape its politics: the Ibadi tradition of consultation (imams are elected in that tradition, for example), and the long rule of the Said family. Partly because of these dual traditions, as Jones and Ridout claim, "political parties, if they were to be formed, would be constrained to observe the constitutional status of the al-Sa'id family."[30]

Oil wealth created a newly educated elite, who encouraged the development of both political institutions and social groups. In partial response to their interests, Sultan Qaboos created the State Consultative Council in 1981, replacing it with the Majlisa al-Shura in 1991. Both those who ran for seats on the Majlis and a majority of voters who selected them comprised members of the political elite; the majority of Omani citizens have much less input.[31]

The Omani Executive

Sultan Qaboos rules largely through decree, although in November 1996 he issued an order, the Basic Law, which can be characterized as a constitution. The Basic Law provides for a prime minister, establishes a bicameral Omani council, and sets down a set of basic civil liberties. However, Qaboos appointed himself prime minister and has no cabinet. There are very few rulers who govern with virtually no executive branch, but Qaboos is one of them.

Qaboos's successor, according to the Basic Law, must be a male descendant of Said Turki ibn Said ibn Sultan and a legitimate son of Omani Muslim parents. The Basic Law also requires the Ruling Council to name the successor within three days of a vacant throne, and, if unable to reach a decision, the Defense Council can then confirm the appointment of the person designated by Sultan Qaboos.[32] The succession issue is critical in Oman, as Sultan Qaboos is unmarried and has no children.

The Omani Legislative System

The Omani legislature consists of two houses. The former legislature, the State Consultative Council, was replaced by the Majlis Oman, with an upper chamber, or Majlis al-Dhowla, created in 1997 and a lower house, or Majlis al-Shura, formed in 1991. The citizens of Oman elect the Majlis al-Shura, which has eighty-three seats and was last elected in October 2003. The Consultative Council has seven permanent substantive committees: legal, economic, health, social affairs, education and culture, services and development of local communities, environment and human resources, and follow-up and implementation. The sultan chooses the second body, the Majlis al-Dhowla, or Council of State, with forty-eight seats, from nominations submitted to him. The Majlis al-Dhowla plenary session meets four times a year. These bodies are not truly legislative, since they neither propose nor draft laws. Rather, they advise the sultan on matters of state.[33]

There are no political parties in Oman, but there is also no legislation prohibiting their formation, and the Basic Law permits Omani citizens to form associations. Should parties be established, they would have to respect the status of the al-Said family, as noted above, but also respect freedom of religion (thus religious-based parties would appear to be illegal) and advocate an economic free market.[34]

The Omani Judicial System

Oman has a nominally independent legal system, though the sultan appoints all the judges in the Omani court system. The court system itself is a combination of civil courts (for criminal cases), Islamic courts (for family cases), the Authority for the Settlement of Commercial Disputes, the Labor Welfare Board, and the Real Estate Committee for tenant-landlord disputes. At the criminal court level, punishment can include a sentence of execution, but Sultan Qaboos reviews all capital punishment sentences. There is also a State Security Court, which can hold trials in secret, to try those suspected of subversion against the state. In 2005, for example, two Omanis came before the State Security Court for critical remarks against the state, and were sentenced to prison terms, though the Omani Court of Appeals reduced one sentence and the sultan pardoned the other.[35]

The Structure and Performance of the Omani Economy

Oman has a private economy as stipulated in the Basic Law of 1996. Although the economy is not burdened by a large state-run sector, it is hampered by a relatively small petroleum reserve compared to its Gulf neighbors. Oman has around 4 billion barrels of crude, which represent a twenty- to fifty-year supply at present rates of production. While Oman is not one of the world's major oil producers, oil revenues count for almost 90 percent of export earnings, and close to 40 percent of its overall GDP. That may change, however, as one of the major investors in Omani oil, Royal Dutch Shell, found that it had overestimated Omani reserves by 40 percent and that the enhanced oil recovery efforts were dramatically increasing production costs.[36] The Petroleum Development Oman, Oman's national oil company, plans an ambitious program to recover at least 50 percent of that oil through enhanced recovery techniques, which is unusual for most Gulf countries but necessary in Oman given its oil geology.[37] Oman has taken a major step to decrease its oil dependency by developing its natural gas reserves.

Oman's population of 3 million has a GDP per capita of around $13,500, high for the Arab world, though the unemployment rate for 2006 stood at 15 percent. Oman runs a positive balance of trade and has a relatively low external debt unique for a developing country.

Oman has been preparing for the day that petroleum is no longer commercially viable with an ambitious plan called Vision 2020. It calls for expanding Port Salahah and building a $2.4 billion aluminum smelter. Oman has also worked to develop a major seaport, Salalah, in the southern region of the country. According to plans, this joint venture with Sealand-Maresk will make it the tenth largest seaport in the world.[38] There are also plans to ship from Port Salahah to India ammonia and urea extracted from gas fields.[39] Oman has also changed its tax law to allow non-Omanis the same favorable benefits from investments that Omanis enjoy, and Oman hopes to attract foreign investment in telecommunications, tourism, financial services, and mineral extraction.[40] Petroleum Development (Oman) is also planning to expand downstream operations, moving into marketing finished petroleum products.[41] There are also plans to reduce the oil share of the GDP from 40 percent to only 9 percent by the year 2020, while increasing manufacturing from 5.4 percent to 15 percent and natural gas from 1 to 10 percent.[42] The Omani government is also developing tourism and real estate with policies allowing foreign ownership of land in certain tourist areas, and Oman expects to benefit from a designation by the United States as a free trade area.

For the future, Oman must find more employment for Omani citizens, since illegal expatriate workers fill many jobs in the country. In 1998, the Ministry of Labour and Social Affairs attempted to boost "Omanization," partially by ousting thousands of expatriate workers (many from South and Southeast Asia). The consequence was that the number of Omanis working in the private sector rose from 33 percent in the first half of 1998 to 40 percent by the fall of the year.[43] According to Sultan Qaboos, the goal for the year 2020 is 90 percent Omani worker participation in the private sector.[44] That also means training thousands of Omanis in the skills left by the expatriates, something that several ministries are initiating.

The Status of Women in Oman

Women may vote and run for the Majlis. A number of women challenged for positions in the Majlis al-Shura in the 1997 elections, with two incumbent women re-elected. In his first appointment of the Majlis al-Shura, Sultan Qaboos selected women to fill four of the forty-one positions. Women also hold three portfolios in the cabinet, including Tourism and Higher Education. In addition, women hold significant positions through Oman's governmental departments and serve in the military (predominantly in the Royal Air Force of Oman), and constitute 8.9 percent of the Omani civil service. Women now constitute a majority of students at the Sultan Qaboos University, which opened in 1986.[45]

Omani Foreign Policy

For decades, Oman relied exclusively on Great Britain to provide for its security. Although Sultan Qaboos continues to maintain a strong link to the United Kingdom, he recognizes the predominate role that the United States plays in the region. Qaboos has also tried to balance Omani foreign relations in an effort not to rely too heavily on any one power. This means that while Oman maintains good relations with the United States, it has also striven for good relations with Iran. While committing forces to Operation Desert Storm, it maintained diplomatic relations with Iraq, and maintained a relationship with Israel.[46] Of all the Gulf countries, Oman has taken the lead in supporting Arab-Israeli peace negotiations, and has participated in all the peace process working groups created by the Madrid Peace Conference in 1991.[47] Oman has also tried to maintain good relations with Iran, especially important given its position right across the Gulf. Oman tried without success to mediate the Iran-Iraq war, and more recently supported efforts to bridge the gap between the Gulf Arab countries and Iran.[48] In August 1998, Oman and Iran discussed holding a joint military exercise between their two navies after the commanders of both countries' navies met in Tehran.[49] Oman balances these ties by maintaining strong ties to its Arab neighbors, both within and outside of the GCC. Consistent with this position, Oman supports the UAE's claim to the three islands in the lower Persian Gulf occupied by Iran since 1971.[50] Oman has also tried to mediate between Saudi Arabia and the UAE over UAE displeasure with Saudi overtures toward Iran.[51] Oman has also tied its economic future to outside interests, investing in the Caspian Basin Pipeline Consortium and other projects in South Korea, Thailand, and India.[52]

IMAGES

The Omani air force transport plane drones slowly out over the water from Muscat, and as it gains altitude, the panorama of ships below fans out into the Indian Ocean. They are oil tankers of every size and shape, and most are headed eastward, their white wakes trailing behind. As the plane approaches the narrow mouth of the Straits of Hormuz, the ships become more numerous as they vie for position to enter the Gulf, some at anchor until a slot opens. The cinnamon-colored mountains sweep down to the waters as the plane approaches the Musandam peninsula, a tiny disconnected slice of Oman at the mouth of the straits. Here at the lower end of the Gulf, Oman controls one side of the waterway where perhaps 70 percent of the world's oil flow transits, one of the most strategic spots on earth. For all its importance, though, the place is almost unpopulated, and that becomes apparent as the plane banks sharply through a narrow canyon and lands at a tiny gravel-covered strip facing the Gulf waters, barren except for a windsock and an empty wood frame shack with a sign in Arabic and English, "Welcome to Goat Island International Airport" and smaller signs proclaiming "this way to subway, taxis, customs, duty-free stores." Even here, someone has a sense of humor.

THE UNITED ARAB EMIRATES

The United Arab Emirates is one of the more interesting Gulf countries, a collection of seven small sheikdoms located between Qatar and Oman on the Arabian side of the Gulf. There were originally nine sheikdoms that were collectively known as the "Trucial Coast." However, after the British terminated the nineteenth-century treaty two of the sheikdoms decided on autonomy (Bahrain and Qatar), while seven others, specifically Abu Dhabi, Dubai, Sharjah, Fujairah, Umm al-Quwain, Ajman, and Ras al-Khaimah, joined into the United Arab Emirates in 1971.

The Modern History of the United Arab Emirates

The history of the federation now known as the United Arab Emirates is both ancient and recent. In ancient times, the area on the Arabian Peninsula side of the southern Gulf was known as Hormuz. It was the home of the Qawasim, a confederation of tribes who turned to piracy as a source of income. They operated a fleet of over 900 ships and plied the southern Gulf in search of the rich trade passing between northern Gulf ports and the Straits of Hormuz. British sea power put an end to this activity, forcing the Qawasim sheik to sign a treaty with Britain giving them protectorate status in 1853.

Oil production began in the late 1950s, and Abu Dhabi and Dubai developed oil fields that accelerated their economic growth ahead of the other emirates, creating the foundation for the wealth that followed. In 1971, Britain withdrew from the Gulf and the lower Gulf emirates agreed to form the UAE, all except Ras al-Khaimah, whose ruling sheik attempted to stand independently from the others until he found himself in a conflict with Iran over the Greater and Lesser Tunb Islands and the island of Abu Musa. After Iran took the islands just after the British left,[53] Ras al-Khaimah quickly joined the other emirates.[54]

The United Arab Emirates' Political System

The largest member of the United Arab Emirates is Abu Dhabi, and when the emirates gained independence from Britain in 1971 the leaders selected Sheik Zayid bin Sultan al-Nahyan of Abu Dhabi as the president of the confederation, and he ruled until his death in November 2004. The vice president and prime minister is

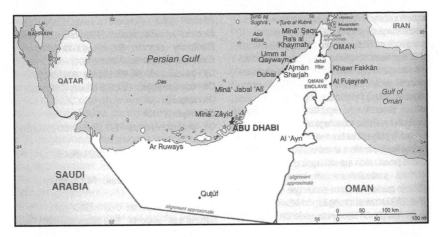

MAP 6.3   UNITED ARAB EMIRATES

the ruler of Dubai, and that title passed to Sheik Mohammed Bin Rashid al-Maktoum in December 2005 upon the death of his older brother. The Federal Supreme Council (FSC), comprised of the seven emirs from each emirate, elects the head of state, most recently in October 2001. The UAE is ranked as "not free" by Freedom House, although the regime appears to stay in place largely because of its popularity rather that its use of traditional political measures to prevent opposition.

Sheik Zayid was quite popular with his subjects. He claimed he liked to meet his subjects in person, "because our secret police don't get it right half the time."[55] His family tried to prevent him from driving, which he liked to do, because it took him a long time to get from place to place, making stops along the way at his subjects' houses, inquiring as to their welfare and needs.[56] He continued to work from his wheelchair until he died in November 2004. His son Khalifa ibn Zayid al-Nahyan succeeded him.

Perhaps the popularity of Sheik Zayid and the overall wealth of the country helped avoid protests over the lack of democracy, where the UAE lags behind the other Gulf Arab countries. Said one observer, "It's hard to demonstrate behind the wheel of a Mercedes." However, the press has become more willing to criticize the regime and there is discussion about holding local elections.[57]

The guiding document for a political structure was a provisional constitution signed by six of the seven emirates (Ras al-Khaymah signed a year later), to be replaced after five years by a permanent constitution. However, disagreement over substantive issues like contributions to the budget and responsibility for defense remained, and consequently the government extended the provisional constitution for five years when the time came to replace it. The UAE political structure finally ratified it in 1996.

The constitution separates power into an executive, a judicial, and a legislative branch. It also separates political responsibility into emirate and combined authorities, reserving foreign and security policy to the combined authorities while reserving certain other powers to the emirates. However, the FSC along with the Council of Ministers and the presidency performs the executive and legislative functions. It formulates general policy, ratification of federal laws, budget, and financial policy, ratification of treaties, and the approval of appointments for the prime minister. It requires the agreement of at least five members on what are regarded as important issues, and the rulers of Abu Dhabi and Dubai have veto power over Supreme Council decisions.[58]

The Council of Ministers administers combined affairs with a membership of twenty-five ministers. The Federal National Council is the primary legislative body, and the emirate rulers appoint its membership for two-year terms. It is largely limited to consultation.

The Status of Women in the United Arab Emirates

The constitution declares that women are equal to men before the law and guarantees other rights to women, like forty-five days paid maternity leave and four months paid leave at the death of a husband. Education is widely available to women in the UAE, making it one of the few Arab countries where the literacy rate for women (79.8 percent) is higher than that for men (78.9 percent). The UAE also has an officially sponsored UAE Women's Federation that, among other things, seeks to increase the employment of women in government. It also works to reduce the number of unmarried women in the UAE by reducing the number of second wives and by reducing the dowry price fathers must pay to marry off their daughters. The head of the UAE Women's Federation is Sheika Fatima bint Mubarak, wife of the late Sheik Zayid; in addition to that role, she holds open majlis for women.[59] In November 2004, Lubna al-Qasimi became the first woman member of the twenty-one-member UAE cabinet, with the portfolio of planning and economy.[60]

The Ministry of Labor and Social Affairs has established a network of Social Development Centers that train women in a number of fields while providing child care for those who need it while attending classes. However, most training concerns traditional areas such as housework, handicrafts, and agriculture.

There are areas where women face challenges. The UAE does not permit civil divorce, which is carried out instead through Islamic law. That means that men can declare unilateral divorce, and they normally gain custody of any children from the marriage.

The Structure and Performance of the United Arab Emirates Economy

The UAE is one of the wealthiest countries in the world, with its combination of a small population and large oil production. Its total wealth is largely due to its petroleum industry. However, credit is due to the merchant class who built much of the structure on which that wealth is built. The development of the port of Dubai, the development of a central administration, the establishment of telephone service, electricity, and education were all stimulated by the merchant class, which remains important today, particularly in Dubai.[61]

While the official population of the UAE is around 2.6 million, only 19 percent of them are emirati citizens; the rest are foreign workers. They often live in squalid conditions, earning between $4 and $7 per hour for long hours, and get few rights from the various emirates governments.[62] The GDP per capita of $45,200 is particularly high since only the emiratis benefit from it, and the international workforce is not generally well remunerated for its labor. Inflation is a low 2.4 percent, the government budget is overbalanced, and exports are almost twice the value of imports even though the emirate imports high technology and high-value goods for its wealthy national population.

The 98 billion barrel oil reserves that supply the country with almost one-third of its GDP should last for more than 100 years. As long as oil prices remain stable, the UAE should continue to prosper.[63]

The UAE has planned lavish expenditures that seem to match plans for a post-oil future oriented toward tourism, and a need for increased status. Dubai is building such things as the world's largest artificial island ($3 billion for the palm-shaped creation, which is visible from space), the Dubai marina ($10 billion), Festival City ($1.6 billion), the world's largest shopping mall, a $150 million new zoo, Dubailand, to become the Disneyland of the Middle East, among other attractions.[64] The foundations for what will be the world's tallest building have been laid, and the UAE is increasing the amenities that attract tourists, including more golf courses, thousands of new hotel rooms, and sports attractions like offshore powerboat racing and the world's largest indoor ski jump. Ferrari enthusiasts can whet their appetite at the $360 million theme park on Yas Island where they can enroll in, among other attractions, a Ferrari driving school. Another ambitious project is the expansion of Emirates Air (owned by Dubai), which ordered over $15 billion worth of new Boeing and Airbus civilian aircraft, fifty-eight in all.[65] The emirates hope that these new planes will carry hundreds of thousands of tourists from Europe, Asia, and the former countries of the Soviet Union to the UAE. Importantly, this growth pattern departs from the normal growth led by Abu Dhabi and Dubai in that the other emirates are also beneficiaries and engines for development.[66]

This investment could sustain the UAE long after the oil runs out if it generates revenue from tourism and business travel. However, should oil revenues dip as they did in much of the 1990s, the United Arab Emirates could be saddled with a huge debt and forgone opportunities for investments elsewhere. At the same time, investments in tourism (particularly in high-end tourism) hold higher promise for the future than do investments in industry, as Saudi Arabia is doing. Still, the economy must accommodate the growing population (half of which is under 21 years old) and medium and long-term job creation is essential.[67]

IMAGES

> *It is a rainy, misty night in the UAE, but even through the low clouds it looms impressively above the darkening sands. The Burj al-Arab, the world's tallest and probably most expensive hotel, seems to float on the Gulf waters, with its traditional sail-like shape soaring close to the height of the Empire State Building. Inside the towering atrium narrows in soft blue light until the top is no longer visible. Massive aquariums line the expansive stairs to the main floor. Each suite has two floors, decorated in lavish furnishings, rotating beds, gold-plated bathroom fixtures, and museum-quality paintings. The most inexpensive suite costs close to US$1,000 a night with tax and transportation, but the price of the multiroom royal suites at the top is discussed only in hushed voices. "It probably will never make a profit," notes a well-placed official, "but that is not the point. The point is the image that it gives the UAE—that is what will stay in visitor's minds forever."*

The Foreign and Security Policy of the United Arab Emirates

The United Arab Emirates faces a situation that is similar to Kuwait's. It is very small in comparison to its neighbors and cannot hope to maintain its own security using its own resources. It also faces a dangerous neighbor across the southern part of the Gulf—Iran—which it regards as its most serious threat, and that assessment predates the Iranian revolution of 1979.[68] Shah Muhammad Reza Pahlavi indicated during his reign that Iran would play a significant role in the Gulf, and that clearly worried the small UAE, as the shah seized three small islands between Iran and the UAE, Abu Musa and the Greater and Lesser Tunbs.[69] Iran continues to occupy them, claiming them as historically Persian.

Sheik Zayid built close relations with the United States, while criticizing US support for Israel. The Gulf War of 1990–1991 strengthened UAE-US relations, and these ties resulted in cooperation on the peace support operations in Somalia, protection of intellectual property rights in the UAE, and a significant number of port calls by US naval ships in UAE ports, more visits than the US Navy paid to any other port since the Gulf War. The UAE also hosts significant American military forces.

BAHRAIN

Modern Bahrain may be located on the site of Dilmun, an ancient civilization mentioned in many old records. Exhibits in the national museum reveal a long occupation of the island by peoples who depended largely on fishing for a livelihood. Given the harsh climate of the land—no sources of fresh water other than rain and thus very limited arable land—the culture never progressed beyond a fishing economy until oil was discovered in the twentieth century. There has been a Twelver

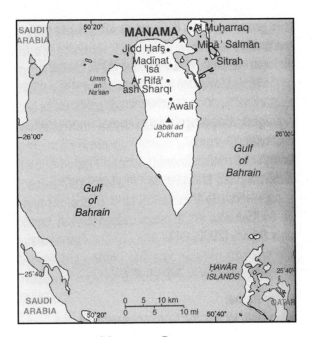

MAP 6.4   BAHRAIN

Shiite community in Bahrain for centuries, and the capture of the island by Persian Shah Abbas I in 1602 solidified their position. Thus Bahrain has the largest percentage of Shiites of any Arab country, around 75 percent of the total population.

The Modern History of Bahrain

In the sixteenth century, the Persians occupied Bahrain, but the Matareesh family replaced them in 1602. The Matareesh family was Omani by birth but loyal to the Persian Empire. The al-Khalifa family moved up the Gulf in the seventeenth century, drove the Matareesh out of Bahrain in 1783, and have ruled the island ever since. In 1861, members of the ruling al-Khalifa family signed a pact with Great Britain to protect themselves from rival families in the region and, like the other Gulf states, gave the British long-term control over the area.

The economy of Bahrain remained tied to the sea, but the introduction of cultured pearls in the mid-1930s all but wiped out the economy of the island. Fortunately Bahrain was the site of the first discovery of oil on the Arab side of the Gulf, in 1932.

In December 1971, Britain granted Bahrain full independence, and in June of the following year, Sheik Issa ibn Salman al-Khalifa announced that the country would be governed by a constitution with a Constituent Assembly. However, debate in the National Assembly grew sharp over the emir's efforts to pass a new state security measure, and two political blocs in the Assembly, the Religious and People's Blocs (see below) joined forces to try to defeat the measures, which they believed were targeted at them and their electoral base. However, in August 1975, the emir capped off the debate by dissolving the National Assembly. Despite a constitutional provision calling for new elections within two months, the emir chose not to do so, and the National Assembly disappeared from the political scene. The arrest of a popular Shiite cleric in 1994 led to bursts of unrest through 1995, resulting in more arrests.

After Sheik Issa died in 1999, his son Hamad assumed power and began a reform process leading to a referendum election in February 2001 declaring Bahrain a constitutional monarchy. The measure passed by a 98 percent margin, authorizing the reestablishment of a bicameral parliament to open in 2003. In February 2002, Issa proclaimed Bahrain to be a monarchy instead of an emirate, declaring himself His Majesty Shah Hamad bin Isa al-Khalifa, the king of the kingdom of Bahrain.

The Bahraini Political System

The royal family is Sunni even though around 70 percent of Bahrainis are Shiite. There is an elected parliament, as a result of political reforms in the early 2000 period, and limited political expression, earning Bahrain a rating of "partly free" from Freedom House.

The Bahraini Executive

The chief executive and head of state is King Hamad bin Isa al-Khalifa. All cabinet members receive their appointments from the king, including the prime minister, who is the emir's uncle, Khalifa ibn Salman. The minister of defense is Gen. Khalifa ibn Ahman, the king's great uncle, and his first cousins serve as interior minister and foreign minister. Of the eighteen ministers in the cabinet, seven come from the ruling family, and the others are split between the Sunni and Shiite communities. The Shiites have six cabinet posts, but some claim that these are less important and less powerful than the other cabinet positions.[70] There are few Shiites in the Bahraini military, reflecting the reality that the Sunni who run the military do not trust the Shiites, particularly since Iran is a potential opponent.[71]

The Bahraini Legislature

The National Assembly opened in 1973, but Emir Issa closed it only two years later, as noted above. In its place, the government established a thirty-member Consultative Council (Majlis al-Shura) in 1992. That body consists of twenty-two elected members and twenty appointed members (eight appointed directly by the emir and twelve appointed by the Council of Ministers. The twenty-two members were elected in December 1972, Bahrain's first election. A second election, held a year later, elected the thirty-member National Assembly, an advisory body, for four-year terms, and the Council of Ministers. In 1995, Emir Isa expanded the Consultative Council to forty members, and allowed up to half of the members to be elected indirectly from cultural or professional organizations. Some saw the move as an effort to curtail Shiite protests about their exclusion from power.[72] The expansion did not seem to change the Consultative Council's unwillingness to challenge the regime on meaningful issues.

The National Assembly members did not officially have party affiliations since the government bans parties, but three blocs emerged in the first elected assembly:

- The People's bloc, consisting of eight members who wanted the legalization of labor unions
- The Religious bloc, made up of six Shiite members who demanded a ban on the sale of alcoholic beverages and labor reform
- The Government bloc, a group of sixteen members who generally supported positions taken by the emir

After Isa's death, King Hamad allowed elections for municipal governments in 2002 and restructured parliament in 2003, supplementing the Consultative Council (40 appointative seats) with a House of Deputies, also with forty seats. Hamad opened the new parliament in December 2002. Some parliamentarians complained that the new assembly still lacked power, while the executive worried that the Religious bloc, held over from the past parliament, would demand an end to alcohol sales in Bahrain and the exit of American forces based there.[73] The political blocs, or associations, were also restructured, as reform advocates tried to transform them into political parties. The proposed revisions would require the parties to comply with the constitution, "work on national cohesion and patriotism, and shun sectarian orientations," leading one member of the Islamic bloc to denounce the proposal, saying, "It is yet too soon for such a project."[74]

The 2006 elections saw the Islamic National Accord Association, a Shiite group, gain sixteen seats in the first electoral round, supported by the left-wing National Democratic Action Association, while Sunni Islamists gained eighteen seats, with the remainder going to independents. The opposition, now headed by the Shiite al-Wifaq and its leader, Ali Salman, has joined with some liberal Sunnis to broaden participation, though they understand that in the next election they can win a bare majority at best, which the royal family can then dilute with appointments to the unelected upper house.[75]

The Bahraini Judiciary

Bahrain, like many other Arab states, has a judicial system featuring both secular and religious courts. Given the mix of Sunni and Shiite, the religious law comes from several sources, including the Maliki and Shafii Sunni schools of law and the Jaafair school of Shiite law. The religious courts of first instance exist in most Bahraini communities and there is a Sharia Court of Appeal. At the apex of the court system is the Supreme Court of Appeals, where both civil and religious cases are sent if appealed. That court is not independent from the royal family.

The Bahraini judiciary had wide powers under Isa. The government could detain anyone without charges by the authorities for up to three years if suspected of subversive activities.[76] After Hamad assumed leadership, he announced a general amnesty for political prisoners, although a three-judge panel challenged his decision by sentencing a Shiite cleric to a ten-year prison sentence and a $15.4 million fine for allegedly spying and inciting unrest.[77] Two days later, though, Hamad suspended the entire sentence.[78] In October 1999, he established the Bahrain Human Rights Committee to examine human rights issues, selected from the Shura Council but reportedly independent from the council.[79] Most political prisoners not only went free but also found themselves consulted by the emir on policy issues. The result has been a marked decrease in political violence, and other Arab Gulf countries now watch Bahrain as an example of political liberalization.[80] The judiciary also upheld other freedoms: a man banned from writing critical editorials in a local newspaper sued the paper and won his case in the courts.[81] That freedom was reinforced with the establishment of the first independent newspaper in a GCC country, Bahrain's *al-Wasat*, which adopted a moderate tone toward the Bahraini government but stridently criticized the United States and Israel.

The Status of Women in Bahrain

Women in Bahrain are not required to veil themselves, and they can drive vehicles and work in the presence of men. They also have the right to vote and to participate in politics. In March 2002, two Bahraini women made history by being the first of their gender to drive in the grueling Bahrain International Auto Rally, and a Bahraini woman competed in the 2004 Olympics. The first women's society in the Gulf started in Bahrain in 1955, and the key women in the al-Khalifa family have been active in supporting women's groups and women's issues.[82] In 2002, King Hamad directed that the Ministry of Justice investigate and resolve problems concerning the rights of women in divorce cases, including reports of unfair alimony and child custody cases and long delays in settlements.[83] Still, in April 2004, a number of women petitioned to reform the personal status laws that favor men, but no changes resulted. In 2006, 16 women out of 2,006 total candidates ran for parliamentary seats, but none advanced past the second round.[84]

The Structure and Performance of the Bahraini Economy

Bahrain once prospered on its oil resources, but those reserves have dwindled over the past decade. Bahrain's population of around 700,000 (including 235,000 non-Bahraini) has a GDP per capita of $23,000, high by world standards. Inflation is low and the government budget is in the black. Bahrain's oil reserves are miniscule by Gulf standards (124 million barrels), and other resources are limited. Bahrain once relied on agriculture as a principal source of income, with dates as the most significant product. However, by the 1980s other kinds of agriculture replaced the date palm groves as Bahrain tried to diversify its food sources. But rainfall is sparse, and the ruling al-Khalifa family owns much of the best land. Thus only about one-fifth of the land under cultivation at independence remained so by the mid-1990s. Fishing, also an important source of jobs and food, also has declined, despite government efforts to expand the fishing industry infrastructure, including building new processing plants and motorizing some of the fishing fleet.

In recent years, there have been attempts to diversify the Bahraini economy. Infrastructure projects are ongoing in the areas of communications and desalination of seawater, including the construction of a $450 million plant on the island of Muharraq.[85] Other developments involve a new industrial zone and new port facilities and hotels, along with ship repair, battery production, aluminum, and paper production (interesting for a country without many trees).[86] Bahrain has also developed a significant banking industry, including its own banks plus branches from a number of other countries. The growth of Islamic banks, including branches of both Arab and non-Arab banks (Citicorp, Banque National de Paris, and the Gulf International Bank), is emphasized. In December 2003 the Bahraini cabinet approved the privatization of electrical generation.[87] Like other Gulf countries, Bahrain is also encouraging tourism and took the bold step of building a multimillion dollar automobile race track, which in April 2004 hosted the first formula one grand prix race in the Middle East.

In September 2004, the United States and Bahrain signed a free trade agreement, which allows 100 percent of consumer imports and 80 percent of agricultural imports from the United States to enter Bahrain duty-free; likewise Bahrain's exports to the United States would be duty-free. The arrangement, reportedly intended in part to reward Bahrain for supporting US policy in the region, drew criticism from other GCC countries as a violation of the GCC treaty and reflected fears that lower-priced goods imported into Bahrain from the United States might be illegally resold in other GCC countries.[88]

The Foreign and Security Policy of Bahrain

Bahrain, along with the other Gulf Arab countries, has pursued relatively close relations with the West and the United States. The country serves as a naval facility for a number of US naval vessels (the Fifth Fleet is headquartered at Manama), and American and British military aircraft use Bahraini airfields. While that presence produces strains between the two countries, the rift can be exaggerated. For example, when an Iraqi Exocet antiship missile hit the frigate USS *Stark* in 1988, the injured crewmembers were rushed to Bahraini hospitals.[89]

Bahrain faces a particular challenge with its Shiite population, who have both religious and historical ties to Iran. In 1981, Iran reportedly sponsored a coup attempt, which the regime suppressed, and arrests followed throughout the 1980s.

QATAR

Qatar is close to Bahrain on the eastern side of the Persian Gulf. Like most of these small political entities, it is a remote place where pearl diving and trade formed the substance of its economy until the discovery of oil and natural gas.

The Modern History of Qatar

The peoples who began permanent settlements in Qatar probably came from the central part of the Arabian Peninsula. Two powerful families, the al-Jalahim and the al-Khalifa, came around 1766, and engaged in fishing, pearling, and piracy, building small villages on the beaches to support their maritime activities. Some of these encampments grew into fortified towns, and one, al-Bida, later became the capital city of Doha. When the Bani Utub conquered Bahrain, which had more fresh water than did Qatar, most of the al-Khalifa left for that island, taking their political institutions with them. Thus, as Crystal observes, "Qatar was left with no strong central authority, but instead was saddled with a series of violent power struggles and weak rulers."[90] The al-Thani family arrived in Qatar sometime during the nineteenth century. Later the British would come, hoping to keep the Gulf free for British navigation since British Empire trade flowed through it. They adopted a dual strategy, offering the General Treaty of Peace, signed with tribal leaders along the Gulf in 1820. But to enforce their message of determination, British naval forces destroyed many pirate ships and attacked pirate ports in 1819. In 1868, the British recognized for the first time that Qatar was distinct from Bahrain, and acknowledged the al-Thani tribe's claim to rule Qatar. Later the al-Thani family ended its tenuous Ottoman connections and adopted the Wahab interpretation of Islam, thus putting it under the protection of the al-Saud family in the land that would later become Saudi Arabia. The Ottomans officially accepted the situation in 1913 by renouncing sovereignty over Qatar.[91] Qasim's son, Abd Allah ibn Qasim al-Thani, then signed a treaty with the British in 1916 placing Qatar under the same British protectorate system initially offered in 1820. In 1935, Britain offered promises of assistance to Qatar in exchange for drilling rights for the Anglo-Persian Oil Company.

As oil revenues began to flow into impoverished Qatar, the British held the upper hand, ultimately offering to support Abd Allah's son as ruler against his relatives, who were clamoring for a large share of the incoming oil revenues. However, Ali ibn Abd Allah al-Thani was inexperienced in governance and turned to his patrons, the British, for help. The British trained his police to help keep him in power, but oil revenues allowed Ali to buy off his opponents. Ali finally abdicated in 1960 and passed the reins of power to his son Ahmad ibn Ali. Ibn Ali also turned to the al-Thani family as he staffed important government positions, galvanizing rival families to form the Country Unity Front in 1953. Ahmad ibn Ali responded by exiling and jailing the opposition leaders. Such actions could have led to the ouster of the al-Thani family, had it not been for the political skill of Khalifa ibn Hamad, who had lost out as ruler to Ahmad Ali's father, but remained as heir apparent and

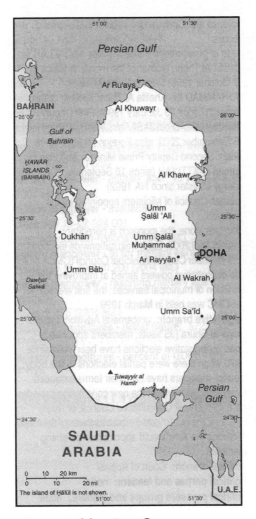

MAP 6.5   QATAR

prime minister. Khalifa ibn Hamad built up Qatar's economic infrastructure and attempted to diversify Qatar's economic base, actions that provided economic
prospects for the opposition families and a respite in political tensions.

In 1968 the British announced that they planned to withdraw from the Gulf,
and in April 1970, Qatar got its first constitution. Ahmad ibn Ali al-Thani became
emir and Khalifa ibn Hamad took the prime minister post. Seven of the ten ministers in the newly formed Council of Ministers were from the al-Thani family. The
family also put its support behind Khalifa ibn Hamad when he deposed Ahmad
ibn Ali, who was hunting in Iran in February 1972 when he learned of the coup.
The coup may have been inspired by rumors that Ahmad ibn Ali was planning to

impose his son Abd al-Aziz as heir to the throne, which would have gone against the consensus of most other al-Thani family members. But many in and out of the al-Thani family were growing tired of Ahmad ibn Ali's frequent visits to his chalet in Switzerland and his opulent living style that he afforded by taking around one-fourth of all Qatar's oil royalties for his personal expenses. In launching the overthrow, Khalifa ibn Hamad, perhaps unwittingly, set a precedent for his own ouster more than twenty years later. On June 27, 1995, Hamad ibn Khalifa al-Thani overthrew his father while the latter was on a trip to Europe, and has served as Qatar's emir ever since. His rule has not gone unchallenged; in February 1996, political opponents attempted a coup and then fled to Yemen and the UAE when it failed. Both those countries returned some of the coup plotters, who were sentenced to prison terms after being found guilty at trial. In May 2001 an appeals court sentenced nineteen of the plotters, including the emir's cousin, to death, and an additional thirty-three to life in prison. In the last few years, though, there have been few political challenges to Hamad's rule.

The Qatari Political System

The al-Thani family has ruled Qatar almost since they arrived in Qatar. Change was slow until 1995, but with the accession of Emir Hamad, reforms opened the Qatari political system to a level of participation not seen previously in the Persian Gulf. In November 1995, Hamad announced general elections for membership in the Central Municipal Council. In 1997, he opened voting to that body to women, and in November 1998, he announced that he was amending the Qatari constitution to allow for an elected parliament.[92] That has not happened, although there have been elections for municipal councils. Qatar has no viable civil society, and political parties are banned.[93] Qatari citizens have the right to elect local governments, and the government does not generally interfere with freedom of expression, though Qatar is "not free" according to Freedom House.[94]

Despite the ranking, Qatar has embraced some liberal ideas, to include a closer relationship to Israel than other Gulf countries. In 2005, Emir Hamad al-Thani donated land to build the first Christian church in Qatar, despite the country's conservative Sunni Muslim leanings.[95] There are few signs of discontent in Qatar, and state officials have persuaded mosques preaching an antiregime message to moderate their messages.[96]

The Qatari Executive

The head of state is Emir Hamad ibn Khalifa al-Thani, who also serves as minister of defense and commander in chief of the Qatari military. The prime minister was his brother, Abdullah ibn Khalifa al-Thani, but Abdullah resigned in April 2007 and Hamad bin Jassem al-Thani, the previous foreign minister, replaced him. A younger brother, Muhammad ibn Khalifa al-Thani, is deputy prime minister. In October 1996, the emir designated his third son (actually the second son by his second wife), Jassim ibn Hamad ibn Khalifa al-Thani, as the crown prince. If previous patterns hold, Jassim will someday assume the title of emir.

While the al-Thani rule supreme, they do rely on the Council of Ministers and Advisory Council, which at least give the appearance of consultation. The Qatari constitution gives the ruler the power to appoint and discharge ministers, to issue decrees, to command the armed forces, and almost any other power the ruler wants to assume. The constitution also provides for a prime minister with responsibility for the budget and other administrative duties. The Advisory Council debates proposed laws from the Council of Ministers, and offers advice on such matters to the emir. Ministers have the constitutional right to attend Advisory Council meetings and address matters within their ministry's purview, but that is a perfunctory right since members of the Council of Ministers are also members of the Advisory Council. In practice, the Advisory Council is selected from nominees from the ten electoral districts created by the constitution in 1971. Each district nominates two persons, and the emir selects one of them, for twenty "elected" members. The Advisory Council was expanded to thirty-five members in 1988, and the emir selects the other fifteen members without input from the electoral districts. Members of the Advisory Council were initially to serve for three years, but in May 1975, membership was extended for all members for an additional three years, and again extended to four years in 1978. However, every four years membership is again extended for four years, so in practice, members serve until they die, retire, or are dismissed by the emir.

Under the ministers is a large state bureaucracy, some of which was inherited from the British, particularly to cover financial matters. Other state ministries run state-owned industries, while yet others manage civil and foreign affairs. With thirteen ministries in all, the Qatari regime has ample levers of power to control almost all aspects of Qatari politics.

The Qatari Legislature

There is no legislature in Qatar, but, as noted above, the emir allowed elections in March 1999 for a municipal council, the first elections in Qatar since 1970. With that precedent established, the emir appointed a commission to draft a constitution that would allow for a directly elected parliament; however, it has never materialized.

The Qatari Judicial System

The constitution created a judiciary with a dual court system. The civil courts include criminal and civil courts administered through secular procedures. A labor court and a court of procedures are also part of the secular court system. A Sharia court administers law interpreted through the Hanbali school of jurisprudence and considers cases involving family matters like divorce, property, and Islamic behavior.

In 1990, the emir established the Permanent Committee for Legal Affairs to coordinate the workings of the Ministry of Justice with the other ministries. A subcommittee or Permanent Committee represents the government in all legal proceedings, and Qatar in international legal matters.

One potential source of political instability is the nonresident worker population of Qatar, mostly from South Asia or Middle Eastern countries like Egypt, Palestine, or Jordan. They make up almost 80 percent of Qatar's total population. While they have caused no serious incidents, their sheer size and relative poverty make them a potential source of political unrest, particularly if oil prices continue to decline.

The Status of Women in Qatar

Qatar, like Saudi Arabia, is influenced by Wahhabist teachings, which influence the role and status of women, though to a lesser extent than in Saudi Arabia. For Qatari women, arranged marriages are less common than in earlier years, but the divorce rate is growing and divorced women with children have a difficult time remarrying.[97] Women got the right to vote in 1998 and may drive and travel abroad (but only with permission of a male relative) and run for office in municipal elections.[98] Six women ran among the 227 candidates, although none were elected in the February 1999 elections despite the fact that women constitute 45 percent of total voters.[99] A second round of elections in 2003 saw one women elected.

The Structure and Performance of the Qatari Economy

Like the rest of the Gulf states, Qatar is dependent on oil revenues, which account for around 30 percent of its GDP and 70 percent of government revenues.

Qatar's tiny population of just more than half a million accounts for the high GDP per capita of $28,300, with the perhaps 120,000 Qatari citizens the prime beneficiaries. Inflation is very low, unemployment almost does not exist, and the foreign debt burden is very small. Qatar, like most oil-producing Gulf countries, has deficit spending that contributes to social projects like education, medical care, infrastructure, and other things that help political and economic stability.

Qatar oil reserves are dwindling, but its natural gas reserves are among the largest in the world. In the North Field alone, there are gas reserves estimated at over 350 trillion cubic feet, and more than 900 TCF total. As demand for natural gas continues to increase (partially because it burns more cleanly than does liquid petroleum), companies like Shell and Exxon/Mobil have decided to join Qatar Petroleum to invest heavily in infrastructure to liquefy and transport Qatari gas.[100] Qatar may see its hydrocarbon wealth continue into the twenty-first century, although privatization of that sector has been very slow.[101] Still, state investment in the petroleum sector is growing rapidly, with a planned tripling of liquefied natural gas production by 2011, and oil production up 25 percent, partly as a result of the half billion dollar al-Shaheen field development offshore.[102]

Qatar, like the UAE, plans to increase tourism as a way to diversify the economy. A major expansion of Doha's international airport will rival the huge airport in

Dubai, and Qatari Airways is planning to double its fleet of large passenger planes to bring tourists to the country.[103]

Qatari Foreign Policy

As a very small country in an unstable area, Qatar has followed a prudent foreign policy. It has maintained a good relationship with its former protector, Great Britain, and many Britons serve as advisers on economic and military matters. Qatar's relationship with the United States has also been generally good, but marred occasionally by problems, such as when American-made Stinger antiaircraft missiles appeared at a military parade in Doha in March 1988. The United States demanded that the missiles be returned since they had been obtained by unauthorized means, and Qatar refused.

Qatar is a strong supporter of the GCC and committed troops to the defense of Saudi Arabia during the Gulf War of 1990–1991, engaging Iraqi troops at the battle of Ras al-Khafji.[104] However, Qatar has also had disputes with other GCC members. In 1995, Qatar walked out of a GCC meeting to express its dissatisfaction that no Qatari had received a high position in the organization since its founding.[105] Qatar has strained relations with Saudi Arabia, which have been worsened by articles appearing in *al-Jazeera* critical of Saudi Arabian leadership. There is also concern in Qatar about the disintegration of the al-Saud leadership and the possibility that Qatar could be drawn into the subsequent conflict.[106]

Qatar is one of several Gulf countries that have given support to the Arab-Israeli peace process, believing that peace will result in economic stability for the entire Middle East. However, Qatari leadership is disappointed by the consequent breakdown of the process and has returned to denouncing Israel for its treatment of the Palestinian population.

IMAGES The glittering lights of Doha fade into the distance amid the enveloping desert. The tent is warming in the cool night air, and the white desert outside seems to glow in the starlight. Warm fresh camel milk comes in bowls and is served in hollowed-out dates, along with bitter cardamom coffee. The herders crouch in front of the tent, knowing that their life is mostly reenacted for the tourists, and that they are among the last to escape the lure of Doha's lights.

The Gulf emirates are still struggling to establish their identity in some parts of the Arab world. The other large state on the Arabian Peninsula, Yemen, has no such problem. Yemen has a unique culture and history as one of the oldest countries in the world. Mountainous and remote, Yemen is unique among Arab countries.

SUGGESTED READINGS

Kuwait

Crystal, Jill. *The Transformation of an Oil State*. Boulder, CO: Westview, 1992.

Tétreault, Mary Ann. *Stories of Democracy: Politics and Society in Contemporary Kuwait*. New York: Columbia University Press, 2000.

Oman

Allen, Calvin H. *Oman: The Modernization of the Sultanate*. Boulder, CO: Westview, 1987.

Allen, Calvin H., and W. Lynn Rigsbee II. *Oman Under Qaboos: From Coup to Constitution, 1970–1996*. London: Frank Cass, 2000.

Kechichan, Joseph A. *Oman and the World*. Santa Monica, CA: Rand Corporation, 1995.

United Arab Emirates

Davidson, Christopher M. *The United Arab Emirates: A Study in Survival*. Boulder, CO: Lynne Rienner, 2005.

Peck, Malcolm C. *The United Arab Emirates: A Venture in Unity*. Boulder, CO: Westview, 1986.

Bahrain

Khuri, Fuad Ishaq. *Tribe and State in Bahrain: The Transformation of Social and Political Order in an Arab State*. Chicago: University of Chicago Press, 1980.

Lawson, Fred H. *Bahrain: The Modernization of Autocracy*. Boulder, CO: Westview, 1989.

Qatar

Anscombe, Frederick F. *The Ottoman Gulf: The Creation of Kuwait, Saudi Arabia, and Qatar*. New York: Columbia University Press, 1997.

Crystal, Jill. *Oil and Politics in the Gulf: Rulers and Merchants in Kuwait and Qatar*. Cambridge: Cambridge University Press, 1990.

Zahlan, Rosemarie Said. *The Creation of Qatar*. London: Croom Helm, 1979.

7

YEMEN

IMAGES | *The mountains are stark here, with buff-colored crags separated by deep valleys where the qat trees appear as the only green. Watchtowers occupy strategic locations so that one tribe can observe a pending raid by another tribe. The small mountain villages all have one thing in common: a stone silo in the center. When a visitor asked if the silo stored grain, the answer came that it was a last sanctuary for the villagers from attacks by other villages. When it was noted that all the silos had been reduced to mere stumps, the answer came back, "Yes, we have unstable times here."*

THE COUNTRY ON THE SOUTHEASTERN CORNER of the Arabian Peninsula occupies one of the most fabled lands in the Middle East. Some believe that Yemen was the home of the legendary Queen of Sheba, who traveled to Jerusalem to rendezvous with King Solomon in biblical times.[1] Yemen is the land of frankincense and myrrh, the highly prized resins burned as incense. The old Yemeni port of Mokka (or Mocca) has given its name to both a coffee bean and a coffee brand (MJB once stood for "Mocca Java Blend"). For most people, Yemen is a remote and mysterious place of tall mountains and canyons rivaling the American Grand Canyon. Yemeni men wear curved daggers called *jambayyas* in their belts, and both men and women in Yemen chew qat, a narcotic plant capable of stimulating both passive and violent behavior. Yemen has a rich cultural and historical tradition, and in modern Yemen, democracy and human rights exist in ways that are still uncommon in the Arabian Peninsula.

THE MODERN HISTORY OF YEMEN

The Zaydi imamate began in Yemen when Yahya ibn al-Hussein migrated from the Caspian to Yemen and took Sanaa in 901, establishing an imamate that lasted until the 1962 civil war and leaving behind significant political traditions. It is the only country where the Zaydi, or "Fiver," tradition of Shiite Islam is influential.

175

The Ottoman Empire tried to incorporate Yemen in the sixteenth century, but the Zaydi around Sanaa drove them out a century later. The British came to the south Arabian Peninsula in 1839, claiming the port city of Aden as a British protectorate. They drew up what was called the Violet Line to divide this territory from the Arab parts of Yemen to the north. The Ottoman Turks returned to Yemen in 1872, but the Zaydi contested the Turkish forces between 1916 and 1919 before finally ousting them. The British recognized Yahya Muhammad Hamidaddin, who became known as Imam Yahya, in the Treaty of Sèvers in 1920 as the king of Yemen. They declared Yemeni independence in 1925, though retaining their protectorate in Aden until the 1960s. The British then divided the country into North and South Yemen along the old Violet Line of 1839. Yemen also lost Asir to Saudi Arabia in 1934.

The Beginnings of Independence

Yemeni opposition to Yahya coalesced into the Free Yemeni movement in 1944. Yahya's eighth son joined the movement in 1946, and a decision was made to assassinate Yahya. The first attempt in January 1948 to break into Yahya's palace failed, but an ambush followed later in the month, and Yahya died in his Cadillac, which was riddled with more than fifty bullet holes. Following Yahya's assassination, the crown prince, Ahmed ad-Din, fled to the mountains of Hajjah as the leaders of the revolution selected Abdullah ibn Ahmed al-Wazir as the "secular imam" and leader of the country. They stormed into Sanaa and took over the city, but their revolution was hardly established. The ninth son of Yahya, al-Abbas, formed an army and attacked the rebel stronghold at Sanaa, beheading al-Wazir.

The Origins of Civil War

Ahmed ad-Din proclaimed himself the new imam and ruled for fourteen years, as assassins made numerous attempts on his life. He died in September 1962, either from an assassination attempt or from a morphine overdose, and his son, Muhammad al-Badir, succeeded him. However, the imam's death gave opportunity to Abdullah al-Sallal, the chief of the Royal Guards, to overthrow the regime. But Muhammad al-Badir escaped and fled north, where he organized efforts to resume power. That sparked the Yemeni civil war, which was joined by two other Arab countries anxious about events there. To the north, Saudi Arabia worried about the establishment of a republican regime on the Arabian Peninsula, while Egypt's Nasser looked on the event as a chance to weaken his Saudi Arabian rival. The Soviet Union recognized the republican regime in Sanaa in October 1962 and began to supply aid to both al-Salla and the Egyptian forces entering the country to support it against the royalists in the north.[2] Sallah invited the Egyptians, who landed on the Red Sea at Hudaydah in 1964. However, the act of calling in foreign forces alienated Sallah from his republican allies, including former Minister of Defense al-Ahadi Abdarrahman al-Iryani and the commander in chief of Republican forces

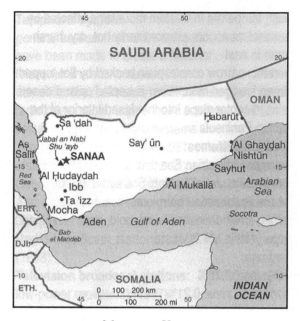

MAP 7.1   YEMEN

Gen. Hasan al-Amri. Sallah sent them to Cairo on a political mission to get them out of the country, and Egyptian President Nasser placed them under house arrest, releasing them three years later.

Egyptian forces remained in Yemen, fighting an increasingly frustrating and deadly war with Yemeni fighters, who used the rugged territory of Yemen to ambush and wear out the Egyptians. Finally, out of desperation as much as anything else, Egypt began chemical weapons attacks against the Yemeni opponent. The first probably occurred in July 1963, with larger attacks coming in January 1967 against the area where Royalist Prince Hasan bin Yahya located his headquarters.[3] The attacks provoked strong criticism of Egypt by Saudi Arabia, Iran, Israel, the United States, and Great Britain, but they only ended when Israel defeated Nasser in the 1967 war, and Egypt sought to repair relations with Saudi Arabia.[4] Egypt probably wanted to reduce the huge cost of this operation, which at its peak had around 60,000 Egyptian troops in Yemen.

Upon his return, al-Iryani forced Sallah aside and created a position for himself, the first chairman of the Republican Council. Al-Amri became the prime minister. They had little time to prepare to face their most serious challenge in the civil war, the siege of Sanaa by Royalist forces. From December 1, 1967, to February 8, 1968, Royalist armies surrounded the city, threatening to destroy it. Finally, Hasan al-Amri led his forces through the siege and freed the city, with considerable assistance from Soviet-supplied equipment. To capitalize on their victory, the Republican forces attempted to win converts to their side. In the summer of 1968, they got their biggest prize when Qasem Munassar, a leading Royalist general, brought himself and his Beni Husheich tribe to the Republican side. On March 8, 1969, Imam al-Badr fled to Saudi Arabia, and a week later al-Iryani called a constitutional convention to unify Yemen. Saudi Arabia finally recognized the Arab Republic of Yemen in July 1970, temporarily ending the long civil war.

The civil war was not the only conflict tearing at the country. The British found themselves under increasing opposition from Yemeni nationalists, inspired partially by Nasser. Two organizations, the National Liberation Front (NLF) and the Front for the Liberation of South Yemen (FLOSY), worked to overthrow British occupation of Aden. In 1963 the British sent in Sir Richard Trumbull, who had led the British against the Kenyan Mau Mau rebels, to Aden. Trumbull failed to crush the Yemeni resistance, and Lord Humphrey Trevelyan replaced him in 1967. Trevelyan reportedly reached a secret agreement with the NLF (who preferred a negotiated settlement to violence) and crushed FLOSY. Thinking that they would at least avoid a Nasserite regime in Aden, the British withdrew in November 1967. Aden became the capital of South Yemen, and Sanaa the capital of North Yemen. The division started by the British with the old Violet Line would further complicate Yemeni politics.

In June 1969, the leftist wing of the NLF overthrew Qahtan ash-Shaabi, the president of South Yemen, and Salim Rubaia Ali replaced him. Rubaia Ali, who advocated unification with North Yemen, was toppled in a coup the following year, largely due to the poor economic conditions in South Yemen. He tried to regain power in June 1978 through another coup, but was arrested and executed. The new president, Abdul-Fattah Ismail, attempted to further "scientific socialism" as the guiding economic principle for South Yemen. Others in the ruling party opposed his ideas, and Ismail found himself exiled to Moscow, only to return in 1985, and appointed again to high political office by President Ali Nasser Muhammad. That provoked still another crisis as members of President Muhammad's government opposed Ismail. In a violent struggle between government members Ismail was shot dead while Ali Nasser Muhammad was forced to flee into North Yemen in January 1974 with 20,000 of his followers. Some 10,000 Yemenis died in the brief but bloody struggle and the fighting destroyed much of Aden. Colonel Haider Abubaker al-Attas became president of South Yemen.

Events were not much more peaceful in North Yemen. Conservative tribal opposition and Saudi Arabian pressure forced President al-Iryani out in June 1974. Colonel Ibrahim Muhammad al-Hamdi tried to organize a government, but an opposition group assassinated him in October 1977. His successor, Col. Ahmed Hussein al-Ghashmi, got the national parliament to elect him president in April 1978 but a South Yemeni left a bomb in his study, which exploded and killed Ghashmi. The new president was Ali Abdullah Saleh, an army officer and colleague of Ghashmi. Saleh's first challenge was the escalating war between North and South Yemen, which was going badly for North Yemeni forces until Kuwait intervened in 1979 and a stalemate followed. Saleh was reelected by the national parliament for another five-year term in May 1983.

Unification

The bloody civil war persuaded both north and south that unification was the only way to avoid further violence. A National Committee formed to explore unity in 1981, but the death of South Yemen President Ali Nasser Muhammad in a coup attempt delayed unification. However, Ali's successor, Ali Salim al-Bidh, and Saleh met in April 1988 to revive the unification process. The talks produced a demilitarized zone between the two Yemens, with joint economic initiatives following.[5] By November 1989, the two parties reached agreement on unification principles, and in May 1990 the Yemeni Arab Republic and the People's Democratic Republic of Yemen unified into the Republic of Yemen. The inspiration for this unity effort may have been the reduction in economic assistance from the former Soviet Union to the PDRY, and its consequent inability to stand alone, particularly in the face of its inability to produce enough food to feed its population. It had fallen behind the YAR to become an economic backwater.[6] Still, the YAR remained impoverished, and Saleh realized that the possibility of oil in the PDRY could lift both countries should they become unified.[7]

Unification would not end Yemen's political violence. The People's Democratic Congress (PDC) ruled the former Yemeni Arab Republic and the Yemeni Socialist Party, led by Ali Salim al-Beedh, ruled the former People's Democratic Republic of Yemen. Upon unification, both parties agreed to split all government positions on a fifty-fifty basis. However, since the Yemeni Arab Republic had a larger population than did the People's Democratic Republic of Yemen, the actual split was delayed until the April 1993 elections. The Yemeni Socialist Party lost seats to the newly formed Islah (Yemeni Congregation for Reform), and, fearful of northern hegemony over the south, Ali Salim al-Beedh left Sanaa and moved to Aden. President Saleh and his new allies in Islah organized to prevent a breakaway southern state, and in May civil war broke out again. Fighting lasted until July, when the secessionist leaders fled the country. A period of relative stability followed, and in the September 1999 elections President Saleh won the first public election for president with over 96 percent of the vote against two opposition candidates. In 2005, Saleh announced that he would not run for reelection, potentially ending his twenty-seven-year rule. However, he reversed himself and ran for president again in 2006, garnering 77 percent of the total vote.

Although much of this history focuses on the development of the Yemeni state, it would be misleading to suggest that all or most Yemenis identify with the state as a legitimate political entity, or that state building is complete. Many Yemenis express primary loyalty to their tribe, and tribal identity has often hampered the creation of a strong central state. In many parts of rural Yemen, tribal order and tribal politics are far more significant than is the government in Sanaa.[8]

THE YEMENI POLITICAL SYSTEM

The Zaydi ruled Yemen for most of its Islamic history, and the legal traditions of this Shiite branch, the so-called Qasimiyya-Hadawiyya school of jurisprudence that

emphasizes a rationalist theology, is still important in understanding Yemeni politics.[9] So is the Marxist underpinning of the PDRY, still influential in southern
Yemen.

Unification in May 1991 brought a new political structure to replace the two
systems previously in place. The Unification Agreement, ratified by referendum on
May 16, 1991, with 99 percent approval, provided for a constitution to establish
political structures, as well as political rights and responsibilities. The Yemeni Constitution chartered a legislature with 301 members elected by universal suffrage, an
executive branch, and an independent judiciary. The Supreme Elections Committee, consisting of seven members selected by the president from a list of fifteen candidates submitted by parliament, supervises the provisions of General Election Law
27 of 1996. The Supreme Elections Council members must refrain from political
or party activity during their term on the council, and may not nominate themselves for public office during that time. This law governs the conduct of Yemeni
elections. Yemen is "partly free" in the 2006 Freedom House ratings. While there
are certainly democratic advocates in Yemen, Schwedler argues that their primary
obstacle to further democratic reform is neither the Islamists nor tribal leaders but
the regime itself, since it depends on considerable patronage from bureaucrats to the
economic elite who might lose control of resources and trade.[10]

The most important parties in Yemen are the General People's Congress (GPC),
which holds the presidency and a majority in parliament, and Islah, or Islamic Reform Party. Other parties include the National Arab Socialist Baath Party, the
Nasserite Unionist Party, and the Yemeni Socialist Party (YSP). Elections for parliament have occurred twice in Yemen, first in April 1993 and again in April 1997.
Members of parliament represent single-member electoral districts. The president
of Yemen calls parliamentary elections, required at least sixty days before the conclusion of a parliamentary term. Candidates representing a party or an organization must secure the official endorsement of that party or organization's
secretary-general.

The parliament selected the president of Yemen until 1999, when provisions for
the presidential direct election went into effect. Parliament still plays a role, but under the new law it votes approval on nominees for the office, and any candidate
must get at least 10 percent of members to vote for him or her. Parliament then
transmits a list of approved candidates to the Supreme Elections Committee, which
the president appoints from a list of fifteen candidates nominated by at least two-
thirds of parliament. For the 1999 election, four candidates submitted their names
to parliament, but only two—Saleh, with 182 votes, and Najib Qahtan Muhammad Nassere al-Shabi, with 39 votes—made the 10 percent cut.[11] Saleh became the
nominee of both the PCC and Islah, while the opposition parties failed to agree on
a nominee. In the end, to provide some competition, Saleh's supporters nominated
al-Shabi and helped fund his campaign. Saleh even sent his own cabinet speakers to
speak at al-Shabi appearances.[12] In September 2006, Saleh again ran for president,
this time against Faisal ibn Shamlan, winning with 77 percent of the popular vote
in a disputed election that opponents called "laughable."[13] In many ways, though,

the outcome was predictable. For one thing, the GPC's domination of political and economic life is rentier-like, although Yemen is not a major oil state. The Islamist Islah could not hope to compete with a party apparatus that controlled such a resource base, as Longley noted, "Saleh had a free hand to use public funds for his campaigns and to promote the GPC in general. . . services poured into poverty stricken areas in the name of Saleh and his party."[14]

Yemen has a relatively free press in accordance with Press and Publication Law 25 of 1990. The law ensures freedom of expression and requires that, within reason, public organizations must provide information to journalists. Rather than banning critical newspapers, President Saleh has denounced them when they print critical news, as he did in May 2004 over published charges that Saleh and other high officials in his administration were plotting to install their sons in positions of succession.[15] In June 2007 Yemeni security agents arrested former editor in chief of Al-Shoura.net, Abdulkarim al-Khaiwani, claiming he had links to terrorist bombings, but other journalists suspected that it was Al-Khaiwani's criticism of the regime that landed him in jail.[16]

Political Parties and Organizations

Law 66, passed in 1991, allows for the formation and operation of political parties. The law provides for a Committee for Political Parties headed by the minister for parliamentary affairs, and includes as members the minister of justice and minister of the interior, and four other independent members chosen from the Supreme Court judges or lawyers. The committee considers applications by those wishing to form a new party, and if the committee has no objection to the proposal, the party becomes legal in forty-five days. Any new party must have at least 2,500 founding members. Once a party receives a charter, it is eligible for government funding to support its activities.

The reality in Yemeni politics, though, is that no single party has been able to challenge the GCC's hold on power. For some analysts, the decline of the middle class, as well as the growth of corruption and governmental inefficiency, is propelling Yemen towards the status of failed state. Only a coalition of parties like the Joint Meeting Parties (JMP), including Islah, the Yemeni Socialist Party, and several smaller parties can effectively challenge the GCC and prevent political collapse.[17]

The Yemeni Executive

The president of Yemen is Ali Abdallah Saleh, who served as the president of North Yemen until unification. His party, the GPC, also controls the ministries—out of the thirty ministerial positions, ministers affiliated with the GPC head twenty-five. That does not mean that there are not significant policy differences within the GPC. For example, Prime Minister Abd al-Aziz abd al-Ghani, who served in that position since 1994, resigned in April 1998 because of differences with President Saleh over political reform. Abdul-Karim al-Iryani replaced him in May 1998.

President Saleh has some informal political allies in the "Afghan Arabs," who left Yemen to fight the Soviet Union in Afghanistan in the 1980s and then returned to Yemen. Saleh recruited many Afghan Arabs in his final unification push in 1994, and he provides government protection and subsidies to supporters of Saudi Arabian exile terrorist Osama bin Laden. While some argue that Saleh would like to rein in the Afghan Arabs, others claim that they remain a powerful factor that limits Yemen's ability to strengthen its ties to the West.[18] Their presence also suggests that the Yemeni government lacks the ability to control large areas of the country. In rural Yemen, radical Islamist clerics preach against the United States, Jews, and Arab governments that do not agree with their position, including the Yemeni government.[19] After the September 11, 2001, attacks against the United States, the Saleh government tried to clamp down on followers of Osama bin Laden and other militant groups. In early 2002 Yemeni forces swept into areas like remote Marib to capture both terrorists and kidnappers, whose actions against foreigners deprive Yemen of needed foreign investment. The operation generated opposition from the Islamist Islah Party (with 64 of 301 seats in parliament), whose leader stated that "when the government. . . behaves according to US pressure or interests, Yemenis will fight back."[20]

The Yemeni Legislature

In 1997, President Saleh appointed the fifty-nine-member Consultative Council to advise him on a variety of issues, and the council does include some of the president's critics.[21] In January 1999, the Ministry of Legal Affairs amended the Yemeni constitution to transform the Consultative Council into the upper house of the Yemeni legislature.[22] The house became Yemen's single chamber legislature, with its 301 members elected by popular vote. Yemen thus became the second country on the Arabian Peninsula after Kuwait to have a democratic legislature. According to the constitution, the president cannot dissolve parliament except by emergency decree and even then only after approval by a nationwide referendum. Members represent single-member districts chosen by equal population size as determined by the general central census.

In the April 1997 elections, the General People's Congress (GPC) got 189 seats, the Yemeni Congregation for Reform (Islah) 52, the Nasserite Unionist Party 3, the Baath Party 2, and independent candidates 54.[23] The Yemeni Socialist Party boycotted the election and thus has no parliamentary representation. In April 2003 the GPC increased its seats to 229, Islah garnered 47, and the YSP 7.

The parliament has shown streaks of independence, as when it engaged in extensive debate with the executive over the budget in 1996, and as a forum for YSP and Islah members to push for favorite programs. The Islamists, for example, pushed for legislation mandating Islamic banking practices, forcing President Saleh to pressure GPC members to sustain his veto of the measure.[24] Islah also pushed for control over the Ministry of Education, increased school time for Quranic studies, and a designation of Islamic law as Yemen's unique law source.[25] Parliamentary committees may investigate complaints against the government, as they did in visiting a prison to probe charges of inhumane treatment of inmates.[26] Still, the Yemeni parliament is short of resources necessary to challenge the executive and internal divisions between parties in parliament limit its effectiveness as a viable political challenge to the executive.[27] It is still an important political forum in an increasingly vibrant Yemeni democratic system. It may not propose legislation on its own, but as one report noted, "It is here that most of the country's business gets done."[28] This is because many legislators also hold positions as minor regional sheiks who wield considerable regional influence and can get things done in the regions beyond the reach of central authorities in Sanaa. That factor is a limiting factor in Yemeni democracy, as parties grew under powerful personalities and not as institutions. But in recent years party policy is increasingly shaped by democracy inside the party and not by the dictates of the party leader.[29]

The Yemeni Judiciary

Unification produced a judicial court system that has many of the divisions familiar in other countries. Each of Yemen's eighteen political districts has a court of first instance, which covers all kinds of cases. There are no specialized courts. Each province also has an appellate court that receives appeals from the court of first instance. The eighteen provincial courts of appeal have branches that are divided into civil, criminal, matrimonial, and commercial. At the top is the Supreme Court of the Republic, which has jurisdiction over:

- The constitutionality of laws and regulations
- Conflicts between jurisdictional bodies
- Investigations of petitions referred by members of parliament
- Appeals (only on points of law, not fact) from the district courts of appeals
- Cases brought directly against the president or other high government officials

The Supreme Court is divided into constitutional, appeals scrutiny, criminal, military, civil, family, commercial, and administrative divisions. In each division, five judges consider appeals based on points of law or procedural violations. They also have the power to review capital punishment cases and punishments involving amputation or flogging.

Yemenis have certain rights stemming from State Law 6/1995, including the assumption of innocence until proof of guilt. Reasonable doubt must be in the favor of defendants, there is no punishment before trial, all are equal before the law, torture is not used to gain confessions, and every defendant has the right to counsel. Flogging is generally applied for sexual crimes (100 lashes for fornication, for example), and the right hand is amputated for theft (for the first offense; left foot for the second). Those arrested for political activity are treated with more leniency, as indicated in December 2003 when Yemeni security authorities released over 180 individuals suspected of membership in al-Qaeda or other extreme Islamic groups.[30]

The Supreme Judicial Council selects members of the Yemeni judiciary, who get lifetime appointments based on good behavior. The Supreme Judicial Council is made up of the president, the chief justice of the Supreme Court and his two deputies, the attorney general, the minister of justice and his deputy, the chair of the judicial inspection commission, and three senior Supreme Court judges.

However, much of Yemen lies beyond the official justice system. In rural areas, justice is often administered by tribal sheiks who mete out penalties through personal negotiation. The tribute often consists of Kalashnikov assault rifles for a murder victim's family, and the agreements are kept only during rare times of truce.[31]

CIVIL SOCIETY IN YEMEN

A flourishing civil society exists outside of the formal governmental structure, which is common for a country where tribal identity remains important. Local mutual aid societies, tax collection and dissemination, and village improvement projects exist as replacements for central government involvement in local politics and economics. Urban clubs and associations serve as vehicles for both communication and political involvement. Yemen also has a long tradition of labor union activism and independent news media that serve as alternatives to government involvement in economic development and news dissemination.[32] Some argue that since the Yemeni government is resistant to significant change, civil societies are the catalyst for Yemen's future, particularly since a number of them are led by women who advocate political change.[33] On the other hand, there are those who argue that many civil society leaders are more interested in attracting funds for their personal gain than for the members or interests of the group.[34]

Political insurgency exists in Yemen, though it is sometimes difficult to distinguish between insurgency and banditry. For example, the jihad movement began in Yemen in the early 1990s when Sheik Tariq al-Fadli returned to Yemen from Afghanistan, where he worked with Saudi Arabian exile Osama bin Laden. In the late 1990s reports indicated that the jihad movement organized the Aden-Abyan Islamic Army to carry out antigovernment actions in the belief that the regime was about to grant the United States military facilities on the island of Socotra.[35] The group's ties to Osama bin Laden again appeared, though suggestions also surfaced that the Aden-Abyan army helped President Saleh's victory in the Yemeni civil war.[36]

Yemen has tried to crack down on terrorists operating in the country. Yemeni leaders publicly stated that Osama bin Laden is not welcome in Yemen and in August 1998 stated, "Yemen will accept no terrorists or wanted persons in its territory."[37] However, the government's inability to police the remote tribal areas makes such a statement difficult to support with actions. The terrorists who attacked the American destroyer USS *Cole* in October 2000 apparently had bases in rural Yemen. Some parts of the country are home to veterans of the war in Afghanistan against the Soviet Union, and the Islah Party recruited many of them. They served with Saleh during the 1994 civil war and Islah and its so-called Afghan Arabs replaced the defeated socialists in some of the southern political regions.[38]

THE STATUS OF WOMEN IN YEMEN

Before unification, the YAR and the PDRY took different approaches to the status of women. The YAR emphasized traditional Arab and Islamic approaches to the status of women, while the PDRY adopted a secular code with defined rights for women. In the YAR, polygyny and divorce by *talaq* (divorce by the husband's decree) was permitted, though there were some general protections for women, and practices toward women differed between the more conservative Zaydi parts of the north and the more orthodox Shafii regions. The PDRY required all divorces to go through the courts, denied men automatic child custody, and banned *talaq*.[39] Unification resulted in the earlier YAR law of 1979 being applied to the whole country, thus costing women some rights they had held in the former north, although not to the degree desired by the Islah.[40] Islah has welcomed women members, though it has no platform to advance them to higher positions within the party. Still, women constitute 18 percent of Islah's total party membership, actually giving Islah one of the highest women memberships of any party in Yemen.[41] Other parties have followed: the GPC agreed to a 10 percent quota for women in parliament, the Socialist Party called for a 30 percent membership for women, while the Nasserite Party advocated proportional membership over a quota.[42]

Article 27 of the constitution that followed unification states that "all citizens are equal before the law. . . There shall be no discrimination between them based on sex, color, ethnic origin, language, occupation, social status, or religion." The General Election Law of 1996 gives women the right to vote and run for political office, and Article 5 of the constitution specifies that the Supreme Committee "shall take all appropriate measures to encourage women to exercise their voting rights." In the 2006 presidential elections, 3.9 million women voted out of a total electorate of 9.3 million. There are no women, however, on the thirty-member cabinet. The highest-ranking woman in government is Undersecretary of Information Amax Aleem al-Sosowa, who successfully objected to a measure lifting the ban on marriage for girls under fifteen.[43] Women have some access to the government through the Women's National Committee, which is a consultative technical committee founded in 1996. They also have membership on the Permanent Committee of the GPC, although there are only thirty-three women on the 700-member body. Women campaigned for parliamentary elections in 2006, but of the 199 candidates, only thirty-three won seats, and numerous women either suffered personal attacks or were divorced for attempting to enter politics.[44]

The State Department human rights report for Yemen notes "spousal abuse is reportedly common, it is generally undocumented."[45] The report also notes that men may take as many as four wives (though few do, for economic reasons), that in practice women divorce their husbands only when they do not provide for them, and that most women in Yemen have little access to health care.[46] Education for women still lags behind that for men, a fact reflected in the literacy rates, 53 percent for men and only 26 percent for women.

THE STRUCTURE AND PERFORMANCE
OF THE YEMENI ECONOMY

Yemen is the poorest country in the Arab world. It has very little oil and a high population growth rate, swelling its 21 million population by 3.5 percent each year, and contributing to high unemployment (35 percent) and 45 percent of the population below the poverty line.

A highly centralized economic decisionmaking system is partly to blame for Yemen's economic problems, as are continuing political divisions hindering economic consolidation. The poorer north is now economically dependent on the south, and tensions remain between the two formerly separate countries. The consequences of the 1990–1991 Gulf War did not help Yemen either; Saudi Arabia expelled around 750,000 Yemeni workers when Yemen refused to oppose Iraq, and the families of these workers lost their remittances, though some left to work in other oil-rich Gulf states. Yemen preserves a strong state sector as a legacy from its Arab socialism and influence of the PDRY. Efforts to privatize are under way, though, as in the sale of 45 percent of Yemen Mobil telecommunications system to private investors in December 2006.[47]

Yemen has a significant external debt, about 75 percent of it owed to Russia. Given the precarious nature of the Russian economy, there may be a willingness to reschedule at least some of the debt, particularly if the alternative is for Yemen to renounce it. On the other hand, Russia clearly needs the money and may be unwilling to wait for it. Another alternative is for the United States to pay off some of this debt in return for Yemeni support for the global war on terrorism, but thus far no such offer has been made.

Yemen has limited oil and gas reserves (around 4 billion barrels of oil and 16.9 trillion cubic feet of natural gas), and is developing an infrastructure to produce and export petroleum products. Oil sales constitute 40 percent of Yemen's total revenues, and the French firm Total is exploring a scheme to develop the Marib region where significant petroleum deposits may lie; Saudi Arabia is helping finance port facilities in Aden to export petroleum products. Such financing may continue to depend on Saudi Arabian–Yemeni relations, which remain somewhat tense (see below). However, NatWest Capital Markets did finance a $180 million reconstruction of a refinery in Aden, so Yemen is clearly trying to avoid depending too much on country-to-country economic agreements. However, Yemen has problems in attracting significant foreign investment, partly because Yemeni laws do not protect investors who get into disputes with the government and partly because of its poor reputation for protecting foreigners, who are frequently kidnapped for ransom by poor tribes.[48] China may be an exception, as it has expressed an interest in investing in Yemeni petroleum facilities.[49] The Yemeni regime has also tried to draw foreign tourists to its spectacular and rugged scenery and long history, but the security issues noted above, as well as the July 2007 killings of nine Spanish tourists, will make this quest difficult at best.

Yemen has attracted international developmental aid, receiving an International Monetary Fund (IMF) credit worth $191 million in 1996. In addition, in 1996, the World Bank lent $80 million to the Yemeni government for reform of trade policy, privatization, and the phasing out of price controls. Later in the same year, the World Bank advanced another $365 million in loans over a three-year period to 1999. Moreover, the European Union pledged grants of almost $62 million. All these institutions have offered further aid contingent on government efforts at economic reform. Those reforms have been slow in coming, and in December 2005, the World Bank concluded that Yemen had failed to combat corruption and, moreover, skewed subsidies from oil revenues disproportionately away from Yemen's poor. The World Bank subsequently reduced its assistance to Yemen by 34 percent.[50] Yemen also lost its contributions from the US Millennium Challenge Account in 2005 because of its failure to abide by the requirements of that program, including combating corruption and engaging in political transparency.

Such reform often is politically dangerous in developing countries. It can mean an end to price controls, which keep goods and services affordable to the population, even while discouraging innovation and competition. This occurred in Yemen when the government discontinued subsidies on oil and electricity in March 1995, effectively doubling the prices; violent protests immediately ensued. In January 1996 more subsidies were ended, including those for water and oil, followed by more protests, particularly by farmers dependent on subsidies. In 2006, riots again swept many Yemeni cities as the regime further cut fuel subsidies.

An additional problem unique to Yemen is the substitution of food production by qat. Qat leaves produce a mild narcotic stimulation when chewed in large quantities, and the habit permeates Yemen. A 1999 survey by the Central Statistical Organization revealed that, on average, qat and cigarettes together take 17.3 percent of the total family budget.[51] The north is now dependent on exports for food because so much land is planted with qat as the habit spreads. There is no market for qat outside of Yemen, so the resources devoted to growing and harvesting it contribute nothing to Yemen's trade balance. Qat takes an estimated one-fourth of the irrigated land in Yemen (after coffee, sesame, and tobacco).[52] While qat cultivation increases, other crops decrease. Wheat production, for example, dropped from 117,000 tons in 1995 to 40,000 tons in 2001.[53] Floods in June 1996 further weakened Yemen's agricultural capacity, causing considerable loss of topsoil. Water shortages also limit agricultural production, and are sometimes so critical that fighting breaks out between tribes over access to water wells.[54] Environmental degradation, including depleted aquifers, denuded hillsides, and the consequences of overgrazing, may be so severe in Yemen that the damage is not reversible.[55]

Yemen's economic problems are likely to persist unless the Yemeni economy can grow at rates exceeding Yemen's birth rate. That will be difficult, since Yemen has the highest birth rate in the Arab world, which will propel Yemen's population to almost 50 million by the year 2031.[56]

IMAGES | *Yemenia Air Flight 742 to London climbs gracefully from Sanaa Interna-*
          | *tional Airport to 50,000 feet, with cabin service beginning almost im-*
          | *mediately. The spotless Airbus A340 soars above khaki-colored ridges*
          | *dotted with tiny villages. The in-flight movie begins on time, the service*
          | *is continuous, and the plane finally descends into foggy London right on*
          | *time. The baggage is all accounted for. American passengers who may*
          | *have been initially nervous that Yemenia Air maintains its own aircraft*
          | *("Jordan used to do it but now we do, right here in Sanaa," says a proud*
          | *Yemeni pilot), begin to wonder if their own country and its troubled in-*
          | *ternational air carriers might learn something about how to run an air-*
          | *line from the poorest Arab country.*

YEMENI FOREIGN POLICY

In recent years, Yemen has been embroiled in disputes with its neighbors, including Oman, Saudi Arabia, and even Eritrea, over borders or territorial limits. Yemen has territorial disputes with Saudi Arabia dating from the 1930s that remain contentious. In July 1998, Saudi Arabian and Yemeni forces fought on the small Red Sea island of Duwaima off the Yemeni coast. While the fighting lasted only five hours, it could have easily escalated. Both Yemen and Saudi Arabia have attempted to put the best verbal face on areas of contention. After Saudi Arabian Prince Nayif ibn Abdul Aziz visited Yemen in November 1998, he claimed that "the leaders and wise men in the Yemeni side have always affirmed the loftiness and special characteristics of the relationship (with Saudi Arabia), especially with regard to the border issue."[57] In July 2004, Saudi Arabia returned some territory to Yemen and a German firm finished a final demarcation of the border between the two countries.[58] This has not stopped Saudi Arabia from interfering in Yemeni politics, including sending cash payments to some Yemeni groups and attempting to spread its Wahhabist version of Salamis Islam, reportedly reaching some influential leaders of Islah.[59]

The United States began improving relations with Yemen in the mid-1990s, partly because it wanted access to Yemeni port facilities to resupply naval ships supporting military patrols in the Persian Gulf. American military personnel worked with Yemeni authorities to combat terrorist forces in the country, and Yemen asked for US assistance in building a coast guard to help keep terrorists from penetrating the country.[60] However, these efforts did not protect the United States from terrorism in Yemen. After more than twenty US Navy ships resupplied in the port of Aden, the destroyer USS *Cole* came under attack from terrorists, who rammed a bomb-laden small boat into it, killing seventeen Americans.

That tragedy, coupled with the September 11, 2001, attacks against the US homeland, did improve US-Yemeni relations. Yemeni security forces provided much information to the CIA and have adopted strict visa requirements designed to prevent terrorists from seeking refuge in Yemen.[61] Yemeni-American relations suffered a blow when the United States sent an unpiloted Predator drone armed with missiles over the skies of Yemen, which blew up a car and killed Abu Ali al-Harithi, a senior al-Qaeda leader and one of the terrorist network's top figures in Yemen. Yemeni officials were angered that the United States carried out the operation without informing or consulting with them. In November 2003, Yemen reportedly arrested Muhammad Hamdi al-Ahdal, a top al-Qaeda official, but refused to let American officials interrogate him.[62]

Across the Gulf from the Arabian Peninsula lies Iran, a country with a modern name but an ancient past. The Persian civilization differs in so many ways from the Arab culture a short distance across the Gulf that countries on both sides of the Gulf cannot agree on even what to call it—the Persian Gulf or the Arab Gulf.

SUGGESTED READINGS

Badeeb, Saeed M. *The Saudi-Egyptian Conflict over North Yemen, 1962–1970.* Boulder, CO: Westview Press, 1986.

Carapico, Sheila. *Civil Society in Yemen: The Political Economy of Activism in Modern Arabia.* Cambridge: Cambridge University Press, 1998.

Dresch, Paul. *Tribes, Government, and History in Yemen.* New York: Oxford University Press, 1989.

———. *A History of Modern Yemen.* Cambridge: Cambridge University Press, 2000.

El Mallakh, Ragaei. *The Economic Development of the Yemen Arab Republic.* London: Croom Helm, 1986.

Gause, F. Gregory. *Saudi-Yemeni Relations: Domestic Structures and Foreign Influence.* New York: Columbia University Press, 1990.

Kostiner, Joseph. *South Yemen's Revolutionary Strategy, 1970–1985: From Insurgency to Bloc Politics.* Boulder, CO: Westview Press, 1990.

———. *Yemen: The Tortuous Quest for Unity.* London: The Royal Institute of International Affairs, 1996.

O'Ballance, Edgar. *The War in Yemen.* Hamden, CT: Archon Books, 1971.

Peterson, John. *Yemen: The Search for a Modern State.* Baltimore, MD: Johns Hopkins University Press, 1982.

Schwedler, Jillian. *Faith in Moderation: Islamist Parties in Jordan and Yemen.* Cambridge: Cambridge University Press, 2006.

Wenner, Manfred W. *The Yemen Arab Republic: Development and Change in an Ancient Land.* Boulder, CO: Westview Press, 1991.

Zabarah, Muhammad Ahmad. *Yemen: Tradition vs. Modernity.* New York: Praeger Publishers, 1982.

8

IRAN

IMAGES | *The milk chocolate-colored mountains stretch to the horizon, lightly frosted with January snow. In the deep valleys lie tiny villages with mud and stone buildings, next to sheep pens and dirt roads. These tree-less mountains have been the home to endless generations of Persians who preserve the lifestyles of their ancestors, far removed from the bustle of Tehran or even the smaller cities over the mountains. Those living there today still remember the feared Assassins, who dwelled in these very mountains at the time of the Crusaders. They would find these areas literally unchanged should they magically return to them.*

IRAN IS THE ONLY non–Arabic speaking country in the Persian Gulf area, with a distinct language and a unique history and culture. Modern Iran has at least three sources of influence in regard to its culture and politics: Persian, Shiite, and Western. Iran was once ancient Persia, with a long and proud heritage lasting thousands of years. It is one of only a few countries with a large Shiite majority, leaving it with both conservative and reformist traditions.

Iran lies across the Persian Gulf from Saudi Arabia and the Gulf emirates, south of the Islamic countries of the former Soviet Union. It borders on Pakistan, Iraq, Turkey, and Afghanistan. (See Map 8.1 on page 192.)

THE MODERN HISTORY OF IRAN

The Qajar dynasty ruled Persia from 1796 to 1925, but its power diminished after prolonged rule and growing unrest, particularly by the Islamic leadership, or *ulama*.[1] As the Qajar rulers became increasingly preoccupied with domestic problems, outside countries, particularly Britain and Russia, began to press closer to Persia. The two powers ultimately collaborated to weaken Persian power. When the British demanded a share of the Persian economy, they gained a tobacco monopoly and the right to establish banks. Reaction in Persia from the religious groups and merchants crystallized into the Constitutional Revolution of 1906, resulting in a *majlis* (or parliament) and limited political freedoms.[2] The British imposed the Anglo-Persian Agreement of 1919 on a weak Persian regime, stimulating strong nationalism that remains to this day.

Pahlavi Nationalism

Opposition to the 1919 agreement took several forms, but the most influential resistance was secular and modernist, like that led by Reza Khan, who overthrew the government in February 1921, establishing journalist and fellow conspirator Said Zia ad Din Tabatabai as prime minister. However, Reza Khan soon moved Tabatabai aside and assumed the post himself. In 1925, Reza Khan officially declared the end of the Qajar dynasty.[3] Taking the title "Reza Shah" in 1926, he inaugurated the Pahlavi dynasty, which lasted until 1979. Inspired by Kemal Ataturk of Turkey (see Chapter 11), Reza Shah built a large military and a strong state bureaucracy, along with a Western system of education, civil law, schools for women, and the prohibition of the veil for women. He also replaced the Muslim lunar calendar with a solar calendar, took over public functions (public baths, hospitals, and orphanages that the religious elite ran) and even tried to ban the *hajj*. These acts consciously challenged the power of the religious leadership. In 1935, he changed the name of the country from the Greek-origin name "Persia" to "Iran," a derivation of "Aryan," to emphasize the difference between Iranians and their Arab neighbors.

As criticism of Reza Khan grew, particularly from the conservative religious leadership, he imposed harsh measures on his critics, either jailing or exiling them. He also challenged the Russian and British influence over his country by opening Iran to Germany. In response, Great Britain and the Soviet Union invaded Iran in August 1941 and occupied it throughout the war. Reza Shah abdicated the Peacock Throne in favor of his son, Muhammad Reza Shah, and fled the country to South Africa, where he died in July 1944.[4]

Nationalism Continues

Reza Shah's departure left a vacuum in Persian politics. Britain considered restoring Qajar rule but was dissuaded by the inexperience of Crown Prince Hamid and his inability to speak Persian. The Soviet Union also meddled in Persia, working to gain support in Iran through the Iranian communist Tudeh Party.[5] Several parties with links to the Tudeh declared autonomous republics in the north of Iran, ready to grant oil concessions to the Soviet Union.[6] After the end of the war, Soviet troops remained in Iran even as American and British forces evacuated. However, after Muhammad Mossadeq was elected Iranian prime minister by the Majlis (first established in 1906 but closed in 1908 and reopened in 1943), Iranian and American pressure forced the Soviet Union to withdraw its forces, and the government banned the Tudeh Party.[7]

The agreement between Iran and Britain over the Anglo-Iranian Oil Company (AIOC, originally the Anglo-Persian Oil Company, formed in 1909) kindled Iranian

MAP 8.1   IRAN

nationalist sentiments, and in March 1951, the Majlis voted to nationalize AIOC. The loss of British technology caused a drop in oil-generated income, and Mossadeq took more powers to himself in the face of mounting political unrest. He also turned for support to his old enemies in the Tudeh for support. This connection drew attention from the United States, which was concerned about potential Soviet designs on Iran. Thus the Central Intelligence Agency organized the ouster of Mossadeq in 1953, an event that continues to stimulate anti-American sentiment in Iran today.[8]

The American Footprint

The American-led coup returned Muhammad Reza Shah Pahlavi, the son of Reza Shah, to the throne he had inherited after his father's abdication. The shah, like his father, drew inspiration from Ataturk, envisioning a secular Iranian republic with close ties to the West in general and the United States in particular. The United States encouraged Iranian membership in the Baghdad Pact (see Chapter 1) in October 1955. Muhammad Reza Shah strengthened his political hand by appointing a series of prime ministers supportive of his positions. He suppressed the Tudeh and other antimonarchy parties and established a secret police, known as SAVAK. The shah also tried economic reform, including land reforms and profit sharing for workers. He also granted women the right to vote (arousing the ire of the religious elite), and signed a status of forces agreement allowing special status for American military units advising the Iranian armed forces.

The shah drew opposition from a number of quarters in Iranian society, notably Ayatollah Said Ruhollah Khomeini, a religious leader from the northern city of Qom. Khomeini began organizing against the shah in the 1960s, and in response the shah exiled Khomeini, to Turkey and then Iraq. After Saddam Hussein ousted him from Iraq, he went to Paris, France, where he would continue to agitate against the shah until his return to Iran in 1979.[9]

The shah opened opportunities for foreign oil companies. In October 1954, British Petroleum obtained 40 percent of the Anglo-Iranian interests, while Royal Dutch Shell got 14 percent. A consortium of five American companies (Gulf Oil, Socony Vacuum, Standard Oil of California, Texaco, and Standard Oil of New Jersey) got another 40 percent. The French Compagnie Française des Pétroles got 6 percent.[10] Although Iran received 50 percent of the revenues as tax intake, the profits accruing to foreign oil companies remained a cause of disagreement between the shah and his critics.

For the United States, the shah's Iran appeared as a bulwark against the spread of Soviet influence. However, American presidents worried about the shah's political flaws, including his harsh methods of rule and the economic difficulties that, in the words of one adviser, "might drive the non-Communist opposition into the arms of the Soviet Union."[11] Still, the Kennedy administration responded to the shah's exaggerated threat estimates that were intended to pry assistance from the United States, setting a pattern followed by future American administrations.[12]

Several assassination attempts and the murder of his prime minister in 1965 alarmed the shah, who opened the political system slightly and attempted to improve economic performance. He undid earlier efforts to create a party system (originally creating the ruling Mardom and the "loyal opposition" Melliyun Parties in 1957) by disbanding both and chartering the Resurgence Party in the 1970s. The shah continued to retain central power despite creating an appearance of political liberalization.

Between 1964 and 1973, Iran experienced significant economic growth under the so-called White Revolution, which included land reform, public sale of state-owned factories, worker profit sharing, and efforts to increase literacy.[13] While the shah portrayed the White Revolution as a modernizing revolution that would transform Iran into the equivalent of a Western industrial country, it may have had more to do with his personal ambitions. Ansari claims that "the White Revolution was. . . a strategy for legitimization, through the use of rationalization, universalization, and eternalization. Socio-economic benefits were emphasized in an effort to disguise the real political gains."[14]

The economy improved even more between 1973 and 1976, growing by more than 50 percent as average per capita income reached $2,000, a third world record.[15] Yet opposition to the shah's regime only increased. Some of it came in reaction to the presence of Westerners, who often dressed and behaved in ways that Iranian Muslims found offensive. The shah's pro-American policies also fueled this opposition, alienating many politically active Iranians.[16] Opposition increased as the Iranian economy slowed in the late 1970s, burdened by expensive investments in industry and the Iranian military. Religious leaders and rural landlords suffered when the shah distributed their land to peasants.[17] The shah's price controls on essentials such as food favored city dwellers at the expense of the peasants. As unemployment grew in the countryside, many peasants fled to the city, fueling the opposition to the shah.[18] Large demonstrations in Qom and elsewhere were met by a government crackdown, which in turn fueled more demonstrations. The actions of the SAVAK were particularly brutal and helped galvanize the opposition.

Opposition to the shah's rule came from several sources. Some was secular and modernist in orientation, like the remnants of the old National Front, which reformed several times to emerge as the Third National Front in 1965.[19] It also included the freedom movement of Iran, led by Mehdi Bazargan, who would later head the provisional government after the shah's departure. Opposition also came from groups whose tribal identity was challenged by the shah's efforts to "Persianize" them, including the Baluch, Kurds, Turkmen, and Qashqai.[20]

Other opposition leaders like Ali Shariati attacked both the regime and the *ulama,* linking modern problems to the Safavid dynasty of the sixteenth century, when the Shiite faith became subservient to the state.[21] Another influence was Abu Al Hassan Bani-Sadr, who would become the first president of Iran in the post-shah period. He ultimately moved beyond Shariati to advocate violence and social regimentation.[22] Many Shiite leaders had lost power to the shah as he secularized the schools and the judicial system, which, among other things, cost the *ulama* their jobs.[23] These leaders and their rhetoric outflanked the moderate opposition, and the shah rejected advice to launch an all-out campaign against the religious forces. As Keddie notes, the shah was more effective at eliminating the moderate opposition, which left the radical Islamists in position to alter the country.[24] The resistance got the upper hand, and the shah left the country "on vacation" in January 1979, never to return. His ouster came at the hands of a temporary political coalition of moderate reformers and conservative Shiite clerics, who then formed the basis of the government that followed the death of Ayatollah Khomeini.

The Iranian Revolution

Ayatollah Ruhollah Khomeini arrived in Tehran in January from his Paris exile, greeted by a tumultuous crowd. He named Mehdi Bazargan as prime minister and then established the Revolutionary Council of Islamic clerics, which rivaled the civil government of Bazargan. Khomeini also created the Revolutionary Guards as a counterforce to the army, which Khomeini did not trust because of its American influence. Few in these groups had political experience, though, and Iranian problems multiplied, partly because Islamic radicals anxious to cleanse Iran of its immediate past sent many of Iran's business, political, and military elites to the firing squads or prisons, thus eliminating those with experience in running the economy and preparing for war.

Another reaction to the revolution was an outbreak of violence by Iranian minority ethnic groups, including the Turkmen, Arab-speaking Iranians, and Iran's Kurds, who feared Shiite political dominance. In response, the Revolutionary Guards imposed a general crackdown throughout the country. They shut down newspapers and arrested both real and suspected opponents. The Revolutionary Council also acted, appropriating private holdings and transferring them to state control. None of this was done under any constitutional authority, but the resulting chaos suggested that a constitution might be necessary. The constitution that was finally approved in December 1979 gave considerable power to the clerics, weakening Bazargan's power. For Bazargan, though, the worst was yet to come.

Iran Confronts the United States

When news that the ousted shah, seriously ill with cancer, petitioned Washington for permission to enter the United States for medical treatment, student protestors marched on the US embassy and seized it on November 1, 1979, subsequently holding its staff hostage. Bazargan resigned two days later. The so-called hostage crisis continued for more than 400 days, and revealed much about the chaotic nature of Iranian politics after Khomeini seized power. The hostage takers were allegedly students who had invaded the embassy on their own. Nevertheless, Khomeini gave his approval for the action, and the Iranian government appeared to be either incapable or unwilling to intercede against the students. The United States responded by severing diplomatic relations with Iran and freezing Iranian assets in the United States, estimated to be around $30 billion. However, Iran continued to hold the hostages until the day of President Ronald Reagan's January 1981 inauguration as final insult to President Carter.

The Radicalization Continues

Shortly after the 1979 revolution began, the religious leadership replaced the position of prime minister with that of president. Two candidates, Ahmad Madani and Bani Sadr, ran for the new office; Bani Sadr, a scholar of Islam and politics, won by a large margin. However, Bani Sadr failed to get Islamic Revolutionary Party (IPR) backing and found himself increasingly at odds with the speaker of the Majlis, Akbar Hashemi Rafsanjani, a founder of the IRP. A new purge confronted Bani Sadr, resulting in thousands of firings and executions, as well as a continuing Kurdish problem. Khomeini tried to mediate between Bani Sadr and the IRP leadership, but a rising chorus of Islamic militants called for Bani Sadr's ouster, and he fled to Paris in June. He left behind growing chaos and bloodshed as rival groups contended for influence. In June 1981, a bomb destroyed the IRP headquarters, killing Ayatollah Muhammad Beheshti, a Khomeini rival, and many other high IRP officials. Prime Minister Javad-Bahonar died in a similar bomb blast two months later. The bombings were followed by more executions of guerrilla leaders, and by 1982, the situation had deteriorated to the point where

Khomeini again tried to rein in the unrest, perhaps alarmed by the growing crisis with Iraq.[25]

The Iran-Iraq War

Iraqi President Saddam Hussein, eyeing the growing political turmoil in Iran and apparently calculating that disorder had paralyzed his neighbor, abrogated the 1975 agreement between the two countries on sharing the Shatt al-Arab, the waterway separating Iran and Iraq. In September 1980, Iraq followed this action with a large-scale invasion of Iran, after Iranian efforts to stir opposition in Shiite areas of Iraq and to assassinate Iraqi minister Tariq Aziz. Iraq's initial aim in the war apparently was to gain Iranian respect for Iraqi military might.[26] The attacks quickly escalated, with each belligerent striking the other's oil resources in the first days of the war. Internal discussion in Iran about the release of the Americans froze as Iranian leaders concentrated on defending their country. Iraqi hopes for a quick victory ended after a week as their forces bogged down on the front, and the war dragged on for eight years. In July 1988, a US warship accidentally shot down an Iranian civilian airliner over the southern Gulf. Iranian leaders, fearing that the United States was getting ready to enter the war and knowing they could not also fight America, acceded to a peace plan that left both Iran and Iraq largely with the territory they had when the war started. For Iran, the cost may have been more than 500,000 dead and $369 billion by the end of 1986.[27] A vast cemetery on the outskirts of Tehran typifies Iran's war losses, where the graves extend over the horizon while a huge fountain spews blood-red water to memorialize the war's victims.

The protracted war allowed the Iranian regime to forestall discussions of democracy or pluralism.[28] The economic cost was uneven; rising oil prices allowed Iran to pay for the war, although rationing and shortages caused problems.[29] The opportunity cost of the war is more difficult to calculate, but the cost in lives and property as well as money, combined with an inefficient cleric-run economy, contributed significantly to the economic crisis that followed the war for years after.

The Moderates Gain Influence

Iran's course appeared to outsiders as locked in the direction of Islamic militancy, but the May 1997 presidential election of Muhammad Khatami, a relative moderate, suggested that Iran's political system was more flexible than its critics might have believed. Khatami made statements indicating a desire to reestablish ties to the West and to Iran's Arab neighbors. In February 1999, Iran held local elections, the first since 1979. Numerous parties and candidates contested these elections, including conservatives, liberals, reformers, and traditionalists. The result was a sweeping victory for the reformers, as they received around 80 percent of the vote, with religious conservatives far behind. Elected representatives controlled power at the local level for the first time in 2,500 years, thus effectively diluting the political control of the clerical elites.[30]

However, both internal and external change appeared constrained by the remaining power of the religious elite. Student demonstrations at Tehran University briefly flared during the summer of 1999, but both the police and young, self-appointed Islamic vigilantes quashed them. The restive mood appeared to spread beyond the students, as the results of parliamentary elections held in February 2000 showed. Reformers won between 60 and 70 percent of the 270 seats in parliament, and the conservative clerics appeared willing to abide by the results. Ayatollah Khamenei said as much in a quote in a conservative paper: "The real winners are the great people of Iran."[31] However, the rule of the clerics remained firm, with the conservative Council of Guardians voiding the results of ten provincial constituencies. In April 2000, Tehran courts under clerical control closed twelve reformist newspapers.

In June 2001, Khatami again swept presidential elections, after apologizing for the failures of his first term and promising to bring more democracy to Iran. He exceeded his 69 percent margin in 2001, sweeping aside nine challengers with a 78 percent victory. Still, the religious elite continued to hold considerable power in Iran, and with their control of the media, the judiciary, and other institutions, they retained the ability to block future reforms. However, the newer generation born during the Iran-Iraq war is reaching political maturity, and it brings a new set of demands. Young Iranians want jobs, access to secular education, and increased freedom. One sign of the impact of their demands is regime compromise on culture, including an official rock and roll industry to combat illegal rock and roll coming in from Iranian immigrant groups in Los Angeles and elsewhere.[32]

After the 2001 terrorist attacks on the United States, Iran found itself in a difficult situation, caught between its desire to see an end to the Taliban regime in neighboring Afghanistan and fear of the growing American influence in Central Asia. Iran offered to rescue downed American aircrews during the attacks on Afghanistan and avoided criticism of US policy in confronting terrorism. However, when President George W. Bush included Iran in an "axis of evil" in his 2002 State of the Union Address, he paradoxically hurt the very reform movement the United States hoped would prevail in Iranian politics. As one Western diplomat noted from Tehran, "This was immensely damaging. It really, really hurt Khatami," who withdrew from politics before the June 2005 elections.[33]

The Conservatives Return

The elections in mid-June 2005 produced a runoff between the two top candidates, Expediency Council Chairman Rafsanjani and Tehran Mayor Mahmoud Ahmadinejad. Ahmadinejad won 62 percent of the runoff election, gaining support from the poor, while Rafsanjani got votes largely from the wealthy, who feared that Ahmadinejad would clamp down on the limited social reforms dating from Khatami.[34] When a predictable cabinet of conservatives won appointment from Ahmadinejad, Iran appeared to be on a course that rejected the tradition of reform that dated back to the 1906 constitutional revolution and instead emphasized the political and economic status quo.

Shortly after winning the election, Ahmadinejad aroused considerable ire in the West by arguing that ". . . the regime occupying Jerusalem should vanish from the pages of time," which was interpreted in the U.S. and Israel to mean that Israel should be wiped off the map. The remarks might have indicated that the divide between pragmatists and conservatives was not resolved by the president's apparent electoral landslide. Rafsanjani remained as leader of the Expeditionary Council, and, after Ahmadinejad's election, that body moved to strip the presidency of some of its powers and give them to Rafsanjani and his organ. Thus Ahmadinejad's harsh comments may have been an effort to win public support in the face of the Expeditionary Council.[35] That body continued on the path taken since 1979, to ensure that religious zeal continued as the cornerstone of contemporary Iranian politics. Those caught on the other side of that zeal faced harsh measure. For example, In June 2007 a young man accused of having Western hair was marched down the street by the religious police with a jerry can used by Iranians to cleanse their private parts stuffed into his mouth.

THE IRANIAN POLITICAL SYSTEM

Iran's political system was rebuilt after the 1979 Islamic revolution. It is a two-tiered system at the top, with a "supreme leader" as head of state and an elected president as head of the government. Ayatollah Khomeini was the first "supreme leader" followed by Ayatollah Ali Khamenei, after Khomeini's death.[36] The supreme leader appoints military leaders, the head of the security forces, the judiciary, and the members of the Guardian Council of the Constitution, otherwise simply known as the Council of Guardians, a body of senior clerics that can over-rule any action by the legislature it finds in violation of Islam. The president is popularly elected for a four-year renewable term. The president has little power relative to the unelected clerical elite, resulting in a "not free" stamp from Freedom House for Iran. Noted one commentary, "Though its political structure incorporates elements borrowed from the modern nation-state, and some of its traits evoke the Soviet system, it cannot be identified with either model. It is a theocracy founded on the political privileges of a clerical oligarchy."[37]

Political participation in Iran increased dramatically during and after the 1979 revolution, partly due to Shiite traditions, and partly because of manipulation of the population by Khomeini.[38] That tradition continues as each presidential and parliamentary (Majlis) election attracts a large turnout of voters. Over 80 percent of eligible voters turned out for the May 1997 election, and 77 percent in the election of 2001, though the 2005 participation level dropped to around 60 percent.

In some ways, Iran is divided between conservative traditionalists and moderate reformers. The moderates, whom Khatami reputedly represented, gained the presidency for at least four reasons: the continued vigor of Iranian civil society even after twelve years of religious rule, interregime factionalism that divided the religious conservatives, fortuitous events like an endorsement of Nateq-Nuri by Khamenei that backfired, and Khatami's reputation as a more moderate candidate than the conservative Nateq-Nuri.[39] Khatami also emphasized governmental accountability, a more equitable distribution of wealth, and an end to the abuse of women by men.[40] In an interview, Khatami emphasized the dual need for religion and freedom: "When religion and freedom are put at odds, both suffer. Without democracy, religion becomes extreme. With religion, democracy becomes more spiritual."[41] However, the 2005 election vaulted the conservatives back into total control of the political system, though arguably they had control anyway through the power of the judiciary and the Council of Guardians. Iran's political pendulum swung back, as reformers were exhausted by conservative resistance.

Political divisions in Iran go beyond a divide between reformers and conservatives, however. Frustrated with the glacial pace of reforms, the reformers split into those supporting Khatami and those pushing for faster and more radical reform. The conservatives also split, with some like Ayatollah Ahmed Jannati and Ayatollah Muhammad Yazdi openly supporting despotism while others call for modest reform if only to preserve their influence from more radical reform.[42] Seifzadeh argues that there are actually three primary factions in Iranian politics now, including:

- Fundamentalists, whose social basis in traditional society informs their opposition to modernity but divides them into transitional fundamentalists (modernizers who are fearful of the consequences and residual fundamentalists who are steadfastly opposed to modernity)
- Pragmatists, who oscillate between the fundamentalist and reformist factions
- Reformers, who understand Islam through a combination of scientific rationality, philosophy, and spiritual gnosticism[43]

These faction labels do not adequately explain Iranian politics, though. In the 2005 presidential election, 17 million Iranians voted for Ahmadinejad, supposedly the conservative candidate compared to Rafsanjani (who got 10 million votes). However, only 6 million Ahmadinejad voters were considered to be regular conservative voters, with the other 11 million (many former Khatami voters) supporting Ahmadinejad because they preferred his personal frugality over that of the reported extravagance of Rafsanjani.[44] Still the regime mustered its resources to assure Ahmadinejad a majority and the staying power to survive growing unrest among Iran's citizens, as might be expected in a traditional rentier state, bolstered by ever-rising oil prices in 2006 and 2007.

Religion and Politics in Iran

Shiite Muslims make up 89 percent of Iran's population; Sunnis, only about 10 percent.[45] Thus it is not surprising that the political fire that fueled the 1979 revolution was its Shiite identity. According to Halm, the Twelver Shiite tradition of *kalam*, or reasoned argumentation in jurisprudence and theology, has shaped modern Iranian politics: "The successes of the Iranian Shi'a today cannot be understood without taking this into account."[46] Others argue that religion actually plays a lesser role in Iranian political life. Olivier Roy comments that "politics rule over religion,"[47] noting that the appointment of Khamenei as guide divided clerical circles, since he was not an ayatollah but a lower-ranking hojatolislam[48] (see Chapter 2), and that the constitution of 1989 and the reform of the Expediency Council in 1997 reduced the role of religious leadership.[49] It remains to be seen whether the results of the 2005 election reflect a return to a stronger religious foundation for Iranian politics, a reaction to Western opposition to Iranian policy, or simply the ability of the conservatives to finally cement their original 1979 preferences for a truly Islamic Iran. The conservatives have constructed an elite power base with token mass participation, and the role of religion in Iran's political life may cloak elite ambitions of the clerical elite who also manage the economy.

The Iranian Executive System

The executive branch is divided between the spiritual leadership of the leader of the Islamic revolution, Ayatollah Ali Hoseini-Khamenei, who took the title in June 1989, and President Mahmoud Ahmadinejad and the Iranian cabinet. The ayatollah, because of his religious status, has checked the power of the president. Khamenei limited Khatami's reform efforts, as noted above, and, more recently, obliquely criticized Ahmadinejad for his emphasis on Iran's nuclear program, noted below.[50]

Islamic political leadership consists of the leader (Rahbar), the Council of Guardians (Shouraye Negahban), and the Assembly of Experts (Majlis-e Khobregan). The Assembly of Experts is a popularly elected body of eighty-six religious scholars who monitor the supreme leader and in theory can replace him. It is a weathervane for the tone of Iran's political direction. So when senior cleric Muhammad Taqi Mesbah Yazdi packed the assembly with his conservative pupils in December 2006, the expectation was that the body would become highly authoritarian.[51] The Council for Ascertaining the Interest of the Regime (Shouraye Tashkhis-e Maslehat-e Nezam), created in 1988 and otherwise known as the Expediency Council, serves to balance interests across the branches of state.[52] The Expediency Council chairman is veteran political figure Akbar Hashemi Rafsanjani. The Council of Ministers, appointed by the president with legislative approval, serves as a cabinet. The president serves a four-year term, while the Council of Experts, a religious body, appoints the leader of the Islamic revolution for life.

The executive also controls the Revolutionary Guards and the Basij militia, which Khamenei strengthened in response to reformist gains in 1997. The top leaders of the Revolutionary Guards have moved beyond security responsibilities to assume top posts in foreign and national security policymaking, as well as economic positions.[53] Ahmadinejad replaced some forty senior ambassadors with ideologues close to him, and put militarists favorable to him in senior management positions, regional governorships, and state-owned banks, thus deeping his authoritarian hold on Iranian policy.[54]

The Iranian Legislative System

Iran opened its first parliament, or Majlis, in 1906. It was revived in 1943 but had little power under Reza Shah. The 1980 constitution revived it as a single-chamber Islamic Consultative Assembly, or Majlis al-Shura-e-Islami, with 270 members elected by popular vote to four-year terms. Since the Council of Guardians must screen all candidates, those running under the banner of the Islamic Revolutionary Party (IRP) won heavily in the first Majlis election in 1980. The first act of this Majlis was to impeach President Bani-Sadr, though his supporters retaliated by bombing IRP headquarters, killing twenty-seven Majlis deputies.[55] Factions consisting of followers of rival ayatollahs, representatives from different regions, and differing interpretations of Islam continued to mark the succeeding Majlis. Consequently the Majlis did not always support the president, rejecting ministerial appointments and differing widely over policies in foreign affairs, economic policy, and social conditions.[56] They also disagreed over land reform, with a reformist element arguing for land distribution to poor peasants while conservatives pushed for the preservation of private property.[57]

Such disagreements increased after the moderate victory in the February 2000 parliamentary elections gave the speakership to Ayatollah Mehdi Karrubi, making him the third-ranking member of Iran's government. He was a reformer, stating that people's homes should be free from searches, that women not wearing the hijab should not be attacked, and that "reform means freedom of thought, participation. . . the rule of law, and no monopolization of economics or politics," statements that obliquely criticized the hard-line position of Khamenei.[58] However, Khamenei demonstrated his control over the legislative agenda when he blocked a bill granting extensive press freedom. The action reinforced the weakness of the parliament, whose measures require approval by the Council of Guardians. The legislature can appeal bills rejected by the Council of Guardians to the Expediency Council, but since conservatives dominate both bodies, they continued to reject reformist measures. The conflict stopped with the 2004 Majlis elections that, due the disqualification of eighty reform-minded parliamentarians, brought victory to the conservative Islamists, who won 190 seats to 50 for reformers, the remaining seats going to religious minorities and independents.

The Iranian Judicial System

The Supreme Court heads the judicial branch, with a judicial code based largely on Islamic law. The judicial system enforces a system adopted by the regime in 1981 called the code of retribution, which removes the state as the prosecutor in the commission of crimes and establishes procedures for compensation of victims. Ayatollah Mahmoud Hashemi-Shahrudi, a political conservative, heads the Supreme Court. One critic described Shahrudi as "the most detested man in Iran today" because of his draconian rulings (criminalizing all discussions with the United States, for example) and his secret policies and a vast budget larger than that of the presidency.[59] Shahrudi's power seems to extend beyond the judiciary as he comments frequently on a variety of issues, including the alleged unifying impact of foreign criticism of Iran's nuclear program.[60]

Iranian revolutionary courts do not make distinctions between normally independent functions, like judge and prosecutor. The judge is also the prosecutor, and attorneys for the defense get less information about their cases, as revealed in a trial involving thirteen Iranian Jews accused of espionage. Their lawyer claimed that despite a confession by one of the defendants, he had no access to the classified information that the prosecution used to accuse the defense.[61]

The struggle between the clerics and the moderate reformers carries over into the judicial system, which conservative judges operate. As religious conservatives failed to dampen the power of reform at the polls, they shifted to the courts, attacking reformers through religious law. In 1999, the Special Court of the Clergy tried and convicted two high-ranking officials for such things as insulting Islam and Khomeini.[62] Since both were supporters of President Khatami, the court may have had a political as well as a religious agenda. By early 2002, the courts summoned more than sixty reformist members of Iran's parliament and charged them with a variety of crimes, including plotting to overthrow the government and influence peddling. It was unclear whether the charges had merit or represented a politically motivated campaign of intimidation against parliamentary moderates.

There are a few signs that the courts are becoming more liberal on certain social issues. Some transsexuals seeking sex change operations have found greater willingness to permit such procedures despite the fact that homosexuality is considered a violation of the Islamic faith.[63] Nevertheless, caution continues. Iranian authorities recently cracked down on Internet sites, with efforts by the judiciary to define cyber crimes and to punish "anyone who disseminates information aimed at disturbing the public mind through computer systems."[64] In 2007 the Iranian Supreme Court exonerated six members of the Basiji militia for killing an engaged couple who, they claimed, walked together in public and thus demonstrated moral corruption, a justification based on an interpretation of Islamic law and on Iran's penal code, which permits murder in response to moral corruption.[65]

Minority Groups in Iran

While Iran is officially a Persian or Farsi country, only about 51 percent of its population consists of Persian speakers, with the rest divided among numerous minority groups, including Kurdish, Arabic, Turkmen, Baluchi, and Azeri language groups. The Azeris are the largest group, almost 23 percent of Iran's population.

There are around 4 million Kurds in Iran, making 9 percent of the total population. A religious ruling by Ayatollah Khomeini declaring the Kurds to be atheistic continued efforts to prevent Kurdish independence or autonomy. Moreover, Iran's Kurds live in economically undeveloped parts of Iran and have little political recourse to development, partly because they have avoided participation in Iranian politics. They attempted an opposition group, the Democratic Party of Iranian Kurdistan, but government forces eliminated it. However, another group, the Free Life Party of Kurdistan, clashed with Iranian troops near the Turkish border, raising fears of a spreading effort by the Turkish *Partiya Karkeren Kurdistan* (PKK), a Kurdish revolutionary group, to spread influence across the Iranian and Iraqi borders.[66]

Around 7 percent of Iran's population are Arabic speakers, with many living in oil-rich Khuzestan on the Persian Gulf. Despite the wealth the area generates, these Arabs are among Iran's poorest population.[67] The Azeri also have not benefited from Iran's oil wealth, and live under official regime suspicion that their loyalties lie with Azerbaijan, whose independence has spurred some of Iran's Azeri to demand more rights themselves.[68]

Religious Minorities in Iran

There are several significant religious minorities in Iran, including the Sunni Muslims (mostly Arabs and Kurds) and non-Muslim minorities: Zoroastrians, Christian Assyrians and Chaldeans, a small population of Jews, and the Bahai. All these minorities have faced obstacles under the revolutionary government, particularly the Bahai, whom the Shiites regard as heretics. The other religious minorities have a small representation in the Majlis, though each group also faces challenges. The regime has executed Jews occasionally on charges of treason; Armenians and Chaldeans have only one representative in the Majlis, and Shiite religious authorities have sometimes stopped Zoroastrian religious celebrations.[69]

CIVIL SOCIETY IN IRAN

Civil society in Iran has been targeted by all regimes since 1953. The shah attacked those who advocated alternative political and social choices, and the post-1979 regime has echoed that stance. Says Omid Memarian, "The hardliners cite the collapse of the Soviet Union and the fall of Eastern European regimes as a direct result of the expansion of civil society and international and aid organisations. The suppression or control of civil society, they argue, is essential for the survival of the regime, and it can be attained through sporadic arrests of activists, accusations of espionage against NGO members, and increasing the price of activism in general."[70] Hen-Tov notes that while there are purportedly voluntary *bonyads* that administer civil society–like missions (social services, veterans affairs, women's groups, for example), the bonyads are really "the preferred tool of social engineering for the clerical establishment."[71]

THE STATUS OF WOMEN IN IRAN

Before the overthrow of the shah in 1979, women were treated more liberally in Iran than in most other Middle Eastern countries. In 1910, women gained access to education, something previously denied to them. In 1936, the shah banished the veil, and in 1966 women got the right to vote. By 1973, women were granted the right to petition for divorce (previously only men could initiate divorce) and the right to contest custody of children following divorce. The shah legalized abortion in 1974, and by 1976 the state passed laws banishing polygamy and allowing alimony payments to women after divorce. Laws also granted women more access to the workplace, and because they worked for less than men, women flooded the workplace, sometimes driving men out in the process. This caused friction, as males resented losing their jobs to those they regarded as inferiors.

Women were an important constituency of the Islamic leaders, and significant numbers revolted against the shah's reforms for women, wearing the veil illegally at demonstrations against his rule.[72] Therefore, when women protested their loss of rights and freedoms, the regime could not ignore them. Thus women gained back some of their rights, including some property and child custody rights in divorce, and access for women to education and employment increased. Khomeini praised their role, referring to them as the "lion-heart women whose great effort saved Islam from the captivity of the foreigners."[73] Iranian women's role in Iran's war with Iraq also drew praise from Iranian revolutionary leaders, and women entered military training (but not actual combat). Women also received training as Islamic leaders and did significant work in Islamic social welfare organizations.[74] Women had the right to vote from the days of the shah. Women continued to have access to education, and the gender gap in literacy decreased from 33 percent in 1976 to 10 percent in 1995,[75] and it is reportedly 3 percent for women between the ages of fifteen and twenty-four.[76] Other reports put the literacy rate for women at 75 percent, compared to 37 percent in 1979.[77] Finally, women in Iran have access to birth control; in other Islamic countries the lack of birth control means that women spend much of their lives raising large families. Birth control, denied initially under the clerics as un-Islamic, is now readily available, and couples getting married are required to be informed about birth control.

The Islamic Revolution reinstituted the requirement that women wear the chador in public. The Islamic regime passed laws restricting women to half-day work, repealing access to abortion, closing the Family Protection Courts established under Muhammad Reza Shah to protect women in divorce cases, and restricting women's access to education.[78] Government authorities can arrest women for appearing in public without proper attire and forced marriage is tolerated. The government closed nurseries, considered corrupting influences by Islamic purists, making it more difficult for women with young children to take jobs outside of the home. Women hold second-class citizenship under the Iranian legal system. Article 33 clearly states that a woman's testimony is worth no more than half of a man's testimony, and intentional murder convictions can only be obtained on the basis of testimony by two male witnesses.[79] Polygamy has returned, and divorce for women is almost impossible. One filmmaker had her work banned for portraying an eight-year-old female character in her films without a headscarf.

However, clerics like Mohsen Kadivar argued for a contextual vision of Islam emphasizing individual rights, and Khatami appeared to embrace the essence of such a vision.[80] It is unsurprising, therefore, that a large number of women voted for Khatami. Some changes did occur after Khatami assumed the presidency; for example, women returned to the state universities, outnumbering men for the first time in 2003.[81] Unemployment remains much higher for women than men and many of the changes made after 1979 remain.[82] A significant legal change in November 2003 occurred when the Expediency Council headed by former President Akbar Hashemi Rafsanjani backed a parliamentary change granting divorced women custody of both male and female children until age eleven, reversing a previous law limiting maternal custody of boys to two years and under. The change came in the face of opposition from the Revolutionary Council, suggesting the influence of the pragmatists, noted above.[83] By the spring of 2006, however, the fashion police were cracking down on women they considered improperly dressed. According to justice minister Jamal Karimi-Rad, "women who do not observe the veil can face 10 days to two months imprisonment or a fine."[84]

THE STRUCTURE AND PERFORMANCE OF THE IRANIAN ECONOMIC SYSTEM

With one of the world's largest deposits of natural gas and considerable oil reserves, Iran has the potential for significant economic growth, but mismanagement and inefficiency have limited it. According to one study, Iran's booming population required the addition of over 800,000 jobs annually, but the regime was able to generate only half that many.[85] Iran's almost 69 million people have a GDP per capita of $8,900, higher than many Arab non–oil producing countries, but the country's leadership does not distribute the wealth equally (no regime or economic system does). In Iran's case the income is so unequally allocated that over 40 percent of the population lives below the poverty line. The public debt is almost 25 percent of total GDP and the almost 16 percent inflation rate indicates that the combination of economic inefficiency and foreign economic sanctions is creating significant shortages.

IMAGES *The tiny boats hurtle through the choppy seas at the entrance to the Straits of Hormuz, their wakes visible miles away. They come in groups, sometimes as many as twenty at a time, each crewed by several people who appear in constant jeopardy of being thrown into the sea. They wear no lifejackets, and the boats carry no safety equipment. Their cargo is mostly sheep, which lie motionless in the bottom of the boats, to be delivered to the Arabs in the small Omani ports across the Straits of Hormuz. The sailors are Iranians who make this perilous journey several times a day, risking their lives to get a small payment in cash or cartons of cigarettes to take back to their families in Iran. Omani officials report that at least six bodies a month wash up on their beaches. Iran's dire poverty drives these brave souls to risk death on a daily basis.*

The leaders of the Iranian Revolution attempted to Islamicize the economy after they took power in 1979, yet they had little to work with, since the concept of an Islamic economy is incomplete. It prohibits charging interest and puts abstract limits on wealth accumulation. However, as Roy notes, "The Islamization of the Iranian economy is superficial."[86] The religious trusts, or *waqfs*, are functioning once again after the shah tried to eliminate them, but are in reality closer to holding companies, while the financial system has not been Islamized.[87] In Khomeini's view, a true Islamic society must stress the spiritual over the material and thus economics must play a secondary role to the spiritual.[88] Khomeini paid little attention to the economic system, once claiming that "economics is for donkeys."[89] This was possibly one factor explaining the inchoate performance of the Iranian economy since the 1979 revolution, with periods of recession (1979–1982) and growth (1982–1986).[90] The other factor that greatly hampered economic growth was the disastrous Iran-Iraq war of 1981–1988, which diverted resources away from investment.

Iran's economy suffers from mismanagement by clerics who lack training in economics. For example, efforts to privatize many of Iran's public enterprises failed to plan for the massive corruption that followed, and the regime suspended the program.[91] Yet there are few specifics advanced in regard to economic reform, or even clear economic goals from the regime. With the announcement of the fourth five-year development plan, Ayatollah Khamenei announced that "the population should enjoy healthy environment, health service, welfare, food security, social security, equal opportunity, foundation of family should be reinforced, poverty, corruption and discrimination should be removed within the next 20-year planning."[92] He did not elaborate on what economic plans might accomplish such goals. Four years later, the words rang hollow for most Iranians as unemployment rose and prices increased substantially; tomatoes rose threefold in the past year and housing prices in Tehran doubled, as foreign investment dried up.[93]

Iran has oil reserves estimated at 132.5 billion barrels, and the world's second largest natural gas reserves.[94] Iran depends on these revenues for around 30 percent of its GDP, putting it in the rentier category (see Chapter 3). As Hen-Tov observes, "The state-managed sector has dominated investment decisions, thus crowding out both the private oil sector as well as other industries. Moreover, heavy state investment has led to rent seeking. . . which in turn has wasted resources and lowered overall investment."[95]

However, a slow pace of investment has dampened hopes that Iranian energy sales could boost a lagging economy, with some investors deterred by the fear of American sanctions against them.[96] Recognition by the Oil Ministry of the necessity for integration with foreign companies may finally spur investment in Iran's natural gas industry, which is behind countries like Qatar and Nigeria in such capacities as liquefying natural gas for transportation to markets.[97] That could feed China's growing appetite for natural gas, as evidenced by Chinese plans to export some 110 million tons of liquefied natural gas at a cost of $20 billion by 2008.[98] Currently, though, both oil and natural gas shortages exist in Iran, despite the size of its reserves, and the regime has set consumption rationing to limit shortfalls.[99] By June 2007, rationing began in Tehran, as the price of dairy products rose at least 20 percent.[100] This despite the reality that Iran spends the equivant of billions of dollars purchasing around 40 percent of its oil on foreign markets. Gasoline subsidies still exist, costing billions more and allowing for considerable waste: "A quarter of a million litres of petrol is sploshed daily on to filling station floors daily by careless motorists."[101]

In 1984, the United States listed Iran as a supporter of terrorism, and in 1987, the Reagan administration reimposed economic sanctions on the country (initiated by President Carter and ended in 1981). Those sanctions had only a modest impact on the Iranian economy compared to problems posed by poor management and low oil prices, with their total cost estimated at $777 million per year, or around 2.7 percent of total Iranian gross national income. Partly because the overall economic cost to Iran is small and because they are not multilateral, US sanctions have not succeeded in causing Iran to end support for groups the United States denounces, open its nuclear program, and democratize.[102] Sanctions have produced tertiary problems, though, by raising pressure on Western companies not to do business with Iran, by drying up overseas investment, and by making dollar sales for oil difficult. Iranian banks countered by switching oil sales from dollars to euros, which, may actually benefit Iran as the euro was higher than the dollar in 2007.[103]

Iran has worked to expand foreign trade with Russia and China as well as the Arab Gulf countries, although a mid-2005 outbreak of cholera in Iran caused a sharp drop in food sales across the Gulf.[104] Iran has also attempted to reduce reliance on trade by expanding its own production. This apparent contradiction may reflect the schism between reformers and conservatives, with reformers wanting to expand trade while conservatives, fearful of the potential negatives associated with foreign association, push for self-sufficiency. Thus Rafsanjani, in his role as head of the Expeditionary Council, called for new development in Iranian agricultural infrastructure, insisting that "Iran's reliance upon others for agricultural products and in scientific and industrial sectors will inflict a great loss."[105]

One consequence of Iran's economic problems may be a wider gap between poor and rich. The poor have to work two or three menial jobs to survive, while, as one report notes, "Many well-connected businessmen have accumulated massive wealth over the years through real estate and currency speculation and trading."[106] If this gap continues to grow, it could sow even more political discontent on top of what already exists, particularly among the young. Another possible consequence is that Iran now has the world's highest opiate addiction rate in the world, with estimates as high as 4 million regular opiate users, partly because opium and heroin mask despair caused by high unemployment, particularly for young people.[107] High levels of heroin use may also be responsible for a rise in AIDS/HIV infections, as around 4 percent of injecting drug users tested positive for HIV in 2003. Since a third of these users report extramarital sex, the possibility for a rapid growth in the overall AIDS/HIV rate is considerable.[108]

IRANIAN FOREIGN POLICY

After the 1979 revolution, Iranian foreign policy shifted from a pro-Western, anti-Soviet emphasis to reflect the views of Ayatollah Khomeini. Khomeini talked about spreading the fruits of the Iranian revolution to other Islamic areas, causing a considerable reaction in the Arab Middle East, which is largely Sunni. However, Iranian foreign policy under Khomeini also reflected ancient Persian-Arab discords. Iran supported minority groups in some Arab countries, including Bahrain and Lebanon, where Iran aided Hizbollah, the Lebanese Shiite group that waged guerrilla war against Israel from southern Lebanon.

Iranian forces occupy several small islands in the Gulf claimed by the UAE, Abu Musa and the Lesser and Greater Tunb (called Jazireh-ye Tonbe Kuchek and Jazireh-ye Bonb-e Bozorg in Persian). Iran fortified these islands, and in 1992 tried to use them to deny UAE access to a third island, Abu Musa, which Iran and the UAE administer jointly. The UAE obtained considerable diplomatic support for its position, and Iran retracted its position, but the issue remains significant (see Chapter 6 for discussion of the UAE-Iran dispute).

After a long period of isolation from most Arab counties except Syria, Iran began a slow process of opening up. President Khatami called for Iranians in Saudi Arabia to stop demonstrations for the *hajj*, a practice that had continued since 1979,[109] and Iran publicly abandoned its goal of exporting Islamic revolution.[110]

For years, Iran reportedly funneled support to Hizbollah, the Shiite group operating out of southern Lebanon, in planes that flew in supplies and money from Iran to Damascus; then it was brought overland to Lebanon (see Chapter 13 for more on Hizbollah). Tehran provides Hizbollah with around $100 million annually, and Hizbollah senior military operatives maintain close ties to Iranian intelligence and to other groups connected to Khamenei.[111] Iranian support for Hizbollah may be a reflection of Iranian domestic politics, with the conservative clerics using their support for Hizbollah as a means to support their right to rule because of their support of a revolutionary Shiite movement. Moderates, on the other hand, may see Iranian support for Hizbollah as interfering with improved relations with other countries that Iran needs to expand its economy. The Israeli withdrawal from southern Lebanon in May 2000 may have strengthened the hands of the clerics in this regard, since it handed a symbolic victory to Hizbollah.

Iranian-American Relations

After the 1997 Iranian elections, moderates considered ways to improve relations with their neighbors, as well as with the United States. In January 1998, President Khatami called for exchanges with the United States to break down "the bulky wall of mistrust between us and the US administration."[112] That statement opened discussions in Washington on how to respond. However, the events following the September 11, 2001, attacks on the United States altered Iranian-American relations. Fearing that a post-Taliban Afghanistan might swing toward the West, Iran reportedly worked to counter the impact of American-backed programs.[113] Relations with the United States worsened when Israeli special forces intercepted a ship, the *Karine A*, in the Red Sea loaded with arms designated for the Palestinian Authority. Iran reportedly supplied the arms and thus drew swift condemnation from the United

States. When President George W. Bush included Iran with Iraq and North Korea in an "axis of evil" in his January State of the Union message in 2002, he fueled Iranian anger, and large crowds reminiscent of 1979 took to the streets, burning American flags and once again denouncing the Great Satan.

During the 1990s, reports surfaced about Iran developing weapons of mass destruction. In late 1997, Israeli intelligence claimed that Iran was close to obtaining nuclear weapons, from six to twenty-four months in their estimation. Iran appeared to accelerate its nuclear weapons program after the US military operation against Saddam Hussein in 2003. Evidence surfaced in mid-2003 that Iran had possibly accelerated its nuclear weapons program on the assumption that the American attack against Saddam would not have happened had that regime had nuclear weapons.[114] It was unclear if earlier reports of Iranian nuclear activity were incorrect or if the inchoate Iranian political system had once again shifted position and decided on a long-term rapprochement with its neighbors and with the United States. Iran's willingness to open a suspected nuclear site at Parchin to International Atomic Agency inspectors was also a potential effort to improve Iranian-American ties.[115] However, swings in Iranian policy ended this overture, and the Bush II administration responded by calling for more economic sanctions against Iran in 2006, though some Iranian reformers argued that the Bush policies were only strengthening the conservatives: "You are harmful for us. We try to tell politicians in Washington, D.C., please don't do anything in favor of reform or to promote democracy in Iran. Because in 100% of the cases, it benefits the right wing," said Saeed Leylaz, a business consultant and advocate of economic reform and greater dialogue with the West.[116] In late 2006, the UN Security Council approved a basket of economic sanctions against Iran for refusing to open nuclear sites for inspection, an act that may have produced cleavages within Iran's leadership, as noted above. In February 2007, the IAEA suspended twenty-two of its fifty-five technical aid programs, though one American expert argued that the suspensions were mostly symbolic.[117]

The administration also renewed Iran's status as a state supporter of terrorism, while paradoxically giving tacit support to a radical group known as the Mujahedin-e Khalq (MEK), which claimed to work for the ouster of Iran's regime. Yet it also appeared on the State Department terrorist list.[118] Nothing is simple about the web of US-Iranian relations.

Iran is the only Persian country in the Middle East, but its culture has influenced those around it for thousands of years. One of those areas of influence is the Levant, or eastern Mediterranean, whose soil was tramped numerous times by Persian soldiers who left footprints but did not replace the strong influence of the Arab peoples.

SUGGESTED READINGS

Abrahamian, Ervand. *Iran Between Two Revolutions*. Princeton, NJ: Princeton University Press, 1982.

Adelkhan, Faribah. *Being Modern in Iran*. New York: Columbia University Press, 2000.

Al-Suwaidi, Jamal S. *Iran and the Gulf.* London: I.B. Tauris, 1997.

Chubin, Shahram, and Charles Tripp. *Iran and Iraq at War.* Boulder, CO: Westview, 1988.

Keddie, Nikki R. *Modern Iran: Roots and Results of Revolution.* Updated ed. New Haven, CT: Yale University Press, 2006.

Kurzman, Charles. *The Unthinkable Revolution in Iran.* Cambridge, MA: Harvard University Press, 2004.

Moaddel, Mansoor. *Class, Politics, and Ideology in the Iranian Revolution.* New York: Columbia University Press, 1994.

Standish, John F. *Persia and the Gulf.* New York: St. Martin's, 1998.

Takeyh, Ray. *Hidden Iran: Paradox and Power in the Islamic Republic.* New York: Times Books, 2006.

9

IRAQ

IMAGES | *The grainy images of a body stripped naked, dismembered, and hanging from a lamppost horrified readers of Newsweek in July 1958. This image of the remains of Iraqi crown prince Abdul Illah ibn Ali ibn Hussein tattooed an impression of Iraq on the American imagination that would never fade. A mob burst into the presidential palace in Baghdad and murdered the entire royal family, initiating decades of Baathist rule. That ended in 2003, but the paradox for those who remember 1958 is the grainy image of Saddam Hussein in December 2006 about to meet the same fate as another Hussein whom his party had brutally killed.*

IRAQ OCCUPIES some of the most significant historical ground in the world. Watered by the Tigris and Euphrates Rivers, modern Iraq is the site of the ancient kingdoms of the Fertile Crescent, including the fabled cities of Babylon with its hanging gardens, and Ur, the reputed birthplace of Abraham. (See Map 9.1 on page 213.)

THE MODERN HISTORY OF IRAQ

The Turkish Ottoman Empire ruled Iraq from the sixteenth century until the end of World War I as three provinces, Mosul in the north, Baghdad in the center, and Basra in the south. Great Britain developed a growing interest in modern Iraq after Turkey offered Britain's rival Germany a chance to build a railroad from Konya in southern Turkey to Basra in 1902. British interests grew even keener in 1914 when Turkey entered World War I on the German side. British troops landed at al-Faw at the mouth of the Shatt al-Arab, and after a considerable struggle, the British took Baghdad from Turkish forces. Subsequently Britain controlled almost all of Iraq except for the Kurdish north. Many Iraqis celebrated the end of Ottomans, as they would celebrate the end of Saddam decades later, but such jubilation did not translate into support for the conquering powers.

Britain's interest in Iraq focused on access to the Gulf and Iraqi oil. That commodity became increasingly valuable as the Royal Navy shifted from coal to petroleum use.

In 1914, Britain took over the Turkish Petroleum Company facilities in Iraq. The year before the British and the Turkish regimes defined the border of Kuwait in the Anglo-Turkish Convention. That agreement would prove fragile in years to come.

Sir Percy Cox, the first British high commissioner, found himself with a myriad of problems left over from centuries of Ottoman rule. (See Chapter 1 for a discussion of the British Mandate after World War I.) The local citizens demanded that the British provide order, build roads and canals, and provide seeds and livestock. Tribal fighting, suppressed somewhat by the Ottomans, broke out anew, paralyzing much of western Iraq. Nationalism reared up against British mandatory policy, which was managed by inexperienced officers, leading to resentment by Iraqis who saw the British as intent on turning Iraq into a British colony.

Nationalist and Islamist groups began to grow, including the League of Islamic Awakening, the Muslim National League, and the Guardians of Independence. With the announcement of mandate status for Iraq in May 1920, anti-British fervor grew, with the Grand Mujtahid of Karbala, Imam Shirazi, calling for jihad against British rule. The Shiites and Sunnis briefly joined forces in the Revolt of 1920, which the British suppressed with forces sent from Iran and India, including Royal Air Force bombers and seaplanes. For the British, the cost of maintaining Iraq in its unruly state was too high to bear on top of the costs of World War I. The 1921 Cairo Conference and events on the Arabian Peninsula would provide a solution.

At Cairo, Britain carved modern Iraq from the Kurdish north, the Sunni center, and the Shiite south (the former Ottoman provinces of Mosul, Baghdad, and Basra). A Sunni-led army and the Anglo-Iraq Treaty were to hold it all in place. The British installed Faisal, the son of Sharif Hussein of Mecca, as the king of Iraq. Faisal had played a part in the Arab revolt of 1916 against the Ottoman Turks, so the British hoped he would be acceptable to Iraqi nationalists. To reinforce the image of independence from Britain, the Treaty of Cairo created the Electoral Law providing for an elected Constituent Assembly, which met for the first time in March 1924 and ratified the treaty. However, Iraqi nationalists opposed the treaty as nothing but a cover for British imperialism. Their position gained credibility when the British attempted to gain oil concession rights in Mosul province for the British-controlled Turkish Petroleum Company. Iraqi negotiators tried to gain a 20 percent participation in the company (later renamed the Iraqi Petroleum Company) but failed, and in March 1925 Britain gained a seventy-five-year lease for 100 percent of the assets of the Iraqi Petroleum Company. In 1930, Iraq signed a treaty granting Britain lease rights to Iraqi air bases in case of war and mutual defense rights. Faisal's close adviser, Nuri al-Said, negotiated for Iraq and forced the treaty through the Iraqi parliament despite strong opposition. However, British public support for the growing cost of maintaining control of Iraq was waning, as threats from both inside and outside (the Ikhwan tribes from Arabia and the Turkish threat to Mosul) grew beyond Britain's ability to stabilize the country. Britain withdrew its troops in 1927, raising questions about whether it should have remained to continue stabilizing and rebuilding efforts.[1]

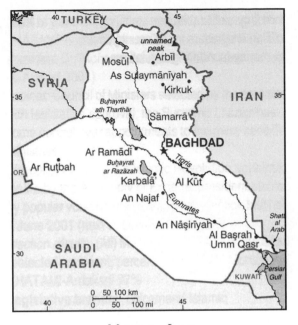

MAP 9.1   IRAQ

Iraq Gains Independence

Iraq gained independence from Britain in October 1932, although both British influence and the British-imposed governance structure remained. Britain sought a ruler who might pacify the otherwise unruly country, and decided on Faisal Hussein, crowning him as Faisal I. Faisal I inherited a number of problems from the British, in particular the long-standing divisions within Iraq's borders. The Sunni, who had been favored by the Ottoman Turks and the British, dominated the political system, leading to Shi'a fears of Sunni oppression. Years later, the Iraqi Shiite population claimed that they were deprived of power after having played a significant role in the revolt, and would never again allow the Sunnis to marginalize them.[2] Other conflicts grew from the British-drawn borders. They cut the city of Mosul in the north from its trade with Syria, and Basra in the south in a similar way from its Iranian trade. The Kurds in the north resisted Arab rule, as did the largely Christian Assyrians, who had sided with the British against the rebellious Kurds.

Faisal had little time to cope with these divisions, dying from heart problems in September 1933. His inexperienced son Ghazi took over but lacked his father's ability to create the appearance of stability. His government lasted only three years before Iraq experienced its first coup, launched by Gen. Bakr Sadqi, a Kurdish officer; Hikmat Sulayman, a Turkmen; and Abu Timman, a Shiite. Sulayman formed a cabinet, banishing Prime Minister Yasin al-Hashimi in the process.

King Ghazi had no choice but to accept Sulayman's regime. Ghazi died in an automobile accident in April 1939 and his infant son Faisal II succeeded him, with the country administered through the regency of Nuri al-Said until Faisal II became an adult. The British demanded that Nuri al-Said sever ties with Germany in 1939. This provoked Iraqi nationalist Rashid Ali al-Kailani, the prime minister, to launch a coup d'état against Nuri in April 1941. In response, the British landed forces at Basra and ousted the Rashid Ali regime a month later.[3] British troops then reimposed the regency for Faisal II, who dutifully declared war against the Axis powers in 1943.

The pro-British Nuri al-Said dominated Iraq following World War II.[4] His continued efforts to strengthen Iraqi-British ties (like the Treaty of Portsmouth of January 1948) increased nationalist resentment against him, climaxing in the 1948 uprising that strengthened the hands of the nationalists. The poor performance of the Iraqi army in the 1948 war served to strengthen their position. Further protests broke out in 1952 as the economy deteriorated, burdened by high inflation and corruption. Al-Said's decision to join the Baghdad Pact in 1955, binding Iraq in a mutual defense alliance with Britain, Pakistan, Iran, and Turkey, also provoked nationalist opposition, which crystallized on July 14, 1958, with a coup against the monarchy and the government. That opposition formed around the Baathist Party, founded in 1954 through the merger of the small Baathist movement and the Arab Socialist Party.

The Military Takes Power

General Abd al-Karim Qasim and Col. Abd al-Salaam Arif were ordered to mobilize their troops on the morning of July 14, 1958. Qasim was sent to Jordan to bolster the regime of King Hussein, who King Faisal believed was threatened by events in Lebanon (see Chapter 1). But Qasim led his troops to the royal palace instead, where the soldiers killed both King Faisal II and regent Abd al-Illah. The king's aides wrapped his body in a carpet and secretly buried it, but a mob threw Illah's body out a window and dragged it through the streets, mutilated it, and suspended it from a lamppost. Nuri al-Said attempted to escape disguised as a woman, but he was caught and killed.

Fighting between Arif and Qasim hampered the new leader's ability to build a political consensus, and ultimately Arif was removed, charged with treason. Qasim developed ties to the Iraqi Communist Party, and his increasingly left-wing policies (like nationalizing the Iraqi Petroleum Company) provoked opposition in the conservative Sunni ranks. However, a March 1959 coup effort against Qasim failed, and Qasim only strengthened his ties to both the Iraqi Communist Party and the Soviet Union. However, more problems erupted, including violence in northern Iraq between Kurds and Turkmen. Baath leaders decided to dispense with Qasim and appointed a young Baathist functionary named Saddam Hussein to do the deed in 1959. Hussein and his small band of followers failed, and he was apparently shot several times, caught in the fire of his conspirators across the street. The attack left Qasim's Chevrolet riddled with bullet holes, but he escaped unscathed.

Qasim weakened his ties to his communist allies and turned his attention to foreign adventures. In 1961, he claimed Kuwait, reviving an old Iraqi claim based on the unratified Anglo-Ottoman Convention of 1913 declaring Kuwait an autonomous district of the Ottoman Empire.[5] Around 7,000 British troops quickly entered Kuwait to block Iraqi forces. The crisis was ended for the moment in November 1963 when Qasim was ousted and executed by his partner in the 1958 coup, Colonel Arif. Arif initially included Iraqi Nasserites along with Baathists in his ruling coalition, but ultimately the Nasserites gained power at Baathist expense. Arif originally planned to use his Nasserite ties to join the United Arab Republic (UAR), the union of Syria and Egypt fostered by Nasser, but the merger never actually took place. Arif also nationalized most of Iraq's business enterprises, including cement, steel, insurance, and others, modeling his efforts after Nasser. However, Arif began to lose enthusiasm for a union with Egypt and ousted several ranking Nasserite officers from leadership positions, provoking Iraqi Nasserites to attempt their own coup against him. Their September 1965 coup effort failed, but in April 1966 Arif died in a helicopter crash and his brother Abd al-Rahman Arif took over. He attempted to improve relations with Iran, which had been supporting attacks by Iraqi Kurds against the regime, and visited Teheran in the spring of 1967. However, just as one crisis seemed to be lifting, another erupted, this time with Syria. The Iraqi Petroleum Company transported oil in pipelines running through Syria to the Mediterranean, and in the winter of 1966–1967 Syria demanded that Iraq pay Syria for what Damascus claimed was a pattern of Iraqi underpayment of fees dating back to 1955. Internal strife and economic mismanagement so weakened the regime that it chose to stay out of the Arab-Israeli war of 1967, giving fuel to its critics that it could not mount a military operation against the Israeli enemy. Another coup came in July 1968 led by Col. Razzaq al-Nayif and Ibrahim al-Daud. After only a few weeks they were replaced by a group of military officers from the Baath Party. They were Sunnis from Tikrit in the north central part of the country, and they distrusted the politicians in Baghdad. Two of these leaders emerged to lead the Baath, Ahmad Hasan al-Bakr and Saddam Hussein. Their first opportunity to consolidate power came in a countercoup led by Nasserites and Arif supporters: Bakr and Hussein outflanked them by arresting hundreds of suspected Nasserite supporters and executing them. Saddam prepared to assume sole authority by having his relatives installed in powerful positions in the regime; his brother-in-law, Gen. Adnan Khayr Allah Talfah, became minister of defense. In July 1979 Bakr, suffering from declining health, resigned, and Saddam took the top positions, including president, secretary-general of the Baathist Party, and commander of the military. He promptly centralized power by arresting and executing as many as 500 senior Baath Party officials in 1979 in a televised session shown around the country.[6] Saddam then embarked on a campaign to consolidate power by eliminating potential and real rivals and inculcating his regime with images from Iraq's historical memory. In many ways he emulated earlier Iraqi nationalists in an effort to personalize power and bring unity to a fractious political entity.[7]

The War with Iran

Soon Saddam Hussein initiated war against Iran, with which Iraq had a border dispute. Since 1979, Khomeini had supported efforts to undermine Hussein, calling on Iraqi Shiites to jihad against him and breaking the 1975 Algiers Accord. Saddam decided to strike first, apparently believing that the war would be short because the Iranian Islamic revolution had weakened the Iranian military. Hussein aimed to eliminate Iraqi dissidents operating out of Iran (including Iraqi Shiites ousted from Iraq earlier) and get control of the Shaat al-Arab. He also proclaimed his intent to curb the perceived threat of the Iranian Islamic revolution spreading into the Arab world.

After a bloody eight-year war (see Chapter 1 for details), Saddam had little to show for his efforts except a depleted treasury, hundreds of thousands of dead soldiers and civilians, and small slices of Iran, which he would keep only temporarily. However, Saddam did get the grudging support of the Gulf Arab states, which also feared Iranian efforts to stimulate Islamist opposition against their deeply entrenched monarchies. They advanced Saddam billions of dollars to support his war against Iran, ironically sowing the seeds of Saddam's next military operation against one of the Gulf Arab countries that supported him against Iran. The United States viewed Saddam as the "enemy of my enemy" and thus at least a potential friend. Under the Reagan and Bush I administrations, the United States removed Iraq from the state-supported terrorism list and shared selected intelligence with it. The United States offered the Saddam Hussein regime $400 million in agricultural credits despite the fact that Iraq had used chemical weapons against Iraqi Kurds and Iranian troops, significant violations of human rights, and despite Saddam's constant denunciations of the United States.[8]

Iraq Invades Kuwait

In early 1990, Saddam began to complain that Kuwait refused to forgive debt Iraq had incurred and was drilling into Iraqi territory from a shared oil field. On August 2, 1990, Saddam's forces moved across the Kuwaiti border and quickly occupied the small country (see Chapter 1). In the end, Iraq would lose much of its military force as well as its hold on Kuwait when other Arab countries joined the coalition led by the United States to crush Iraqi forces and drive them out of Kuwait. As Iraqi forces appeared to dissolve, the Bush I administration hinted at support for an uprising of the Iraqi Shiite and Kurdish populations but never provided actual assistance; Saddam Hussein crushed the uprisings. That failure only added to the sufferings of both groups, particularly the Kurds, whom Saddam attacked with chemical weapons in May 1988. Thousands of Kurds were either killed or driven into exile.[9]

Iraq After the Gulf Wars

In the immediate aftermath of the invasion of Kuwait, the United Nations imposed economic sanctions on Iraq, including continuing sanctions on trade originally imposed at the start of the war, limiting it to foodstuffs and medicines for humanitarian purposes, and sanctions against aircraft flights into Iraq. The sanctions were meant to get Iraq to recognize its border with Kuwait and agree to international conventions prohibiting the stockpiling and use of weapons of mass destruction (WMD).[10] Given Iraq's use and development of WMD, the termination of such programs became a war objective. The UN-brokered agreement ending the war provided a mechanism to detect and destroy Iraqi WMD research and production facilities (see below for details of the Iraqi WMD programs). What resulted was a cat-and-mouse situation between the UN inspectors and the Iraqi government, resulting in a series of crises between the United Nations and Iraq, and drawing in the United States and Britain to enforce UN inspection rights.

By December 1998, the United States and Britain had wearied of constant Iraqi efforts to stymie UN inspections, and President Clinton ordered a large buildup of military force. This time, unlike previous clashes, Saddam received little support for his obfuscation, and so Iraqi leaders backed down from their refusal to allow inspections and promised full cooperation. In February 2000, Iraq gave permission for a team from the International Atomic Energy Agency to inspect the country for nuclear weapons, but the inspectors claimed that constant efforts by Iraqi officials to conceal possible weapons sites made their job impossible.

Saddam's position remained insecure after 1991, with efforts directed against his life from both within and outside Iraq. He faced external challenges from Iraqis who either fled or were exiled to Iran. Inside the country, Shiites engaged in a brief flurry of protest, led by Grand Ayatollah Muhammad Sadeq Sadr, in Najaf, but that ended violently after Ayatollah Sadr, along with two of his sons and two other senior Shiite clerics, were murdered in February 1999. Riots broke out in Najaf, which Saddam's forces crushed with their usual brutality. Saddam remained in power, much to the frustration of his enemies at home and abroad. Even his old nemesis, the United States, appeared to relax its posture somewhat, despite continuing its support for UN sanctions and bombing Iraqi targets daily. By mid-2000, the United States was buying more oil from Iraq than it had before the Gulf War, almost 7.3 percent of total US imports.[11] By early 2001, senior US military leaders discussed relaxing both economic sanctions and enforcement of the no-fly zone.

Despite oil revenues, conditions inside Iraq remained grim. According to relief officials, repressive political conditions made it almost impossible for aid workers to operate. Reports also surfaced that Saddam Hussein took control of the aid materials and sold them outside Iraq. Iraq reportedly sold medical supplies given as aid to Lebanon and food to Syria, using money from these diversions to buy cigarettes and whiskey for Saddam Hussein's associates.[12] Saddam also spent money on numerous presidential palaces decorated with imported marble, fine woods, and luxurious furnishings and surrounded by lavish gardens. Others reported that Saddam built a huge resort for his family and supporters, including 625 homes, stadiums, amusement parks, hospitals, and a safari park stocked with wild animals.[13] Observers felt that Iraqi complaints about the effect of sanctions might have been a cover for its leader's expenditures.

Iraqi power potential grew as world oil supplies diminished by mid-2000, increasing Iraqi oil revenues and allowing Iraq to do considerable damage by suspending oil exports. Some countries that previously supported the UN embargo were openly trading with Iraq, including Turkey, Dubai, Qatar, and Oman, and Iraq once again charged Kuwait with stealing Iraqi oil as it had before the 1990 invasion.[14] While UN sanctions continued, it was becoming clearer than ever that, in Niblock's words, "the evidence suggests strongly that the dynamics underlying the Iraqi policy have not been changed positively by sanctions and the potential for the Iraqi state to interact effectively with its neighbors has not been enhanced."[15]

There was evidence that Iraq continued to work on weapons of mass destruction and it reportedly developed, for example, enough botulism toxin to kill the population of the earth several times over.[16] Iraqi scientists also developed 528 gallons of aflatoxin, a known carcinogenic agent, mixing it with riot control agents and spraying it in Iraqi Kurdish areas, as noted above. Iraq produced enough anthrax to kill billions of people, and even experimented with ricin, a deadly toxin distilled from castor beans.[17]

In December 1998, Iraq again refused renewed inspection plans and ousted the UN inspectors. This time the United States and Britain responded with a fierce bombardment of suspected Iraqi WMD facilities. Iraq responded by renouncing its 1990 agreement to allow Allied aircraft to patrol the no-fly zones in northern and southern Iraq. The United States flew these missions anyway, but as Iraqi radar sought these flights, American pilots responded by bombing antiaircraft sites in both no-fly zones. Those strikes reportedly claimed the lives of more than 300 Iraqis and wounded more than 800, according to Iraqi sources.[18]

Iraq tried belatedly to reinstate UN inspections in 2003, but, as noted above, the United States led attacks against Saddam that ousted his government. Although the presence of Iraqi WMD was the primary justification for the attack, by the fall of 2003, no real evidence of such programs emerged despite determined searches by US personnel. President Bush acknowledged the mistake more than two years later but argued that if faced with the decision to invade in late 2005, he would still have ordered the operation.

The End of the Saddam Hussein Regime and the American Occupation

The George W. Bush administration changed the equation on Iraq. After the September 11 attacks, Bush singled out Saddam's regime as the most dangerous state in the region. Even though both European and Middle Eastern countries urged caution, Bush II pushed ahead with plans to combine military and diplomatic means to oust Saddam. By August 2002, the Bush administration began to target Saddam's regime directly, stepping up bombing attacks against select targets and threatening military force if Saddam did not accept the return of UN weapons inspectors. As the military pressure increased, it was accompanied by political pressure, especially from other Arab governments, for Iraq to readmit UN weapons inspectors, which the regime reluctantly agreed to in November. This time Iraq seemed willing to co-operate with the inspectors, who, despite their new access to sites they wanted to visit, did not find evidence of ongoing Iraqi WMD by the end of the year. American impatience with the process grew and by January 2003, Bush administration officials were openly talking about "regime change," independently of the WMD inspection results. American forces flowed rapidly into the region, using bases in several Gulf Arab countries as staging areas. By mid-March, under the banner of Operation Iraqi Freedom, they crossed from Kuwait into Iraq while American warplanes launched a crescendo of attacks against Baghdad and other Iraqi cities.

Saddam Hussein's regime fell in a matter of days after the Iraqi military dissolved under the combined attack by American, British, and Australian forces. Saddam vanished as mobs, sometimes aided by US soldiers, dragged down his statues and looted his many palaces. However, initial Iraqi jubilation at Saddam's demise gave way to frustration and violence as the country descended into economic and political chaos. The Americans brought in Ahmed Chalabi, a Shiite Muslim and leader of the exiled Iraqi National Congress, a group favored by the Bush administration despite allegations that neither its leader nor its members represented the general interests of the Iraqi people. American officials under the inexperienced L. Paul Bremer governed Iraq after the fall of Saddam, and actions like denying participation in Iraqi reconstruction to countries not involved in Iraqi Freedom and giving almost total control over Iraqi administration to American military forces only reinforced that fact. The Americans dismantled the whole Baath structure and discharged Baath Party members and the Iraqi military, creating a vast unemployed army seething with resentment. The sense of humiliation felt by many Iraqis was only reinforced by the capture in December 2003 of a ragged, bearded Saddam Hussein, whom American troops forced from a small hole at a farmhouse near his hometown of Tikrit. He emerged submissively without firing a shot or taking his own life after earlier urging his Iraqi subjects to resist to the death. However, Iraqis throughout the country continued to resist American policy, and rampant lawlessness, high unemployment, and a loss of faith in Iraq's future combined to keep American forces in the country with no end in sight. Disorder broke out in Najaf, where Moqtada al-Sadr, the son of Ayatollah Muhammad Sadeq Sadr, led a Shiite insurgency that was also an act of defiance against the older Shiite leadership of clerics like Ayatollah Ayat Allah Ali al-Husayni al-Sistani, who outranked al-Sadr.

The United States created the Coalition Provisional Authority (CPA) to rule Iraq until an Iraqi government was formed that was favorable to the Americans. The CPA tried to build a relationship with Chalabi, but by May 2004, he had fallen out of favor, accused of leaking classified information to Iran. In June the United States officially turned over power, and the CPA became the Iraqi Governing Council, appointing Ayad Allawi, a Shiite and former CIA operative, as interim prime minister and Sunni tribal leader Ghazi Yawar as president. An effort to draft a constitution for the country in 2005 showed the strains between the disparate ethnic and religious groupings when the draft language identified Iraq as guided by an Islamic (but specifically non-Arab) identity. Sunni opposition mobilized in large demonstrations and some claimed that the loss of Arab identity would remove the glue that had held Iraq together.[19] Some Sunni political leaders threatened to derail the constitutional draft by organizing to vote against it, but a Shiite-Kurdish coalition in parliament changed the rejection rules from two-thirds of the vote to two-thirds of registered voters, thus almost guaranteeing approval. Frustrated Sunni leaders then threatened to boycott the election, a tactic that failed them in the previous parliamentary elections.[20] The parliamentarians reversed the decision the next day, indicating how much confusion remained as Iraq tried to transition from centuries of autocracy to some semblance of democracy. When the December 2005 parliamentary elections did take place, the results revealed how divided Iraqis remained since the British conceived the country in 1920. Nine out of ten Iraqis in the Shiite Muslim provinces of the south voted for religious Shiite parties, nine out of ten Iraqis in Sunni Muslim Arab areas of central and western Iraq voted for Sunni parties, and nine out of ten Iraqis in the Kurdish provinces of the north voted for Kurdish candidates. Nationwide, only about 9 percent of the total Iraqi population voted for tickets that purported to represent all Iraqis.[21] That alone indicated the depth of Iraq's problems in finding national unity, which seemed no closer to some than it was at the country's founding decades before. Moreover, one study published in late 2006 put the Iraqi death toll since 2003 at over 600,000.[22]

THE IRAQI POLITICAL SYSTEM

Prior to March 2003, Saddam Hussein ruled Iraq through the Baathist Party, which he stocked with his supporters after eliminating rival Baathist leaders and members he considered disloyal to him. He tolerated no dissent, and his personal security apparatus worked to eliminate all opposition in Iraq. Suspected opponents were tortured, murdered, or purged. The end of the Saddam Hussein regime in the spring of 2003 created a considerable power vacuum that the United States tried to fill by importing members of the Iraqi National Congress to use as the foundation for a new Iraqi government.

One facet of the Saddam government was a forced unity of Iraq's disparate population, but that artificial accord began to break down after coalition forces eliminated Saddam's ruling apparatus. Reports of violence between factions grew—Sunni against Shiite, Sunni against Kurd, Kurd against Turkmen—as different groups tried to settle old scores and as property claims became increasingly enforced with weapons.[23] Now the Kurds have constructed a regional central Iraqi government, the Kurdistan Regional Government (KRG) that makes laws, pushes for economic autonomy, and exercises as much independence from Baghdad as the constitution (which permits federalism) allows.[24] Additionally, the CPA disbanded the Iraqi military, which had potentially negative connotations for Iraqi unity. As Hashim notes, "While the history of the Iraqi army has not been covered with martial glory, the vast majority of Iraqis take pride in their army."[25] The United States not only created a vast unemployment problem but also cast aside one of the few symbols of Iraqi unity.

Iraq is clearly transitioning from despotism to democracy, despite the continuing violence; Freedom House still ranks Iraq as "not free" in its 2006 assessment.

The Iraqi Executive

In the wake of Saddam's overthrow, American and British officials hoped to replace the entire Iraqi Baathist structure with a functioning democracy. However, a combination of the economic wreckage left by Saddam and the war, lingering antiforeigner sentiment from the past, and poor postwar planning left the country in political chaos after President Bush announced an end to the fighting in May 2003. American and British troops were the most visible sign of "government," even as local town councils tried to restore some form of governance. The national executive was the American ambassador, Bremer, who headed the CPA, which included UN officials from various UN bodies, reconstituted organizations like the Iraq State Oil Marketing Organization and the Office of Human Rights and Transitional Justice, and numerous American officials from the different executive branch agencies involved in Iraqi reconstruction. Without a formal constitution or other legal authorization, the executive struggled to resolve short-term problems like energy and police shortages. In September 2003, American officials, through the CPA, engineered a temporary cabinet consisting of twenty-five members, mostly Western educated, to assume at least titular control over some government functions. The cabinet consisted of thirteen Shiites, six Kurds, five Sunnis (with one Turkman and one Assyrian Christian), and only one woman.[26] Its senior member, Ahmed Chalabi, as noted above, had long ties to conservatives in the Bush administration but had not actually lived in Iraq since 1958. The group, constituted in August 2003, appeared paralyzed, owing to lack of governing experience or to internal divisions. By the following November, an American official stated bluntly that the council had done "nothing of substance" and further claimed that the board was "inept" in its efforts to reach out to the populace.[27] Still the Americans pressed on with a Transititional Administration Law as a precursor to a new Iraqi constitution and provincial committees established to provide local governance and select a national assembly.[28] In May 2004 the Americans and UN envoy Lakhdar Brahimi tried to install Adnan Pachachi, formerly the Iraqi foreign minister, as president. But after experiencing internal pressure, he refused the post, which went instead to Ghazi al-Yawar, a Sunni. Ayad Allawi, a Shiite, former interim prime minister, became prime minister. The cabinet included Hoshiyar Zebari, a Kurd, as foreign minister, and Adel Abdul Mehdi, a Shiite, as finance minister. The 2005 elections resulted in a new government headed by Prime Minister Ibrahim al-Jafari, also a Shiite, and Jalal Talibani, who was a part of a powerful Iraqi Kurdish family, became president. In May 2006, the parliament selected Nuri al-Maliki as prime minister. Al-Maliki, of the Dawa Party, prevailed over Abdul Aziz Hakim of the Supreme Islamic Iraqi Council Party, when Moktada al-Sadr, the influential Shiite leader, backed al-Maliki.

Al-Maliki has struggled in his job, failing to bring about even a fiction of unity between the parties and facing factious rivalry within the Shiite party structure.

Political favoritism abounds, and, as one report stated, "ministries have been doled out in rough proportion to the number of seats each party had in Parliament, with the result that some completely unqualified people became ministers and some crucial ministries were run almost as fiefs with large numbers of jobs given out to party members. One result has been a crumbling of basic services across Iraq."[29]

The Iraqi Legislature

Under Saddam Hussein, Iraq's legislature consisted of a National Assembly (Majlis al-Watani), with 250 seats but no independent power. After March 2003, American authorities created a Governing Council to function like a legislature. The Governing Council, with twenty-five members, including each of Iraq's religious and language groups, faced an uncertain future at the beginning of 2004, with some Americans wanting to preserve it as an upper parliamentary chamber while other Americans and Iraqis wanted to end it in favor of a democratically elected body. By the summer of 2004, those plans were finalized by a call for nationwide parliamentary elections at the end of January 2005. Those elections resulted in 128 seats of 275 total to the Shiite parties, ten short of a majority, with Kurdish parties obtaining 53 seats and the largest Sunni parties getting 44 and 11 seats respectively. Former Prime Minister Allawi's party only received 25 seats, indicating the potential fate of any politician who appeared too pro-American.[30]

The Iraqi Judiciary

The reconstruction of the Iraqi judicial system came on the ruined foundations of the Saddam system. However, after the ouster of Saddam, American military forces administered most judicial functions, including penal institutions where individuals were frequently held without any legal protections and, as revealed in the spring of 2004, under conditions of extreme abuse. The interim government did attempt to construct a judicial system after crime increased dramatically in the wake of the Baath ouster, but critics charged that its operation (defendants charged with capital crimes often had no lawyers) and outcomes (judicial punishment included execution by hanging) did not meet even the most basic human rights criteria. Its defenders, though, argued that the severity of crime in Iraq mandated swift and deadly punishment as a means of criminal deterrence.[31]

Criminal proceedings were embroiled in turmoil, and the Central Criminal Court became a hybrid of Iraqi justice and American incarceration of suspects. A lack of training in judicial procedure, distrust between Americans and Iraqis, and a rush to try the thousands of suspects produced a system that barely functions.[32] The trial and subsequent hanging of Saddam Hussein in early 2007 demonstrated the Iraqi judicial system's numerous flaws, from beginning to end. Many groups take justice into their own hands, arresting and killing suspects; dozens of bodies frequently appear throughout Iraq, beheaded and bearing signs of torture. Self-appointed Islamist vigilantes also patrol society to find and torture those whose conduct they deem un-Islamic, as in the case of a young man beaten and forced to drink his own urine and chicken blood for having downloaded a pornography site at an Internet café.[33]

CIVIL SOCIETY IN IRAQ

Saddam Hussein eliminated all groups not controlled by the Baath, so in post-2003 Iraq, there was virtually no civil society. After 2003, civil society emerged from two directions, one from local leaders and one from the occupying American forces. Local leaders brought Islamic traditions of local accountability, while organizations like America's Development Foundation (ADF) and the US Agency for International Development (USAID) bring in small grants for anticorruption activities, democratization, women's protection, and media activities. Iraqi civil society has often tried to organize local neighborhoods around a strict understanding of Islamic customs, where neither the Iraqi government nor the occupying forces has much reach. Women's civil society organizations have done much to advance short-term causes despite considerable Islamist opposition.[34]

THE STATUS OF WOMEN IN IRAQ

Iraqi women had numerous rights before the Baathist takeover, with the first Iraqi woman judge and ambassador named in 1948. The Baath increased women's rights as a way to emphasize the secular aspect of the Baath Party. The General Federation of Women, founded in 1968, served to advance women in literacy, education, and access to the workplace. A 1978 change in the personal status laws actually gave the courts authority to overrule the male members of a women's family in certain legal matters.[35] Women entered medicine, law, and engineering, and voted for candidates and served in the legislature.[36] With a shortage of skilled workers, Iraq decided to educate women and bring them into the workforce, instead of importing thousands of foreign workers, as most Persian Gulf countries did (and still do).[37] However, during and after the Gulf war Saddam needed the support of the Islamic clerics and thus found it expedient to put restrictions on women. Many began to wear *hijab* (headscarves) and withdrew from the more active role they played in Iraqi society before the Gulf war. As Bengio notes, there was virtually no civil society in Iraq during Saddam Hussein's rule, so women had no independent means of organizing to support their political interests or creating associations responsive to women's needs.[38]

In the post–Saddam Hussein era, some Iraqi women hoped to find new freedoms, and some actually went out in public without their *hijab* or *abaya*, but they found that old discrimination continued.[39] In addition, as noted above, even the US-supported Coalition Provisional Authority appointed only one woman to a seat in the twenty-five-member cabinet. Amnesty International reports that violence against women has significantly increased since the defeat of Saddam Hussein, both by armed gangs and elements of the outside occupation forces, and women in cities like Basra report being afraid to leave home alone. Women also report increased attacks against anyone not wearing the *hijab*.[40]

KURDS IN IRAQ

Like Turkey, Iran, and Syria, Iraq has a Kurdish population, and like other Middle Eastern countries with such a minority, Iraq's Kurdish situation has spilled over into its foreign and security policy. Iraqi Kurds live largely in the northern part of Iraq, where there are significant deposits of oil.

Iraqi Kurds received an unexpected windfall from the UN-imposed economic sanctions against Iraq. Many engaged in smuggling prohibited goods into the country while receiving cheap oil from the regime in exchange for allowing Iraqi oil to slip over the borders in Kurdish areas to neighboring countries.[41] This situation led to a greater degree of Kurdish autonomy in northern Iraq. Kurds used their own currency, flew their own flag, developed their own school curriculum, and expressed loyalty to their own leaders and opposition to Saddam.[42] The Kurdish windfall complicated US efforts to use the Kurds in its effort to overthrow Saddam Hussein. Given their improved situation, Kurdish leaders were reluctant to side with a sometimes unpredictable United States and possibly lose the roughly $1.5 billion per year that flowed into their region.[43] However, when American forces entered the region in 2003, many Kurdish fighters joined them and were effective against a group of Ansar al-Islam members camped in a valley next to the Iranian border. Their status, as well as the question of Kurdish autonomy, remained unresolved many months after the United States ended Saddam's reign. However, as Iraq continued in chaos after the Iraqi Freedom operation, the Kurdish areas drifted away from the rest of the country, with more than half of the Kurdish population signing a petition demanding a referendum on Kurdish independence.[44] Iraq's Kurds are more supportive of a continuing American role than are other elements of the population, and, as noted above, a Kurd, Jalal Talibani, is president of Iraq.

THE STRUCTURE AND PERFORMANCE
OF THE IRAQI ECONOMY

Iraq sits on one of the world's largest oil fields, and two of the world's largest rivers water its land. Its oil reserves are estimated at 100 billion barrels, and 12 percent of its land is arable. However, a combination of massive military spending by the Saddam regime and the impact of international economic sanctions led the country to economic ruin after 1991.

The 2003 coalition military operation devastated an already weakened Iraqi economy. The overthrow of the Saddam regime shut down Iraq's largest employer. Thus thousands of people on Saddam's payroll as soldiers, police, and other government functionaries found themselves out of work, and unemployment jumped to around 60 percent.[45] To make matters worse, Iraq had a foreign debt of almost $50 billion prior to the Gulf war, and that figure did not include an estimated $35 billion owed to the Gulf Arab countries to support Iraq in its war with Iran. American construction firms began to rebuild Iraq's ruined oil infrastructure, but decades of neglect meant years of reconstruction in the face of uncertain oil prices. How to repair the damage became a priority issue for the CPA, which adapted privatization as a partial answer. Initial privatization plans targeted the state-owned oil industry, to be followed by additional transformation to private ownership in other sectors. However, some critics warned that the conditions for successful privatization were absent in Iraq and that the real beneficiaries might be the "crony capitalists" who enriched themselves under Saddam.[46]

The US military tried to reconstruct Iraq's damaged and neglected infrastructure, and by the summer of 2004, most services were back to prewar levels. However, the impact of Baath neglect under Saddam took longer to address. In one move, the American military put over 15,000 Iraqis to work on basic tasks, like cleaning out clogged sewer lines in Sadr City where the streets were covered in inches of raw sewage.[47] Given the disregard of basic services under Saddam, such conditions might supply years of work, as long as funding continued to flow from the United States. The recovery was slow, however, and by the fall of 2004 troubling signs of economic despair remained, including a report that the rate of malnutrition in Iraqi children had doubled to over 400,000 individuals, since the start of the US-led invasion.[48] Moreover, Iraq's primary export potential continued to be oil, and at the end of 2004, oil production reached around 2 million barrels a day, 20 percent below prewar levels but enough to begin pumping revenue into the country.[49] By mid-2005, the first IMF report on Iraq in twenty-five years found that oil production had reached prewar levels of 2.5 million barrels per day.[50] But it fell off from that point, dropping to 2.2 million barrels in August 2005, amid charges of mismanagement by the prime American contractor, KBR (a subsidiary of the Haliburton Corporation), the Army Corps of Engineers, and Iraqis themselves, including those who divert water intended for oil injection into irrigation. There is concern that Iraq will be able to eventually recover only 15–25 percent of the oil in southern fields due to delays and damage.[51] The problem is illustrated by the twenty-hour wait motorists had to endure in Kirkuk, a city above a lake of oil so large that the stench of it is everywhere. However, there is no capacity to refine oil because of insurgency attacks, insufficient infrastructure, and governmental inefficiency.[52] A May 2007 report indicated that billions of dollars in oil is disappearing through smuggling and corruption, depriving the country of badly needed revenue.[53]

Per capita income for 2007 was around $1,900, far below most other Arab countries, even those without oil reserves. Unemployment hovered between 25–30 percent and an inflation rate of 50 percent indicated that key shortages remained.

Oil has the dual dangers of price instability and the rentier state problems (see Chapter 3) that oil-rich countries often suffer. Birdsall and Subramanian suggest that some mechanism to distribute Iraqi oil revenues directly to the population might help avoid the latter problem, though devising a trustworthy mechanism for doing so will be tricky at best.[54] Iraq's banking sector showed a slight recovery from prewar levels as it formed partnerships with international banks to handle billions of dollars of reconstruction money, but the state banking sector continued to dominate the industry, controlling around 80 percent of total deposits and refusing to modernize.[55]

Iraq's agriculture benefited briefly from the economic sanctions but fell into disrepair after the regime change, as a 2006 report indicated: "Across much of Iraq, the practice of agriculture today has the look of Dust Bowl era desperation. World War II-era pumps smoke and clatter as they suck water from canals that are clogged or drying up. Irrigation ditches are filled with muck that barefoot farmhands remove with shovels. Tractors and harvesters are few and antiquated. Women in black robes bundle harvested crops to carry home on their heads or on donkeys' backs. Irrigation water is often tainted by sewage and industrial pollutants."[56]

IRAQI FOREIGN POLICY

Between 1958 and 2003, Iraqi foreign and security policy focused on expansion of Iraqi power and prestige in the region. The Baath Party embraced pan-Arabism and emphasized Iraq's particular struggle against foreign forces. Iraq also turned to the Soviet Union for support and foreign assistance, particularly in areas of military technology and sales. The end of Saddam's regime brought an opportunity for a shift in foreign policy, but in the absence of a viable government, a viable foreign policy became impossible as Iraqis struggled to restore their domestic political situation.

Iraq is a new country in its present state compared to many in the world. The next section, by contrast, covers some of the oldest countries in the world, starting with Egypt, one of the few Arab countries familiar to almost every schoolchild because of its enduring civilization.

SUGGESTED READINGS

Axelgard, Frederick W. *Iraq in Transition: A Political, Economic, and Strategic Perspective.* Boulder, CO: Westview, 1986.

Baram, Amatzia. *Culture, History, and Ideology in the Formation of Bathist Iraq.* New York: St. Martin's, 1991.

Davis, Eric. *Memories of State: Politics, History, and Collective Identity in Modern Iraq.* Berkeley: University of California Press, 2005.

Dodge, Toby. *Inventing Iraq: Nation Building and a History Denied.* New York: Columbia University Press, 2003.

Feldman, Noah. *What We Owe Iraq: War and the Ethics of Nation Building.* Princeton, NJ: Princeton University Press, 2004.

Haj, Samira. *The Making of Iraq, 1900–1963: Capital, Power, and Ideology.* Albany: State University of New York Press, 1997.

Karsh, Efraim, and Inari Rautsi. *Saddam Hussein: A Political Biography.* New York: Free Press, 1991.

Khalil, Samir. *Republic of Fear: The Inside Story of Saddam's Iraq.* Berkeley: University of California Press, 1989.

Marr, Phebe. *The Modern History of Iraq.* Boulder, CO: Westview, 2004.

Nakash, Yitzhak. *The Shi'is of Iraq.* Princeton, NJ: Princeton University Press, 2003.

Rezun, Miron. *Saddam Hussein's Gulf Wars: Ambivalent Stakes in the Middle East.* Westport, CT: Praeger, 1992.

Tripp, Charles. *A History of Iraq.* Cambridge: Cambridge University Press, 2002.

Wiley, Joyce N. *The Islamic Movement of Iraqi Shi'as.* Boulder, CO: Lynne Rienner, 1992.

Section III

THE COUNTRIES OF THE EASTERN MEDITERRANEAN

Dusk on the road from Petra to Amman. This is the long way, winding through the Jordan Valley, following steep mountain roads that descend below sea level. The deepening gloom veils the massive hulk of an ancient castle perched atop a hill overlooking a small town below. It is Kerak, one of the largest Crusader castles in Jordan. The road winds around the bottom of the hill and through the narrow streets of the town, making the ghostly ruins appear to dominate the area below it. The stronghold withstood two efforts by Salal al-Din to oust the Crusaders under Renauld of Champollion, the first in 1135 during the marriage of Renauld's fifteen-year-old stepson to his eleven-year-old bride. Salal al-Din started his attack by bombarding the castle walls. But after the bride's mother took food from the wedding out to Salal al-Din and his troops, he complied with her request to aim away from the tower where the couple was to spend their first married night.

The fortress remains there today in stark testimony to the fact that Europeans came to the Levant as invaders and occupiers, carving out Crusader states to protect with their castles. There are scores of these castles: high lofts above the land where the Crusaders ruled for almost two centuries, until driven out by the Mamluk armies. The Turkish Ottomans would come less than 300 years later to the same lands. After 400 years of Ottoman domination (1516–1917), Europeans returned to the Levant as occupiers and ultimately state makers, creating the modern states of Palestine, Syria, Lebanon, Iraq, and Trans-Jordan. Sometimes those states incorporated peoples who had been traditional rivals. Separated by

*their own borders, they learned to avoid each other, at least most of the
time. Put together into one Iraq or one Lebanon or one Jordan, they found
themselves fighting each other, which was exactly what the foreign occu-
pier wanted. Collective memory recalled the immense Crusader castles as
the new "Crusaders" repeated the Crusader past. It is perhaps not surprising that people of the region give modern Europeans (and their American cousins) only a guarded welcome.*

What makes the eastern Mediterranean special is the tremendous span of
history that has played out here over the millennia. The Levant was the home
of ancient Phoenicia, the ancient Israelite kingdom, and the Syriac cities of
Ugarit and Ebla. The world's three monotheistic religions have their origins in
the eastern Mediterranean, and all three have sacred places here. Today it is
the location of the modern countries of Egypt, Syria, Turkey, Israel, Lebanon,
and Jordan.

This area of the world is regarded as one of the cornerstones of human civilization. The geography is not as harsh and forbidding as is the Arabian
Peninsula, and it is watered by numerous rivers fed by snowmelt from mountains that wear a mantle of white into late March. Two of these rivers, the
Tigris and Euphrates, originate in the mountains of Turkey and have sustained human activity along their banks for thousands of years. The mountains of Lebanon produce the Jordan River, the Litani River, the Orontes
River, and the Barada River which flows through Damascus. The Nile runs up
from deep in central Africa, its ancient course interrupted by human structures, perhaps to the detriment of Egypt's modern inhabitants.

Storied cities of antiquity grew up here: Troy, Jerusalem, Damascus, Baal-
bek, Thebes, Luxor, and Palmyra. Discoveries in the fields of mathematics,
medicine, law, and theology somehow survived the destruction of their great
cities, to be carried on to later generations. Later the great Hebrew kingdom
of David and Solomon would populate Jerusalem, and the Phoenicians settled
Lebanon. These civilizations are long gone now, and there is little visible connection between them and the people who live in the Levant or Egypt now.
The Arabic language and the Islamic religion have replaced cuneiform, hiero-
glyphs, and the pantheistic religions of the ancients. However, there is a deep
sense of pride in ancient accomplishments in most modern countries today.
Their museums are filled with artifacts dug up from the piles of rubble and
sand covering the ancient cities, and the old monuments have been restored
and serve as magnets for tourists. The National Museum in Damascus, for

example, contains a small piece of a clay tablet from the buried city of Ugarit, containing twenty-six letters, the basis for the modern Latin alphabet. The museum curators claim it is the oldest such evidence of an alphabet, and they show it with great pride, along with such treasures as a tiny 3,000-year-old cameo of a face whose eyes seem to move and follow the viewer across the room.[1]

The following chapters focus on Egypt, Turkey, Syria, Lebanon, Israel, Jordan, and Palestine. While the discussion emphasizes current politics, each country has roots that are embedded in thousands of years of history. People often seem to take the grand legacies of their past for granted as they rush by them, but ask anyone on the street late at night where a particular monument is, and he can tell you without hesitation, along with supplying the details of its history.

10

EGYPT

IMAGES

The modern republic of Egypt lives in the shadows of its remarkable past. The capital city, Cairo, spreads westward from the banks of the Nile River to the edge of the Giza plateau, where the three Great Pyramids and the Sphinx stand. These ancient monuments loom large as the sun sets over the Western Desert, reminders to citizen and visitor alike of Egypt's ancient glory. Its grand span of history marched on after the end of the pharonic dynasties, and Cairo grew to replace the ancient cities of Memphis and Thebes. Minarets of many styles now grace Cairo's skyline, some stretching hundreds of feet into the haze. They represent significant periods of Islamic Cairo: the Abbasid, the Fatimid, the Ayyubid, the Mamluk, and the Ottoman. The grandeur of al-Azhar University, the mosque of Kait Bey, the citadel of Muhammad Ali, the mosque of ibn Tulun, and the al-Husseini mosque soar above the buildings around them, their Islamic styles inspiring the gothic architecture of Europe.

Below these spires, Cairo grew and decayed over the centuries. Drab concrete blockhouses stained with grime replaced the graceful Islamic architecture of the past. Today Cairo's citizens can only imagine what it once was. Nevertheless, everything from the grand mosques to the ornately carved niches in ancient walls serves to remind. While few modern Egyptians expect Cairo to regain the glorious days of the past, they take pride in knowing that Cairo was once one of the greatest cities in the world.

EGYPT IS A PART OF THE MIDDLE EAST, the Islamic world, and North Africa, though in many ways it stands apart from the countries around it. Its passion for culture—including its vibrant film industry, its music, its intellectual fervor, and its support for individual achievement—has made it home to some of the world's greatest artists and thinkers. As the late scholar Edward Said put it, "Most Eastern Arabs, I believe, would concede impressionistically that the dour Syrians and Jordanians, the quick-witted Lebanese, the rough-hewn Gulf Arabs, the ever-so-serious Iraqis never have stood a chance next to the entertainers, clowns, singers and dancers that Egypt and its people have provided on so vast a scale for the past several centuries. Even the most damaging political accusations against Egypt's governments by Palestinians or Iraqis are leveled grudgingly, always with a trace of how likeable and charming Egypt—specially its clipped, lilting dialect—as a whole is."[1] Egyptians take tremendous pride in these artists, including Naguib Mafouz, the 1988 Nobel laureate for literature, Umm Kulthum, considered one of the world's greatest singers, cinema stars like Noor al-Sherif, Tahia Carioca, famous dancer and actress (in whose memorial Edward Said made the comments above about his fellow Arabs), singer Mohammed Abdul Wahhab, and Hassan Fathy, whose architectural innovations have been copied around the world.[2]

Culture is just one of the things that sets Egypt apart from other Arab countries. Egypt is a critical political actor in the Middle East, and Cairo is now a mandatory stop for diplomats, soldiers, and state leaders desiring to influence the Middle East.

A map of Egypt on the facing page shows its primary features.

Egypt is about the size of New Mexico, a vast expanse of desert broken only by the green ribbon of life along the Nile River and a few oases in the desert. The Nile is the reason for life in Egypt, and almost 95 percent of its population lives on the 5 percent of land next to that great river.

THE MODERN HISTORY OF EGYPT

Few countries can boast of a history as grand as Egypt's. The ancient Egyptians built a civilization along the Nile River and beyond that ranks as one of the greatest in history. However, in 332 BCE the Persians conquered Egypt, beginning a long period of foreign rule; from 332 BCE to 1952 CE no native Egyptian ruled Egypt. The Ottomans controlled Egypt until the British made it a protectorate between 1914 and 1922, which ended in the face of widespread anti-British violence in Egypt.[3] While Britain technically granted Egypt sovereignty, it continued to influence the policies of King Fuad (whom the British helped install as king of Egypt) and of his son Farouk, who succeeded Fuad in 1936.

Egyptian Nationalism and the Road to Independence

The Wafd, Egypt's first significant nationalist movement, rose when Britain and King Fuad reluctantly accepted a constitution in 1923 permitting parliamentary elections. The elections occurred the next year, and the Wafd won 179 out of 211 seats in the new legislature. However, both the Wafd and the legislature were weakened by subsequent events, including the 1930 constitution that strengthened the power of the king, and the 1936 Anglo-Egyptian Treaty that failed to give full independence to Egypt. Demonstrations broke out against the Wafd, which demonstrators blamed for not challenging the treaty and for failing to address the chronic problems of Egypt's sluggish economy. Many of those who broke with the Wafd joined the Muslim Brotherhood, founded in 1928. In the 1930s, Egyptian nationalism rose in response to a number of currents. As Egyp-

MAP 10.1   EGYPT

tians traveled more, some acquired an anti-Western and pan-Arab outlook.[4] These ideas would form the basis of Egypt's role in a nationalist pan-Arab movement after World War II.

The Israeli declaration of independence in 1948 brought Egyptian and other Arab troops into Palestine to block the creation of Israel. But lacking any coordination between armies, the Arab forces were defeated. King Farouk's strategic objective seems to have been to join Syria and Lebanon in blocking the Hashemite ambitions of the Iraqi and Jordanian monarchies rather than liberating Palestine.[5]

The 1948 war galvanized both pro-Arab and anti-Western nationalism in Egypt, and brought to prominence a young officer named Gamal Abdul Nasser, who became the leader of the nationalist Free Officers movement. Other groups mobilized by the 1948 defeat included the Muslim Brothers, founded by Hassan al-Banna in 1928. The Wafd took power again in January 1950 and abolished the treaty with Britain. In January 1952, anti-British riots tore through Cairo and other Egyptian cities. The British pressured King Farouk to intervene, but the Free Officers, waiting in the wings, decided to pre-empt the monarch. On July 23, 1952, they launched a coup against him.

As King Farouk sailed out of Alexandria on a yacht for the last time (he would die in exile in Italy in 1965), the Free Officers formed the Revolutionary Command Council (RCC) and invited former Prime Minister Ali Mahir to head a new government, electing Gen. Muhammad Naguib as president. When Ali Mahir resigned as prime minister, Naguib took that post as well, and led the RCC into the first of a number of sweeping reforms to oust the old elite. The agrarian reform law limited land ownership in an effort to break the political power of rural landlords. In January 1953, the RCC banned all political parties, intending to weaken the power of both the wealthy and the political left. Gamal Abdul Nasser became president in 1954, and the Revolutionary Command Council, renamed the Arab Socialist Union, replaced the king's bureaucracy with its own.

Egyptian Nationalism Grows

Foreign relations remained a problem for the Free Officers, with the Suez proving to be intractable. Nasser found himself pulled between the British, who offered him membership in the newly formed Baghdad Pact, and Egyptian nationalists, including the Muslim Brotherhood, who demanded that Nasser nationalize the Suez Canal.[6] Nasser refused the British offer and moved toward the Soviet bloc after Egypt was humiliated by a powerful Israeli raid on Gaza in February 1955. Nasser also found that the initially promising relationship with the United States (which refused to support King Farouk during the coup) began to sour as Egyptian–British tensions grew. Secretary of State John Foster Dulles initially offered Egypt $20 million in aid, including funds to construct a new dam at Aswan. However, Egypt was shopping for arms from Soviet bloc countries and arranged a purchase from Czechoslovakia in September 1955, reflecting anger over Western support for regional rival Iraq.[7] This caused the United States to withdraw an offer to fund construction of the Aswan High Dam.[8] The Soviet Union quickly made its own loan offer for the project, and, perhaps bolstered by his new patron, Nasser turned his attention to what he regarded as a remnant of foreign influence: the Suez Canal. Although a private company operated the Suez Canal, British forces protected it.

Nasser nationalized the holdings of the Suez Canal Company in July 1956. He anticipated a negative reaction but hoped to avoid war.[9] However, war erupted (see Chapter 1), but the United States forced Britain out of the operation, and, without British support, the French and Israelis retired from the war. Nasser emerged victorious, portraying the win as a crowning moment for Arab nationalism. But it was not to last.[10]

Nasser's acceptance of a Syrian proposal for Arab union led to the short-lived United Arab Republic (UAR) between 1958 and 1961. While Syria initiated the proposal, Syrian leaders grew to resent Egyptian dominance of the UAR and Egyptian interference in Syrian politics, and consequently the United Arab Republic fell apart in September 1961. Yemen also became associated with the Egyptian-Syrian effort in 1958, launching a vague federation known as the United Arab States. The pact did not last, but the enterprise was costly to Egypt, which placed some 75,000 troops in Yemen attempting to defend an antiroyalist revolution. Those troops were absent from the front lines when Egypt and Israel engaged in their third war in 1967, contributing to the outcome of that conflict.

Nasser Shapes Egypt

At the height of his power, Nasser nationalized almost every major industry and carried out drastic land reform in the countryside. Part of the motive for this was import substitution industrialization, intended to reduce Egyptian dependence on imported goods. New public sector industries were created to produce cement, steel, and ships, which quickly contributed to Egypt's heavy public debt.[11] Nasser also imposed a high tax (over 90 percent) on persons in upper income ranges in the name of leveling wealth. One consequence was that many of Egypt's wealthy left the country, taking their wealth with them. In addition, given the growing stridency of Nasser's anti-Israel rhetoric, so did most of Egypt's Jewish families.[12]

Challenges to Nasser came from the Muslim Brotherhood, and its leading intellectual, Said Qutb, the author of works calling Nasser an infidel, demanded that his rule be replaced with an Islamic regime. After purported Muslim Brotherhood efforts to assassinate Nasser, the president arrested Qutb and had him executed in 1966. Government authorities arrested many other members of the Muslim Brotherhood and kept them in prison for years to come. Nasser also feared that communism could compete with Arab nationalism as a basis for unifying the Arabs and consequently jailed members of the Egyptian Communist Party even as he courted the Soviet Union, which turned a blind eye to the imprisonment of Egyptian Marxists.

The Arab-Israeli Wars

For reasons that remain controversial and disputed (see Chapter 2), Israel initiated an attack against Egypt, Syria, and Jordan on June 5, 1967. The whole operation ended six days later with the defeat of Arab forces on all fronts.[13] Nasser announced his resignation, but mobs of people gathered outside his residence chanting his name and the National Assembly refused to accept his departure as president.[14]

The 1967 defeat dealt Arab nationalism a crucial blow, and Islamist organizations enjoyed a membership spurt. Nasser purged several top officers, attempted to reform some of the more drastic economic measures, and added a measure of competition to his single-party rule. However, many citizens regarded the reforms as largely cosmetic, and discontent with Nasser grew. So did tensions with Israel, which were finally mediated by the United States and the Soviet Union.[15] Nasser never had a chance to benefit from the peace that followed, since he died of a heart attack in September 1970.

The Sadat Years

Upon Nasser's death, Vice President Anwar Sadat became acting president. Sadat was widely regarded as a weak political figure, but in October 1970, he won over 90 percent of the election to succeed Nasser and quickly established a power base of his own. In May 1971, he arrested a number of Arab Socialist Union officials and charged them with plotting a coup against him. Sadat's act distanced him from Nasser and, by replacing Nasser's old guard of pro-Soviet loyalists, Sadat was finally able to chart his own political course. He tried a peace initiative in September 1971, offering to recognize Israel for a partial Israeli withdrawal from the Sinai. Although that effort did not evoke a response in Tel Aviv, Sadat kept trying. He secretly communicated with the United States, and American officials told him that the United States would pressure Israel into a peace accord only if Sadat ousted his Soviet military advisers. He did so in July 1972, but the United States still remained noncommittal to peace.[16] Sadat felt at that point that he had no choice but to implement his alternative plan.

On October 6, 1973, Egyptian forces launched an attack across the Suez that surprised the Israelis as much as they had surprised the Egyptians in 1967. While Israel ultimately gained the advantage in the 1973 war, the Arab forces fought well, redeeming their dismal 1967 performance. The war was also a turning point for superpower relations and for Middle East politics. The United States and the Soviet Union initiated a peace process that produced what Egypt had sought in the 1973 war: a graduated Israeli withdrawal from the Sinai, as well as the June 1975 opening of the Suez Canal, blocked by mines and war wreckage. That progress climaxed in Sadat's unexpected trip to Jerusalem in November 1977.

Sadat introduced a new constitution to begin his separation from the Nasser era in 1971. He also dismissed many of Nasser's advisers and chose his own loyalists. He allowed a modicum of competition for seats in the National Assembly, although the ASU (now renamed the National Democratic Party) won the vast majority of seats in the October 1976 election. Sadat also increased participation for the Muslim Brotherhood, which he saw as a check against leftist influence. He tried to liberalize the state-controlled economy, allowing limited importation of foreign goods and currency. However, these measures did not win enough support to stave off violent political demonstrations in January 1977 when Sadat announced a suspension of food subsidies in response to conditions demanded by the International Monetary Fund for a loan. After some 800 people died in countrywide rioting, Sadat had to roll back the price increases and raise wages. As there seemed to be no easy solution to Egypt's continuing economic crisis, Sadat decided that one answer lay with Israel.

Egypt Initiates the Peace Process

In November 1977, Sadat arrived in Israel at the invitation of Israel's new Prime Minister Menachem Begin, which in turn led President Jimmy Carter to invite Sadat and Begin to the presidential retreat at Camp David in the Maryland mountains in 1979 for negotiations on disengagement. After days of painstaking negotiations the parties agreed on a peace treaty.[17] While Sadat hoped to gain back the entire Sinai (which he did), he also hoped that peace with Israel would reduce Egypt's heavy defense burden and free up money for domestic economic improvement. The Carter administration tried to oblige by offering a long-term foreign aid package to help sell the peace process. However, the economic dividend from peace ultimately disappointed the Egyptian population, partially because subsidies to Egypt from the wealthy Gulf Arab countries were cut off after the Camp David agreement. Moreover, cutting the Egyptian military budget risked throwing soldiers into the ranks of the unemployed. Ultimately, frustration over the laggard economy mounted throughout Egypt. Fearful of losing power to this frustration, Sadat began to rule increasingly by decree, pushing through the so-called Law of Shame that criminalized a whole variety of vague acts and allowed arrests almost at will. In 1981, regime authorities rounded up almost 1,500 suspects, many of them members of the Muslim Brotherhood. Government forces closed their paper and arrested other figures as well, including some former Wafd leaders. The growing repression, along with Sadat's opulent lifestyle and corrupt aides, only increased popular discontent with his rule. The growing number of wealthy Egyptians with ties to Sadat added fuel to the growing popular resentment of the president.[18]

On October 6, 1981, Sadat was watching a military parade honoring the 1973 war when a small band of radical Islamic assassins leaped from a military truck and sprayed his seat with automatic weapons fire, killing him instantly. The depth of Sadat's unpopularity among the majority of the Egyptian people became clear: throughout Egypt the Islamic celebration of Id al-Adha (the feast following the *hajj*) continued as if nothing had happened. Few Egyptians mourned him.

The Mubarak Presidency

Sadat had endorsed a successor as his vice president, Hosni Mubarak, the former head of the Egyptian air force, and a national referendum approved that choice. Mubarak realized that he could not repeat Sadat's mistakes and allowed a gradual opening of the political system. By the time elections were scheduled in 1984, five parties contested the NDP for seats in the National Assembly and the Wafd won 57 seats, though the NDP swamped the opposition by winning 391 seats. However, despite the appearance of more openness, the 1984 election law excluded smaller parties by requiring an 8 percent minimum vote to get a seat in the National Assembly. Moreover, the new law redefined electoral districts so that each district was now multimember, thus allowing the National Democratic Party to overwhelm the opposition.

In response to a growing wave of Islamist demonstrations, Mubarak called for early elections in 1987, along with a reform of election laws. Those changes included adding forty-eight seats in the National Assembly for independent candidates. However, the appearance of change did not persuade most Egyptians that the change was substantive; in the 1987 election, voter turnout was only 25 percent. Despite this, the New Wafd Party won thirty-five seats, while the Islamic Alliance gained sixty, making it the largest group of opposition members.[19] However, elections held in 1990 and 1995 saw widespread arrests and harassment of Islamist and other opposition candidates. The National Democratic Party won 93.6 percent of National Assembly seats in an election denounced as "one of the most fraudulent elections conducted during Mubarak's reign."[20] Mubarak ran up similar numbers in the September 1999 presidential referendum with 93.8 percent of the vote, and, as of 2004, appeared to be grooming his son to take control of the NDP. Opposition mounted in Egypt in the summer of 2005 as Mubarak seemed set to run for yet another term. However, a terrorist attack against foreign tourists and Egyptians in Sharm al-Sheik seemed to dampen the potential negative reaction to his July 2005 announcement that he would run for a fifth term. The main reaction appeared to be a cynical joke making the rounds in Cairo: Mubarak's aide asks if Mubarak does not think it is time for him to write a farewell speech to the Egyptian people. Mubarak, looking confused, asks, "Where are they going?"[21] In September 2005 he campaigned for reelection against nine candidates in Egypt's first multicandidate presidential election, but the Muslim parties remained officially banned, eliminating what might have been his stiffest competition. Officially Mubarak won almost 89 percent of the vote in an election marked both by low turnout (no more than 15 percent of eligible voters, by one estimate) and confusion over poll watching.[22] Still, it was the first time in Egyptian history that a president ran in a contested election.

THE EGYPTIAN POLITICAL SYSTEM

The Egyptian political system has evolved slowly, and power reamins concentrated in the executive and among Egypt's elites. The pinnacle of political power in Egypt is the presidency, institutionalized by the constitution of 1971. It grants the president authority to appoint vice presidents, prime ministers, and the cabinet, and thus the power to run the vast Egyptian bureaucracy, and with it the power of patronage. The president also chairs the National Security Council, which is responsible for defense and military policy. Given the lack of genuine checks on the power of the executive, Egypt is rated as "not free" in the 2006 Freedom House rankings, despite the language of its country report: "Egypt witnessed its most transparent and competitive presidential and legislative elections in more than half a century and an increasingly unbridled public debate on the country's political future in 2005."[23]

Egyptian political power lies in the hands of several key interlocked elites, including the military (the origin of all of Egypt's modern presidents) and the commercial elites, who share a mutual antipathy of Egypt's various opposition movements. The military, the political backbone of the regime, remains outside of direct governance, but, as Cook notes, "the officers have grown comfortable with arrangements in which one of their own remains the head of state and a range of pseudodemocratic institutions and representative structures insulate them from politics."[24]

The elites control the media (the editor of *al-Ahram*, Egypt's oldest newspaper, was a close friend of Nasser), the ministries, research organs (including the al-Ahram Center for Political and Strategic Studies, affiliated with *al-Ahram* newspaper), and their ties to foreign elites, who sometimes supply funding to Egyptian projects, as noted below in the water development sector. Al-Azhar University may also be understood as a tacit supporter of the political elite, as al-Azhar's religious scholars often denounce antiregime Islamist movements while giving Islamic sanction to government actions (see below). Even when the National Democratic Party tried to mobilize voters to approve a pro-regime constitutional vote in early 2007, only 25 percent of more than 370,000 party workers turned out.[25]

The Egyptian Executive

Under the provisions of the 1971 constitution, a two-thirds majority of parliament selects Egypt's president for a six-year renewable term, confirmed by a popular referendum. The ruling National Democratic Party has almost monopoly control partly because of government power, and partly due to the weakness of the opposition.

The president appoints the prime minister, who has considerable responsibility for the day-to-day running of the government and the implementation of policy. Under both Nasser and Sadat, the prime minister wielded substantial influence in domestic policy. Mubarak tried to reduce the power of the prime minister and the ministries by bringing in his own inner circle of advisers, including some from the diplomatic corps and the private sector.

Political Parties in Egypt

The dominant party in modern Egyptian politics is the National Democratic Party (NDP), which holds a commanding lead in parliamentary seats. The NDP is a holdover from Nasser's Arab Socialist Union and remains a vehicle for those elites rewarded by fidelity to the party and its leadership.

Both Sadat and Mubarak allowed other parties to form, partly to provide a safety valve for the opposition. The regime also cultivated a number of voluntary associations to serve as magnets for political grievances, but since opposition parties have no links to these groups, they are relatively ineffective in responding to discontent.[26]

The primary opposition parties are:

- The Muslim Brotherhood (see below), which is not permitted to run as a formal political party; its members campaign as independents.
- The Liberal Party, formed in 1976 as a right-wing party, with its primary emphasis on unrestricted capitalism and foreign investment in Egypt's economy.
- The National Progressive Unionist Party (NPUP), which became a reservoir of leftist opposition.
- The Tomorrow Party, headed by Ayman Nour.
- The New Wafd Party, founded by former Wafd Party members and headed by Noman Gomaa for five years until his removal in January 2006.

The Egyptian Legislature

The legislature in Egypt comprises two houses, the lower People's Assembly (Majlis al-Shaab) and the upper Consultative Council (Majlis al-Shura). The People's Assembly has 454 seats, with 444 elected by popular vote, and 10 appointed by the president. The Consultative Council, an advisory body, has 264 seats; 176 elected by popular vote from 222 electoral districts, and 88 appointed by the president. While members of the People's Assembly serve five-year terms, the Consultative Council members serve indefinite terms, potentially for life. The Egyptian constitution gives the legislature the power to pass laws, question the prime minister, and monitor the actions of the executive branch, including the right to level criminal accusations against the president.

Egypt was the first Arab country to have a legislative body, electing a parliament in 1866. With such a long tradition, Egyptian parliaments might have emerged as an independent check on the power of the executive. However, the Egyptian legislature has little power relative to the executive. Egyptian laws give the executive power over the legislature in many areas, for example, to order decrees in place of laws that must pass the parliament. The legislature has little real budget power and must either reject or accept the budget from the president in its entirety. Moreover, the president's party, the National Democratic Party, dominates the legislature, and most legislators are dependent on the government: many work for the state.

This is not to say that the parliament has no independent power—the constitution delegates less important matters to the body, and occasionally some significant issue gets debated in the legislature. The parliament may also withdraw confidence from a cabinet minister or from the entire cabinet. However, it cannot pass a vote of no confidence or even vote against a government-supported budget.

In the 2005 elections, the National Democratic Party won 311 seats (down from the 421 seats in 2000) in the 444-seat body. Independents won 112 seats, the New Wafd party 6; splinter parties hold the remainder.

The Egyptian Judiciary

While the president often influences the legislature, Egypt's judiciary system is relatively independent from executive influence. This system enforces a composite of religious and civil law, the latter a remnant of the Napoleonic period when judges were imported from France to run the Egyptian judiciary.[27] In the modern system, judges are appointed for life, and law prevents the president from interfering with their role and decisions, something that Presidents Sadat and Mubarak have largely abided by.

In 1956 Egypt abolished the religious courts (including Islamic, Jewish, and Christian courts) and folded their jurisdiction into the civil court system. However, civil courts can apply religious as well as civil law in its cases.[28] During the Nasser years, the courts used mainly secular law in its casework. There is evidence, however, that Islam increasingly influences the Egyptian court system. In 1980 Sadat added some components of Sharia to Egypt's constitution, claiming that Sharia is "the main source" of Egyptian law. There is also evidence that judges are increasingly relying on Sharia as a legal basis for their decisions, as when a professor's wife was ordered by the court to divorce him because he stood accused of apostasy.[29]

The district tribunals form the lowest level of the court system, serving as courts of original jurisdiction. There are courts in each of the twenty-six governorates to hear appeals from the district tribunals. Higher-level courts exist in seven cities to hear appeals from district courts, and appeals from these courts go to the Court of Cassation in Cairo. A number of special courts exist as well, including the Supreme State Security Court for political and military security, and a series of administrative courts headed by the Council of State.

Although the Egyptian court system mainly enforces civil and criminal law, it is also a part of the political system. The Ministry of Justice exercises a heavy hand over dissent, particularly when it became violent. During Mubarak's rule a record sixty executions have taken place, many for acts of violence during protests. The military courts, which gained power under Mubarak to arrest and try civilians, imposed many of these executions. Between 1992 and 1996, military courts imposed seventy-four death sentences on civilians.[30]

There are laws preventing criticism of the government, although the courts often dismiss those charged with violating such laws if the violations were minor. The act of writing critical graffiti on a village wall is likely to gain a dismissal, although publishing an opposition newspaper may result in jail time. Sometimes the government arrests its critics, as in the case of human rights activist Saad Eddine Ibrahim, whom the police accused of illegally accepting foreign funds. Ibrahim claimed that the regime targeted him because he found widespread fraud in the 1995 elections.[31] The court sentenced Ibrahim to seven years in prison for his criticism of the Mubarak government, raising doubts about both Egypt's standards of civil rights and the fairness of the judicial process.[32] In December 2002, the authorities released Ibrahim from jail, and in March 2003 the Supreme Court reversed the guilty decision. It was unclear if American threats to not increase Egyptian foreign aid over the Ibrahim case influenced the decision.[33] However, as of early 2004, Egyptian citizens were still imprisoned for belonging to banned organizations while American aid continued to flow into the country.[34]

The courts have challenged Mubarak on several issues, for example, overturning his ban on the New Wafd Party and the Sadat-era decree granting women certain political and civil rights. On the other hand, the Ministry of Justice, charged with enforcing court orders, has ignored such orders when so directed by the president.

Both the regime and the courts have had difficulty responding to criticism generated by an increasingly independent press, particularly after Sadat's death. The Islamic papers reported police abuses of Islamist suspects, which ultimately resulted in trials for those accused. While the Islamists accuse the judiciary of being too harsh on dissidents, Copts accuse the same body of being indifferent when Muslims abuse them. They argue that the judicial system largely excludes Copts and that the government was indifferent to attacks against Copts and their property until pressure from the United States forced them to respond.[35]

Egypt's judiciary faces more than just religious strife. Regime efforts at privatizing the economy have led to greater efficiency but also higher poverty levels. Labor strife increased in the 1990s, and fears of a repeat of the bread riots of the 1970s and 1980s contributed to regime decisions to deliberalize the political climate.[36]

Religion and Egyptian Politics

Around 90–94 percent of Egyptians are Muslims and about 6 percent Coptic Christians. The large majority of Muslims are Sunni. Egypt nonetheless has a long tradition of secular rule, and thus regimes attempt to strike compromises with Islamic tradition in areas of policy and law. However, multiple factors, including governmental accountability and efficiency, in addition to economic privation, push many Egyptians to embrace Islam as a vehicle to produce political change. Because underdevelopment was one source of grievance against the government in Cairo, Islamist movements gained support in areas like Egypt's southern areas. A lack of services, a traditional social distance from the urban north, and the ability of Islamists to provide more and better services than the government contributed to the rise of political Islam there.[37] The role and recruitment skills of Islamist organizations are also instrumental in gaining adherents. As Wickham notes, social mobility theory suggests that the narrative of successful mobilizers involves a combination of correlating individual self-interest with group values and addressing resentment over elite domination with the Islamic call for moral reform. Social grievances may form the foundation of Islamist recruitment and sustainment, but the ability of Islamist groups to provide alternative voices is also key.[38]

Egyptian Islamists generally divide into three groups:[39]

- The Muslim Brotherhood *(al-Ikhwan al-Muslimin),* a relatively moderate group that dates back to 1928. It espouses gradual and peaceful change, believing that the Sharia prohibits violence.
- The jihadis, including *al-Jamaa al-Islamiyya* and *al-Jihad.* Both groups advocate armed struggle and have directed violence against members of the regime and its supporters. They have also carried out numerous attacks against tourists, hoping to deprive the regime of tourist revenues. Those attacked include a busload of Greek tourists (apparently mistaken by the killers for Israelis), the 1997 Luxor massacre that killed over sixty tourists, and attacks in 2004 and 2005 against tourist resorts in the Sinai. According to one source, al-Jamaa al-Islamiyya is no longer active.[40]
- The *Takfir wal-Hijra* (literally "Excommunication and Emigration"), which believes that all of society is tainted as infidels, a view taken from the notion that pre-Islamic society was *jahiliyya,* or idolatrous. Their potential application of violence extends to all that do not share their visions.

The Muslim Brotherhood, founded in 1928 by Hassan al-Banna, has traditionally tried to work for change inside the Egyptian political system, though it is also interested in issues outside of the country, particularly the Palestinian plight. Egypt's ruling regimes have alternated between bemused tolerance and repression. The Muslim Brotherhood has traditionally eschewed violence, and its vision of Egypt under Islamic influence is generally limited to Islamic laws and curbs on political and economic corruption. According to an Egyptian source, al-Azhar University has persuaded younger members of the Muslim Brotherhood to go them to Iraq for paramilitary training and to Lebanon to join the jihad there.[41]

Islamist groups attract members with similar backgrounds. Many come from Upper Egypt, displaced by poverty and rapid urbanization.[42] They also attract intellectuals and professionals who abandoned their previous support for secular politics after their faith in Egypt's nationalist government waned.[43] Islamist leaders, driven out of Upper Egypt by the security services, organize in the rapidly growing urban slums in Cairo.[44] They may find inspiration from charismatic leaders like Sheik Uman Abd al-Rahman, who preached in the Upper Egyptian city of al-Minya until he illegally entered the United States. An American court sentenced him to life in prison for his part in the 1991 bombing of the World Trade Center. Sheik Ahmad Ismail was another spellbinding preacher who included anti-Christianity and anti-Judaism in the themes of his sermons.[45]

The Egyptian government has responded to Islamic militancy with a combination of repression and social action.[46] The security forces have rounded up many militants, some of whom the courts ordered executed. Mosques have been "nationalized" under the High Committee for Islamic Dawa, popular Islamic radio shows have been taken off the air, and information centers have been established to warn of the dangers of militant Islam.[47] The regime also launched poverty relief and education measures to counter the Islamist appeal of providing social services. Traditionally these compromises start between the government and al-Azhar University, one of the most respected centers of Islamic learning in the world. Nasser, Sadat, and Mubarak all sought favorable religious rulings (or *fatwas*) from the al-Azhar faculty, offering increased financial support in exchange.[48] The government has also granted more authority to al-Azhar in an effort to squelch opposition from the faculty to government policies.[49] These three presidents also nationalized most of Egypt's mosques in an effort to control radical Islamic preachers and their congregational influence.[50] Paradoxically, such efforts may have furthered the Islamicization of Egyptian society, as Islam's message is constantly reinforced through the state media.[51]

These measures have been partially successful, as Islamist violence has declined. They also indicate government willingness to cooperate and fund activities by civic Islamists, who push civic projects like clinics, study circles, schools, and charities.[52] However, the 1997 attack at the temple of Hatshepsut that killed over sixty tourists reminded both Egyptians and the world that the violent Islamists can still strike with devastating consequences. Still, regime actions against al-Jihad and al-Jamaa al-Islamiyya caused them to splinter into cells and factions and, as noted above, their imprisoned leaders called for a truce in July 1997. Moreover, Islamic leaders both inside and outside Egypt denounced the Luxor attack, and Mubarak used this outrage to take the political initiative from the radical Islamists.[53]

In restricting the activities of militant Islam, however, the government has retained its near-monopoly power status. As Gerges notes, "Expanding political space and participation would prevent the further radicalization of the mainstream Islamist movement and hasten the dissolution of al-Jamaa and Jihad, as paramilitary groups, by integrating them into the political process."[54] However, the regime blocked all efforts by mainstream Islamists, along with former leaders of al-Jamaa and al-Jihad, to establish political parties.[55] Abdo argues that government repression of Islamists transforms moderate Islamists into radical Islamists, thus strengthening the Islamist opposition.[56]

CIVIL SOCIETY IN EGYPT

Egyptian civil society organizations include charitable associations, community development groups, the Young Men's Muslim Association, and a number of medical groups that are typical of the role played by civil society. They compete with government hospitals and some believe that they provide superior care.[57]

Civil society groups grew during the Sadat years, and both leftist and Islamist groups found Egypt's universities fertile ground for organizing. Both groups addressed Sadat's growing moves toward the West and free markets, and the Islamists organized against his push for women's rights (see below).[58] Such movements gained traction even as Mubarak amended the constitution in 2005 to allow for multiparty presidential elections. A group of Egyptian intellectuals launched the Egyptian Movement for Change, popularly known as Kifaya, which coalesced with women and minority groups and moved into the expanding public media space with its denunciation of the Mubarak regime for weakness in the face of "American intervention and occupation of Iraq and Zionist's continuing aggressiveness."[59]

THE STATUS OF WOMEN IN EGYPT

Egyptian women were among the first in the Middle East to organize for equality.[60] By 1923, they organized the Egyptian Feminist Union and gained admission to the Egyptian National University in 1928. In the Nasser era, Egyptian women were able to start businesses, enter parliament, and gain appointments to cabinet positions.[61] Several women have become judges in some of Egypt's commercial courts. Law 91 of 1959 prohibits discrimination based on gender, and Law 44 brought changes in women's personal status laws, giving them the right to divorce a husband who takes a second wife and the right to child custody in some cases.[62]

However, women remain largely excluded from the political system. In 1979, a proposed reform gave women thirty seats in the legislature, but the proposal disappeared after Islamists expressed opposition to it following Sadat's death. The ruling NDP slate for the October 2000 elections reflected the continuing marginalization of women; out of 444 NDP candidates on the ballot, eleven were women.[63]

There is a general perception among the lower classes that the Egyptian woman's primary responsibility is to raise a family. In rural areas, the average woman gives birth to 4.5 children in her lifetime, compared to 3.4 for the country as a whole.[64] Despite government and Western pressures for population control, Egypt's Islamic clerics proclaim that procreation is an Islamic duty. Partially in response, the average Egyptian woman has four to five children in her lifetime, with several more pregnancies ending in miscarriage.[65] There has been progress in family planning, and in 2000 more than half of married women in Egypt used birth control. The rate of overall reproduction is down from the 1960s, though Egypt may be decades away from a replacement rate of two live births per couple.[66]

In 1979, possibly due to behind-the-scenes pressure from President Sadat's wife, Jahan, a presidential decree reversed personal status laws allowing a husband to divorce a wife without conditions and child custody laws normally favoring a husband. The decree stated that polygyny was grounds for a woman to sue for divorce, that alimony in divorce could extend for more than one year, and that the wife automatically gained custody after a divorce of sons until they are ten years old and daughters until they are twelve years old. However, following Sadat's assassination in 1981, Egyptian authorities ruled that this decree was unconstitutional because it was declared during a time when the People's Assembly was not in session. A new law negating most of the 1979 reforms replaced the presidential decree, which had sparked resistance among Islamists. By 2000, the moderates in the People's Assembly apparently felt that the Islamic opposition has weakened politically, and thus passed another law granting women the right of divorce. The law did stipulate that in order to obtain a divorce, the petitioning woman had to return any dowry paid by her family to her husband, who was freed from any future financial obligations to her.[67]

Egyptian law does not recognize the citizenship of children born to an Egyptian woman and a foreign father, thus discriminating against women, according to its critics. The roots of the law are partially in Islam (Muslim lineage runs through the father, according to tradition), but also in tribal traditions that exclude members who marry outside of the tribe. Critics of the law argue that it marginalizes women. As one put it, "If children feel that their mothers cannot provide them with the same protection as their fathers, then the whole status of women will remain less important."[68] Gamal Mubarak, the president's son, has managed to push a bill through parliament that would end this practice.[69]

The political status of women in Egypt varies according to area. In urban areas women hold positions in universities, government (there are three women ministers in the cabinet), and the private sector. In rural areas, the possibilities for women advancing beyond traditional roles are limited, and old beliefs persist. This is also often the case in poor urban areas, where veiling is reappearing in response to Islamist pressures.[70]

Discrimination is only one issue women face; another is female genital mutilation. Despite a government ban on it, Amnesty International reported that two young girls bled to death from the procedure. According to UNICEF, an estimated 80 percent of Egyptian women suffered genital mutilation as of 1994.[71] According to another study, 97 percent of ever-married Egyptian women were circumcised.[72] If these numbers are correct, then the government's ban on the procedure is widely violated. The ban itself came under fire from the rector of al-Azhar University, who issued a *fatwa* in 1995 stating that female circumcision was part of adherence to Islam. He claimed that the practice honors women and is necessary for social order.[73]

A group of men and women challenged the ruling in court, and, to the surprise of some observers, won their case, reinforcing the government ban.[74]

The issue of women and divorce also arises in Egypt's Coptic Church. A 1999 effort by Coptic Pope Shenouda to revise Egypt's 1938 personal status code, allowing violence as grounds for divorce, was criticized by human rights activists. However, the pope reiterated his stance that while he personally condemned spousal violence, it should not be grounds for divorce.[75]

THE STRUCTURE AND PERFORMANCE OF THE EGYPTIAN ECONOMY

Egypt's economy, once dominated by agriculture and small crafts, has shown a dramatic shift to the service sector and industry. It was a slow transformation, partly because of Nasser's legacy of Arab socialism, and partly due to the heritage of the past.

During his presidency, Nasser implemented Arab socialism, which placed heavy emphasis on state ownership, central planning, and self-sufficiency. Nasser nationalized a considerable portion of the Egyptian economy and poured substantial investment into shipyards, steel mills, cement plants, and other forms of import substitution. Arab socialism also advocated the equitable distribution of wealth and employment of both the rural and urban poor, resulting in high subsidies. President Sadat, however, reduced the role of Arab socialist ideals in the Egyptian economy, and the role of private investment and private incentive grew over state ownership and state planning. Sadat's peace efforts with Israel brought a commitment of economic assistance from the United States. By 2006, Egypt had received more than $26 billion over twenty-five years, giving a substantial boost to the Egyptian economy. President Mubarak furthered the trends pushed by Sadat, though he also resisted demands for a complete privatization of Egypt's economy. However, opposition developed against Mubarak's policies, both from the conservative business elite and the rural and urban poor, who were increasingly joining Islamist groups partly because of the impact of Mubarak's economic policies. Mubarak thus found his freedom to move limited, and his policies became even more incrementalist.

Egypt's economy shows a mixed picture of progress and problems. The unemployment rate is considerably lower than it was several years ago, when it hovered around 24 percent, but does not include the underemployed or those with temporary jobs. With a rapidly growing population of over 79 million (2007), job creation is a considerable challenge. Many Egyptians work at the margins of the economy, barely making a living carving tourist trinkets, carrying water, or collecting garbage from Cairo's hotels. The GDP per capita in 2007 of $4,200 does not reflect their position, nor does it reflect the wealthy Egyptians who live in Heliopolis or Maadi, prosperous suburbs of Cairo where the walled villas and armed security guards keep out the poor. According to Egyptian estimates, some 2–3 million Egyptians live "by European standards," while the rest live below them, with around 20 percent below the poverty line. The government has tried to lower unemployment and poverty by hiring: one-third of all new jobs are in the government, though the government also tracks two-thirds of all Egyptian students into technical education, which has a much lower employment rate than the college-bound track.[76]

The other figure that stands out starkly is the balance of trade: Egypt imports much more than it exports. This results in a drain on Egyptian financial resources and indicates the dependence Egypt has on the countries that sell it goods. These imports include food (almost half of the food consumed in Egypt is imported) and other essential goods like transportation equipment, machinery, metals, electronics, and military goods. An additional problem is the staggering public debt, which is 103 percent of the GDP.

The Mubarak government has worked to reform Egypt's economy, largely through privatization of state-owned industries and enterprises. The International Monetary Fund approved of Egypt's privatization efforts and the ending of currency controls, and foreign investment has increased. However, reforms did not blunt the impact of the September 11, 2001, terrorist attacks against the United States, which lowered Egypt's tourism revenues, as did attacks against tourists, most recently in the summer of 2005.

Obstacles to Economic Growth

Egypt faces numerous obstacles to steady economic growth. First, the country has few natural resources that are desired on the international market. If the present rates continue, children under fifteen will be 30 percent of the population by 2016, placing a great strain on educational resources and job creation.[77] Third, the legacy of socialism persists in the form of onerous rules and a bloated bureaucracy. Moreover, the Ministry of Industry must approve all business expenditures (even if a factory wants to purchase a car), and government-guaranteed jobs inspire thousands of college graduates to wait years for public employment because of the easy hours and lifetime job security.[78] The economy remains shackled to subsidies, particularly for food, that drain resources from other more potentially productive activities. Subsidies consume two-thirds of the national budget, for bread, gasoline (which is thus priced at around US$1.00 a gallon), sugar, and water.[79] Bread subsidies led to large-scale black marketeering and inefficient practices such as feeding bread to livestock, since subsidized bread was cheaper than animal feed.[80] In 2003, the government spent some $600 million in bread subsidies.[81] Finally, Egyptian banks have a substantial portion of their assets tied up in public debt, itself between 120 and 130 percent of the GDP, thus depriving the country of funds that otherwise could go to finance new business and new jobs.[82]

One of Sadat's reforms was Law 43 of 1974, to engage in *al-infitah*, or "economic openness." The new law gave serious impetus to privatizing Egypt's tourist industry by allowing the Ministry of Tourism to alter taxation and regulation of the tourism industry in hopes of expanding it.[83] One consequence is that tourism has become Egypt's largest source of foreign earnings, surpassing revenues from the

Suez Canal and remittances from Egyptian workers abroad. Enterprises like mortgage banking, air transport, and electrical transmission are also undergoing privatization, although there are signs that some state-owned firms are being sold to other state companies due to fears of foreign domination of some sectors of the Egyptian economy.[84]

Agricultural Development

Egypt is mostly desert, with a narrow ribbon of water sustaining its population; 95 percent of Egyptians live on 5 percent of its land. Traditional methods of agriculture cannot support a population growth rate of close to 2 percent per year.

Efforts to expand cropland have resulted in as many difficulties as benefits. The Aswan High Dam, built in the 1960s with Soviet assistance, was intended to store water in a huge lake (Lake Nasser) to irrigate much of Upper Egypt. However, the dam is located in an extremely hot region where water evaporates quickly, and thus Lake Nasser became increasingly saline as water evaporated from its vast surface. The dam trapped the silt from the central African mountains, and farmers lost invaluable fertilizer. Now the dam generates considerable electricity just to produce fertilizer to replace the lost silt. The fringes of Lake Nasser became breeding grounds for snails hosting parasitical diseases.

The Egyptian government stakes much of its future economic growth on expanding agriculture through water management. Despite earlier problems, ambitious plans continue for irrigating Lower Egypt. They include the al-Salem canal from the Nile to al-Arish in the Sinai and diversion of Nile water to Abu Simbel and then to three branches east, which will expand Egypt's arable land by more than 40 percent.[85] Other projects include the "new delta" in southern Egypt, to pump water from Lake Nasser to irrigate half a million acres at a cost of $1.5 billion. A related project, the Southern Valley Project, is expected to cost $88.5 billion over the next twenty years. Some funds from Abu Dhabi and Saudi Arabia have already been contributed, and Saudi Arabian Prince Walid ibn Talal ibn Abdul Aziz al-Saud is funding a 450,000-acre farm in the area.[86] The East Oweinat Project taps fossil water in the desolate southwestern desert to cultivate up to a quarter of a million acres. In December 1998, President Mubarak visited the area to inaugurate a new airport, power station, and the beginnings of tourist and industrial complexes.[87] Other projects are designed to expand water from the ancient oases in central Egypt.

Problems abound, however. The countries to the south complain that Egypt is already using too much water from the Nile and may attempt to constrict its flow.[88] The East Oweinat Project draws from the same aquifer that Libya is tapping for the Great Man-made River Project (see Chapter 18), and the two countries may also compete over this source of water, which runs under their border.[89] Money is an additional problem. Foreign investors may be hesitant to lend money for such ambitious projects that may not pay off.

Egypt's military has tried to help the Egyptian economy by providing for its own equipment. Therefore, Egypt builds American-designed M1-A1 tanks in a state-of-the-art factory outside of Cairo. The plant, which employs some 5,000 workers, produces a tank that US Army officials rank as better than those made in the United States. However, the Egyptian army cannot afford to buy any more, so at the end of the assembly line is a vast room filled with brand-new tanks. The plant cannot lay off workers, so it continues to produce tanks, and some officials express hopes that they may be sold to Turkey. However, the Turkish military cannot afford them, so they continue to collect at the end of the line. In addition, the Egyptian government continues to pay workers to build more tanks for a nonexistent market.[90]

Tourism generates around $9 billion annually, the largest source of outside revenues for Egypt. The Egyptian economy benefits from three other outside sources: revenues from the Suez Canal ($3 billion a year), income from Egyptian workers abroad, and US assistance, as noted above. Egypt's economy needs investment, both foreign and domestic, to grow faster than Egypt's population. A few years ago, economic conditions were so grim that Egyptians with money tended to invest their funds outside of the country.[91] In addition to the agricultural investment noted above, foreigners are investing in expensive new developments like a new high technology manufacturing section in the northern Sinai, as well as new port facilities at Port Said and Damietta.[92] That will be even more significant since American developmental assistance is scheduled to cease funding infrastructure projects, claiming that such projects must seek investment from international capital markets and not aid.[93]

Some investors are also interested in expanding Egyptian natural gas production, taking advantage of the discovery of large gas fields off Egypt's Mediterranean coast. Gas production was 1,600 cubic feet per day(cf/d) in 1999, but the state-owned Egyptian General Petroleum Corporation expected that figure to double by the end of 2000.[94] However, in 2005 Egypt still consumed all the natural gas it produced, leaving none for export.

EGYPTIAN FOREIGN POLICY

Because of its location, its status as the largest Arab country, and the prestige accorded its leaders, Egypt plays an essential role in Middle East politics. Under Nasser, Egypt appealed to other Arabs on the basis of pan-Arabism; under Mubarak, Egypt has been a voice for stability and peace building efforts.

Egypt and the United States have maintained close ties since Sadat severed his relationship with the Soviet Union. Next to Israel, Egypt receives more US aid than any other country, as noted above. Egypt has purchased some expensive equipment in the past with this funding source, including frigates, artillery pieces, Harpoon antiship missiles, and F-16 fighter aircraft, as well as tanks coproduced in Egypt, as noted above.[95]

Egypt's relationship with the United States is tempered by the attitudes of its citizens, US policies toward the Israeli-Palestinian dispute, US sanctions against Iraq, the operation against Saddam Hussein in 2003, and the US campaign in Afghanistan. All this has led many Egyptians to conclude that the United States is really at war with Islam. By late 2001, Western diplomats suggested that anti-American sentiment was as high as it had been in years, and President Mubarak, probably in response, has permitted attacks on the United States in government-owned media.[96] Mubarak has slowed the pace of his visits to Washington, distancing himself from the George W. Bush administration and allowing other actors like Saudi Arabia to take a more prominent position in Middle East regional affairs.

Relations with Neighbors

Egypt shares a border with Sudan to the south. Although tensions have been high between the two countries, there has been some relaxation recently. Egypt's relationship with Sudan soured after the 1989 Islamist coup in Khartoum, and Egypt accused the Sudanese regime of harboring Egyptian Islamist fugitives and of complicity in a 1995 assassination attempt against Mubarak. Even though both sides have tried to mend relations, disputes remain over the exact location of the border. The key issue remains the free flow of the Nile, which runs through Sudan before reaching Egypt. Sudan has not yet tried to divert or block its flow, which would cause Egypt to suffer considerably.

Egypt has attempted to raise its international profile through the commitment of peacekeeping forces. Egypt commits some 300 troops to peacekeeping in Bosnia and 124 for the same purpose in the Central African Republic. Egyptian forces also covered the US withdrawal from Somalia and participated in the UN mission in East Timor in early 2000.

Egypt has embraced globalization, although conditionally, and with it, challenges to its own image of cultural superiority. McDonald's arrived in Egypt in 1994, and, as one commentator wryly noted, "In Egypt the chain's reputation is very different from the greasy spoon aura the original now exudes on its home turf, the USA. Here a family meal at 'Mac' is a special treat, a symbol of status, the shiny beacon of progress, and the epitome of modernity."[97] Progress indeed.

Egypt has long ties to Turkey from Ottoman days, and even though Turkey is not a member of the Arab world, it sharescultural similarities with the country across the Mediterranean, which is the subject of the next chapter.

SUGGESTED READINGS

Abdo, Geneive. *No God but God: Egypt and the Triumph of Islam.* Oxford: Oxford University Press, 2000.

Badran, Margot. *Feminists, Islam, and Nation: Gender and the Making of Modern Egypt.* Princeton, NJ: Princeton University Press, 1996.

Baker, Raymond William. *Egypt's Uncertain Revolution Under Sadat and Nasser.* Cambridge, MA: Harvard University Press, 1978.

_____. *Sadat and After: Struggles for Egypt's Political Soul.* Cambridge, MA: Harvard University Press, 1990.

_____. *Islam Without Fear: Egypt and the New Islamists*. Cambridge, MA: Harvard University Press, 2003.

Beattie, Kirk J. *Egypt During the Nasser Years*. Boulder, CO: Westview, 1994.

_____. *Egypt During the Sadat Years*. New York: Palgrave, 2000.

El-Mikawy, Noha. *The Building of Consensus in Egypt's Transition Process*. New York: Columbia University Press, 1999.

Gordon, Joel. *Nasser's Blessed Movement: Egypt's Free Officers and the July Revolution*. New York: Oxford University Press, 1992.

Ibrahim, Saad Eddin. *Egypt, Islam, and Democracy: Critical Essays*. Cairo: American University in Cairo Press, 2002.

Kenney, Jeffrey T. *Muslim Rebels: Kharijites and the Politics of Extremism in Egypt*. New York: Oxford University Press, 2006.

Kepel, Gilles. *Muslim Extremism in Egypt: The Prophet and Pharaoh*. Berkeley: University of California Press, 1993.

Marsot, Afaf Lutfi al-Said. *A Short History of Modern Egypt*. Cambridge: Cambridge University Press, 1985.

Posusney, Marsha Pripstein. *Labor and the State in Egypt, 1952–1994: Workers, Unions, and Economic Restructuring*. New York: Columbia University Press, 1997.

Sagiv, David. *Fundamentalism and Intellectuals in Egypt, 1973–1993*. London: Frank Cass, 1995.

Starrett, Gregory. *Putting Islam to Work: Education, Politics, and Religious Transformation in Egypt*. Berkeley, CA: University of California Press, 1998.

Sullivan, Denis J., and Sanaa Abed-Kotob. *Islam in Contemporary Egypt: Civil Society vs. the State*. Boulder, CO: Lynne Rienner, 1999.

Wickham, Carrie Rosefsky. *Mobilizing Islam: Religion, Activism, and Political Change in Egypt*. New York: Columbia University Press, 2002.

11

TURKEY

IMAGES *The moonlight emphasizes the grandeur of the minarets towering above stylized domes. Every Middle Eastern country has mosques, but those high on the slopes by the Golden Horn off the Bosporus seem both larger and more significant, particularly at night. They reflect the classic Ottoman architecture, with multiple domes spilling down from the center, some with a single minaret, others with four or more, all illuminated by soft lighting like slender spears piercing the Istanbul skyline. This is a city that straddles the divide between Europe and Asia, and wants to be a part of both. In that sense, the graceful minarets are reminders of both Europe's fears and Turkey's pride.*

TURKEY IS A FASCINATING and important country in the Middle East, standing between Europe and Asia both geographically and historically. Its culture embraces the traditions of ancient Greece and Rome and its land was home to such legendary figures as St. Nicholas, Helen of Troy, King Midas, and Saul of Tarsus, who would become the Apostle Paul. Much of Turkey contains the ruins from classic civilizations, including several sites of the so-called Seven Wonders of the World and ancient Troy. Istanbul, once known as Constantinople, is one of the world's most historic cities.

Turkey's political system reflects its dual identity between Europe and the Middle East—a vibrant if imperfect democracy where an Islamist-oriented party won the largest number of seats in the Turkish parliament and then pledged to work for Turkey's admission to the European Union. Turkey was an early member of the North Atlantic Treaty Organization, the only Muslim country in the alliance, and has had a close relationship with the United States since the end of World War II. It is a country ripe with contradictions. (See Map 11.1 on page 256.)

THE MODERN HISTORY OF TURKEY

Turkey's Ottoman period dates from the fifteenth century, and ended during the last days of World War I. The Ottoman period placed Turkey at the apogee of Middle

Eastern politics with control over a vast sweep of land from Tunisia in the west to the Persian Gulf in the east, and much of the Balkans in Europe. Ottoman efforts to conquer Austria and beyond in the sixteenth and seventeenth centuries launched a European political force to limit Ottoman expansion which ultimately destroyed it. During their long period in power, the Ottomans contributed considerably to both Turkey and the greater Middle East. Their accomplishments included a widely adopted model of Islamic governance (including respect for the rights of other religious communities, which were given the status of millets under Ottoman rule),[1] mass education, and an extraordinarily rich culture, nurtured over centuries and spread over the vast sweep of the modern Middle East.[2] Neither Turkey nor the former Ottoman Empire can be thoroughly understood outside of the Ottoman context.

The Ottomans contributed to their own downfall through overexpansion, harsh occupation policies, and an increasingly incompetent regime in Istanbul.[3] The Ottoman Empire reached its zenith in the sixteenth century and then entered a slow decline. Internal decay and a continuing series of wars depleted its morale and its power, until reform, unsuccessfully tried since the eighteenth century, finally brought the so-called Young Turks to power.[4] The Young Turks traced their political ideas to Europe, where many of them went into exile and learned about political reform. They took power in 1908 under the guise of the Committee for Union and Progress, but they reacted ruthlessly to resistance against their efforts to "Turkify" Turkey's Arabs, Albanians, and Kurds.[5] This, together with the negative consequences of the two Balkan wars (1912–1913, and 1913) for Turkey, discredited the Young Turks and by 1913 the military took power and ended the experiment in reform. Turkey sided with Germany in World War I, and when the Allies finally triumphed in November 1918, the last vestiges of the old Ottoman Empire vanished, with the British and French dividing up much of the spoils in the Sykes-Picot Agreement. The new Turkish Republic rose from its ashes.

The Ataturk Period

Mustafa Kemal, the founder of modern Turkey, was born in Salonika in 1881 and rose through the ranks of the Turkish military to prominence at the battle of Gallipoli, where Turkish forces decisively defeated British efforts to invade Turkey. Allied with Germany in 1915, Kemal led victorious Turkish troops against Greek forces that invaded Anatolia in 1919 to reclaim the old Christian Greek parts of Turkey for Greece. In May of that year, Kemal presided over a meeting in Samsun of nationalist-minded Turks who opposed the Ottoman capitulation to the victorious Allies. When the Ottoman government refused to accept their demands for a new Turkish identity based on the Anatolian peninsula and Istanbul, he resigned from the army. In April 1920, the nationalists chartered the Grand National Assembly and elected Kemal its president. In October 1923, he was elected president of the new Turkish republic. Kemal quickly moved to bring Turkey closer culturally and politically to Europe. He changed the Turkish alphabet from Arabic to Latin, abolished the positions of caliph and sultan, and banned the wearing of the

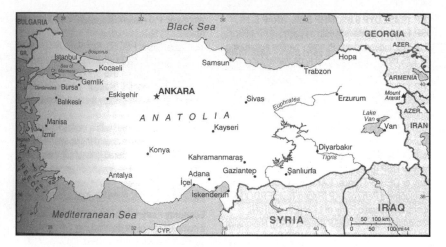

MAP 11.1   TURKEY

fez (the distinctive headgear worn by men) and the veil. He closed religious schools and adopted the Gregorian calendar to curb the influence of Islam as he tried to secularize Turkish society and politics. He instituted a secular legal code that ended the religious court's control over issues involving women, marriage, and family. In an effort to break with Turkey's past, Kemal moved the capital from Istanbul to the small city of Ankara. In 1934 the Grand National Assembly gave Mustafa Kemal the name Kemal Ataturk ("Father Turk") for his accomplishments.

Ataturk defined his purpose for modern Turkey in six principles: republicanism, nationalism, populism, reformism, statism, and secularism, and together they became "Kemalism." They formed the bedrock of Turkey's republican constitution, and they remain a keystone of modern Turkish political identity, although opposition groups have challenged some of the Kemalist principles since the founding of the republic. "Secularism" is generally interpreted as "antireligious," although Davison argues that it may also be understood as anticlerical or laicist, literally the elevation of lay or "lower" persons of religious belief.[6] Given Ataturk's effort to shift political power in Turkey away from religious leadership in favor of modernism in a heavily Muslim country, the laicist understanding conforms to a power replacement mode rather than an effort to challenge fundamental belief. As Ayata notes, Ataturk "saw that Islam was a significant part of Turkish society, that religious faith was important for national unity and mobilization, and that it could contribute to social and moral welfare."[7] Still, the concept of secularism came under fire from Islamists fearing a loss of power and faith, and the nationalistic emphasis gave rise to Kurdish resentment, since Ataturk advanced Turkish nationalism even as he abolished the old Ottoman millet system that gave limited autonomy to minority groups. This identity reinforced the Turkish preeminence over non-Turkish minorities, including the Kurds and Turkey's minority Arabic-speaking population. The statist principle also became the foundation for the role of state planning in the Turkish economy.

Ataturk developed the Republican People's Party (CHP) as a vehicle to govern Turkey. Despite the language of reformism and populism, the CHP became a one-party system enabling Ataturk to govern without institutionalized challenges until his death in 1938.[8]

IMAGES

| *The sharp click of military heels tap along the stone pavement as the procession moved slowly toward the Ataturk mausoleum. Soldiers in white helmets and leggings standing at attention line the route as the foreign visitors ascend the stairs to the burial site, accompanied by the lilting sound of the Muslim call to prayer from a nearby mosque, as they lay a wreath over the resting site of Turkey's most celebrated lay leader. One moment, two Turkeys: the sacred and the secular.*

The End of One-Party Rule

Ataturk hoped that his six principles would become universal in Turkey, but an Islamist society without the tradition of separation of church and state found secular politics hard to accept; likewise Turkish nationalism in a country with important minority groups (particularly the Kurds). Additionally, the Kemalist hope that the army would be the ultimate guardian of Ataturk's legacy almost ensured a Turkish future rife with civil-military tension. It is in this context that the post-Ataturk period must be understood.

Following Ataturk's death, Ismet Inonu became president and maintained Ataturk's model of strong one-party rule. Inonu kept Turkey neutral during World War II despite German pressure, largely due to fear of the Soviet Union.[9] Realizing that neutrality would not be an option after the war, Turkey joined the United Nations as one of the original fifty-one members in 1945.

After World War II, resentment of one-party rule under the CHP and Inonu grew, and in 1946 former Prime Minister Mahmut Celal Bayar and Adnan Menderes founded the Democrat Party (DP), which gained 62 seats out of 465 in July 1946. Landowners, peasants, the commercial class, and non-Muslim minorities found common grievances against the CHP, objecting to land reform and heavy-handed centralism. The election of May 1950 demonstrated the broad-based appeal of the DP when it won 408 seats, ending the hold of the CHP on Turkish politics and giving Bayar the presidency.[10] Bayar tried to move Turkey beyond its largely socialist economy by emphasizing private enterprise and reform of the Turkish civil service. But after further increases in the CHP parliamentary majority in 1954, the military toppled Bayar in 1960 and sentenced him to death a year later for "crimes against the state" by a military tribunal. The military later commuted his sentence.

The military coup of 1960 resulted in the creation of the Committee of National Unity consisting of the senior officers who conducted the coup, with General Cemal

Gursel taking the positions of president, prime minister, and defense minister. However, all that concentrated power proved incapable of handling Turkey's growing economic problems, and General Gursel indicated that the committee would call for new elections. The military, in the meantime, tried to gut the DP by placing over 600 of its officials on trial (hanging Menderes and two cabinet members), so new parties and some old ones competed for seats in the October 1961 elections, with the CHP winning 173 seats and the new Justice Party (AP) getting 158 seats. The Grand National Assembly named General Gursel president and he, in turn, asked former President Ismet Inonu to serve as prime minister; he filled the post between 1960 and 1965.

By 1965, voters gave the DP a clear majority, bringing one of Turkey's better known political figures, Suleyman Demirel, to serve as prime minister. Demirel continued the tradition of the DP as a broad-based party encompassing the peasantry, business classes, and moderate Muslims, while maintaining the Kemalist legacy. In the meantime, Bulent Ecevit succeeded Inonu as leader of the CHP and set out to reform the party by expanding its political base.

Demirel's majority began to erode as several parties normally allied with him deserted the coalition. Defections from Demirel's own party reflected Turkish polarization away from the center and toward the religious end to leaders like Necmittin Erbakan, a moderate Islamist, or the sometimes violent Turkish nationalism of Alparslan Turke, who took over the Republican Peasants National Party and later transformed it into the xenophobic Nationalist Action Party.[11] In March 1971, Demirel resigned under pressure from the army, which demanded a stronger government. Nihat Erim became prime minister, imposing strict law-and-order policies and bowing to American demands to curtail Turkish opium poppy cultivation. Two other weak prime ministers followed Erim in a government of national unity, which struggled along until 1974 when Ecevit persuaded the head of the Islamist-oriented party, MSP (*Milli Selamet Partisi,* or National Salvation), Necmittin Erbakan, to join his coalition. The coalition did not last long, but it set the stage for further cooperation with the moderate Islamists. The coalition fell apart in late 1974 and the president had to persuade an independent to run Turkey with a nonparty government until Demirel cobbled together enough parties to form a weak coalition. The CHP did even better in the 1977 elections while the DP won but a single seat, illustrating once again the dramatic swings for Turkish parties and Turkish politics. The economy was often a factor, as it quickly eroded the earlier gains of the CHP. Demirel lost a vote of no confidence and Ecevit tried to continue, but the ensuing political crisis caused him to quit in October 1979. The president replaced him with Demirel.

Demirel faced a mounting political crisis as Ecevit aligned himself with Erbakan to push Turkey away from its pro-Western stance, while Turkey's Islamists organized a large rally in Konya demanding the return of Islamic law. Additionally the Turkish economy was plagued with both high unemployment and high inflation. The Turkish military had had enough, believing that despite a reluctance to overthrow a democratically elected government, they, as the ultimate guardians of the

Turkish state, had to intervene.[12] In September 1980, they once again ousted the civilian government and took power, dissolving the Grand National Assembly, jailing both Demirel and Ecevit, and banning political parties and trade unions. Charges of political repression, torture, and political executions soon followed, and the Council of Europe suspended Turkey's membership.

The military moved cautiously to restore some of Turkey's party system, but wiped the previous slate clean by banning politicians active before the coup. The military did certify three political parties to compete, the Motherland, or *Anavatan Partisi* (ANAP), the Populist Party (*Halkci Partisi,* or HP), and the Nationalist Democracy Party (*Milliyetci Demokrasi Partisi,* or MPD), the party favored by the military. In the first election after the coup, the ANAP won 45 percent of the vote, indicating dissatisfaction by Turkey's voters with military rule. The leader of ANAP, Turgut Ozal, became the new prime minister. Both economic problems and foreign affairs issues (the first campaign against Iraq in particular) dogged his administration, and his popularity slipped. However, Ozal proved to be a hardy political survivor, engaging in such risky behavior as a state visit to Athens in 1989, after Greece and Turkey had clashed over oil drilling rights in the Aegean Sea two years earlier. Ozal also took steps to strengthen Turkey's ties to Europe by formally applying for full membership in the European Community (later to become the European Union) in 1987, renewing Turkish efforts to join the old European Economic Community (later the EU) beginning in 1959. However, the European community rebuffed Turkish membership (although Turkey was an associate member of the European Community), beginning a long and difficult struggle for full membership in the European Union.

The First Religious Party Success

Even though Ozal relinquished the prime ministership in 1989, he was appointed president and served until his death in 1993. Mesut Yülmaz became prime minister, but nagging corruption charges brought about his downfall, and once again, Demirel served as prime minister between November 1993 and May 1993, when he resigned to assume the presidency. In the elections of 1993, Tansu Çiller's True Path Party (*Dogru Yol Partisi,* or DYP) won the election and Çiller, an American-educated economist, became prime minister. She formed a coalition with the Motherland Party, and Yülmaz succeeded her as prime minister. Çiller devalued the Turkish lira, and subsequently the Turkish stock market fell dramatically. The coalition collapsed two years later in the face of growing Kurdish insurgency. Once again, critics charged corruption, and the Islamist-oriented Welfare Party (Refah) headed by Necmittin Erbakan won the election in December 1995 but could not put together a coalition, thus allowing the two center-right parties to form an anti-Islamist bloc in parliament. That coalition fell the next year, and Erbakan became Turkey's first Islamist prime minister by inviting Çiller to join his party in a coalition. The Welfare Party probably benefited from the electorate's belief that it was at least honest. Erbakan realized that the Constitutional Court would likely ban the party, and thus changed its name to the Virtue Party (Fazilet) in December. Turkey's military viewed the Welfare Party with alarm, fearing a departure from the Kemalist tradition. The rise of Islamist splinter groups, fund-raising by Islamic groups outside of Turkey from expatriate Turkish workers, and the growth of illegal Islamist schools was especially worrisome to the military.[13] Said one Turkish general, "Destroying fundamentalism is of life or death importance," as the military worried aloud about the visible symbols of Islam in government that "could give Turkey a bad name."[14] In 1997, the military orchestrated the collapse of the coalition, which led to a new coalition led by the Motherland Party of Mesut Yülmaz. That coalition found itself also under scrutiny for corruption, and Yülmaz resigned in January 1998, and Bulent Ecevit replaced him as prime minister.[15] Ecevit was helped in part by the capture of PKK leader Abullah Ocalan. However, the effect was brief. In the 1999 elections, the right-leaning Nationalist Action Party gained votes, and the Virtue Party ended its two-year existence when one of its women candidates for parliament was banned from the chamber before being sworn in because she wore a headscarf.

The Virtue Party itself was banned in May, and its discontented members turned from Erbakan to Recep Tayyip Erdoğan the former mayor of Istanbul, who helped found the third incarnation of a Turkish Islamist-oriented party, the Justice and Democracy Party (*Adalet ve Kalkünma Partisi*, or AKP). Erbakan and some of his followers then created the Felicity Party, but that organ failed to capture the Islamist vote once enjoyed by its predecessors. With the end of his Islamist rival, Erdocan capitalized on the growing public dissatisfaction stemming from internal strife and the Turkish economy.

For Turkey, the decade of the 1990s was marked not only by political instability but also the rekindling of a Kurdish revolt. This time the Kurdistan Worker's Party (*Partiya Karkeren Kurdistan*, or PKK) rose up. The PKK espoused a violent Marxist ideology, and its resulting struggle with the Turkish military would cost over 30,000 lives by the time it ended in the late 1990s. The inability of successive Turkish governments to cope with the PKK problem helped undermine the traditional political structure, as did the nagging doldrums of the Turkish economy.

By November 2002, Turkey's economy plunged into recession, and voters apparently tired of the revolving door of the old parties and leaders, and Prime Minister Ecevit's Democratic Left Party fell behind in the polls for the national election in that month, paving the way for the Justice and Development Party (*Adalet ve Kalkünma Partisi*, or AKP).

Islam Revived?

Erdoğan, along with Abdullah Gul, a former economics professor, distanced AKP from radical Islam (denouncing the September 11 attacks against the United States, for example), and by November 2002 the AKP won a sizable victory with 34 percent of the total vote, giving it a majority of seats in parliament. Only the Republican People's Party won enough votes to keep seats in the Grand National Assembly;

the other parties lost heavily. The parties making up the previous ruling coalition all fell below the threshold of 10 percent of the total vote, with Ecevit's Democratic Left Party receiving only 1.2 percent of the total ballots. However, despite the overwhelming win, Erdocan, the head of the AKP, could not assume the post of prime minister because of a previous conviction for reading a poem deemed subversive. Erdocon's Islamist past raised questions both inside and outside Turkey, since as mayor of Istanbul, he had banned alcohol and had discussed openly the possibility of Turkey withdrawing its application for membership in the European Union. Erdoğan had also refused to shake women's hands and had once reportedly said of democracy, comparing it to a streetcar, "You ride it to your destination, then you step off."[16] However, he tried to reassure both Turkish voters and the outside world that he would remain a moderate and continue to campaign for Turkish admission to the European Union.[17] Because of his conviction, Erdoğan could not serve as prime minister, so Gul took the post until January 2003.

The election results indicated a deep-seated public rejection of the Turkish political status quo, with one poll indicating that one-third of the 2002 voters wanted to "try out a new party." Subsequently the former coalition parties DYP and ANAP plus the other two centrist parties fell from 83 percent of the 1991 vote to only 36 percent in 2002.[18] Turkish voters clearly reacted to charges of corruption, the boom-and-bust economy, and the overall inefficiency of the government that was demonstrated in particular after the devastating earthquake of August 1999.[19] Old-line party leaders like Bulent Ecevit began to step aside as party heads, as the eighty-year-old former prime minister resigned as head of the DSP in December 2003. Others continued to be dogged by charges of corruption, like Mesut Yülmaz.[20]

Religiously observant Muslims remained the core of the AKP, with another poll indicating that 90 percent of AKP supporters prayed at least once a day, 99 percent observed Ramadan, 81 percent saw themselves as Muslims first and Turks second, and 60 percent said that religious values took precedence over national values.[21] However, Erdoğan continued to pay symbolic homage to Kemalism, stating on National Day in 2003, "The Republic of Turkey, by marching resolutely along the path of enlightenment based on Ataturk's principles of popular sovereignty, independence, national unity, modernity, secularism, and peacefulness, has made important progress over the past 80 years. The goal that Mustafa Kemal Ataturk pointed out to us was not the goal of reaching contemporary civilization, but rather that of rising above it."[22] While several terrorist bombings in Istanbul in the fall of 2003 reminded Turks that Islamic militancy remained an issue, they did not appear to shake the faith that most Turks have in a moderate Islamic country with a secular government.[23] Erdoğan appeared to turn more to those Islamist traditions when he appointed an Islamist banker as head of the central bank (President Sezer rejected the nomination), and inviting leaders of Hamas and Iraqi Shiite leader Muqtada al-Sadr to Turkey. Those moves may be popular with the Turkish public, which will decide in 2007 if Erdoğan and his party get another term.[24]

THE TURKISH POLITICAL SYSTEM

Turkey is a parliamentary multiparty democracy that continues in many ways the legacy of Kemal Ataturk. It is also a part of the legacy of the Ottoman Empire, which, as Ozbudun notes, "held that the social order was of divine origin and hence immutable. . . . Political power did not derive from the society, but was imposed on it by the will of God."[25] Thus when Ataturk dismantled most of the formal religious structure comprising much of the Ottoman state, he created a power void, which allowed another Ottoman tradition, a strong military presence in politics, to emerge as a power in Turkish politics.

Turkey has had three constitutions since the founding of the republic; the 1924 constitution set forth the basic structure of the state, the 1961 constitution provided for an independent judiciary, and the 1982 constitution, among other things, abolished the 150-member Republican Senate.

Islam, the religion of almost all Turks, has played a clear role in Turkish life, but secular Kemalism continues to trump the currents of Islam in Turkish political life. There are pockets of radical Islamists in Turkey, but their activity has been restricted to scattered, if deadly, terrorist bombings.[26] Since 1967 Turkish authorities have periodically arrested members of the caliphate-oriented group Hizb ut-Tahrir (see Chapter 2), but since the EU-oriented judicial reforms, the authorities have ceased the arrests.[27] Perhaps radical Islam has little attraction for the larger Turkish population. As White observes, though, "Radical Islam in Turkey as inspired by transnational trends died because of a general realization that a shari'ah-based state was not a practicable goal due to state and military resistance, a popular lack of support for Islam in politics, and the recognition that Arab Islam differs from Turkish Islam, which is more individualistic and tolerant."[28] Turkey's public divisions between Islamic and secular continues, with a 2006 survey indicating that while 47 percent of Turks describe themselves as "quite religious," compared to 25 percent in 1999, the number of women wearing headscarves dropped from 53 percent to 49 percent over the same period, and those favoring Islamic rule declined from 21 percent to 9 percent.[29] More of these observant Turks have moved into Turkey's middle class because of economic growth, and, as one report noted, the selection of AKP foreign minister Abdullah Gul as president "will boost Turkey's new political class—modernizers from a religious background."[30]

Turkish identity continues to inspire currents in Turkish politics, as evidenced by passage of Article 301 of the Turkish Penal Code in June 2005. The law criminalizes "insulting Turkishness," and Turkish authorities have used it to punish commentary on Turkish history, particularly on narratives about the Armenian massacre of 1915, convicting, among others, Hrant Dink, editor of the Armenian-language newspaper *Agos* in May 2006.[31] Article 301 may prevent Turkish admission to the European Union; it has drawn widespread condemnation from outside of Turkey (including Amnesty International) as well as from inside. Former President Demirel said that "lifting 301 may lead to confrontation. Illegal paramilitary forces may step in. However, 301 may be amended in a manner that won't offend the people."[32]

The Turkish Executive

Like most parliamentary systems, Turkey has a titular president (Ahmet Necnet Sezer, a secular politician, expected to be replaced by Abdullah Gul, a member of the AKP). Although the power of that office is limited, the president chairs the National Security Council, a powerful body consisting largely of senior military officers, and can veto cabinet nominations and constitutional amendments. The National Assembly elects the president for a seven-year term, though the AKP is maneuvering to change to a direct election, this after Turkey's Constitutional Court annulled the first round of the presidential election in May 2007. Erdoğan then proposed direct presidential elections, with a five-year renewal term, and Sezer vetoed the proposal; parliament passed it again in June 2007. The crisis revealed the growing tension beween Turkey's laicist and religious politics, as the laicist forces tried to hold on to the one element they controlled in national politics.[33]

The Turkish Military in Politics

The Turkish military formed the backbone of the Kemalist movement, and, having sustained Ataturk in power, undertook to guard the Kemalist legacy of secularism. As Candar puts it, "The army, which is the most respected institution of the Turkish state, vigorously defends the republic against what it perceives as imminent threats from Islamic fundamentalism."[34] In this way, the military in Turkey plays a role unlike that in most other Middle Eastern countries, where the military may be the locus of a particular movement (particularly the Baathist movements in countries like Syria) but rarely intervenes to rule as an antidote to Islamic politics.[35]

Turkey's armed forces have several political vehicles for influencing political outcomes. One is the direct assumption of power, which has happened twice in the modern era. The second is a more subtle message of dissatisfaction which, given the military's public status, can often bring about the desired changes. The military also gets considerable attention from the news media, and these sources often quote Turkish senior officers on political matters. The third is through one of the most powerful bodies in contemporary Turkish politics, the National Security Council (NSC). Created in 1961 when the military was in power, NSC saw its power increased in 1983 through the National Security Council Law that the Council of Ministers give "priority consideration" to its recommendations.[36] The military holds five of the ten seats on the NSC, including the chair, but its added authority comes from the definition of national security as including the preservation of the Kemalist heritage; thus almost all aspects of Turkish politics by definition involve the military.[37] Still, as Heper and Guney note, the contemporary Turkish military preferred "to stay on the sidelines and obey political rulers. If they thought they had to come into the picture they preferred the role of arbiter to that of exercising a veto power, and the latter to actual intervention."[38] They have largely played that role on one of Turkey's most controversial issues, joining the European Union, although it puts Turkey's military in the difficult position of both welcoming an official entry into Europe (a Kemalist tradition) and maintaining Turkish stability and security with sometimes undemocratic methods (also a Kemalist tradition).[39]

Turkey's Political Parties

Turkey is one of a few Middle Eastern countries to develop a competitive party system. A combination of republican-secular oriented competitive parties and the necessities of the cold war helped ensure the evolution of a competitive party choice for Turkey's voters after an initial monopoly by the Republican People's Party.[40] Between 1946 and 1960, Turkey had a two-party system, dominated by Ataturk's CHP and the Democratic Party (which later became one of the foundations for the DYP).[41] However, the first military intervention of 1960 ended that system, and multiparty coalitions in parliament became a regular feature of Turkish politics until the election of November 2002 when a single party, the AKP, won an outright majority of seats. Now Turkey's numerous political parties span the ideological gap from right to left and from secular to religious. The more significant parties, their leaders, and the percentage vote received in the November 2002 elections are:

- Democratic Left Party or *Demokratik Sol Parti* (DSP) (Bulent Ecevit); center-left nationalist (1.2 percent)
- Justice and Development Party (*Adalet ve Kalkünma Partisi* or AKP) (Recep Tayyip Erdoğan); moderate Islamist (34 percent)
- Motherland Party or *Anavatan Partisi* (ANAP) (Ali Talip Ozdemir); pro-European orientation (5.1 percent)
- Nationalist Action Party or *Milliyetçi Hareket Partisi* (MHP) (Devlet Bahceli); right-wing nationalist (8 percent)
- Republican People's Party or *Cumhuriyet Halk Partisi* (CHP) (Deniz Baykal); center-left, founded by Ataturk (19.4 percent)
- True Path Party (sometimes translated as Correct Way Party) (*Dogru Yol Partisi*) or DYP (Mehmet Agar) (9.6 percent)
- Young Party or GP (*Cem Uzan*); conservative nationalist (7.2 percent)

Some parties in Turkish politics have risen to prominence only to disappear suddenly. Some change their name, as in the Islamist-oriented Welfare Party, which was abolished by the military and then re-formed, first as the Virtue Party (again banned by the military) and finally as the Justice and Development Party (Turkish law prohibits a religious title for a party). This is part of the dilemma for religiously oriented parties in a country that spans a Kemalist-inspired tradition with a yearning by some to return to a more religious political life. In 1950 only one religious party (the Nation Party, or MP) was able to hold seats in parliament, and only in 1970 did an explicitly religious party, the *Milli Selamet Partisi* (MSP), gain ground by offering a program of rapid industrialization, indicating, as Toprak states, that voters care more about economic than religious issues in Turkey.[42]

Some Turkish parties are little more than vehicles for individual leaders, whose electoral fortunes rise and fall with the fortunes of those leaders. The DSP, whose power is tied to Bulent Ecevit, won the largest percentage of the vote in 1999 but plummeted to a tiny fraction of that vote in 2003 as Ecevit's health and public standing faded.[43] The ANAP was founded by Turgut Ozal as a "middle-class" organization. Although ANAP was already in decline when Ozal died of a heart attack in 1993, and under Ozal's successor, Mesut Yülmaz, ANAP's identity as a party "started to fade, and no new one could be easily established."[44] Even parties that are not direct reflections of their leadership are vulnerable to leadership whims, as in the case of the DYP, which almost evaporated after Tansu Çiller's political miscalculations.[45] Other parties float in Turkey's turbulent political climate, as in the case of the Nationalist Action Party (MHP), which rose in the Ozal liberalization period in the 1980s. This climate gave an opening to Turkey's cleavages that were submerged by Kemalism, and thus an old-line Turkish rightist like Alparslan Turkes shaped the MPH with a rigid nationalistic bent, concentrating on both real and imagined Turkish enemies.[46] The MHP rose from insignificance to gather 18 percent of the vote in the 1999 elections and then dropped again to less than half that in the November 2002 elections. It is possible that the sudden success of the AKP drew voters who only three years before had gravitated to the MHP.

The Turkish Parliament

While Turkish parliamentary tradition dates back to 1876, the modern legislature dates to 1920. It is officially called the *Turkiye Buyuk Millet Meclisi* (Grand National Assembly) and has 550 seats. Under Turkey's most recent constitution of 1982 (superseding the constitutions of 1921, 1924, and 1961), the legislature has the power to enact, change, and repeal laws, to declare war, to supervise the ministers in the executive, and to pass the budget. It also has the power to change the Turkish constitution. The parliament is divided into both party groups and functional committees, including a constitutional committee, a national defense committee, and a human rights committee (seventeen in all). Representatives from political parties constitute the Grand National Assembly, though the constitution limits participation to members of parties that get 10 percent or more of the total vote, a floor twice as high as most other European parliaments. It may be argued that this restriction is designed to keep out the most radical parties, but Turkish law forbids parties from both the extreme left and right, and thus the 10 percent rule may serve to limit the rise of new parties and to stabilize the parliamentary system by avoiding the plethora of parties in Israel that renders the formation of a majority government almost impossible for any duration.

The results of the November 2002 elections gave the AKP 363 seats and the CHP 180 seats, meaning the AKP had a solid majority in the Grand National Assembly, since no other party received the required 10 percent or better of the total vote. That vote translated into the AKP winning 363 seats in the Grand National Assembly, the CHP with 178, and independents holding 9 seats. The CHP probably benefited from being the outsider party as voters rejected those in power, and from the decision of the popular modernizer Kemal Dervi to join the party just before the election.[47]

The election was the first time in twenty-five years that a party gained an outright majority in the Assembly, and thus the AKP did not have to form a coalition. The AKP now has the chance to govern without having to make compromises with other parties to gain a majority on an issue. This gives it considerable leeway to influence policy but also removes the traditional excuse for the largest party that it could not effectively govern because of the need to water down measures to gain the support of other party coalition members.

The Turkish Legal System

With the establishment of the Turkish Republic in 1923, Turkey borrowed heavily from the Swiss system. Turkey's highest court is the Constitutional Court, whose members are appointed by the president. Below the Constitutional Court are the Court of Appeals and the Council of State. The Turkish legal system also features the Court of Jurisdictional Dispute, the Court of Accounts, and the Supreme Council of Judges and Public Prosecutors. The Turkish judiciary is theoretically independent from parliament and the ministries. Although several AKP parliament members repeated the oft heard charge that the judiciary is not independent, little evidence emerged.[48] Given the judicial role in addressing governmental corruption, it is perhaps unsurprising that members of the party in power might charge the judicial branch with being influenced by the parties out of power, as has been the case historically.

The Turkish legal system has drawn criticism from several sources, including Amnesty International, which held that "torture and ill-treatment by law enforcement officials continued to be reported. Reports of torture or ill-treatment of individuals detained for political offences decreased. However, people detained on suspicion of committing ordinary crimes such as theft or for public disorder offences were particularly at risk of ill-treatment."[49] Previous reports were also critical, the Human Rights Association alleging over 500 deaths from torture in 2003, including 44 women.[50] In October 2003, interior minister Addulkadir Aksu argued that Turkey must do more to gain judicial independence for its legal system, to abolish the State Security Courts, and to end the practice of torture.[51]

CIVIL SOCIETY IN TURKEY

Civil society languished in Turkey until the 1990s, when it grew, partly in response to the growth of Islamist political space. A number of Kemalist-oriented groups joined pro-Kurdish groups coming out of hiding in reaction to both political liberalization on the Kurdish issue and fears of the marginalization of traditional secular politics. Other organizations such as the Turkish Industrialist's and Businessmen's Association and the Union of Chambers became more like members of civil society in their growing criticism of the government.[52] However, given the relative newness of civil society as a political entity in Turkey, it is premature to speculate on how effective it is in translating its members' desires into policy or as an alternative vehicle to the existing party system.

The Kurdish Issue

Kurds have lived in Turkey for many centuries. However, during Ottoman times, they were part of a larger Sunni community and not recognized as a distinct minority, as were, for example, Christians and Jews. They gained relative independence in the sixteenth century, when the Ottoman sultan created semiautonomous fiefdoms for them. But the collapse of the Ottoman Empire and the emphasis on Turkish national identity in Kemalist Turkey engendered Kurdish resentment and a series of bloody revolts, particularly in the 1930s. The Democrat Party decade between 1950 and 1960 saw Turkey's Kurdish population enjoy relative freedom, but that ended with the military coup of 1960 and the rise of Kurdish leader Molla Mustafa Barzani. The military coup leaders threatened that "the army would not hesitate to bombard (Kurdish) towns and villages" should Kurdish unrest rekindle. The 1960s and 1970s saw the creation of the Democratic Party of Turkish Kurdistan and the Eastern Revolutionary Cultural Hearths, which formed the core of the PKK.[53] The 1980 military coup brought a crackdown against the Kurds by the military, helping to radicalize the PKK, which by 1984 advocated Kurdish independence and a pan-Kurdish state reaching beyond Turkey to include Kurdish areas in neighboring countries. The Marxist-oriented group, led by Abdullah Ocalan, launched a violent revolution in hopes of creating an independent Kurdistan. It adopted classic insurgent tactics, killing local leaders, teachers, security forces, and Kurds who refused to support PKK objectives. The number of suicide attacks increased dramatically, with many women participants.[54] The Turkish military responded violently against suspected PKK members, and tens of thousands died in the spasms of violence. By 1995, the PKK orientation shifted away from Marxism and demands for a Kurdish independent state. Instead, Ocalan claimed to envision a collection of Kurdish federations with the countries containing significant Kurdish populations: Turkey, Iran, and Iraq.[55] Ocalan moved to Damascus, and Turkey threatened military reprisals against Syria unless they turned Ocalan over to Turkey.

Turkish forces arrested Ocalan in February 1999 in Kenya after Syria finally agreed to evict him, and Turkish television showed pictures of a confused-looking captive sitting between two masked Turkish soldiers, tied up and blindfolded, appearing not to understand that he faced over 400 pages of charges against him.

Turkish policy shifted to a mix of force and compromise after Ocalan's arrest, which led to a cease-fire between Turkey and the PKK (which changed its name to the Kurdish Freedom and Democracy Congress, KADEK, in April 2002). In September 2003, KADEK called off the four-year cease-fire as it rejected a partial amnesty offered by the Erdoğan government. The Ankara government also opened cultural and language doors for Turkey's Kurds as the EU accession talks grew closer, allowing limited Kurdish-language broadcasting and language instruction, although there are signs that this support may be fading.[56]

In November 2003, KADEK announced that it was dissolving as an organization to seek a peaceful settlement with the government, though the Turkish government dismissed the declaration as a ploy to improve the Kurdish image.[57] In 2004, after Kurds charged that Turkey was continuing conflict against Kurds, the PKK reformed, and by 2005, armed clashes between PKK members and the Turkish military resumed in southeastern Turkey.[58] They continued through 2006 as a bloody weekend in April 2006 claimed fifteen lives and many in central Turkey wondered if the violence of the early 1990s was returning.[59]

The Alevis

While they get less public attention than do the Kurds, Turkey's Alevi (see Chapter 2) population may be larger than the Kurdish, at around 25 percent, though the two populations overlap since some Alevi are also Kurdish speakers. The Alevi and the Turkish majority sometimes had a tense relationship, but the Alevi tendency to view religion as a personal choice rather than a state matter helped them embrace Turkish nationalism. As Poyraz notes, "When confronted with Kurdish nationalism, they [Alevi Kurds] tend towards the principle of the nation state."[60]

THE STATUS OF WOMEN IN TURKEY

In 1934 women gained the right to vote and to hold political office, and they have been included in the political system ever since. Other Kemalist changes included abolishing Sharia law, the *hijab,* and polygamy, as well as passing new laws that give women equal opportunity in almost all walks of life. The number of women physicians in Turkey tripled between 1953 and 1970, as did the number of women lawyers.[61] Turkey is one of a handful of countries where a woman has served as state leader (women have also served as head of state or government leader in three other Muslim countries—Pakistan, Bangladesh, and Indonesia). Turkey retained certain laws that benefited men, such as a legal stipulation that men are the head of the family, but those laws were repealed in January 2002, giving Turkish women full legal equality with men some sixty-six years after women won the right to vote. Turkey legalized abortion in 1983, laws against rape and other forms of sexual and domestic violence were stiffened in the 1990s, and the 1982 constitution gives full equality to women. Turkish women serve in the armed forces and may assume combat roles.[62]

As Islamic identity grew in Turkey, so did reaction to the restrictions on public Islamic identity. Headscarves began to reappear as some Turkish women chose to express themselves in ways that were, to some, uniquely Turkish, neither reflecting the image of Iran or Saudi Arabia nor the republican strictures, but instead viewing their headscarves as a public form of liberation.[63]

THE STRUCTURE AND PERFORMANCE
OF THE TURKISH ECONOMY

Turkey's economy has swung dramatically from impressive growth rates to serious recession, high unemployment, and an unstable currency, and back to high growth rates. Turkey's population of just over 70 million has a GDP of around $670 billion for 2007, with a GDP/capita of almost $9,000. The economic growth rate is 5.3 percent, which is clearly an improvement over the laggard years of the 1980s and late 1990s. The GDP/capita places Turkey around the middle of other Middle Eastern countries, below the wealthy Gulf oil-producing countries but above non–oil countries like Egypt or Morocco. Turkey's public debt is 65 percent of Turkish GDP. While Turkey still has a large state economic sector, the private sector has grown dramatically in the past several decades. Some 40 percent of Turkish workers labor in the agricultural sector, which hampers overall economic growth given the slow growth of this sector. Turkey's largest industry is textiles and clothing, where competition from other developing countries has squeezed Turkish access to the international market.

The Turkish economy has historically been the source of turbulence, stagnation, and high inflation—the latter often a product of the Turkish political system that used the economy to boost the popularity of the party or coalition in power. Populist programs to increase economic growth and jobs that appealed to the average Turkish voter did not often have a sound treasury behind them, and inflation would follow, but not before the immediate benefits of the policies (subsidies, tax breaks, new government projects and the like) fell to the ruling groups. High inflation led to a loss of confidence in the Turkish lira, and substitution by other currencies (the US dollar or German deutschmark, for example) became common. Therefore Turks found it cheaper to import goods priced in foreign currency, and Turkish production suffered, further damaging the economy.[64]

Turkey launched an economic reform program in January 2000, attempting a currency reform effort to reduce inflation. The program failed, and the International Monetary Fund had to intervene with a loan as interest rates rose and the Turkish lira fell precipitously.[65] Turkey thus became dependent on international institutions for economic and political stability. While this gave Turkey a sort of economic safety net, it also meant that outside institutions like the IMF shape what used to be sovereign economic decisions.[66] Turkey also reformed the role of the central bank by giving it independence and thus severing it from government control and the cycle of printing money and providing "soft" loans to buy votes before an election.[67] Structural reform also eliminated the weaker banks and encouraged foreign direct investment; as a result, more than 1,200 foreign companies set up shop in Turkey in 2003–2004.[68]

When the AKP won a convincing victory in the 2004 elections, it adopted a relatively populist attitude toward the economy, potentially putting it on a collision course with the IMF. However, facing opposition from Turkish secular politicians (including then-President Sezer), possible problems with EU membership, and burdened with a lack of experience in managing the economy, Erdoğan accepted IMF policies. As Patton notes, "By toeing the IMF line, the AKP's economic policies have been successful in servicing debt, bringing down inflation, and reining in fiscal discipline; however these steps have neither improved income distribution nor addressed the problem of unemployment."[69] How this may affect the future of the AKP remains to be seen, but in other countries, adherence to IMF policies that threatened slower economic growth by curbing regime acceleration policies often meets with popular resistance.

Turkey turned to the United States in hopes that agreement on strategic interests in the region would draw in American economic assistance. However, Turkish hopes for a large loan were dashed when the government refused to allow American and Allied forces to use Turkish bases to launch Operation Iraqi Freedom in March 2003. The Bush administration agreed to a smaller $8.5 billion loan package in September 2003. The news of this loan, along with the appreciation of the Turkish lira against the US dollar (thus lowering Turkish public debt, which is in dollars), gave new life to the Turkish economy.[70] However, while the United States has extended free trade privileges to a few Middle Eastern countries such as Jordan, Morocco, and Bahrain, it refuses to extend such an arrangement to Turkey. Thus items like clothing imported to the United States from Turkey carry a 20 percent duty.[71]

Successful privatization in some sectors helped also, particularly in the airline industry, where Turkish Airlines was one of the few international carriers to show profitability and expand its routes, giving the Turkish economy the additional boost of increased Arab tourism, which in 2003 increased 27 percent over the previous year.[72] However other efforts at privatization met with determined resistance, as in the case of the Tupras oil facilities, where workers recently chased potential private investors away from plant gates in Izmir. That action did not dissuade a London-based investor from arguing that, "if Tupras and the [state-owned] tobacco company can be sold successfully this year, Turkey may be free from financial troubles in 2004," noting the country's stretched 80 percent debt to gross national product ratio.[73]

TURKISH FOREIGN POLICY

Turkey's geographical position alone ensures that foreign policy will be a priority for any Turkish government. Turkey lies astride the waterways linking the Black Sea to the Mediterranean, and thus Russia and Turkey have historically viewed each other with suspicion, which sometimes kindles into war. Turkey and Greece both have historical claims on the small islands lying between them in the Aegean Sea, though most of those claims are now settled. Turkey has land borders with Syria and Iraq, and partially because the Turkish-Iraqi border lies in an area populated by Kurds, it is also a tense area where Turkish troops have often crossed the line between the two countries to ensure that Iraqi Kurds do not offer support to Turkish Kurds.

Ottoman history still plays a role in Turkish foreign policy, as evidenced when Iraq's post–Saddam Hussein government refused Turkey's offer to send peacekeepers to help maintain order. Iraq's new leaders argued that such a move would only rekindle memories of the harsh Ottoman occupation of the lands currently constituting Iraq. The 1915–1916 reports of the massacre of up to 1.5 million Armenians by Ottoman forces still affects Turkish relations with its newly independent neighbor, the Republic of Armenia (and, to an interesting extent, Americans of Armenian descent).[74] The vast outpouring of Turkish sympathy for a murdered Armenian journalist in Istanbul in January 2007 may have been a symbolic indication that Turkey (because senior Turkish officials attended the funeral) wants to mend Turkish-Armenian relations.[75]

After World War II, Turkey quickly retreated from the studied neutralism of its post-Ottoman past. The onset of the cold war quickly engulfed Turkey as the Soviet Union, eager to gain unrestricted access to the Mediterranean from the Black Sea, pressured Turkey in 1946 to agree to Soviet bases in the Dardanelle Straits. That pressure, along with other Soviet moves in the Middle East, ultimately led to the Truman Doctrine of 1947[76] and Turkey's decision to join the North Atlantic Treaty Organization (NATO) in 1952. Turkey has a seat at the NATO table, the only predominantly Muslim nation to be there. Turkey's most significant foreign (and domestic) policy objective is full membership in the European Union, which has continuously raised barriers to Turkish membership since the first application in 1987.[77] These patterns may be changing, though. As Larrabee argues, "The pro-Western elite that has shaped Turkish foreign policy since the end of World War II is gradually being replaced by a more conservative, more religious, and more nationalist elite that is suspicious of the West and has a more positive attitude towards Turkey's Ottoman past."[78] The AKP party elite is a part of this replacement group, and changes in Turkey's foreign policy reflect the new AKP compass.

Turkish foreign policy under the AKP took some unpredictable turns as the new leadership grappled to unify Turkey's historical interests with its moderate Islamist followers. Erdoğan refused to allow the United States to use Turkey as a staging ground for Operation Iraqi Freedom, likely in response to the Turkish public's overwhelming opposition to the United States in Iraq. When the Bush II administration asked Turkey to provide peacekeepers after toppling the Saddam Hussein government, Turkey refused, this time because of Iraqi objections. Some American observers felt that the United States handled the entire affair poorly. "This whole episode has angered and embarrassed Turkey. Three years ago, 60 percent of Turks said America was its best friend. Now that number is down to the teens. This is a fiasco," stated former US Ambassador Richard Holbrooke.[79]

The AKP also appeared eager to continue relations between Turkey and Greece, which had gradually improved after the earthquake diplomacy in 1999. Disputes over islets in the Aegean Sea have largely been resolved and bilateral trade between the two countries now exceeds $1 billion annually.[80] The most significant issue dividing Greece and Turkey today involves the politics of the island of Cyprus (see below).

Turkey imports most of its energy, and Turkish leadership increasingly focuses its attention on the oil and natural gas deposits in the so-called Caspian basin.[81] Since the Caspian basin lacks natural access to the sea, energy pipelines are important to both the producers and consumers. Consequently Turkey worked to build a pipeline to bring Caspian energy into and through Turkey. The pipeline runs through Azerbaijan and Georgia into Turkey, and then to Turkey's Mediterranean port of Ceyhan, thus giving Turkey considerable prominence in the region. To further this relationship, Turkey has reversed the long-standing Kemalist principle of negating pan-Turkism, and increased contacts and, in some cases, given military aid to Kazakhstan and Uzbekistan (predominately Turkic-speaking countries) and expanding trade and economic cooperation with historical rival Russia.[82] Turkey is also expanding and revising its ties to Iran and Syria, long chilled by those countries' support for the PKK.[83]

Given this list of foreign concerns and potential opportunities, Turkey's foreign policy interests have expanded, and Turkey's military capacities have expanded in response.[84] Turkey now has its own modern aircraft facilities capable of producing the American-designed F-16 fighters along with other modernization efforts.[85]

Cyprus

The island of Cyprus, right below Turkey in the Mediterranean, has a mixed population of Turks and Greeks, who lived in relative harmony until the crisis of 1974, when Greece engineered the ouster of Archbishop Makarios III. Believing that Greece organized the coup as a first step in unifying Cyprus with Greece, Turkey sent 30,000 troops to the island. Turkish forces took the northern third of Cyprus before the United Nations brokered a cease-fire and a dividing line between the Republic of Cyprus in the south holding the Greek population and the newly proclaimed Turkish Federated State of Cyprus. Now called the Turkish Republic of North Cyprus (TRNC), the Turkish part is almost entirely subsidized by Turkey, the only country to recognize it as a legal entity. In December 2003, Turkish Cypriots voted on unification but produced a split vote, again delaying a decisive move one way or the other. In May 2004, the Greek Cypriot population voted against unification, sending the issue back to the proverbial drawing board.

Turkey and the European Union

In 1959, Turkey applied for associational membership in the European Common Market (later to become the European Union) and was finally granted this limited membership in 1963. During the next two decades, Turkey pursued an industrial development strategy that precluded trade as a major part of Turkish economic development, and it was thus disinterested in joining the European Union. However, as Turkish economic priorities changed toward increased trade, Turkey applied for full membership in 1987. But Turkey missed the shift in EU priorities, believing that it would reward economic changes like free market reform over political considerations such as rewarding countries like Spain, Portugal, and Greece for their efforts to stabilize democracy.[86] Turkey did gain the Customs Union Agreement in 1995 that opened the Turkish market to European companies, but the Turkish aspirations for full membership were dashed again in 1997.

After the AKP won the elections in November 2002, Erdoğan reiterated his commitment to Turkish EU membership. But at Copenhagen the next month, Turkey's bid was rejected, amid promises to reopen the membership question in 2004. Erdoğan traveled to Copenhagen in December 2002 (even before his status as prime minister was official) and bluntly criticized EU members at the annual meeting for holding anti-Islamic views. He also threatened that Turkey might petition to join the North American Free Trade Agreement (NAFTA) if rejected for EU membership again.[87] In turn, the EU rejection cited the Copenhagen criteria as the benchmark that it claimed Turkey still failed to meet, including the full legislative adoption of all EU legislation and regulation and a reduction of the role of the Turkish military in Turkish politics, to include the abolition of the National Security Council.[88] In Cizre's words, the Turkish military "produced an ever-growing void between Europe and Turkey."[89] The European Union is also troubled by the military power on the NSC, leading to speculation that a civilian chair might emerge just before the EU vote on Turkey.[90]

There were several other reasons for the rejection, according to Robins, including a poor Turkish negotiating effort, a heavy-handed American effort to get Turkey into the European Union in exchange for Turkish support for the US attack on Iraq, and missed signals on Turkish cooperation on EU defense issues.[91] It is also significant that the European membership of the EU fears that hundreds of thousands of Turkish workers will migrate north to their countries to take jobs, joining the already 11–12 million Muslims living in Europe whose assimilation into European culture is, at best, incomplete.[92] Moreover, even though Turkey belongs to many European organizations, some Europeans argue that Turkish culture is too Islamic to allow Turkey to qualify in Europe's most significant political organization.[93] As signs of further rejection continued (a report from the European Parliament again claiming that Turkey "has not done enough" in political reform areas, for example), many Turks wondered if they would ever be "European enough" to win EU admission.[94] Said the prime minister in May 2004, "If the EU does not want to be viewed as a union of geography, or as a Christian club, they have to give us a date."[95] In December 2004, Turkey got that invitation, though it came with strings: strict EU monitoring of Turkey and threats to restrict Turkish farm products and workers from Europe even if Turkey did gain EU membership.[96] For Turkish leadership and the Turkish population, gaining admission to the European Union reaffirms Turkey's very identity as a European nation-state, and the issue will continue to dominate Turkish headlines until it is resolved in Turkey's favor. However, rising nationalism and the long delays have soured many Turks on EU membership, with support dropping from the 60 percent range to the low 50s, and now more Turkish citizens believe that Turkey should stop asking and wait for the European Union to ask Turkey to join.[97]

Turkish-Israeli Relations

No strategic partnership for Turkey has drawn more political heat than its relationship with Israel. The cooperation began in 1991 when Turkey exchanged ambassadors with Israel and grew to include military cooperation, intelligence sharing, and defense industrial cooperation. Arab countries have strongly criticized the partnership, but, as Israeli scholar Efraim Inbar notes, "The two countries share similar regional concerns regarding Syria, the proliferation of weapons of mass destruction. . . the challenges of Islamic radicalism, concerns over potentially aggressive policies from Iran or Iraq, and the geopolitical destiny of Central Asia. At the global level, they display a strong pro-American orientation, have a problematic relationship with Europe, and are suspicious of Russian schemes."[98] In another move that indicated that relations with Israel continue after the election of the AKP, Israel announced that it was planning to buy 15 million cubic meters of water per year from Turkey, and that it had future plans to purchase natural gas and electricity from Turkey as well.[99] Turkey did not comment then, but in 2007 announced plans to build such a network of pipelines for gas, oil, and water to Israel.[100]

Turkey and Iraq after 2003

Turkish leaders received the chairman of the Governing Council of Iraq, Ahmed Chalabi, in September 2003 to ask for a contingent of no more than 10,000 Turkish peacekeeping troops to be stationed in the western parts of Iraq. In October 2003, Prime Minister Erdoğan announced that Turkish troops would deploy to Iraq, making Turkey the first Muslim nation to contribute troops. However, the plan drew opposition from members of parliament and the public, as polls showed more than 64 percent opposition to sending Turkish soldiers to Iraq.[101] Apparently the cabinet agreed to the move after the United States reportedly promised Turkey that it would remove the threat of PKK resurgence in northern Iraq, although the United States provided no details about its exact plans for doing so.[102] By mid-2005, Turkey demanded the right to send troops to Iraq to combat PKK forces there, but the United States refused, and Turkish public opinion soured considerably toward the United States. A June 2005 poll of AKP voters revealed that 72 percent considered themselves anti-American.[103] A July 2005 poll that asked Turks to distinguish between "America" and "George W. Bush" found that while 71 percent of respondents did not trust Bush, only 16 claimed that they were "opposed to the United States in every respect."[104]

Turkey's main influence in the modern Middle East came from Ottoman times when Turkey, as the capital of that empire, exercised tremendous political, economic, and cultural influence over a region stretching from the eastern Arabian Peninsula to modern Algeria. Turkey's political and economic influence diminished as Turkey turned to the West in the twentieth century. As one small indicator, nightlife in Ankara and especially Istanbul is more like Madrid or Paris or Rome than, say, Amman or especially Jeddah. However, the civilization the Ottomans left remains visible through much of the Arab world, as the Turkish-inspired pencil-shaped minarets that dot the skyline in Damascus, Turkey's southern neighbor, clearly attest.

SUGGESTED READINGS

Barkey, Henri J., and Graham E. Fuller. *Turkey's Kurdish Question*. Lanham, MD: Rowman & Littlefield, 1998.

Cinar, Alev. *Modernity, Islam, and Secularism in Turkey: Bodies, Places, and Time*. Minneapolis: University of Minnesota Press, 2005.

Howard, Douglas. *The History of Turkey*. Westport, CT: Greenwood, 2001.

Ibrahim, Ferhad, and Gülistan Gürbey, eds. *The Kurdish Conflict in Turkey: Obstacles and Chances for Peace and Democracy*. New York: St. Martin's, 2000.

Kedourie, Sylvia. *Turkey Before and After Ataturk: Internal and External Affairs*. Portland, OR: Frank Cass, 1999.

Larrabee, F. Stephen, and Ian O. Lesser. *Turkish Foreign Policy in an Age of Uncertainty*. Santa Monica, CA: RAND Corporation, 2003.

Lewis, Bernard. *The Emergence of Modern Turkey*. 3rd ed. New York: Oxford University Press, 2002.

Martin, Lenore G., and Demitris Keridis, eds. *The Future of Turkish Foreign Policy*. Cambridge, MA: MIT Press, 2004.

Ozbudun, Ergun. *Contemporary Turkish Politics: Challenges to Democratic Consolidation*. Boulder, CO: Lynne Rienner, 2000.

Robins, Philip. *Suits and Uniforms: Turkish Foreign Policy Since the Cold War*. Seattle: University of Washington Press, 2003.

Rubin, Barry, and Metin Heper. *Political Parties in Turkey*. Portland, OR: Frank Cass, 2002.

White, Jenny B. *Islamist Mobilization in Turkey: A Study in Vernacular Politics*. Seattle: University of Washington Press, 2002.

Yavuz, M. Hakan. *Islamic Political Identity in Turkey*. New York: Oxford University Press, 2003.

_____. *The Emergence of a New Turkey: Democracy and the AK Party*. Salt Lake City: University of Utah Press, 2006.

12

SYRIA

The first things to appear are the minarets, deep blue in the afternoon sun. The streets are clogged with cars, dusty overland buses, and pedestrians, all seemingly drawn to this place. Nearing the shrine, the dome comes into view and then the gates, in varying shades of color, from azure to robin's egg blue. Islamic designs in careful tracery decorate the tiles. Through the entrance is a vast prayer hall with a lace-covered cenotaph in the center. Light streams through the windows onto the seated worshipers, most of them women, who speak quietly in Persian as they grip the wrought-iron gates around the cenotaph.

This is the tomb of Zaynab bint Ali, the granddaughter of the Prophet Muhammad and the sister of Hussein ibn Ali. She was one of the few to survive the slaughter of Shiites at Karbala in 680 CE, throwing herself on the frail son of Hussein Ali and thus saving his life. She would die later, accidentally, at the hands of a farmer. In his remorse, the farmer started constructing the shrine that has become a magnet for Shiites throughout the Middle East. They come from Iraq, Bahrain, and Egypt. Many of the dusty buses parked outside have "Tehran" on their license plates.

Remarkably, this site is in Syria, perhaps the most secular of all Middle East countries, where the Shiites are probably around 5 percent or less of Syria's total population. Call it religious tolerance, or commercial crassness, or the ruling al-Asad family's effort to embrace a community of which they claim to be a part. But whatever the reason, the fact that the secular Baathist regime allows and supports this particularly holy Shiite site says much about religious forbearance in Syria.

NEAR THE ANCIENT UMAYYAD MOSQUE in Damascus it is possible to walk into neighborhoods that appear untouched by time since, say, the eighth century. Narrow lanes meander past earthen-colored buildings and tiny courtyards where the laughter of children seems to echo from the distant past. The clamor of business in the old Hamidiyya souq and the pungent scent of exotic spices seem to underscore the word "oriental." Damascus is the world's oldest continuously inhabited city. It at once underscores the city's irresistible charm and Syria's modern problems.

Syria lies in the center of the Levant, sharing borders with Turkey, Iraq, and Lebanon, as well as Israeli-occupied Golan, as shown on Map 12.1 on page 278.

THE MODERN HISTORY OF SYRIA

The modern country of Syria dates back to the collapse of the Ottoman Empire in 1919 (see Chapter 1). Faisal Hussein captured Damascus near the end of the war and declared himself the king of Syria and Lebanon. However, the British abandoned him when they signed the Anglo-French Declaration in 1919, thus turning Syria over to France. Faisal, under pressure from Arab nationalists in Damascus, tried to negotiate independence from France, signing an agreement with French Premier Georges Clemenceau granting France the right to provide for Syrian security and foreign policy and to house a high commissioner in Aleppo as the representative of the Mandatory power.[1] Faisal, himself an outsider in Syria, tried to rally Syrian citizens to the flag of Arab nationalism, organizing large rallies and supporting mass movements supporting both the Arab cause and his role as its Syrian leader.[2]

At the 1920 San Remo Conference, France and Britain divided the area, giving Syria and Lebanon to France and Palestine to Britain. In July, French troops invaded Syria and by August had established a puppet regime in Damascus. French policy favored the rural elites and Christian religious minorities, and along with Faisal's efforts to stimulate Syrian nationalism initiated the Great Revolt of 1925–1927. The uprising began in the Druze area in southern Syria and spread to the cities, and the French responded with massive artillery and bombing campaigns against civilian areas, killing thousands. The French finally quelled the revolt, but nationalist feelings continued to simmer.[3]

Other French actions also fueled Syrian nationalism. In 1922, France carved Lebanon out of Syria and made it a separate country, purportedly to protect the Maronite Christians there, who had ties to France since at least 1648. In 1939, the French cut off Hatay province on the northern part of the Syrian coast and gave it to Turkey, partially to encourage Turkey to remain neutral in Europe.

Syria Gains Independence

France granted Syria formal independence in 1941, and Shukri al-Quwwatli assumed the presidency two years later. But the real power fell to Jamil Mardam Bey, a Syrian nationalist who became Syria's premier and defense minister in 1947. He introduced a number of governmental reforms in an effort to build a Syrian political structure free from French influence.[4]

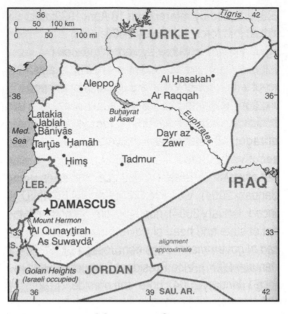

MAP 12.1   SYRIA

The French left no real political structure for Syrians to build upon after independence. Most political power resided with a small wealthy elite who owned land and businesses, and who had benefited from French favors. In 1946, members of this elite formed the National Bloc, which split into industrial and agricultural interests a year later. The Syrian People's Party formed around Aleppo, Syria's second largest city. Its power base was Aleppo's merchants and landowners, reflecting Aleppo's traditional rivalry with Damascus. The National Party formed in Damascus, led by that city's economic elite. Both parties had considerable resources but no broad base of support, despite controlling the parliament and its leaders. Largely left out were Syria's peasants, small business owners, and the military. The Syrian system has not changed appreciably since that time.

A third party movement began around this time, aimed largely at this excluded population. The Baath (meaning "renaissance" in Arabic) Party represented the ideas of two Damascus educators, Michel Aflaq and Salah al-Din Bitar. Aflaq was a Christian, while Bitar was a Sunni Muslim. Both had studied in Europe and absorbed the ideas of Mussolini on fascism and Lenin on revolution. The Baathist movement was the result of this fusion. Inspired by Italian fascist hopes for a restored Roman Empire, Baathist nationalism combined Arab nationalism with a strong political party (from Lenin) to mobilize national resources. The memory inspiring it was the Arab Umayyad and Abbasid caliphates. The nationalist impulse was from Europe and typified the thinking of the time that rejected religion as a basis of unification and progress.[5]

In 1944, the Baath Party formed along the ideas of Aflaq and Bitar, and its first party congress in 1947 saw both Aflaq and Bitar elected to senior party positions. The party grew slowly in these years, still trying to sort out its belief system. However, events would soon help its rise to prominence.

The 1948 war represented the first test for the new Syrian army. Syrian President Shukri al-Quwwatli defined the threat of a Hashemite "greater Syria" led by Jordan's King Hussein as greater than the threat from Israel. Thus the Syrian military, which was disloyal to al-Quwwatli, did not fight in coordination with the other Arab armies, and the overall result was an Arab defeat.[6] Partly in response, Gen. Husni al-Zaim launched a military coup against the government in early 1949, ousting al-Quwwatli as president. Zaim gained considerable support for the action because the civilian regime had performed poorly both economically and militarily in the 1948 war against Israel. Zaim rebuilt the Syrian military into a political force and tried to introduce progressive political reform, even giving literate women the right to vote.[7] However, his efforts failed to prevent his overthrow in a coup in December 1949 led by Lt. Col. Adib al-Shishakli.

During this time, the Baath Party grew and other new parties appeared amid mounting political chaos.[8] One was the Syrian Social Nationalist Party (with strong fascist leanings), the Arab Socialist Party, and the Syrian Communist Party. The Arab Socialist Party joined forces with the Baath Party in 1953, and the two parties eclipsed the Syrian Social Nationalist Party after one of its followers assassinated a leading Baathist official. In 1957, the Baath merged briefly with the Communist Party and in 1958, the Baath concluded a political union with Egypt, apparently hoping that Egyptian President Nasser would eliminate the Syrian Communist Party as a political force, as he had done with Egyptian Communists. The ploy succeeded, resulting in the creation of the United Arab Republic (UAR). However, Nasser also clipped Syrian Baathist power in the arrangement, and the rise of Egyptian power in Syria led to a 1961 Syrian military coup to end the relationship. The UAR experiment greatly weakened the nationalist and socialist parties in Syria, and the People's Party and the National Party grew again in power. A December 1961 election gave both parties control of the National Assembly, and People's Party head Nazim al-Qudsi gained the presidency.

Once conservative parties brought the urban and rural elites back into power, however, Nasser's authoritarian leadership in the UAR discredited mainstream Baathists and allowed new actors to come to power. That group came primarily from the military, which organized a secret military committee that opposed Syria's incorporation with Egypt. These senior military officers launched a coup in 1963 that toppled both the Qudsi presidency and the UAR. Hafiz al-Asad, a young Alawi air force officer, served on the military committee and used that post to rise to power.[9]

The Baathist plotters first installed Salah al-Din Bitar as Syria's new president. However, the Baath membership had moved far to the left of Bitar, and his rule ended three years later. Both he and cofounder Michel Aflaq were expelled from the party and from Syria, and Salah Jadid took over as chief of state.[10]

The disastrous consequences of the 1967 war with Israel challenged Baath power (see Chapter 1) and political rivals criticized al-Asad, the minister of defense at the time, for the debacle. He survived politically and began to scheme against Jadid. With the help of his brother, Rifat, Hafiz al-Asad had Jadid arrested and confined to a long prison term. In November 1970, Hafiz al-Asad took power as president of Syria.

As the member of a small and suspect religious minority, al-Asad realized that he needed to legitimize his standing as a Muslim in a predominately Muslim nation. He initially tried to reduce the role of Islam in Syria by eliminating references to it in the draft 1973 constitution. However, this decision provoked demonstrations in several Syrian cities, and in response, al-Asad turned to Musa al-Sadr, who was then head of the Higher Shiite Council in Lebanon. Musa al-Sadr overlooked the Alawi veneration of Ali and issued a *fatwa* that the Alawi were a genuine form of Shiite Islam.[11]

To expand his power base, al-Asad created the National Progressive Front in 1972, bringing in the remnants of the Syrian Communist Party, the Syrian Arab Socialist Union, and several other smaller leftist groups. Al-Asad also reached beyond the political party structure to expand his influence, advancing both Sunni Muslim and Christian officers to high positions in the military. He made peace with Syria's Christian leadership and tried to broker good relations with Syria's Kurds. Al-Asad also attempted to win the loyalties of the peasants from the old elites through a system of land reform, making the peasants dependent on the state instead of the rural landowners.[12] Al-Asad also made sure that Syria had virtual control of Lebanese politics, reinforcing his nationalist claims that Lebanon was actually a part of Syria.

Domestic groups rarely challenged Syria's secular Baathist rule with the significant exception of the Muslim Brotherhood revolt in the early 1980s. Following a failed assassination attempt against al-Asad in June 1980, Baathist forces allegedly massacred Muslim Brotherhood prisoners in Palmyra. Undeterred, the Muslim Brothers formed a broader Islamic Front in Syria, inspired partially by a desire to expand Islam into the Syrian political structure. The Islamic Front in Syria launched a series of bombings and assassinations against Baath officials, and the Baath responded by attacking the Islamic Front's stronghold city of Hama in February 1982, killing somewhere between 5,000 and 25,000 people by simply leveling parts of the city with military firepower.[13] That operation almost eliminated Islamist opposition to the Baath, even more than twenty-five years later.

Hafiz al-Asad died in June 2000, and his son Bashar succeeded him after the parliament amended the Syrian constitution to lower the age eligibility for president from forty to thirty-four, Bashar's age.[14] Bashar was disinterested in politics, preferring to practice medicine in London, but Hafiz al-Asad's oldest son Basil, the designated successor, had died in a car crash in 1993.[15] In July 2000, Bashar received around 97 percent of the vote in a referendum election to replace his father as president of Syria. Bashar al-Asad opened his presidency with calls for both economic and political reform, but after the arrest of critics, the hoped-for Damascus spring became quiet. The only disruption to a quiet, stagnant rule came in April 2004 when police apparently squelched a terrorist attack in the Mazza district of Damascus, which followed a spate of violence in Syria's Kurdish north. In June, the Baath Party banned all other political parties and associations, including Kurdish political associations (see below).[16] It was a clear indicator that Syria was hardly ready to open its closed political system despite the hopes of Syrian reformers. The assassination of former Lebanese Prime Minister Rafik Hariri in February 2005 caused ripples in Damascus (see Chapter 13). The reported suicide of Gen. Ghazi Kanaan, the interior minister, in October 2005 only clouded the Harari investigation, as he had been in charge of intelligence in Lebanon from the 1980s until 2003, and presumably had information of interest to UN investigators, who had interviewed him.[17] As the possibility of US force against Syria grew after the UN report fingered high-ranking Syrian officials (including Bashar al-Asad's brother-in-law) as responsible for the Lebanese bombing, Syrians gathered in the streets of Damascus to rally against the United States, with a fervor reminiscent of their 1920 support for the Arab nationalism of Faisal.[18]

THE SYRIAN POLITICAL SYSTEM

The Baath Party dominates Syrian politics. It is officially secular, retaining the mantle of Arab nationalism, the only such bastion since the ouster of Saddam Hussein. Hafiz al-Asad banned religious symbols (including women's headscarves) and forbade soldiers from praying in mosques (measures his son Bashar rescinded after assuming office). While the Baath tolerate religious observance, all faiths are limited from political participation.

The Baath regional command directs the party from the top, with twenty-one members, including party representatives from Aleppo and Hama. Hafiz al-Asad wanted representatives from these two cities in particular to be at the center since Aleppo and Hama were traditional centers of opposition and whoever was in power in Damascus. Baathist influence in local areas was further increased in 1980 by the creation of the Central Committee, made up of representatives from counties, districts, and towns across Syria. While power rested largely within the regional command, the Central Committee members were links to the far corners of the country, and thus could be mobilized to extend Baathist influence. Freedom House considers Syria "not free."

Baath Party leaders are all al-Asad loyalists, transferring their loyalty from Hafiz to his son Bashar. Baathist newspapers are the only public source of information, and Baathist public affairs outlets—radio, television, magazines, and such—poured out a steady stream of effusive praise for al-Asad and his top lieutenants. Portraits and statues of al-Asad dot Syria, often executed in the stark socialist realism school, with a smiling leader walking among his adoring followers.[19]

The al-Asad family was at the top of the power structure through the 1990s. Hafiz's younger brother Rifat commanded the Defense Companies, an elite military force responsible for internal security. His older brother Jamil also commanded a paramilitary group. However, in the 1980s Jamil and Rifat fell out of favor when they challenged the president for power. Rifat was accused of trying to launch a coup when the president's health failed in 1982.

In addition to Bashar, other sons and daughters of Hafiz al-Asad remain influential. Bashar's sister Bushra married Asef Shawkat, who became head of Syrian intelligence and was implicated in the Hariri murder. Bashar's younger brother Maher is also highly influential in Baath politics.[20] He serves as the effective head of the Republican Guard, along with the son of former Defense Minister Mustafa Tlass.

The Baath Party reaches into all areas of Syria. It sponsors training camps for young Syrians to indoctrinate them into the Baathist organization. It has party branches everywhere, particularly in rural areas where the Peasants Federation brings in members and in the schools. The peasant base is vital for the Baath, and conditions for peasants have generally improved under Baathist rule.[21] Universities have strong Baathist ties, particularly at the Universities of Damascus and Aleppo.

The Baathist leadership typifies al-Asad's penchant for bringing in others from outside his family circle to solidify his party's rule. Since Sunnis make up almost three-quarters of Syria's population, it is hardly surprising that al-Asad picks leaders from the Sunni ranks to guide Syrian policy. However, al-Asad also brings in members of the unorthodox Islamic sects like the Druze and the Ismaili. Even Kurds, treated as enemies by most other Middle Eastern countries, received protection under al-Asad, though the relationship has deteriorated in the last few years.

As Bashar al-Asad settled into the job of presidency, there was some evidence that he might expand Syrian political space. For example, the Baath under Bashar al-Asad discussed allowing the National Progressive Front to engage in limited activity, to include the publication of NPF newspapers.[22] Al-Asad also allowed the Syrian Social Nationalist Party to hold a plenary meeting, its first since it was banned in 1955, though the government stopped short of allowing the party to compete in elections.[23] The state-owned media briefly published mild criticism of domestic policy, but denigration of Syrian foreign policy remained nonexistent.[24] Bashar al-Asad put definite limits on expression. In February 2001 he sharply criticized dissidents and limited political forums that might criticize the regime.[25] The government apparently went so far as to arrest a group of activists trying to discourage Syrians from smoking cigarettes.[26] However, either the apparent growth of Islamic identity after the downfall of the Saddam Hussein regime signals a new openness by the Baath, or it was orchestrated by Bashar al-Asad as a way to energize the population in light of the languid response of most Iraqis to the American attack of 2003. "This is an attempt at mobilization," noted one Syrian writer, but others saw it as a reflection of al-Asad's inability to improve on the inefficient regime he inherited from his father.[27] Some in Syria argue that Bashar allows family members or close friends to control immense business empires and challenges any effort at economic reform that would break their economic power.[28]

How this will develop over the long run is not clear, but it does appear that Bashar al-Asad is more than just a "correctionalist" who believes that while his father made a few mistakes, continuity is most important. He appears to fall into a group of "reformers" who emphasize reform and technological communications as symbols of modernization and globalization.[29] He also vacillates between control and reform, first emphasizing limited reform after his assumption of the presidency, only to veer to control again a year later. For example, Bashar al-Asad pushed the appearance of reform in 2005 after the Lebanon fiasco, but then reverted to control a year later, arresting human rights activists and closing an EU human rights center. There was also a new religious emphasis (appointing a religious leader instead of a secular Baathist to head the Religious Ministry), as former Vice President Khaddam became a threat to Bashar al-Asad by courting the banned Muslim Brotherhood.[30]

The Syrian Executive

In an effort to liberalize the Syrian economy, President Bashar al-Asad shifted membership in the cabinet several times. In December 2001, he replaced his prime minister, choosing Mustafa Mira in the hope that Mira would find ways to energize economic modernization. Bashar al-Asad chose Muhammad al-Imadi as minister of economy and foreign trade, a major supporter of economic liberalization. However, Syria's economic growth continued to disappoint, and in February 2002 al-Asad replaced Imadi with Ghassan al-Refae, previously an adviser to the Bank for the Middle East. In October 2004, al-Asad again changed cabinet membership, with Muhammad Naji Itri becoming prime minister and Muhammad al-Hussein appointed as finance minister. The problem was that al-Asad did not show willingness to make dramatic changes like significant privatization or a sound banking system or currency reform, but instead chose to buy time by shuffling ministers. In 2006, al-Asad again changed his cabinet, replacing Foreign Minister Farouk al-Shara, elevated to vice president, with Walid Muallem and elevating Fuad Issa Joni as minister of industry, along with ten other new appointments. As one report noted about the governmental crisis, "The crisis has highlighted how Mr. Assad's efforts to bring young, forward-looking technocrats into the government have largely failed, and how isolated Syria has become. And it has demonstrated, perhaps most disturbingly to many younger, reform-minded Syrians, how tone-deaf the leadership can be."[31] In May 2007, Bashar al-Asad ran unopposed in a national referendum for another seven-year term.

The Syrian Legislature

The People's Council, or *Majlis al-Shaab,* consists of 250 members, elected by popular vote and serving for four years. The dominant party structure in the People's Council is the National Progressive Front (NPF). This coalition includes the ruling Arab Socialist Renaissance (Baath) Party, the Syrian Arab Socialist Party, the Arab Socialist Union, Syrian Communist Party, the Arab Socialist Unionist Party, and the Socialist Union Democratic Party (headed by Ahmad al-al-Asad). Since Bashar al-Asad is both secretary-general of the Baath party and chairman of the National Progressive Front, it is apparent that what appears to be a multiparty system is in reality controlled by the Baath.

The Syrian Judiciary

The court system in Syria begins with the State Security Courts and continues through the Court of Cassation, the High Judicial Council, and the Supreme Constitutional Court. The president appoints members of these courts for four-year terms, and thus judicial independence is rare. The laws stem from both religious and civil traditions, but most religious matters are referred to special religious courts.

Human rights groups have long criticized Syria for the judicial process it follows, and crimes against the state include political criticism and dissention. Political prisoners were long held in detention without trial or legal representation. In November 2000, President Bashar al-Asad pardoned over 600 political prisoners, suggesting a relaxation of regime pressures against nonviolent dissent.[32] Yet apparently torture and other forms of prisoner abuse continue to exist in Syria, and even the United States and Canada may have taken advantage of this when a Syrian-born Canadian citizen was turned over to Syria to allow the Syrians to extract information from him through torture.[33] Syrian authorities also stand accused by human rights groups of arresting the wives of suspected members of the Islamist group Jund al-Sham when the members themselves eluded arrest.[34]

CIVIL SOCIETY IN SYRIA

Baathist rule allows for the existence of civil society. Hafiz al-Asad's balancing act was to allow such things as unions (which occasionally challenge state ministries) and to avoid control of the economy so that independent merchants and artisans could enjoy a certain autonomy; this limited autonomy continues under Bashar al-Asad.[35] With the exception of the crackdown on Islamic extremism, Hafiz al-Asad allowed civil society to serve as a kind of escape valve for political pressure, though there were clear limits on what would be tolerated. After Hafiz al-Asad died, civil society underwent a brief resurgence, with civil society groups springing up in Damascus and elsewhere and the licensing of Syria's first private newspaper. By the fall of 2001, however, the regime clamped down, apparently influenced by former Vice President Khaddam, and the arrest of prominent civil society activists dampened the movement.[36] By 2005, civil society reappeared, perhaps because of Khaddam's resignation, but also possibly inspired by Lebanon's Cedar Revolution (see Chapter 13). In October of that year, a dozen political groups that had been at odds with each other united to sign the so-called Damascus Declaration demanding greater political freedom and an end to political repression.[37] But Damascus Spring was followed by "Damascus Winter," with the regime shutting down almost all civil society organizations. Still, as Landis and Pace argue, a coalition of Islamists, Kurdish activists, and leftists united under a demand for democratic change, and such a force can become a viable opposition if the regime does not eliminate it through force.[38]

Still, civil society in Syria has not acquired the influence that it has in some Arab countries, but under Bashar al-Asad, the Syrian political system seems willing to accept a legitimate role for civil society, particularly now that his wife, Asma, heads a civil society group.[39]

THE STATUS OF WOMEN IN SYRIA

Syria is officially a sectarian state under Baathist rule that minimizes the role of religion in politics. Consequently there is no official pressure on women to abide by a conservative Islamist interpretation of their societal role. The electoral law of 1949 granted the voting franchise to women as well as men, the first time in the Arab world that women got the right to vote.[40] Women are not restricted as to dress and general interactions with men. Syrian women drive automobiles and work in a variety of jobs. Women in Syria have made progress in advancing through the Syrian political system, with 25 women holding seats out of 250 total in the Syrian parliament, which is second only to Morocco as a percentage of women holding parliamentary memberships. In the Syrian cabinet, women hold the positions of social affairs and labor, out of thirty-one total cabinet posts.

The impact of Islam and its practices is not absent in Syria. There is gender segregation in ways not found in the West. While women and men sit in the same university classrooms, for example, the women group on one side of the room and the men on another. A majority of women wear the *hijab,* though the practice is not universal. A majority of young women are encouraged to marry men their parents approve of, and arranged marriages are common. Many women may not object to such decisions, though, as a growing number of Syrian women are becoming vanguards in Islamic revival. Syrian women are forming what are known as Qubaisiates, or secret Islamic societies, where members study the Quran and other Islamic traditions, partly in hopes of influencing the men in their families to embrace Islamic traditions.[41]

Political discourse about women was noticeably absent in Syria until several years ago, when the subject of honor killings surfaced. A 2006 UN study revealed that around a fourth of Syrian married women were beaten by their spouses, but, according to one advocate, there were few remedies available. "As it is now, there are still no mechanisms to report violence against women," said Abdul Salam. "We hope that this study will soon lead to practical action on the ground."[42]

THE STRUCTURE AND PERFORMANCE OF THE SYRIAN ECONOMY

Baathist Syria featured an economy modeled roughly after that of the former Soviet Union, with a large state sector in agriculture and manufacturing. Small business also makes up a significant portion of the Syrian economy. Under Bashar al-Asad, privatization evolved at a slow pace. Syria's roughly 18 million people have a per capita GDP of around $4,000, with an 8 percent unemployment rate.

As in many Middle Eastern countries, Syria's population growth necessitates both new jobs and more education. Syria had one of the highest levels of population growth in the world for years, and this contributes to endemic unemployment as the bulge of young people reaches employment age in a country where there are not enough resources to create adequate jobs.[43] By one estimate, Syria will have to create at least 300,000 new jobs a year and sustain an average annual growth rate of 7 percent just to sustain the present level of employment.[44]

During the 1970s, investment flowed into plants that depended on imported raw materials, and Syria lacked the expertise to run them.[45] Syrian agricultural development favored middle-class farmers rather than peasants, thus contributing to unemployment in the country.[46] There was some progress; according to Lawson, the Syrian balance of trade moved into the black after the European Community rescinded its 1986 ban on economic assistance and advanced a $200 million loan arrangement.[47] The Syrian gross domestic product rose by around 6 percent, and inflation dropped from 70 to 40 percent.[48] Syria also enjoyed a period of economic growth after its participation in the Iraqi operation of 1990–1991, as the Gulf oil-producing countries rewarded Syria with roughly $2–3 billion. Syrian oil sales also helped, and Syria profited on Iraqi oil that ran in a pipeline through Syria. Although limited oil reserves in Syria are running out, Syria does have around 240 billion cubic meters of natural gas, but, as one analyst notes, "rent income from oil or gas will only buy time."[49] Reforms are still needed to reduce the role of state economic planning and the poor policymaking that led to a lost decade of development. Kiernam indicates that Syria's economic growth rate for 1995 was 6.9 percent, 2.2 percent in 1996, 0.5 percent in 1997, and –1.5 percent in 1998.[50]

To complicate matters further, the United States imposed trade sanctions against Syria in May 2004 in response to charges that Syria supported groups linked to terrorism. While Syrian-American trade was never significant, even a small reduction in Syrian foreign trade was a problem for a struggling economy. In January 2005, the United States threatened further sanctions, including prohibitions on US firms dealing with Syrian banks, unless Syria clamped down on former associates of Saddam Hussein who were allegedly raising terrorist-related funds in Syria.[51]

Syria's 2005 withdrawal from Lebanon may also hurt Syria's economy. Lebanon employed large numbers of Syrian workers, possibly over 300,000, which both alleviated Syrian unemployment and remitted around $12 million per day back to Syria.[52]

Privatization

In May 1991, Syrian leadership announced Law 10, which was intended to privatize much of Syria's economy. The hope was that the estimated $60 billion in savings Syrians had banked abroad would return. However, little of that money has returned to Syria, and there is very little foreign investment there. Part of the problem is that few follow-up reforms have come after Law 10, such as currency reform and renovation of the highly inefficient and undercapitalized banking system.[53] The lack of a stock market also limits capital for business ventures. Moreover, there are no private banks in Syria, which inhibits new investments. Law 10 has also failed to privatize the large state-managed enterprises making steel, cement, and other products. These enterprises are important sources of employment, and to either privatize them or allow them to compete with new private enterprises would inevitably result in large-scale layoffs. Moreover, implementation of Law 10, if successful, might bring in large multinational firms whose activities might drive the smaller business owners, one pillar of the al-Asad regime's support, out of existence.[54] Finally, privatization threatens the existing economic order, dominated by the top managers in the public sector, the small entrepreneurial class, and the security and military elite who protect them. This group enriched itself through corruption during the elder al-Asad's rule, and it will be resistant to any change that threatens its status.[55] So parts of the state sector remain operative, and, in some cases, expanding. The Ministry of Industry announced that for the first time, Syria would produce an automobile in partnership with Iran. The Sham started production in March 2007, built by the state's General Institution for Engineering Industries, despite the fact that Syria had no automobile building experience in a global market dominated by better established auto producers.[56]

Bashar al-Asad has called for greater Internet connectivity, stating that soon "the internet is going to enter every house."[57] In April 2000, Syria liberalized rules against the possession of foreign currency, relaxed rules governing business, and announced plans for investment by two cellular telephone companies to invest in a pilot telephone project.[58] That was a start into the modern global era, but Syria still has a way to go. While there has been growing pressure since Hafiz's death to liberalize the economy, Bashar al-Asad is unlikely to engage in it. He is particularly unlikely to privatize the major public sector assets, since to do so might cause social unrest because of the resulting unemployment.[59]

SYRIAN FOREIGN POLICY

Syria faces potential or real enemies on each border. To the north is Turkey, where a vast water project threatens to reduce Syrian access to the Euphrates River. To the east is Iraq, where the American military operation to oust Saddam Hussein's regime left American forces on the Syrian-Iraqi border. To the south is Israel and Lebanon, where Syrian forces have done battle numerous times in the post–World War II era. Syria moved forces into Lebanon initially in 1976, and their role increased following the 1989 Taif accord.[60] Syrian forces remained in Lebanon until the spring of 2005, when the assassination of Lebanese leader Rafiq Hariri led to their withdrawal.

Syria's foreign policy style used to be more strongly tied to Baathist ideology, producing a rigid policy. However, as Sadowski notes, the decline of ideology and the rise of capitalist thinking now allows the Syrian regime more flexibility, as when it sided with the United States against Iraq in 1990–1991 and offered to discuss a peaceful resolution with Israel over Golan.[61]

Syrian-Israeli Relations

The Golan Heights, under Israeli occupation with around 18,000 Israeli settlers, remains one of the highest priorities for Syrian foreign policy. Early negotiations on Golan were held in Washington in 1995, and further negotiations took place in early 1996 at the Wye Plantation in Maryland. According to Syrian sources, some

80 percent of the issues were resolved, including an Israeli agreement to return to the June 1967 border.[62] The election of Prime Minister Benjamin Netanyahu in May 1996 put discussions of the Golan on a distant back burner. The election of Ehud Barak as Israeli prime minister in May 1999 opened the door again to Syrian-Israeli peace talks over the Golan. Formal talks resumed in December 1999, as Foreign Minister Shara met Prime Minister Barak in Washington after pressure from the United States to restart talks. However, by January 2000, the parties had made no progress and the talks broke off after the Israeli newspaper *Haaretz* leaked trial drafts of an agreement that suggested Syrian concessions. There is also evidence that Barak did not consult with his cabinet or with the Israeli military, and some Israeli military officers privately blamed Barak instead of al-Asad for the failed talks.[63] A May 2000 meeting between President Clinton and al-Asad only highlighted the obstacles to peace. For example, any future agreement on the Golan most likely will have to account for water sharing. Israel views the area as critical because the headwaters of the Jordan River rise there. Israel resisted Syrian efforts to divert water from Jordan tributaries in July 1966, and one reason Israel gave for the 1967 war was fear of a repeat effort. The fate of the roughly 18,000 Israeli settlers is another issue that will not be easily resolved, since any agreement returning Golan to Syria will require them to leave. Finally, Syrian leaders are skeptical that peace with Israel will bring economic reform; they look at the Egyptian and Jordanian economies after peace, and recognize that the hopes for peace bringing prosperity were not realized in these two cases.[64] Hafiz al-Asad believed that war is no longer a viable policy option but still demanded nothing less than a full resolution of the issues dividing the two countries.[65] Bashar al-Asad seems to take a different tack, however. In a December 2003 interview, he called for the resumption of peace talks with Israel, calling for no preconditions and stating that it was possible for Syria, in the end, to have full diplomatic relations with Israel. Possibly the American ouster of Saddam Hussein in neighboring Iraq has leveraged al-Asad to reengage the peace process, and possibly reductions in Syrian support for Hizbollah might allow the United States to try to reengage Syria and Israel.[66]

Syrian-Turkish Relations

Syrian relations with her northern neighbor Turkey involve several disputes, some of them predating Syria itself. In 1939 French occupation leaders gave Hatay province in northern Syria to Turkey, as noted above. Today modern Syrian maps still show this part of Turkey as Syria, although few believe that Syria will use force to regain the territory.

Turkey began constructing a series of dams on the Euphrates River in the 1960s. The project, known collectively as the Guney Doğu Projesi (GAP), is scheduled for completion in the early 2000s. It is intended to capture more water from the Euphrates and Tigris Rivers and divert it to the Anatolian plateau to stimulate economic development. Initially Turkey tried to keep the flow of the Euphrates into Syria and Iraq at around 500 cubic meters per second (m³/s). In 1987 Turkish

Prime Minister Turgut Ozal negotiated an agreement with Syria to keep the flow of the Euphrates at 500 m³/s and Syria in turn agreed to cooperate on curbing PKK activities in Syria. Only months later Ozal complained of Syrian complicity with the PKK, while Syria claimed that it kept its part of the bargain by restricting PKK activities to the Beqaa Valley, in Syrian-occupied Lebanon.[67] After the Gulf war, Turkey and Syria signed a security agreement in April 1992, partly out of fears that the victorious Allies might create Kurdistan in northern Iraq. By 1995, PKK activity in Hatay province increased, raising suspicions in Ankara that Syria was again supporting PKK operations.[68] But Turkey was turning to Israel as a strategic partner and the specter of facing combined Turkish-Israel military and political power became more ominous in Damascus. Turkey also raised its own water issue with Syria over the Orontes (or Asi) River, which flows through Syria before entering Turkey. Turkey claimed that Syria was leaving only 10 percent of the Orontes water by the time the river reached Turkey.[69] The water issue is likely to become more serious after the GAP becomes fully operational around 2030. Syrian (and Iraqi) shares of the Euphrates could fall from 500 m³/s to 300 m³/s, accompanied by climatic changes and increases in both salinity and pesticides from Turkey's upstream use.[70] Syrian construction of the Martyr Basil Hafiz al-Asad Dam on the Khabour River, a tributary of the Euphrates, allows Syria to store more water should Turkey eventually restrict the flow of the Euphrates.[71] Moreover, the Euphrates is not the only river that Syria claims Turkey is blocking; in northeast Syria authorities claim that Turkey is blocking and draining the numerous streams that feed the Khabour River, another source of water in that arid part of the country.[72]

Syria and Turkey have cooperated more recently on several measures. After the November 2003 bombings in Istanbul, Syria turned over to Turkey some twenty-two Turkish citizens suspected in the attacks, and in mid-December of that year Syria and Turkey signed a measure on cooperation in combating cross-border crime and terrorism. In January 2004, Syrian President Bashar al-Asad made the first Turkish visit for a Syrian president, where he and Prime Minister Erdoğan discussed mutual economic interests and the possible restart of the Middle East peace process.[73]

Syrian Support for Terrorist Organizations

Syria remains on the US State Department list of countries that allow terrorists to operate from within its borders. Syria appeared to end state-operated terrorism after April 1986, when a Palestinian serving as a Syrian intelligence operative in London persuaded his pregnant Irish girlfriend to board an Israeli El Al plane with a bomb (authorities arrested her before the bomb exploded, and the woman was reportedly unaware of the bomb). Syria allegedly still supports the Shiite militia Hizbollah, operating in southern Lebanon, although Syria has repeatedly denied such involvement. Syria has allowed Iranian transport aircraft to land at Damascus with supplies bound for Hizbollah.[74] In May 2004, after many months of threats, the US government tightened economic sanctions against Syria in response to these activities.

Bush II administration officials began an increased verbal attack on Syria, accusing it of both allowing Syrian nationals to infiltrate the Syrian-Iraqi border to fight American troops there, and also of developing weapons of mass destruction.[75] Syrian-American tensions escalated even more after the Hariri assassination, particularly when a subsequent UN investigation into the murder led to Syrian intelligence authorities who were tied to Bashar al-Asad. While the United States called for tough measures to force the Syrian regime to collaborate with the investigation, Syria's response was to deny responsibility, which triggered a unanimous UN Security Council resolution demanding Syria identify those responsible for the Hariri killing.

IMAGES | *The dim lights of the ancient city of Damascus stretch to the horizon as the five climbers ascend Jabal al-Qassun, the mountain range behind the city where houses and narrow alleys cling to the steep sides of the slopes. The night makes the climb difficult, as each step on the ancient stone paths must be placed with care. Up beyond the dim green neon of the minaret loom massive stones above the last row of tiny houses. Suddenly a voice cries out. "Hello, hello, welcome," as the surprised Americans are led to a small patio beside a humble dwelling. Plastic chairs appear as a man and his friend offer water and cigarettes and the wife appears with a plate of sweet konafa. "Welcome to my house, although it is very small," says the host, who wears a T-shirt emblazoned with the words "Baseball Coach." "I can practice my English," he continues, and the discussion ensues, about the city, about America, about small but memorable things until the guests somewhat awkwardly depart, with well wishes all around. The fact that American-Syrian relations have been chilly for decades does not stop this humble man, his wife, and his friend from inviting in five American strangers. He does not ask if they are military, nor does he know that one is about to assume command of one of the mightiest warships in the world. He just offers traditional Arab hospitality to strangers. Indeed, as the guests descend the steep stone path back to greater Damascus, they wonder aloud what the fate of five Syrians climbing the hills of Boston or San Francisco or any other city after 11:00 at night might be.*

Syria shares a border with Lebanon, a country with a rich and often tragic history that Syria has frequently been a party to. Lebanon's story follows next.

SUGGESTED READINGS

Gelvin, James L. *Divided Loyalties: Nationalism and Mass Politics in Syria at the Close of Empire.* Berkeley: University of California Press, 1998.

George, Alan. *Syria: Neither Bread Nor Freedom.* London: Zed, 2003.

Lawson, Fred H. *Why Syria Goes to War: Thirty Years of Confrontation*. Ithaca, NY: Cornell University Press, 1996.

Lesch, David W. *The New Lion of Damascus: Bashar al-Asad and Modern Syria*. New Haven, CT: Yale University Press, 2005.

Moshe, Maoz, and Avner Yaniv, eds. *Syria Under Asad*. New York: St. Martin's, 1986.

Perthes, Volker. *The Political Economy of Syria Under Asad*. New York: Taurus, 1995.

Rabil, Robert G. *Syria, the United States, and the War on Terror in the Middle East*. Westport, CT: Praeger Security International, 2006.

Seale, Patrick. *Asad of Syria: The Struggle for the Middle East*. Berkeley: University of California Press, 1988.

_____. *The Struggle for Syria: A Study of Post-War Arab Politics, 1945–1958*. New Haven, CT: Yale University Press, 1965.

Tauber, Eliezer. *The Formation of Modern Syria and Iraq*. London: Frank Cass, 1995.

Van Dam, Nikolaos. *The Struggle for Power in Syria*. London: I.B. Tauris, 1996.

Wadeen, Lisa. *Ambiguities of Domination: Politics, Rhetoric, and Symbols in Contemporary Syria*. Chicago: University of Chicago Press, 1999.

Zisser, Eyal. *Asad's Legacy: Syria in Transition*. New York: New York University Press, 2001.

13

LEBANON

IMAGES | *The mountains tower over the landscape, snowcapped in March, with the white giving way to verdant green valleys dotted with little villages. On the Mediterranean side, the crystal beaches stretch on for miles, with sunbathers under colorful umbrellas. Traffic jams up in Beirut on New Year's Eve, and party goers can find no place to park their expensive Mercedes sports cars. But on the other side of the mountains in the green valleys live pockets of Shiite Lebanese who lead a hand-to-mouth existence, tending small farms and often driving hours for medical care. Their children still scan the skies for the jets with bombs, and a loud noise makes them startle. Two populations, two sides of the mountain, both claiming to be Lebanon.*

Lebanon is an anomaly in the Middle East. Mountains, rather than desert, cover most of its land area. It has the largest concentration of Christians in the Middle East, along with other religious minorities. It was home to the ancient Phoenicians and other peoples who left their imprint and their words (including the word "Bible" from the Lebanese city of Byblos) for generations to follow. Map 13.1 on page 294 shows the location and the key areas of Lebanon.

THE MODERN HISTORY OF LEBANON

Lebanon's mountainous terrain provided a good hiding place for vulnerable religious minorities, and over the centuries three groups found sanctuary there. One was the Maronite Christians (see Chapter 3), who take their name from Maron, their patron saint. The Maronites moved into northern Lebanon in the eighth and ninth centuries to escape persecution by other Christian sects. Another group seeking sanctuary in Lebanon was the Druze. In the eleventh century they left Egypt for Lebanon, where they settled in the southern part of the country. The third minority was the Shiites. Many fled Egypt after rival Sunnis replaced the Shiite Fatimid dynasty and extended the Sunni influence into Lebanon (see Chapter 2 for more on these religions).

The Ottoman Legacy

The Ottomans granted the Lebanese semiautonomous status, and during much of the Ottoman period two Druze families ruled in the name of the Ottomans. Relative peace prevailed during much of that time, but sometimes inequities between religious groups produced violent conflicts, as in a civil war between the Druze and Christians in 1860.[1] During World War I, the Ottomans ruled Lebanon directly, imposing a harsh blockade on the entire eastern Mediterranean to deprive British forces of supplies; thousands of Lebanese starved. Ottoman forces cut down great cedar forests to fuel their supply trains and publicly executed Lebanese who revolted against them.

European rule replaced Turkish after the Sykes-Picot Agreement of 1916 (see Chapter 1) as France received a mandate to govern Syria. In 1920, the Council of the League of Nations met at San Remo, Italy, and drafted the San Remo Agreement. The agreement allowed France to separate Lebanon from greater Syria, ostensibly to protect the Christian majority that retained power in the areas around Beirut and the other coastal cities. The French developed Beirut as a cosmopolitan city of banking and tourism, although largely ignoring other parts of the country. A 1932 census showed that Christians outnumbered Muslims and that Maronite Christians were the largest single religious community. During World War II, the pro-German Vichy French gained control of Lebanon. After the war, France recognized the independence of Lebanon, a country that had never before enjoyed full sovereignty.

Lebanon After Independence

Modern Lebanon began in 1943 when the Maronite leader Bishara al-Khoury and Sunni Muslim leader Riad al-Solh agreed to the National Pact. The unwritten agreement called for a Maronite president, a Sunni prime minister, and a Shiite Muslim as speaker of the Chamber of Deputies. The agreement also apportioned the legislature according to the breakdown of religious preference in the country in 1943, with six Christian seats for every five Muslim seats. Positions in the civil service were likewise allocated based on religious proportions. In September 1943, Lebanon held the first national elections for seats in the Chamber of Deputies, and al-Khoury gained the presidency. An effort to end the French mandate resulted in the arrest of Lebanon's national leaders; Lebanese Christians and Muslims were united against the arrests. In November 1943, the French capitulated and Lebanese independence began in earnest. So did Lebanese problems.

Al-Khoury won a second term in 1949, but his increasing remoteness and the country's laggard economic growth provoked opposition to his rule and his policies. In 1952, the Social National Front formed as a coalition of dissatisfied parties that

MAP 13.1   LEBANON

crossed religious lines. It included Kamal Jumblatt, a member of an influential Druze family, Camille Chamoun, a Christian and former Lebanese ambassador to Britain, and Pierre Gemayel, another influential Christian. The Social National Front called a national strike, which effectively ended the Khoury presidency in May 1952. In September of that year, the Chamber of Deputies elected Camille Chamoun to replace Khoury. His administration began peacefully enough, but a growing sense of Arab nationalism spilled over into Lebanon as Egyptian President Nasser became a popular figure throughout the Arab world. In Lebanon, "Arab nationalism" translated into "Islamic nationalism," and Lebanese Muslims increasingly demanded power in the government. Religious tensions mounted in 1957 when Chamoun gained a two-thirds majority in the Chamber of Deputies to run for reelection, causing many to believe that the election was manipulated.

Outside events also influenced Lebanese politics. The July 1958 overthrow of the Iraqi monarchy underscored the fragility of the Chamoun regime. Two months earlier, unknown assailants murdered the anti-Chamoun editor of *al-Telegraph,* and anti-American riots swept through Lebanon, with rioters blaming both Chamoun and the United States for the act. Shortly afterward President Eisenhower dispatched Marines, who startled sunbathers on Beirut's beaches as they stormed ashore to protect the country from possible spillover violence from Baghdad.[2]

As a result of the 1958 events, the Chamber of Deputies selected Gen. Fuad Shihab, the chief of staff of the Lebanese army, to replaced Chamoun as president. Shihab made some changes in the structure of the Lebanese political system, expanding the Chamber of Deputies from sixty-six to ninety-nine seats, and tried to improve Lebanon's economic infrastructure, although there was little money available. He also demanded the withdrawal of US forces from the country. In August 1964, the Chamber of Deputies tapped Charles Helou to replace Shihab as president, but Helou found that the Lebanese political fabric was coming asunder in ways he could not control. Palestinian guerrillas increased their involvement in southern Lebanon, provoking a reaction from the Lebanese army. The fighting drove much of the Shiite population in southern Lebanon to take refuge in Beirut, and their place was taken by a new influx of Palestinians fleeing from the Jordanian decision in September 1970 to oust Fatah members. Lebanon's new president, Suiliman Franjeih, elected in August 1970, found himself governing an increasingly divided and volatile country.

Temporary coalitions formed among various Lebanese groups. The members of the Franjeih, Chamoun, and Gemayel Christian families created the Lebanese Front. The Lebanese National Movement (LNM) formed in opposition. Headed by Kamal Jumblatt, a Druze, the LNM attracted a variety of Islamic militias. The growing power of these groupings became the undoing of Lebanon's delicate political balance by 1975. The Muslim population of Lebanon had grown to majority status and wanted a greater share of Lebanese political power.

Israeli clashes with Palestinian guerrillas on the southern border grew more intense, as did combat between the Shiite militias and the incoming Palestinian refugees. Israeli counterterrorism activities reached into Beirut on several occasions, provoking growing protest from Muslim political figures in the government. However, given the institutionalized weakness of the government, the situation could only grow worse.

Lebanon's Civil War

It was not just outsiders who were adding fuel to the tinderbox that would become Lebanon's civil war. On April 13, 1975, a group of Christian militiamen killed four members of the rival Christian Phalangist militia during an assassination attempt on former President Pierre Gemayel. In the mistaken belief that the attackers were Palestinians, Phalangist gunmen shot up a bus carrying twenty-six Palestinians. The fighting, kindled by decades of smoldering resentment between Christians and Muslims, quickly escalated. Soon images of blasted buildings and bloody bodies filled the world's television screens. Short-lived cease-fires allowed the various militias to rearm and reequip their forces for the next round of shooting. The armament got heavier and deadlier with each round. Militia members fired truck-mounted multiple-barreled antiaircraft guns against buildings and rival fighters, and the shabbily constructed apartment buildings in Beirut crumbled under their shells. As rubble piled up in the streets, public services stopped. Police and fire protection disappeared, and armed militia fighters took over their jobs. Medical care consisted of stretcher bearers dashing toward the Volkswagen minivans pressed into service as ambulances. Garbage was piled high in the streets, providing ready-made material for barricades. Civilians were reduced to living like prisoners in their basements, terrified to come out except to find food. The true horror of the situation was evidenced by a militia vehicle speeding down a Beirut highway dragging a dead enemy body behind, with the passengers casually waving to a rival militia vehicle coming the other way, also with a body bouncing along behind it.

A year after the civil war started, Syria made its first effort to intervene. Hoping for a stalemate in the fighting, the Syrians advanced a proposal for general political reform. However, the Lebanese army virtually fell apart, and many of its members joined a militia group called the Lebanese Arab Army. They attacked parts of Christian Beirut and forced Franjeih to flee to the Shouf region. In response, Syrian forces intervened directly against the Lebanese National Movement but took heavy casualties before withdrawing from the struggle. It was the beginning of Syria's effort to influence Lebanese politics. Syria wanted a pro-Syrian government in Lebanon, dominance over the PLO, and Arab recognition of Syria's paramount role in Lebanese politics.[3] The Israelis assisted the South Lebanon Army to control most of south Lebanon to the Litani River in 1976.

When President Franjeih's term expired in September 1976, the Chamber of Deputies elected Elias Sarkis to replace him. Sarkis had ties to Syria and to Syria's attempt to impose its own solution on Lebanon's civil war. Thus the Druze under Kemal Jumblatt opposed Sarkis out of fear that a Syrian-imposed peace would lead to Syrian domination of Lebanese politics. He had reasons for his concern.

Earlier, in May, Syrian forces again took on the Lebanese National Movement and almost crushed it. Subsequently Syria joined an Arab-led peace conference in Riyadh, Saudi Arabia, in October 1976. The Arab League also held a conference on Lebanon in October to try to build a consensus for stopping the bloodshed, agreeing to dispatch an Arab deterrent force (ADF) to Lebanon, which arrived in January 1977. Despite the name, the real power in the force was Syria, which contributed 27,000 of the 30,000-person force. The Syrians were effective peace enforcers, setting up checkpoints on the so-called green line dividing Muslim and Christian neighborhoods in Beirut. They did not hesitate to use force against those trying to cross the checkpoints and fanned out into local areas searching for violators. Most importantly, Syria became a political force in Lebanese politics.

ADF forces stayed out of the southern part of Lebanon, which was home to Palestinian refugee groups. Several Palestinian factions established bases in southern Lebanon from which they launched guerrilla raids into Israel. In March 1978, around 25,000 Israeli troops drove into the area in retaliation for a bus attack by Palestinians in Tel Aviv. The Israelis rolled up to the Litani River and remained there for three months before returning the area to Saad Hadad. After being forced out of Lebanon's army, Hadad formed his own militia, the South Lebanon Army. The UN Security Council responded by authorizing the UN Interim Force in Lebanon (UNFIL) to help stabilize southern Lebanon, but that force was unable to bring about agreements between the various factions.[4] Intense fighting continued between Palestinians, Christians, and several Shiite militias. PLO militants also used the region to lob shells and rockets into northern Israel, setting the stage for another Israeli intervention in 1982. In Beirut the situation deteriorated when the ADF fought both the Lebanese army and the Christian population, culminating in a massive shelling of the Christian part of the capital. Sarkis resigned in protest but soon returned to the palace, now unable to control his Syrian occupiers. Twice, in 1980 and again in 1981, Syria acted to curb the actions of the Christian Phalange Party, now headed by Bashir Gemayel. Those actions south of Beirut alarmed Israelis, who feared that the Phalange loss would strengthen Syria's position in Lebanon. They flew in aircraft and downed two Syrian helicopters, prompting Syria to introduce antiaircraft missiles into Lebanon, further escalating the crisis.

Israel decided to seek support from the South Lebanon Army. The purpose of this unit, for the Israelis, was to keep Palestinian terrorists away from the Israeli border, although for Hadad it was a source of power and resources. Clashes continued between the Shiite AMAL militia and Fatah, the militant wing of the PLO. The Christian militias also intensified their infighting, with the Gemayel Phalangist militia gaining the upper hand in July 1980 over the rival Chamoun militia.

Israeli Defense Minister Ariel Sharon visited Gemayel in January 1982 and apparently linked assistance for Gemayel's presidential quest to a large Israeli military operation in the south to drive out PLO guerrillas operating against Israel.[5] Israel then launched Operation Peace for Galilee on June 6, 1982. Israeli ground forces moved swiftly up into the Mount Lebanon area and into the Beqaa Valley. As they pressed north, thousands of refugees, mostly Shiites, fled in front of them. Israeli planes destroyed over eighty Syrian combat planes and eliminated Syrian antiaircraft missiles in the Beqaa. Syria, getting no help from Moscow, pressured for a cease-fire that was signed on June 11.[6] However, the PLO remained in Lebanon, and the understanding allegedly reached between Sharon and Gemayel broke down when Gemayel's Phalangist forces refused to attack PLO positions in East Beirut. The PLO forces came under siege in East Beirut from Israeli and Phalangist forces, and Israeli planes repeatedly bombed PLO sites there, inflicting heavy civilian casualties. Criticism against Israeli measures grew, both from the United States and many other countries, as television coverage of the bombing focused on the devastating consequences for Beirut civilians. President Ronald Reagan and Prime Minister Menachem Begin exchanged increasingly harsh words, but the campaign continued. Matters became worse when an assassin killed Bashir Gemayel on September 15, and Lebanese politics broke down completely as Bashir's less experienced brother Amin replaced him. Israeli forces stormed into East Beirut along with Phalange gunmen, who, protected by Israeli military forces, massacred hundreds of Palestinian civilians in the neighborhoods of Sabra and Shatilla.[7] That event rapidly brought in peacekeeping forces from the United States (sent in June to reinforce the cease-fire, then withdrawn to a ship off the coast).[8] French peacekeeping forces joined the Americans, sent because neither France nor the United States wanted to intervene alone.[9] France had its own reasons for joining in the peacekeeping operation, but France's inability to distance itself from American policy and policy objectives helped doom France to fail in Lebanon.[10]

The PLO evacuated Beirut and other parts of Lebanon, but not all PLO members actually left. Yasir Arafat reestablished his headquarters in Tunisia, and the United States and France tried to reestablish order in Lebanon. But in October 1983, simultaneous terrorist attacks on Israeli, French, and American military positions left hundreds dead, and effectively doomed French and American efforts to restore peace and stability to Lebanon. These interventions also formed core support for the Shiite militia Hizbollah, or Party of God, which grew on the weakness of the other Shiite militia, AMAL. The latter supported Israeli incursions, hoping that they would weaken Palestinian influence in Lebanon. Hizbollah developed into one of the most formidable Islamist groups in the region.[11]

At this point Syria was the only potential force for stability. President al-Asad realized that the fighting in Lebanon could again spill over into war between Israel and Syria as it did in 1982. Syria, weakened militarily by declining support from the former Soviet Union, realized that peace in Lebanon might ultimately serve Syrian interests. Saudi Arabia was growing in political importance outside of the Gulf, and willing to use its influence to gain peace accords.

Not all Lebanese supported Syrian intervention. Gen. Michel Aoun, appointed as interim prime minister in 1988, launched a campaign in early 1989 against the Syrians and their Druze allies. Aoun hoped for international support after embarking on his increasingly destructive campaign, but it did not come. In an effort to end the fighting, Saudi Arabia invited representatives of the various Lebanese factions to the summer resort city of Taif in Saudi Arabia and, under Saudi Arabian prodding, Lebanese leaders assented to an agreement giving Syria a predominant role in policing Lebanon. Syrian forces disarmed the rival militias, with the exception of Hizbollah, which they left armed to keep pressure on Israel. More than 25,000 Syrian troops remained in the country even though Taif required them to leave after the arrangement was completed. Nevertheless, their presence there probably made the agreement possible in the first place.[12]

The Post–Civil War Era

In December 1990, Saudi Arabia exercised its diplomatic influence in the city of Taif to broker the Taif Accord of December 1990, which ended the civil war and restructured the Lebanese political system. Under the accord, the president was elected by the legislature, not the people. According to Article 49 of the Lebanese constitution, amended in 1995, a serving president may have his term extended by half. Then-President Ilyas Hrawi, elected the year before, had his six-year term extended for three more years by the National Assembly in 1995, in hopes of gaining political stability. In September 1998, the possibility of abolishing the 1995 amendment surfaced.[13] Initially Speaker Nabhi Berri approved but later relented and indicated that a parliamentary election was in the offing; retired Gen. Elias Lahoud was at the top of the presidential candidate list.[14] Thus Lahoud succeeded Hrawi, a Maronite Christian, in November 1998. Lahoud locked horns with wealthy Prime Minister Rafiq Hariri, who had invested heavily in the reconstruction of Beirut, and

Hariri subsequently resigned. Lahoud replaced him with Salim Huss, who failed to revive Lebanon's sagging economy. Hariri then ran for parliament in September 2000, winning a seat handily and supporting candidates who won nineteen of the twenty parliamentary seats for Beirut, while Huss lost his seat.[15] The Taif reforms gave Christians and Muslims an equal number of seats, sixty-four seats each, but independents fill another 128 seats, thus reducing the influence of the old confessional system of governance. The constitution that followed the Taif Accords also shifted power away from the president and toward the prime minister and the Chamber of Deputies.

Taif did not undo the confessional system of religious apportionment (see below), which was something its most enthusiastic supporters had hoped for, nor did it end Lebanon's tradition of clientalist politics. Political positions still represented religious divisions, and prominent Lebanese families still exercised considerable influence. It was thus expected, for example, that after the assassination of Rafiq Hariri, his son Saad would quickly emerge as his political heir.

With Israeli forces finally out of southern Lebanon, Hizbollah ceased its call for an Islamic Lebanon and now participates formally in Lebanese politics, with some Hizbollah leaders rejecting the forceful imposition of Islam. Hizbollah has also limited its direct attacks on Israel, whle continuing to collaborate with other anti-Israeli groups.[16] Syria remained a significant force in Lebanese politics until February 2005, when a massive car bomb killed Rafiq Hariri, who was considering another run for prime minister. Hariri's assassination sparked huge anti-Syrian demonstrations in Beirut and widespread international condemnation of the Syrian presence in Lebanon, as Syrian operatives were widely suspected in Hariri's death, though other reports fingered Fatah al-Islam, an indigenous terrorist group.[17] After several days of demonstrations and counterdemonstrations by hundreds of thousands of protestors, known as the Cedar Revolution, Syrian forces finally departed, although rumors continued to surface that some Syrians secretly remained. President Lahoud survived the wave of anti-Syrian sentiment, even though he had supported Syria's presence in the country, and in the face of large anti-Syrian gains in the Lebanese parliamentary elections in May and June 2005. The UN Security Council ordered a probe into the Hariri assassination and in September 2005, the chief investigator announced the arrest of three pro-Syrian Lebanese generals who had close ties to Lahoud. Whether or not the investigation would find the real culprits or establish Syrian involvement remained a mystery. Given that most of Lebanon's political assassinations remain unsolved, the answer to who killed Hariri will probably remain unsolved. The divisiveness of Syria's Lebanese role became clearer when Defense Minister Elias Murr announced that Syrian officials had threatened him before he was wounded in a car bombing in July 2005. President Lahoud immediately issued a statement affirming his "brotherly lasting ties to Syria," which was particularly interesting given that Elias Murr is not only his defense minister but also his son-in-law.[18]

The internal and external pressure on Syria to withdraw was too much to resist, and Syrian forces were pulled back to the border, though Syrian intelligence agents reportedly stayed under cover in Lebanon. While Syria did have allies in the Lebanese political system, it was widely reviled. As Ajami notes, "The machinery of extortion had become particularly burdensome, as the Syrians helped themselves to what could be had in Lebanon."[19] In the end, few Lebanese mourned Syria's departure, though its role as a peacekeeper had probably helped Lebanon recover from its violent decades.

If many in Lebanon hoped that Syria's departure would bring stability to Lebanon, they would be sorely disappointed. In July 2006, Hizbollah attacked an Israeli post and kidnapped two Israeli soldiers. Israel responded by a large-scale land, sea, and air campaign against suspected Hizbollah targets throughout Lebanon, killing over 1,200 Lebanese and causing around $7 billion in damage. Hizbollah used areas of Lebanon to launch rockets into Israel, killing scores of Israeli citizens. Israeli military operations against Hizbollah produced surprising losses for the Israelis, and ultimately both sides agreed to UN Resolution 1701, calling for disengagement and peacekeeping, but with few solutions for the roots of the conflict.[20] Hizbollah emerged from the conflict with increased popularity across the Lebanese political space, but the conflict also brought problems for the organization. Notes Talal Atrissi, a political sociology professor at Lebanese University, "They were not expecting the results of instigating against the government to be transformed into sectarian tensions between Sunnis and Shiites in the street, which was about to become an even bigger problem. . . The other party was able to use the sectarian tension to face Hezbollah and to transform the battle to its benefit."[21]

Thus decades after its founding, Lebanon still faces the many conflicts that have inflicted so much damage on this small state and its people. In 2007 rebellion flared from Palestinian refugee camps, car bombs continued to detonate in Beirut and beyond, inspiring one commentator to state, "I can't say we're now in a failed state, but we could become a failed state if assassinations resume, we see more car bombs and if you see no political solution and no president elected in due time. If all this happens between now and November, it means we're in a big mess. And after that, you can say it's a failed state."[22]

THE LEBANESE POLITICAL SYSTEM

Lebanon's national political system has always struggled to unify a factional country. Even its educational system, with its selective portrayal of recent Lebanese history, reifies sectarianism over national identity. As one educator put it, "America used the school to create a melting pot; we used it to reinforce sectarian identity at the expense of the national identity. . . I am forming the student as a sectarian person, not as a citizen."[23]

The postindependence political system was deeply rooted in the old patron-client relationships and splinter group politics of the nineteenth century that preserved the power of local leaders, who provided favors to clients in exchange for political support.[24] Because of the power of these local patrons, Lebanese national unity was difficult to achieve. Former Prime Minister Salim Huss decried the continuing power of factions in a 2004 interview: "Electoral laws, he said, shape the entire political system. . . What this effectively means, he said, is the leaders of these large blocs—who number less than a handful—control Parliament, and therefore the country. The decision is not in the hands of Parliament. It is in the hand of those three or four people, and they have the power to make decisions and jurisdictions pass or fail. This means we are living in an autocratic state, not a democratic one."[25] Lebanon is "not free," according to Freedom House.

Lebanon has a confessional political system in which religion determines the apportionment of power. By custom the president is a Maronite Christian, the prime minister is a Sunni Muslim, and the speaker of the National Assembly is a Shiite, an arrangement dating to the 1943 National Pact.

The Lebanese political system largely excludes the Palestinians, partly because they are relative newcomers to Lebanon who are unable to compete with the traditional power structures. They have no civil rights in Lebanon and are excluded from many professions or occupations.[26] The size of the Palestinian population depends on the sources, which vary between 200,000 and 376,000.[27] Lebanese policy regarding these refugees perpetuates their status, since Lebanese law forbids Palestinian resettlement and bars them from numerous jobs and professions in order to encourage them to migrate elsewhere.[28] Their economic situation worsens with each passing year; the amount given by the UN Relief and Works Agency has dropped from around $200 per refugee per year in the 1970s to around $70 in 2004.[29]

The Lebanese Executive

As noted above, the Lebanese parliament elects the president to a four-year term. The president serves as head of state, commander of the Lebanese military, and head of the Supreme Defense Council. He or she also approves resolutions passed by the Chamber of Deputies. The president has fifteen days to consider chamber resolutions and may request a reexamination of the measure. The president names the prime minister with the concurrence of the Chamber of Deputies. In June 2005, President Lahoud named Fuad Siniora as prime minister.

The Chamber of Deputies and the Party System

The Chamber of Deputies is Lebanon's national legislature. Members are chosen on the basis of religion, with each of the 128 seats assigned to one of the seventeen officially recognized religions, based on the 1932 census. That census, disputed by Muslims even in 1932, was the last census ever taken, so the results of elections based on it are inevitably disputed by the now majority Muslims.[30] Elections for the chamber occur every four years. Because proportional representation is based on religion, most parties are affiliated with a religious faction. Thus in the parliamentary elections held in August and September 2000, Muslim-affiliated parties received 57 percent of the vote (Shiite and Sunni parties split most of the vote with 25 percent each, and the Druze with 6 percent). The Christian parties got 43 percent overall, and the Maronite parties received 23 percent. In the June 2005 elections, the Future Movement Bloc, led by Saad Hariri, won thirty-six seats; the Development and Resistance Bloc, headed by Nabhi Berri, the AMAL Shiite leader, won fifteen positions; and Druze leader Walid Jumblatt's Democratic Gathering also won fifteen seats, with the remainder going to smaller parties. Some districts showed the diversity of their population (northern Lebanon's Akkar district elected two Greek Orthodox, three Sunni, one Maronite, and one Alawi), while others reflected the dominance of one group; Tyre elected four Shiites to parliament.

Members of the legislature elect the presiding officer, the speaker, and the deputy in the opening session. By custom, the speaker is a Shiite, and Nabhi Berri, formerly the head of the AMAL militia, currently holds the position.

For two years after this election, the Chamber of Deputies may vote only once to withdraw confidence in either the speaker or deputy speaker. A passing vote requires a two-thirds majority following the introduction of a no-confidence petition signed by a minimum of ten members. Should that vote pass, the chamber must meet immediately to replace the ousted member. This was designed at Taif to create more stability in the chamber. As noted above, Taif also changed religious membership in the chamber, with the 128 seats split equally between Christians and Muslims. Each seat corresponds to an electoral district from which the deputy is chosen. There are five such districts—Beirut, Beqaa, Mount Lebanon, North Lebanon, and South Lebanon.[31]

Like most legislatures, the Chamber of Deputies is divided into committees; there are thirteen in all, including Budget and Finance, Foreign Affairs and Emigrants, Public Works, Defense and Security, and Planning and Development. The Chamber of Deputies also appoints the prime minister, a Sunni Muslim, as required by law.

The Taif Accords strengthened the Chamber of Deputies in four ways. First, it involved the chamber in the selection of the prime minister. Second, it gave parliament sole authority to remove the prime minister; third, it limits the power of the president to declare a bill urgent; and fourth, the speaker's role has been strengthened.[32] Given the increased representation of non-Maronites in the chamber, the net impact of the Taif-inspired constitution is to increase the power of the majority groups in Lebanon. However, certain minorities like Hizbollah also gained influence. The network of services that Hizbollah provided in impoverished southern Lebanon has helped it to become one of the stronger political parties in Lebanon.

The Lebanese Judicial System

The court system is divided into four Courts of Cassation, three for civil and commercial cases, and one for criminal matters. A higher court, created in 1992, tries senior officials and ministers, and is composed of seven members of parliament and eight judges. The court system also includes special courts, including the Court of Audit, designed to curb corruption by public officials. The Court of Audit, nominally attached to the prime minister's office, is empowered to examine the expenditure of public funds to ensure that they are appropriated as intended. The court can investigate public officials accused of misspending public funds and the procedures to spend such money.

The court's discretion over capital crimes was reduced in 1994 by a law requiring judges to give the death penalty for all murder cases, premeditated or not, and limiting the power to commute such sentences to the president of Lebanon.[33] The court has also come under criticism for its failure to resolve some highly controversial cases, like one involving a five-year-old girl who died after repeated sexual assaults, but with no resolution by the courts.[34]

The power of the judicial system remains unclear relative to other centers of national power. The police fall under the control of the Interior Ministry, which apparently tested its own sense of authority when it rounded up over 200 followers of Michel Aoun (see above). The action appeared to be an independent test of judicial power that drew condemnation and suggestions that the judicial agencies were working against the president.[35] The Lebanese military also plays a significant role in the judicial system, holding military tribunals to try terrorist suspects.[36]

CIVIL SOCIETY IN LEBANON

Like most other Middle Eastern countries, Lebanon has civil society elements. Most civil society organizations have a religious base, but others emphasize a particular cause, like the environment or women's issues.

Hizbollah, or the Party of God, functions as a part of civil society, even though it now participates in the Lebanese political system. While widely known as a terrorist group, Hizbollah dates to the Israeli invasion of Lebanon in 1982.[37] Guided spiritually by the charismatic cleric Said Muhammad Hussein Fadlallah, Hizbollah gained ground in Lebanese politics after Israeli actions drove Shiite Muslims to Beirut from southern Lebanon.[38]

Hizbollah is more than a militia. Augustus Richard Norton has described it as "arguably the most effective and efficient political party in the country."[39] In many of the poor Shiite areas of Lebanon, Hizbollah provides education, medical facilities, community centers, food distribution systems, and other services not provided by the government.[40] There is also evidence that Hizbollah is gradually turning from violence to accommodation with the realities of both Lebanese politics and the Israeli presence to the south. Since the Shiite population is a minority (so, for that matter, is every religious group), it may be wise for an organization drawing support from at least some of Lebanon's Shiites to draw closer to the Lebanese political system.[41] Still, Hizbollah did not miss the opportunity to add to its credibility among (and beyond) Lebanon's Shiite population by its actions against Israel in 2006. It took on even more civil society functions as the rebuilder of the parts of Lebanon destroyed in the fighting. That may have a negative impact on the idea of Lebanese nationhood, though, as one critical essay noted, "their [Hizbollah's] efforts constitute not a boon for the country but rather a serious challenge, and drive Lebanese citizens' attention and loyalties even further away from the national state and healthy democratic politics."[42] That being said, the question remains as to whether the failing state or Hizbollah is responsible for such devolution of public fealty to Lebanon.

Other Lebanese civil society groups include those interested in preserving and improving the environment (the Green Forum and Green Peace, for example), who fill in for the largely inefficient Ministry of the Environment.[43] Other groups focus on women's issues, where they have become a voice in the issues noted below.

THE STATUS OF WOMEN IN LEBANON

Women in Lebanon have not suffered from legally imposed restrictions, but at the same time Lebanese tend to be conservative socially and current conditions facing women there reflect this. Men are a majority of the workforce, except in low-paying jobs.

Women gained the right to vote in 1953, and Lebanon ratified the Convention for the Elimination of All Forms of Discrimination Against Women in 1996. Still, there is resistance to change in the status of women in Lebanon, which is reflected in the personal status codes that each religious group uses to influence the behavior of its followers. In a study of the fifteen different personal status codes in Lebanon, Shehadeh finds that provisions in each cause a woman to lose most of her legal rights relative to her spouse. This means that women receive unequal treatment in such matters as divorce, child custody, postdivorce income, and the right of remarriage.[44] For example, women are entitled to custody of sons in divorce cases until the boy reaches seven years, but often the trial is postponed until the son is over seven, so the mother never actually gets custody.[45]

THE STRUCTURE AND PERFORMANCE OF THE LEBANESE ECONOMY

Lebanon was once known as the "Switzerland of the Middle East" not only for its towering snowcapped mountains, but also for its banking system. Decades of civil war destroyed much of that banking system, and, with it, much of the Lebanese economy. Now much Lebanese political activity is devoted to economic reconstruction, which was progressing until the devastating Hizbollah–Israeli conflict of 2006, which destroyed much of the southern part of Beirut as well as the Shiite communities.

There are a few bright signs. The inflation rate is low, as is the foreign debt. GDP growth is high, and GDP per person of $5,500 is more than twice the poorest Arab countries, although significantly lower than in the oil-producing Persian Gulf states. Unemployment is high at 20 percent, though the exodus of Syrian workers from Lebanon in the spring of 2005 may allow the Lebanese to fill the jobs they once held. Around 28 percent of the population lives below the poverty line.

Other serious problems include the public deficit, with the government spending almost three times what it takes in from revenues, and the massive deficit balance of trade. Under Harari, foreign debt grew to around 186 percent of the total GDP, and although Harari promised that he would raise $5 billion by 2005, not a single dollar was actually generated.[46] The total public debt is over 206 percent of GDP, one of the highest in the world. According to a World Bank economist,

Lebanon's debt creates "a vicious circle which very few countries have been able to successfully come out of."[47] Lebanon's debt burden consumes over 70 percent of government expenditures, leaving little for other government-funded items.[48] Imports are seven times the value of exports. War damage and other factors mean that Lebanon has almost nothing to export, and 25 percent of what it does export goes to Syria. A huge amount of material comes into Lebanon to rebuild the Lebanese economy, so in the end the import-export balance may pay off in higher rates of economic development. Such development needs funds, and banks from some of the wealthier Arab countries are assisting, putting funds in Lebanese banks since those institutions may accrue interest on deposits, unlike the Islamic banks in many Gulf states. Lebanon's banks showed a record profit in 2006, increasing by almost 29 percent over 2005, despite the conflict between Hizbollah and Israel.[49] However, attracting direct foreign investment in Lebanon, a major policy goal under both the Hariri and Huss governments, did not materialize, partly, according to one analyst, because neither government did enough to privatize Lebanon's economy.[50]

The ambitious economic rebuilding plans of Prime Minister Rafiq Hariri under the Investment Development Authority of Lebanon represented an effort to reindustrialize the country. Companies investing in the special industrial zones would get tax holidays and be exempt from customs duties, among other things.[51] However, the high costs of these and other development projects provokes anger especially among Lebanon's poor, who see these future projects taking away from present needs.[52] Such projects also contribute to Lebanon's deficit, as noted above.

Lebanon is benefiting from increased tourism, particularly from the Gulf states and Europe. Its national airline, Middle East Airlines, one of the region's oldest, was restructured by its chair and is now on the road to privatization, showing a profit in 2002 for the first time in twenty-five years.[53] Continued success may pave the way for further privatization in a country with a heavy state-controlled economy. That step poses its own problems, though, since some candidates for privatization are very inefficient. Lebanon's state-owned electric company, Electricite du Liban, is running an annual loss of $800 million, raising the question of who would buy it.[54]

LEBANESE FOREIGN POLICY

As a small country in a difficult area, Lebanon has long had its foreign affairs either dictated or influenced by outsiders. Thus, Lebanon has rarely been able to influence even its own foreign relations, so its role as an actor in the larger foreign relations of the eastern Mediterranean is limited at best. Moreover, Lebanon has a very small military and thus can barely defend itself from outside forces or, for that matter, from the threat of militia forces inside Lebanon, should they once again reconstitute as armed gangs.

Peace between Israel and Lebanon

Talks between Israel and Lebanon have stalled since February 1994. Both sides have indicated that since Syria is a party to the issues in Lebanon, there can be no progress on peace discussions about Lebanon without a peace agreement between Israel and Syria. However, after the election of Ehud Barak in May 1999, the Hizbollah guerrillas in southern Lebanon slowed their attacks against Israel to their lowest level in years. A year later, Barak withdrew Israeli forces from southern Lebanon unilaterally with no peace agreement, but fighting between Hizbollah fighters and Israeli troops continued over a disputed farm area that Israel took from Syria in 1967.

Lebanon's troubles come largely from its internal population makeup and its neighbors, who frequently influence favored Lebanese groups. Lebanon's southern neighbor, Israel, the subject of the next chapter, has influenced both Lebanese history and current affairs.

SUGGESTED READINGS

Cobban, Helena. *The Making of Modern Lebanon.* Boulder, CO: Westview, 1985.

Collings, Deirdre, ed. *Peace for Lebanon? From War to Reconstruction.* Boulder, CO: Lynne Rienner, 1994.

Dagher, Carole. *Bring Down the Walls: Lebanon's Postwar Challenge.* New York: St. Martin's, 2000.

Deeb, Marius. *Syria's Terrorist War on Lebanon and the Peace Process.* New York: Palgrave/Macmillan, 2003.

El-Khazen, Farid. *The Breakdown of the State in Lebanon, 1967–1976.* Cambridge, MA: Harvard University Press, 2002.

Evron, Yair. *War and Intervention in Lebanon: The Israeli-Syrian Deterrence Dialogue.* Baltimore: Johns Hopkins University Press, 1987.

Hamizrachi, Beate. *The Emergence of the South Lebanon Security Belt: Major Saad Hadad and the Ties with Israel, 1975–1978.* New York: Praeger, 1988.

Khalaf, Samir. *Civil and Uncivil Violence: The Internationalization of Communal Conflict in Lebanon.* New York: Columbia University Press, 2002.

Longrigg, Stephen Hemsley. *Syria and Lebanon Under French Mandate.* London: Oxford University Press, 1958.

Makdisi, Samir. *The Lessons of Lebanon: The Economics of War and Development.* London: Tauris, 2004.

Norton, Augustus Richard. *AMAL and the Shia: A Struggle for the Soul of Lebanon.* Austin: University of Texas Press, 1987.

Phares, Walid. *Lebanese Christian Nationalism: The Rise and Fall of an Ethnic Movement.* Boulder, CO: Lynne Rienner, 1995.

Rabil, Robert. *Embattled Neighbors: Syria, Israel, and Lebanon.* Boulder, CO: Lynne Rienner, 2003.

Rabinovich, Itamar. *The War for Lebanon, 1970–1984.* Ithaca, NY: Cornell University Press, 1984.

Salem, Elie Adib. *Violence and Diplomacy in Lebanon: The Troubled Years, 1982–1988.* New York: Tauris, 1995.

14

ISRAEL

The view is almost ghostly from the windows of the van as it speeds through the nighttime streets of Tel Aviv: broken glass sparkling in the dim light, splintered wood, people probing through wreckage for any trace of human flesh, which has to be collected and buried as quickly as possible, according to religious custom. This is mostly the flesh of small children, who were laughing in their Purim costumes when the Palestinian bomber, stopped by security guards from entering a mall, simply ran across the street and detonated his deadly knapsack. Their laughter vanished in the shattering roar of the explosion, replaced by the silence that so often follows a terrible act. The candles, hundreds of them, now burn everywhere near the site, left by hundreds of people who come to stand speechless at the results of unimaginable hatred.

Fences define the desolate land, covered mostly with scrub. Someone entering from Jordan passes through an electric fence and walks across a carefully raked patch of sand, which Israeli soldiers inspect frequently for footprints. Someone leaving Israel passes through a gate in another electric fence. For non-Palestinians, there is one gate. However, Palestinians must wait in long lines at another gate, and being turned back means losing a day's pay. Queried at length by uniformed Israelis, the older men wear a look of resignation and defeat. The face that captures the moment is that of a small child at his father's side, a mask of fear and anger at the humiliation that a parent must suffer. When the papers are thrust back into the man's hand, he and his child must then return to one of the tin shacks that lie below the small hillocks topped by Israeli settlements. These outposts are landscaped with the traditional spears of cedar trees planted along the winding roads leading to condominiums often worthy of Southern California. Many funded with the assistance of foreign money, these elegant stone and brick structures seem to mock the impoverished Palestinians who live in their shadows.

ISRAEL IS LOCATED on the eastern Mediterranean coast, south of Lebanon and west of Jordan.

Map 14.1 on page 309 shows Israel proper, consisting of the borders set after the 1948 war and the area called the West Bank, taken by Israel after the 1967 war.[1] There are also Israeli settlements in the Golan Heights area, taken from Syria in the same war.

The land of Israel goes back for millennia, yet modern Israel dates only to 1948. For most Jews, Israel is a constant reminder of their past, as well as a signal of hope for the future. As David Grossman notes, almost every holiday is the remembrance of some past injustice; the Hebrew struggle against the Greeks, the flight from Egypt, freedom from Babylonian bondage, the destruction of the Second Temple, Holocaust Remembrance Day, and so on.[2] The State of Israel has incorporated many Jewish core values and myths, including the commitment of labor, asceticism, equality, military heroism, exile and redemption, and Zionist socialism as a way of cementing a country around religious foundations.[3] Israel has also incorporated the memory of the Nazi Holocaust, which is a central event in both Israeli identity and the identity of its neighbors, where selective recall allows Arab neighbors to be equated with Hitler and the Nazis.[4] These efforts represent an effort to provide a national identity to a people who for centuries had no national identity other than their religion.

THE MODERN HISTORY OF ISRAEL

In the nineteenth century, a number of events in Europe rekindled the identification of European Jews with the ancient land of Israel, including separateness from Christian Europe and attacks against Jewish communities, particularly in Poland and Russia. In response, Jewish writers and organizers founded the Zionist movement in Europe in the early 1800s, drawn from one of the early names for Jerusalem. Zionism was initially inspired by the writings of Rabbis Yehuda Solomon Alkalay and Zvi Hirsch Kalisher, who observed a loss of faith among Jews worldwide in the nineteenth century. Both Alkalay and Kalisher advocated a rekindling of a self-sufficient Jewish community in Palestine, with Hebrew as the common language. The Zionist movement gained momentum in the mid-nineteenth century, and European Jews began organizing to return to the area. The most notable of these organizers was Theodor Herzl, a journalist who wrote of his plan for a Jewish state in Israel to serve as a refuge for Jews who were coming under increasing persecution in Europe.

Herzl and his followers met in Basel, Switzerland, in August 1897 and formed the first World Zionist Congress. The momentum of the Basel conference carried over into Herzl's dealings with Great Britain, which issued the Balfour Declaration in November 1917 (See Chapter 1), calling for the creation of a Jewish homeland.

Britain, which received control over Palestine in the League of Nations Mandate of 1922, faced parallel pressures from Jewish leaders and from its Colonial Office, which feared that support for Zionism would inflame the Muslim populations of

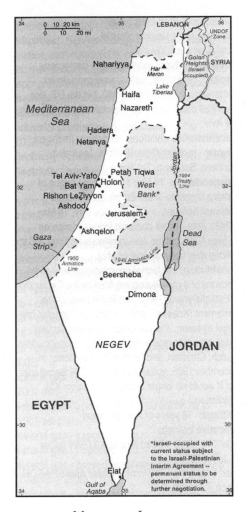

MAP 14.1   ISRAEL

the British Empire. Britain tried to limit Jewish immigration to Palestine that had been ongoing since the end of the nineteenth century (see Chapter 1), but found itself increasingly powerless to stop it. In April 1947, a special session of the UN General Assembly attempted to create a partition plan satisfactory to both Arabs and Jews. Jewish Palestinians accepted partition, but the Arab governments in the region rejected the plan, and both the Arab and Jewish sides then prepared for conflict. Several Jewish groups organized military forces, including the Haganah (the militia force under the Yishuv, or Jewish settlement), the Irgun Zvai Leumi (better known as Irgun), and the Lochamei Herut Yisrael (known as the Stern Gang).[5] The smaller groups carried out acts of violence against Palestinian Arabs and the British

(Irgun blew up the King David Hotel in Jerusalem in 1946, killing 91 people, mostly British officers). The British, weakened by their effort in World War II, gave up the mandate and let matters take their own course.

The *Yishuv,* or Jewish community, formed the political roots for the State of Israel. One of the most stalwart institutions of the Yishuv was the political party, and the strongest party was Mapai, the Labor Party, led by David Ben-Gurion, who arrived in Palestine from Russia with the second *aliya* (see Chapter 1).[6] The national labor union, Histadrut, also emerged during the Yishuv period, in order to channel new immigrants into the labor pool.[7] However, there was no mechanism for enforcing political decisions during the Yishuv period, so those disenchanted with a particular decision would simply form a new political party. This development gave rise to the multiplicity of parties seen in modern Israel and the pattern that would be repeated again and again; during the Yishuv time no party received a majority in elections.[8] The Jewish Agency, a secular organization, carried out fund-raising and planning for the Jewish community, and it evolved into the government of Israel after independence.

As the Jewish community in Palestine grew, Palestinian Arabs became increasingly alarmed about the potential loss of their land to the new settlers. As violence spread between the two groups, the Jewish community debated how best to defend and expand their area in the face of this hostility. Initially defensive, the Zionists shifted to expansive and offensive tactics in the 1930s, and this tradition would shape the security and foreign policy of Israel after its founding.[9]

Israel Becomes a State

David Ben-Gurion, as head of the provisional government, proclaimed the birth of the new country of Israel by radio in May 1948, as the sound of gunfire echoed in the background. Israel's Arab neighbors refused to accept a Jewish entity in their midst and consequently initiated the 1948 war, the first of a series of conflicts that would fill cemeteries on both sides.[10] After intense fighting, the war ended with Israel in control of more territory than allotted to it by the UN partition.[11]

While the Zionist-oriented sector of Israel's population wanted to make Jerusalem the capital, the Jewish Agency established the capital instead in coastal Tel Aviv, to avoid alienating the United States and the Catholic Latin American countries whose votes were needed to approve the UN partition plan establishing a Jewish state.[12] The Israeli government formally designated Jerusalem as the capital in 1949, although most countries do not recognize the claim and maintain embassies in Tel Aviv.

Having won a country, Israel's leaders would now have to form a government. There was no constitution, and although Ben-Gurion promised one, no version was ever ratified because of lingering disagreement over the role of religion in state affairs. Following independence, Ben-Gurion became prime minister and appointed Chaim Weizmann as president. Ben-Gurion's first action as prime minister was to try to integrate the many Jewish militia forces into the Israel Defense Forces (IDF), but he met resistance from Irgun. Ben-Gurion had to order an attack against the Irgun ship *Altalena* carrying guns to finally establish control over rival military forces.[13]

Israeli Population Changes

In July 1950, the Israeli Knesset (legislature) passed the Law of Return, allowing anyone claiming to be a Jew to immigrate to Israel and obtain citizenship, triggering a flow of Jewish immigrants from Arab countries and Turkey. Between 1948 and 1952 around 300,000 non-European Jews came into Israel. They were called Sephardim (or Sephardic Jews) to distinguish them from the European Jews, or *Ashkenazim*. The *Sephardim* (or *Mizrachim*) were largely uneducated and more likely to be religious than were the mostly secular Ashkenazim. The Ashkenazim were more familiar with the democratic traditions of Europe, and many had been members of socialist parties in their former countries. A second wave of Sephardim from Tunisia, Morocco, Algeria, and Egypt after the 1956 war increased the growing division between the Ashkenazim and the Sephardim. Egypt expelled many Jews after allegations that the Israeli intelligence service, Mossad, had recruited them to conduct sabotage against Egyptian targets.[14] By 1961, around 45 percent of Israel's population was Sephardic.

After the 1948 war, around 170,000 Palestinian Arabs remained in Israel. Their status in Israel was questionable at best, since they were not Jews (most were Muslims, with a small percentage of Christians). Israeli authorities placed the areas where they lived under military control and restricted their movements. The military expropriated some of the land they owned and transferred it to Jewish *kibbutzim* (collective farms where workers shared both labor and revenues). The Arabs could not purchase land even if they could afford it, since Israeli law prohibits most non-Jews from buying land. (In Israel, the state itself owns much of the land.) They got limited political rights partially because Ben-Gurion hoped they would affiliate with Mapai instead of joining the Israeli communists.[15]

Labor Shapes Israel

Labor's socialist roots also influenced Israeli policy through Histadrut, the labor federation created by the Zionists in 1920. Under Mapai, Histadrut became a central planning agency, running many industries, banks, the national health care system, and much more. Private business was allowed, but it was taxed heavily if it competed with Histadrut activities. Under this system, the Israeli economy grew rapidly, although high inflation became a problem in a managed economy with high levels of defense spending.

The Labor Party also sought to expand Israel's Jewish population as fast as possible, appealing in particular to Jewish people living in Arab countries. In 1949, 45,000 Yemeni Jews migrated as a part of Operation Magic Carpet, and beginning in May 1950, 123,000 Iraqi Jews participated in Operation Ali Baba.[16] After 1967, the Labor Party encouraged Israeli Jews to settle in sparsely populated areas in the West Bank and Gaza Strip, largely for security reasons.

By the mid-1970s, a combination of factors weakened Labor's hold on the prime ministership. Internal divisions split Labor leadership on significant issues, and Labor positions on domestic economic policy alienated many of the more conservative and less socialist-oriented Sephardic Jews. Labor's high levels of defense spending fueled inflation, which sometimes reached triple digit rates. Corruption and mismanagement also plagued the Labor Party, reaching even to the highest levels, including Prime Minister Yitzak Rabin's wife, who was caught with an illegal American bank account. Finally, the Israeli right wing blamed Labor for being unprepared for the 1973 war, and despite Labor's effort to divert the criticism by firing several top military officers, a majority of Israelis voted for a relatively new party in 1977, Likud. Likud was formed in 1973 by a merger of Herut and the Liberal Party, and led by one of Israel's more controversial leaders, Menachem Begin. Likud gained forty-three seats in the Knesset, while Labor lost nineteen.

Likud Takes Over

Menachem Begin brought a distinctly conservative ideology to the policy issues he faced. On the domestic front, Begin tried to reduce the power of Histadrut, but its roots were deep, and even nine years later Histadrut generated 27 percent of Israel's economic activity.[17] Inflation continued to soar until the mid-1980s, when the government reduced the defense burden by almost half. Begin would make his mark more on foreign policy than on the economy.

Begin appointed Ariel Sharon as defense minister and allowed a considerable increase in Israeli settlements in the occupied territories. But Israel continued to suffer security problems, as Palestinian and other Arab groups were now building up a force in southern Lebanon, and Begin's Likud Party was taking increasing criticism in Israel for its perceived lack of response. In June 1982, after an attack on an Israeli embassy official in London by Abu Nidal's Fatah Revolutionary Council (FRC), Israeli forces marched again into southern Lebanon (they first intervened in 1978), and that operation was one factor in the extremely close election of 1984. Again a government of national unity had to be formed when neither major party could form a majority in the Knesset.[18] Shimon Peres from the Labor Party served as prime minister for two years, then rotated with Yitzhak Shamir of Likud, who served as foreign minister. Another government of national unity formed in 1988, but this time Shamir remained prime minister until the elections of 1992, when Yitzhak Rabin challenged Peres for the head of Labor. After Rabin won, his party then obtained a narrow majority. When Rabin was assassinated by an Israeli extremist in November 1995, Shimon Peres replaced him as prime minister. Peres tried to shore his position against anti-Israeli violence by launching yet another Israeli military operation into southern Lebanon (Operation Grapes of Wrath); four separate terrorist bombings in Israel in early 1996 undercut his support. In May 1996, Benjamin Netanyahu, former Israeli ambassador to the United Nations, won the prime minister's post for Likud, defeating Peres by less than a percentage point.

One Israel

Netanyahu had criticized Peres for the peace process, and proceeded to delay implementation of a number of essential points of the Oslo Agreement. (See Chapters 1, 3 for a discussion of the Oslo Accords.) He refused to reopen talks with Syria (broken off after Grapes of Wrath) and delayed the removal of Israeli forces from Hebron. It took eighteen months to implement the return of 13 percent of land in the West Bank to the Palestinian Authority, and that happened only after a tense week-long meeting at the Wye River Plantation in Maryland in November 1998. Largely because of these actions (and inaction) Netanyahu saw his majority in the Knesset drop to the point where a vote of no confidence was just a matter of time (see below for an explanation of the vote of no confidence measure). He called for new elections in May 1999 but lost to One Israel's Ehud Barak, who promised to restart the peace process.[19] After months of hesitation and confusion, and with encouragement from the United States, Israel and the Palestinian Authority agreed on a further 11 percent land transfer to the PA in September 1999. However, Barak had less success with negotiations on the Golan Heights. In early 2000, Israeli and Syrian negotiators met in West Virginia to discuss a variety of issues, but the talks broke off after the Israeli newspaper *Haaretz* leaked details of draft proposals. To complicate matters, the Lebanese situation was unraveling and Barak withdrew Israeli forces in May 2000, contributing to the growing political chaos in south Lebanon.

Barak also hoped that his election would galvanize peace talks with the Palestinian Authority. However, those ended with no agreement, with the fate of Jerusalem as the capital of a Palestinian state as the major obstacle. In September 2000, Ariel Sharon, head of Israel's Likud Party, toured the Haram al-Sharif/Temple Mount, setting off a new episode of violence.[20] The besieged Barak faced Sharon in the February 2001 elections, and Sharon soundly defeated Barak, forming a government of national unity with Likud (19 seats in the Knesset), One Israel (26 seats), and Shas (17 seats), and two other ministers for 64 seats total.

Sharon Takes Over

As the violence between Israelis and Palestinians mounted in the spring of 2002, Sharon decided to pre-empt a possible slide in popularity by calling early elections in January 2003, gaining 17 more seats for 38 total, while Labor lost 6. The growing split between the Orthodox and Shiniu grew as well, as Shiniu gained nine seats while Shas lost six. Amram Mitzna, the new head of Labor, refused another government of national unity and resigned as Labor leader, allowing Sharon to form a coalition with Shinui, the National Union Party, and the National Religious Party. The lineup allowed Sharon to exclude both Labor and Shas from his coalition. Israel had clearly changed directions politically, with right-wing Knesset seats up to forty-five in 2003 from twenty-seven in 1999, while the religious parties dropped from twenty-seven to twenty-two seats and the left from thirty-eight to twenty-eight during that time.[21] By the fall of 2003 the Israeli public seemed weary of long-term stagnation both in Palestinian relations and in the economic realm. A poll taken then indicated that less than one-third of Israeli respondents would vote for Sharon.[22] However, Sharon did not moderate his approach to Palestinian relations, and in the spring of 2004 Israeli missiles killed Hamas leaders Ahmed Yassin and Abdul Aziz Rantisi within weeks of each other, provoking criticism throughout the Arab world and from Europe. At the same time the Knesset Finance Committee reported that since Sharon's election in 2001, 70,000 workers had become unemployed.[23]

Sharon surprised friends and foes by announcing a planned closure of Israeli settlements in Gaza in mid-2004, and found himself facing a Likud Party rebellion and a rupture of his ruling coalition. He responded by dismissing both rebel Likud and coalition members from his cabinet and, in need of a supporting majority, turned once again to a government of national unity. Veteran Labor Party member Shimon Peres again found himself in government, this time with the new title of vice premier.[24] In August 2005, Netanyahu resigned his cabinet post, creating the potential for more turmoil, even as Israeli troops prepared for the Gaza disengagement. At the end of the month he challenged Sharon for the leadership of Likud, a first for Israeli politics.[25] That challenge failed, but another test brewed for Sharon when Amir Peretz, a labor organizer and former head of Histradrut, defeated Shimon Peres as Labor Party chief in November 2005, and announced that he would pull Labor out of the government. Realizing that this would bring down his government, Sharon again surprised observers by quitting the very Likud Party he had helped to found more than three decades earlier and forming the new National Responsibility Party (Kadima) to support his run for the prime ministership in March 2006. Shimon Peres followed Sharon's resignation by resigning from the Labor Party whose original party he had joined in 1944, only to resign and then rejoin Labor later. In January 2006, Sharon lapsed into a coma from a massive stroke, ending his political career.

Kadima and Lebanon

In March 2006 the elections produced twenty-eight Knesset seats for Kadima and twenty for Labor in an election marked by a historic low turnout of 63 percent, revealing perhaps a growing dissatisfaction with the political status quo. Likud fell to fifth place, suggesting that Netanyahu no longer swayed voters with his security above all else approach. Kadima's leader and vice prime minister Ehud Olmert became prime minister, and Amir Peretz of Labor became defense minister. Neither had significant military experience, and both found a significant challenge when Hizbollah guerrillas kidnapped two Israeli soldiers in July 2006, triggering Israeli land, air, and sea attacks against southern Lebanon, and Hizbollah rocket attacks against much of northern Israel. Hundreds of Lebanese and scores of Israelis died in the fighting, and the Israeli military fared somewhat poorly against stubborn Hizbollah resistance. The United States at first did little to restrain Israeli forces in Lebanon, but as the conflict stretched into weeks and casualties mounted on both sides, the United States and France brokered a cease-fire. The consequences for Israeli leadership did not stop, however, as both Olmert and Peretz received considerable criticism for Israeli performance. Whether the new Kadima Party (without Sharon) could survive was another matter. Labor voters angrily ousted Peretz as head of the Labor Party in late May 2007, and former Prime Minister Barak replaced him with a plurality of votes. The stalemate for both parties suggested that there was no new guard to replace aging political veterans. Israel faced the future without twenty-first-century leadership.

THE ISRAELI POLITICAL SYSTEM

The Israeli political system is similar to the European political systems that many of Israel's founders knew before they came to Israel. It is a parliamentary system with a prime minister, a cabinet, a legislature, or Knesset, and an independent judiciary. Israel's founders did not draft a constitution, as noted above, since the political divide between those desiring a secular state versus those favoring a religious state was too wide to bridge. What followed was a compromise structure with a secular government that included provisions of Jewish law enacted as state law. Israel is ranked in the 2005 Freedom House survey as "free," the only Middle East country to achieve that status.

As in the case of Turkey, the political imagination of Israel is partly a reflection of its founding prime minister. Ben-Gurion feared that a religious state, as opposed to a state with a religious identity, would fracture the Jewish community, and perhaps cast aside democracy in favor of immutable religious law. The sociology of Western European Jewry, shaped more by Holocaust images than by religious fervor, provided the founding organizational principles, but as Israel's Jewish population became less Western European, pressure mounted for more a more Jewish state from those whose Jewish identity had been sublimated in their previous homelands. These Jews also did not share the heritage of parliamentary democracy that their Western European counterparts had, at least in some cases. Their views of Israel's neighbors were conditioned by their former life in Arab countries, in the former Soviet Union, or in the eastern bloc, where political compromise was not commonly practiced. Consequently Israel's political system became more fractious as the older generation of Zionists fought to maintain the Ben-Gurion image in the face of challenges from those who scarcely remembered him.

Political Demographics

The Israeli population reflects not only its current status but also future problems. The Muslim population of Israel is growing at 3.5 percent, compared to a 1.9 percent increase among Jews. That factor, combined with the impact of the second intifadah, has worsened already poor relations between Jewish and Arab Israelis, stoking fears among some Israeli Jews that Israeli Arabs might ultimately join forces with Palestinians in the occupied areas.[26] Some accused Ariel Sharon of capitalizing on such fears, citing both inflammatory statements by his ministers against Israeli Arabs along with provisions making it more difficult for Israeli Arab parties to compete in Israeli elections.[27] While economic statistics do not separate Israeli Arabs from Israeli Jews relative to economic prosperity, Israeli Arab children receive considerably less education (9.6 years) that do either Ultra-Orthodox children (14.5 years) or non-Hareidi Jewish children, at 12.6 years.[28] This is reflected in comparative poverty levels: there are three times as many Arab Israeli families living in poverty as there are Jewish Israeli families, though the state spends an average of NIS378 (new Israeli shekel) on each Jewish welfare family compared to NIS246 on each Arab family.[29]

Another political division is the Ashkenazi-Sephardim (Mizrachim) distinction. The Sephardim, finding themselves excluded from Israeli politics by the Ashkenazi-dominated Labor and Likud Parties, formed Shas in 1983, which quickly became one of the fastest growing political parties in Israel, winning seventeen seats in the 1999 elections. Shas sought to redefine Zionism to bring it more in line with Sephardic understandings of Judaism.[30]

Another source of potential division is the Russian population, largely arriving since 1990 and now constituting almost one-fifth of Israel's population, and gravitating to the Israel B'Aliya Party. In the 2003 elections the Israel B'Aliya Party, led by former Soviet dissident Natan Sharansky, lost four of its six Knesset seats, possibly a sign that the Russian olim (immigrants) are becoming more integrated into Israeli society and thus less in need of their own party.[31]

The divisions within the Knesset and, more broadly, within the Israeli population trouble many Israelis: between Ashkenazi and Sephardic Israelis, between Reform, Orthodox, and Ultra-Orthodox, between recent immigrants and third- or fourth-generation families, between urban and kibbutzniks, and so forth.[32] Many secular Jews are increasingly troubled by the growing influence of religious Jews and their demands for a society based solely on Jewish religious law, as well as exemption from both labor and military service.[33]

The Prime Minister

In most parliamentary systems, the real power goes to the prime minister. The model for Israel was Ben-Gurion, who founded both Mapai and the Histadrut, thus becoming both party leader and manager of what would become a largely socialist economy. The role of prime minister has evolved since that time, but it remains that of party leader and, increasingly, coalition manager due to the necessity of coalition government. As Arian, Nachmias, and Amir have noted, Israel's increasingly fragmented party system has weakened the power of the Knesset and further increased the relative power of the prime minister.[34] After 1977 and the election of a Likud majority in the Knesset, the prime minister has had less power to regulate the economy, since government ownership of firms was largely terminated then. However, the prime minister is still held accountable for the state of the economy, and his or her coalition may fall should the economy perform poorly, unless security concerns outweigh economic performance in the minds of the Israeli electorate.

The Cabinet

The prime minister's cabinet is composed of the heads of the ministries, who are usually appointed for party ties, not expertise. The general cabinet consists of seventeen members, with at least eight votes needed for a majority. While the prime minister selects the cabinet members, he or she is never assured of a supportive majority, since ministry leaders often come from coalition parties needed by the leading party to form a majority. Ehud Barak, for example, saw six of his cabinet ministers vote for early elections in May 2000; consequently he fired all six, reducing his cabinet from twenty-two to sixteen members. In governments of national unity, the post of foreign minister generally goes to the head of either Labor or Likud.

Given the makeup of the cabinet, it is hardly surprising that it is vulnerable to charges of weakness. Maoz argues that the cabinet has frequently been mesmerized by military arguments in favor of force, as in the case of Lebanon in 1983.[35] The cabinet seemed equally flummoxed by the 2006 war with Hizbollah.

The Knesset

The Knesset predates the establishment of Israel as a representative body. Jewish settlers founded it in 1920, and the British mandatory authorities recognized it in 1928. Israel's proclamation of independence in May 1948 created a Constituent Assembly to draft a constitution. However, it failed to produce a constitution and instead adopted the Transition Law that transformed the Constituent Assembly into the Knesset. Today the Basic Law (a series of acts that serves as a kind of constitution) does not actually define the powers of the Knesset. The 1958 Knesset Law specifies that it is the official legislature of the State of Israel and that it shall include 120 members. The Knesset Law also specifies that election law can be amended only by a majority of sixty-one members. Amendment 9 (passed in July 1985) states that no party can participate in Knesset elections if it denies the existence of the state of Israel or advocates racism.[36]

The Knesset has 120 seats, with members elected by popular vote to serve four-year terms. It has exclusive authority to enact laws, which may be initiated by the government, by individual Knesset members, by groups of members, or by a Knesset committee. The Knesset also supervises the work of the government and has the power to remove the president of the state. In November 2004 the Knesset added a measure to the Basic Law giving itself subpoena powers.[37]

Political wrangling in the Knesset is almost a given, since no single party has ever won a majority of seats. Thus the parties with the most number of votes must scramble to win over smaller parties in order to form a coalition. This is done through the assignment of cabinet positions, which become available to minor party members as a reward for supporting the party of the prime minister. For example, Hussniya Jabara (the first Arab woman to serve in an Israeli cabinet) ran as a member the Meretz Party, winning the seat although Meretz won only 8 percent of the 1999 vote, because adding Meretz contributed to a Labor-led majority. Likewise, Benjamin Elon became minister of tourism even though his Yisrael Beiteinu Party won only 2.6 percent of the vote in 1999, for the same reason.

Because Israel has so many parties, they form lists of candidates sponsored by parties or party coalitions that stand for election. In order to maximize votes, a candidate for prime minister or the Knesset will try to list himself or herself with more than one party; in 1996, Benjamin Netanyahu ran on the Likud-Tzomet-Gesher list.[38] In 1999, Ehud Barak won on the One Israel list. Smaller parties form lists around joint platforms, as the National Religious Party and the National Union did in 2006 to oppose territorial compromise with the Palestinian Authority. There are many such lists; for example, in 1981, thirty-one lists competed for Knesset seats.

The Knesset is composed of parliamentary groups, which are combinations of two or more parties that maintain a single group in the Knesset. Given the number of political parties in the Knesset, it is unsurprising that there has been almost no case where one group had a majority. Amendment 12 limits Knesset members from moving across parliamentary groups for material benefits. This is designed to prevent the collapse of parliamentary groups by members deserting them for political rewards. The effort was intended to try to stabilize the Knesset, but it failed. In the ninth Knesset, there were thirteen groups at the start of the session, but they broke into twenty groups at the end of that same session. New groups form when members break away from their original group to either form a new group or to join another Group. During the thirteenth Knesset, for example, the Yiud broke away from the Tsomet, and the Third Way broke from Labor, and David Levy's Gesher split from Likud. The 1990 election law attempted to reduce the splits, but it has had limited success at best. This may be connected with factional divisions within the parties, often linked to personalities. Factions may also form from ethnic origins. For example, in Likud during the 1980s (then Herut), Israelis of Western origin were more inclined to back Yitzhak Shamir, while those of Asian or African background were more likely to support either Ariel Sharon or David Levy (born in Morocco).[39]

In 1996, the Knesset passed a direct election law to strengthen the post of prime minister. The winning candidate needs at least 50 percent of the vote in the first round, and if no candidate gains that majority, the two top candidates run in a second round.[40] However, it became clear in early 2001 that the 1996 reforms did not achieve the hopes of their supporters. Instead of strengthening the larger parties, the law resulted in more votes for the smaller parties. Instead of increasing the legitimacy of the prime minister, it led to three prime ministerial elections in five years. Critics of the direct system, who claimed it led to an unstable combination of the American presidential system and European parliamentarianism, ultimately won the argument.[41] Barak's tenure in office was the final straw, and in March 2001, Israel returned to the pre-1992 system with slight modifications.[42] It was a painful recognition of the difficulties of sustaining a workable democracy in an increasingly fragmented political society.

Israeli Political Parties

The Knesset is organized around political parties. The following list includes the most significant parties and their membership in the 2006 Knesset (compared with the 2003 Knesset):

- Likud, rightist, relatively pragmatic: eleven (38 in 2003)
- Labor, left-center: twenty (19 in 2003)
- Shinui, secular, avowed policy of challenging Ultra-Orthodox influence: zero (15 in 2003)
- Shas, Ultra-Orthodox Sephardic: thirteen (11 in 2003)
- National Union: (6 in 2003) (combined with the National Religious Party in 2006), Ultra-Orthodox (7 in 2003) for a total of nine seats
- Meretz, left-wing, peace oriented: four (6 in 2003)
- United Torah Judaism, (Torah and Sabbath Judaism in 2006), Ultra-Orthodox Ashkenazim: six (5 in 2003)
- Kadima, founded by former Prime Minister Sharon and led by Deputy Prime Minister Ehud Olmert after Sharon became disabled: twenty-eight
- Arab parties (Hadash, Balad, and the United Arab List/Arab renewal, reformed for 2006): ten seats total
- Pensioners Party (Gil) (new in 2006): seven

These are the most significant parties, but there are many others. The Knesset often has more than fifty parties represented, since a party must get only 1.5 percent of the total vote to hold seats in the Knesset. Many other parliamentary systems require a 5 percent minimum to gain parliamentary seats. Parties come and go and leaders scramble to find new allies and abandon old friends. Disgruntled party members abandon their parties and start new ones in opposition to the party they left. Some die and then reappear, as in the case of Shinui, formed in 1973. Shinui merged with the Citizens Rights Movement and Mapam to form the leftist Meretz in 1992, but Shinui's founder, Uriel Reichman, left Meretz seven years later to reconstitute Shinui, and persuaded television personality Yosef (Tommy) Lapid to become its leader. Under Lapid, Shinui positioned itself as a balancing party between Likud and Labor.[43] In January 2006 Lapid resigned from the party, saying, "Shinui, in its present incarnation, doesn't deserve the public's faith."[44] It disappeared in the 2006 election. Some in Israel wondered aloud whether Kadima would stay together long, with its only virtue being its centrist cast in a environment where most Israelis are tired of both the right and the left.[45]

Israel's Arab minority is underrepresented, with almost 19 percent of the population but only 2 percent of seats in the Knesset. In the 2003 elections, only three of the five Arab parties received enough votes to exceed the 1.5 percent Knesset threshold. At the same time, the religious parties hold twenty-four Knesset seats, almost 24 percent of the total, although they represent around 10 percent of the Israeli population.

The change in Israeli electoral law had an impact on party strength and composition. When the direct election of the prime minister law was in effect, there was a considerable increase in the number of parties, especially in secular parties. However, with a return to the former single vote system in 2003, the smaller parties lost ground to the two major parties, and the sectarian parties (with the exception of Shas) lost strength.[46] It is possible that Prime Minister Sharon's evacuation of Gaza (see below) in 2005 happened because the smaller parties that would have opposed the move had weakened in the Knesset.

Not all parties are in the Knesset. There are several smaller parties which represent the extreme end of the Israeli right wing, including the Gush Emunim or Bloc of the Faithful, Kach, and Khane Chai (Kahane Lives). All three get their inspiration from radical figures (Gush Emunim from Rabbi Avraham Isaac Kook[47] and both Kach and Kahane Hai from Rabbi Meir Kahane).[48] Kach (founded by Kahane) and Kahane Chai (founded by his son) are both banned from electoral competition because of their racist positions on Arabs.[49] Gush Emunim advocates permanent Jewish settlement of the West Bank and the rebuilding of the Second Temple, which would necessitate the destruction of both the Dome of the Rock and Al-Aqsa Mosque.[50]

The Israeli Judicial System

The Basic Law establishes the Israeli judiciary with three tiers: the Supreme Court, district courts, and magistrate courts. The first two are trial courts while the Supreme Court is a court of appeals. The Supreme Court consists of fourteen judges, chosen by a special committee with two Knesset legislators serving as members. The chief justice, or president of the Supreme Court, heads the Supreme Court, with the next senior judge holding the rank of deputy supreme justice. The Supreme Court may also sit as the High Court of Justice, which covers judicial matters not under the clear jurisdiction of another court. The High Court of Justice may issue orders to officials, release prisoners wrongfully imprisoned, or lift the immunity of a Knesset member. The court also has authority over the military, as it demonstrated when it ordered the military to turn over to the Palestinian Authority bodies of Palestinians killed in the Jenin refugee camp in April 2002.[51] The Supreme Court also adjudicates Israel's death penalty law, which specifies death only for crimes against humanity, and was used only once, for the execution of Nazi war criminal Adolf Eichmann in 1961.

The magistrate courts are the first step in the Israeli judicial system, with jurisdiction in criminal matters for cases with a possible maximum punishment of seven years or in civil matters up to NIS1 million in value. There are twenty-nine such courts in Israel, each with a single judge. The president of the magistrate court, however, has the authority to empanel a three-judge body to hear a case.

District courts make up the next judicial layer, holding original jurisdiction for criminal cases with possible penalties of more than seven years or civil matters over NIS1 million in value. The district courts also have appellate power over the magistrate courts, and a single judge commonly chairs them, except when ordered by the president or deputy president of the district courts to form a three-judge panel. There are five district courts, located in Jerusalem, Tel Aviv, Haifa, Beersheba, and Nazareth.

The president selects the judges for all courts in the system after nomination by the Judicial Selection Committee, consisting of the minister of justice (who chairs the committee), another cabinet minister, the president of the Supreme Court, two other Supreme Court justices, two Knesset members, and two representatives of the Israel Bar Association.[52] Thus all three branches of government plus a nongovernmental body take part in the judicial selection process. The purpose is to ensure an independent judiciary. Since Israel has no jury system, judges make all the legal decisions, and consequently competence and experience is even more important than it is in countries with jury systems. Once an appointment to the Israeli court system is made, it is permanent until age 70. Judges cannot be removed from the court system except by a decision of the Court of Discipline, consisting of judges appointed by the president of the Supreme Court or the Judicial Selection Committee. In the latter case, seven of the nine members must support a decision for removal for it to take effect.

Israel also has religious courts. Rabbinical courts cover matters of marriage and divorce for Jews, or other religious matters referred to the courts by consent of all parties, while Sharia courts handle a broader range of issues for Israeli Muslims. Christian and Druze courts perform functions similar to the rabbinical courts.[53] Some of the religious sects in Israel that do not recognize the State of Israel (see above) run their own court systems. Agudath Yisrael, for example, maintains its own court system, as does Edha Haharedit and the Hasidim of Belz, although none of these groups recognizes the courts of the other group.[54]

Judicial Review

Critics of the court in the Knesset have threatened to restrict its power; in July 1998 the Knesset speaker warned darkly against judicial activism and suggested legislation restricting or circumventing High Court decisions.[55] Such criticism raises the question of judicial review: the power of a court to overturn legislation or executive decisions based on a finding that they are unconstitutional. As noted above, Israel does not have a formal constitution, but that has not prevented the court from examining decisions to see whether they fall under the framework of the Basic Law. Additions to the Basic Law passed in 1992 (human dignity and freedom of occupation) expanded the court's power of judicial review. Clause 8 of the Basic Law, Human Dignity and Liberty provides the basis for reviewing and possibly declaring unconstitutional legislation that does not conform to that law.[56] For example, in July 1998 the High Court of Justice ordered the Interior Ministry and civil administration to reconsider their policy requiring Israeli Arab women who marry Palestinians to forfeit their citizenship.[57] This may be a halting first step toward judicial review, but it is a step nevertheless.

The President

The president of Israel is officially the head of state, but the office has only limited powers. The president is elected by secret ballot by the Knesset plenum for a seven-year term, and is eligible for a second term. That vote can be a signal of the prime minister's influence, or lack thereof, as happened when the relatively unknown Moshe Katsav of Likud defeated the old Labor stalwart and former prime minister Shimon Peres in a Knesset vote largely taken as a sign of Ehud Barak's weakness after his peace efforts at Camp David in July 2000.[58] Katsav resigned weeks before his term expired, having been charged with sexual harassment, and Shimon Peres replaced him. Generally, the president serves in ceremonial functions and official visits. The president also receives credentials from foreign diplomats and credits Israeli representatives, and appoints judges to the Israeli courts.

CIVIL SOCIETY IN ISRAEL

There is an active civil society in Israel that gained impetus, according to Yishai, when Israel shifted from Zionist ideological inclusion to an emphasis on material wealth beginning in the late 1960s.[59] In response, a variety of interest groups formed, many taking positions on the occupied territories. Others took up the cause of women, the environment, and Jews of Moroccan origin, for example. While some of these civil society movements still exist, others, like Kach, evolved from a civil society group to a political party.[60]

Israeli civil society includes a variety of groups that cover almost all causes: peace with Palestinians (the Israeli Information Center for Human Rights in the occupied territories and Peace Now, for example), human rights (Rabbis for Human Rights), Israeli Arab issues (Palestinian Nongovernmental Organizations Network), women's issues (Woman's Affairs Technical Committee, Bat Shalom, and the Israeli Women's Network, for example). It is unclear, though, how much influence civil society has on political outcomes. Civil society activity may serve as a safety valve for those frustrated with the often slow and compromised policy outcomes of the government.

THE STATUS OF WOMEN IN ISRAEL

Both tradition and religious views affect the status of women in Israel. Traditional Jewish belief largely holds that women should be separate from men though they should have equal rights with them. Jewish myth features stories of women as the source of evil, as in the case of Salome and Jezebel. Yet in modern Israel women enjoy the right to vote, serve in political office, and run businesses. Abortion under certain conditions is legal.[61] Women fought in the 1948 war and have served in the Israeli military since then. When Golda Meir became prime minister, it was an indication that Israel might be pursuing a more progressive approach toward women and politics than was the case in much of the rest of the world. In 2004 the percentage of women in the Knesset was 15, compared to over 40 percent in Scandinavian countries, but around 6 percent in Arab countries. Golda Meir was one of only six women to serve in the cabinet. In the seventeenth Knesset, only one women, Tzipi Livni of Likud (until 2006, when she joined Kadima), held cabinet rank, though she held the important post of foreign minister. There have been women's political parties in Israel since the 1920s, but in the Knesset election of 2003, none made the qualifying 1.5 percent threshold to get Knesset seats.[62]

Traditional Jewish law affects women's rights in Israel. Religious courts, where the rabbis are all male, are the only venue available for a divorce. Though a woman may sue for divorce, these courts do not always view complaints by women about spouse abuse as sufficient grounds to grant the woman a divorce. A number of women have died from spousal violence, and, according to one figure, emergency wards have treated around 40,000 women a year for domestic violence.[63] In one case, a rabbinical court jailed a woman for asking to discuss alimony when her husband filed for divorce. She left him because he allegedly beat her.[64]

One solution is a prenuptial agreement binding both parties in a marriage to the choice of a civil court should divorce arise. The director of rabbinical courts, Rabbi Eli Ben-Dahan, announced that rabbinical authorities agree in principle with such a prenuptial agreement. However, an amendment to the Inheritance Law early in 1998 strengthened the power of rabbinical courts over divorce issues. The measure forbade family courts from hearing questions on child custody, alimony, or division if either party to the divorce action had sued on any of these issues in a rabbinical court. In short, should the husband file suit in rabbinical court, his wife could not gain recourse from the family court. This state of affairs generally favors the male, since rabbinical courts typically award settlements that are 30 percent lower than those awarded by family courts.[65]

Other issues involving women in Israel involve gender equality in the workplace. In July 1998, 60 percent of Israeli women responding to a poll on women's issues answered that lack of equality in the workplace was their most significant concern, compared with 34 percent of American women answering the same question.[66] Moreover, statistics indicate that Israeli women in comparable jobs earn just 68 percent of what men earn.[67]

Military service has been open to women since the founding of the IDF. However, contrary to popular belief outside Israel, women were excluded from combat roles until 1997, when the Israeli Supreme Court struck down the combat training exclusion rule for pilots. In January 2000 the military abolished the rest of the restrictions on women serving in combat units.

THE STRUCTURE AND PERFORMANCE
OF THE ISRAELI ECONOMY

The Israeli economy consists of two primary parts: large state enterprises including El Al, the state-owned airline of Israel, and Israeli Aircraft Industries, along with a growing private sector.[68] The average Israeli enjoys a standard of living comparable to that of most Western European countries, with a GDP per capita of $26,200, which is the highest in the Middle East outside of the oil-producing Gulf countries. The inflation rate is low by Israeli standards at barely 2 percent, and unemployment is 8.5 percent, with around 23 percent of the population living below the poverty level.

Israel's status as an advanced economy is shown by the fact that around 70 percent of activity comes from the service sector (tourism, financial, health care, and so on), while industry is less than 30 percent and agricultural less than 3 percent. The economy is also export oriented, with around 30 percent of GDP coming from foreign trade. The European Union and the United States are Israel's most significant trading partners.

The state initially controlled a considerable portion of the Israeli economy through a combination of public ownership and government regulation. However, privatization efforts have been under way since the mid-1980s and the state has gradually deregulated the financial sector, although all but one of the major banks remains under state control. The share of the economy controlled by Histadrut, the Labor-affiliated labor federation, also dropped from 26 percent of manufacturing in 1985 to 14 percent in 1998.[69] Still, the public sector employs almost half of the labor force, largely because of the size of the enterprises it operates, like IAI.[70] Efforts by the Sharon administration to continue privatization drew staunch opposition from Histadrut, which in November 2003 organized the largest labor strike in Israeli history. The fight, in many ways, was really about Israel's political future as much as its economic future, with the old soul of Israel's labor foundations fighting to preserve its strongest power base in the face of the conservative opposition. Like Netanyahu, Israeli conservatives are followers of former British Prime Minister Margaret Thatcher who took on British labor tradition and ended much of its political influence.[71]

American financial assistance to Israel totaled $120 million, while defense climbed from around $1.6 billion in 2005 to $2.34 billion in 2006, partly to offset the cost of the 2006 war with Hizbollah. American military assistance replaces money that Israel would spend on defense were it not for American funds. Some Israelis argue that American assistance actually hurts the Israeli economy since the money must be spent in the United States, thus depriving Israeli defense contractors of business.[72]

Politically, the relative health of the Israeli economy made US economic assistance less necessary than it was when Israel was spending heavily on defense. The most significant political aspect of US economic assistance is the perceived association with Israeli foreign and military policy. Arab countries criticize the United States for providing financial help to a country that frequently carries out policies that are counter to Arab interests. There is a belief in many Arab capitals that Israel would be more conciliatory toward its Arab neighbors if it were not sustained by US financial aid. The other side of the coin is the possible leverage that the United States gains from its funding to Israel. It might be argued that Israel is constrained to some degree in its foreign and defense policy by knowing that the United States could eliminate or reduce the aid should Israel stray beyond what Americans believe is prudent. Another criticism is that the aid harms the Israeli economy by interfering with market incentives and invites the continuation of inefficient government expenditures.[73]

There is evidence that the Israeli economy benefits from progress in the peace process. After the election of Prime Minister Netanyahu in May 1996, the Tel Aviv stock market lost 16 percent of its value, largely based on fears that Netanyahu would disrupt progress on peace with the Palestinians and Syria. However, after Netanyahu signed an agreement withdrawing Israeli troops from the West Bank city of Hebron, the stock market gained back 3 percent of its value.[74] Stocks also surged upward on the news that Prime Minister Barak would reopen peace talks with Syria in late 1999. The economy grew by 11.25 percent in the first quarter of 2000, but after the Al-Aqsa intifadah, growth for the comparable quarter in 2001 dropped by 9.8 percent.[75] Several months later the GDP growth rate actually declined by 0.6 percent and GDP per capita dropped by 2.7 percent, and with exports of goods and services down by 27 percent.[76] The number of Israelis living in poverty jumped to one in five.[77] The World Bank found 22 percent of Israelis living in poverty in 2004, a situation that the bank attributed to a combination of the intifadah and to Finance Minister Netanyahu's funding reductions in social programs.[78] In April 2004 the number of children living in poverty jumped to 600,000, or around 30 percent of all children.[79] Tourism also suffered from the violence, dropping 52 percent between September 2001 and January 2002, costing Israel around $2.4 billion in lost revenue.[80] By 2004 the total cost of the second intifadah totaled some $12 billion.[81]

The Israeli economy may benefit from peace in another way, by taking advantage of cheaper labor in Arab countries with which Israel has made relative peace. This is illustrated by Israeli investments in Jordan, which include moving entire industries out of Israel to take advantage of Jordanian wage rates. For example, Caniel, Israel's largest producer of metal cans, opened a joint venture with a Jordanian company (with Caniel holding 50 percent of the shares) in hopes of expanding its exports to Europe.[82] The other side of the issue is the fact that Israel is increasingly employing large numbers of immigrant workers from South Asia to replace Palestinians, who still make up a considerable portion of Israel's labor force, thus depriving thousands of Palestinians of a livelihood.

ISRAELI FOREIGN POLICY

Israel is primarily a security state. Its stated mission is to provide security to its Jewish population, although its means for doing so generate much controversy and thus shape Israeli foreign policy. Israel can count on few friends and thus values its relationship with the world's most powerful country, the United States.

Israeli-American Relations

Israel received support from the United States even before its declaration of independence in 1948, although that support has been conditional. Israel is not a formal American ally. At times American policy has attempted to rein in Israeli policies that Americans associate with regional instability. On other occasions, American leaders found themselves pushing reluctant Israeli leaders toward peace arrangements favored by the United States.[83] American policy under both Republican and Democratic presidents has supported Israel, consistent with American public opinion, which tends to lean toward Israel and away from the Palestinians.

A 2002 Gallup poll noted that 43 percent of Americans expressed sympathy for the Israelis as compared to only 14 percent for Palestinian Arabs, which is consistent with other Gallup polls over five years.[84] While such sentiment does not necessarily correlate with American policies favorable to Israel, it at least provides a political safety net for American presidents to tilt toward Israel without negative domestic political consequences.

Some point to the influence of the so-called Jewish lobby to explain close US ties to Israel and accuse the American Israel Public Affairs Committee (AIPAC) of exercising undue influence over US Middle East foreign policy.[85] Others argue, though, that American support for Israel has been inconsistent at best and at times opposes Israeli objectives. The United States opposed Israeli participation in the 1956 war and put great pressure on Israel to limit its role in Lebanon after the 1982 invasion. The Reagan administration sold advanced airborne warning and control (AWACS) aircraft to Saudi Arabia in the 1980s despite strong opposition from AIPAC.[86] The issue of Jerusalem has been especially vexing for the United States, which has refused to move its embassy there.[87] Moreover, Israel has operated AIPAC for decades, yet US economic assistance to Israel rarely topped half a billion dollars per year (in 1996 constant dollars) until the 1970s. Then it spiked to over $6 billion before dropping back to around $3 billion. According to A. F. .K. Organski, who reported the figures, the dramatic increase was due more to American fears of Soviet gains in the Arab world than to AIPAC political efforts.[88] It was also a reward for an Israeli-Egyptian accord at Camp David in 1979 (Egypt and Israel share almost two-thirds of total American foreign aid), and a lubricant in the hoped-for settlement of the Palestinian issue. The record here has been mixed, as Lasensky notes. Foreign aid was a positive inducement in the peace accords reached by Israel, Egypt, and Jordan, but it was insufficient (including the Clinton offer of $35 billion at Camp David) to save the Israeli-Palestinian peace process.[89]

Israeli-Palestinian Relations

Israel's most significant foreign and security issue is relations with the Palestinian population. That problem originated in the nineteenth century as Jewish immigrants displaced Palestinian Arabs. The 1948 war with its attendant displacement of Palestinians exacerbated the problem, which grew more serious in 1967 when Israeli forces occupied the West Bank of the Jordan River and the Gaza Strip, and thus governing hundreds of thousands of Palestinians. In the early 1970s Israel began to allow Jewish settlers to construct settlements in both territories, and by 2007 almost 187,000 Israelis lived in the West Bank, with an additional 177,000 living in East Jerusalem.

In 1988, the PLO shifted its objectives to claim only the territory of the West Bank and Gaza as the core of a Palestinian state instead of all Israel. (See Chapter 2 for details on the Israeli–Palestinian peace efforts.)

Recently Israel reduced dialog and negotiation in favor of erecting a vast fence between the two populations. The fence, which at its completion will stretch for over 400 miles and cost $1.3 billion, carves off land into Israel claimed by Palestinians, divides Palestinian villages, and, in the words of one Palestinian, "makes hatred between us and them."[90] The fence's defenders argue that a similar fence around Gaza keeps suicide bombers out of Israel, and that it is the only guarantee for Israeli security.[91] Israelis appear more desperate for a solution as the conflict seems even more intractable. In addition, Israelis fear that a precipitous American departure from neighboring Iraq could make the entire region even more unstable.[92] Israel's military shows the strains of three years of combat, with chief of staff Lt. Gen. Moshe Yaalon publicly criticizing Sharon's emphasis on force, some reserve military pilots refusing to fly missions against crowded Palestinian neighborhoods, four former leaders of Shin Bet (the Israeli security service) calling for a quick settlement, and ordinary soldiers beginning to speak out against Sharon's continuing refusal to seek at least a truce.[93] Sharon did act on his own to evacuate Israeli settlers from Gaza in mid-2005, but Sharon's departure in 2006 from Israeli politics cast the future of the peace process into even greater doubt. While Kadima and Labor wanted further negotiations with the PA, the National Union and the National Religious Party formed a party list against such compromise, while the leader of Shas, Eli Yishai, said in February 2006, "The vast majority of settlers understand today that we will have to make territorial compromises."[94] If the Israeli public had its way, though, further peace negotiations would take a political backseat to the resolution of numerous domestic issues. In a January 2007 poll, Israeli respondents indicated that achieving a Palestinian peace agreement ranked fifth on a list of things they wanted Israel to achieve, with fighting corruption ranked first.[95]

Relations with Syria and Turkey

Israel has tense relations with Syria due to the Israeli occupation of the Golan Heights. The Labor government of Yitzhak Rabin started negotiations, but the Netanyahu government suspended them in 1999. They resumed in January 2000 in West Virginia with active US support, but broke off shortly thereafter with mutual recriminations from both sides. One obstacle to peace is continued Syrian support for groups like Hizbollah and the violent Popular Front for the Liberation of Palestine, General Command. Israel has sought a way out of its isolation by strengthening its ties to Turkey. Turkish military leaders recognize that stronger ties with Israel could bring more support from the United States as well as access to Israeli markets for Turkish products.[96] Turkey's closer ties to Israel brought a strong denunciation from Muslim countries meeting at Tehran, but for both Turkey and Israel, the alliance makes sense. Facing powerful common enemies in Iraq and Syria, Turkey and Israel believe that they can work together to offset the Arab advantage. Turkey announced a significant increase in military modernization programs, planning to spend around $150 billion on its armed forces over twenty to twenty-five years, and Israel as a major arms producer could supply some of the new equipment.[97] The Turkish-Israeli agreement benefits Turkey, since it can obtain new US equipment through Israel that it cannot buy directly because of its human rights record and its problems with Greece.[98] The question since 2003 is whether the Turkish-Israeli arrangement will last after the demise of the Saddam Hussein regime in Iraq and the election of a Turkish prime minister from the Islamist-oriented Justice and Development Party.

IMAGES | *The Israeli Golan, seized from Syria in 1967, is a contrast in development. Parts of it are dotted with ranches, vineyards, orchards, and wheat fields. New infrastructure makes it look like modern Midwest America in many respects. Some of the settlers here demand that the government guarantee that they can keep it in perpetuity. They have gone so far as to organize a traveling road show complete with motion pictures of the Israeli-occupied Golan, showing happy Israelis skiing on its snow-covered mountains, drinking wine from its grapes, and riding motorcycles over its twisting roads. What the film fails to show, however, are the stark stone remnants of the people who used to live here. But travel through the area reveals the rubble of a farmhouse or a stone fence appearing off in the distance, faint reminders that Syrians once farmed these fields until Israeli forces drove them away in 1967. Israeli bulldozers leveled much of what the Syrians built, possibly in the hope that they would never return to their old homeland. But bulldozers cannot expunge the memories of the people who now live in the slums of Damascus and dream of returning to their ancestral land.*

Israeli Weapons of Mass Destruction

Israel was the first country in the Middle East to develop a nuclear weapons program, starting in 1956 and gaining deliverable weapons by the 1967 war.[99] Analysts believe that Israel currently possesses as many as 200 nuclear weapons, although that number stems largely from information provided by Israeli nuclear scientist Mordechai Vanunu, whom Israel imprisoned for twelve years for revealing Israeli nuclear information.[100] Israel has never acknowledged its nuclear program and has tried to keep its existence and scope secret. It banned the British Broadcasting Corporation from Israeli cable channels for a July 2003 BBC report on Israel's nuclear weapons capability. Israel has obliquely threatened to use its nuclear weapons, most recently during the buildup to the 2003 Iraq war, when Prime Minister Sharon warned that Israel would strike back "in a due way" (implying with nuclear weapons) if attacked by Saddam's forces.[101] The evidence for a deterrent effect from Israel's nuclear capacity is decidedly mixed, though.[102]

Israel is the only Middle Eastern country that has not signed the Nonproliferation Treaty, which prohibits the sharing of nuclear weapons, technology, or data.[103] The United States, while condemning other Middle Eastern countries for weapons of mass destruction programs, has never criticized the Israeli program or even officially mentioned it. Still, after Iraq's potential for nuclear weapons was forcefully suspended by US and coalition forces in the spring of 2003, and with Iran and Libya both agreeing to nuclear inspection in late 2003, pressure might build for Israel to open its suspected nuclear facilities. What would happen if the United States did put pressure on Israel to match Libya and Iran? Said one commentator, "If Washington made that decision, that would be it. Israel would decide to give it up. Israel would never resist a U.S. policy decision. We'll make the noises of rejection, quarrel, and anger, but basically we would accept it. At the same time, however, I don't see Washington doing so. I don't see the Americans putting that kind of pressure on Israel."[104]

Israel stands apart from its Arab neighbors in the sense that much of its civilization and political system is derived from European models. However, the growing infusion of Arab culture into Israel, brought partly by Jews from Arab countries, and a growing recognition that the future of Israel lies in the Middle East and not in Europe may help integrate Israeli lives with those of the Arabs who live so close and yet still far away. It is still a wide cultural and political step to cross from Israel into Jordan, the subject of the next chapter.

SUGGESTED READINGS

Alimi, Eitan Y. *Israeli Politics and the First Palestinian Intifada: Political Opportunities, Processes, and Contentious Politics*. London: Routledge, 2007.

Arian, Asher. T*he Second Republic: Politics in Israel*. Chatham, NJ: Chatham House, 1998.

Arian, Asher, David Nachmias, and Ruth Amir. *Executive Governance in Israel*. New York: Palgrave, 2002.

Arian, Asher, and Michal Shamir. *The Elections in Israel—2003*. New Brunswick, NJ: Transaction, 2005.

Bergman, Aharon. *Israel's Wars: 1947–1993*. New York: Routledge, 2000.

Cohen, Avner. *Israel and the Bomb*. New York: Columbia University Press, 1998.

Garfinkle, Adam. *Politics and Society in Modern Israel: Myths and Realities*. Armonk, NY: Sharpe, 1997.

Halpern, Ben, and Jehuda Reinharz. *Zionism and the Creation of a New Society*. New York: Oxford University Press, 1998.

Karsh, Efraim. *Fabricating Israeli History: The "New Historians."* Portland, OR: Frank Cass, 1997.

Levey, Zach. *Israel and the Western Powers, 1952–1960*. Chapel Hill: University of North Carolina Press, 1998.

Maoz, Zeev. *Defending the Holy Land: A Critical Analysis of Israel's Security and Foreign Policy*. Ann Arbor: University of Michigan Press, 2006.

Morris, Benny. *The Birth of the Palestinian Refugee Problem, 1947–1949*. Cambridge: Cambridge University Press, 1987.

_____. *Israel's Border Wars, 1949–1956.* New York: Oxford University Press, 1994.

Penslar, Derek Jonathan. *Israel in History: The Jewish State in Comparative Perspective.* London: Routledge, 2007.

Reich, Bernard, ed. *Arab-Israeli Conflict and Conciliation: A Documentary History.* Westport, CT: Greenwood, 1995.

_____. *Securing the Covenant: United States-Israeli Relations After the Cold War.* Westport, CT: Praeger, 1995.

Safran, Nadav. *Israel: The Embattled Ally.* Cambridge, MA: Harvard University Press, 1978.

Schindler, Colin. *Israel, Likud, and the Zionist Dream: Power, Politics, and Ideology from Begin to Netanyahu.* New York: St. Martin's, 1995.

_____. *The Triumph of Military Zionism: Nationalism and the Origins of the Israeli Right.* London: Tauris, 2006.

Sprinzak, Ehud, and Larry Diamond, eds. *Israeli Democracy Under Stress.* Boulder, CO: Lynne Rienner, 1993.

Wright, J. W., Jr., ed. *The Political Economy of Middle East Peace: The Impact of Competing Arab and Israeli Trade.* New York: Routledge, 1998.

Yuchtman-Yaar, Ephraim, and Yochanan Peres. *Between Consent and Dissent.* Lanham, MD: Rowman & Littlefield, 2000.

Zemir, Itzhak, and Allen Zysblat, eds. *Public Law in Israel.* New York: Oxford University Press, 1997.

Zertal, Idith. *Israel's Holocaust and the Politics of Nationhood.* Cambridge: Cambridge University Press, 2005.

15

JORDAN

IMAGES To the uninitiated, the name Jordan connotes a river, not the country that takes its name. However, on the scale of rivers in the Middle East, the Jordan is a small one. It would be called a stream if it were in, say, Ohio. Its brown current cuts a narrow ribbon across an otherwise barren desert between Jordan, Israel, and the West Bank, providing vital water to the parched land. For Christians, it is the river in which John the Baptist baptized Jesus. The place where this event is thought to have happened is now open to tourist traffic on the Jordanian side of the border. It is refreshingly clear of the normal tourist trappings, reachable only by a rutted dirt road, a dusty place to park, and a narrow dirt path leading to the riverbank. Once a bridge spanned the river, but Israeli warplanes bombed it into rubble in one of the several wars fought between Israel and Jordan. To climb up the rubble for a better view of the river is to invite an Israeli response from the opposite bank, which arrives by way of a jeep mounting a large machine gun and carrying soldiers toting automatic weapons. It is late 1998, though, and one hopes that the peace accord between Jordan and Israel restricts their response to a friendly wave.

JORDAN IS ONE OF THE SMALLER Arab countries, lying below Syria and next to Iraq and Israel. Map 15.1 on page 333 shows the major cities and borders of Jordan.

Jordan has traditionally comprised the older Transjordanian population living on the East Bank of the Jordan River and the Palestinian population on the west side. But the West Bank has not been part of Jordan since the 1967 war, and the wave of Palestinian refugees has given Palestinians majority status in Jordan. Nonetheless political and economic influence remains disproportionately in the hands of the Transjordanian population.

THE MODERN HISTORY OF JORDAN

The Ottoman Empire ruled the east bank of the Jordan River from the middle of the sixteenth century to the end of World War I. To maintain order and import people they could trust, the Ottomans moved some Circassian Muslims from the Caucasus Mountains to the East Bank.[1] That did not ensure peace, however, and the Ottomans had to put down several bedouin revolts in the early twentieth century. However, Ottoman rule had only a few years left; when World War I ended, the British supplanted the Ottomans as the new rulers of the East Bank of the Jordan River.

Jordan Under British Influence

The British quickly found themselves facing the renaissance in Arab nationalism that challenged Ottoman rule in the beginning of the twentieth century. To placate that force, Ottoman Sultan Abdul Hamid II appointed an Arab and descendant of the Prophet, Hussein ibn Ali al-Hashimi, as grand sharif of Mecca in 1908. However, Hussein found himself at odds with the so-called Young Turks who had come to power by ousting Abdul Hamid II in the next year. Arab nationalists in Damascus then turned to Hussein as a leader of the Arab cause against the Ottomans. Hussein's son Abdullah visited British high commissioner Lord Kitchener in Cairo in February 1914, hoping for British support for the Arab cause. After Kitchener became secretary of war and the Ottoman Empire sided with Germany, he repaid Abdullah's visit by declaring British support for conditional Arab independence. Hussein then declared the Arab Revolt against the Ottomans in June 1916, and proclaimed that his independent Arab government should rule the Arabian Peninsula, Palestine, Lebanon, Syria, present-day Jordan, and Iraq. Sir Henry McMahon, replacing Kitchener as British high commissioner in Egypt, expressed general support for such an entity in correspondence with Sharif Hussein. At the same time, though, the British were negotiating with the French on how to divide the post-Ottoman world into protectorates, allowing the two European powers to retain influence in the Middle East. The Sykes-Picot Agreement gave Britain a zone of interest in Palestine, while the British also issued the Balfour Declaration in November 1917 declaring support for a national homeland in Palestine for the Jewish people. Those two agreements would counter the provisions of the so-called McMahon pledge of an independent Arab state made to Hussein. However, the Arabs did not know about the Sykes-Picot Agreement until the Russian Bolsheviks revealed it in 1917. Arab armies fought to displace the Ottomans, and at the end of the war their leaders considered themselves to have earned independence. But at San Remo, Italy, in 1920, the British and French finalized the provisions of Sykes-Picot. Hussein realized the false nature of British promises when the Arab nationalist General Syrian Congress selected his son Faisal as king of Syria, who was then exiled by French forces. In the end, however, the British created a new kingdom for him. In 1921, he became king of the newly created state of Iraq.

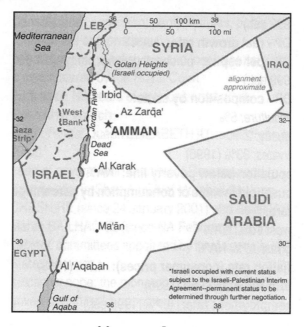

MAP 15.1　JORDAN

In August 1920, Sir Herbert Samuel, the British high commissioner of Palestine, declared that the new entity of Transjordan would be separate from British-mandated Palestine. The purpose was to limit Jewish settlement in Palestine, which even in 1920 was beginning to alarm Palestinian Arabs. The question remained as to who should lead the new country.

Sharif Hussein's second son, Abdullah, was organizing resistance in Syria against the British and French. The British were concerned about the incursion of followers of Wahhabi, or Muwahuddin, from Saudi Arabia, who appeared ready to intervene in Jordan.[2] Realizing that Abdullah might be accepted as an Arab nationalist leader, they proposed granting him the throne of Jordan. He agreed, and the British then declared Jordan a country outside the mandate and barred Jewish settlement there. It was as close as the British ever came to granting the Arab independence promised in 1917.

It is one thing to create the legal necessities of a country; it is another to create a sense of nationalism. The inhabitants of Jordan were tribal, and there was little to unify them as Jordanians. Some were longtime residents of the east bank area of the Jordan River, villagers who either herded or farmed. Others were of Syrian descent, while yet others were Palestinian, Circassian, Chechen, or Druze. They had little attachment to the son of the former sharif of Mecca, and even less attachment to the British advisers who remained to assist in keeping Abdullah in power. In 1928, Britain and Jordan ("Trans-Jordan" until 1949) tried to redefine their relationship

with a new treaty that reduced British oversight on domestic matters (except financial affairs), but continued British control over Transjordanian foreign affairs. That
authority eroded gradually, with the British granting Transjordan the right to open
consular representation in Arab countries in 1934. However, Britain kept its hand
on security affairs, and in 1939 a British officer, John Bagot Glubb, assumed command of Transjordan's military forces. Under Glubb (who took the title "Glubb
Pasha") the Arab Legion became an efficient fighting force which participated in
several campaigns of World War II, including one against pro-Nazi Rashid Ali in
Iraq and another against the Vichy French forces in Syria.

Transjordan Gains Independence

In partial response to the performance of the Arab Legion, Britain and Transjordan
signed the Treaty of London in March 1946. However, the Soviet Union vetoed
Transjordanian admission to the United Nations because Jordan was not fully independent from Britain, and the agreement was modified in 1948 removing all restrictions on Transjordanian sovereignty.

Transjordan was quickly swept up in the reaction against the creation of Israel in
May 1948. Even though King Abdullah was willing to consider the original UN
partition plan, the other Arab countries rejected it, and the Arab League (of which
Transjordan was a founding member) voted to use whatever means to oppose the
Jewish state created after partition. The Arab League gave Abdullah nominal command of the combined Arab forces in that operation, known in Israel as the War of
Independence. While the Arab forces were in the end defeated, Abdullah obtained
the West Bank of the Jordan River and the Old City of Jerusalem, but along with
those significant land acquisitions came some major challenges.

Of the estimated 700,000 Palestinians who fled from Israel, some 500,000
ended up in Jordan, more than doubling its population. In April 1950, Abdullah
annexed the West Bank of the Jordan River, giving him more land to absorb the
refugees from Palestine but also adding the half million Palestinians living there to
his population. However, the problems that this posed, along with Jordan's many
other issues, would have to pass to Abdullah's heir. On a 1951 visit to Al-Aqsa
Mosque in Jerusalem, an assassin gunned down Abdullah, who was with his fifteen-
year-old grandson, Prince Hussein. The issue remained as to who would inherit his
throne.

Abdullah had designated his son Talal as crown prince.[3] But Talal suffered from
schizophrenia, and after assuming the throne in September, his rule was sadly characterized by bizarre behavior. He was deposed in 1952 and exiled to Turkey, where he
died in 1972.[4] Talal's son Hussein formally assumed the throne in May 1953, at age
seventeen. Prime Minister Tawfiq Abul Huda exercised considerable power during
the first year of Hussein's reign, and although Hussein replaced him with Fawiz al-
Mulqi, Hussein had to turn again to Abul Huda after dismissing al-Mulqi. Abul
Huda squelched political opposition and maneuvered for support in politically cre-
ative ways. When he bungled an attempted treaty revision with Britain, Hussein dis-

missed him in May 1955.[5] The next year Hussein dispensed with Glubb Pasha and refused membership in the Baghdad Pact (see Chapter 1). He thus solidified his credentials as a moderate nationalist. Saudi Arabia agreed to make up the financial subsidy from Britain that had kept Jordan's economy afloat. The United States joined Saudi Arabia in 1957 to start an aid program to Jordan that continues to this day.

Jordan's domestic troubles continued, linked both to Jordan's foreign relations and to the fragile nature of the Jordanian political system. In October 1956, Hussein allowed elections, and critics of the Hashemite regime obtained a majority in parliament. Hussein appointed the leader of the National Socialist Party, Sulayman al-Nabulsi, as prime minister, possibly to bring the opposition under control.[6] However, Nabulsi broke ranks with the monarch and Hussein dismissed him in 1957, thus launching the so-called crisis of 1957, when an attempted overthrow of his regime by Jordanian nationalists led Hussein to invoke martial law.[7] A military coup attempt against Hussein followed in July 1958, most likely inspired by Syria. The Syrians may have tried to shoot down Hussein's plane when he attempted to fly out of Jordan for a vacation.[8]

In 1958, regional tensions grew when Egypt and Syria formed the United Arab Republic, and Hussein's uncle, the king of Iraq, was killed. Hussein had to appeal to the United States and Britain for assistance in avoiding the nationalist current sweeping the Middle East, but he became swept up in it when Israel attacked Egypt and Syria in June 1967.

Jordan in the 1967 War

In May 1967 Egyptian President Gamal Abdul Nasser closed the Straits of Tiran to Israeli shipping, and on May 30 Hussein traveled to Cairo to sign a military alliance with Egypt, after a convoluted diplomatic course that saw Egyptian-Jordanian relations deteriorate.[9] That pact placed the Jordanian army under the command of an Egyptian general, making it difficult for Jordan to remain out of the war even after Israeli Prime Minister Levi Eshkol tried to persuade Hussein to do so. Once the Egyptian commander ordered Jordanian units to fire on Israeli forces, there was no turning back. Therefore, Israeli forces fighting in the Old City of Jerusalem and the West Bank defeated the Jordanian forces there, and Jordan lost both areas. For King Hussein, who traced his ancestry back to the Prophet Muhammad, the loss of the Old City with the sites sacred to Islam was a bitter blow. Jordan also experienced a new flood of refugees—Palestinians fleeing the Israeli military from the West Bank, joining other Palestinian refugees from the 1948 war. More than 224,000 West Bank Palestinians fled to Jordan, adding an additional burden to the task of caring for the 1948 refugees. The question loomed as to who would provide financial support for them.

The question was partially answered at Khartoum, Sudan, in August 1967, when the Arab League, at its annual meeting, assessed its members to help with the costs of the Palestinian refugees. Jordan was promised $112 million per year for Palestinian relief. However, the Palestinians, radicalized more than ever by the events of

1967, began organizing in Jordan and elsewhere to recover their lost territory and launching attacks against Israel. King Hussein hesitated to crack down on his Palestinian population, as it was by this time a majority of the people living in Jordan. However, the Israeli military struck retaliatory blows against Jordanian targets. Hussein tried a compromise with the Palestinians in 1968, but that largely failed. Fighting escalated between the Palestinian militias and the Jordanian military. In September 1970, the Popular Front for the Liberation of Palestine (PFLP) hijacked several civilian airliners and blew them up on a remote Jordanian airfield.[10] After this, Hussein decided to evict the Palestinian militia, or fedayeen, as they called themselves. The cease-fire that followed on September 25 required the *fedayeen* to evacuate Jordanian cities. Hussein then appointed Wasfi al-Tal as his prime minister, but Wasfi was assassinated in Cairo after launching a stiff crackdown on the fedayeen.

Jordan would find itself at war again, albeit briefly, in 1973, when Egypt and Syria attempted to gain back the Gaza Strip and Golan Heights, respectively, territory lost to Israel in 1967. Several brigades fought on Syria's side in the Golan, but Jordan managed to remain free from the bulk of the fighting. The postwar environment weakened Jordan's stance on the return of the West Bank, since the Palestine Liberation Organization asserted its own claim to mandatory Palestine.

Jordan and the Palestinians

The aftermath of the 1967 war produced new political fissures between Jordanian nationalists and Pan-Jordanians, with the former somewhat relieved that the West Bank was no longer Jordan's problem and the latter believing that both banks were integral to Jordan's identity.[11] The division within a community that was a power base for the monarchy meant that Hussein had to step even more gingerly on the whole Palestinian issue.

In October 1974, the leaders of twenty Arab states met in Rabat, Morocco, where the PLO demanded that the assembled Arab states recognize the PLO as the legitimate representative of the Palestinian people, and further accept the PLO position that any territory won back from Israel that was once Palestinian be returned to PLO control. Jordan protested since that would include the West Bank, part of Jordan from 1949 to 1967. However, in a compromise Hussein stated that the West Bank would not be considered part of Jordan, and he relinquished his claim to it altogether in 1988. Jordan also lost the water contained in the three underground aquifers located in the West Bank, which now supply water for Tel Aviv and Jerusalem.

Hussein tried to redefine his relationship with the Palestinians on the East Bank. In November he amended the constitution to grant himself the authority to dismiss parliament. He saw the growing tensions between both East and West Bank Palestinians and his own regime, which had, among other things, accepted UN Resolutions 242 and 338 calling for an exchange of peace for land. The Palestinians rejected both resolutions, since they treated the Palestinians as simply refugees instead of people in search of a national homeland, and demanded that 242 contain a reference to a Palestinian "right of return" to the West Bank. Hussein saw the prospect of a Palestinian state as a threat to his own state, and was particularly troubled by the possibility that a Palestinian state might expand to include all of Jordan, which had a significant Palestinian population on the East Bank.

Jordan found itself in a critical position in 1990 following the Iraqi invasion of Kuwait. King Hussein decided not to join or support the coalition against Saddam Hussein for several reasons, including fear of his large Iraqi neighbor and the popular support Saddam received from Palestinians in Jordan. Countries both inside and outside of the Middle East criticized Hussein for his choice, and in the end, his country paid a heavy price for it. Gulf countries immediately ceased their subsidies to Jordan, Jordanian workers were sent home, and thousands of Palestinians working in Kuwait found themselves exiled to Jordan after the war. Therefore, Jordan had a large refugee population to support with no Gulf money to help. That reality is reflected in the economic problems that Jordan still faces years after the Gulf war ended.

The Rule of King Abdullah II

King Hussein suffered from lymphatic cancer and had to leave Jordan in 1998 for treatment in the United States.[12] Crown Prince Hassan took authority in King Hussein's absence, but he continued to play an important role in Middle Eastern politics even in his weakened condition. During a particularly difficult stage of the October 1998 Wye Plantation talks, President Clinton called on the king to help broker an agreement. The king worked to bring the Israelis and the Palestinians to a compact and appeared at the Wye Memorandum signing ceremony, looking weak but invigorated by the small step that Wye represented.

King Hussein returned to Jordan once more in January 1999 to change his line of succession, replacing Crown Prince Hassan with Abdullah, Hussein's son by his second wife. When Hussein died in June 1999, the thirty-six-year-old crown prince became King Abdullah II.[13] The new king, educated in Britain, appeared to be less nationalistic than his father. He denounced Saddam Hussein during the Iraqi dictator's last months in office and did not oppose the American-led effort to topple Hussein in the spring of 2003. King Abdullah II, apparently sharing his father's disdain for the Jordanian parliament, suspended the body in 2001, allowing new elections for the reopened legislature only in June 2003.

Abdullah II began to transform his father's emphasis on political survival to economic reform. He deemphasized the personalized reign of Hussein and turned instead to the advice of young, well-educated advisers. His emphasis on economic development over political liberalization began to alienate groups ranging from moderate Islamic leaders (once allies of King Hussein) to secular liberal forces who had hoped that political and economic reform might go hand in hand.[14] King Abdullah II named Prince Hamzah, the son of Hussein and Queen Noor, as the crown prince immediately after Abdullah assumed the throne.[15]

THE JORDANIAN POLITICAL SYSTEM

Jordan is a constitutional monarchy, with both a crown and a functioning legislature. The constitution defines the relationship between the two bodies, but in reality, a series of compromises specifies the degree to which the legislature is independent from the Crown. Freedom House considers Jordan as "partly free."

Many factors shape the Jordanian political system, including pressures deriving from economic hardship. Jordan has few natural resources and depends on outside income from wealthy oil-producing Gulf countries, giving it the status of a rentier state (one where a large bulk of the state's revenues come from outside as rent; see Chapter 3). Once remittances from Gulf countries dried up in the 1980s, Jordan had to turn to the International Monetary Fund (IMF). However, the secret arrangement requiring Jordan to adopt strict austerity measures had negative economic consequences for most of Jordan's population, and riots ensued in 1989. Largely in response to this turmoil, Jordan began a program of political liberalization, to both respond to political anger over Jordan's economic crisis and, according to Robinson, protect the interests of Jordan's political elite.[16] The first elections came in 1989, but there were no organized political parties and turnout was light. This gave the king's sometime allies in the Muslim Brotherhood an advantage since they had the best organization.[17] They won twenty-two of the sixty-eight contested seats, raising the specter that they would find ways in parliament to oppose democratic principles.[18] The king legalized political parties in 1992, and the newly legalized Islamic Action Front (IAF) won sixteen seats, though Islamists in general lost ten seats from the previous election. This may have resulted from a combination of the arrest of a prominent Islamist member of parliament on trumped up charges and a split between Islamists into social and political camps.[19]

In the fall of 1997, Jordan again held elections for parliament, but this time the Islamic Action Front called for a boycott, partially as a protest against Jordan's 1994 peace treaty with Israel. But the IAF also argued that Jordan's electoral laws largely favor the rural areas where the king's bedouin supporters were strongest, noting that the cities of Amman and Zarqa, with almost half of Jordan's population, get only a quarter of the seats in parliament.[20] The boycott apparently hurt the IAF, since, according to General Secretary Abdel Latif Abariyat, "We lost quite a few of our active members then, as they chose to participate in the elections rather than adhere to the party line."[21]

The Muslim Brotherhood's decision to boycott the elections led to speculation about the political direction of the movement. Some argued that the Muslim Brotherhood was headed in the direction of greater extremism, while others believed that the efficient state security and the investments that the Muslim Brotherhood had in the Jordanian economy would prevent extremism.[22] Those questions were partially answered in the 1998 elections for the Muslim Brotherhood Shura Council, the organization's highest decisionmaking body. Both hawks and doves lost to centrist candidates, who won twenty-five of the forty-five seats contested. Such radical hawks as Ali Ewtoum and Abdul Jalil Awawdeh lost, along with dovish member Ishaq Farhan.[23]

Political participation in Jordan is constrained despite the liberalization effort starting in 1989. The legislature is the only elected body of the three branches of government, and its power is restricted. The king serves as hereditary monarch and appoints the government, including the prime minister and the heads of ministries. This is not to suggest that there is no public involvement in the selection of ministers; recently the prime minister sacked several ministers over complaints about water quality and the accuracy of economic indicators published by the state (see below). However, the process is clearly indirect. As Schwedler notes, King Abdullah II constrained the liberalization started by his father, even as the IAF has moderated its own voice.[24]

The Jordanian polity also divides between the traditional inhabitants of the East Bank (known properly as Transjordanians, although sometimes referred to as bedouins), and the Palestinians who came largely after 1948. While the Palestinian population controls a larger share of Jordan's wealth than does the Transjordanian population (Palestinian-owned companies are 60 percent of total companies, for example), the Transjordanian population has more influence in the public sector and more influence politically, partly due to tribal ties and to control over foreign aid funds.[25]

The Jordanian Executive

The king heads the executive branch, and the prime minister and the heads of the ministries, some twenty-six in all, serve under him. King Hussein frequently shuffled persons in and out of his cabinet; there were eight governments with 143 new members in Jordan between 1989 and 1999.[26] Executive instability continued after King Abdullah II took the reins of power. Three cabinet shuffles followed his coronation, prompted by the king's demand for more sweeping economic and political reforms. In January 2002, Prime Minister Ali Abul-Ragheb resigned, apparently after failing to bring in the technical expertise into the cabinet that might have fulfilled the king's hope for reform.[27] The current prime minister is Marouf al-Bakhit, appointed in November 2005.

The Jordanian Legislature

The legislature, or *Majlis al-Umma,* consists of two houses, the House of Notables *(Majlis al-Ayan)* with forty seats, and the House of Representatives *(Majlis al-Nuwaab)* with a membership of eighty. The monarch appoints the Majlis al-Ayan from a designated list of public figures (business executives, scholars, and other distinguished persons), while the House members serve four-year terms. There are several political parties represented in the Majlis al-Nuwaab (the al-Umma, or Nation Party, the National Constitution Party, and the Arab Land Party), though most members run as independents. The political parties have no formal access to the government and thus a very limited policymaking role.[28] The Islamic Action Front has the largest number of seats at seventeen, and has more influence in part because the other thirty-two parties are in disarray. Notes one Jordanian analyst, "This is the usual pattern in the Middle East. The Islamists are strong by default."[29]

The legislature has increasingly taken independent stances since the 1980s. It can block bills favored by the executive and can dismiss the prime minister or other cabinet members. It has debated such sensitive topics as corruption, economic policy, and civil liberties, and several members have publicly criticized measures taken by the Crown.[30] Some of this new assertiveness comes from the Islamic faction, which probably pushed the regime to tilt toward Saddam Hussein in the 1990–1991 Gulf war. However, its numbers fell after the 1993 elections, and it boycotted the 1997 round. Most of the parliamentary winners in that election were traditional supporters of the monarchy, and the influence of the Islamists is no longer felt there.[31]

The legislature is organized around party membership, but that does not mean that a member elected from one party must remain with it after the elections. Parties may merge or re-form. In 1995, for example, the Jordanian Arab Democratic Party, the Jordanian Democratic Progressive Party, and the Jordanian Socialist Democratic Party merged to form the Jordanian Unionist Democratic Party. In May 1997, the National Constitution Party was created when eight small parties merged. However, independents held the largest bloc of seats in the legislature. The independents could shift their loyalties from party to party, and from opposition to the Crown. The monarchy has an advantage in the sense that the Jordanian political culture favors tribal loyalty to the Hussein dynasty, and this was clearly shown when politicians loyal to Abdullah II won over half the seats in the parliamentary election of 2003.[32]

The reality is that the king can still dismiss parliament, the Palestinian population is underrepresented by a districting system that favors rural over urban areas where a majority of Palestinians live, and parliament lacks the technical expertise to challenge the executive on many policy issues.[33]

The Jordanian Judiciary

The Jordanian judicial system consists of three levels of courts: the civil courts, the special courts, and the religious courts. The degree of judicial independence in such matters as political opposition, women's issues, and press freedom is debatable.

Civil liberties are debated continuously in Jordan, including such areas as freedom of the Jordanian press. Efforts by the government to clamp down on what was considered "unfavorable reporting" were met by a blitz of criticism in the legislature. In the House, a measure specifying monetary penalties for criticism and capital requirements to own media came under fire in June 1998. Some critics noted that part of the law contradicted the stated wishes of the king, who had called for an end on the banning of foreign publications. However, the draft law contained exactly such a ban.[34] This issue is widely expected to generate continuing political heat.

CIVIL SOCIETY IN JORDAN

In countries that restrict political participation, the existence of a viable civil society is an alternative (see Chapter 2 for a discussion of civil society). In Jordan the various ministries regulate the activities included in civil societies. The Ministry of Social Development licenses all charitable organizations, and the Ministry of the Interior regulates political parties, labor unions, and professional associations.[35] Additionally, several laws, including the Law of Societies and Social Organizations of 1966, specifically rule out social organizations that may include political gain as a part of their agenda.[36]

In other cases, secret police patrol civil society activities in order to intimidate those attempting to participate. For example, the secret police questioned members of the Women's Studies, a cultural society, for allegedly discussing election issues, which the police charged they were not licensed to do. In another case, authorities banned the Karak Cultural Forum after it hosted a lecture critical of the government.[37] In another case, the Campaign to Eliminate So-Called Honor Crimes, started in 1999, found that its efforts to repeal Article 340 of the Jordanian Penal Code (which reduces penalties for honor crimes against women) drew opposition from the legislature and silence from the executive.[38]

There has been some change, with the state trying to invigorate a stronger relationship between the state and civil society, sponsoring, for example, a workshop to foster more state relationships with Jordanian civil society to push economic development.[39] However, a viable civil society that might challenge state policies and directions is lacking in Jordan.

THE STATUS OF WOMEN IN JORDAN

The status of women in Jordan has changed considerably since the founding of the country, but challenges remain. Tensions continue between interpretations of the Sharia that appear to restrict women's rights and the constitution of Jordan that appears to give women equal rights. Jordan is the only country in the Middle East to ratify all four conventions on women's rights, something that even the United States has not done.[40]

The Jordanian Woman's Alliance, formed in 1954, gained educated women the right to vote in 1955.[41] The alliance was close to obtaining greater rights for women when authorities closed it during a general crackdown in 1957. The women's movement largely went underground until the alliance reappeared as the Women's Union in 1974, but was shut down by the government in 1981. The government created the General Federation of Jordanian Women in 1982. In 1992, Princess Basma bint Talal al-Husseini, the sister of King Hussein, formed the National Committee on Women's Affairs (now renamed the Jordanian National Committee for Women), which formulated the National Strategy for Women in 1993. The strategy was somewhat ambiguous in wording, and its implementation was largely in the hands of the royal family. Some critics charge that it reflects the general preference of the royal family to avoid radical solutions to problems, but, at the same time, it shows more regime involvement in women's issues than is the case with most other Middle Eastern countries. Moreover, the studies done by the Jordanian National Committee for Women did result in policy changes favorable to women. Those changes include the provision of medical insurance, the appointment of women to village councils, the granting of maternity leave, and other changes.[42] Later efforts by Jordanian women to form the Center for Women's Studies in 1996 were met by detention and a ban on their activities by the Mukhabarat, or security services.[43]

Jordanian women gained the right to vote in 1974, but their numbers have not translated into power in the Jordanian parliament. While Tujan Faisal became the first woman elected to parliament in the 1993 elections (and later was charged with apostasy), none of the seventeen women candidates who ran in the November 1997 elections won. In frustration, some women in Jordan wanted a parliamentary quota of at least 20 percent of seats reserved for women.[44] The idea generated considerable opposition, but at the same time, the lack of women parliamentarians brought a measure of support even from women who previously had not wanted quotas. Women found a more open political venue in the Islamic Action Front Party. The IAF platform clearly acknowledged the rights of women to participate and lead in politics, although no woman has run as an IAF parliamentary candidate.[45]

Women in Jordan are more likely to face poverty than are men, partially because more women than men are likely to marry before age 18 (around a third), and thus be unable to finish school. Traditionally they are occupied with raising a large family. While that is still true in rural areas, birth control is now available in urban areas, allowing women to plan for smaller families.[46]

Female genital mutilation is still performed in a Jordanian tribe living in the south of the country. In response to a report on it, Jordan's Mufti Said Abdul Hafeez al-Hajawi referred to the practice as a "noble trait," arguing that it "safeguards women's chastity" in addition to protecting them from "malignant diseases."[47] This statement is evidence that a wide gap remains between those who seek to advance the status of women and those who prefer the status quo.

Jordanian women serve in the army and air force, and some 3,000 women serve in uniform, around 3 percent of the total military. While they do not serve in combat-related positions, one woman is a member of the elite Royal Guard that protects the royal family.

THE STRUCTURE AND PERFORMANCE OF THE JORDANIAN ECONOMY

Jordan's location limits its potential for economic growth. Jordan has no exploitable oil reserves, and the only natural resource is phosphorus. Desert covers much of the country, and the semiarid grazing areas provide only sparse vegetation, requiring the bedouins who feed their animals there to move frequently in search of adequate pastures. More than two-thirds of the population lives in Amman.

The monarchy embarked on a number of capital-intensive projects that were probably based more on highlighting the Husseini monarchy than on principles of economic efficiency. Some of these projects were quite wasteful, as in the case of Queen Alia Airport (built beyond all usage factors), the massive Jordan Phosphates

Mines Company, and Royal Jordanian Air, the national airline that ran up an $850 million debt (around 11 percent of Jordan's total GDP).[48]

External events have had considerable impact on the Jordanian economy. For example, the 1967 war cost the economy dearly, not only because of the military expenses but also because of the loss of the West Bank and Jerusalem. The West Bank contributed almost one-fourth of Jordan's GDP, and Jerusalem brought in tourist revenue; both disappeared after Israel won the 1967 war.[49] The war also produced between 250,000 and 300,000 Palestinian refugees who needed emergency food and housing, further depleting scarce Jordanian resources.[50]

Jordan borrowed heavily to modernize its economy, and by 1989, the debt became too burdensome to carry without assistance. Jordan turned to the IMF and agreed to the budget deficit reductions and economic structural reform imposed on it. Those reforms resulted in riots and demands for the finance minister's resignation.[51] However, the Gulf war of 1990–1991 badly damaged Jordan's economy by interrupting Jordanian worker remittances and Gulf Arab assistance due to Jordan's refusal to support the anti-Iraq coalition. In addition, since much of Jordan's economy was built to supply Iraq (the port of Aqaba, for example), the economic sanctions against Iraq compounded the impact of the war on Jordan.[52]

A flood of Palestinian refugees from Kuwait further burdened Jordan's economy, with many arriving without much besides the clothes on their back. They joined earlier generations of Palestinians living in squalid refugee camps, taking menial jobs where they could. Since the few job openings tended to go to those with some longevity in Jordan, the new refugees frequently ended up unemployed and frustrated.

The GDP per capita of $4,900 for 2007 is twice that of some of the poorer Arab countries like Yemen, but considerably less than that of the oil-producing countries. Unemployment is 15 percent, with around 30 percent of the population of around 6 million under the poverty line. One critical problem is the foreign trade deficit, which reflects the low value of Jordan's exports compared to the expense of imports. Jordan exports phosphates, potash, and other mined products, while it must import crude oil, machinery, food, and almost all manufactured goods. Jordan benefited from cheap oil imports from Iraq, but the 2003 war ended that relationship, and Jordan had to switch to more expensive oil from the Persian Gulf countries. Jordan also benefits from increased trade with the United States, along with almost $800 million annually in US aid.[53] Jordan is developing port facilities and tourist attractions, and foreign investment from the Arabian Gulf countries fuels growth in Amman.

The figures do not indicate how wealth is distributed and do not reflect the economic position of the Palestinian population, noted above. Jordanians in the southern part of the country also have lower living standards than those in Amman. In Maan, for example, the per capita income is around half of the national average (inflated because almost two-thirds of the population live in the capital), and unemployment hovers around 30 percent, leading to considerable instability and an increase in Islamic insurgency.[54]

Like most Middle Eastern countries, Jordan is vulnerable to water shortages that limit its economic growth. Jordan receives 60 percent of its water from rainfall, and the remainder comes from rivers and aquifers. This is why a water-sharing arrangement with Israel is so important to Jordan (see below). All of Jordan's rivers originate outside of the country and run through Israel. However, Jordan's future outlook remains bleak. Its rapidly growing population requires some 1,257 million cubic meters (mcm) of water a year, but resources will provide only 960 mcm.[55] Moreover, the antiquated water supply system is plagued with leaks and pilferage, which, according to one estimate, costs about 55 percent of the water pumped to Jordanian citizens.[56] Finally, Jordan does not price water in ways that would encourage conservation: urban water is priced at cost level and rural water is free.[57] Thus when Yarmouk River water became available in the 1990s, one response was to plant banana trees, which require a lot of water, in the Jordan Valley, instead of less thirsty plants like vegetables.[58]

JORDANIAN FOREIGN POLICY

Jordan's location shapes its foreign policy and security concerns. With Israel on its southwest border, Iraq on its eastern frontier, and Syria to the north, Jordan lives in a volatile neighborhood. Possessing a small (albeit highly professional) military, Jordan had to rely on the skill of its diplomats in general and the diplomatic skill of King Hussein in particular. Jordan's dual identity between its Transjordanian and Palestinian elements may preclude a more decisive foreign policy, though a more open political system might have responded to the Palestinian element in Jordan's relations with Israel and with the West, making compromise more difficult.[59]

Another factor affecting Jordanian foreign and security policy is Jordan's economy. As noted above, Jordan has few natural resources, and consequently it must depend heavily on outside support to maintain its economy. This is why Laurie Brand argues for a strong link between Jordanian economic requirements and Jordanian foreign policy.[60]

Such efforts require delicate balancing. On the one hand, Jordan refused to support coalition forces against Saddam Hussein. On the other hand, Jordan sent observers to joint Israeli-Turkish-US military maneuvers in early 1998, much to the disdain of opposition political groups in the country.[61] More recently, King Abdullah II gave support to US positions on both the Israeli-Palestinian peace process (arguing that both sides must do more), and called on Saddam Hussein to readmit UN weapons inspectors into Iraq.[62] When the United States terminated the Saddam Hussein regime, King Abdullah did not oppose the war as vigorously as his father did in 1991, believing that the Iraqi leader had lost support in the Arab world in general, as well as among Jordanian Palestinians.

Peace Between Jordan and Israel

Israel and Jordan signed a bilateral agreement in September 1994 known as the Israeli-Jordanian Common Agenda. That agreement ended the state of hostility existing between the two countries, which paved the way to establish diplomatic relations in November in 1994. Jordan and Israel share the waters of the Yarmouk

River because of the 1994 peace agreement, although both the Yarmouk and Lake Tiberias, which the Yarmouk feeds, are declining.[63] The agenda also established direct telephone links between Israel and Jordan, joint electrical grids, the opening of an international air corridor, and border crossings.[64] For the first time Israeli tourists could cross over the Allenby Bridge spanning the Jordan River and visit the many historic sites in Jordan, while Jordanians could reciprocate in Israel. Further progress came in August 1995, when the Jordanian parliament abandoned a boycott of Israeli goods. That in turn paved the way for further economic cooperation between Israel and Jordan that would ultimately include the prospect for joint economic ventures and development of the Irbid Qualifying Industrial Zone. Here Israeli-Jordanian joint ventures could take advantage of Jordanian labor rates, and by 1998, a few Israeli firms were moving to Irbid to take advantage of this.

The 1994 accords attempted to build lasting institutions to preserve and further the peace process. The agreement established both a crisis prevention center and a regional security center to allow for discussion and possible resolution of future conflicts and crises before they escalate into full-blown war. The main center is located in Amman, Jordan, with secondary centers in Qatar and Tunisia. Another institution stemming from the Oslo and Madrid talks (see Chapter 1) was the Arms Control and Regional Security Working Group (ACRS), which brings together leading military and political leaders from the region and beyond to discuss critical issues. The conferees divided ACRS into two tracks, II and I, with track I designed to address substantive military issues, and track II to continue dialog. However, ACRS track I became paralyzed over Egyptian objections to Israel's reported nuclear weapons programs being excluded from the nuclear proliferation treaty, and thus only track II is operative.

The death of Yasir Arafat in November 2004 may have paved the road for a further Jordanian effort at peace building between the Israelis and Palestinians, a role largely abandoned by King Abdullah II because of the distrust he feels for both parties. With a new Palestinian leadership, though, Abdullah II might have a chance to replace Egypt as the region's peacemaker, and, at the same time, relieve the Jordanian burden of having to care for thousands of Palestinian refugees who may be able to return to a viable Palestinian state.[65]

IMAGES

The reviewing stand at Um Qais in Jordan's northwestern corner offers a panoramic view of the entire lower Galilee. Off in the haze to the west are the Horns of Hattin, where Salah al-Din defeated the Crusaders for the control of Jerusalem in 1187. South of the Sea of Galilee was the site of the battle of Yarmouk, where Islamic armies defeated the Byzantines in September 636, ending one of the last vestiges of the Roman Empire. Farther south along the Jordan River hidden behind the shadowy hills is Ayn Jalut, where legend holds that David defeated Goliath, and later, in 1260, the Mamluk army under Baybars ended the Mongol reign of terror in the Middle East. One place on the hill gives a view to four of the great battlefields of history. These battles happened a long time ago,

though, and the blood spilled on these fields has long since dried and the screams of the dying faded into the wind. Could history repeat itself here?

A Jordanian soldier who has been marking these places on a map in front of the stand places a new map on the podium. It shows the territory returned to Jordan by Israel as a part of the peace treaty signed by the two nations. The two countries agreed to channel the Yarmouk River into Jordan, giving some relief to chronic water shortages there. Israelis and Jordanians too have spilled each other's blood on many a battlefield, but this map suggests that even in the shadow of these historical fields of fire, peace may be possible in the end.

Jordan is a young state by world standards, but next to it is an entity that still lacks formal statehood, Palestine. The Jordanians and the Palestinians share a common heritage, since a majority of Jordanians are of Palestinian descent. However, to travel from the suburbs of Amman to the refugee camps in Palestinian territory is to travel from relative affluence to dire poverty and despair.

SUGGESTED READINGS

Braizat, Musa S. *The Jordanian-Palestinian Relationship.* London: Tauris, 1998.

Dann, Uriel. *King Hussein and the Challenge of Arab Radicalism, Jordan, 1955–1967.* New York: Oxford University Press, 1989.

Dann, Uriel, ed. *Studies in the History of Transjordan, 1920–1949: The Making of a State.* Boulder, CO: Westview, 1984.

Majali, Abdul Salam, Jawad A. Anani, and Munther J. Haddadin. *Peacemaking: The Inside Story Of the 1994 Jordanian-Israeli Treaty.* Norman: University of Oklahoma Press, 2006.

Massad, Joseph A. *Colonial Effects: The Making of National Identity in Jordan.* New York: Columbia University Press, 2001.

Mutwani, Samir. *Jordan in the 1967 War.* Cambridge: Cambridge University Press, 2002.

Piro, Timothy J. *The Political Economy of Market Reform in Jordan.* Lanham, MD: Rowman & Littlefield, 1998.

Robins, Philip. *A History of Jordan.* Cambridge: Cambridge University Press, 2004.

Satloff, Robert B. *From Abdullah to Hussein: Jordan in Transition.* New York: Oxford University Press, 1995.

Schwedler, Jillian. *Faith in Moderation: Islamist Parties in Jordan and Yemen.* Cambridge: Cambridge University Press, 2006.

Shlaim, Avi. *The Politics of Partition: King Abdullah, the Zionists, and Palestine, 1921–1951.* New York: Oxford University Press, 1998.

Vatikiotis, P. J. *Politics and the Military in Jordan: A Study of the Arab Legion, 1921–1957.* New York: Praeger, 1977.

Wilson, Mary C. *King Abdullah, Britain, and the Making of Jordan.* Cambridge: Cambridge University Press, 1987.

16

PALESTINE

The Church of the Nativity in Bethlehem dates back to the time of the Emperor Constantine and his mother, Queen Helena, who attempted to find the places sacred to the life of Christ over 300 hundred years after the crucifixion. Whether the site of Christ's birth is actually in Bethlehem (the site of the Church of the Nativity was formerly a temple dedicated to Aphrodite, the Greek goddess of love) or near Nazareth, far to the north, no longer matters. Thousands of Christian pilgrims flock to the church, particularly during the Christmas season. It does not seem to occur to most until they disembark from their bus that Bethlehem lies in the Palestinian Authority, the quasi-governmental body that administers land returned by Israel to the Palestinians.

The Palestinian Authority police at the Church of the Holy Sepulcher wear impressive military-style uniforms and speak perfect English as they guide the jet-lagged tourists toward the front entrance of the church. The area around the church is spotless, cleaned up by the Palestinian Authority to commemorate the 2000th anniversary of the nativity. Across the street and down the road, a Palestinian restaurant owner puts his sons to work serving a large gathering, inviting his guests into the kitchen to inspect the fresh lamb he is cooking. Everything is modern, up to the standards of even the strictest New York restaurant kitchen. "Things are much better now," he says, as the buses flow by his front window. Of course Bethlehem is not Gaza, or Ramallah, or many other Palestinian areas where deep pockets of poverty bring both despair and support for radical and sometimes violent politics. As Israeli soldiers surrounded the church and destroyed or damaged surrounding buildings during Palestinian uprisings in the spring of 2002, one had to wonder if such expressions of hope would arise anytime soon in Bethlehem. By the summer of 2004, such hopes lay shattered in the ashes of many of the buildings that once surrounded the Church. By early 2006 Hamas won half of the seats allotted to Bethlehem in Palestine's first parliamentary election.

THE OTHER CHAPTERS IN THIS BOOK are about countries—nation-states with the trappings of currency, postage stamps, passports, flags, ambassadors, and recognition as a nation-state by other nation-states. The Palestinians, for most of their history, have had none of these things, remaining just a people. Like the Kurds, the Palestinians identify themselves as a separate national group, although unlike the Kurds, they also are considered Arabs, since Arabic is their language. They base their separate identity not on language but on geography: the land of Palestine. Those who live in the West Bank and Gaza Strip have a partial state because of the peace process initiated formally in Madrid, Spain, in 1991. It came close to reality in July 2000 when Palestinian and Israeli negotiators met at Camp David, Maryland, to discuss the creation of such an entity, although the meeting ended in failure. Therefore the Palestinian state is incomplete in that it has not yet declared itself a state.

Yet, in most other respects, it is a state, with a democratically elected government, ministries, a flag, and most of the other mechanisms of a state. It has long been recognized as such by numerous governments, even before Madrid. While it still uses the Israeli shekel as its currency, it is in many ways close to a real state. That itself is a major achievement; in their long history, the Palestinians have never enjoyed such a thing as their own state. Instead, they are the largest refugee community in the world, according the United Nations, with between 3.5 and 4.9 million living outside the Palestinian Authority, mostly in refugee camps, almost half of the total Palestinian population.[1] This chapter focuses on Palestinians living in the area now controlled by the Palestinian Authority, although the creation of a Palestinian state would leave a majority of Palestinians as refugees living in squalid camps in Lebanon, Jordan, Syria, and elsewhere in the Arab world.

The Palestinian Authority administers some of the land once occupied by the Philistines of Roman times (from "Philistinia" gradually came "Palestine"). Palestine covers the coastal region of the Levant roughly from Gaza next to Egypt to the Lebanese mountains. It once stretched into what is now Jordan. It borders were fluid over time, shifting continuously, both expanding and contracting, to include modern Jordan. The Ottoman Empire divided the area into two separate regions: Syria and Palestine, and included modern Syria, Lebanon, Israel, and sometimes parts of modern Egypt. However, the people who have centuries-old roots there identify themselves as Palestinians, regardless of whether or not they ever lived in a formal Palestinian state, and that sense of identity gives rise to their longing for their own state.

One constant is the city of Jerusalem. It is a natural capital for the region, rich with history and religious significance.

The Palestinian area encompasses the West Bank of the Jordan River and the Gaza Strip (or simply Gaza). Map 16.1 shows both areas.

The West Bank includes Jewish settlements under the protection of Israel and enclaves that the Palestinian Authority administer in accordance with the 1992 Oslo Accords and the more recent 1998 Wye River Accords. As of 2007, Pales-

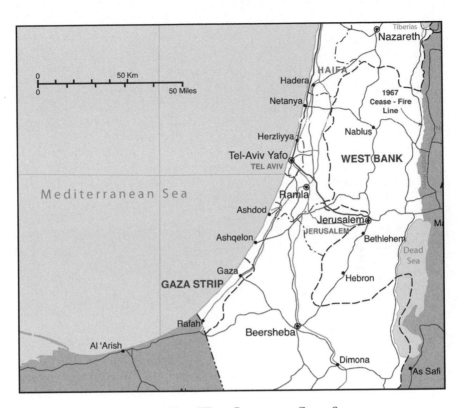

MAP 16.1   THE WEST BANK AND GAZA STRIP

tinians controlled about 40 percent of the West Bank, and all of Gaza. In December 1998, President Bill Clinton visited Gaza, the first American president to do so. He watched as the Palestinian National and Legislative Councils voted to repeal a covenant in the original PLO charter calling for the destruction of Israel. Prime Minister Binyamin Netanyahu had demanded as much as a condition for further Israeli withdrawal from West Bank territory. However, the action by the PA provoked strong opposition from rival Palestinian groups that met in Damascus, Syria, along with Hizbollah representatives to organize opposition to the proposed changes. Leaders of these groups, including Ahmed Jibril of the Popular Front for the Liberation of Palestine, Nayef Hawatmeh of the Democratic Front for the Liberation of Palestine General Command, and Said Hassan Nasrallah of Hizbollah, all called for Palestinians to reject changes in the charter.[2] Since these various Palestinian groups have around 100 representatives on the Palestinian National Council, these demands could have some impact on future PA actions.

THE MODERN HISTORY OF PALESTINE

Prior to World War I, the area now known as Palestine was part of the Ottoman Empire. Ottoman officials conscripted many Palestinians against their will into military service (some 300,000 total served). Ottoman officers often hanged deserters.[3]

Palestinian and Israeli politics began to intertwine in the nineteenth century as Jews started migrating to Palestine from Europe. While in some cases Jewish settlers and Palestinians engaged in an uneasy cooperation, conflict was more likely. Efforts by Jews and Muslims to refurbish holy sites in Jerusalem led to bloody riots in August 1929. Things got worse with the Arab Revolts of 1936 and 1939, sparked by the murder of a Jewish woman by Palestinians and subsequent Jewish retaliation. Finally Britain, with its treasury drained by World War II and growing unrest in much of the British Empire, announced the evacuation of its forces from Palestine. The 1948 war followed (see Chapter 1), ending Palestinian hopes for a quick state.

The Palestinian Exodus

There is some uncertainty about how many Palestinian Arabs lived in mandatory Palestine before 1948. British records indicate that around 1.3 million Arabs lived in Palestine and that somewhere between 700,000 and 900,000 lived in the area that became Israel after 1949. After the 1948 war, around 170,000 Arabs remained in Israel, while approximately 700,000 left. Around 300,000 of these refugees moved to the narrow confines of Gaza, while 400,000 others fled to the West Bank of the Jordan River. Some remained in these areas, while others moved on to Jordan, Syria, Lebanon, Egypt, and the Persian Gulf countries.

These stateless Palestinians did not initially develop their own leadership but turned to Arab countries to take up their cause. However, for many Arab countries, Palestinian refugees became a problem. Many Palestinian settlers lived (and still live) in fetid settlements on the fringes of Arab cities, and despite the efforts of the UN relief work, most remained mired in poverty. Even in wealthy countries like Kuwait, overcrowding, lack of educational opportunity, and poverty marked the Palestinian communities.[4] Similar conditions existed elsewhere in the Arab world, fueling Palestinian resentment against Arab governments that seemed unwilling to further the Palestinian cause.

Creating the PLO

Some Arab leaders argued that if the Palestinians directed their grievances against Israel and the West instead of against the Arab world, they would be less likely to take over their host countries. Thus in 1964, the League of Arab states chartered the Palestine Liberation Organization (PLO) with Ahmad Shuqayri as its head. But Palestinians who had belonged to underground organizations since the early 1950s (including Yasir Arafat, founder of Fatah, and George Habash, founder of the Popular Front for the Liberation of Palestine) opposed Shuqayri from the start. Early on, Syria (with Hafiz al-Asad as Syrian air force chief) allowed Fatah to establish training camps in Syria. However, opposition from most Arab regimes prevented the PLO from mounting anything more than guerrilla attacks against Israel. However, those attacks themselves were one basis for the Israeli decision to launch the 1967 war, and the bitter end to that war opened a new chapter for the PLO.[5] That war created thousands more Palestinian refugees, who fled advancing Israeli forces into neighboring Arab countries.

The 1967 war placed Palestinians in the West Bank and Gaza under Israeli occupation, and Israeli settlers moved into both regions. The 1967 war ended the career of Shuqayri, whose opposition to guerrilla operations led to his forced resignation in December of that year. In July 1968, the Palestinian National Council (the umbrella group of PLO subgroups) met, and Yasir Arafat's Fatah faction won 38 seats of the 100-member PNC. Arafat, the champion of guerrilla resistance, rose to the position of PLO chairman, and his forces quickly amended the PLO Charter to call for "armed struggle" as "the only way to liberate Palestine."[6]

For Arafat and his supporters, the question involved how to conduct such a campaign. Initial attempts called for operations out of the occupied West Bank and Gaza. However, Israeli forces made such operations almost impossible, arresting thousands of Palestinians suspected of supporting the PLO and other Palestinian organizations. There were some fights like that at Karamah, in Jordan, in March 1968, where Palestinian and Jordanian units fought an Israeli raiding party to a standoff, and the Israeli response to that event drove Palestinians deeper into Lebanon and Jordan.[7] Life for Palestinians continued under Israeli occupation, and the Israelis allowed a few concessions, such as the selection of Arab city mayors, but forbade any activity that would challenge Israel's hold on the territories.

In 1974, the PLO gained some status in the territories when the Arab League summit in Rabat, Morocco, declared the PLO to be the "sole legitimate representative of the Palestinian people." But contesting this view was the Democratic Front for the Liberation of Palestine, led by Naif Hawatma, who broke with the Popular Front for the Liberation of Palestine to form his own movement, the Democratic Front for the Liberation of Palestine (DFLP).

Palestinians Abroad

More than 700,000 Palestinians became refugees after the 1948 war. Around 180,000 Palestinians fled to Lebanon after the 1948 war, but Lebanese authorities refused to allow for the integration of Palestinians into Lebanon's population.[8] This was partly because of Christian opposition and partly due to an Arab consensus that the Palestinians must not integrate anywhere, so that they would form the basis of a return movement. Palestinian activists began to operate on their own from Lebanon, as the PLO launched a series of aircraft hijackings, but Israeli retaliation for the hijacking of an El Al aircraft in December 1968 destroyed thirteen Lebanese planes at the Beirut airport. That began a political crisis that continued through the Lebanese civil war.[9] Palestinian activity in Jordan also grew until it threatened the government of King Hussein. After Palestinian commandos hijacked several civilian airliners, flew them to Jordan, and blew them up, Jordanian forces mobilized to drive out Fatah and other Palestinian guerrillas in September 1970. By July 1971, Jordanian forces drove most Palestinian guerrillas from Jordan to Lebanon, increasing Lebanese instability in the process. Some became parties to the Lebanese civil war, as well as victims of it. Others were caught up in the Israeli invasion of Lebanon in June 1982, which intended to evict Palestinian fighters from southern Lebanon. Many Palestinians died or were wounded in attacks against their refugee camps, as occurred at Sabra and Shatilla in 1982 when Lebanese Christian militiamen entered areas controlled by Israeli forces and massacred hundreds of Palestinians.

First Efforts at Compromise

In an impromptu interview in 1989, Arafat emphasized the renouncement of armed struggle and claimed that he needed the United States to broker agreements with Israel.[10] Although PLO operations gained the organization considerable notoriety, they failed to gain back even one square inch of land for the Palestinians at a time when Egyptian President Sadat won the return of the Sinai Peninsula through negotiations with Israel. The PLO headquarters was ousted first from Amman and then from Beirut, to remote Tunis, far away from the bulk of the Palestinian population. Even there it was not safe from Israeli raids.

The First Intifadah

In December 1986, an Israeli military vehicle hit and killed several Palestinians in Gaza. This incident ignited decades of frustration and anger, resulting in the *intifadah,* or "shaking off." The intifadah was a series of sporadic but continuing demonstrations against Israeli occupation in the West Bank and Gaza, fought mostly through strikes and hit-and-run attacks against Israeli troops. Most of the participants were young Palestinians who had lost hope of obtaining a future under Israeli occupation. They consumed a considerable part of the Israeli military's effort, and resulted in growing numbers of casualties for both sides. The Israeli military operated patrols in Palestinian areas, which often found themselves under attack by Palestinian youth wielding stones or Molotov cocktails. They retaliated by shooting tear gas and rubber-coated bullets at the demonstrators, who died in increasing numbers. Despite the Israeli response, the demonstrations continued, resulting in a growing chorus of criticism from outside Israel to act on some of the Palestinian demands. The PLO appeared removed from the intifadah and in some ways, the demonstrations also appeared to challenge the remoteness of the PLO and its leadership from the day-to-day struggle under Israeli occupation. Both the PLO and the Israeli government came to believe that the only road out of the endemic violence was a peace agreement.

Peace Again?

The Oslo-Madrid peace process offered an end to the unrest, and in many ways, the whole Oslo-Madrid peace offerings attempted to bring to closure the continuing violence in the West Bank and Gaza. The Madrid Declaration of Principles laid out a systematic method intended to disentangle Israelis and Palestinians under occupation (see Chapter 1 for details). In June 2005, Israel withdrew all settlers from Gaza. The number of Israeli settlers in the West Bank is far larger, with over 230,000, twice the number at the start of the Oslo-Madrid talks designed to return the occupied territories to the Palestinians.[11]

In June 2000, Yasir Arafat and Israeli Prime Minister Ehud Barak met at Camp David, Maryland, to attempt a final settlement of the differences between the two polities. The effort failed, fueling frustrations on both sides. A visit to Jerusalem holy sites in September 2000 by future Prime Minister Ariel Sharon only reinforced Palestinian frustrations, and the resulting violence led to the collapse of the peace process.

The Second Intifadah

The second intifadah (often referred to as the Al-Aqsa intifadah) saw different tactics used by both Palestinian activists and Israeli forces. Rather than burning tires and throwing rocks, followed by Israeli rubber-coated bullets and tear gas, this one became far deadlier for both sides. Palestinians turned to suicide bombings and sniper attacks, while Israel escalated to using heavy weapons (including American-supplied F-16 fighter aircraft and Apache helicopters) against activists in the crowded cities and refugee camps in the occupied territories. Patchwork efforts by the United States and others failed to bring about progress, and peace remained as elusive as ever. President George W. Bush hoped that a new Palestinian prime minister might rejuvenate the talks. However, in the face of over 700 Israeli and over 2,000 Palestinian dead since September 2000, the prospects remained dim. Polls indicated that the Palestinian population was turning away from Yasir Arafat and the Palestinian Authority and toward the Islamists, with Arafat's support slipping from almost 32 percent in June 2000 to 21 percent in April 2003 while support for the Islamist parties increased from 12 to 30 percent during the same period.[12] As Israeli attacks continued (assassination targets included Sheik Yassin, the spiritual head of Hamas, in March 2004), Palestinian resistance seemed deeper than ever, although powerless to resist the Israeli military. Arafat's death in November 2004 only increased Palestinians' sense of hopelessness, as their most recognized symbol was gone. Others, though, felt that a new style of Palestinian leadership might replace the autocratic and shortsighted ways of Arafat.[13] That chance occurred in January 2005 with the overwhelming election of Mahmoud Abbas with a margin of over 65 percent of the total vote.[14] A year later, though, Palestine held its first parliamentary elections, and the voters swept Abbas's Fatah Party from power, as Hamas gained seventy-six seats compared to Fatah's forty-three.

The Palestinians gained a small but valuable piece of land when Prime Minister Sharon ordered Israeli settlers evacuated from Gaza in the summer of 2005. The Palestinians benefited from the real and symbolic value of the withdrawal, but the violence between Israeli soldiers and the settler supporters that marred the withdrawal indicated that a much larger (and thus more politically difficult) spasm of violence would mark any Israeli withdrawal from the West Bank, which was a larger, if now more elusive goal for most Palestinians. Palestinians also lost land in 2005 and later as Israel erected a "security obstacle" (defenders call it a fence, detractors call it a wall) to prevent attacks against Israeli targets from Palestinian areas. According to one ranking Palestinian official, Gaza and the West Bank represent 22 percent of the original Palestine, and the barrier, which snakes through Palestinian lands near the Israeli border, takes 15 percent of the 22 percent, leaving Palestinians with even less land for a state.[15]

In January 2006, the Palestinian Authority held another round of parliamentary elections, and Hamas took a majority of the 132 seats with 76, leaving Fatah with 43. Even Hamas leaders seemed surprised by the scope of their victory, and it took a while to begin the selection of a government. As both the United States and Israel cut off their limited aid to the Palestinian Authority, the need for a functioning government was perhaps the less serious problem the new government faced. The differences between Hamas and Fatah were increasingly settled by violence, and in June 2007, Hamas virtually took over Gaza by force. The prospects for a peaceful settlement in Gaza diminished as Hamas also expanded its influence in the West Bank. Said one Fatah member, reflecting the grim situation, "I know Hamas. I believe there may not be a dialogue; the resolution may be unfortunately by force."[16]

THE PALESTINIAN POLITICAL SYSTEM

The political structure of the Palestinian Authority came from the Declaration of Principles on Interim Self-Government Arrangements (DOP), signed in Washington in September 1993. The DOP provided for an interim self-government that was to transition to permanent status over a period not to exceed five years. The problem is that no final status agreement exists after the final talks began in May 1996. Consequently the Palestinian Authority operates under interim status. Palestine is not ranked by Freedom House as a country, but in both categories of "Israeli occupied territory" and "Palestinian Authority–administrated territories," the rankings are "not free." While there are state structures (ministries, institutions, and other trappings), true state formation remains largely strangled by poverty, occupation, isolation, corruption, and deep factions within the Palestinian nation.

Political Divisions Among Palestinians

Factions fill the Palestinian political space. Even in the Arafat era, chasms across this space became increasingly wide; with Arafat's death, they became almost a paralyzing condition for Palestinian unity and statehood. These factions formed against the backdrop of a lack of integral forces in Palestinian history, as early occupiers divided the Palestinians with real and imagined boundaries. Current political actors both inside and outside of the Palestinian community reinforce those early bloc divisions, usually to their own perceived advantage.

One reason for Palestinian divisions is the different history of their two respective territories, Gaza and the West Bank. Egypt occupied Gaza between 1949 and 1967, and Egypt's Muslim Brotherhood became an inspiration for Gazans who studied and traveled to Egypt, giving Gaza a more religious cast than the West Bank. Jordan controlled the West Bank, also until 1967, and its political dialect came about more through Jordanian-inspired Arab nationalism. It is hardly surprising now that the religious-based Hamas holds sway in Gaza while the more nationalistic Fatah is dominant in the West Bank.

The Palestinian population is hardly unified on the peace accords, or, for that matter, on many other things. It generally separates into three camps: the mainstream nationalist center, a leftist opposition, and Islamist opposition.[17] The center supports a secular Palestinian state in the West Bank and Gaza, with at least some democracy, and its followers are likely to be young, male, and less educated. The left opposition, largely the PFLP and the Democratic Front for the Liberation of Palestine (DFLP), accepts Israeli-Palestinian peace but not the Oslo Accords. They are largely young and well educated. The religious opposition favors a religious state, opposing the peace process and the legitimacy of Israel. It permits some religious practices (like veils for women) while favoring limited democracy. Adherents range from illiterate to well educated.[18]

The political mainstream got support after Oslo, holding at around 38 percent. The left had around 5 percent and the Islamists about 15 percent as of 1998.[19] However, the results did not reveal the depth of support for any position, and some commentators claimed that Hamas itself had 35–45 percent of Palestinians in the PA-controlled areas.[20] Arafat's own support continued to erode, slipping from 47 percent at the time of Camp David to 33 percent a year later, while Fatah dropped from 37 percent in July 2000 to 29 percent in July 2001.[21] By 2007 new Islamist groups were filling Palestinian life, imposing draconian measures on society (raiding Internet cafés and destroying the computers), and criticizing Hamas for participating in the government. One Hamas official stated, "There is a central problem and that is al-Qaeda, and they are spreading. The Islamic awakening has been going on for 25 years now. But this, now, is going to become a huge problem for us."[22]

Hamas arose after the start of the first intifadah in 1987, its followers inspired by the sermons of Sheik Ahmed Yassin.[23] Its objective is to create an Islamic state in the former Palestinian mandate and eliminating Israel. Its functions are both military and social, with members involved in both the provision of social services within the occupied territories and in strikes against Israel. The latter often involves suicide attacks inside Israel carried out by the militant Izzedine al-Qassam Brigades. The attackers often strike civilian targets in an effort to demoralize the Israeli public, although one Hamas leader claimed that they were legitimate since "no one in Israel who reaches eighteen can bypass the Army," leaving the impression that

Hamas considers everyone in Israel a soldier and thus a legitimate target.[24] Hamas has generally opposed the Palestinian-Israeli peace process, and the attacks are apparently designed to thwart further peace progress. Hamas moved into the Palestinian political sphere in 2005, declaring its intention to compete for parliamentary seats, which it swept in January 2006, as noted below.

Palestinian Islamic Jihad arose around 1979 in the occupied territories, largely inspired by the Islamic revolution in Iran. Its founders, Fathi Shqaqi, Abd al-Aziz Odah, and Bashir Musa, were Palestinian students in Egypt who became disenchanted with the Egyptian Muslim Brotherhood's gradual moderation on the Palestinian issue, and moved to the territories to organize Islamic resistance to the Israeli occupation. The Palestinian Islamic Jihad originally competed with Hamas for influence, but the two groups now occasionally cooperate. After Israeli agents reportedly killed Fathi Shqaqi in 1995, the Palestinian Islamic Jihad weakened. Hamas apparently no longer sees it as a rival organization.

The Palestinian Authority (PA) under Arafat had to contend with staggering problems at its onset as a political organization. The area under its control suffered from deep poverty, and political divisions were difficult to bridge. By some estimates, around 40 percent of the Palestinian population living in Gaza and 20–25 percent in the West Bank supported Hamas. Hamas used PA territory as a base of operations to launch attacks against Israeli targets, and Arafat had to clamp down on Hamas supporters in his territory. PA courts did hand down stiff sentences (including execution by firing squad) for Hamas members arrested in connection with acts of violence both against Israel and against PA officials. The PA also found itself struggling to make the transition from opposition group to governors, dealing with not only the Israelis and radical Palestinian groups, but also with the day-to-day struggles to govern a poor area where hope was sometimes a scarce commodity.

When the PLO became the Palestinian Authority, its leadership and its political structure were oriented toward revolution rather than governance. The transition to the PA thus required a transformation of the organization. The PLO had no trained administrators who understood how to manage public organizations and carry out public functions. There were, for example, no trained police and no mechanisms to train them. Thus Jordan trained Palestinians in police functions in order to implement Oslo.

The Palestinian Executive

The chairman of the Palestinian Executive wields the most political power in the Palestinian Authority areas. Yasir Arafat, the first chairman, molded the executive in ways that both enhanced his authority and gave the appearance of power sharing. Arafat gained legitimacy through his position as leader of the Palestinian revolution, though many Palestinians argued that he lost much of it in his role as peace negotiator and security cooperator with Israel. By winter 2000, he appeared to gain back some authority as peace with Israel floundered amid violence, and Arafat's tougher stance regained lost popularity among Palestinians.[25] But it would not last. As violence from both sides continued into the winter of 2001, a poll conducted by Nader Said of Bir Zeit University showed that Palestinian support for Islamist groups rose to 31 percent from 23 percent, while Arafat's Fatah organization dropped from 33 percent to 20 percent. Support was particularly high for Hamas, which women favored for its support of schools and other social services.[26] One quote summed up the situation: "On the ground, after years of Israeli military raids and blockades and Palestinian political paralysis, the economy is growing more dependent on foreign donors, and the institutions of statehood are crumbling."[27] It was hardly surprising, therefore, when Hamas won national elections handily in 2006.

The Palestinian Executive includes thirty-one ministers, some at the head of various ministries, while others serve without portfolio. The Palestinian Charter did not establish the number of ministers, so Arafat increased its size arbitrarily. In August 1998, he added ten ministers and reappointed some previously accused of corruption. There was reported consternation within the Palestinian Legislative Council over the announcement, particularly when Arafat announced the reappointment of three ministers accused of spending government money on personal items such as luxury cars and furniture.[28] In the wake of this action two cabinet ministers resigned, included Palestinian negotiator Hanan Ashrawi, who had been initially transferred from the Higher Education Ministry to the Tourism and Antiquities Ministry.[29] In mid-2003, both the United States and other Arab countries put increasing pressure on Arafat to do something he had refused to do—appoint a prime minister as an alternative source of influence in Palestinian Authority politics. Finally he reluctantly appointed Mahmoud Abbas (otherwise known as Abu Mazen) to the position, and the United States immediately urged Abbas to start peace talks with Israel.[30] For a brief period progress seemed possible, and Abbas and Ariel Sharon talked on several occasions, with Abbas agreeing to rein in the violent Palestinian groups held accountable for numerous suicide bombings in Israel. However, by August 2003, the process appeared to fall apart as both sides once again exchanged violence. Abbas resigned in September, blaming Israelis, Americans, and the Palestinian legislature for failing to back him.[31] Arafat then nominated the speaker of the Palestinian parliament, Ahmed Qureia, as prime minister, although some observers argued that his closeness to Arafat might limit his independence.[32] Palestinian militants deeply dislike Qureia, faulting him for the failed peace plan of 2000.[33] In October 2003 Arafat named a new cabinet, but there were few changes except the naming of Nasser Yousef to the Interior Ministry, which has charge of the security forces.[34]

Arafat's leadership style hampered the Palestinian Authority. He did not appear to have a long-term strategy but rather relied on short-term improvisation.[35] Arafat also relied on a small circle of senior Palestinian Authority officials who served with him in Tunisia. This small group controlled access and information reaching Arafat, shielding him from both the Palestinian public and negative news.[36] The consequence was that Arafat and the old leadership lacked the ability to set new directions for Palestinian policy.

Arafat's death in November 2004 led to the appointment of Mahmoud Abbas as chairman of the Palestine Liberation Organization as well as Fatah, while Rawhi

Fattouh, speaker of the Palestinian Legislative Council, became acting president until elections could be held within sixty days. Abbas faced a considerable challenge as
he had lived under Arafat's shadow, as had much of the Palestinian governing apparatus, leaving considerable uncertainty about its future.[37] Palestinian voters ultimately rejected both Abbas and Arafat's legacy in January 2006, giving Hamas an
outright majority in the Legislative Council. The results were as much a consequence of political skill as of popularity. Hamas only got 44 percent of the total
vote, but it ran only one candidate for each seat, while Fatah candidates often competed against each other (39 candidates for six seats in Jerusalem, for example).[38] In
March 2006, the parliament chose Ismail Haniyeh as prime minister, Said Siyam, a
popular Hamas lawmaker from Gaza to head the Interior and Civil Affairs ministries, and Mahmoud Zahar as foreign minister. Fatah refused to take part in the
government, and its self-exclusion led to bitter fighting, exacerbated by a funding
cutoff by Western countries, led by the United States. Saudi Arabia intervened, calling both Fatah and Hamas leaders to Mecca, after which they returned to Palestine
to hammer out yet another government, with Fatah getting at least six cabinet seats.
One political figure held out little hope that things would change. A Palestinian
lawmaker, Rawya Shawa, said, "In principle I support power-sharing, but it won't
be easy for Hamas and Fatah to get along together, and I'm not sure a unity government will last long."[39]

The Palestinian Legislative Council

Under the Basic Law that serves as the Palestinian Authority, the Palestinian Legislative Council has the largest grant of political power. However, since Arafat never
signed the Basic Law, it remains in suspense. Should that law become official, the
president of the Palestinian Authority would have to sign a bill granting legislative
authority to the Palestinian Council into law within thirty days of the third reading
of the measure.

Elections for the first Palestinian Legislative Council were held in January 1996,
with eighty-eight seats contested. The results gave Fatah forty-nine seats, Fatah-
affiliated legislators fifteen seats, independent Islamic-affiliated legislators four, with
independents gaining seventeen seats, with three belonging to breakaway legislators
who dropped their affiliation during the election. The January 2006 elections reversed Fatah's dominance, as that party won only forty-three seats (sixteen from
election districts and twenty-seven from national lists) compared to Hamas's seventy-six seats (forty-six from electoral districts and thirty from national lists). Thirteen seats went to smaller parties or independent candidates. The elections of
January 2006 changed that lineup dramatically, with Hamas winning an outright
majority of seats, reducing Fatah to the role of opposition party.

The Oslo Accords link the Palestinian Legislative Council to another Palestinian
legislative body, the Palestinian National Council. While the PLC represents just
the Palestinians living in the PA-administered areas, the PNC claims to represent all
Palestinians, including those under Israeli occupation. The PNC, a 422-member

body, elects the Executive Committee of the PLO that serves as its leadership. The PNC also has the power to change the Palestinian National Charter, and did so in April 1996, deleting the parts of that charter denying Israel's right to exist. The PNC repeated that vote in December 1998 in the presence of President Clinton after Israeli Prime Minister Benjamin Netanyahu demanded the vote as a condition to his continuing engagement in the Israeli-Palestinian peace process.

The Palestinian legislature attempted to carry out independent functions, including approving prime ministers and cabinets, but also took the somewhat unusual step of voting a no-confidence motion against the government in September 2005 for failing to stop Hamas-inspired violence in Gaza following the Israeli pullout. That vote, 43 to 5, was accompanied by visiting Palestinian police, who entered parliament with guns firing into the air in protest over their lack of bullets in coping with Hamas the week before.[40] The incident suggested that democratic norms were not fully accepted in all Palestinian political quarters.

The Palestinian Judiciary

The PA has yet to establish a formal court system, so the Palestinian police authority has taken much of the responsibility for the administration of justice. One of those responsibilities is security policing. The PA wanted the authority to police citizens without interference from Israel. So one of the first steps in creating the structure of the PA was security force training, provided mostly by Jordan. More recently, that training has included a role for the American Central Intelligence Agency. Building on a long history of ties with the PLO, the CIA began a program in 1996 to train PA security forces in interrogation of suspects, intelligence gathering, and other practices designed to help PA forces combat Hamas.[41] That has been a considerable responsibility. Hamas is the declared enemy of the PA as well as the Israelis. Hamas regards the Palestinian acceptance of the Oslo Accords as a sellout of Palestinian aspirations calling for the elimination of Israel.[42] The Palestinian police detained Hamas leader Ahmed Yassin under house arrest after a car bomb exploded in Jerusalem in October 1998. However, PA police even turned on Fatah, Arafat's own Palestinian party, when they stormed a Fatah headquarters in October 1998 in search of illegal weapons.[43]

THE STATUS OF WOMEN IN PALESTINE

Even after incorporation as the Palestinian Authority, the role of women in the new political entity was not clear.[44] Women were significant participants in the intifadah, often organizing demonstrations and supporting males in their families. This role raised questions about what rights would women have in a Palestinian political entity. Would the marriage age be raised to eighteen so girls could finish high school before marriage? Could a woman seek a divorce if her spouse took another wife? Would women be allowed full participation in the Palestinian political system?

In 1998, the Women's Center for Legal Aid and Counseling organized a mock parliament. Deputies to the parliament voted to remove gender discrimination in existing Palestinian laws, shocking Islamists, who claimed that the event was a "conspiracy against Islam."[45] PA officials gave the session their sponsorship and protection, and denounced the Islamists statements as "terrorism of the mind."[46] A more recent effort on the part of some Palestinian women to reform marriage laws (requiring the father's permission for women to marry and permitting males more than one wife) were met by stiff resistance from Islamic leaders. A cleric from Ramallah accused the women of advocating adultery because they wanted to decriminalize it.[47] An organization of Islamic women, Hansah Society, opposed their efforts claiming that the problem was not with Islamic law but with how it was interpreted.[48]

Palestinian women were traditionally underrepresented in the higher levels of PA government. One study found that while women constitute 46 percent of the positions in the lower levels of PA institutions, women hold only 14 percent of the higher positions in these same organizations; in six ministries, no woman is a deputy minister.[49] Women were active in the 2006 Hamas campaign for parliament, registering voters and going to homes to mobilize Hamas supporters. In that election, women candidates won six of the seventy-four Hamas seats in parliament (thirteen total seats, up from five previously), including one mother whose three sons died in suicide attacks. By some accounts, Hamas opened doors for women: "Before Hamas, women were not aware of the political situation. However, Hamas showed and clarified what was going on. Women have become much more aware."[50]

Women in Gaza also face the burden of high birth rates, as noted above. Women who want to limit their families find opposition from both Islamic clerics and from the remnants of the PLO policy that encourages Palestinians to have more children than Israelis do and thus overwhelm Israel through demographics. Thus women in Gaza average 7.0 children in their childbearing years, and in the West Bank 5.6.[51]

THE STRUCTURE AND PERFORMANCE
OF THE PALESTINIAN ECONOMY

The Palestinian economy is really three economies: Gaza, West Bank, and East Jerusalem. In both the West Bank and Gaza the GDP per capita is $1,500, one of the lowest in the Middle East. Unemployment in both Gaza and the West Bank is at over 20 percent, with around 46 percent of the population below the poverty line. These numbers are estimates, and the unemployment rate may be higher than reported.

The Palestinians suffer from a laggard economy, poor infrastructure, and continued dependence on the Israeli economy. The economy will have to grow dramatically to support population growth, something that seems unlikely for the next several years. The consequences of the second intifadah have decimated the Palestinian economy. According to one source, the GDP dropped by more than 24 percent, while GDP per capita declined by 40 percent between 1999 and the end of 2002, while the Palestinian population in the occupied territories increased by more than 10 percent.[52] An Israeli study in 2004 estimated that the accrued cost of the intifadah to the Palestinians was $4.5 billion and that the Palestinian GDP dropped by 30 percent over that period.[53]

Economic problems are particularly serious in Gaza. Even before Israeli occupation, the area was poor and underdeveloped. After Israel took the area in 1967, the economic situation was transformed by what Roy calls "de-development."[54] This policy prevented the development of the resources and institutions necessary for economic growth, curtailing banks and education, and siphoning off a large part of the Gazan population to work in Israel.[55] Many residents of Gaza (around 25,000) work in Israel, where the wages are higher than at home. However, the Israeli government has cut those numbers by two-thirds in the past decade, partially because the numerous border closings by the Israeli government have caused Israeli employers to seek a more reliable labor source.[56] Israeli policies have turned Palestine from an exporting to an importing economy.[57] While the resulting labor shortage in Palestine prevented substantial investment there, Palestinian workers also found themselves replaced in Israel by workers from eastern Europe and South Asia, resulting in the dual dilemma of high unemployment and a lack of foreign investment.[58] The high unemployment is likely to continue, since the staggering birth rate in Gaza will cause its population of 1.1 million to double by the year 2014. The population of the West Bank, at just over 3 million in 2000, should reach 5.5 million over the same time.[59]

Other problems abound. In the summer of 1997, a report by a committee of the Palestinian Legislative Council allegedly found widespread corruption among PA officials responsible for managing public budgets. While the report (and the street rumors that exaggerated its findings) found fiscal mismanagement and inefficiencies, one critic of the report argues that it highlights the extraordinary difficulty of public management in the absence of a state and its necessary structures and laws.[60] There is no subsequent evidence that the problems have abated since the report.

In 2000, explorers found deposits of natural gas off the coast of Gaza, and Israel, which has control over that coast, tacitly permitted the Palestinian Authority to treat the find as its own. The PA issued a concession to the BG Group of Great Britain to drill an exploration well that revealed recoverable gas, valued at between $2 and $6 billion. According to BG, the gas might provide ten to twenty years of power for electrical generation, relieving the Palestinians from having to buy most of their energy from Israel, and leaving some to sell on the international market.[61] The income from the gas could also help the Palestinian Authority push economic development, although there is no assurance that it will not end up in the pockets of Palestinian officialdom.

The Role of Outside Aid

Outside aid helps the territories sustain a minimal level of existence and offers some hope for economic growth. In late 1998, a number of international donors pledged $3 billion to the PA, including $2 billion from the European Union and

$900 million from the United States. While some of the money is earmarked for roads and housing, some is intended to bolster the Palestinian public payroll. [62] That may buy short-term political support, but it may also prevent the PA from trimming an already expensive public sector. Aid from the Arab world, by contrast, was a scarce commodity until early 2001, when several Gulf oil-producing countries donated $300 million to keep the PA from going bankrupt.[63]

PALESTINIAN FOREIGN POLICY

Recognition of a Palestinian national entity came slowly, but even before the Oslo-Madrid process, all Arab countries and some countries outside of the Middle East recognized Palestine as a nation-state and even accorded it diplomatic status, complete with embassies in many Arab capitals. Palestinian foreign policy also began before the formal recognition of the Palestinian Authority as the legitimate agency governing land occupied by Palestinian citizens.

The agreement finalized in 1993 between the Israelis and the PLO was designed to form a framework for a Palestinian political entity short of an actual state and create a climate of trust for both sides in order for negotiations to proceed. The agreement, known as the Declaration of Principles (DOP), specified a political framework for a Palestinian political entity by specifying elections for a Palestinian Council. International observers and the Palestinian police were to supervise compliance of the agreement after the DOP took force. The Palestinian Council's jurisdiction includes the Gaza and the West Bank, except for "issues that will be negotiated in the permanent status negotiations."

The Palestinian Council received specific authority over particular issues, including education and culture, health, social welfare, direct taxation, and tourism. The agreement also authorized the Palestinian police to control crime. Sometimes the Palestinian police resorted to unorthodox methods that smacked of punishment without trial. For example, Palestinian police arrested suspected drug dealers in areas under Palestinian control and shot them in the kneecaps. Even more dramatically, the PA executed two police officers for the alleged murder of two brothers after a thirty-minute trial held two days after the murder.[64]

The DOP attempted to build a permanent international connection to the agreement, inviting the governments of Jordan and Egypt to participate in facilitating liaisons between both their governments and the Palestinian Authority and the Israeli government and the Palestinians. The DOP also recognized that disagreements between Israelis and the Palestinian Authority would inevitably result and thus established a Joint Liaison Council to address such problems when they occurred.

A Future Palestinian State?

There are few other issues that arouse as much controversy and passion as the question of a Palestinian state. For Palestinians, statehood remains an ultimate dream—something they have never had but have sought for a century. It would provide for them what the Israelis, the British, the Ottomans, and all others who once ruled

Palestine did not give them—a social services system, sovereignty, their own leaders, their own currency, their own postage stamps, and all other things that people living nation-states take for granted.

For Israel, a Palestinian state represents another Arab state that becomes the basis for organized enmity against the Jewish state. It becomes a potential ally for other hostile Arab states. A Palestinian state might represent so much of a compromise with Palestinians that it could fuel the fires of Palestinians who demand nothing short of the elimination of the Jewish state. A Palestinian state would demand that its capital be Jerusalem, and ultimately it would deny access for Jews to the sacred sites, as Jordan did before 1967.

Others argue that a Palestinian state might actually enhance Israeli security. Such a state would reduce the incentive for Palestinians to resort to anti-Israeli violence. It is also possible to conceive of a Palestinian state with a police force for internal order, but not large enough to pose a threat to Israel.

The cohesion of such a state is problematic. If it were restricted to the West Bank and Gaza, it would encompass Israeli settlements in the West Bank. By all accounts, these settlements are growing, with over 364,000 settlers in both the West Bank and East Jerusalem in 2007. As the settlements are located in Israeli-controlled areas of the West Bank, consolidation of either a Palestinian or Israeli population would be difficult at best.

The proposed Palestinian state also raises questions about where its capital should be. Palestinians have been adamant that the capital must be Jerusalem, a position just as staunchly opposed by Israelis. For the Palestinians, Jerusalem is the natural choice of a capital since it is considered sacred to all Muslims. However, Israelis recall that they were not allowed access to the Western Wall between 1947 and 1967, and vow that Israel must never give up control over it. Some argue that the Israeli government is trying to make it impossible for Jerusalem to become the capital of a Palestinian state by surrounding it with Jewish settlements. The other part of the Israeli strategy seems to involve keeping Jerusalem as Jewish as possible by urging Jews to live in the city and discouraging Palestinians. However, some Israeli Jews have left because they find Jerusalem too dirty, too crowded, too expensive, and too Orthodox. Those who can afford it are increasingly choosing to move to the suburbs, bringing about a 4 percent decline in the Jewish population since 1967.[65]

The plight of the Palestinians, as a stateless people, is felt widely in the larger Arab world. Even across the Maghreb, the broad expanse of land stretching from Egypt to the Atlantic Ocean which is covered in the next section, people express sympathy for the Palestinian cause because, even though the Maghrebi cultural heritage is distinctive, it is also Arab, and Arab unity remains the key factor linking the Maghreb with the other regions covered in this book.

SUGGESTED READINGS

Beinin, Joel, and Rebecca L. Stein, eds. *The Struggle For Sovereignty: Palestine and Israel, 1993–2005*. Stanford, CA: Stanford University Press, 2006.

Brand, Laurie A. *Palestinians in the Arab World: Institution Building and the Search for a State.* New York: Columbia University Press, 1988.

Brown, Nathan J. *Palestinian Politics After the Oslo Accords: Resuming Arab Palestine.* Berkeley: University of California Press, 2003.

Cobban, Helena. *The Palestinian Liberation Organization.* Cambridge: Cambridge University Press, 1984.

Farsoun, Samih K., with Christina E. Zacharia. *Palestine and the Palestinians.* Boulder, CO: Westview, 2006.

Fischback, Michael. *Records of Dispossession: Palestinian Refugee Property and the Arab-Israeli Conflict.* New York: Columbia University Press, 2003.

Hunter, F. Robert. *The Palestinian Uprising: A War by Other Means.* Berkeley: University of California Press, 1991.

Khalid, Rashid. *The Palestinian Identity: The Construction of a National Consciousness.* New York: Columbia University Press, 1998.

_____. *The Iron Cage: The Story of the Palestinian Struggle for Statehood.* Boston: Beacon, 2006.

Kimmerling, Baruch, and Joel S. Migdal. *Palestinians: The Making of a People.* Cambridge, MA: Harvard University Press, 1994.

Matthews, Weldon. *Confronting an Empire, Constructing a Nation: Arab Nationalists and Popular Politics in Mandate Palestine.* London: Tauris, 2006.

Mishal, Shaul. *The PLO Under Arafat: Between Gun and Olive Branch.* New Haven, CT: Yale University Press, 1986.

Mishal, Shaul, and Avraham Sela. *The Palestinian Hamas: Vision, Violence, and Coexistence.* New York: Columbia University Press, 2000.

Pappe, Ilan. *A History of Modern Palestine: One Land, Two Peoples.* Cambridge: Cambridge University Press, 2006.

Seikaly, May. *Haifa: Transformation of a Palestinian Arab Society, 1918–1939.* New York: Taurus, 1995.

Zahlan, A. B., ed. *The Reconstruction of Palestine: Urban and Rural Development.* New York: Columbia University Press, 1996.

Section IV

THE COUNTRIES
OF NORTH AFRICA

IMAGES *An ancient solitary pine tree frames the view from the hotel window of the Algiers harbor, under a sky filled with scudding dark clouds. One floor below is the Eisenhower Room, once the headquarters of the Allied commander. This ancient hotel holds the echoes of many conversations over the centuries, in Berber, French, English, German, and Arabic. Elegantly dressed Algerians come into the hotel bar, sample some Algerian wine, smoke a few cigarettes, and then disappear into the night, down the narrow lanes that lead to the harbor. They seem to have stepped out of a history book, briefly passing by the Americans sitting at the bar drinking Tango beer, before stepping back into the past. So much history here, so many memories, so little time to contemplate it all.*

The part of North Africa between Egypt and the Atlantic Ocean is called the Maghreb. It lies west of Egypt, which is also geographically a part of North Africa. The exact dividing line is not clear because it is as much cultural as geographical. Perhaps the best definition comes from the former president of Tunisia, Habib Bourguiba, who notes that west of the line the main dish is couscous (the wheat-based staple of the Maghreb diet), while on the other side of the line people eat rice.

The long Mediterranean coast of North Africa has been home to people who probably migrated there from central Africa and parts of the Middle East. Signs of human habitation indicate settlements may date back to 4000 BCE. Yet just below a fertile belt only a few kilometers wide lies the vast Sahara. The

Sahara is covered by endless dunes and stony outcrops, yet it is also the home to a civilization that struggled and grew in the oases, mountains, and small villages that supported both sparse agriculture and the caravan trade passing from sub-Saharan Africa and the eastern Sahara to North Africa's ports and into Egypt and beyond. To the uninitiated, it is barren and hostile, but to those who look closely, it is vivid colors, sharp-edged mountains, tawny scrub contrasted by salt marshes and oases.

Along the narrow ribbon of North African coast, great civilizations flourished thousands of years ago. Carthage was the seat of one of those civilizations, settled by Phoenician sailors in 814 BCE to provide a base for Phoenician ships sailing from Lebanon. Carthage became the seat of a significant civilization in North Africa, and it was from there that the great leader Hannibal attacked Rome by crossing the Alps and descending to Rome. The Romans won the conflict after several wars with Carthage, sacking the city in 146 BCE. They built over the rubble of Carthage, and now there is almost nothing left of this ancient city by the sea.

The Phoenicians were not the only newcomers to settle in North Africa. A people called Berbers by the Greeks moved into North Africa and settled along the coast from Libya to Morocco. Their language (actually a collection of languages commonly called Berber) distinguishes them. Berbers were the majority population when the Arab armies of the seventh century came through spreading Islam and Arab culture. Some Berbers intermarried with Arabs, and almost all adopted the Arab language and Islam. They did not adopt it easily, though, particularly when Islamic rulers from afar imposed hardships on them. The Berber revolt in 740-741 against Umayyad governor Ubayd Allah ibn al-Habhab was suppressed only with heavy losses among the Syrian troops sent in to quell it.[1]

In the nineteenth century, the Maghreb was caught in the competition between European states for colonies. France took the bulk of the central and western part, although Spain marked off for itself the extreme western part and called it Spanish Sahara. Italy grabbed what is now Libya. The old colonial empire died hard in some places, but today independent countries sit atop its remains. The colonial influence remains, however. The French language is still widely spoken in the former French North Africa. Most trade in the Maghreb is with Europe, and many people from the new countries migrate to Europe seeking jobs. Agriculture dominates the economies of most North African states, and thus their exports are generally closed to a Europe protected by the European Union, which rejected Morocco's application as an associate member.

For many in North Africa today, that rejection is indicative of the relationship they have with the Europe that once colonized them, as second-class citizens. While the 2007 per capita income of France is close to $30,000, Morocco's is around $4,400, and in Algeria, it is about $7,700. Algerians and Moroccans fleeing the poverty of their respective countries get an increasingly hostile reception when they try to migrate to France. Those who do live in France write back home of the relative wealth enjoyed by French citizens. The makings of an increasingly cross-Mediterranean political climate are possible, but strident differences in culture remain. Differences also remain among Maghreb members. An effort to create an Arab Maghreb Union in 1990 failed when, for the second time in two years, the disputes between Morocco and Algeria, the positions taken by Libya, and the Western Sahara issue forced a cancellation of the Arab Maghreb Union summit in Algiers.[2]

The history of the Maghreb goes back for thousands of years, although the current state system dates largely from European colonial times. In each country chapter, therefore, the term "modern" is used in conjunction with each nation-state in times before its actual nation-state status. That simply reminds the reader that "modern Algeria," for example, dates back centuries as a place of importance, but that place was not always called "Algeria."

17

TUNISIA

IMAGES | *The helicopter sweeps low over the rolling hills covered with new grass, passing over tiny farmhouses and cattle. Gravel roads lead to small towns, each with a mosque and its distinctive square minaret. Outside of the picturesque villages along the coast that attract tourists, this rural farmland is another side of Tunisia, small farmers living much tas their ancestors did, eking out a living from this ancient land, depending on the rains that bring life or destitution.*

TUNISIA OCCUPIES A SMALL CORNER of the southern Mediterranean coast, wedged between Algeria and Libya. It is a modern country that retains strong connections to its past and its unique aesthetic tastes, including a penchant for painting the doors and windows of its stucco buildings a colorful blue and preserving the hauntingly beautiful Maluf music that dates back to Islamic Spain. Map 17.1 on page 371 shows Tunisia's location.

THE MODERN HISTORY OF TUNISIA

Once a part of French North Africa, the area now occupied by Tunisia has a rich history. Ancient Carthage dominated much of the Mediterranean region from a site that is now in modern Tunisia. The Romans destroyed so much of the city after the Second Punic War that little remains today.

The French Colonial Period

French influence in Tunisia began when French forces crossed into Tunisian territory from neighboring Algeria to stem border raids by Algerians opposed to French rule.[1] Tunisians initially resisted, but during the 1880s, they tended to adjust to the French and jockeyed for positions within the French administration system. French colonial policy relied on local officials under French supervision, while gradually increasing French power. Therefore, for example, in 1881 the bey's overseer was the

French resident minister, who was elevated to the post of foreign minister and, as Ling notes, "guardedly, but surely, power was transferred from the Bey to the resident-minister."[2] France placed Tunis under a treaty of protection rather than incorporating it into the republic as a *département*, since the French had already learned much from their Algerian experience. In this way, the French were able to minimize Tunisian opposition to their rule. They also offered opportunities for Tunisians to become at least symbolically important. Thus elite Tunisians learned French and established French-style schools to prepare them for employment in the colonial service. However, the French settlers, or *colons*, resisted, and opportunities for Tunisians diminished. The *colons* took the most productive land for themselves, leaving the Tunisians with marginal land and high taxes, to offset the untaxed activities of the French.[3] After World War I, resistance to French rule grew, and Tunisian nationalists founded the Destour, or constitutional movement (recalling the 1861 constitution) toward independence. Most Destour followers were from the higher social groups, the *khass* who were important by virtue of genealogy and education. Their ties to the remainder of Tunisian society were tenuous at best. By the late 1920s, the Destour movement was on the decline, challenged by a militant nationalist faction. In 1934, Habib Bourguiba, who had studied law in Paris, led a rump congress at Ksar Hilal in March 1934 to form the Neo-Destour (or New Constitutional) Party. The Neo-Destour appealed to the masses in Tunisia and became the foundation for the broad-based Tunisian independence movement.[4]

The Neo-Destour formed the locus of resistance against the French, which came to a bloody climax on April 9, 1938, when the police fired on a crowd of demonstrators in front of the French residence, killing 122 and wounding 62.[5] French colonial officials outlawed the Neo-Destour, and during World War II, they imprisoned Bourguiba, whom the Italians later freed. After the war, Bourguiba, exiled by the French in Cairo, made trips to many countries, including to the United States, to argue the cause of Tunisian independence. With Bourguiba absent from Tunisia, Ben Youssef assumed the leadership of the Neo-Destour Party.

The French hold on Tunisia tightened after the 1952 appointment of resident-general Jean de Hautecloque (known as "Jean the Terrible" in Tunisia). Hautecloque also cracked down on the Neo-Destour, arrested Bourguiba, and insisted that the French population of 30,000 would have political representation equal to that of the 300,000 Tunisians. Such a demand only institutionalized the preponderant representation of the colonial power, dashing the hopes of Tunisian nationalists that the French would ultimately increase Tunisians' political representation. Violence erupted, fueled by weapons left over from World War II, and the French responded with violence in turn.[6] French atrocities, including killing, rape, and mass arrest, were particularly severe in the Cape Bon area south of Tunis in early 1953. The situation became so grim that it, combined with other problems in the French empire, brought about the fall of the French government of Prime Minister Joseph Laniel, whom Pierre Mendès-France replaced in June 1954. Mendès-France offered Tunisia internal autonomy in the hope of retaining some French influence there. However, with the granting of complete sovereignty to Morocco, it became almost

MAP 17.1   TUNISIA

impossible for France to deny the same to Tunisia. The resulting Franco-Tunisian Protocol of March 20, 1956, gave complete independence to Tunis, allowing France to concentrate on Algeria. The structure of government defined at independence largely remains to this day.

Tunisia after Independence

Unlike other former colonies, Tunisia made what L. Carl Brown called an "elegant" transition to independence. Where violence wracked Algeria, Kenya, and much of

Portuguese Africa, Tunisia transitioned to a modern country without turmoil, and in many ways that was due to Bourguiba's leadership.[7]

The first task was to establish the mechanisms of government, and to determine who would run them. The Tunisian elite who were educated in Franco-Arab schools and identified with the Neo-Destour Party became the administrative elite. The Sadiki College produced leaders steeped in secular education on the theory that only knowledge and application of secular methods and thinking could resist Western encroachment.[8] It became the basis for the secular government that continues today.

Bourguiba, under the Neo-Destour banner, became president in 1956 after the French departed. He won a challenge over Ben Youssef, who took an Arab nationalist position in contrast to Bourguiba's secular liberalism.[9] The nationalists who once followed Ben Youssef gravitated to political Islam, but Tunisia became a reflection of Bourguiba himself, and by the late 1950s, he held command of all state institutions. In 1959, Bourguiba pushed through a constitution containing laws for elections, emphasizing straight majority voting, and thus allowing the Neo-Destour party lists to win handily.[10] The Tunisian president held considerable power relative to the National Assembly, according to the constitution, becoming in reality a rubber stamp for Bourguiba's policies. The Tunisian judiciary was theoretically independent from political control, but in reality members of the Neo-Destour could and did interfere with its rulings.[11] The Neo-Destour had successfully incorporated other elites and much of the labor movement.[12] However, that mantle did not extend across Tunisia, and particularly to the Islamic faith and small farmers.

Bourguiba's rule emphasized his nationalist background over the Islamic setting of Tunisia, and sometimes his challenges to Islamic practice caused problems. For example, in 1960 Bourguiba decided to circumvent the Ramadan fast because he argued that it inhibited national development. He drew on Islamic teaching to show that the war against underdevelopment was really a holy war, or jihad, and thus Muslims fighting this war were exempt from observing Ramadan. However, this line of thinking disturbed Tunisia's population, and ultimately Bourguiba abandoned it.[13] Bourguiba nevertheless kindled Islamist opposition, inspired by leaders like Rachid Ghannouchi, whose own writings reflected the thinking of Islamist thinkers like Hassan al-Banna and Said Qutb. Bourguiba had Ghannouchi arrested, but he failed to stem the influence of his somewhat modest interpretations of an Islamic alternative to Bourguiba (and later Ben Ali's) socialist vision of Tunisia.[14]

Bourguiba found support for the Neo-Destour slipping in the countryside after 1977, when unemployment doubled for a variety of factors. The police quelled riots, and the national labor union (UGTT) broke with the government and became a source of opposition to it. Despite government efforts to shore up the agricultural sector, disturbances continued through the 1980s, and Islamism as a political force grew as well.[15] The regime responded by arresting the leadership of the Islamic Tendency Movement (MTI). When lenient sentences resulted, Bourguiba was enraged and ordered a retrial. The interior minister, Zine el Abine ben Ali, recognized the danger of Bourguiba's actions, and may have used the incident to finalize his decision to orchestrate Bourguiba's removal.[16]

In 1964, the Neo-Destour Party became the Destourian Socialist Party, only to be relabeled the Democratic Constitutional Assembly in 1988 after Zine el Abine ben Ali replaced the ailing and ineffectual Bourguiba as president of Tunisia the year before. In that same year the National Assembly abolished the president for life provision in the old constitution, reflecting the frustration stemming from Bourguiba's thirty-one-year-long rule.

Tunisia's period of colonialization was brief, and it is Tunisia's earlier history that shaped its character and identity. As Waltz notes, Tunisia developed the mechanisms for a strong state long before the French arrived, but the modern state is not inclusive. The power hierarchy remains small and there are few alternative avenues of participation.[17] Moreover, Tunisian nationalists tacitly cooperated where necessary with the French, and thus managed to avoid the chasms that developed between France and Algerian nationalists, for example. Moreover, it is reasonable to speculate that Tunisia became the homogeneous country it is today partially because its population avoided such a struggle.

THE TUNISIAN POLITICAL SYSTEM

Habib Bourguiba used the party he founded, the Neo-Destour Party, to gain power and to govern as president from 1956 to 1987. Bourguiba renamed his party the Destourian Socialist Party (PSD) in 1962. The Destourian Socialist Party was renamed the Constitutional Democratic Rally Party (RCD) in 1987, and it holds a large majority in the unicameral Chamber of Deputies. Of the seven legal parties in Tunisia, the RCD holds 144 seats out of 163 in the legislature, while the Movement of Democratic Socialists (MSD) has only ten seats that were given to it by the ruling party to foster the appearance of a competitive party system. The other eight are divided among the five other legal parties. This 98 percent majority for the RCD gives the president almost unfettered rule without legislative interference. Tunisia is judged to be "not free" by the 2005 Freedom House survey.

Zine el Abidine ben Ali seized power from Bourguiba on November 7, 1987, claiming that Bourguiba was too ill to continue serving as president. Ben Ali had been an army brigadier general and chief of military intelligence who, because of his successful suppression of Islamist demonstrations, achieved the post of interior minister in April 1986 before he seized power. He was reelected in March 1994 to a second term without opposition, winning 99 percent of the total vote, and to a third term in October 2004 (Tunisia has no presidential term limits). There was little resistance from Tunisia's other parties. While the MDS is legal, its leadership has endured harassment from Tunisian authorities. In February 1996, MDS party leader Muhammad Mouada was convicted and imprisoned for alleged espionage, and in July of the same year the chief MDS deputy, Khemais Chamari, was sentenced to five years in prison on the same charge. The government released both from prison on January 2, 1997, reportedly on humanitarian grounds. Chamari's wife, Alya Sharif-Chamari, was seriously injured in an automobile accident in February 1996. Witnesses reported that a vehicle from the Tunisian state security service deliberately rammed her car.

The electoral laws for president were changed in time for the scheduled 1999 election to allow for multiple candidates, and 20 percent of the Majlis seats are designated for opposition parties. In June 1999, the cabinet approved changes in the election laws allowing any party with one or more seats in the Chamber of Deputies to advance a presidential candidate.[18] In the October 1999 election, two other candidates ran against Ben Ali in one of the first contested elections in the Arab world. However, in the face of the RCD dominance of the Tunisian political system, it was not surprising that Ben Ali again won 99 percent of the election.

Tunisia has a smattering of smaller parties, but they have almost no influence. While the Tunisian Communist Party (renamed the Renewal Movement in April 1993) is legal, the regime has outlawed the Islamist party al-Nahdah. The regime has also jailed Communist Party members for their activities, but President Ben Ali released several of them in 1993 and 1995.

Outside of the party structure, other political actors play significant roles in Tunisian politics. One is Union Générale des Travailleurs Tunisiens (UGTT), the Tunisian trade union organization. As noted above, Bourguiba cracked down on the UGTT in 1985–1986. Before that, the UGTT was probably the strongest labor organization in North Africa and the Middle East. Bourguiba's actions did not break the organization, and Ben Ali managed to coopt its leaders after his rise to power. After that, the UGTT tended to cooperate in curbing radical influence in its membership from both the political left and from al-Nahdah, which had tried to gain influence in the labor organization.[19]

Al-Nahdah (or rebirth), the Islamist movement, is the other political force outside the formal structure of the state. It began as the Mouvement de la Tendance Islamique (MTI) in the 1970s and its locus was Zaytuna University. The Bourguiba regime responded to political Islam with a mix of conciliation and pressure, jailing its leaders while engaging in a program of mosque building.[20] MTI metamorphosed into al-Nahdah and ran candidates in the 1989 elections, leading to state repression, as noted below.

There are three other Islamic groups in Tunisia—the Daaw, the Movement of the Islamic Way, and the Progressive Islamists, all of which call to a return to Islamic roots, or purity and virtuousness. Their members tend to emphasize personal and community faith rather than political action, though in one sense they are a possible reaction to Bourguiba's emphasis on Tunisian secularism.[21]

According to Articles 21 and 22 of the constitution, all citizens twenty-five years or older and holding Tunisian nationality for at least five years are eligible to vote in national and local elections. Any voter born of a Tunisian father (lineage is patrimonial in Islamic societies) is eligible to run for the Chamber of Deputies.

The Tunisian Executive

The president is directly elected by universal adult suffrage for up to three five-year terms. The president serves as head of the government. The prime minister serves under him, presiding over a cabinet of twenty-nine ministers, including Interior, Religious Affairs, Finance, Education, National Defense, and Foreign Affairs. Ben

Ali created the Religious Affairs Ministry in March 1992, arousing speculation that it was created to give the president cover for his crackdown on al-Nahdah.

Ben Ali tends to retain his ministers but shuffles them across ministries, very much as Bourguiba did. For example, in 1996, Ben Ali named Abdullah Kallel as defense minister, a position he had previously held in 1989 through 1991. But in January 1997 he moved Kallel to the post of justice minister, replacing Sadok Chaabane, and Habib Ben Yahia was named defense minister. Ben Ali also appointed Abderrahim Zouari as foreign minister, moved over from his position as minister of youth and childhood. Expertise is apparently less important than loyalty. Moreover, one way to ensure loyalty is to move loyal ministers across ministries to sweep out those whose loyalty may be in question.

However, even loyalty has its limits in times of political stress. In June 2000, Ben Ali found himself facing two camps in his administration as protests against his regime and attacks on journalists eroded Tunisia's image abroad. Some in his cabinet, including Interior Minister Adbellah Kallal and presidential advisers Abdelaziz Ben Dhia and Abdelwahab Abdallah, counseled a continuation of soft authoritarianism. Others, including Defense Minister Mohamed Jegham and former head of the Tunisian Human Rights League Dali Jazi, advised Ben Ali to relax his pressure against the Islamist movement.[22] There were a few signs of relaxation (the release of al-Nahdah member Toufik Chaib after a 52-day hunger strike).[23]

The Tunisian Legislature

The Tunisian legislature is a unicameral body, the Chamber of Deputies (Majlis al-Nuwaab), with a membership of 163. Legislators serve five-year terms. A 1993 law raised the number of seats from 144 to 163, and provided 19 seats selected by proportional representation. The constitution stipulates that the chamber meets at least twice a year for sessions lasting no more than three months, but also allows that either the president or a majority of members may extend sessions. Those sessions begin during October and end during July, except that the first session of every legislature begins during the first fifteen days of November, according to Article 29 of the constitution.

The Chamber of Deputies also has the power of censure (Article 62), where a vote is triggered by a motion of censure signed by at least half of the members. The vote, which must be delayed for forty-eight hours after the motion is approved, results in the resignation of the government if approved by a two-thirds margin. Should the legislature adopt a second motion of censure during the same legislative session, the president of Tunisia must either accept the resignation of the government or dissolve the chamber, and then call for new elections within thirty days.

The Tunisian Judiciary

The Tunisian judiciary consists of a Court of Cassation, with one criminal and three civil sections. Under the Court of Cassation are three courts of appeal, thirteen courts of first instance where cases originate, and fifty-one cantonal (or local) courts. The Council of State serves as an administrative court to handle disputes be-tween individuals and the state.[24]. The Council of State also contains a Court of Accounts, which monitors government compliance with laws regulating public funds. The military maintains its own separate military tribunals, which may try both military members and civilians accused of violating national security. The Tu-nisian constitution stipulates an independent judiciary; however, the judiciary itself falls under the Ministry of Justice and thus the executive branch. Moreover, the president is head of the Council of Judges and can pressure judges in politically sen-sitive legal issues. The Sharia courts—once divided into two systems, one for the followers of the Hanbali school and one for the Malaki school (see Chapter 2)—be-came one system in 1956 as Bourguiba merged them under the Personal Status Code, allowing women new rights.[25]

Ben Ali swiftly abolished several institutions associated with state repression of human rights after his ascent to power. First, he got the legislature to abolish the policy of incommunicado pretrial detention, and then he disbanded the positions of general prosecutor and the state security court.[26] After the 1989 election, how-ever, the pendulum began to swing the other way, with limits on press freedom and a clampdown on Islamists after an attack on an RCD office in the town of Bab Souika in February 1991 allegedly carried out by al-Nahdah.[27] In July 1992, the regime put 279 accused Islamists on trial, and in July, the regime sentenced 167 to prison terms ranging from three to twenty years. The regime held the trials under the scrutiny of Amnesty International, and sentences were less severe than feared.[28]

More recently, charges of short-term detention, harassment, torture, telephone taps, and other measures against political dissidents have surfaced.[29] Groups like Amnesty International, the Association Tunisienne des Femmes Democrates, and other groups are under surveillance and security forces disrupt or ban their meetings.[30]

According to the State Department report on human rights, the government's human rights record remains poor and it persists in committing serious abuses. However, the government continues to demonstrate respect for the religious free-dom of minorities, as well as the human rights of women and children.[31] The re-port also cites restrictions on freedom of the press.[32] Tunisian security forces monitor electronic communications, and, as one report holds, "Tunisia has proven itself to be perhaps the most repressive Arab government" in filtering access to In-ternet communications and in punishing those who find ways to get around the ban, although the government claims to be filtering out militant Islamic sites.[33]

Ben Ali has banned the al-Nahdah Party and severely repressed identified Islamists. However, Ben Ali justifies these acts as counterterrorist measures, and Tunisia has been relatively free from terrorism, at least originating in the Islamist movement.

THE STATUS OF WOMEN IN TUNISIA

President Bourguiba was an early modernizer, and his reforms included the emanci-pation of Tunisian women. He attacked such traditions as the veil and encouraged women to vote in elections.[34] As Micaud notes, "It took the explosion of triumphant nationalism to brush aside ancient customs sacralized by Islamic Law."[35] Today Tunisia is one of only two Arab countries (Jordan being the other) to have ratified all four human rights conventions on women's rights.[36] Tunisia is almost the only Arab country where abortion is legal and women have easy access to the procedure.[37] In the November 1999 elections for parliament, women won 12 percent of the seats.[38] Still, Tunisia is an Islamic country, and Islamic practices affect women living there. The Islamist movement is outlawed, and President Ben Ali has attempted to show progress for Tunisian women, if largely to demonstrate how he has controlled political Islam. In August 1998, for example, he presided over Tunisian Women's Day, celebrated in Tunisia to mark the anniversary of Code of Personal Status (CPS), put into law in 1956. The CPS resulted from Bourguiba's personal belief in the importance of advancing the interests of women in society.[39] The Code of Personal Status abolishes polygamy, sets a minimum marriage age for women, and allows both spouses to seek a divorce.[40] In 1992, new laws required the mother's consent for underage daughters to marry, created a fund to support alimony payments, and required judges to be educated in the area of women's rights. In 1996, the regime passed another law strengthening women's rights to property, but inheritance laws still favor the male spouse in divorce proceedings. Women make up around 45 percent of the workforce, which is very high for an Islamic country. School enrollment for girls is among the highest in the Arab world at 97 percent. Even more unusual is the percentage of women judges in Tunis, 60 percent of the total, as is the 43 percent of women university students. Few women hold powerful positions, however; for example, there is only one woman, Neziha Zarrouk, minister of Women and Family Affairs in the thirty-eight-member cabinet; traditionally, the position itself represents "women's work" in Tunisia.

Several women's groups exist in Tunisia, the largest being the National Union of Tunisian Women, which focuses largely on issues of women and the economy. However, as noted above, the regime bans women's groups that focus on human rights. The Tunisian Association of Democratic Women operates the only counseling center for battered women, and while there are stiff penalties for spousal abuse, police are reportedly reluctant to intervene and courts often regard it as a family problem.[41]

THE STRUCTURE AND PERFORMANCE OF THE TUNISIAN ECONOMY

The region now occupied by Tunisia once supplied the Roman Empire with grain and other agricultural products. Now, while agriculture remains an important component of Tunisia's economy, other sectors are rapidly replacing it.

The economic growth rate for the 1990s was around 4.4 percent (compared to the US growth rate of 4.1 percent in the same period). That appears to be a relatively healthy rate, but it has not kept pace with the large number of young people desiring to enter the workforce; thus the unemployment rate is more than 16 percent. The Tunisian economy is highly dependent on its agricultural sector and thus can fluctuate from year to year based on weather and other factors affecting agricultural production. In the 1950s, for example, economic growth ranged from −7.2 to +12.4 percent, depending on the amount of rainfall, and the economy suffered a deep depression in 1994 during a drought year.[42] In 2007, Tunisia had a 4 percent growth rate, and a GDP per capita of $8,600, higher than its other North African neighbors. Part of that growth reflects a shift away from agriculture (around 12 percent of employment) and toward services, around 22 percent.

When Tunisia became independent, its leadership had to choose a method to develop the economy, either a strong state role emphasizing the public sector or allowing the private sector to use market forces to build the economy. After considerable discussion Bourguiba first chose a liberal development strategy, emphasizing private capital and state assistance to capitalist projects and financial institutions.[43] However, after a disappointing performance, the state took the lead, and during the 1960s, the public sector accounted for 72 percent of fixed capital investment.[44] Economic conditions remained poor, though, and in January 1978 the UGTT called a general protest strike. The army repressed the strike harshly (47 dead in the official account, over 200 unofficially), but little was done by the regime to address the grievances.[45]

Prime Minister Hedi Nouria directed that the private sector again take the lead in Tunisia's economic development, and the regime created new institutions to foster private growth. The economy grew rapidly, setting the stage for the relatively healthy economy that followed.[46] Ben Ali built on ongoing reforms to reduce budget deficits, reform the tax system, and reduce price controls.[47] Privatization also encouraged private investment, which increased threefold in the first part of 2000.[48]

The statistics reflect few problems in the overall picture of Tunisia's economy. Inflation is relatively low, and the GDP per capita is comparable to that of other Arab countries without significant supplies of oil. While unemployment is relatively high, it is much lower than in Lebanon or Egypt, by comparison. More than eight in ten Tunisians own their homes, 75 percent of the population is middle class, and Tunisia is the third largest recipient of foreign direct investment in the Middle East despite having no oil.[49] Tunisia has also made significant progress in dismantling trade barriers, signing free trade agreements with the European Union, Turkey, Egypt, Jordan, and Morocco. However, there are structural problems remaining from the days when the state managed things from Tunis, and the government continues to intervene in ways that discourage individual initiative.

Tourism from Europe, in particular, is growing as more people discover the scenic beauty of the country, and investments from other Arab countries in Tunisia's tourism sector are expanding it even more.[50] Tunisia also benefits from another European connection; thanks to intervention by Italy, Tunisia gained access to part of the European Union market, and Tunisian olive oil now flows into Europe. The European Union signed its first Mediterranean partner agreement with Tunisia in April 1995, allowing certain Tunisian agricultural products to be exported into EU member countries. Tunisia is the EU's fifth largest foreign textile supplier.[51] The EU connection also bolsters Tunisia's tourist economy, since European tourists find Tunisia's beaches and historic ruins attractive. The government-run Union Touristique Internationale brings around 300,000 tourists from the European Union to Tunisia each year, and the director of that organization expected a 10 percent increase in 1999.[52]

Tunisia has small deposits of oil and natural gas, first exploited in 1949. The Cap Bon gas field was developed in that year to supply Tunis with gas, and in 1964 oil-field production began at El Borma. More discoveries came in 2005 and 2006, but thus far proven reserves add up to only around 1.5 billion barrels.

TUNISIAN FOREIGN POLICY

Tunisia is a small country between two larger and unstable ones and attempts to maximize its security by maintaining a strict policy of neutrality. Wedged between Algeria and Libya, Tunisia must watch to ensure that the aspirations of Muammar Qadhafi and the violence of Algeria do not spill into the country. Therefore Tunisia maintains ties to France and the United States, and received limited economic support from both. Tunisia's leadership realizes that economic prosperity is one vehicle to resist both the temptations of Qadhafi and the seduction of radical Islam.

IMAGES

> The hooded men descend on ropes from the helicopter and quickly over-power the surprised men inside the small building. Other commandos suddenly appear out of nowhere, storming another building and ripping it apart with automatic weapons, leaving bodies on the ground in their wake. Then helicopters arrive and drop men into the sea, who surround and destroy a small boat trying to land invaders in the surf. Live rounds turn the water into angry columns of white froth as body fragments fly into the air.
>
> This is only a drill, orchestrated by Tunisia's elite special forces. American special forces soldiers, watching the exercise, pay the Tunisians the ultimate compliment: "I'd fight on their side any time." Tunisia is a small country, wedged between the turmoil of Algeria and the unpre-dictability of Libya. It is clearly outgunned by its larger neighbors, and diplomacy goes only so far. Therefore the soldiers have to be good.

Another device Tunisia uses to minimize pressure from its neighbors is the emphasis on the Maghreb as a system, recognizing Mauritania's independence in 1960, for example, to expand the Maghreb system and reduce the roles of Algeria and Morocco.[53] For perhaps similar reasons, Tunisia reached out to Libya in 1970 after Egypt tried to exclude Libya from the Permanent Consultative Committee of the Maghreb.[54]

In December 1994, Tunisia was one of a number of Arab countries and actors signing an agreement with Israel to reduce military tension in the region. In January

1996, Tunisia and Israel signed an accord establishing special interest sections in each other's capitals (special interest sections are a form of international contact—a step short of full diplomatic recognition). That pact was implemented in April 1996 when Israel's first diplomat arrived in Tunis to run the Special Interest Bureau. That development comes on top of a tense history between Tunisia and Israel, as noted above.

Tunisian actions against al-Nahdah raised tension between Tunisia and some other Muslim countries that tried to support the outlawed group. In July 1992, Tunisia suspended diplomatic relations with Sudan, accusing the regime of supporting al-Nahdah activities. Some link Libya to support for al-Nahdah, although that support may have ceased when Libyan leader Qadhafi needed Tunisian support in challenging the UN embargo imposed against Libya for terrorist support. Tunis did call for an end to sanctions in 1991, and in January 1996, Ben Ali and Qadhafi met in Tunisia to discuss greater bilateral cooperation. Islamist support outside of a government also appeared when members of the Algerian-based Armed Islamic Group crossed into Tunisia from neighboring Algeria in February 1995. They attacked a border town and killed six Tunisian soldiers before escaping back to Algeria. Tensions over support for al-Nahdah also reached outside the Muslim world. In 1993, Britain sanctioned al-Nahdah leader Rached Ghannouchi after a Tunisian court gave him a life sentence in absentia, and a French national was arrested in Tunisia for allegedly inciting Islamic unrest. Demonstrations at French universities and a protest by the French government followed, while Tunisia strongly protested Britain's decision on Ghannouchi. In 2007 Tunisian authorities battled militants from the Algerian-based Salafist Group for Preaching and Combat (GSPC), which had planned to attack the British and American embassies in Tunis along with hotels and nightclubs.[55]

Despite their proximity, Tunisia and Libya have quite different political and historical experiences, as the next chapter shows.

SUGGESTED READINGS

Anderson, Lisa. *The State and Social Transformation in Tunisia and Libya, 1830–1980.* Princeton, NJ: Princeton University Press, 1986.

Bellin, Eva. *Stalled Democracy: Capital, Labor, and the Paradox of State-Sponsored Development.* Ithaca, NY: Cornell University Press, 2002.

Hamidi, Muhammad al-Hashimi. *The Politicization of Islam: A Case Study of Tunisia.* Boulder, CO: Westview, 1998.

Hermassi, Elbaki. *Leadership and National Development in North Africa.* Berkeley: University of California Press, 1972.

Laroui, Abdallah. *A History of the Maghreb: An Interpretive Essay.* Princeton, NJ: Princeton University Press, 1977.

Ling, Dwight L. *Tunisia: From Protectorate to Republic.* Bloomington: Indiana University Press, 1967.

Murphy, Emma C. *Economic and Political Change in Tunisia: From Bourguiba to Ben Ali.* New York: St. Martin's, 1999.

Perkins, Kenneth J. *A History of Modern Tunisia.* Cambridge: Cambridge University Press, 2004.

Waltz, Susan. *Human Rights and Reform: Changing the Face of North African Politics.* Berkeley: University of California Press, 1995.

Zartman, I. William, ed. *Tunisia: The Political Economy of Reform.* Boulder, CO: Lynne Rienner, 1991.

18

LIBYA

The ghostly remains of the Lady Be Good *were found in 1959, after years in the Libyan desert.* Lady Be Good *was an American B–24 bomber that lost its way back to its Libyan base from a raid on Italy in 1943 and crashed in the desert after running out of fuel. Its crew bailed out before the plane bellied into the desert sand, but their long trek northward in search of help led them nowhere, and they died in a few days.*

The vast Sahara Desert had claimed more victims in its trackless wastes. It is one of the most hostile places on earth, countless thousands of miles of sand and rock where not even the hardiest of plants or animals can survive. Yet clinging to its edges were some of the more fabled civilizations in history, and some of the epic events that marked that history. Here the Egyptians carved out a civilization, here the Phoenicians built magnificent Carthage, which the Romans destroyed after the Second Punic War. Here were fought the famous World War II battles of el-Alamein and Operation Torch. In 1989, American warplanes streaked over Tripoli to bomb in retaliation for alleged acts of Libyan terrorism. War seems to be an integral part of North Africa.

The remains of the Lady Be Good *were stripped of anything useful, and some of its parts were installed on other aircraft. Its propeller synchronizers went into a C–54, which then had propeller trouble, its radio found its way into a C–47, which ditched in the sea; its armrest went into an army Otter aircraft that crashed in Libya's Gulf of Sidra; all was lost except the armrest, which washed ashore. One of the engines, still containing a bullet from apparent combat, is on display at the Air Force Museum in Ohio. However, the hulk of the stripped plane remained in the desert where it fell.*

Libyans, despite deep political differences with the United States, still respect the memory of those who died in desert warfare. In 1996, thirty-five years after the Lady Be Good *was found in the Libyan desert, Libyan trucks loaded up the remains of the bomber and took it to a military museum in Tripoli.*

LIBYA IS RECOGNIZED today in most of the world as the country ruled by Col. Muammar Qadhafi, the mercurial leader whose unpredictable behavior masks Libya's importance in North Africa, with a significant history and a meaningful role to play in North African politics. Libya must be understood in terms that go beyond Qadhafi. It is an oil-exporting country centrally located on the southern coast of the Mediterranean Sea, although the quantities of oil in Libya are considerably smaller than are Gulf oil reserves.

Map 18.1 on page 385 shows the location of Libya and its major sites.

THE MODERN HISTORY OF LIBYA

Libya's Ottoman rulers attempted to develop Libya's economy in the latter nineteenth century with agricultural products, ore, and slaves (the slave trade did not end in Libya until the mid-1890s) as primary exports. However, high taxes and a lack of arable land made farming difficult except for the wealthiest landholders.[1] Another form of Libyan economic endeavor, piracy, drew foreign intervention. Libyan rulers built an economy on raiding ships in the Mediterranean, particularly American ships, since the United States had little in the way of a navy after independence. It dispatched a Marine Corps expedition to Tripoli in 1801 (thus "to the shores of Tripoli"), but in the end paid $18,000 a year to the pasha of Tripoli to keep hands off American ships. However, no sum of money could keep foreigners away from Libya.

Compared to Morocco, Tunisia, or Algeria, Libya was less attractive as a potential colony. It had less arable land and remained divided between the southern desert region and the northern regions of Cyrenaica and Tripolitania. However, Italy, which had just become unified into a modern country in 1850, sought colonies in Africa. Libya lay directly south, occupied by the deteriorating Ottoman Empire. In 1911, Italy accused Turkey of arming Libyans against Italian businesses in Libya, and used this pretext to launch an invasion. Italy and Turkey fought a brief war over Libya but Turkey had to withdraw, and in the Treaty of Lausanne in October 1912 it gave Italy title to the country.

The vast majority of Libyans rejected Italian rule, and war broke out. Germany and Turkey armed some of the Libyan revolutionary factions after Italy joined the Allied side in World War I in 1915. That war also brought to prominence a leader of the Sanusi Order, Muhammad Idris as-Sanusi, who established a power base in Cyrenaica before fleeing to Egypt in 1921.[2] Fighting intensified during the 1930s, as the Italian forces ruthlessly attempted to quell the rebellion, destroying entire villages, uprooting entire populations, and summarily executing prisoners. In 1934, Italian forces largely crushed Sanusi resistance and forcibly unified Tripolitania and Cyrenaica into the colony of Libya, with roughly half of the population perishing in that effort. Italy moved settlers to Libya, claiming some of the best land for them, which only fueled Libyan anti-Italian sentiment. Idris, still in Cairo, obtained a British agreement for him to lead Libyan resistance against Italy after World War II broke out. That war ended Italy's occupation of Libya as British forces expelled Axis forces from the country in February 1943.

After Independence

Following a contentious effort by the United Nations to resolve Libya's status, Idris (who had returned to Libya in 1944) proclaimed himself King Idris I in December 1951. Under the constitution adopted in that same year, a prime minister headed the executive branch and a bicameral legislature composed of a Senate (half the members to be nominated by the Crown) and a Chamber of Deputies, though Idris banned political parties in 1952. The United States initiated economic assistance in exchange for access to Wheelus air force base, where the US Air Force based military aircraft until 1969. By 1960, American and British foreign aid constituted almost 35 percent of the Libyan economy.

In 1952, the United Nations ranked Libya as one of the poorest countries in the world, despite US and British assistance. Part of the reason for Libya's poverty was its lack of natural resources, but King Idris was also a factor as he rewarded his Cyrenaican elite at the expense of the rest of the country. However, in 1959, geologists discovered oil in Cyrenaica, bringing wealth to the country for the first time. The role of British and American oil companies also grew, stimulating nationalism and a growing resentment as American and British petroleum companies dominated the Libyan economy. Libyan nationalism intensified after Arab losses in the 1967 war with Israel, which many Libyans blamed on the United States for supporting Israel. Idris remained pro-Western and kept Wheelus AFB open, compounding the difficulties he faced as a Cyrenaican who was hardly accepted as the king of Libya in Tripolitania. When Idris sought medical treatment in Greece in June 1969, Crown Prince Hasan al-Rida, the regent, suddenly found himself king. He had one of the shortest reigns in history, as the Libyan military launched a coup in September 1969 that ended the monarchy.

Qadhafi and the Revolution

The coup brought a group of military men to power whose Nasserist influence was obvious from their name—the Free Officers Movement. It consisted mainly of junior officers with no real political experience. They formed a Revolutionary Command Council (RCC) and announced that they were promoting Capt. Muammar al-Qadhafi to colonel and assigning him command of the Libyan armed forces. He rapidly rose to head the RCC and used his position to remake Libyan politics. He disbanded the Sanusi order that had provided King Idris's power base and created the Arab Socialist Union to unify Libya under its mantle. He watched the United States evacuate Wheelus AFB, fulfilling an agreement made under King Idris. He turned to the Soviet Union for military assistance, and soon Soviet and Eastern European military equipment flowed into the country.

Qadhafi fancied himself as a political theorist rather than a political leader. So while he kept the titles of power, he turned over the actual functioning of Libya to the RCC, later renamed the General People's Congress (GPC). In 1973, he announced what he called the "third universal theory," which substituted Islamic reform measures for the four pillars of socialism: socialism, popular democracy, Arab

MAP 18.1   MAP OF LIBYA

unity, and progressive Islam.[3] In 1977, Qadhafi further reorganized the Libyan political system through the creation of revolutionary committees to supervise the Basic People's Congress, the local bodies that were supposed to provide input into the
GPC. The result was a confusing grant of power to groups often dominated by revolutionary zealots. The paradox was that while other revolutionary leaders tried to
strengthen the state, Qadhafi worked to avoid state creation, constructing instead a
polity mobilized from below, though, as Vandewalle wryly observes, Qadhafi "un-
leashed upon Libya a further wave of contradictory policies that put the state in
charge of all economic and social activity, while simultaneously trying to make it ir-
relevant as a focus for political identity."[4]

Qadhafi also tried to abolish the tribal groups that remained an integral part
of Libyan society. Qadhafi and his close circle viewed tribal identity as a potential bastion of conservative tendencies, and thus an obstacle to Qadhafi's vision
of revolution.[5] Consequently many local governors with tribal ties were dismissed and replaced by government bureaucrats with no connections to the old
structure.[6]

Many Libyans who ran afoul of Qadhafi fled abroad, and after ordering them to
return, Qadhafi apparently had many of them assassinated. However, opposition
came not only from those wealthy enough to own property, but also from Islamists
who objected to Qadhafi's unorthodox pronouncements on Islam and from his fellow soldiers. Qadhafi executed several senior officers who objected to his economic
changes, and some officers apparently attempted coups in response.

Qadhafi left his mark on Libyan foreign affairs in particular. He supported a variety of terrorist groups around the world, and the United States blamed him for a disco bombing in 1986 in Berlin, Germany, that killed a member of the US military. In response, American military aircraft bombed Libya and killed Qadhafi's adopted daughter in the raid.[7] However, Libyan involvement in terrorism apparently continued. In 1988, an American airliner blew up over Scotland, and investigators implicated Libyan agents in the act. For years, the Libyan government refused to surrender the suspected bombers to either the United States or Britain, and thus the United Nations imposed economic sanctions against the country in 1992. While the sanctions did not ban the sale of Libyan oil, they did forbid foreign investment in Libya and prohibited the sale of oil-producing equipment. While Qadhafi initially defied the sanctions, the economic toll that resulted may have persuaded him to reconsider his domestic and foreign policies.

Qadhafi has changed his radical direction for Libya in a number of ways, however. He has tempered his radical rhetoric against the West, and emphasized the importance of foreign investment and globalization, instead of Libyan self-reliance and pan-Arabism. He shifted away from his emphasis on the Arab world, and instead stressed his connection with Africa. In April 1999, Qadhafi accepted a compromise on the Lockerbie suspects offered by the United Nations, and in January 2001, a tribunal held in the Netherlands found one Libyan agent guilty of the airliner bombing. While the United States decided to continue sanctioning Libya, the United Nations lifted its sanctions, and the Libyan economy began to grow slowly. Qadhafi moderated his rhetoric, even toward his old nemesis, the United States. After the 2000 US presidential election, he voiced the opinion that President George W. Bush "seemed nice," and after the terrorist attack against New York and Washington in September, 2001, Qadhafi said "Everyone should put human considerations above political differences. . . and offer aid to the victims of this gruesome act."[8]

When Qadhafi opened Libya's reported weapons of mass destruction facilities for full international inspection, the West rewarded him by dropping all remaining economic sanctions against Libya. In April 2004, Qadhafi embarked on a diplomatic visit to Europe. Quartered at an estate in Brussels, he erected a black tent on the estate grounds and lectured the assembled European diplomats who visited him on their colonial misadventures in Africa.[9] Some things had apparently not changed.

THE LIBYAN POLITICAL SYSTEM

While most Arab leaders strove to build a modern state following independence, Qadhafi promoted a stateless manifesto, as Vanderwalle describes it, "The *Green Book*'s central tenet is that ordinary citizens can directly manage the bureaucratic and administrative decisions that shape their lives, and devise their own solutions to their economic and social problems."[10] This ideational construction did not last, but it sent Libya on a bizarre course of political modernization.

Qadhafi dominates the political system of Libya, and his use of Islam reveals the extent of that domination. He set himself up as interpreter of Islam, denouncing Islamic clerics as reactionaries and claiming that "Muslims have strayed from Islam," and thus a review was in order.[11] He published his Green Book, he claimed, in response to the need for such a review. It consists of three volumes: *The Solution to the Problem of Democracy* (1975), *Solution of the Economic Problem: Socialism* (1977), and *Social Basis of the Third International Theory* (1979). However, since the last two volumes omitted any reference to Islam, they appear to stem more from the mind of Qadhafi than from interpretations of the Quran or the Sunna.[12] For many Muslims, the Green Book suggested apostasy, since it set aside the Sharia, or Islamic law, for its own text, among other departures from orthodox Islam.[13] Others point out that the Green Book received more inspiration from the French philosopher Jean-Jacques Rousseau than from Islamic thought.[14]

Qadhafi allows little if any dissent, and the other bodies in the Libyan system have little power. Libya is categorized by Freedom House as "not free."

The Libyan Executive

Muammar abu Minyar al-Qadhafi holds the title of Revolutionary Leader, which makes him the de facto head of state. The head of the government is the secretary of the General People's Committee, a position held by Ab al-Majid al-Qwaud from 1994, until Qadhafi replaced him in June 2003 with Shukri Muhammad Ghanem, who is reportedly more reform-minded than was his predecessor. Serving in the place of a cabinet is the General People's Committee, elected by the General People's Congress in unscheduled elections. However, most political power rests with Qadhafi. He does not have a monopoly of power within his own executive, however. In the mid-1990s, during Libya's economic crisis, some of the more pragmatic members of the cabinet, led by former General Secretary Umar al-Muntasir and the minister of energy, Abdallah Salim al-Badri, argued that Libya required economic reform and international investment to bring both economic growth and political stability. Opposing them were close associates of Qadhafi, including Addelssalem Jalloud, who argued for continuing defiance of the outside world. By 1998, Qadhafi sided with the reformers and purged some of the more radical members of the ruling Revolutionary Committee.[15]

Qadhafi's son Saif al-Islam has emerged from his father's shadow to strike a forward-looking image for Libya: fluent in English, educated in the West, and interested in democracy in Libya and the rest of the Arab world. His vision for Libya, though, seems to be a federal system with more powerful elected regional governments sharing power with a tribal leader who would apparently have the same powers as his father.[16]

The Libyan Legislature

The General People's Congress is a unicameral (single chamber) legislature of unknown size, indirectly elected by local People's Committees. All Libyan citizens over eighteen years are required to vote for the local People's Committee members. Since political parties are illegal in Libya, it is widely believed that the General People's Congress is totally loyal to Qadhafi.

The Libyan Judiciary

There is a Supreme Court in Libya, which appears to be a vehicle for enforcing Qadhafi's policies. The Libyan legal system is based generally on Italian civil law and Islamic law (largely for civil cases). There are separate religious courts to enforce religious laws, although the role of religious leaders on these courts is minimal.

According to Amnesty International, hundreds of political prisoners are detained in Libyan prisons, some without trial. In 1999, Amnesty International also reported torture and ill treatment in prisons.[17] But in 2004, Qadhafi specifically referred to the Amnesty International report and called for reforms to stop the alleged abuses. Amnesty International responded, "We welcome Colonel al-Gaddafi's speech. We hope that it will give impetus to reforms in laws and practice that will secure institutional change, as well as to accountability for perpetrators and full redress for victims of human rights violations." Further, "the Libyan authorities have taken some positive steps on human rights in recent years. These include the release in 2001 and 2002 of nearly 300 prisoners, including prisoners of conscience detained since 1973, and the recent opening of the country to a degree of international scrutiny. However, a pattern of human rights violations continues, often justified under the new rhetoric of the 'war on terror.'"[18] Recently the murder of a Libyan journalist who had written about official corruption in Libya aroused suspicion that the state security forces were still terminating critics of the regime by any means.[19]

The Libyan Supreme Court intervened in a controversial case involving Bulgarian and Palestinian nurses who received death sentences for allegedly infecting children with AIDS in 1999. Critics charged that the allegations were made to cover up conditions in Libya's health system that allowed AIDS to spread, and, in the face of international condemnation of the charges, the court sent them for retrial in December 2005.[20] In July 2007, Libya released them.

CIVIL SOCIETY IN LIBYA

The Libyan regime does not allow rival political groups, so opposition exists underground. Numerous groups oppose Qadhafi for differing reasons. The Libyan Militant Islamic Group (LMIG) has criticized Qadhafi for both corruption and what it calls "futile wars."[21] Oher groups include Islamic al-Islami (Islamic Struggle), al-Jama al-Islamiyya Libya (Islamic Group-Libya), Hizb al-Tahrir al-Islami (Islamic Liberation Party), and al-Haraka al-Islamiyya Libya (Islamic Movement-Libya). Qadhafi also faces opposition from the military, which reportedly launched a number of coups against him, tribal opposition (particularly from Cyrenaic), and secular opposition. The largest secular opposition movement is the National Front for the Salvation of Libya (NFSL), which serves as an umbrella group and has a military wing. However, internal divisions render the NFSL largely ineffective.[22]

Some groups have targeted Qadhafi himself. Several underground Islamist groups, including the Islamic Fighting Movement, the Islamic Martyrdom Movement, and the Libyan Islamic Group, have been recruiting veteran Islamic fighters from Afghanistan. In June 1996, the Libyan Islamic Group attacked a police station, killing eight officers. Other attacks followed, with increasing severity. Qadhafi was the target of several of these attacks, and one reportedly killed a bodyguard.[23] While the violence does not match that in Algeria, it continues to escalate, fueled apparently by Islamic (and secular) unhappiness with Qadhafi and his policies.

THE STATUS OF WOMEN IN LIBYA

Libya before Qadhafi was a deeply traditional society, which did not accord women anything like equal status with men. The 1969 Constitutional Proclamation gave women total equality with men. Qadhafi has attempted to improve the condition of women and has opened education to them. Although schools remain segregated by gender, Libyan colleges are integrated.

Official Libyan delegations praise the progress made by Libyan women. According to the Libyan delegation to the Committee on Rights of the Child held in Geneva, Switzerland, in January 1998, Libyan women "fully enjoy all rights and there is no discrimination against them."[24] Moreover, the report claimed, "Women also attended general congresses and participated in political decisionmaking."[25] On the other hand, even defenders of the system note that women rarely run for or win public office, and one of the few women members of the General People's Congress noted that it is still very difficult for women to win a parliamentary election.[26]

THE STRUCTURE AND PERFORMANCE
OF THE LIBYAN ECONOMY

Libya's economy depends heavily on petroleum revenues, as only 2 percent of its land is arable. There is some groundwater for irrigation, but Libya is using it, mostly for agriculture, at eight times its replacement rate. Libya has spent some $25 billion on the world's largest water development project to bring water from an aquifer on the Libyan-Egyptian border to increase crop acreage, although the project may have alternative uses (see below). However, until Libya expands its cropland, it will continue to depend on foreign sources for its food, about 75 percent of total consumption.

Libyans enjoy a GDP per capita of $12,700, one of the highest in the Arab world outside the Gulf. The unemployment rate is 30 percent, however, though only 7 percent of Libyans live below the poverty line.

After Qadhafi assumed power, he nationalized most of the Libyan economy, including banks, insurance companies, and agricultural land. By 1973, he had completed the process, with even small-scale industries and enterprises coming under state control. Those who controlled the economy (and thus understood it) lost power to new bureaucrats who did not. The National Oil Company took charge of all oil production, and public corporations took over most of the infrastructure and the national airline. The government also nationalized the remaining Jewish and Indian-owned banks and exiled their former owners. The regime also took over all import and export functions.[27] The consequence was political and economic disorder.

Libya is a classic rentier state (see Chapter 4). Even before Qadhafi came to power, Libya derived considerable revenues from selling oil to other countries. The massive oil revenues allowed Libyan authorities to bypass the normal state economic regulatory institutions that guide economic development. Instead, Qadhafi and his small circle of close political allies could decide on economic distribution without the accountability that state agencies might provide.[28] As Vandewalle notes, the ministries distributed almost 80 percent of the state budget, which not only enhanced the power of the state (despite efforts by Qadhafi to abolish it) but allowed the ministries to become instruments of considerable corruption.[29]

Qadhafi changed economic policy again when he created the Jamahiriyya in 1977, meaning roughly people's government (mentioned in the Green Book). The Jamahiriyya, among other things, placed all private commerce, including wholesale and retail, in the hands of "people's committees," thus reducing the role of both the remaining private sector and the state administration. The government seized all individual bank accounts in 1981, and all employees, even in households, had to be given partial ownership.[30] Qadhafi's second Green Book on socialism called for the elimination of the merchant class and an equitable distribution of wealth. However, the inexperienced people's committees were unable to manage the economy, and as shortages and inefficiency resulted from Qadhafi's efforts at reform, private markets appeared again. Yet Qadhafi continued to tinker with the economy. In 1988, more than 140 companies joined the list of "self-managed" firms. The problems emerging from all these "reforms" were bad enough, but they were about to get worse.

The United Nations placed Libya under economic sanctions in April 1992 for refusing to turn over suspects in the Pan American Airlines bombing over Lockerbie, Scotland, in 1988. Those sanctions did not harm the Libyan economy as badly as they did Iraq, since they allowed Libya (unlike Iraq) to export oil.[31] The Libyan standard of living fell sharply during the sanctions period, partly because sanctions caused high inflation. However, the sanctions allowed the government to apportion blame to them for Libya's poor economic performance and thus escape the consequences of mismanagement, falling oil prices, and the huge investment for the "great man-made river" (around 15 percent of total government spending for this project, discussed below).[32]

Under the dual impact of sanctions and declining petroleum prices, Libya tried to diversify its economy, expanding into steel, cement, aluminum, and petrochemicals. However, so-called Revolutionary Committees manage these new enterprises, resulting in considerable bureaucratic inefficiency.[33] The Libyan government has also attempted to expand agriculture, a difficult challenge in one of the driest countries of the world. It has invested heavily in the Great Man-Made River Project to carry water under the desert from Tunisia to Egypt. After many years and over $24 billion, the first phase was completed in 2001. By the time Libya completes the project, it may supply around 2 cubic kilometers of water per year for fifty years. Agricultural diversion was not enough, though, for the International Monetary Fund, which argued that Libya needs more market reform, including a restructured banking system and streamlined management and fiscal policies, to continue to grow economically.[34]

The UN sanctions were supposed to end in 1999 when Libya turned over the Lockerbie suspects to a Scottish court, but disagreement over compensation to the victims' families delayed the end until September 2003.[35] Despite the sanctions, the Libyan economy showed signs of reviving. Reports indicated new construction activity in Tripoli and shops filled with luxury goods not seen recently. In 2007, Qadhafi's son Saif al-Islam announced that Libya would become a new construction hub for the region and planned to build hundreds of hotels and office buildings.[36] Tourism is one factor fueling the growth, with European tourists taking advantage of both new hotels and the numerous historical sites in Libya.[37] The growth rate may increase as the Libyan government is investing over $35 billion in mineral exploitation, transportation, and other infrastructure.[38] Such investments may also allow Libya to reduce its heavy dependence on oil revenues, now estimated to generate around 95 percent of foreign exchange earnings and 70 percent of government revenues.[39] Still, Vandewalle notes that classic rentier states stunt the traditional systems for wealth distribution to the point where economic liberalization is very difficult to achieve.[40]

LIBYAN FOREIGN POLICY

Libyan foreign policy is a reflection of its leader, Muammar Qadhafi, who emphasizes pan-Arabism, as well as opposition to Israel and the West. Qadhafi turned against the latter shortly after assuming power, nationalizing the holdings of both the British Petroleum Company and the American-owned Occidental Petroleum Company. He also pushed for Arab unity in his effort to join Egypt, Syria, and Libya in something called the Federation of Arab Republics (FAR), but it never progressed beyond the talking stage.

Undeterred, Qadhafi next tried unity with Tunisia but found no support. A second effort with Syria briefly succeeded after both countries found common ground in castigating Egypt for its peace efforts, and Qadhafi offered to pay off Syria's $1 billion debt to the Soviet Union. But that alignment put Qadhafi in an awkward position when Syria supported Iran against Iraq, and Qadhafi had to follow suit, making Libya only one of two Arab regimes to support Iran against a fellow Arab country. Qadhafi also had to contend with the strange disappearance of Lebanese Shiite leader Musa al-Sadr, who disappeared on a visit to Libya in 1978. Arab members of the Shiite faith held Qadhafi responsible for the disappearance, further tarnishing his reputation as an Arab standard-bearer.[41] Qadhafi also quarreled with Saudi Arabian Crown Prince Abdullah during a February 2003 Arab summit meeting, and, reportedly incensed by Abdullah's remarks to him, allegedly ordered Abdullah's assassination.[42]

Qadhafi's foreign policy also led him south to Chad, Sudan, and Uganda. In 1973, Libyan forces occupied a part of Chad that Qadhafi regarded as historically Libyan. He also interfered in the prolonged tribal warfare that plagued Chad, and ultimately France, Chad's former colonial power, sent in forces to oust Libyan troops.[43] Qadhafi also interfered in Sudanese politics, and Chad accused Libyan agents of bombing the Chadian embassy in the Sudanese capital of Khartoum. In the 1990s, Qadhafi reached out to sub-Saharan Africa, calling for the elimination of borders and the integration of African national economies. Libya's most notable effort in foreign policy involved support for a variety of terrorist organizations around the world. Libyan support, training, and arms went to the Irish Republican Army, the Palestine Liberation Organization, the Japanese Red Army, the Philippine Moro National Liberation Front, the Baader-Meinhof gang in Germany, and a host of other groups. Qadhafi's agents were also associated with blowing up Pan American flight 103 over Lockerbie, Scotland, in December 1988, as noted earlier. Consequently, the United States and many other countries imposed a complete economic and political boycott on Libya while suspects in that bombing remained in Libya. In April 1999, after long negotiations, Libya turned the suspects over to UN officials and had them flown to the Netherlands, where a Scottish court found two of them guilty as charged. Libyan foreign policy shifted considerably after the Lockerbie incident, moving to establish political and commercial ties with European countries and terminating support for terrorist groups that had been a part of its foreign policy in the early Qadhafi years.[44]

The Libyan economy is dependent on foreign workers, who constitute almost 280,000 out of a total labor force of 1 million. Many of these workers are Egyptians, who send at least part of their earnings home to Egypt rather than spend it on the Libyan economy. The presence of these Egyptian workers in Libya is one factor in Egypt's efforts to keep good relations with its neighbor, since Libya provides a source of employment for Egyptian workers who might otherwise bring instability to the Egyptian political system.

Libyan WMD

In March 1990 American intelligence discovered a suspicious facility near the town of Rabta, which analysts concluded was designed to make chemical weapons.[45] American officials released photographs of the buildings at the site, which Libya claimed was for manufacturing pharmaceuticals. Analysts observed, though, that the plant was heavily guarded and that the materials going into the plant were not ingredients for making aspirin.[46] Later Libyan officials claimed that fire destroyed the plant, and released their own photos showing what appeared to be fire damage. American officials concluded that the Libyans had stacked old tires around the buildings and torched them to give the appearance that the plant had burned.

Rabta, as it turned out, was only the tip of Libya's chemical weapons iceberg. In March 1996, the CIA reported locating what it described as "the world's largest underground chemical weapons plant" near the town of Tarhuna.[47] The plant was built into the side of a mountain, and, according to intelligence estimates, could be destroyed only by a direct hit from a nuclear weapon.[48] The site covered some 15 square kilometers and was potentially capable of making tons of toxic gases each day.[49] Initial reports also indicated that the plant at Tarhuna would be completed by the end of the decade, and the United States warned that it might bomb the site. Egypt tried to pressure Qadhafi to open the site for European inspectors, but the

Libyan leader refused, claiming that Israel would have to open its suspected nuclear weapons sites in reciprocity.[50] In December 1997, Clinton administration officials claimed that work on the facility had stopped.[51] Whether or not that assessment was correct is unclear, as is the purpose of another suspected plant at Sabha. There is evidence that Libya sought outside technical assistance for a chemical weapons program. In October 1996, Lebanese officials arrested a German national in Beirut upon arrival from Paris and charged him with smuggling chemical materials destined for Libya.[52]

The United States, concerned about Libya's ongoing WMD programs, embarked on a long-term dialog with Libya on dismantling its programs. In December 2003, Libya agreed to allow UN inspectors into the country to inspect and dismantle Libyan WMD programs. They included a rudimentary nuclear weapons effort which was, according to British officials, close to developing a weapon.[53] The Bush administration praised Libyan cooperation and indicated that the remaining economic sanctions on Libya would be lifted as soon as the United Nations declared Libya compliant with its pledge to end WMD programs. The Bush administration also claimed that the 2003 Iraq invasion had pushed Qadhafi to dismantle his WMD program. Other evidence suggests, though, that Libyan leaders seriously considered ending their WMD program in the early 1990s, and that a combination of carrots and sticks from the outside eventually terminated the programs.[54] In September 2004, the United States ended sanctions on Libya.

Libya is in some ways a transition state between the Middle East of Egypt and the Maghreb world of Morocco, which is the focus of the next chapter.

SUGGESTED READINGS

Ahmida, Ali Abdullatif. *The Making of Modern Libya: State Formation, Colonialization and Resistance, 1830–1932.* Albany: State University of New York Press, 1994.

Allan, J. A., ed. *Libya Since Independence: Economic and Political Development.* New York: St. Martin's, 1982.

Anderson, Lisa. *The State and Social Transformation in Tunisia and Libya: 1830–1980.* Princeton, NJ: Princeton University Press, 1986.

Bearman, Jonathan. *Qadafi's Libya.* London: Zed, 1986.

Davis, John, *Libyan Politics: Tribe and Revolution.* Berkeley: University of California Press, 1987.

Deeb, Marius, and Mary Jane Deeb. *Libya Since the Revolution: Aspects of Social and Political Development.* New York: Praeger, 1982.

El-Kikhia, Mansour O. *Libya's Qadhafi: The Politics of Contradiction.* Gainesville: University Press of Florida, 1997.

Gurney, Judith. *Libya: The Political Economy of Oil.* Oxford: Oxford University Press, 1996.

Vandewalle, Dirk, ed. *Qadhafi's Libya: 1969–1994.* New York: St. Martin's, 1995.

_____. *Libya Since Independence.* Ithaca, NY: Cornell University Press, 1998.

_____. *A History of Modern Libya.* Cambridge: Cambridge University Press, 2006.

19

MOROCCO

The open square of the Marrakech souq is filled with exotic sights and sounds; snake handlers, dancing monkeys, fortune-tellers, and whirling dervishes. Here all forms of business gather. A dentist squats on a carpet in front of a table advertising his skill—rows of pulled teeth. Near him are tables piled high with fresh fruit, nuts, and dried beans. A huge man ladles tiny clams in their shells from pots of boiling water into the bowls of eager customers. The whole square is scented by spices, grilling meats, and exotic perfumes. Beyond it are bustling alleys lined with shops selling everything imaginable. Ceramics line the walls of some stalls, along with brassware, shoes, candles, and imitation Gucci handbags. Tourists flock to the souq in Marrakech for all these things and then retreat to their hotels or to the nearby fields to be photographed on a camel. What they miss, though, is the other world of Morocco that lies within and beyond the walls of the souq. Small, dimly lit passages lead away into the surrounding neighborhood, lined with walls painted the traditional Moroccan light blue and packed with children. They are everywhere, dashing through the narrow lanes into the dark in search of a tourist who will give them a few coins for carrying their purchases. They reflect both the hopes for Morocco as well as its burden. Like most Arab countries, Morocco has a rapidly growing population, with around 31 percent of its population under fourteen. The country will need more schools, more jobs, and more food and water as these young people grow to maturity. Morocco emphasizes its growing tourist industry as a key to its future. Tourists do create jobs, but they are often nothing more than holding a camel for a tourist or carrying their packages through the souq.

IN RECENT DECADES MOROCCO has become a favorite vacation spot for tourists. Its Mediterranean beaches and fabled cities like Casablanca and Marrakech are magnets for foreign visitors who are drawn to images of a romantic world; the labyrinthine alleys of the old souqs, the High Atlas Mountains, and Morocco's beaches. However, Morocco is much more than a tourist attraction. It occupies a strategic location at the southern entrance to the Mediterranean Sea, and its history is rich with tradition. Its mix of Arab, Berber, and French culture make it a cultural bridge between Europe and the Arab world. Map 19.1 on page 396 shows Morocco's location on the northwest coast of Africa.

THE MODERN HISTORY OF MOROCCO

The Ottoman Empire reached to the current Algerian-Moroccan border but stopped short of Morocco, thus exempting Morocco from the stormy history that ultimately consumed the Ottomans. In 1804 Spain and France divided Morocco between them, realizing the value of Morocco and the dangers to each should they fight over its control.[1] France got the northern part with its Mediterranean coast while Spain took some coastal enclaves and a large chunk of the southern part of the country. The small enclave of Ifni fell to Spain after Morocco lost the 1859–1860 Hispano-Moroccan war.

By 1912, Moroccan fears about possible German expansion led it to become a French protectorate. The French got access to Moroccan goods and control over Moroccan incursions into neighboring Algeria, which the French considered part of France. France also cooperated with Spain to quell the revolt by Abd el-Krim in Spanish Morocco in 1926. That uprising spread to French-occupied Morocco and ultimately required over 200,000 French troops under General Pétain (who led the Vichy French government during World War II) to cope with the movement.[2] Paradoxically the French occupation broke the power of the local *marabouts*, or religious leaders, which opened Morocco to more outside ideas. Those ideas included, as Eickelman notes, the "ideological currents in the Arab east, where Muslims had an earlier and in some cases protracted experience with the problems of foreign domination that now faced Morocco."[3]

France also faced a violent reaction in Morocco to its rule. In the early part of the twentieth century, resistance hampered French occupation to the point where France divided Morocco into two parts, "useful" and "useless," with the latter part given de facto independence. Resistance continued into the 1920s and 1930s, with the Moroccan opposition becoming more skilled at guerrilla warfare.[4] France tried to find a compromise, allowing Mohamed Ben Youssef to proclaim himself as King Mohamed V in November 1933. French authorities hoped that he would not directly challenge French authority, but the king met with World War II Allied leaders Churchill and Roosevelt, and refused to bend to the Vichy French anti-Jewish policies.[5]

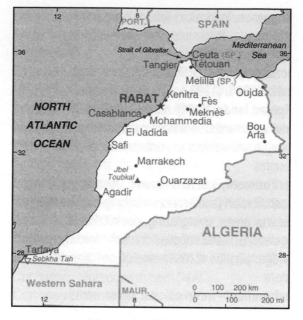

MAP 19.1   MOROCCO

The Beginnings of Independence

After World War II, agitation for Moroccan independence began, both in Morocco and among Moroccan exiles in France. The Istiqlal (Independence) Party issued a manifesto in 1944 demanding postwar independence for Morocco, but the French largely ignored the issue. In 1953 France ousted Mohamed V and replaced him with Muhammad ben Aarafa, widely seen as a French puppet. France cracked down hard on nationalist sentiment, and by 1954 "Morocco resembled a large collection of prison camps."[6] However, the high cost of repressing nationalist sentiment led French officials to allow Mohamed V to return in 1955, paving the way for Moroccan independence in 1956.[7] The next year Mohamed V became king.

Independence under Mohamed V did not bring much change to the political structure of Morocco, which continued the same central organization as it had under the French protectorate system. Istiqlal, Morocco's first nationalist party became more important in the second Council of Government in October 1956, while the king centralized power in the palace with the creation of the private Crown Council.[8] Istiqlal did not challenge Mohamed V's personal primacy or his claim to the throne, realizing that for any Moroccan party to do so would be tantamount to sacrilege.[9] Tension within the government increased as minister after minister resigned from the Council on Government. A new body, the Superior Council of the Plan, came about in mid-1957, but problems remained, some exacerbated by drought and the resulting poor performance of the economy.

Above much of this stood King Mohamed V. His Alawite dynasty traced its legitimacy to the Prophet Muhammad, gaining the king considerable allegiance among his subjects.[10] Coupled with his ties to Moroccan nationalism, a cross-section of the Moroccan public venerated Mohamed V.[11] However, he faced challenges from within his ruling circle and outside of it.

The king realized that the goal of Istiqlal was to create a one-party state with the monarch reduced to a figurehead. The 1956 government had nine Istiqlal members, six from the small and conservative Democratic Party of Independence (PDI), and six nonparty members. Nevertheless, Istiqlal was the best organized of Morocco's new political parties and drew considerable power from the urban upper class. The party would continue to challenge Mohamed V's policies and choice of leadership while remaining loyal to him on the surface. More serious resistance came from various Berber groups in the Middle Atlas Mountains, the Rif, and Tafilalt. Berber uprisings in these areas began in the mid-1950s, partly out of concern for the growing power of Istiqlal. They were also an expression of Berber frustration at being excluded from the main currents of Moroccan politics, largely because they could not break the dominance of the urban political elite.[12] While Moroccan security forces ultimately quelled these uprisings, the Berbers were joined by the Popular Movement (MP), a leftist party formed by other dissident Berbers. Since Mohamed V believed in broadening his power base, he allowed the MP to register as a legal party in 1959, against the wishes of Istiqlal. He also assumed direct leadership of the government in 1960 (thus reducing the role of the parties), and named his son Mulay Hassan as his deputy, after initially naming him as chief of staff of the Royal Armed Forces in April 1957. He also increased the political participation for Morocco's Berbers, elevating their participation in the military and the security police.[13]

During the early 1950s, the United States negotiated with France to use airfields in Morocco for strategic nuclear bomber bases.[14] King Mohamed decided to renegotiate the 1948 French-American agreement in 1959, asking the United States to remove its bombers and turn the bases over to Morocco. The king also decided to diversify Morocco's sources for military weapons, buying from both the United States and the Soviet Union, along with France, Morocco's traditional supplier.

The death of Mohamed V in 1961 brought Hassan II to the Moroccan throne. Hassan II announced that he intended to implement the Charter of 1958 in which Mohamed V promised to transform Morocco to a constitutional monarchy. The king submitted the constitution to a referendum in December 1962, which received widespread approval. However, the aura of King Mohamed V did not pass easily to Hassan II. In June 1965, riots broke out across Morocco, triggered by economic difficulties, and the king invoked Article 35 of the constitution to crack down. He assumed all legislative and judicial powers, declaring a "state of exception" in justifying the grant of power. In July 1970, Hassan II drafted another constitution granting the monarch even more power, which voters eventually approved.

The challenges for Hassan II were not just in the domestic arena, but also extended into Morocco's relations with its neighbors. As Algeria finally obtained independence from France after a bloody struggle, it attempted to define its borders with Morocco. The French had not delineated the border between Morocco and Algeria between Bechar and Tindouf, a line of almost 1,000 kilometers. Both countries rushed forces to the area in the early 1960s out of fear that the other would try to adjust the border in its favor. By 1963, matters had grown worse as Algeria joined the socialist world while Morocco retained a conservative monarchy. Morocco accused Algeria of attempting to overthrow Hassan II, and Moroccan and Algerian forces fought a series of brief conflicts on the border in October of that year.

On the domestic front, Hassan II reorganized his government, appointing Ahmed Bahnini as prime minister. Bahnini headed a government comprised of parties that supported the royal family, the Front for the Defense of Constitutional Issues (FDIC). However, the FDIC was plagued by internal conflict, with some members bolting to join the opposition Istiqlal.

Hassan had considerable difficulty stabilizing the political climate. Students rioted in Casablanca over educational reform and fourteen Moroccans were executed for gunrunning. In June 1965 Prime Minister Bahnini resigned and Hassan II assumed the post. He later appointed Ahmed Laraki as prime minister; Laraki resigned in August 1971 and was replaced by Mohamed Karim Lamrani. Riots also followed the Arab defeat in the Arab-Israeli war of 1967. The king had sent Moroccan troops to the fight, although they arrived too late to see action.

Hassan II found himself increasingly at odds with his military, facing a coup effort in July 1971 when Moroccan army officers stormed his palace at Skhirat. Other officers led by Colonel Muhammad Ababou took over army headquarters in Rabat, but the attempt soon fell apart, and four generals, five colonels, and a major went before a firing squad. The event pushed the king to put yet another constitution before the voters in early 1972, but that did not prevent a second coup effort by air force officers, who tried to shoot down the king's plane in August 1972.[15] The king also found himself in disagreement with his powerful interior minister, Gen. Muhammad Oufkir, over participation of the opposition parties in the elections. This military opposition, according to Hammoudi, reflected a military attitude that placed "defending ideals. . . above partisan squabbles: God, the motherland, and the king."[16] Worse, for the king, was the revelation that Oufkir had been party to both the 1971 and 1972 coup efforts. When confronted, Oufkir reportedly committed suicide, although reports surfaced of four bullet wounds in his body.

Shaken by events, Hassan II reached out to the opposition, which rejected his overtures. Frustrated, he turned to his own family and appointed his brother-in-law, Ahmed Osman, as prime minister. The king headed up the armed forces himself, for understandable reasons. Those forces went to the Golan in the 1973 Arab-Israeli war, performing credibly against the Israeli military and taking high casualties in the process. However, the king's decision to send forces to help the Arab cause did not buy Hassan II much goodwill at home. Problems simply shifted from the military to the academic community, where left-wing demonstrations spread through several cities in early 1973. The turmoil increased when terrorist groups, apparently trained in Libya, infiltrated Morocco to sow disorder. Part of the reason for the uprisings was the sharp increase in world oil prices, which rippled through Morocco's vulnerable economy, and part was a reflection of the continuing perception among many Moroccans that the regime was increasingly out of touch with their demands. The king declared martial law and had the courts hand out more than eighty death sentences to those suspected of creating the disorder.

The king realized that the political disorder reflected a widespread loss of confidence in his reign. He scheduled elections for November 1976, and a number of new parties formed to take advantage of the shift. Independent royalist parties won 45 percent of the seats, while Istiqlal took 22 percent. A new constitution in 1992 expanded the powers of the legislature, which in turn curtailed some of the powers of the executive.

King Hassan died in July 1999, and his son Sidi Mohamed succeeded him at age 36, taking the title Mohamed VI. Though seen as inexperienced, Mohamed VI had served as coordinator of the Bureaux and Services of the Royal Armed Forces and thus had good ties with the Moroccan military. He showed his independence from his father's legacy when he dismissed Interior Minister Driss Basri, regarded as the second most powerful figure in Moroccan politics and an opponent of political reform. Mohamed VI also released almost 8,000 prisoners, many of them jailed for suspected membership in the Islamist group Adl wal Ihsane.[17] His efforts to liberalize, however, did not appear to appease members of Salafiyya Jahadia, a group of militant Muslims in Morocco, Tunisia, Algeria, and Europe, who claimed responsibility for the May 2003 bombings in Casablanca that took twenty-nine lives and presented Mohamed VI with the continuing dilemma of controlling the most violent Islamists while modernizing his country.[18]

THE MOROCCAN POLITICAL SYSTEM

The foundations of the Moroccan political system are deeply rooted in an authoritarian tradition, reinforced by both rituals (such as gift giving between subordinate and superior) and genuine political power that, in the Moroccan case, lies primarily within the military.[19] The ruling Alawi dynasty draws on the power of religious legitimacy. Members of the dynasty claim to be descended from the family of the Prophet Mohamed, and claim that they are empowered with *baraka*, a belief that God endowed all descendants with a beneficial force that is both spiritual and material (capable of bringing rain, for example).[20] Against this tradition, democracy developed slowly in Morocco, and the pressure for further openness from both inside and outside Morocco compete with traditions that enforce monarchial power. Nevertheless, Morocco is a relatively open society compared to other traditional countries in the Arab world, generating a "partly free" rating from Freedom House.

Morocco is a constitutional monarchy. The first constitution was proposed in December 1962 and the first elections under that constitution were held the following year. However, political unrest in June 1965 pushed King Hassan to invoke Article 35 of the constitution, which granted an exception to democratic rule under conditions of turmoil. This gave the king both executive and legislative powers which he then exercised freely. He pushed through a referendum on a new constitution in July

1970 that gave him even more political power, and this in turn provoked opposition from the military. As previously noted, members of the military launched their first coup effort in July 1971, which propelled the king to draft a second constitution in early 1972 enlarging the number of democratically elected members of parliament by one-third. However, the military (especially the Moroccan air force) remained unsatisfied and the second coup followed in August 1972. The king, increasingly embroiled in the Western Sahara issue (discussed later in this chapter), recognized the need for widespread support for what promised to be an expensive and controversial policy of taking on both Spain and Algeria for control of the region. By 1976, the king again expanded suffrage to include elections for local councils, and parliamentary elections were held in 1977, with the Istiqlal and Popular Movement Parties gaining a two-thirds majority. The king continued to vacillate between concessions to participatory politics and heavy-handed treatment of opponents. He suppressed labor strikes in January 1983 and a potential opponent, Gen. Ahmed Dlimi, the commander of the Western Saharan forces and the intelligence services, mysteriously died in an automobile accident. The king also scheduled parliamentary elections twice, in 1983 and again in 1984, but canceled them both times, claiming that they could only be held after the referendum on the Western Sahara. The parliamentary elections ultimately resulted in a victory for the Constitutional Union Party.

Further reforms led to another constitution in September 1992. It provided for an Economic and Social Council, reinforced governmental accountability of members of parliament, and strengthened the position of prime minister. The new constitution got an overwhelming majority in the referendum elections that followed, with a reported 99.6 percent endorsing the new constitution, which, in the face of a campaign to abstain launched by the king's political opponents, suggested the possibility of electoral manipulation. However, elections for constitutional change continued; they were again held in September 1996, and the results created a parliament whose members were all directly elected for the first time.

Political reform in Morocco has come slowly, usually in response to outside pressures. As Layachi notes, "The main purpose of the political reform was to calm the rising tide of popular discontent, of social tensions, and of international criticism. Far from affecting the nature of the political system, those reforms had all the marks of a 'regime survival strategy.'"[21]

The Moroccan Executive

The king is head of the executive, and the constitution holds that "he shall be the protector of the rights and liberties of the citizens, social groups, and communities," and "shall guarantee the independence of the Nation and the integrity of the Kingdom within its authentic borders."[22] At the administrative level, the prime minister heads the government and serves as chief minister over the other ministers. The king appoints the prime minister, who has responsibility to initiate laws, issue regulatory power, and coordinate ministerial activities.

In 1998, the Moroccan Crown further accommodated the opposition by appointing Abdurrahman Youssoufi as prime minister. Youssoufi was exiled for criticizing the Crown, but in an act of reported liberalization, King Hassan allowed him to return to Morocco. Hassan appointed another former opposition figure, Fathallah Oualalou, as economics and finance minister at about the same time.[23] In 2002, the king appointed Driss Jettou as prime minister.

The Moroccan Legislature

The parliament consists of two chambers, a Chamber of Counselors with 270 seats (restored by the 1996 constitution) and a lower Chamber of Representatives with 325 seats. Local councils, professional organizations, and labor groups indirectly elect the Chamber of Counselors for nine-year terms. One-third of the Chamber of Counselors membership is elected every three years. The Chamber of Representatives is elected by popular vote for five-year terms, with seats apportioned according to the percentage of the popular vote each party receives.

The 1992 constitution expanded parliamentary power far beyond what existed before, including new budgetary power. The constitution also requires the Crown to act on a law passed by parliament within thirty days, thus eliminating the old power of the king to avoid signing or rejecting legislation.[24]

Morocco's party structure has evolved since independence, and the main parties now include the following:

- Social Democratic Movement, headed by Mahmoud Archane (pro-government).
- Istiqlal, the oldest party; it remains strongly pronationalist and is active on pan-Arabist issues (opposition).
- The Union of Social Popular Forces (USFP), headed by Prime Minister Abderrahmane Youssoufi. Established in 1974, it is a leftist-oriented party and finds strength in urban areas and among organized labor. It is now the ruling party.
- The Popular Movement, a Berber-based party that emphasizes protecting Berber language and culture.
- The Justice and Development Party, an Islamist party that proposes a Sharia-based political system.
- The National Rally of Independents, founded in 1977 as a personal vehicle for then Prime Minister Ahmed Osman.
- The Constitutional Union Party, founded in 1983.
- The National Democratic Party, formed in 1983 by Arsaleane el-Jadidi; the party is largely based in rural areas.
- The Party of Progress and Socialism is technically Morocco's oldest party; earlier the Moroccan Communist Party. Legalized in 1974, it counts among its followers the economically and politically disaffected.
- The Organization for Democratic and Popular Action, a leftist-oriented party that strongly supports Morocco's claim to the Western Sahara.

There is some degree of coordination among opposition parties, not including the Islamist movement or the Democratic Action Party, which is not represented in the government but supports it. The Moroccan Popular Movement Party, the Constitutional Union, and the National Democratic Party coordinate on some matters, and the leader of the Moroccan Popular Movement Party once claimed that there was more harmony between the opposition parties than within the pro-government parties.[25] After the Chamber of Counselors elections in December 1997, the party representation saw the National Rally of Independents with forty-two seats, the Social Democratic Movement with thirty-three, the Constitutional Union with twenty-eight, the Popular Movement with twenty-seven, the National Democratic Party with twenty-one, Istiqlal with twenty-one, the Socialist Union of Popular Forces with sixteen, and the Labor Party with thirteen. Other parties hold the remaining seats. The 2002 elections saw Youssoufi's Socialists lose three seats, and Istiqlal, four.

In the Chamber of Representatives the Socialist Union of Popular Forces won fifty-seven seats in the December 1997 elections, followed by Constitutional Union Party with fifty seats, the National Rally Party with forty-six, the Popular Movement with forty, Istiqlal with thirty-two, the National Popular Movement with nineteen, and the remainder of the seats split among the smaller parties.

While the election of October 2002 saw the USFP win fifty seats and al-Istiqlal forty-eight, the surprise was the forty-two seats gained by PJD, up from fourteen before the election. While the PJD advocated such policies as segregated beaches for women and men, a ban on alcohol, and Islamic banking, some analysts saw their rapid rise in seats as more a reflection of disenchantment with the present government's performance than a swing toward Islamic politics.[26] The Casablanca bombing may have produced a backlash against the PJD, although there is no evidence that it was connected in any way with the tragedy. However, in the municipal elections of September 2003 it scored only 1 percent of the total vote, and won only 87 seats of 6,952 total, whereas both the USFP and Istiqlal did much better.[27]

The Moroccan Judiciary

Morocco's judiciary consists of a Supreme Court, with the Council of the Judiciary appointing the judges. The king presides over the court. Below the court are communal and district courts (handling small claims), administrative tribunals (claims between government organizations and citizens), tribunals of original jurisdiction (criminal and civil cases), and appellate courts. The Supreme Court reviews cases from lower courts, appeals from government agency actions, and suits covering alleged bias of lower court judges. There is also a Special Court of Justice for cases against government members charged with fraud or embezzlement.

In 1990, King Hassan II created a Consultative Council on Human Rights (CCDH). On paper an independent body, the CCDH was composed of thirty-six members drawn from a cross-section of the community, including human rights groups, representatives from political parties, academics, and other leading citizens.[28] Although the CCDH has complained about reported human rights violations, it has distanced itself from issues that could reflect badly on the monarchy.[29]

King Mohamed has released one of King Hassan's most ardent critics, leader of the Islamist Justice and Charity Group Abdassalam Yassine, who was under house arrest for ten years.[30] At the time, Mohamed seemed to be adopting a more liberal attitude toward critics. However, his decision to shut down three leading independent newspapers in December 2000 indicated that limits to toleration remain.[31] The arrest and trial of Nadia Yassine, Abdassalam's daughter, for proclaiming that Morocco would be better off without a king, was another sign of limits on the regime's tolerance of free expression.[32]

The 1992 constitution (Articles 76–77) created a Constitutional Council, which was implemented in 1994. The king appoints the president of the Constitutional Council, who, like the other members, serves for six years. The king also appoints four of the regular members and the speaker of the Chamber of Representatives appoints the other four. The Constitutional Council judges the constitutionality of elections and determines whether organic laws and statutes passed by the legislature meet constitutional standards. In this sense, the Constitutional Council performs a function similar to that of the US Supreme Court.

Minorities receive some protection in Morocco, including the Amazigh or Berbers (though it is questionable whether Berbers are a minority, as over 60 percent of Moroccans claim some Berber blood). Due to concerns that the Berber language (or Tamazight) was disappearing, broadcasts in Tamazight increased in both the radio and television media, and over 350 schools added Tamazight classes in 2005.

CIVIL SOCIETY IN MOROCCO

Reforms have only partially met popular expectations, and civil society has grown in response to disillusion over the slow pace of transformation. Other factors spawning civil society organizations include the rise of an urban elite, relative freedom of speech, and Morocco's need to cultivate a liberal image for potential international investors.[33] The result has been the growth of nongovernmental organizations that serve as alternative means of political participation from those offered by the regime. They include an Amnesty International office in Rabat and over 4,000 others, addressing health care, education, culture, and women's rights.[34] Some of the growth may also be attributable to King Mohamed VI's practice of keeping control of the key ministries to himself, and thus, according to some, stifling ideas and vision, in turn necessitating more civil society.[35]

Despite such modernization efforts, limits on political discourse remain. In November 2004, the government sentenced three journalists to prison terms after finding them guilty of "lack of respect due to the king, undermining the monarchy."[36]

THE STATUS OF WOMEN IN MOROCCO

Morocco was one of the first Arab countries to reform the old religious laws on marriage and divorce. In the spring of 1958 new civil laws officially discouraged Islamic divorce (without an outright ban), and passed new restraints on the husband's rights in marriage, leaving only the right of inheritance from his family. King Mohamed V gave considerable support to the changes, though Hassan II was more ambivalent about the place of women in Moroccan society. While he encouraged his sisters to participate in several public forums for the advancement of Moroccan women, his wife lived in seclusion and the press never mentioned her. Hassan did expand women's access to education and health care, policies that King Mohamed VI developed further, partially in response to the terrorist bombings in Casablanca in May 2003. The reforms under Mohamed VI included the establishment of a modern family court system, a minimum age for marriage, and expanded divorce rights for women.[37]

Today Moroccan women share the workplace with men and have access to considerable legal protections in work and family areas. Sexual harassment in the workplace is a crime. Women are entitled to a civil divorce, and laws protect them against spousal abuse. Yet women have not achieved anything close to parity with men on the political front. There are four women ministers in the cabinet of thirty-six. Women held 34 of the 325 seats in the Moroccan parliament after the October 2002 election, up from just two before, giving them the largest share of seats of any legislature in the Arab world. Morocco has taken another innovation in the Muslim world: the first women priests, or *mourchidat* as they are formally called, who can minister to Muslims and lead religious discussions (leading prayers is still reserved for men).[38]

Tradition has its impact on gender relations in Morocco as it does in many other parts of the world. A study of the garment industry in Fez indicated that women laborers are generally regarded as immoral, and although the garment factories employ large numbers of women, most are young and single. This is because husbands expect their wives to devote themselves to the home.[39] Partly in response to lingering tradition, Prime Minister Youssoufi issued his Plan for the Integration of Women, which attempted to address such issues as polygamy, unequal pay, and male guardianship. The plan produced considerable political activity on both sides of the issue. Around 100,000 women marched on the 2000 International Women's Day, while an even larger march against the plan took place in Casablanca organized by Islamists. King Mohamed VI then established a commission comprised of civil society members, magistrates, and Islamic theologians to study women's issues.[40]

THE STRUCTURE AND PERFORMANCE
OF THE MOROCCAN ECONOMY

Data on Morocco's economy reveal a generally positive picture for 2007, with GDP per capita at $4,400 and unemployment at around 8 percent, though almost 20 percent of Moroccans live below the poverty line. The import-export balance is negative, though, and the foreign debt exceeds $17 billion. The budget deficit is 1.7 percent of GDP, down from 4 percent in 2004.[41] While the economy is not in crisis, there are some troubling signs that could lead to political instability if things do not improve. For one thing, the crime rate shot up in the past several years, reflecting the growing gap between Morocco's wealthy and poor.[42] According to one estimate, that gap is wide, with around 5 percent of the population owning 80 percent of the country's wealth.[43]

Agriculture is an important component of Morocco's economy (around 20 percent of total economic activity), with the relatively fertile north contributing much of the crops and meat. There is cannabis production in northeastern Morocco, and both marijuana and hashish find their way to Spain and France. The manufacturing sector in Morocco is connected to agriculture in that many products use agricultural raw materials. The garment industry, for example, weaves animal and plant fibers into cloth. That industry contributes some 25 percent of the manufactured goods exported by Morocco.[44] Those goods, along with the products of Morocco's fields and farms, face stiff barriers when Morocco looks abroad for export potential. In hopes of finding export markets, King Hassan II formed the Arab Maghreb Union to create a free trade area like the European Union. However, the experiment has brought little fruit; in 2007, Morocco's trade exchange with the other four members of the Maghreb Union (Algeria, Libya, Mauritania, and Tunisia) ranked below Morocco's first five trade partners.

Morocco would like to export its agricultural products to Europe, but the European Union restricts access to its markets by nonmembers. Morocco produces many of the same products grown in southern Europe, and the farm interests of those countries are not supportive of allowing Maghreb countries access to EU markets. Moreover, if Morocco did join the EU, it would be required to accept imports of European wheat and barley, which, with their lower prices, would devastate Moroccan agriculture.

Morocco made an approach to the European Union in 1991, but the next year the European Parliament criticized Morocco for its human rights record and its stand on the Western Sahara. Morocco then skillfully exploited the divisions within the EU, and ultimately renewed the Moroccan-EU fishing accord, gained an expansion of EU economic assistance and continuing discussions on the creation of a free trade agreement.[45] Morocco signed a free trade agreement with the United States in July 2004, which allows more Moroccan goods into the US economy, but the real beneficiary of the arrangement is the United States, which will be able to sell more grain to Morocco after the trade agreements eliminate the 20 percent duties on US goods.[46]

Morocco has made considerable progress in privatizing its economy, partly because the government began stimulating the private sector at the time of independence, followed by structural adjustment policies supervised by the IMF and the World Bank in the 1980s.[47] Beginning in the late 1980s, King Hassan II led the movement to transform a largely state-owned economy into the hands of the private sector. In accordance with Article 45 of the Moroccan constitution, a Transfer Commission oversees the process that is to privatize state-owned companies, companies where the state holds the capital, and public establishments by the end of 1998. As of the summer of 1996, some twenty-five companies were privatized, including Shell Oil, the Banque Marocaine du Commerce Extérieur, and seventeen

hotels.[48] Some transfers went to foreign companies, as in the case of power production, where one company went to two Western companies and Casablanca out-
sourced its production of electricity to a French company.[49] The state-run tobacco
firm, Regie des Tabacs, was privatized in July 1997 and both Spanish and French
tobacco firms expressed interest in investing in it and expanding its factories.[50] Private banks are taking an increasingly large share of banking from the state-owned
Banque Centrale Populaire, which now accounts for one-fifth of bank deposits.[51]

While privatization has not done much to redistribute wealth, it has stimulated
the Moroccan stock market and has drawn a considerable number of new share-
holders.[52] That in turn may stimulate the nonagricultural sector of the Moroccan
economy and draw in more foreign investment. It was perhaps reflective of such
hope that the Chamber of Advisers refused to extend the deadline for completion of
the privatization program. The 1993 goal was to privatize 113 firms at the end of
1998, but by the end of that year, only 54 were fully privatized.[53]

Morocco is a favorite tourist attraction for Europeans (only 4 percent of Morocco's tourists come from the United States), and currently the 2.25 million
tourists account for around 8 percent of total Moroccan GDP. However, the state
plans to expand tourism to 20 percent of GDP by building six new resort sites
along the Mediterranean coast. The multibillion dollar plan may help Morocco's
economy grow, but any plan to expand foreign tourism is vulnerable to terrorism;
Morocco's tourist numbers dropped sharply following both 9/11 and the May 2003
suicide bombings in Casablanca that were aimed largely at Western interests.[54]

Morocco's economic doldrums might improve if the significant oil reserves announced by the king prove to be real. In a speech on his birthday, he announced
that oil explorers found "copious and high quality" oil in the eastern desert. Mohamed VI suggested that this came because of his *baraka* (he had earlier claimed
that rains and the 2001 World Soccer Cup would come to Morocco, and when neither did, some Moroccans became suspicious), but foreign oil company interests
gave some credence to the claims.[55] Government estimates of 15–20 billion barrels
may be high,[56] but exploration continues along the Algerian border and off the
coast, where the state oil company Onarep opened bidding on eleven blocks for ex-
ploratory drilling.[57]

A clear strategy might help Morocco's economic future, as it did for Tunisia.
However, the government has failed to provide such a strategy, preferring to concentrate on fiscally sound but unimaginative economic policy. Denoeux suggests
that "the future of Morocco's democratic transition will hinge on the kingdom's economic performance."[58]

MOROCCAN FOREIGN POLICY

Morocco lies at a strategic crossroads—at the Atlantic entrance to the Mediterranean Sea. A considerable portion of the world's seaborne traffic passes north of Morocco, which is one of the reasons why European powers retain such an interest in
Morocco, and one of the reasons why the United States has such an interest now.

However, Morocco has other important issues, including attempting to reinforce a long-standing claim to the Western Sahara, and often tense relations with Algeria and Mauritania.

Possibly because Morocco became independent in a relatively peaceful way, the country has maintained close ties to the West in general, and to France in particular. Morocco, as one official put it, is far away from the centers of conflict in the Middle East, and thus can serve as a place to bring the warring parties together.[59] Morocco has also pursued a relatively moderate line with Israel, at least until the election of Israeli Prime Minister Netanyahu in May 1996, after which Morocco joined other Arab countries in criticizing Netanyahu's stance toward the Palestinians.[60] Morocco was one of a very few Arab countries to support Egyptian President Sadat's opening to Israel, which King Hassan II laid groundwork for in secret meetings with Egyptian and Israeli diplomats. Israel and Morocco maintain liaison officers in their respective capitals, and there are reports that Israel supplied Morocco with around 100 tanks during its border war with Algeria.[61] Morocco also maintains close relations with Saudi Arabia and other Arab Gulf countries, and benefits from financial contributions from those countries. Morocco quickly supported Kuwait after it was invaded by Iraqi troops in 1990 and committed troops to the Allied coalition.

Morocco has enjoyed generally close relations with the United States, and Moroccans take pride in the fact that their country was the first to recognize American independence in 1777, and a Moroccan-US treaty negotiated in 1836 is the longest-standing unbroken treaty in US history. In the 1950s and 1960s, Morocco allowed US nuclear-armed strategic bombers to use Moroccan military bases, and US Navy vessels call regularly at Moroccan seaports. Despite these ties, Morocco views its future economic success as connected to Europe and continues to seek stronger ties to the European Union.

Some of Morocco's foreign policy issues are legacies from European colonial times. Spain still holds small enclaves on the coast—Ceuta and Melilla and the coastal islands of Penon de Alhucemas, Penon de Velez de la Gomera, and Islas Chafarinas. Morocco contests the Spanish claims, but there is no movement to renegotiate them. Morocco also maintains strained relations with Algeria, and Moroccan officials claim that Algeria supports the Polisario in the Western Sahara.[62] Algeria, for its part, accuses Morocco of allowing the Armed Islamic Group (see Chapter 20) to seek safe haven in Morocco.[63]

The Western Sahara

While Morocco has several pressing foreign and security problems, the one that gets the most attention in Rabat is the status of the former Spanish Sahara, claimed historically by Morocco and occupied by Moroccans since 1981. It is an unlikely place for a serious North African conflict, but it is significant.

Western Sahara is located south of Morocco and borders Mauritania, with a small corner touching Algeria. It is one of the more remote areas in the world. The primary inhabitants include at least four varieties of poisonous snakes, several species of vultures, and the Oran lizard that sometimes attacks camels if hungry enough. Its long seacoast is a graveyard for thousands of ships sailing around the African continent. The population consists of around 382,000 people divided across 22 tribes, largely nomadic and illiterate. Its only export is phosphate.

Moroccan claims to the Western Sahara are long-standing. Moroccan dynasties, such as the Almoravid dynasty, ruled parts of the Western Sahara in the eleventh and twelfth centuries.[64] They also claim that Western powers recognized Moroccan claims to the Western Sahara through such instruments as the Treaty of Fez in 1912 and the Spanish-Moroccan Treaty of 1861.[65]

King Hassan II quickly laid claim to the region, citing evidence that historically Morocco encompassed the territory taken by Spain. In 1974, Morocco and Mauritania agreed to partition the Western Sahara, which Algeria recognized at the time. In 1975, Morocco took its claim to Spanish Sahara to the International Court of Justice, but that claim was rejected, with the court concluding that while historical ties existed between the inhabitants of the region and Morocco, that relationship was insufficient for Morocco to claim sovereignty. In a compromise, the region was then divided into three parts, one administered by Spain, one by Morocco, and one by Mauritania. Algeria also played a role in support of the Polisario Front, a rebel group that originally fought for independence from Spain.[66] Some Polisario units established bases in Algeria, and Morocco threatened to pursue them back into Algeria from the Western Sahara, potentially triggering conflict between the two countries.[67]

King Hassan II believed that only a dramatic action would legitimate Morocco's claim as the sole ruler of the land, and thus launched the Great Green March in November 1976. That event mobilized 300,000 Moroccans, who marched over the border between Morocco and Spanish Sahara (now renamed Western Sahara) and occupied the territory. At the same time, the Polisario Front, formed in the Western Sahara in 1969 to combat Spanish occupation of the region, also claimed it. The Polisario claimed to be comprised of natives from Western Sahara. Morocco argued that Algeria and Mauritania supported the Polisario Front, and citizens of those countries consisted mostly of guerrillas. However, irrespective of exactly what the Polisario was, Morocco found itself facing a costly and bloody struggle with it for control of Western Sahara. In hopes of preventing such violence, Spain, Mauritania, and Morocco agreed to administer the Western Sahara jointly. However, Spain quickly withdrew from the territory, and Mauritania signed an accord with the Polisario and withdrew from Western Sahara in 1979. That left Morocco as the sole claimant besides the Polisario, and the Moroccan military found itself caught up in a protracted conflict that sapped its resources. In a desperate effort to isolate the Polisario guerrillas, Moroccan troops constructed huge sand walls around the Western Sahara to both prevent Algerian and Mauritanian assistance from getting in and Polisario guerrillas fleeing to sanctuary in those two countries. The walls were begun in 1981 and took years to build, stretching over 2,000 kilometers, and did limit the Polisario's ability to maneuver in the area. King Hassan also hoped that the death of Algerian President Boumedienne in December 1978 might end Algerian support for the Polisario. Although Boumedienne's successor, Chadli Bendjedid, wanted to reduce tensions in the Western Sahara, he was not prepared to abandon the Polisario.[68]

In 1987, the United Nations sent a fact-finding mission to the Western Sahara and the next year presented a cease-fire proposal coordinated with the Organization for African Unity (OAU). By 1991, fighting had become so costly that both sides agreed to a cease-fire that the parties have generally observed since then. In addition, both sides agreed that a referendum should determine the ultimate fate of Western Sahara, which they initially scheduled for 1992. The OAU and the UN were to monitor the voting, and the UN promised to commit a peacekeeping force. The UN implemented a peacekeeping force called the Mission for the Referendum in Western Sahara (MINURSO). The efforts of MINURSO, however, are limited by Moroccan nonrecognition of the Polisario, by French and American leanings toward Morocco, and by incomplete planning on a future outcome.[69] Those plans also called for a referendum election to determine the final status of the region, to be conducted under MINURSO auspices in 1991. The election did not take place, though, because of differences in the means of implementation.

Efforts to break the long impasse came in 1996 when former Secretary of State James Baker offered to host negotiations in Houston. The resulting Houston Accord reinforced the need for a referendum by the citizens of Western Sahara, but acceded to Morocco's concerns about exactly who those citizens were. Morocco believed that the Polisario Liberation Front was bringing in thousands of Mauritanians to vote under the pretext that they were in fact Sahrawis (the term for people living in Western Sahara).[70] Other Moroccan officials indicated that the referendum did not matter because Morocco would never relinquish title to Western Sahara no matter what a vote determined.[71] Others blamed either the United States or the United Nations, with Moroccan roving ambassador Brahim Hakim claiming that the United States was more concerned about the stability of the Algerian government (which allegedly supported the Polisario) than the rights of legitimate Sahrawis.[72] He also criticized MINURSO for sharing responsibility for the crisis.[73] For their part the Saharan president sounded equally determined to gain independence from Morocco with or without a referendum: "We will regain our independence come what it may."[74] In November 1998, UN Secretary-General Kofi Annan visited the Western Sahara, but some charged that Morocco bused thousands of supporters to greet him while he was at the same time denied access to reported detention camps for dissident Sahrawis.[75] Annan also tried to persuade Morocco to agree to a new referendum by December 1999, but it refused.[76] After Annan departed, Morocco did agree to continue registering would-be voters.[77] An electoral roll of more than 86,000 names was compiled by January 2000. However, Moroccan authorities promised to challenge every name on the list, a process that could add two more years of delay to the referendum.[78] James Baker returned to the scene in May 2000, bringing the two parties together in London for another effort at resolution, but the meeting ended in failure.[79] Algeria largely abandoned its support for a referendum, apparently concluding that improving relations with Morocco was more important.[80] The UN also backed away from the referendum, and thus the ultimate beneficiary was Morocco, which had hoped that the long conflict would exhaust its participants, leaving the Western Sahara with Morocco by default.[81] King Mohamed VI has declared that his top priority is "the defense of the nation's territorial integrity," making it clear that he would continue Morocco's claim over the Western Sahara.[82] The deadlock led both Annan and Baker to seek a third way that excluded both independence and integration, but the Polisario refused to discuss the possibility in May 2003, leaving Zoubar and Benabdallah-Gambier to note dolefully that "few options, except a referendum, can break the stalemate."[83] King Mohammed VI tried to expand the idea of wider autonomy and announced investments worth $220 million in March 2006, but the head of the Polisario, Mohamed Abdelaziz, rejected the idea and demanded full autonomy.[84]

In recent years, Morocco has become a transit point for illegal migrants from sub-Saharan Africa seeking jobs in Europe. Morocco, in an effort to rid the country of these migrants, reportedly drove many into the Western Sahara and abandoned them. The exodus gave yet another mission to MINURSO forces, who tried to round up the refugees and remove them from an area made even more inhospitable by the thousands of land mines scattered about where they had been dropped off.[85]

Morocco lies at one end of the Maghreb; at the other lies Algeria. Though they share the same general area, they are quite different countries. Morocco managed to avoid a violent end to its colonial period, while Algeria's struggles against French colonialism cost hundreds of thousands of lives. Morocco has a reputation in the period that followed for peace, while Algeria's postcolonial period was marked by violence and isolation from its neighbors.

SUGGESTED READINGS

Bourqia, Rahma, and Susan Gilson Miller. *In the Shadow of the Sultan: Culture, Power, and Politics in Morocco.* Cambridge, MA: Harvard University Press, 1999.

Cook, Weston F., Jr. *The Hundred Years War for Morocco.* Boulder, CO: Westview, 1994.

Hammoudi, Abdellah. *Master and Disciple: The Cultural Foundations of Moroccan Authoritarianism.* Chicago: University of Chicago Press, 1997.

Howe, Marvine. *Morocco: The Islamist Awakening and Other Challenges.* New York: Oxford University Press, 2005.

Layachi, Azzedine. *State, Society, and Democracy in Morocco: The Limits Of Associative Life.* Washington, DC: Center for Contemporary Arab Studies, Georgetown University, 1998.

Pennell, C. R. *Morocco Since 1830: A History.* New York: New York University Press, 2000.

Slyomovics, Susan. *The Performance of Human Rights in Morocco.* Philadelphia: University of Pennsylvania Press, 2005.

White, Gregory. *A Comparative Political Economy of Tunisia and Morocco: On the Outside of Europe Looking In.* Albany: State University of New York Press, 2001.

20

ALGERIA

  The narrow road winds along the coast, damp from the light drizzle. The thin ribbon of land between the road and the Mediterranean is plotted into tiny squares of crops separated by fences woven from reeds. Small children sit on boxes by the road selling the green onions culled from these little patches. There is something timeless about the road, which lies above an ancient highway built of great stones by the Romans and traversed by conquerors marching across North Africa. They have left their mark on Algeria: the Berbers, the Romans, the Muslims, the French, their words, their faith, their tombs, and their columns still standing in groves of trees along the road. These children along the roads are their distant descendants, and one can only imagine their forbears sitting on boxes selling onions in the mist to other travelers who have come this way for thousands of years, passing through but leaving their footsteps behind.

ALGERIA TODAY IS A COUNTRY with a history of turmoil dating back to its days as a French colony, where the roots of the current political strife lie. Algeria's long occupation by France produced a postcolonial population that remains divided across cleavages that existed before the French arrived, though widened by the colonial experience. Algeria has transitioned to democracy in its more recent history, offering hope to Algerians that a more peaceful and prosperous future may lie ahead. Algeria's future includes the possibility that its petroleum resources may one day provide the springboard for sustained economic development and political stability.

Map 20.1 on page 413 shows modern Algeria.

THE MODERN HISTORY OF ALGERIA

Algeria consists of a coastal area with fertile farmland, seaports, and cities along a narrow Mediterranean strip, and a Saharan region covered by desert and mountains.

It is thus not surprising that the foreigners who shaped so much of Algeria's history controlled the coastal area, and the rebellions against them began and continued in the Sahara.[1] For centuries, the lands south of the coast were the home to pastoral nomads who herded animals, grew crops, and gathered dates in the lowland desert and the mountains that coursed through it. Those on the coast fished and traded, and the cities of Algiers and Oran became important centers of commerce linking the desert to the Mediterranean and to the rest of the world.

The French Colonial Period

Napoleon planned to invade Algeria in 1808, but his downfall prevented it. However, French soldiers finally carried out his plan in 1830 when France responded to insults that the bey of Algiers directed at the French ambassador by landing 34,000 troops at Sidi Ferruch. They captured Algiers and ransacked the city, beginning an occupation that lasted more than 130 years. In 1834, France annexed the area of French occupation, and French setters arrived. Many were of peasant origin from the poor southern part of France or other poor areas of southern Europe. Some were criminals or political deportees sent to Algeria to complete their sentences or simply exiled there. The French government encouraged such settlement by granting free land to the immigrants, particularly during the 1840s and 1850s. Wealthy French settlers also migrated to Algeria and founded great estates or urban enterprises.

The French occupation produced almost instant opposition, organized by Muhyi ad Din, an original opponent of the dey's rule, who launched attacks against the French from the port city of Oran in 1832. After that attack, his son Abd al-Qadir took his father's place and built an Islamic state in the parts of Algeria not occupied by the French. France viewed this state as a clear threat to its own Algerian holdings. After the French brokered a treaty in 1836 with Abd al-Qadir, their forces defeated the Muslim state in 1843, forcing Qadir to flee to Morocco. After surrendering to the French in 1847, he was granted safe passage and ultimately traveled to Damascus, where in 1860 he arranged with local Ottoman officials to protect an estimated 12,000 Christians from a planned Ottoman massacre. Though he never returned to Algeria (his remains were moved there in 1966), the colors of his battle standard became the official colors of the Algerian flag, and he is revered in Algeria as an Islamic hero.

In 1845, the French divided Algeria into areas of self-administration for the French settlers, or *colons*, mixed communities of French and Arabs, and areas under military control. However, after Louis Philippe's constitutional monarchy was overthrown in 1848, the Second Republic declared that the French-occupied part of Algeria was an integral part of France. A long period of increasing hostility between the French and the Arabs in Algeria then began in earnest. France outlawed the slave trade in 1848, undercutting the economic basis of some local elites.[2] In other areas, local religious leaders led revolts against the French occupation; one such revolt in Zaatsha led by Bu Ziyan was crushed in 1849 with extreme brutality.[3]

Arab Algerians gradually lost power in the mixed areas as French settlers continued to stream into Algeria, driven by the loss of Alsace-Lorraine in Germany in

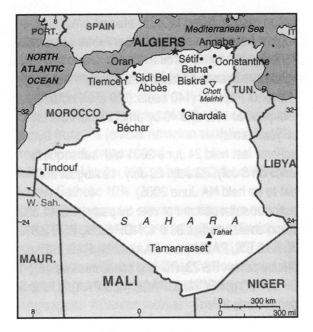

MAP 20.1   ALGERIA

1871. A decision to grant French citizenship to Algeria's 40,000 Jews advantaged them over Muslims. A drought in 1866 brought economic calamity, and pent up Muslim anger led to a revolt in 1871. The French responded swiftly to the uprising, and the Muslims found themselves facing increasingly harsh measures. The violence and the famine that followed the drought may have cost the lives of almost 20 percent of Algeria's Muslim population.

Algeria's Muslims faced other difficulties. They made up almost 90 percent of the population and produced around 20 percent of Algeria's wealth but paid close to 70 percent of direct taxes. Their schools were underfunded to the point where fewer than 5 percent of Muslim children attended school in 1870. France created an Algerian National Assembly, but Algerian Arabs had no seats. By 1915, the French allowed only 50,000 Muslims to vote in local elections. Eleven percent of the population, the *colons,* held 42 percent of the jobs. One Muslim child in ten went to school, while nearly all of the *colon* children did.[4]

Challenges to the French domination of Algeria continued, fueled partially by the 173,000 Algerians who served French interests in World War I. They observed France and its wealth, its democratic traditions, and its professed respect for equality and liberty. Those who survived the war carried those ideas back to Algeria, although they took different forms. Some who served in France would form the basis of the Algerian revolution. Others believed that it was necessary to work with France for ultimate Algerian autonomy under a framework emphasizing equality and social reform.[5] Yet others, believing that assimilation with France was impossible, chose the radical road.[6] Hope flowered briefly for the moderates when the Popular Front, led by Socialist Léon Blum, came to power in France in May 1936. Blum appointed Maurice Viollette as minister of state, and together they sponsored the Blum-Viollette bill to grant French citizenship to Algerians who qualified, around 30,000 in all. However, the bill died in the Senate in 1938, dashing the hopes of Algerians who wanted to assimilate with France.[7] While some radicals hoped to unite with the liberals, French violence against Muslim rioters in May 1945 ended such hopes. France tried to settle the growing tension between Muslims and Europeans by creating an Algerian Assembly in 1947, but in the following year, French authorities arrested many Muslims elected to the assembly for advocating Algerian independence.

Several key Algerian political factions emerged. One faction leaned toward accommodation with the French, typified by such men as the Emir Khaled and Ferhat Abbas. Khaled called for Algerians to be granted citizenship equal to the French, and Abbas believed that compromise would preserve both French Algeria and an Algerian Muslim identity. Abbas headed the Front de Liberation Nationale's (FLN) first provisional government in 1958, but found himself tarred by accusations of collaboration with France.[8] Other Algerians turned to communism and tried to affiliate with the French Communist Party. Messali Hadj emerged to lead the Marxist Etoile Nord-Africaine (ENA), which, while losing its class-struggle orientation, would become a foundation of the social commitment inherited by the modern Algerian state.[9] The *colons* in turn formed the *Organisation Armee Secrete* (OAS), a paramilitary organization that responded to FLN terror with terror of its own.[10]

In November 1954, the FLN launched attacks across Algeria against French military targets, and the violence escalated quickly. The French attempted to eliminate the FLN as a force, and for the next five years violence spread throughout Algeria and into France itself, where FLN supporters killed over 5,000 people through bomb attacks. All sides in the conflict attacked civilians as well as fighters, and the death toll soared. Torture and ritualistic murder became commonplace. French violence reached its peak during the battle of Algiers, between January and March 1957, which France won militarily. But as French citizens learned about the atrocities committed by their troops, public support for the war waned. More than four decades later France remains troubled by the behavior of its soldiers in Algeria.[11] The conflict took on international overtones, as the United States feared that Algerian rebels might become part of what they believed was a growing international communist movement in the Third World. French leaders sought American assistance in ending the conflict but that possibility became more distant when Charles de Gaulle assumed power in Paris.[12]

The *colons* hoped that Charles de Gaulle's assumption of the French presidency in 1958 would result in a French victory over the FLN. Instead, de Gaulle proposed a new constitution establishing Algeria as a French partner rather than as a part of France. The FLN organized a campaign of intimidation against the proposal, and, despite its wide approval in Algeria, de Gaulle abandoned it in 1959 and publicly stated that an independent Algeria was inevitable.[13] That resulted in a surge of violence between the *colons* and Algerian nationalists, a purge of disloyal French from the administration, and secret talks between de Gaulle and the FLN. Some French military officers reacted by starting the OAS, which launched a brief revolt against de Gaulle before independence was finalized in the Evian Accords of March 1962. Even then, the violence did not stop; the OAS turned on French soldiers in late March, then escalated to truck bombings, raids on hospitals, and attacks on Muslim women, killing thirty on May 10.[14] In a futile effort to separate Algeria's population from independence leaders, the army's Sections Administratives Specialisees (SAS) moved thousands of Algerians to resettlement areas, provoking even more resentment against the French.[15] When Algerians won their independence, they made an impact on international relations in doing so. As Connelly observes, Algerian independence "accelerated decolonization in Morocco, Tunisia, and Sub-Saharan Africa; it contributed to France's decision to back Israel and confront Nasser; it triggered the fall of the Fourth Republic and the return of de Gaulle; and it provoked de Gaulle into beginning the withdrawal of French forces from NATO commands."[16]

Algeria After Independence

Algeria's history as a modern country dates back only four decades. It begins with an effort to transition the FLN from a revolutionary organization to a political leadership organ for the country. However, this transition effort was marred by growing factions within the movement that had been masked by the fervor of revolution. The leading candidate for president, Col. Houari Boumedienne, linked up with Ahmed Ben Bella, who formed a cabinet that Ben Bella hoped would join the army (Boumedienne), the party (himself), and the government. However, the Algerian army ousted Ben Bella in June 1965, partially because he signed an agreement with King Hassan II of Morocco in which he agreed to consider giving up Algerian territory to Morocco.[17]

The predominant political group in Algeria after independence was the FLN, but growing internal fissures weakened its unity. Consequently the Algerian military dominated postindependence politics, with a series of officers taking the title of president. Ahmed Ben Bella led from 1962 to 1965, when Boumedienne replaced him and ruled until his death in 1978. Colonel Chadli Bendjedid assumed office and attempted to clean up the FLN, which had been joined by some who were more interested in profiting from political office than continuing FLN political programs.[18] Bendjedid efforts were apparently not enough to clean up the FLN's reputation, as the army forced his resignation in 1992 after the dismal performance of the FLN Party in the 1991 elections. The military has long been a key player in Algerian politics, largely unified by its vision of Algeria as a modern state free and capable of defending its own interests.[19]

Arrayed against the military were the Islamists, whose power grew after the 1979 Iranian revolution. The foremost Islamist party was the *Front Islamique du Salut* (FIS). Its power base grew in the 1980s along with failed promises of national wealth, along with the corruption associated with the FLN. The leadership correctly calculated that the popularity of the FIS was high enough to win a legislative election in 1991. Gaining victory in 188 out of the 430 electoral seats in the first round of the election, FIS alarmed the FLN and the military so much that the military canceled the planned second round of elections.[20]

In an effort to rally the populace behind the FLN, Muhammad Boudiaf, a founder of the FLN who went into self-imposed exile in Morocco, returned to Algeria. He threw his support to the High State Committee (HCE), the collegial presidency replacing Bendjedid. Boudiaf tried to mediate the increasingly unstable political climate by criticizing Bendjedid for corruption and the Islamists for politicizing the mosques. However, unknown assassins murdered him before the results of these efforts spread to the population.[21] The Islamists gained strength after the canceled elections, but their movement also had factions. Those had already appeared in 1992 with the first congress of the Armed Islamic Movement (MIA), distinct from the Armed Islamic Group (GIA). The two violence-prone factions attacked secular society and each other. Escalating instability, in the meantime, ended the ineffective HCE, and the military chose former retired general and defense minister Liamine Zeroual. In 1992 President Bendjedid resigned under pressure after the first round of legislative elections. When the Islamist FIS won 188 of the 231 seats, the military suspended the results. The military appointed Zeroual president in January 1994, and a national election held in November 1995 ratified the appointment.

Zeroual attempted to open negotiations with the FIS in 1994, and those efforts ultimately resulted in a conciliation effort in the Community of Sant Egidio in Rome in late 1994. Attended by a broad slice of Algerian parties and organizations, the group agreed on a set of broad principles of nonviolence, respect for human rights, and democracy. What followed that agreement was the Platform of Rome consisting of a broadened definition of the first agreement. However, while parties representing more than 82 percent of the voters signed the final declaration in 1991, they could not gain adherence from the more violent Islamic groups.

In 1997 the regime again tried to hold parliamentary elections, but when the government party won a majority of seats, the opposition charged fraud. Therefore, in an effort to bring calm to Algeria, Zeroual announced his early resignation and called for new elections in 1999. Initially six candidates declared their interest, but five of the six dropped out, leaving only former foreign minister Abdelaziz Boutiflika to run for president. Boutiflika disappeared from politics after spending time in office in the 1960s and 1970s, but suddenly emerged as the candidate of three of the four parties in the government coalition. He amassed a war chest of money from unspecified sources and received disproportionate time on state-owned Algerian television. Before exiting the presidential race, the other candidates demanded a meeting with Zeroual, but the president refused to see them. The ballots went out with the six names still printed on them, but the opposition supporters urged voters to stay away from the polls. Although Boutiflika won an uncontested election, the event simply reinforced Algerian cynicism about politics.[22] The election turnout produced disputed numbers; the government claimed that almost 61 percent of eligible voters participated, while the opposition stated that between 70 and 80 percent boycotted the election.[23]

In early June 1999 President Boutiflika responded to an offer by the AIS (Islamic Salvation Army; the military wing of the FIS) to lay down their arms by asking parliament to grant amnesty to FIS members. On June 14, parliament passed the measure. However, unknown assailants murdered FIS leader Abdel Kader Hachani in his dentist's office in November 1999, and while the government blamed the GIA for the killing, suspicion focused on Algerian security forces.[24] Still, Boutiflika pressed on with his civil concord initiative, which some viewed as a vehicle to rally support to his leadership rather than pacify the country.[25] Indeed Boutiflika may be less interested in pacifying the country than he professes. Henry and Springborg balefully argue that "the regime depends on violence to stay in power. . . The major source of regime cohesion remains the war itself."[26] The revitalization of the FIS with a program of economic reconstruction rather than religious zeal and an end to the bloodshed may be one avenue out of the political impasse. But, as Takeyh observes, "The tragedy of Algeria is that the FIS, having won elections, was unable to reach a modus vivendi with the ruling establishment, especially the military."[27]

Relative peace returned to Algeria in the early 2000s, as Boutiflika kept pressure on the violent Islamists while working to improve Algeria's faltering economy. In April 2004, he stood for election and won handily with 83 percent of the vote. While charges of voting fraud rang out again (mostly from former prime minister Ali Beflis, who garnered only 8 percent of the vote), the army did not appear to influence the vote, and Boutiflika appeared to have won the first popular mandate in Algeria's long history.[28] With that outcome, and the accompanying surrender of one of the most violent groups, the Salafist Group for Preaching and Combat, might at least signal internal peace for Algeria.[29] In June 2004, Algerian security forces killed both the founder and the leader, Nabil Sahraoui, of the Salafist Group for Preaching and Combat near Kabylie, possibly reducing the threat of a renewal of Islamist violence, though bombs again hit Algiers in the spring of 2006.

The question remains about dealing with the fissures that remain from Algeria's civil war, which, by Boutiflika's reckoning, have claimed 150,000 lives. In 2005, the president announced the Charter for Peace and National Reconciliation offering amnesty to the Islamists who participated in the violence, forgiveness for the security services who countered them, and money for the victims of both sides.[30] In September 2005, over 80 percent of Algeria's voters went to the polls and approved the measure by 97 percent.[31]

Why the Violence?

Why is there such violence in Algeria? Different answers emerge depending on the framework. Serfaty argues that French colonialism and the following revolution severed the link between the old Arab Algeria, and that the old revolutionary generation was in turn replaced by a younger generation with no memory of the revolution. They blamed the old revolutionaries for the corruption and mismanagement characterizing the postrevolution economy.[32] However, after Boumedienne died in 1979 the old left and the army could not fill the vacuum left by the previous leadership. Thus the Islamists got a significant role almost by default.[33] Quandt, however, suggests that a lack of Algerian identity itself may be part of the problem. "After all, in the minds of nearly all Frenchmen an Algerian country never existed. Much of the drama of the Algerian nationalist movement stems from the fact that large numbers of Algerians shared the belief that an Algerian country was a fanciful idea devoid of reality."[34] In this sense, as Waltz notes, "Thirty years of independent rule have not been able to erase a long history of social division. Politics remains the purview of a few, and the state is held hostage to rivalry among its leaders."[35]

THE ALGERIAN POLITICAL SYSTEM

After a faltering start, Algeria may have made a successful transition to a democracy, with three branches of government in the classic model, although the executive is clearly the dominant wing. The elections of 2004 indicated that Algeria may become North Africa's first full democracy, though Freedom House still ranks the country as "not free."

As noted above, Algeria has a tradition of authoritarianism embedded in its populist ideology. The primary pillar of this prevailing belief system is the Algerian military, and while Algeria is not a military dictatorship, the military and its tradition legitimize Algerian authoritarianism.[36] Thus the military dominate power in a country where other elites, including the commercial elite and the various Islamist branches, must contest with the armed forces for political, commercial, and social influence.

The Algerian Executive

The 1989 constitution strengthened the office of president at the expense of both the legislature and the military. Consequently, the executive branch is the most powerful part of the Algerian political system. This is consistent with the rentier economy Algeria ran while oil prices were rising in the 1970s and 1980s. The executive branch distributed the "rent" from oil revenues, and its role thus expanded. As Quandt observes, "The state would provide security, order, welfare, education, and jobs in return for political passivity, or at least controlled access to the political arena."[37] The strong administrative arm remains today.

President Boutiflika heads the executive, and the prime minister (since 2003) is Ahmed Ouyahia. The prime minister in turn appoints the Council of Ministers, which operates with little legislative oversight or accountability.

The Algerian Legislature

Algeria's first legislature opened under constitutional authority in September 1962, but President Boumedienne suspended the body three years later. Boumedienne reopened it in 1976, and the first multiparty elections were held in 1991.

Algeria's legislature consists of two chambers, the National People's Assembly (*Majlis Ech-Chaabi al-Watani*) with 389 members elected by popular vote to serve five-year terms, and the Council of Nations (144 seats; one-third of the members appointed by the president, two-thirds elected by indirect vote). Members of the Council of Nations serve six-year terms and the constitution requires half the council to be renewed every three years. According to the constitution, the Algerian legislature has the power to legislate laws on personal status, budgetary and other financial matters, customs duties, and public health, among other things. Parliament also has the power to question members of the executive and, on the motion of one-seventh of the members, vote to censure the government. Should the members pass the motion by a two-thirds majority, the prime minister and the cabinet must resign.

Algeria has a multiparty system, which includes the following parties:

- Algerian National Front (ANF)
- National Entente Movement (MEN)
- Islamic Salvation Front (FIS) (outlawed April 1992)
- Socialist Forces Front (FFS)
- Al-Nahdah
- National Liberation Front (FLN)
- National Reform Movement (Islah)
- Rally for Culture and Democracy (RC)
- Socialist Forces Front (FFS)
- Society of Peace Movement (MSP)
- Workers Party (PT)

In June 1997, elections were held for the 389 seats in the National People's Assembly. The National Democratic Rally (RND), an ally of the government, won 156, or about 41 percent of those seats. The other eleven parties took the rest, with Movement for a Peaceful Society getting 18 percent and the FIS 17 percent. The regime refused to allow the religious parties to run candidates in this election. The May 2002 elections for the National People's Assembly saw the FLN win 199 seats, the RND 48 seats, slah 43 seats, PT 21 seats, and al-Nahdah gaining only 1 seat, a clear blow for the Islamist movement. The May 2007 elections saw the FLN lose 36 seats, but the party still retained 136 seats, in an election marked by a tepid 37 percent voter turnout.

The Algerian Judiciary

The human rights issue existed in Algeria long before the 1992 elections. As Waltz notes, "The Algerian government did not readily embrace the idea of human rights."[38] The regime did make some small gestures, largely to avoid outside criticism, but after the crackdown, the HCE empowered special courts in October 1992 to try those accused of antiregime activities. The Algerian League of Human Rights spoke out against the procedures, and some of the worst practices ceased; torture

ended and the government released some political prisoners.[39] Reports of detain-
ment without trial, though, continued. In its 1998 report, Amnesty International
charged that Algeria continued to hold FIS and other suspects in detention; they
frequently disappeared for long periods while held in custody.[40] A 2006 update
states that "while there has been a decrease in reports of torture and other ill-
treatment in the custody of police and gendarmerie, torture and other ill-treatment
continue to be used systematically by the 'Military Security,' an intelligence agency
which specializes in interrogating individuals who are believed to have information
about terrorist activities."[41]

Political Opposition in Algeria

Several forms of opposition exist in Algeria, and while most opposition is Islamist in
nature, some comes from the minority Berber community (see below).

Algeria's Islamist movements draw their inspiration from a mix of sources, but
the largest Islamic movement, the FIS, had its foundations in Islamic modernism.
As the Algerian state began its slide toward failure in the 1980s, the FIS emphasized
a message of social justice, emphasizing in particular the state's inadequacy in education, housing, and employment.[42]

The wave began when President Bendjedid was ousted in 1992 and the successor
regime blocked the 1992 electoral results. The Islamist groups contributing to the
resulting violence include the Islamic Salvation Front, the United Company of Jihad, the Armed Islamic Group, the Armed Islamic Movement, the Army of the
Prophet Muhammad, the Movement for an Islamic State, the Salafi Group for Call
and Combat, and some smaller local groups. In 2007, the Armed Islamic Group became al-Qaeda in the Islamic Maghreb (AQ-M). Not all of these groups have ties to
the FIS, the largest Islamist movement in Algeria, and the Armed Islamic Group has
attacked the FIS on occasion; AQ-M seems to be linked to the larger al-Qaeda
group.

By 2004, estimates of lives lost to terrorism and other conflict exceeded 100,000,
and tragically much of it came during holy month of Ramadan. In the first week of
Ramadan for 1998, for example, some estimate that 1,000 people died during the
first week alone.[43] The attackers in many cases were not content to simply kill their
victims; many were mutilated, burned, or had their throats slit. Television news pictures of such atrocities (including a bloody streak running down a wall to a baby
bottle on the floor) horrified audiences around the world. Says one expert, "This is
unbearable to the international community. . . . They can't just keep on doing business in the south while blood flows in the north."[44] But no one in the "international
community" really knew what to do about the terrorism. Nor was there a clear understanding of why it occurred, with explanations ranging from religious fanaticism
(killing those perceived to have less religious zeal) to a systematic method of preventing defections from the Islamist movements.[45]

Support for these groups probably comes from inside Algeria and from Algerian
expatriates living mostly in Western Europe. The GIA, for example, operates in

France, drawing on the large Islamic community there to raise funds and recruit members. GIA operatives carried out a terrorist campaign in France in the early 1990s, but a strong French response apparently halted the operation.[46] Some additional support might come from such countries as Sudan, Iraq, and Iran. The Algerian government formally accused Iran of supporting Islamic terrorist groups and severed diplomatic relations with that country in 1993.

By 1998, the regime seemed to be winning the war against Islamist violence, at least to the point where the survival of the state seemed more assured. Revulsion by a large majority of Algerians against the violence appeared to drive the FIS armed wing, the Army of Islamic Salvation, to declare a truce with the government. That resulted in collaboration between the FIS and the regime against the GIA, and its numbers reportedly have dwindled to a few hundred.[47] However, as one group declined, another splinter faction, the Salafi Group for Call and Combat led by Hassan Hattab, announced in 2000 that it would limit attacks on civilians, thus pushing it in popularity above the GIA.[48]

Not all terrorism originates from Islamist groups. The military may also be involved, as suggested by attacks against civilians that occur near army camps. Some of this may be the work of anti-Islamist death squads like the Organization of Free Algerians and the *Organization Secrete de Sauvegarde de la Republique del'Algeria,* which are probably made up of former security force members.[49]

Islamists are not the only opposition group in Algeria. By some estimates, Berbers populate almost one-third of the country. The government decided in mid-1998 to make Arabic the official language in Algeria, which threatened to marginalize Berber culture. Berber demonstrators responded with an attack on government buildings in the Berber region of Kabylie that resulted in four deaths. The protest that followed was the largest in decades, but, as Blanche notes, there is no indication that the government plans to introduce political, social, or economic reforms that would address the causes of the unrest.[50] Protests spread to neighboring cities of Annaba and Skikda, leading the government to cut off services like power and water to these areas. In May 2002 the Rally for Culture and Democracy, the main Berber party, left the government to protest the government crackdown at Kabylie, where eighty people may have died.[51] Protests erupted again in Kabylie in March 2004 as President Boutiflika paid an unusual visit to the city to court Berber votes.[52] In 2006, apparently in response to Christian missionary activity in Berber areas, Algeria passed a law forbidding efforts to convert Muslims, with the minister of religious affairs stating, "Ten sects are active in Algeria, [referring to Christian groups]. They do not respect our laws. And some of these sects called for revolt in the Kabylie region."[53]

THE STATUS OF WOMEN IN ALGERIA

The role of Algerian women traditionally was shaped both by traditional Arab beliefs and by French efforts to dispense with such beliefs. Like most women in traditional Arab society, Algerian women lived most of their lives isolated from men outside their family. Many veiled themselves in public and found job opportunities outside the home highly restricted. French policy during the colonial period aimed at overturning these restrictions, but Algerians resisted. After independence, however, opportunities for women increased; by 1989 women held around 7 percent of urban jobs, with larger numbers holding jobs in the rural areas.

If ever there was a visible difference between the new modernizers and the Islamists, Algeria portrays it. The French experience emphasized freedom for Algerian women, and their lives were relatively unfettered. However, the Islamist opposition demanded that the status of women be returned to include covering and segregation where possible. The more violence-prone Islamists attacked women who failed to meet their expectations, and even young schoolgirls had their throats slashed for appearing in public without headscarves and veils. The majority of violence against women appears to be committed by relatives, and has grown to the point where the General Directorate of National Security has attempted to recruit more women police officers to aid in the investigation of family violence against women.[54]

The current legal status of women seems to reflect this political cleavage. Articles 39 and 42 of the constitution clearly state, "All prejudicial discrimination based on sex, race, or work is forbidden." However, the Family Code, passed in 1984, contains statutes that define women as inferior to men in rights, meaning that family courts can legally deny women such things as alimony or child custody in divorce cases. The Family Code also legitimizes the practice of a marriage dowry to be paid by the husband's family, and the bride is obligated to return the dowry should she seek divorce outside of the acceptable reasons. The Family Code also continues to recognize polygamy for males.[55] It is thus not surprising that women's organizations have campaigned for the elimination of the Family Code or at modification of its most severe articles.[56]

Progress on political participation for women is mixed. The election of eleven women to the National People's Assembly in June 1997 indicated that Algerians were prepared to examine the strong traditions that kept women as second-class citizens for centuries. However, these women won because they were party candidates, since no independent woman can win on her own.[57]

THE STRUCTURE AND PERFORMANCE
OF THE ALGERIAN ECONOMY

Algeria's economy depends on revenues from oil and especially natural gas, of which Algeria has the world's fifth largest reserves, supplying 57 percent of government revenues and one-quarter of the GDP. Given this dependence, the drop in world oil prices beginning in 1986 pushed the country into a deepening recession, which the government tried to counter by centralizing the economy. That was not a surprising decision since central planning was the only experience that they had to draw on. Moreover, Algeria tried to fund an ambitious industrialization program under Boumédienne's rule, which resulted in inefficient production and also drove much of the private sector underground.[58] Algeria turned to the IMF in 1989 and received a stabilization and deindustrialization package, but the impact of this agreement came too late to forestall the turmoil of 1992.

Algeria's economic problems began in earnest after a drop in world oil prices plunged the country into a severe recession. The government tried to implement a stabilization program in 1989, but political discord stymied the program, fueled by opposition to reforms required by the International Monetary Fund. According to one estimate, the restructuring required by the IMF between 1994 and 1999 eliminated between 200,000 and 400,000 jobs.[59] Debt rescheduling in 1995 and a bumper harvest helped stave off disaster. Algeria announced the privatization of much of its economy, but it will affect only the faltering sectors, raising concerns about its ultimate success.[60]

Algeria's almost 33 million people have a GDP per capita of around $7,200. The unemployment rate is 17 percent, which is high but an improvement over the 31 percent several years before. When the foreign debt of almost $20 billion is added, the reasons for Algeria's political instability become more evident. The difficulty for Algeria in transitioning its state-centric economy to privatization has only compounded the country's economic problems. The foreign debt is declining as a percentage of Algerian GDP, from 72 percent a decade ago to around 33 percent in 2004, and foreign exchange reserves are rising to $36 billion, largely due to sales of natural gas.[61] Algeria's national oil company, Sonatrach, along with foreign partners, plans to drill over 300 exploration wells between 1999 and 2000 in an effort to increase revenues from oil exports.[62] Expanding its pipeline capacity to Europe should allow Algeria to increase sales of its natural gas resources and thus improve the unemployment picture.

ALGERIAN FOREIGN POLICY

Algeria shares borders with Morocco, Tunisia, Libya, Niger, Mali, and Mauritania. With the exception of Morocco, Algeria's borders are relatively uncontested. A brief war on its border with Morocco flared in 1963, but both countries signed a treaty in 1969 demarcating the border. However, that treaty did not address another issue dividing the countries—Algeria's role in the Western Sahara. Algeria directly supported the Polisario front, partly due to domestic politics. This problem would strain Algerian-Moroccan relations. Algeria charged that Morocco gave support to Algerian Islamic radicals partly to pressure Algeria to stop interfering in the Western Sahara. Algeria in turn increased its support of the Polisario.[63] The tension continues between the two neighbors as the conflict in the Western Sahara continues to fester. Morocco's gesture in donating humanitarian aid to Algeria after devastating floods in the fall of 2001 was one indicator, though, that King Mohamed VI of Morocco desired to improve relations.[64]

The United States largely pursued a hands-off policy toward Algeria after the 1991 coup. But toward the end of 1998, the US Navy joined with Algerian forces in a naval rescue exercise, the first American-Algerian exercise since 1962. The United States also doubled its military training budget for Algeria from $61,000 to

$125,000 in 1998.[65] These moves provoked criticism about the United States cooperating, even in small ways, with a regime accused of human rights violations. However, Adm. Thomas J. Lopez, commander of US naval forces in Europe, claimed that, in his view, "Algeria. . . is turning the corner" on human rights abuses, noting a sharp drop in the killings in late 1998.[66] Algeria's President Bouteflika expressed sympathy for the September 11, 2001, terrorist attacks on the World Trade Center.[67]

Algeria retains ties to France despite its painful colonial history, although French military officials are reluctant to consider intervening in Algeria's domestic troubles, citing difficult memories of the past.[68]

SUGGESTED READINGS

Bonora-Waisman, Camille. *France and the Algerian Conflict: Issues in Democracy and Political Stability, 1988–1995.* Burlington, VT: Ashgate, 2003.

Connelly, Matthew. *A Diplomatic Revolution: Algeria's Fight for Independence and the Origins of the Post-Cold War Era.* New York: Oxford University Press, 2002.

Joffe, George. *Algeria: The Failed Revolution.* London: RoutledgeCurzon, 2008.

Martinez, Luis. *The Algerian Civil War.* New York: Columbia University Press, 2000.

McDougall, James. *History and the Culture of Nationalism in Algeria.* Cambridge: Cambridge University Press, 2006.

Naylor, Phillip Chiviges. *France and Algeria: A History of Decolonialization and Transformation.* Gainesville: University Press of Florida, 2000.

Phillips, John, and Martin Evans. *The Killing Fields of Algeria.* New Haven, CT: Yale University Press, 2008.

Quandt, William B. *Between Ballots and Bullets: Algeria's Transition from Authoritarianism.* Washington, DC: Brookings Institution, 1998.

Ruedy, John. *Modern Algeria: The Origins and Development of a Nation.* Bloomington: Indiana University Press, 1992.

Shah-Kazemi, Reza. *Algeria: Revolution Revisited.* New York: St. Martin's, 1998.

Stora, Benjamin. *Algeria 1830–2000: A Short History.* Ithaca, NY: Cornell University Press, 2001.

Wall, Irwin M. *France, the United States, and the Algerian War.* Berkeley: University of California Press, 2001.

NOTES

PREFACE AND ACKNOWLEDGMENTS

1. There is a dispute over the term "Persian Gulf," when referring to the body of water between the Arabian Peninsula and Iran. It is customarily referred to as the Persian Gulf in most Western news media reports, but the Arab countries bordering it prefer "Arabian Gulf," and the United States Central Command, which has geographical responsibility for the region, now officially refers to it as the "Arabian Gulf." The term can be used interchangeably.

2. Some claim that Arab identity must go further, to include descendants of Ishmael, Abraham's son by his Egyptian servant Hagar.

INTRODUCTION: THINKING ABOUT THE MIDDLE EAST

1. One of the best books on the history and religious symbolism of Jerusalem is Eric H. Cline, *Jerusalem Besieged: From Ancient Canaan to Modern Israel* (Ann Arbor: University of Michigan Press), 2004.

2. "In the Heart of Muslim Belief," *International Herald Tribune*, February 10, 2006.

3. Quoted in "The Crusader's Giant Footprints," *Washington Post*, October 23, 2001.

4. Europeans could not pronounce the name of Abu Jafar Muhammad ibn Musa al-Khawarizmi, who wrote ten books on mathematics, so his name came out in Europe as Alogrismus, which later was adapted to the logic of stepwise computation of numbers, familiar to computer operators as "algorithms."

5. These developments are chronicled in Francis Robinson, "Knowledge, Its Transmission, and the Making of Muslim Societies," in *The Cambridge Illustrated History of the Islamic World* (Cambridge: Cambridge University Press, 1996), pp. 228–229.

6. Ibn Khaldun, *The Muqaddimah: An Introduction to History* (Princeton, NJ: Princeton University Press, 1967).

7. See Joshua Parens, *Metaphysics and Rhetoric: Alfarabi's Summary of Plato's 'Laws'* (Albany: State University of New York Press, 1995).

8. See Ross E. Dudd, *The Adventures of Ibn Battuta: A Muslim Traveler of the Fourteenth Century* (Berkeley: University of California Press, 1986).

9. See Bryan S. Turner, *Orientalism, Postmodernism, and Globalism* (London: Routledge, 1994), p. 46. See also Richard E. Rubenstein, *Aristotle's Children: How Christians, Muslims, and Jews Rediscovered the Ancient Wisdom and Illuminated the Dark Ages* (New York: Harcourt, 2003).

10. André Raymond, *Cairo* (Cambridge, MA: Harvard University Press, 2000), p. 101.

11. For an insightful discussion on the varying images of Islam in the West, see Zachary Lockman, *Contending Visions of the Middle East: The History and Politics of Orientalism* (Cambridge: Cambridge University Press, 2004).

12. Edward W. Said, *Orientalism* (New York: Pantheon, 1978), p. 3.

13. Flaubert does not mention his soliciting prostitutes in Egypt, Syria, or Turkey.

14. Said, *Orientalism*, pp. 295, 308–328. Curiously, Said does not mention Karl Wittfogel, whose *Oriental Despotism* (Cambridge, MA: Harvard University Press, 1957) argues that "hydraulic societies" (those dependent on water management) require centralization of power (thus the title) and the elimination of countervailing groups to survive.

15. Douglas Little, *American Orientalism: The United States and the Middle East Since 1945* (Chapel Hill, NC: University of North Carolina Press, 2002).

16. Lockman, *Contending Visions*, pp. 248–251.

17. Martin Kramer, *Ivory Towers on Sand: The Failure of Middle Eastern Studies in America* (Washington, DC: Washington Institute for Near East Policy, 2001).

18. Halim Barakat, *The Arab World: Society, Culture, and State* (Berkeley: University of California Press, 1993), p. 42; Michael Bonner, *Jihad in Islamic History* (Princeton, NJ: Princeton University Press, 2006), p. 160.

19. Raphael Patai, *The Arab Mind* (New York: Scribner's, 1973), critiqued by Dag Tuastad, "Neo-Orientalism and the New Barbarian Thesis: Aspects of Symbolic Violence in the Middle East Conflict(s)," *Third World Quarterly*, August 2003, esp. p. 592.

20. Tuastad, "Neo-Orientalism," pp. 593–596.

21. Kramer, *Ivory Towers*, p. 123.

22. Kramer, *Ivory Towers*, pp. 96–97.

23. "Revisionist" historians Benny Morris, *Righteous Victims: a History of the Zionist-Arab Conflict, 1881–1999* (New York: Knopf, 1999, and Avi Shlaim, *The Iron Wall: Israel and the Arab World* (New York: Norton, 2000), largely blame Israel for initiating the Palestinian exodus, while Israeli scholars like Efraim Karsh accuse the revisionists of selective documentation. *Fabricating Israeli History: The "New Historians"* (Portland, OR: Frank Cass, 1997).

CHAPTER 1:
THE MODERN HISTORY OF THE MIDDLE EAST

1. See Joan Peters, *From Time Immemorial: The Origins of the Arab-Jewish Conflict over Palestine* (New York: Harper & Row, 1984), pp. 402–403. Kimmerling and Migdal claim that Peters's account is based on erroneous information, taken out of context. See Baruch Kimmerling and Joel S. Migdal, *Palestinians: The Making of a People* (Cambridge, MA: Harvard University Press, 1994), p. xvii.

2. For a debate on evidence supporting or refuting the existence of the First Temple, see Margreet Steiner, "It's Not There: Archaeology Proves a Negative"; Jane Cahill, "It Is There: The Archaeological Evidence Proves It"; and Navav Na'aman, "It Is There: Ancient Texts Prove It," *Biblical Archaeology Review*, July-August 1998, pp. 24–46.

3. James Reston, "The Issue in Cairo: Israel a US 'Base,'" *New York Times*, June 5, 1967, p. 1.

4. Shahrough Akhavi, "Islam and the West in World History," *Third World Quarterly* 3 (2003): 553–554; Saad Eddin Ibrahim, "An Open Door," *Wilson Quarterly*, Spring 2004, p. 37.

5. Earl Wavell, *The Palestine Campaign* (London: Constable, 1931), pp. 28–32.

6. David Fromkin, *A Peace to End All Peace: The Fall of the Ottoman Empire and the Creation of the Modern Middle East* (New York: Avon, 1989), p. 174.

7. The title "caliph of the Hijaz" was initially proposed by Arabs as early as the fifteenth century, though it was offered to Hussein by Lord Kitchener, the British Agent in Cairo. When Hussein realized that the British were not going to recognize him as king of Arabia, he attempted to gain their support for a more limited suzerainty where he would at least have power over rival Arab tribes (like the al-Saud). But he failed to get even this and was exiled to Cyprus by Abdul Azziz al-Saud. See Joshua Teitlebaum, "Sharif Hussein ibn Ali and the Hashemite Vision of the Post-Ottoman Order: From Chieftaincy to Suzerainty," *Middle East Studies*, January 1998, pp. 103–122.

8. See Fromkin, *Peace to End All Peace*, pp. 338–339.

9. The Sykes-Picot Agreement conflicted with American statements supporting self-determination and opposing secret treaties as a part of President Woodrow Wilson's Fourteen Points following World War I. Wilson ordered the King-Crane Commission to the eastern Mediterranean to attempt an alternative settlement. While the findings of the King-Crane Commission were not used to challenge Sykes-Picot, they may have unintentionally instigated an outburst of Syrian nationalism that left hundreds of dead when the French repressed nationalist demonstrations. See James Gelvin, "The Ironic Legacy of the King-Crane Commission," in David W. Lesch, ed., *The Middle East and the United States: A Historical and Political Reassessment* (Boulder, CO: Westview, 1996), pp. 11–28.

10. Fromkin, *Peace to End all Peace*, p. 191.

11. See F. W. Brecher, "French Policy Toward the Levant, 1914–18," *Middle Eastern Studies*, October 1983, pp. 641–664. France recognized the Maronite religion as part of Catholicism and thus sought to continue the "protected" status that France had granted the Maronites since the sixteenth century.

12. See John Fisher, "Syria and Mesopotamia in British Middle Eastern Policy in 1919," *Middle Eastern Studies*, April 1998, p. 140.

13. Notable Islamic nationalist Shakib Arslam said that "Arab nationalism. . . is not racist and which has no need of German national-socialist theories." See William L. Cleveland, *Islam Against the West: Shakib Arslam and the Campaign for Islamic Nationalism* (Austin: University of Texas Press, 1985), p. 144.

14. In June 2005, Sotheby's auctioned off two surviving copies of the Balfour Declaration for $884,000.

15. Balfour Declaration, 1917, Avalon Project, Yale Law School, www.yale.edu/law/web/avalon/balfour.htm.

16. British White Paper of 1922, Avalon Project, Yale Law School, www.yale.edu/law/web/avalon/balfour.htm.

17. British White Paper of 1939, Avalon Project, Yale Law School, www.yale.edu/law/web/avalon/balfour.htm.

18. Michael J. Cohen, *The Origins and Evolution of the Arab-Zionist Conflict* (Berkeley: University of California Press, 1987), p. 45.

19. Charles D. Smith, *Palestine and the Arab-Israeli Conflict* (New York: St. Martin's, 1988), p. 90. As in most cases, the exact death toll is disputed by both sides.

20. Ironically the grand mufti was appointed by Herbert Samuel, the British high commissioner to Palestine, himself a Jew. Grand Mufti al-Hajj Amin al-Husaini was responsible for the restoration of the Dome of the Rock and Al-Aqsa Mosque, raising his status as an Islamic leader. After his dismissal in 1936, he agitated among Arabs for Nazi Germany. See

Philip Mattar, *The Mufti of Jerusalem: Al-Hajj al-Husani and the Palestinian National Movement,* rev. ed. (New York: Columbia University Press, 1992).

21. A good history of these societies is in Eliezer Tauber, *The Emergence of the Arab Movements* (London: Frank Cass, 1993).

22. Michael N. Barnett, *Dialogs in Arab Politics: Negotiations in Regional Order* (New York: Columbia University Press, 1998), pp. 59–60.

23. Barnett, *Dialogs in Arab Politics,* chap. 3.

24. William Roger Lewis, *The British Empire in the Middle East, 1945–1951: Arab Nationalism, The United States, and Postwar Imperialism* (Oxford: Clarendon, 1984), chap. 2.

25. See Oles M. Smolansky with Bettie M. Smolansky, *The USSR and Iraq: The Soviet Quest for Influence* (Durham, NC: Duke University Press, 1991), pp. 15–17.

26. See Alvin Z. Rubinstein, *Red Star on the Nile* (Princeton, NJ: Princeton University Press, 1977), esp. chaps. 3, 5–6.

27. See Bruce Robellet Kuniholm, *The Origins of the Cold War in the Near East* (Princeton, NJ: Princeton University Press, 1980), esp. chap. 6.

28. Philip Robins, *A History of Jordan* (Cambridge: Cambridge University Press, 2004), pp. 62–64.

29. Michael J. Cohen, *Palestine and the Great Powers, 1945–1948* (Princeton, NJ: Princeton University Press, 1982), p. 275.

30. S. Ettinger, "The Modern Period," in H. H. Ben-Sasson, ed., *A History of the Jewish People* (Cambridge, MA: Harvard University Press, 1976), pp. 1065–1066.

31. Ettinger, "Modern Period," p. 1056.

32. Roger Friedland and Richard Hecht, *To Rule Jerusalem* (Berkeley: University of California Press, 1996), p. 246.

33. See Eugene L. Rogan and Avi Shlaim, *The War for Palestine: Rewriting the History of 1948* (Cambridge: Cambridge University Press, 2001).

34. Rashid Khalidi, "The Palestinians and 1948: The Underlying Causes of Failure," in Eugene L. Rogan and Rashid Khalidi, eds., *War for Palestine: Rewriting the History of 1948* (Cambridge: Cambridge University Press, 2001), pp. 12–36.

35. See Amitzur Ilan, *The Origin of the Arab-Israeli Arms Race* (New York: New York University Press, 1996), chap. 5.

36. The actual figures for the Arab armies remain difficult to document, since all the Arab countries contributing forces still have not declassified their historical archives. The figures are disputed by Depuy, who claims 40,000 for the combined Arab armies and 30,000 Jewish fighters. See Trevor N. Depuy, *Illusive Victory, The Arab-Israeli Wars, 1947–1974* (New York: Harper & Row, 1978), p. 19.

37. See Kenneth M. Pollack, *Arabs at War: Military Effectiveness, 1948–1991* (Lincoln: University of Nebraska Press, 2002), pp. 15–27, 269–284, 448–457, 1449–1455.

38. "Plan Dalet" is discussed in Ilan Pappé, *The Making of the Arab-Israeli Conflict, 1947–51* (London: Tauris, 1992), pp. 89–99.

39. Nadav Safran, *Israel: The Embattled Ally* (Cambridge Harvard University Press, 1978), p. 62.

40. See, for example, Abbasi's study showing that Plan D succeeded in driving Arabs out of the town of Safad despite threats by Arab leaders to destroy the property of any Arab who fled. Mustafa Abbasi, "The Battle for Safad in the War of 1948: A Revised Study," *International Journal of Middle East Studies,* February 2004, p. 33.

41. Ali E. Hillal Dessouqi, "Nasser and the Struggle for Independence," in William Roger Louis and Roger Owen, eds., *Suez 1956: The Crisis and Its Consequences* (Oxford: Clarendon, 1989), pp. 33–37.

42. For an elaboration of Israeli motives for participating in the Suez operation, see Mordechai Bar-On, "The Influence of Political Considerations on Operational Planning in the Sinai Campaign," in Selwyn Ilan Trone and Moshe Shemesh, eds., *The Suez-Sinai Crisis, 1956* (New York: Columbia University Press, 1990); Netanel Lorch, "Ben-Gurion and the Sinai Campaign, 1956," in Ronald Zweig, ed., *David Ben-Gurion: Politics and Leadership in Israel* (London: Frank Cass, 1991), pp. 293–312.

43. This initial collaboration between France and Israel was the basis for later French assistance to Israel's nuclear weapons program. See Avner Cohen, *Israel and the Bomb* (New York: Columbia University Press, 1998), pp. 53–54.

44. See Keith Kyle, *Suez* (New York: St. Martin's, 1991), p. 459.

45. Idith Zertal, *Israel's Holocaust and the Politics of Nationhood* (Cambridge: Cambridge University Press, 2005), p. 182.

46. Zeev Maoz, *Defending the Holy Land: A Critical Analysis of Israel's Security and Foreign Policy* (Ann Arbor: University of Michigan Press, 2006), p. 110.

47. Interviews, Tel Aviv, April 1986, March 1995.

48. Interviews, Damascus, April 1994, March 1997, March 1998.

49. See Jerome Slater, "Lost Opportunities for Peace in the Arab-Israeli Conflict: Israel and Syria, 1948–2001," *International Security*, Summer 2002, pp. 91–92.

50. Either the Soviets had bad information or they were purposely deceiving the Egyptians and their Arab allies. They may have wanted to prevent Israel from striking Syria, or they may have believed that the Arab forces could have beaten Israel should they attack with surprise. See Richard B. Parker, *The Politics of Miscalculation in the Middle East* (Bloomington: Indiana University Press, 1993), chaps. 1–3.

51. Israel had around 275,000 to 300,000 in uniform, with around 450 military aircraft and 650 tanks. Syria had around 100,000 troops, approximately 400 tanks. Jordan had between 70,000 and 80,000 soldiers and around 50 military aircraft. Egypt had some 300,000 troops (around 40,000 in Yemen), around 1,200 tanks, and some 500 aircraft. See "Combatants in Mideast," *New York Times*, June 6, 1967. These numbers, though, vary from estimate to estimate.

52. "Israeli and Arab Forces Battling," *New York Times*, June 6, 1967.

53. At that time the United States supplied around 85 percent of its own oil.

54. Israel claimed that it attacked the *Liberty* by accident, though a later investigation showed that the ship number and American flag were clearly visible and the attack took place in clear visibility. Perhaps most damaging to the Israelis' claim was the fact that their torpedo boats attacked the ship again after it sent out distress calls from the first attack. The alleged motive was Israeli suspicion that the *Liberty* was listening in on secret Israeli military communications revealing the aggressive purpose of the war. See James Ennes Jr., *Assault on the Liberty* (New York: Random House, 1979). Bamford claims that Gen. Moshe Dayan ordered the attack to conceal Israel's Syrian invasion plans from the US. See James Bamford, *Puzzle Palace* (New York: Penguin, 1983), pp. 291–293. For an Israeli denial, see Ephraim Evron's statement in Richard B. Parker, ed., *The Six-Day War: A Retrospective* (Tallahassee: University Press of Florida, 1996), p. 270.

55. When Defense Minister Moshe Dayan visited the Old City of Jerusalem after the Israeli military occupied it, he ordered that the Israeli flag be taken down from the Dome of the Rock and reassured the Islamic leaders of Al-Aqsa that the Islamic holy places would remain

under Muslim control. See Lawrence Wright, "Forcing the End," *New Yorker,* July 20, 1998, p. 46.

56. Pollack, *Arabs at War*, pp. 58–88, 293–330, 457–478.

57. See Yaacov Bar-Siman-Tov, *The Israeli-Egyptian War of Attrition* (New York: Columbia University Press, 1980), chap. 3.

58. Bar-Siman-Tov, *Israeli-Egyptian War*, pp. 59–71.

59. Helena Cobban, *The Palestinian Liberation Organization* (Cambridge: Cambridge University Press, 1984), p. 143.

60. The PFLP and the PLO were ideological rivals. The PFLP was largely Marxist oriented and Christian led; the PLO emphasized Palestinian nationalism and was largely Sunni Muslim.

61. Samih K. Farsoun with Christina E. Zacharia, *Palestine and the Palestinians* (Boulder, CO: Westview, 1997, pp. 217–218.

62. Maoz, *Defending the Holy Land*, p. 141.

63. Ariel Levite, *Intelligence and Strategic Surprise* (New York: Columbia University Press, 1987), p. 153; "Israel Knew Attack Was Coming, Envoy to the US Asserts," *New York Times*, October 11, 1973, pp. 1–18.

64. Richard K. Betts, *Surprise Attack* (Washington, DC: Brookings Institution, 1982), pp. 68–70.

65. The double agent was Dr. Ashraf Marwan, who had buried into Egyptian society so deeply that he married Nasser's daughter. Later Marwan moved to London, where he engaged in some shady arms deals. In July 2007 the police found him dead beneath his apartment balcony and deemed the death "suspicious." "Revealing the Source," *Jerusalem Post*, July 8, 2007.

66. Gordon, *Arabs at War*, pp. 98–131, 478–513.

67. Most of the houses in al-Qunaytirah collapsed as if they were cut by cables, which is how Syrians allege that Israelis destroyed them, connecting such cables between two bulldozers and driving them down two streets, destroying the houses in between. The hospital is pocked with shell holes (from the war, claim Israelis; from Israeli target practice, claim Syrians), and other buildings appear to have been dynamited. The city remains abandoned twenty-five years later. Interviews, *al-Qunaytirah,* March 1994, April, 1995, March 1998, March 1999.

68. The best work on Camp David is William B. Quandt, *Camp David: Peacemaking and Politics* (Washington, DC: Brookings Institution, 1986); and the revised edition, *Peace Process: American Diplomacy and the Arab-Israeli Conflict Since 1967* (Washington, DC: Brookings Institution; Berkeley: University of California Press, 2001).

69. Evidence shows that the attack was the work of the Popular Front for the Liberation of Palestine, which was not tied to the PLO. However, once Israel entered Lebanon, its primary target was the PLO.

70. Maoz, *Defending the Holy Land*, p. 174.

71. The person arrested for the bombing was an anti-Phalange Christian Lebanese who was alleged to have Syrian connections, at least according to Dilip Hiro, *Lebanon: Fire and Embers* (New York: St. Martin's, 1992), p. 92. The Phalange was a Lebanese Christian party that dated to the 1930s.

72. For details of the accord and its implementation, see Augustus Richard Norton and Jillian Schwedler, "Swiss Soldiers, Ta'if Clocks, and Early Elections: Towards a Happy Ending?" in Deirdre Collings, ed., *Peace for Lebanon?: From War to Reconstruction* (Boulder, CO: Lynne Rienner, 1994), pp. 45–68.

73. Shahram Chubin and Charles Tripp, *Iran and Iraq at War* (Boulder, CO: Westview, 1988), pp. 22–23.

74. For a discussion of these claims, see Majid Khadduri and Edmund Ghareeb, *War in the Gulf, 1991: The Iraq-Kuwait Conflict and Its Implications* (New York: Oxford University Press, 1997), chaps. 1–5.

75. See Shibley Telhami, "Between Theory and Fact: Explaining American Behavior in the Gulf War," *Security Studies*, Autumn 1992, esp. pp. 108–109; 115.

76. See Khaled bin Sultan, *Desert Warrior* (New York: HarperCollins, 1995).

77. David A. Lake, "Ulysses' Triumph: American Power in the New World Order," *Security Studies*, Summer 1999, p. 61.

78. This account draws largely from William B. Quandt, *Peace Process: American Diplomacy and the Arab-Israeli Conflict Since 1967* (Washington, DC: Brookings Institution; Berkeley: University of California Press, 1993), chap. 15.

79. "Hussein Was Sure of Own Survival," *Washington Post*, November 3, 2003. Some of these reports come from former Deputy Prime Minister Tariq Aziz, whose accuracy may be questionable.

80. "Bin Laden Images Mesmerize Muslims," *New York Times*, October 9, 2001.

CHAPTER 2:
RELIGION IN THE MIDDLE EAST

1. George N. Sfeir, "Basic Freedoms in a Fractured Legal Culture: Egypt and the Case of Nasr Abu," *Middle East Journal*, Summer 1998, p. 403.

2. Halim Barakat, *The Arab World: Society, Culture, and State* (Berkeley: University of California Press, 1993), p. 130.

3. Ira Sharkansky, *The Politics of Religion and the Religion of Politics: Looking at Israel* (Lanham, MD: Lexington, 2000), p. 11.

4. The name "Allah" is not restricted to Islam; Christian Arabs also use the term "Allah" when referring to God.

5. For more on the *hajj*, see F. E. Peters, *The Hajj: The Muslim Pilgrimage to Mecca and the Holy Places* (Princeton, NJ: Princeton University Press, 1994).

6. Some Islamic economists argue that *zakat* is a more effective means of state revenue generation than taxes because Muslims recognize a religious obligation to pay *zakat,* but not taxes. See Timur Kuran, *Islam and Mammon: The Economic Predicaments of Islamism* (Princeton, NJ: Princeton University Press, 2004), pp. 41–42.

7. A Saudi Arabian who was drinking alcohol in a Bahrani hotel bar noted that, in his view, "God does not watch what I do while out of Saudi Arabia." Interview, Manama, Bahrain, March 2001.

8. "Apostasy" in its strictest sense means to be unfaithful to Islam. However, some Muslims declared that those outside of their branch or their school of jurisprudence were apostates, and called for their excommunication (*takfir*) from the Islamic community. In a possible effort to unify that community, the session of the 2005 International Islamic Conference, held in Jordan, issued a statement condemned the doctrine of *takfir* and instructed all eight Islamic schools to establish a principle whereby only qualified clerics could issue religious edicts. "Islamic Conference Concluded with Statement Endorsing Religious Edicts," *Amman Petra JNA*, July 6, 2005, FBIS. The eight schools are the four Sunni schools noted below, and the Jafari, Zaydi, Ibadi, and the Thahiri Shiite schools.

9. See Kuran, *Islam & Mammon*; Ziauddin Ahmed, Munawar Iqbal, and M. Fahim Kham, *Money and Banking in Islam* (Jeddah: International Centre for Research in Islamic Economics, King Abdul Aziz University, 1983), esp. chap. 1.

10. During Ottoman times Muslim art depicted the Prophet, but with his face hidden (sometimes by a veil or by emitted light) and Shiite art still depicts Ali and other caliphs.

11. See Sharhrough Akhavi, "Islam and the West in World History," *Third World Quarterly* 24, no. 3 (2003): 548.

12. Akhavi, "Islam and the West."

13. For an enlightening discussion of the validity of a particular hadith, see Richard W. Bulliet, *Islam: The View from the Edge* (New York: Columbia University Press, 1994).

14. Moojan Momen, *An Introduction to Shi'a Islam* (New Haven, CT: Yale University Press, 1985), chap. 2.

15. According to legend, Umar was visiting the Church of the Holy Sepulcher when prayer was called. Invited to pray in the church, Umar declined, noting that had he done so, it would be made into a mosque. He instead prayed outside, and the spot is marked today by a small niche.

16. An anonymous review made this point.

17. According to the story, Aisha was on a caravan when she lost a necklace. After searching fruitlessly for it, she returned to the place where the caravan was resting, only to find that it had moved on without her. She was found by a stranger, who gave her a ride on his camel to her caravan. But Ali, her stepson-in-law, hinted that she might have committed adultery with the stranger. Though the Prophet claimed that Allah revealed her faithfulness to him, she never forgave Ali for his accusation.

18. Fouad Ajami, *The Vanished Imam: Musa al Sadr and the Shia of Lebanon* (Ithaca, NY: Cornell University Press, 1986), p. 138.

19. Abdulaziz Abdulhussein Sachedina, *The Just Ruler: (al-sultan al-'adil) in Shi'ite Islam* (New York: Oxford University Press, 1988), esp. chaps. 3–4.

20. Adapted from W. Andrew Terrill, *The United States and Iraq's Shi'ite Clergy: Partners or Adversaries?* (Carlisle, PA: Strategic Studies Institute, 2004), p. 5.

21. John L. Esposito, *Islam: The Straight Path,* expanded ed. (New York: Oxford University Press, 1991), p. 76.

22. In February 2006, unknown assailants bombed the shrine marking the tombs of al-Hadi and al-Askari in Samarra, Iraq. Bombers attacked the minarets of the same mosque in June 2007.

23. Momen, *Introduction to Shi'a Islam*, p. 75.

24. Heinz Halm, *Shi'ism,* 2nd ed. (New York: Columbia University Press, 2004), p. 49.

25. Esposito, *Islam*, pp. 47–48.

26. For a discussion of the early development and spread of the Hanafi school, see Nurit Tsaftir, *The History of an Islamic School of Law: The Early Spread of Hanafism* (Cambridge, MA: Harvard University Press, 2004).

27. See Earl L. Sullivan, *Women in Egyptian Public Life* (Syracuse, NY: Syracuse University Press, 1986), p. 26.

28. Before the twelfth century there was considerable rivalry between the Shafii and Hanafi schools, particularly when some Hanafis elevated the importance of *ijtihad* (reasoning) above the hadith. Some Sufis adopted the Shafii, which caused consternation among the followers of the Hanafi school, who believed that mystic visions and legalism could not be mixed. See Bulliet, *Islam*, pp. 110–111.

29. Antony Black, *The History of Islamic Thought: From the Prophet to the Present* (New York: Routledge, 2001), pp. 33–36.

30. It is left to the community of Islamic scholars *(ulama)* to determine what an "unacceptable innovation" is, but some have interpreted it to mean that the innovation did not exist at the time of the Prophet. This is why Saudi King Ibn Saud's conservative Ikhwan allies in the Saudi campaign demanded in 1902 that he destroy his phonograph machine. Later, Abdul Aziz had to read the Quran over the radio to get the device accepted by the religious community in Saudi Arabia. Other Hanbali jurists do not take such a strict stance on innovation.

31. Sanford Lakoff, "The Reality of Muslim Exceptionalism," *Journal of Democracy*, October 2004. Lakoff notes, though, that Islamic religious scholars have declared *ijtihad* "closed" since the tenth century to avoid ending a consensus reached between the four religious schools on the concept. Saudi Arabian reformer Abdullah al-Hamid criticizes those in his country who refuse to recognize Ibn Hanbal views that included *ijtihad*. Stéphane Lacroix, "Between Islamists and Liberals: Saudi Arabia's New Islamo-Liberal Reformists," *Middle East Journal*, Summer 2004, p. 349.

32. Eleanor Abdella Doumato, "Women and Work in Saudi Arabia: How Flexible Are the Margins?" *Middle East Journal*, Autumn 1999, p. 576.

33. Nikki R. Keddie, *Modern Iran: Roots and Results of Revolution* (New Haven, CT: Yale University Press, 2003), pp. 13–14.

34. See Madawi al-Rasheed and Louloluwa al-Rasheed, "The Politics of Encapsulation: Saudi Policy Towards Tribal and Religious Opposition," *Middle Eastern Studies*, January 1996, esp. pp. 109–114; and Madawi al-Rasheed, *A History of Saudi Arabia* (Cambridge: Cambridge University Press, 2002), esp. pp. 146–148.

35. Parvin Paider, *Women and the Political Process in Twentieth-Century Iran* (Cambridge: Cambridge University Press, 1995), p. 35.

36. Paider, *Women and the Political Process,* p. 105. Jalaluddin Rumi founded the Whirling Dervish Sufi sect in the Turkish city of Konya in the thirteenth century.

37. Some of the best work on Sufi philosophy is by William C. Chittick. See *Sufi Path of Knowledge: Ibn al'Arabi's Articulation of the Cosmos* (Albany: State University of New York Press, 1989); *Faith and Practice in Islam: Three Thirteenth Century Sufi Texts* (Albany: State University Press of New York, 1992); *The Self-Disclosure of God: Principles of Ibn al-'Arabi's Cosmology* (Albany: State University of New York Press, 1998); and *The Heart of Islamic Philosophy: The Quest for Self-Knowledge in the Teachings of Afdal al-Din Kashani* (Oxford: Oxford University Press, 2001).

38. John L. Esposito, *The Islamic Threat: Myth or Reality?* (New York: Oxford University Press, 1995), p. 37.

39. For an excellent discussion of the Sufi in modern Egypt, see Valerie J. Hoffman, *Sufism, Mystics, and Saints in Modern Egypt* (Columbia: University of South Carolina Press, 1995).

40. Emory C. Bogle, *Islam: Origin and Belief* (Austin: University of Texas Press, 1998), p. 44.

41. Sencer Ayata, "Patronage, Party, and State: The Politicization of Islam in Turkey," *Middle East Journal*, Winter 1996, pp. 48–49.

42. The Fatimid Caliph al-Hakim bi'Amr Allah ruled Cairo during those years, and Darazi was his vizier. Darazi's beliefs shocked so many in Cairo that a mob surrounded Hakim's palace demanding his head. Al-Hakim had to smuggle Darazi out of the palace and he fled to Lebanon, where he founded the Druze sect. Another version of the story is that

al-Hakim executed Darazi. In 1021, unknown persons (possibly on orders from his sister) assassinated al-Hakim, whose body was never found, leading to suspicion that his followers intended for him to be "hidden" like the Twelfth Imam in Shiite tradition.

43. One of the best works on the Druze is Robert Benton Betts, *The Druze* (New Haven, CT: Yale University Press, 1988).

44. Laila Parsons, "The Druze and the Birth of Israel," in Eugene L. Rogan and Avi Shlaim, eds., *The War for Palestine: Rewriting the History of 1948* (Cambridge: Cambridge University Press, 2001), p. 75.

45. Sometimes Muslim reaction against the Alawi, or Alevi, can turn violent, as it did in Turkey in July 1993, when thirty-seven people died in a hotel fire set by Islamists protesting an Alevi cultural festival in the town of Sivas. The Islamists claimed that they were protesting both the Alevi festival and the presence of a Turkish writer who had published excerpts from Salman Rushdie's *Satanic Verses*. See "Court Sentences 86 for Their Part in Islamic Riot," Anatolia News Agency, December 26, 1994; and "Turkish Militant Rioters Jailed for 15 Years," Reuters News Service (Middle East), December 26, 1994.

46. In the custom of the Twelvers, each of the eleven imams had a gate (*bab*), beginning with Salman al-Farisi, who served as *bab* for Ali ibn Abi Talib, and ending with Abu Suayb Muhammad ibn Nusayr, *bab* for the Eleventh Imam. Since the Twelfth Imam "disappeared," ibn Nusayr served as his *bab* during the period of occultation. He is considered the founder of the Alawi sect.

47. Their testament of faith differs considerably from the orthodox (see above). It is, "I testify that there is no god but Ali ibn Abi Talib, no veil but Muhammad, and no gate but Salman al-Farisi." Most Muslims would consider this testament an apostasy.

48. For more background on the Bahai, see Juan R. Cole, *Modernity and the Millennium: The Genesis of the Baha'i faith in the Nineteenth-Century Middle East* (New York: Columbia University Press, 1998).

49. "Bahais Mourn Iranian Leader Jailed for His Faith," *Washington Post*, January 31, 2006.

50. For the reasons why the Bahai selected the site at Haifa, see Idit Luzia, "The Bahai Center in Israel," in Ruth Kark, ed., *The Land That Became Israel: Studies in Historical Geography* (New Haven, CT: Yale University Press; Jerusalem: Magnes, 1990), pp. 120–132.

51. L. Carl Brown, *Religion and State: The Muslim Approach to Politics* (New York: Columbia University Press, 2000), p. 55.

52. Nazih N. Ayubi, *Political Islam: Religion and Politics in the Arab State* (London: Routledge, 1991), pp. 14–15.

53. Bassam Tibi, *Islam Beween Culture and Politics,* 2nd ed. (New York: Palgrave, 2005), pp. 42–45.

54. See Esposito, *Islam*, pp. 43–45.

55. Brown, *Religion and State*, chaps. 10–11.

56. Vali Nasr, *The Shia Revival* (New York: Norton, 2006), p. 95.

57. Gilles Kepel, *Jihad: The Trail of Political Islam* (Cambridge, MA: Belknap, 2002), pp. 23–27.

58. Sayyid Qutb, *Social Justice in Islam*, trans. John B. Hardie (1953; Oneonta, NY: Islamic Publications International, 2000), p. 262.

59. See Ahmad S. Moussalli, *Moderate and Radical Islamic Fundamentalism: The Quest for Modernity, Legitimacy, and the Islamic State* (Gainesville: University Press of Florida, 1999), chap. 5.

60. Abd al-Aziz ibn Baz, the religious adviser to the Saudi royal family, criticized Qutb on several areas, including Qutb's criticism of the Prophet's companions, and substituting metaphors for *tahwid*, thus arguing that Qutb's reasoning was unacceptable for the Wahhabist understanding of Islam. David Commins, *The Wahhabi Mission and Saudi Arabia* (London: Tauris, 2006), pp. 149–150.

61. Momem, *Introduction to Shii Islam*, p. 196.

62. Nasr, *Shia Revival*, p. 126.

63. Quoted in Geneive Abdo, *No God but God: Egypt and the Triumph of Islam* (Oxford: Oxford University Press, 2000), p. 64.

64. Radwan A. Masmoudi, "Struggles Behind Words: Sharia, Sunnism, and Jihad," *SAIS Review*, Summer-Fall 2001, p. 22. This is true for the Sunnis but not for the Imamiyya (or "Twelver") Shiites, as noted elsewhere in this chapter.

65. Tibi, *Islam Between Culture and Politics*, p. 161.

66. "In Turkey, a Sign of a Rising Islamic Middle Class," *New York Times*, April 25, 2007.

67. Sharrough Akhavi, "Islam and the West in World History," *Third World Quarterly* 24, no. 3 (2003): 553–554; Nikki R. Keddie, *Sayyid Jamal ad-Din "al-Afghani": A Political Biography* (Berkeley: University of California Press, 1972).

68. Esposito, *Islam*, pp. 115–116, 131–132. Ibn Taymiyya drew his inspiration from the conversion of the Mongols to Islam after their conquest of Baghdad in 1258 and the argument that such conversions were based on political expediency; thus Islam must be cleansed of such false Muslims.

69. Michael Scott Doran, "Somebody Else's Civil War," *Foreign Affairs*, January-February 2002, p. 28.

70. "Local Hands Accused in Morocco Blast," *Los Angeles Times*, May 19, 2003. The practice of throat slitting stems from the Salifiyyist belief that only weapons available at the time of the Prophet are appropriate for killing those who depart from their vision of Islam.

71. Khaled Abou El Fadl, "The Orphans of Modernity and the Clash of Civilizations," *Global Dialog*, Spring 2002, pp. 1–16.

72. Other Salafiyya groups include the highly ascetic Ikhwan, who live in southern Saudi Arabia and Yemen.

73. "Bin Laden's Followers Adhere to Austere Form of Islam," *New York Times*, October 7, 2001.

74. See, for one example, Hala Fattah, "Wahhabi Influences, Salafi Responses: Shaikh Mahmud Shukri and the Iraqi Salafi Movement, 1745–1930," *Journal of Islamic Studies*, May 2003, pp. 127–148.

75. "Reformers in Saudi Arabia: Seeking Rights, Paying a Price," *New York Times*, June 9, 2005.

76. David Commins, *The Wahhabi Mission and Saudi Arabia* (London: Tauris, 2006), p. 172.

77. Quoted in Kepel, *Jihad*, p. 146.

78. See Zeyno Baran, "Fighting the War of Ideas," *Foreign Affairs*, November-December 2005, pp. 68–78.

79. See Cheryl Benard and Zalmay Khalilzad, "Secularization, Industrialization, and Khomeini's Islamic Republic," *Political Science Quarterly*, Summer 1979, pp. 229–242.

80. Doran, "Somebody Else's Civil War," p. 34.

81. Bernard Lewis, "The Revolt of Islam," *New Yorker*, November 19, 2001, p. 54.

82. Michael Bonner, *Jihad in Islamic History: Doctrines and Practice* (Princeton, NJ: Princeton University Press, 2006), pp. 21–27, 49–51.

83. Reviewer's comment.

84. Hans Wehr, *A Dictionary of Modern Written Arabic* (Ithaca, NY: Spoken Language Service, 1999), p. 169.

85. John Esposito, *Unholy War: Terror in the Name of Islam* (New York: Oxford University Press, 2002), p. 5.

86. David Cook, *Understanding Jihad* (Berkeley: University of California Press, 2005), chap. 2.

87. Sura 2, verses 190, 193.

88. This argument is made by Emmanuel Sivan, "The Holy War Tradition in Islam," *Orbis*, Spring 1998, pp. 171–194.

89. Yohanan Friedman, *Tolerance and Coercion in Islam: Interfaith Relations in the Muslim Tradition* (Cambridge: Cambridge University Press, 2003), pp. 59–60.

90. Fred McGraw Donner, *The Early Islamic Conquests* (Princeton, NJ: Princeton University Press, 1981), pp. 96–97.

91. Donner, *Early Islamic Conquests*, p. 98.

92. Franco Cardini, *Europe and Islam* (Oxford: Blackwell, 1999), pp. 10–11. Creasy argues that the Muslim army lost the seminal battle of Tours in central France in 732 because of false rumors that the Frankish army was plundering their loot. When the Muslims rushed to protect it, they exposed their flanks to counterattack, and the Muslim drive into western Europe was thus halted. Edward Shepherd Creasy, *Fifteen Decisive Battles of the World* (New York: Military Heritage Press, 1987), p. 166.

93. "Saudi Arabia Wrestles with 2 Views of Islam," *Washington Post*, December 15, 2001.

94. "Bin Laden Stirs Struggle on Meaning of Jihad," *New York Times*, January 27, 2002.

95. Fawaz A. Gerges, *The Far Enemy: Why Jihad Went Global* (Cambridge: Cambridge University Press, 2005), chap. 5.

96. Bonner, *Jihad in Islamic History*, pp. 74–75.

97. Nasra Hassan interviewed numerous Palestinians involved in the planning and exercise of "martyrdom." See Nasra Hassan, "An Arsenal of Believers," *New Yorker*, November 19, 2001, pp. 36–41.

98. Peter Partner, *God of Battles: Holy Wars of Christianity and Islam* (Princeton, NJ: Princeton University Press, 1998), p. 37.

99. Cited in Cook, *Understanding Jihad*, p. 143.

100. The term obviously springs from the Protestant Reformation, which was directed against the power and doctrine of the Catholic Church. There is no such church in Islam, so perhaps the term "Islamic renaissance" would be more appropriate since many of the early discussions of Islam emphasized the moderation that those advocating an "Islamic reformation" hope for.

101. Quoted in Dale F. Eickelman, "Inside the Islamic Reformation," *Wilson Quarterly*, Winter 1998, pp. 80–89.

102. Radwan A. Masmoudi, "The Silenced Majority," in Larry Diamond, Marc F. Plattner, and Daniel Brumberg, eds., *Islam and Democracy in the Middle East* (Baltimore: Johns Hopkins University Press, 2003), p. 258.

103. Raymond William Baker, *Islam Without Fear: Egypt and the New Islamists* (Cambridge, MA: Harvard University Press, 2003).

104. Bahman Baktiari, "Dilemmas of Reform and Democracy in the Islamic Republic of Iran," in Robert W. Hefner, ed., *Remaking Muslim Politics: Pluralism, Contestation, Democratization* (Princeton, NJ: Princeton University Press, 2005), pp. 119–120.

105. Kenneth J. Perkins, *A History of Modern Tunisia* (Cambridge: Cambridge University Press, 2004), pp. 136–137.

106. Janine A. Clark, "The Conditions of Islamist Moderation: Unpacking Cross-Ideological Cooperation in Jordan," *International Journal of Middle East Studies*, November 2006, pp. 539–560.

107. Jillian Schwedler, *Faith in Moderation: Islamist Parties in Jordan and Yemen* (Cambridge: Cambridge University Press, 2006).

108. April Longley, "The High Water Mark of Islamist Politics? The Case of Yemen," *Middle East Journal*, Spring 2007, pp. 240–260.

109. Daniel E. Price, *Islamic Political Culture, Democracy, and Human Rights: A Comparative Study* (Westport, CT: Praeger, 1999), pp. 27–28.

110. See Ronald L. Nettler, "Islam, Politics, and Democracy: Mohamed Talbi and Islamic Modernism," in David Marquand and Ronald L. Netter, eds., *Religion and Democracy* (Oxford: Blackwell, 2000), p. 55.

111. See John L. Esposito and John O. Voll, *Makers of Contemporary Islam* (New York: Oxford University Press, 2001), chap. 5.

112. "Turkey, on Road to Secularism, Fears Detour," *New York Times*, January 8, 2002.

113. Christians from select countries (22 total), and Muslims selected from Albania, Algeria, Azerbaijan, Bangladesh, Egypt, Indonesia, Iran, Jordan, Morocco, Pakistan, and Turkey agreed on the desirability of "democratic performance" (both at 68 percent), and on democratic ideals (86 percent Christian, 87 percent Muslim), but disagreed on gender equality (82 percent Christian, 55 percent Muslim), on the desirability of divorce (60 percent Christian, 35 percent Muslim), and on the acceptability of homosexuality (53 percent Christian, 12 percent Muslim). See Ronald Inglehart and Pippa Norris, "The True Clash of Civilizations," *Foreign Policy*, March-April 2003, pp. 62–70.

114. Elie Kedourie, *Democracy and Arab Political Culture* (London: Frank Cass, 1994), pp. 6–7.

115. "Democracy's Uneasy Steps in the Islamic World," *New York Times*, November 23, 2001. The term *fatwa* means a religious opinion issued by a Muslim scholar or judge.

116. Ray Takeyh, "Islamism in Algeria: A Struggle Between Hope and Agony," *Middle East Policy*, Summer 2003, pp. 67–68.

117. Price, *Islamic Political Culture*, p. 28.

118. Alfred Stepan, "Religion, Democracy, and the Twin Tolerances," *Journal of Democracy*, October 2000, p. 47. As noted earlier, though, Freedom House 2006 counts Morocco, Jordan, Kuwait, and Yemen as "partly free," denoting at least partial democracies in these Arab countries.

119. Charles E. Butterworth, "Philosophy, Stories, and the Study of Elites," in I. William Zartman, ed., *Elites in the Middle East* (New York: Praeger, 1980), pp. 10–48. Tibi notes that Islamists regard both Averroes and Avicenna as heretics because of their distinction between religious and philosophical truth. Bassam Tibi, *Islam Between Culture and Politics* (New York: Palgrave, 2001), p. 49.

120. Lewis, *What Went Wrong?* p. 57.

121. Bernard Lewis, *The Jews of Islam* (Princeton, NJ: Princeton University Press, 1984).

122. Abdulaziz Sachedina, *The Islamic Roots of Democratic Pluralism* (New York: Oxford University Press, 2001), esp. p. 100.

123. Quoted in André Raymond, *Cairo* (Cambridge, MA: Harvard University Press, 2000), p. 46. However, another Fatimid caliph, al-Hakim, showed the limits of such thinking

when he persecuted Cairo's Jews and Coptic Christians, and when he ordered the burning of the Church of the Holy Sepulcher in Jerusalem.

124. Abdou Filali-Ansary, "The Sources of Enlightened Muslim Thought," *Journal of Democracy*, April 2003, pp. 31–32.

125. Muhsin S. Mahdi, *Alfarabi and the Foundation of Islamic Political Philosophy* (Chicago: University of Chicago Press, 2001), p. 145.

126. Friedman, *Tolerance and Coercion in Islam*, pp. 59–60.

127. Lewis, *Jews of Islam*.

128. See Zvi Cahn, *The Philosophy of Judaism* (New York: Macmillan, 1962), p. 21.

129. E. P. Sanders, *Judaism: Practice and Belief, 63 BCE–66 CE* (London: SCM Press, 1992), chap. 12.

130. The definitions that follow draw heavily on *The Encyclopedia of Judaism* (New York: Macmillan, 1989).

131. David S. Ariel, *What Do Jews Believe? The Spiritual Foundations of Judaism* (New York: Schocken, 1995), p. 42.

132. The Israeli Labor Party has challenged this exemption, but bills introduced into the Knesset to end the exemption have failed. See "Bills to Draft Yeshiva Students Expected to Fail," *Jerusalem Post*, July 8, 1998, p. 6. Later, after the election of Ehud Barak in May 1999, his party reached a compromise with Shas, the party that wanted the exemptions, for Yeshiva students to take some kind of military training without actually joining the Israeli military. Prime Minister Sharon did not follow through on the compromise after his 2000 election, though.

133. Kalman Neuman, "At Kfar Maimon, the State of the Faithful was Founded," *Haaretz*, July 28, 2005.

134. Hillel Fradkin, "Judaism and Political Life," *Journal of Democracy*, July 2004, p. 131.

135. Harvey Sicherman, "Judaism and the World: The Holy and the Profane," *Orbis*, Spring 1998, pp. 197–200.

136. An Israeli archaeologist claimed to discover the remains of King David's palace, rekindling the debate about the role of that city as the mythical "capital of the Jews," with the project funded by a conservative Israeli think tank and an American financier hoping to prove that "the Bible reflects Jewish history." "King David's Palace Is Found, Archaeologist Says," *New York Times*, August 5, 2005.

137. Sicherman, "Judaism and the World," p. 200.

138. Sicherman, "Judaism and the World," p. 200.

139. Kalman Neuman, "The Land Is a Value in and of Itself," *Haaretz*, August 3, 2005. The senior Kook taught that the coming of the Messiah would follow the establishment of Israel, unlike other strains of Orthodox Judaism. Believing that returning to biblical lands would help that return, Kook's followers moved to cities in the West Bank with particular religious significance, like Hebron and Nablus.

140. Sicherman, "Judaism and the World," p. 203.

141. Much of the following information is based on *The Christian Coptic Orthodox Church of Egypt*, http://cs-www.bu.edu/faculty/best/pbub/cn/Home.html.

142. "Monophysite" refers to the concept that Jesus Christ was a single divine person rather than both divine and human, as held by the Orthodox and Catholic Churches at the time of the Council of Chalcedon.

143. Notable evangelical leader Jerry Falwell voiced this view. See Lawrence Wright, "Forcing the End," *New Yorker*, July 20, 1998, p. 50.

CHAPTER 3:
THE POLITICAL ECONOMY OF THE MIDDLE EAST

1. See Thomas F. Homer-Dixon, *Environment, Scarcity, and Violence* (Princeton, NJ: Princeton University Press, 1999).

2. Manochehr Dorraj, "State, Petroleum, and Democratization in the Middle East," in *The Changing Political Economy of the Third World* (Boulder, CO: Lynne Rienner, 1995), pp. 122–123.

3. Halim Barakat, *The Arab World: Society, Culture, and State* (Berkeley: University of California Press, 1993), pp. 76–78.

4. James L. Gelvin, *Divided Loyalties: Nationalism and Mass Politics in Syria at the Close of Empire* (Berkeley: University of California Press, 1998), p. 37.

5. David S. Landes, *The Wealth and Poverty of Nations* (New York: Norton, 1999), p. 402.

6. Landes, *Wealth and Poverty*, p. 410.

7. Landes, *Wealth and Poverty*, pp. 410–414.

8. Bernard Lewis, *What Went Wrong? Western Impact and Middle Eastern Response* (New York: Oxford University Press, 2002), chaps. 1–2.

9. Timur Kuran, *Islam and Mammon: The Economic Predicaments of Islamism* (Princeton, NJ: Princeton University Press, 2004), p. 146.

10. Ross E. Dudd, *The Adventures of Ibn Battuta* (Berkeley: University of California Press, 1986); George Hourani, *Arab Seafaring* (Princeton, NJ: Princeton University Press, 1995).

11. Stephen O'Shea, *Sea of Faith: Islam and Christianity in the Medieval Mediterranean World* (New York: Walker, 2006).

12. Halim Barakat, *The Arab World: Society, Culture, and State* (Berkeley: University of California Press, 1993), p. 76.

13. Economic growth may stem from many factors, and economic *growth* and economic *development* are not necessarily related. Economic growth may be stimulated by a grant of foreign aid or a change in currency policy, for example, but economic *development* is something more than just positive economic growth. It can mean improvements in economic *structure*, to include power supply, communications infrastructure, advanced education, and a transportation network.

14. United Nations, *Standard Country or Area Codes for Statistical Use,* Series M, No. 49, Rev. 4 (United Nations publication M.98.XVII.9). Available in part at http://unstats.un.org/unsd/methods/m49/m49regin.htm.

15. Ian M.D. Little, *Economic Development* (New York: Basic, 1982), pp. 20–21.

16. Timothy Taylor, "Export Diversification in Latin America and the Caribbean," *International Trade Journal,* Summer 2003, p. 101. This strategy became difficult for many developing countries that had to compete with the subsidies provided by rich countries that both competed with their export products and undercut their domestic production. It was this factor that led to the collapse of the WTO talks in Mexico in the summer of 2003.

17. *Arab Human Development Report, 2002* (New York: United Nations Regional Development Program, 2002), p. 89. Thirty developed countries make up the OECD, including Australia, Belgium, Canada, Finland, France, Japan, Mexico, Poland, and the United States. The only Middle Eastern country in the OECD is Turkey, which is not counted in the UN report on Arab countries.

18. *Arab Human Development Report, 2000* (New York: United Nations Development Program, 2002), p. 85.

19. Paul Collier, *The Bottom Billion: Why the Poorest Countries Are Failing and What Can Be Done About It* (New York: Oxford University Press, 2007).

20. China has grown economically because of population control. One analysis notes that "because Beijing has managed to stem population growth—down to 1 percent a year, from 3 percent during the 1960s—China's growth of output has translated into large gains in income per capita." David Hale and Lyric Hughes Hale, "China Takes Off," *Foreign Affairs*, November-December 2003, p. 39.

21. All population growth rate figures are from the 2006 *CIA World Factbook*.

22. Phillip Longman, "The Global Baby Bust," *Foreign Affairs*, May-June 2004, p. 67.

23. Kenneth J. Perkins, *A History of Modern Tunisia* (Cambridge: Cambridge University Press, 2004), pp. 169–170.

24. Adam Bennett, "Failed Legacies," *Finance and Development*, March 2003, p. 25.

25. Clement M. Henry and Robert Springborg, *Globalization and the Politics of Development in the Middle East* (Cambridge: Cambridge University Press, 2001), p. 144.

26. *Privatization and Deregulation in the Gulf Energy Sector* (Abu Dhabi: Emirates Center for Strategic Studies and Research, 1999), pp. 28–29.

27. "Selling Iraqis on Selling Iraq; U.S. Pushes to Put State Firms on the Block; Skeptics Warn of Unrest," *Wall Street Journal*, October 28, 2003.

28. "On the Rebound: A Stronger Economy Is Reviving Turkish Airlines' Privatization Plans," *Aviation Week and Space Technology*, October 27, 2003, p. 45.

29. Hamed El-Said and Jane Harrigan, "Globalization, International Finance, and Political Islam in the Arab World," *Middle East Journal*, Summer 2006, pp. 227–228.

30. El-Said and Harrigan, "Globalization," p. 230.

31. Samuel P. Huntington and Joan M. Nelson, *No Easy Choice: Political Participation in Developing Countries* (Cambridge, MA: Harvard University Press, 1976), pp. 18–19.

32. Bruce Bueno de Mesquita and George W. Downs, "Development and Democracy," *Foreign Affairs*, September-October 2005, pp. 77–86.

33. Giacomo Luciani, "Resources, Revenues, and Authoritarianism in the Arab World: Beyond the Rentier State?" in Rex Brynen, Bahgat Korany, and Paul Noble, eds., *Political Liberalization and Democratization in the Arab World* (Boulder, CO: Lynne Rienner, 1995), 1:225-226.

34. Joseph T. Siegle, Michael Weinstein, and Morton H. Halperin, "Why Democracies Excel," *Foreign Affairs*, September-October 2004, p. 63.

35. An anonymous reviewer contributed this point.

36. Gilles Kepel, *The War for Muslim Minds: Islam and the West* (Cambridge, MA: Harvard University Press, Belknap Press, 2004), pp. 44–45.

37. U.S. Department of Commerce, Bureau of Economic Analysis, *U.S. Direct Investment Position Abroad on a Historical-Cost Basis, 1998*.

38. *Arab Human Development Report, 2002*, p. 87.

39. Henry T. Azzam, *The Arab World Facing the Challenge of the New Millennium* (London: Tauris, 2002), p. 4.

40. "Foreign Investors Wary of Arab States," *Al-Jazeera*, November 25, 2004. The report also cites bureaucratic complexity and the cost of government welfare systems, particularly in the oil-rich Gulf states.

41. Henry and Springborg, *Globalization and the Politics of Development*, pp. 40–41, 67. Tunisia has reduced tariffs through free trade agreements with the European Union, Egypt, Turkey, Morocco, and Jordan.

42. See Robert Gilpin, *The Challenge of Global Capitalism: The World Economy in the Twenty-First Century* (Princeton, NJ: Princeton University Press, 2000), pp. 88–113.

43. *Building a Knowledge Society: Arab Human Development Report, 2003* (New York: Arab Fund for Economic and Social Development, United Nations Development Program, 2003), p. 134.

44. Philip Robins, *A History of Jordan* (Cambridge: Cambridge University Press, 2004), pp. 142–143, 168.

45. Dirk Vandewalle, *A History of Modern Libya* (Cambridge: Cambridge University Press, 2006), pp. 67–68.

46. Nancy Birdsall and Arvind Subramanian, "Saving Iraq from Its Oil," *Foreign Affairs*, July-August 2004, p. 81.

47. Gawdat Bahgat, "Military Security and Political Stability in the Gulf," *Arab Studies Quarterly*, Fall 1995, pp. 55–56.

48. Gwenn Okruhlik, "Rentier Wealth, Unruly Law, and the Rise of Opposition: The Political Economy of Oil States," *Comparative Politics*, April 1999, pp. 296–297.

49. In the oil-rich sultanate of Brunei, Prince Jefri Bolkiah, the favorite brother of the sultan, spent over $15 billion on luxury items for himself, his wives, and mistresses. The spending spree severely depleted the resources of Brunei, resulting in a huge auction to recover some of the money. Included on the auction block were formula one race cars, fine china, antique cannons, and gold-plated toilet brushes. A government commission surveying the damage from the royal splurge grimly noted "warning signals of fundamental economic problems were ignored." "Brunei: From Oil Rich to Garage Sales," *New York Times*, August 17, 2001.

50. Michael L. Ross, "Does Oil Hinder Democracy?" *World Politics*, April 2001, pp. 325–361.

51. Michael Herb, "No Representation Without Taxation: Rents, Development, and Democracy," *Comparative Politics*, April 2005, pp. 297–316.

52. Meliha B. Altunisik, "A Rentier State's Response to Oil Crisis: Economic Reform Policies in Libya," *Arab Studies Quarterly*, Fall 1996, p. 63.

53. For a good discussion of the American-British rivalry over access to the Gulf during and after World War II, see Michael B. Stoff, *Oil, War, and American Security: The Search for a National Policy on Foreign Oil, 1941–1947* (New Haven, CT: Yale University Press, 1980).

54. See John M. Blair, *The Control of Oil* (New York: Pantheon, 1976), chaps. 1–5.

55. See Stephen D. Krasner, "A Statist Interpretation of American Oil Policy Toward the Middle East," *Political Science Quarterly*, Spring 1979, p. 82.

56. Zuhayr Mikdashi, *The Community of Oil-Exporting Countries: A Study of Governmental Cooperation* (Ithaca, NY: Cornell University Press, 1972), chap. 1.

57. Krasner argues that if the US government had intervened at this point to protect Occidental, the oil price changes that followed might have been avoided. See Krasner, "Statist Interpretation," p. 91.

58. Roy Licklider, *Political Power and the Oil Weapon: The Experience of Five Industrial Nations* (Berkeley: University of California Press, 1988), p. 11. There is another interpretation for the OPEC action, though. As Charles Doran notes, some OPEC members supported the OAPEC embargo. Venezuela and Iran had no reason to punish supporters of Israel, and Iran had been trading with Israelis. The implication is that OPEC took advantage of the war to create the opportunity for price increases. See Charles F. Doran, *Myth, Oil, and Politics: Introduction to the Political Economy of Petroleum* (New York: Free Press, 1977), p. 37.

59. "Iraq-Turkey Pipeline Isn't Secure," *Wall Street Journal*, Far East ed., November 13, 2003.

60. "Pipelines or Pipe Dreams," *Middle East*, June 2003, p. 48. It is unclear if much of the old pipeline remains.

61. Emre Engur, "Turkey Determined to Remain at the Center of East-West Energy Corridor," *Oil and Gas Journal*, January 14, 2002, p. 14.

62. "Libya Buys Israel's Former Stake in Egyptian Refinery," Agence France Presse, June 30, 2003.

63. Colin Campbell and Jean H. Laherrère, "The End of Cheap Oil," *Scientific American*, March 1998, pp. 81–82.

64. Campbell and Laherrère, "End of Cheap Oil," p. 83.

65. John Mitchell with Koji Morita, Mornal Selley, and Jonathan Stern, *The New Economy of Oil: Impacts on Business, Geopolitics, and Society* (London: Royal Institute of International Affairs, 2001), p. 44.

66. Amy Myers Jaffe and Robert A. Manning, "The Shocks of a World of Cheap Oil," *Foreign Affairs*, January-February 2000, pp. 16–29.

67. "Energy Crises Feared If Oil Prices Gyrate," *Washington Post*, November 21, 2000.

68. Mitchell, *New Economy of Oil*, p. 88.

69. Thomas Stauffer, "Natural Gas and Gulf Oil: Boon or Bane," in *Gulf Energy and the World: Challenges and Threats* (Abu Dhabi: Emirates Center for Strategic Studies and Research, 1997), p. 81.

70. Country Analysis Briefs, Energy Information Administration, Energy Administration, International Trade Administration, October 1, 2003.

71. "Middle East Tops Tourism League," *Middle East Economic Digest*, December 5–11, 2003, p. 30.

72. Jan Selby, "The Geopolitics of Water in the Middle East: Fantasies and Realities," *Third World Quarterly* 26, no. 2 (2005): 329–350.

73. "Middle East Faces Water Crisis," *al-Jazeera*, September 21, 2003.

74. "International Water Institute Predicts Shortages," *East London Daily Dispatch*, June 4, 1999.

75. Ashok Swain, "A New Challenge: Water Scarcity in the Arab World," *Arab Studies Quarterly*, Winter 1998, p. 1.

76. "Jordan River May Dry Up," *al-Jazeera*, June 25, 2005.

77. "Jordan River May Dry Up."

78. "Jordan Asks for More," *Economist*, May 17, 1997, p. 52.

79. Mary E. Morris, "Water and Conflict in the Middle East: Threats and Opportunities," *Studies in Conflict and Terrorism*, January-March 1997, p. 3.

80. Warren Singh-Bartlett, "Water," *Daily Star* (Beirut), April 19, 2000.

81. Homer-Dixon, *Environment, Scarcity*, p. 75.

82. "Aquifer That Provides 20% of Water Could Become Unusable," *Haaretz*, February 9, 2007.

83. Wafa Aboul Hosn, "Status and Needs of Water Statistics in the ESCWA Region," IWG-Env. International Work Session on Water Statistics, Vienna, June 20–22, 2005.

84. "Falling Levels, Wastage Make Water Scarce," *Global NewsBank*, March 22, 2004.

85. "Drought Fuels Debate over Agro-Water Subsidies," *Jordan Times*, December 22, 2006.

86. "Israeli Water Use and Exports," http://gurukul.cuu.american.edu/ted/ISRAELH2.htm.

87. Ilene R. Prusher, "Water Lies at Heart of Mideast Land Fight," *Christian Science Monitor*, April 18, 1998.

88. "Israeli Water Use and Exports."

89. "Israeli Water Use and Exports."

90. Morris, "Water and Conflict," p. 7.

91. Helga Haftendorn, "Water and International Conflict," *Third World Quarterly*, February 2000, pp. 56–57.

92. "Lack of Long-Term Solutions to Water Problem 'Will Lead to Catastrophe,'" *Jordan Times*, August 23, 1999.

93. *General Summary Near East*, Aquastat, Food and Agriculture Organization, United Nations, www.fao.org/AG/AGL/AQUSTAT/REGIONS/NEAST/INDEX.STM.

94. "$35 Billion for Withstanding Water Problems in the Arab States," *Arabic.News.Com.*, August 20, 2001.

CHAPTER 4:
POLITICS IN THE MIDDLE EAST

1. Ira M. Lapidus, "Tribes and State Formation in Islamic History," in Philip S. Khoury and Joseph Kostiner, eds., *Tribes and State Formation in the Middle East* (Berkeley: University of California Press, 1990), pp. 25–47.

2. Halim Barakat, *The Arab World: Society, Culture, and State* (Berkeley: University of California Press, 1993), p. 39.

3. Philip S. Khoury and Joseph Kostiner, "Introduction: Tribes and the Complexities of State Formation in the Middle East," in *Tribes and State Formation in the Middle East*, p. 15. See also Faleh A. Jabal, *Tribes and Power* (London: Saqi, 2003).

4. Al-Iraqiyah TV, Baghdad, November 6, 2006.

5. Karl A. Wittfogel, *Oriental Despotism: A Comparative Study of Total Power* (New Haven, CT: Yale University Press, 1957). Popular at the time, Wittfogel's thesis has been challenged by numerous critics who question both its authenticity and its lasting effects.

6. Eric Davis, *Memories of State: Politics, History, and Collective Identity in Modern Iraq* (Berkeley: University of California Press, 2005), pp. 95–96.

7. More on authoritarian regimes may be found in Paul Booker, *Non-Democratic Regimes: Theory, Government, and Politics* (New York: St. Martin's, 2000).

8. Davis, *Memories of State*, p. 186.

9. A discussion of the factors involved in this transformation is found in Samuel P. Huntington, *The Third Wave: Democratization in the Late Twentieth Century* (Norman: University of Oklahoma Press, 1991).

10. Phillippe C. Schmitter and Terry Lynn Karl, "What Democracy Is. . . and Is Not," in Larry Diamond and Marc F. Plattner, eds., *The Global Resurgence of Democracy*, 2nd ed. (Baltimore, MD: Johns Hopkins University Press, 1996), pp. 49–62.

11. Christopher Clague, Suzanne Gleason, and Stephen Knack, "Determinates of Lasting Democracy in Poor Countries: Culture, Development, and Institutions," *Annals of the American Political and Social Science*, January 2001, pp. 16–42.

12. "Arab Summit Meeting Collapses over Reforms," *New York Times*, March 28, 2004.

13. Larbi Sadiki, *The Search for Arab Democracy: Discourses and Counter-Discourses* (New York: Columbia University Press, 2004), esp. chap. 5.

14. Worldwide, Freedom House counted eighty-nine countries as "free," fifty-four as "partly free," and forty-nine as "not free." See "Russia Downgraded to 'Not Free,'" Freedom House press release, December 20, 2004, www.freedomhouse.org/media/pressrel/122004.htm.

15. Iliya Harik, "Democracy, Arab Exceptionalism, and Social Science," *Middle East Journal*, Autumn 2006, pp. 664–684.

16. Harik, "Democracy, Arab Exceptionalism, and Social Science," p. 676.

17. *Arab Human Development Report, 2002* (New York: United Nations Development Program, 2002), pp. 111–112.

18. "Democracy in the Middle East, a U.S. Goal, Falters," *New York Times*, April 10, 2006.

19. Alfred Stepan with Graeme B. Robertson, "An Arab More Than a Muslim Electoral Gap," *Journal of Democracy*, July 2003, pp. 30–44. Harik questions the Stepan and Robertson findings since they are based on Freedom House data, which Harik argues are unreliable at best on Arab political performance. Harik, "Democracy, Arab Exceptionalism, and Social Science," pp. 679–681.

20. Ahmad S. Moussalli, *Moderate and Radical Islamic Fundamentalism: The Quest for Modernity, Legitimacy, and the Islamic State* (Gainesville: University Press of Florida, 1999), pp. 184–185.

21. Islamists prefer Islamist governance, including adherence to Islamic law but not governance by religious leaders. The term is discussed further in Chapter 3. Islamist participation was most visible in Algeria, but Islamist parties also entered candidates in Jordanian elections. See S. V. R. Nasr, "Democracy and Islamic Revivalism," *Political Science Quarterly*, Summer 1996, p. 272.

22. "Islamists Ride Wave of Freedom," *Los Angeles Times*, December 18, 2005.

23. Over 60 percent of Middle Eastern respondents agreed with the statement, topping (in order) Western Europe, other Islamic states, Latin America, sub-Saharan Africa, US/Canada/Aus/NZ, South Asia, Eastern Europe, and Southeast Asia. See *Arab Human Development Report, 2003* (New York: United Nations Development Program, 2003), p. 19.

24. Ranjit Singh, "The Hamas Headache," *Middle East Report*, Spring 2006, p. 11.

25. See Khaldoun Hasan al-Naqeeb, "Social Origins of Authoritarian States in the Arab East," in Eric Davis and Nicolas Gavrielides, eds., *Statecraft in the Middle East: Oil, Historical Memory, and Popular Culture* (Miami: Florida International University Press, 1991), pp. 36–70.

26. Mohamed Talbi, "A Record of Failure," in Larry Diamond, Marc F. Plattner, and Daniel Brumberg, eds., *Islam and Democracy in the Middle East* (Baltimore: Johns Hopkins University Press, 2003), pp. 8–9.

27. Steven R. Dorr, "Democracy in the Middle East," in Robert O. Slater, Barry M. Schutz, and Steven R. Dorr, eds., *Global Transformation and the Third World* (Boulder, CO: Lynne Rienner, 1993), p. 134.

28. This point is made by Najib Ghadbian, *Democratization and the Islamist Challenge in the Arab World* (Boulder, CO: Westview, 1997), p. 32.

29. Kenneth J. Perkins, *A History of Modern Tunisia* (Cambridge: Cambridge University Press, 2004), pp. 27–28.

30. Saad Eddin Ibrahim, "Towards Muslim Democracies," *Journal of Democracy*, April 2007, p. 7.

31. Abbas Milani, "A Historical Perspective," *Journal of Democracy*, October 2005, p. 31.

32. William B. Quandt, "The Middle East on the Brink: Prospects for Change in the 21st Century," *Middle East Journal*, Winter 1996, p. 11.

33. Michele Penner Angrist, "Party System and Regime Formation in the Middle East: Explaining Turkish Exceptionalism," *Comparative Politics*, January 2004, pp. 229–248.

34. Alan Richards, "Modernity and Economic Development: The New American Messianism," *Middle East Policy*, Fall 2003, p. 69.

35. Eva Bellin, "The Robustness of Authoritarianism in the Middle East: Exceptionalism in Comparative Perspective," *Comparative Politics*, January 2004, pp. 139–158.

36. Abdo Baaklin, Guilain Denoeux, and Robert Springborg, *Legislative Politics in the Arab World* (Boulder, CO: Lynne Rienner, 1999), pp. 34–43.

37. The term *majlis* is also used in the region as a word for "parliament" or "legislature," and this term is not to be confused with the form of *majlis* under discussion in this section.

38. Madawi al-Rasheed, *A History of Saudi Arabia* (Cambridge: Cambridge University Press, 2002), p. 81.

39. Sivan notes that many topics, including ideas that run counter to Islamic teachings, are off limited in *shura* discussions. Emmanuel Sivan, "Illusions of Change," in Larry Diamond, Marc F. Plattner, and Daniel Brumberg, eds., *Islam and Democracy in the Middle East* (Baltimore: Johns Hopkins University Press, 2003), pp. 22–23.

40. F. Gregory Gause III, "Can Democracy Stop Terrorism?" *Foreign Affairs*, September-October 2005, pp. 62–76. In a rebuttal essay, Paula J. Dobriansky, Henry A. Crumpton, and F. Gregory Gause III, "Tyranny and Terror," *Foreign Affairs*, January-February 2006, pp. 135–139, two Bush administration spokespersons defend the Bush position without, in this author's judgment, much evidence.

41. Audrey Kurth Cronin, "How al-Qaida Ends," *International Security*, Summer 2006, p. 43.

42. Edward D. Mansfield and Jack Snyder, *Electing to Fight: Why Emerging Democracies Go to War* (Cambridge, MA: MIT Press, 2005), pp. 214–218.

43. See Samuel J. Eldersveld, *Political Elites in Modern Societies: Empirical Research and Democratic Theory* (Ann Arbor: University of Michigan Press, 1993), pp. xiii–xvi.

44. Chris Kutschera, "A World Apart," *Middle East*, February 2000, pp. 21–23.

45. See, for example, John B. Judis, *The Paradox of American Democracy: Elites, Special Interests, and the Betrayal of the Public Trust* (New York: Pantheon, 2000); Thomas Dye, *The Irony of Democracy: An Uncommon Introduction to American Politics* (North Scituate, MA: Duxbury, 1978); and Karl A. Lamb, *The Guardians: Leadership Values and the American Tradition* (New York: Norton, 1982).

46. On this point, see the chapters in Mattei Dogan and John Higley, *Elites, Crises, and the Origins of Regimes* (Lanham, MD: Rowman & Littlefield, 1998).

47. On political armies, see Kees Koonings and Dirk Kruijt, eds., *Political Armies: The Military and Nation Building in the Age of Democracy* (London: Zed, 2002).

48. Mehran Kamrava, "Military Professionalism and Civil-Military Relations in the Middle East," *Political Science Quarterly*, Spring 2000, p. 80.

49. See, for example, Steven A. Cook, *Ruling but Not Governing: The Military and Political Development in Egypt, Algeria, and Turkey* (Baltimore: Johns Hopkins University Press, 2007).

50. Brenda M. Seaver, "The Regional Sources of Power-Sharing Failure: The Case of Lebanon," *Political Science Quarterly*, Summer 2000, pp. 247–272. Since Seaver wrote this, Lebanon has suffered a renewal of sectarian violence.

51. Malik Mufti, "Elite Bargains and the Onset of Political Liberalization in Jordan," *Comparative Political Studies*, February 1999, pp. 100–130.

52. "Rise of the Technocrats Challenges the Powers of Iran's Muslim Clerics," *Christian Science Monitor*, December 8, 1995.

53. Patrick D. Gaffney, "Popular Islam," *Annals of the American Academy of Political and Social Science*, November 1992, p. 38.

54. For more on the concept of civil society, see Michael Waltzer, "The Idea of Civil Society: A Path to Social Reconstruction," *Dissent*, Spring 1991; Jean L. Cohen and Andrew Arato, *Civil Society and Political Theory* (Cambridge, MA: MIT Press, 1992).

55. Larry Diamond, *Developing Democracy: Toward Consolidation* (Baltimore, MD: Johns Hopkins University Press, 1999), p. 1999.

56. See Augustus Richard Norton, ed., *Civil Society in the Middle East* (Leiden: Brill, 1995); Augustus Richard Norton, "The Future of Civil Society in the Middle East," *Middle East Journal* 47 (1993): 205–216; Mehran Kamrava, *Democracy in the Balance: Culture and Society in the Middle East* (New York: Chatham House, 1998).

57. Bassam Tibi, "The Simultaneity of the Unsimultaneous: Old Tribes and Imposed Nation-States in the Modern Middle East," in Philip S. Khoury and Joseph Kostiner, eds., *Tribes and State Formation in the Middle East* (Berkeley: University of California Press, 1990), pp. 127–152.

58. See Richard T. Antoun, "Civil Society, Tribal Process, and Change in Jordan: An Anthropological View," *International Journal of Middle East Studies*, November 2000, pp. 441–463. Antoun criticizes the contributors in the Norton volume cited above for failing to emphasize the connection between the persistence of tribal tradition and civil society.

59. Saad Eddin Ibrahim, "An Open Door," *Wilson Quarterly*, Spring 2004, p. 39.

60. Mustapha Kamel al-Said, "The Concept of Civil Society and the Arab World," in Rex Brynen, Bahgat Korany, and Paul Noble, eds., *Political Liberalization and Democratization in the Arab World*, Vol. 1, *Theoretical Perspectives* (Boulder, CO: Lynne Rienner, 1995), pp. 136–137.

61. Interviews, Kuwait City, April 1994.

62. Isam al-Khafaji, "War as a Vehicle for the Rise and Demise of a State-Controlled Society," in Steven Heydemann, ed., *War, Institutions, and Social Changes in the Middle East* (Berkeley: University of California Press, 2000), p. 260.

63. Amy Hawthorne, "Is Civil Society the Answer?" in Thomas Carothers and Marina Ottaway, eds., *Uncharted Journey: Promoting Democracy in the Middle East* (Washington, DC: Carnegie Endowment for International Peace, 2005), pp. 89–92.

64. "Tunisia's Tangled Web Is Sticking Point for Reform," *New York Times*, June 25, 2004.

65. See Lise Garon, "The Press and Democratic Transition in Arab Societies," in Rex Brynen, Bahgat Korany, and Paul Noble, eds., *Political Liberalization and Democratization in the Arab World*, vol. 1, *Theoretical Perspectives* (Boulder, CO: Lynne Rienner, 1995), pp. 149–166.

66. See Naomi Sakr, *Satellite Realms: Transnational Television, Globalization, and the Middle East* (London: Tauris, 2001); Muhammad El Nawawy and Adel Iskandar, *Al-Jazeera* (Cambridge, MA: Perseus, 2002).

67. Dale F. Eickelman, "New Media in the Arab Middle East and the Emergence of Open Societies," in Robert W. Hefner, ed., *Remaking Muslim Politics: Pluralism, Contestation, Democratization* (Princeton, NJ: Princeton University Press, 2005), pp. 47–50.

68. Universal Declaration of Human Rights, General Assembly, 217A (III), U.N. Doc A/810 at 71 (1948).

69. David Gilles, *Between Principle and Practice: Human Rights in North-South Relations* (Montreal: McGill-Queen's University Press, 1996), p. 44.

70. Mahmood Monshipouri, *Islamism, Secularism, and Human Rights in the Middle East* (Boulder, CO: Lynne Rienner, 1998), p. 19.

71. The State Department publishes annual human rights reports, available at www.state.gov/g/drl/rls/hrrpt/2006. Amnesty International's human rights reports are available at www.amnesty.org.

72. The treatment of Jewish minorities has varied considerably over time and across countries. See Bernard Lewis, *The Jews of Islam* (Princeton, NJ: Princeton University Press, 1984).

73. John L. Esposito, *Islam and Politics* (Syracuse, NY: Syracuse University Press, 1984), pp. 230–231.

74. In June 2007, a mummy in storage for almost a century was identified by DNA as that of Hatshepsut.

75. The tradition appears to have died after the sixteenth century, when Islamic studies became a clearer path to careers in mosques and courts, which prohibited women. See Carla Power, "A Secret History," *New York Times Magazine*, February 25, 2007, p. 22.

76. Marina Ottaway, "The Limits of Women's Rights," in Thomas Carothers and Marina Ottaway, eds., *Uncharted Journey: Promoting Democracy in the Middle East* (Washington, DC: Carnegie Endowment for International Peace, 2005), pp. 118–119.

77. In Lebanon, voting is compulsory for all males over twenty-one years of age, while women must be twenty-one and have at least an elementary education; for them, voting is *authorized* but not compulsory.

78. *Hijab* is discussed in Barbara Freyer Stowasser, *Women in the Quran: Traditions and Interpretation* (New York: Oxford University Press, 1994), p. 122.

79. Moojan Momen, *An Introduction to Shi'a Islam* (New Haven, CT: Yale University Press, 1985), p. 183.

80. Barlas notes that current practice in Islamic countries on divorce negates many of the *Quranic* protections that must be allowed women in the divorce realm. *"Believing Women" in Islam* (Austin: University of Texas Press, 2002), pp. 192–197.

81. *Arab Human Development Report, 2002*, p. 52. A UNESCO report indicates that only five Arab countries achieved parity of gender in education (Palestinian Territories, Bahrain, Jordan, Lebanon, and United Arab Emirates). "Education in the Arab States: Five million girls still denied access to school," UNESCO Institute for Statistics, June 10, 2003.

82. "Fundamental Reforms Needed to Face the Challenges of the Next Century," *Jordan Times*, April 7, 2000.

83. *Arab Human Development Report, 2005: Facts and Figures,* at http://rbas.undp.org/PDF2005/AHDR4_06.pdf.

84. In surveyed Arab countries, less than 20 percent supported a belief in gender equality in the workplace, compared with over 60 percent in the US/Canada/Aus/NZ and Western Europe, See *Arab Human Development Report, 2003* (New York: United Nations Development Program, 2003), p. 19.

85. Elizabeth Fernea, "The Challenges for Middle Eastern Women in the 21st Century," *Middle East Journal*, Winter 2000, pp. 186–187.

86. Janine Astrid Clark and Jillian Schwedler, "Who Opened the Window? Women's Activism in Islamist Parties," *Comparative Politics*, April 2003, pp. 293–312.

87. Catherine Warrick, "The Vanishing Victim: Criminal Law and Gender in Jordan," *Law and Society Review*, June 2005, p. 321.

88. Stowasser, *Women in the Quran*, pp. 127–131.

89. Barlas, *"Believing Women,"* pp. 50–60.

90. Nouha al-Hegelan, "Women in the Arab World," *Arab Perspectives*, October 1980, pp. 1–3.

91. Jenny B. White, *Islamist Mobilization in Turkey: A Study in Vernacular Politics* (Seattle: University of Washington Press, 2002), pp. 228–229.

92. Itamar Rabinovich, *Waging Peace: Israel and the Arabs, 1948–2003* (Princeton, NJ: Princeton University Press, 2004).

93. Ron Pundak, "From Oslo to Taba: What Went Wrong?" *Survival*, Autumn 2001, pp. 32, 39.

94. Pundak, "From Oslo to Taba," p. 33.

95. Scott Lasensky, "Paying for Peace: The Oslo Process and the Limits of American Foreign Aid," *Middle East Journal*, Spring 2004, pp. 210–234.

96. John Quigley, *The Case for Palestine: An International Law Perspective* (Durham, NC: Duke University Press, 2005).

97. Interview, Tel Aviv, March 2006.

98. See Rami G. Khouri, "The Arab-Israeli Peace Process: Lessons from the Five Years since Oslo," *Security Dialog*, September 1998, pp. 333–344.

99. "Mideast Axioms Shaken by Violence," *Washington Post,* May 20, 2001.

100. "All Sides Failed to Follow Road Map," *Washington Post*, August 28, 2003.

101. "Road Map Setbacks Highlight U.S. Pattern," *Washington Post*, October 6, 2003.

CHAPTER 5: SAUDI ARABIA

1. For an excellent analysis of the Ottoman campaign in eastern Arabia and its purposes, see Frederick F. Anscombe, *The Ottoman Gulf: The Creation of Kuwait, Saudi Arabia, and Qatar* (New York: Columbia University Press, 1997).

2. Paradoxically, descendants of al-Sabah would ask the descendants of the al-Saud family to return the favor almost a century later when the ruling Sabah Emir and crown prince fled to Saudi Arabia after the 1990 Iraqi invasion under the protection of the descendant of Muhammad al-Saud, King Fahd ibn Abdul Aziz al-Saud.

3. The Ikhwan's adherence to a pure form of Islam led them to forbid smoking, music, and any item not existing at the time of the Prophet. Thus they objected to Abdul Azziz's practice of playing music records on a hand-cranked phonograph at night. Abdul Azziz had to destroy the instrument in front of his Ikhwan allies to keep their loyalty. See T. W. Gideon, "Sword of Saud and the Birth of a Nation," *Military History*, August 1997, p. 53.

4. Joseph Kostiner, "Transforming Dualities: Tribe and State Formation in Saudi Arabia," in Philip S. Khoury and Joseph Kostiner, eds., *Tribes and State Formation in the Middle East* (Berkeley: University of California Press, 1990), pp. 235–236.

5. See Madawi al-Rasheed's excellent description of the *mutawwa*. She distinguishes them from regular *ulama* by noting that they emphasized religious ritual over theological study. Madawi al-Rasheed, *A History of Saudi Arabia* (Cambridge: Cambridge University Press, 2002), pp. 49–50.

6. Al-Rasheed, *History of Saudi Arabia*, p. 51.

7. Al-Rasheed, *History of Saudi Arabia*, pp. 130–131.

8. Al-Rasheed, *History of Saudi Arabia*, pp. 144–146.

9. Al-Rasheed, *History of Saudi Arabia*, pp. 172–176.

10. "A Man with a Plan," *Economist*, March 23, 2002, p. 44.

11. "Saudi Urges Return of Jihadi Sons," *al-Jazeera*, September 9, 2003.

12. "A Campaign to Rattle a Long-Ruling Dynasty," *New York Times*, November 10, 2003.

13. Abdullah was the only son of one of Ibn Saud's early marriages, and thus he had no full brothers.

14. "Saudi King Pardons 3 Jailed Dissidents and Their Ally," *Washington Post*, August 9, 2005.

15. Joseph A. Kechichian, *Succession in Saudi Arabia* (New York: Palgrave, 2001), chap. 1.

16. Some argued that the Sudayri Seven were taking heroic and expensive methods to keep Fahd alive until Abdullah died, allowing the Sudayri brother to succeed and return the throne to the Sudayri full brothers. Robert Baer, "The Fall of the House of Saud," *Atlantic Monthly*, May 2003, p. 56.

17. "Political Forces," *Economist*, April 28, 2003.

18. Michael Scott Doran, "The Saudi Paradox," *Foreign Affairs*, January-February 2004, pp. 35–51.

19. Doran, "Saudi Paradox," pp. 36–38.

20. Nimrod Raphaeli, "Demands for Reforms in Saudi Arabia," *Middle Eastern Studies*, July 2005, p. 525.

21. Iris Glosemeyer, "Checks, Balances, and Transformation in the Saudi Political System," in Paul Aarts and Gerd Nonneman, eds., *Saudi Arabia in the Balance: Political Economy, Society, Foreign Affairs* (New York: New York University Press, 2005), p. 219.

22. Raphaeli, "Demands for Reforms," p. 529.

23. R. Hrair Dekmejian, "Saudi Arabia's Consultative Council," *Middle East Journal*, Spring 1998, p. 207.

24. Dekmejian, "Saudi Arabia's Consultative Council."

25. Joseph A. Kechichian, "Testing the Saudi Will to Power: Challenges Confronting Prince Abdullah," *Middle East Policy*, Winter 2003, p. 103.

26. "Cruel, or Just Unusual?" *Economist*, June 16, 2001, pp. 45–46.

27. Gwenn Okruhlik, "Empowering Civility Through Nationalism: Reformist Islam and Belonging in Saudi Arabia," in Robert W. Hefner, ed., *Remaking Muslim Politics: Pluralism, Contestation, Democratization* (Princeton, NJ: Princeton University Press, 2005), p. 191.

28. Interview, Jeddah Chamber of Commerce, January 1989.

29. "After Saudis' First Steps, Efforts for Reform Stall," *New York Times*, April 26, 2007.

30. Interview, Riyadh, March 2007.

31. Gwenn Okruhlik, "Rentier Wealth, Unruly Law, and the Rise of Opposition: the Political Economy of Oil States," *Comparative Politics*, April 1999, p. 298.

32. Interview, Saudi Arabia, January 1989.

33. Gawdat Bahgat, "Peace in the Persian Gulf: The Shi'is Dimension," *Peace and Change*, January 1999, p. 79.

34. Author's observations, January 1989.

35. Madawi al-Rasheed and Loulouwa al-Raqsheed, "The Politics of Encapsulation: Saudi Policy Towards Tribal and Religious Opposition," *Middle Eastern Studies*, January 1996, p. 113.

36. Al-Rasheed and al-Raqsheed, "Politics of Encapsulation," p. 114.

37. Stéphane Lacroix, "Between Islamists and Liberals: Saudi Arabia's New Islamo-Liberal Reformists," *Middle East Journal*, Summer 2004, pp. 358–365.

38. David Commins, *The Wahhabist Mission and Saudi Arabia* (London: Tauris, 2006), pp. 170–171.

39. Okruhlik, "Empowering Civility Through Nationalism," p. 203.

40. Lacroix, "Between Islamists and Liberals," pp. 345–366.

41. R. Hrair Dekmejian, "The Rise of Political Islam in Saudi Arabia," *Middle East Journal,* Autumn 1994, pp. 630–632.

42. Dekmejian, "The Rise of Political Islam," p. 633. For more on Ibn Baz, see al-Rasheed, *A History of Saudi Arabia,* pp. 165–168, 171.

43. Howard Schneider, "Calm in the House of Saud," *Washington Post,* weekly ed., January 17, 2000, p. 18.

44. "A Glimpse, Guard Down, of Bin Laden," *New York Times,* December 14, 2002.

45. "Saudi Arabia Wrestles with 2 Views of Islam," *Washington Post,* December 10, 2001.

46. "U.S. Exit Is No Sure Cure for Saudi Royals' Trouble," *New York Times,* April 30, 2003.

47. R. Hrair Dekmejian, "The Liberal Impulse in Saudi Arabia," *Middle East Journal,* Summer 2003, pp. 404–405.

48. Dekmejian, "Liberal Impulse," p. 410.

49. "Saudi King Grants New Powers to 'Parliament,'" *al-Jazeera,* November 30, 2003.

50. "Saudi Intellectuals Appeal for Reform," *al-Jazeera,* December 23, 2003.

51. "3 Beheaded for Sex Offenses," *Bahrain Tribune,* January 2, 2002.

52. "Valentine's Day Ban by Police," *Bahrain Tribune,* February 14, 2002.

53. Interviews, Riyadh, Jeddah, Dahran, Dahman, January 1989; Riyadh, Khamis Mushayt, Arda, March 1996, March 1997.

54. "When Justice Is Seen Not to Have Been Done," *Arab News,* August 1, 2005.

55. "Saudi Women have Message for U.S. Envoy," *New York Times,* September 28, 2005.

56. Eleanor Abdella Doumato, "Women and Work in Saudi Arabia: How Flexible Are Islamic Margins?" *Middle East Journal,* Autumn 1999, p. 569.

57. Doumato, "Women and Work," pp. 577–580.

58. Doumato, "Women and Work," pp. 571, 581–582.

59. Okruhlik, "Empowering Civility," p. 206.

60. Alan Richards, "Modernity and Economic Development: The New American Messianism," *Middle East Policy,* Fall 2003, pp. 65–66.

61. "Plan to Set Up Industrial City Areas for Saudi Women," *Gulf News,* February 6, 2004.

62. Rodney Wilson, *Economic Development in Saudi Arabia* (London: RoutledgeCurzon, 2004), p. 108.

63. See, for example, Osamah al-Siba'i, "Yes, Our Society Is a Society of Men," *Jeddah al-Madinah,* November 28, 1999, FBIS; in Arabic; Thuraya al-Arid, "Two Wings to Fly," *Riyadh al-Jazirah* (in Arabic), November 22, 1999.

64. "Al-Riyadh Rules Out Women's Participation in the Shoura Council," *ArabicNews.com,* January 2, 2002.

65. See the Glossary for a definition of purchasing power parity.

66. Daryl Champion, *The Paradoxical Kingdom: Saudi Arabia and the Momentum of Reform* (New York: Columbia University Press, 2003), chaps. 1–3.

67. Champion, *Paradoxical Kingdom,* pp. 97–113.

68. "Oil Innovations Pump New Life into Old Fields," *New York Times,* March 5, 2007.

69. Some Saudi Arabians express pessimism over the prospects for economic diversification. One fighter pilot said, "My grandfather crossed the desert on a camel at two miles an hour, but today I cross the desert at 700 miles an hour. But my grandson will cross the desert on a camel at two miles an hour." Interview, Saudi Arabia, March 1995.

70. "Saudi-U.S. Trade," www.saudi.net/relations/trade.

71. Rayed Krimly, "The Political Economy of Adjusted Priorities: Declining Oil Revenues and Saudi Fiscal Policies," *Middle East Journal*, Spring 1999, p. 256.

72. "Enormous Wealth Spilled into American Coffers," *Washington Post*, February 11, 2002.

73. F. Gregory Gause, "Saudi Arabia over a Barrel," *Foreign Affairs*, May-June 2000, p. 83.

74. "Report Raises Concerns at High Level of Recurrent Government Spending," *Arab News*, December 22, 2003.

75. "Balance of Payments Estimates," Ministry of Finance, Saudi Arabia, 2003.

76. Krimly, "Political Economy," p. 265.

77. Saudi Arabian Information Resource, n.d.

78. "Saudi Arabia: Saudi Officials View Asian Crisis on SABIC," *al-Riyadh*, May 6, 1998, FBIS-NES–98–126.

79. Press Room, SABIC, July 21, 2003.

80. "Quick Move on Telecoms Is a Breakthrough," *Middle East Economic Digest*, June 12, 1998, p. 37.

81. "Quick Move on Telecoms," p. 38. Privatization of Saudi Arabian Airlines is probably years away, but the airline is undergoing streamlining and modernization that will make privatization a more viable option. See "Privatisation Is Poised for Take Off," *Middle East Economic Digest*, June 2, 2000, p. 25. By April 2006 the Supreme Economic Council approved the privatization plan.

82. "Saudi Arabia's Privatization Pilgrimage," *Air Transport World*, August 2001, pp. 93–95.

83. Gause, "Saudi Arabia Over a Barrel," p. 86.

84. "Shortfall in Saudi Budget May Push Through Reforms," *Middle East Times*, December 18, 2001.

85. "Waiting for the IPO Wave," *Middle East Economic Digest*, July 23–29, 2004, pp. 29–30.

86. "Abdullah and the Ebbing Tide," *Economist*, January 23, 1999, p. 41.

87. "Beyond Oil," *Economist*, p. 17.

88. "A Survey of Saudi Arabia," *Economist*, January 7, 2006, p. 8.

89. Some Koreans demonstrated against harsh working conditions, and in areas where they worked prized Saluki dogs began to disappear. Mindful of national dietary habits, the Saudi Arabians replaced them with Chinese workers from south China, where dog meat is not a part of the normal diet.

90. "People Pressure," *Economist*, March 23, 2002, p. 7.

91. Khaled Almaeena, "Are We a Nation of Clerks?" *Arab News*, July 9, 2004.

92. Interview, Advanced Electronics Corporation headquarters, Riyadh, March 1997.

93. Wilson, *Economic Development*, p. 94.

94. See John L. Esposito, *Unholy War: Terror in the Name of Islam* (New York: Oxford University Press, 2002), pp. 105–115. Evans argues that most madrassas are not preaching radical or violent Islam. Alexander Evans, "Understanding Madrassas: How Threatening Are They?" *Foreign Affairs*, January-February 2006, pp. 9–16.

95. "Senators Push Saudi Arabia to Improve Antiterrorism Efforts," *New York Times*, August 1, 2003.

96. "Oil for Security Fueled Close Ties," *Washington Post*, February 11, 2002.

97. "Arab States, Wary of Iran, Add to Their Arsenals but Still Lean on the U.S.," *New York Times*, February 23, 2007.

98. "After Sept. 11, Severe Tests Loom for Relationship," *Washington Post*, February 12, 2002.

99. "Saudi Arabia: Saudi Prince Views Aftermath of Iraq Crisis," *al-Hayah*, March 25, 1998, FBIS-NEW–98–084.

100. "Saudi Leader's Anger Revealed Shaky Ties," *Washington Post*, February 10, 2002.

101. "Saudis May See U.S. Exit," *Washington Post*, January 18, 2002; "Saudis Feeling the Pain of Supporting the U.S.," *New York Times*, September 24, 2001.

102. "Flow of Saudi Cash to Hamas Is Scrutinized," *New York Times*, September 17, 2003.

103. See Richard L. Russell, "A Saudi Nuclear Option?" *Survival*, Summer 2001, pp. 69–80. According to Russell, the Saudis purchased between fifty and sixty CSS-2 Chinese missiles (p. 73), while other sources give a lower number, thirteen to eighteen. Interview, Saudi Arabia, January 1989.

CHAPTER 6: THE PERSIAN GULF EMIRATES

1. Jill Crystal, *Oil and Politics in the Gulf: Rulers and Merchants in Kuwait and Qatar* (Cambridge: Cambridge University Press, 1990), p. 43.

2. Crystal, *Oil and Politics*, pp. 51–53.

3. See Nigel Ashton, "Britain and the Kuwaiti Crisis, 1961," *Diplomacy and Statecraft*, March 1998, pp. 163–181.

4. Interview, US Embassy, Kuwait City, March 1994.

5. Interview, Kuwait City, March 1994.

6. Sharif S. Almust, "Kuwait and the Dynamics of Socio-economic Change," *Middle East Journal*, Summer 1997, p. 364.

7. Ghanim Alnajjar, "The Challenges Facing Kuwaiti Democracy," *Middle East Journal*, Winter 2000, p. 244.

8. "Kuwaiti Cabinet Sworn in," *al-Jazeera*, February 20, 2006.

9. Crystal, *Oil and Politics*, p. 100.

10. Crystal, *Oil and Politics*, pp. 22–23.

11. "Kuwait Debate: Caution Urged," *al-Jazeera*, December 21, 2004.

12. "Unholy Row," *Economist*, May 8, 1999, p. 48.

13. Mary Ann Tétreault, "Kuwait's Unhappy Anniversary," *Middle East Policy*, June 2000, pp. 73, 75.

14. "Kuwait Seeks Role 10 Years After Invasion," *Washington Post*, July 31, 2000.

15. Michael Herb, "Emirs and Parliaments in the Gulf," in Larry Diamond, Marc F. Plattner, and Daniel Brumberg, eds., *Islam and Democracy in the Middle East* (Baltimore: Johns Hopkins University Press, 2003), p. 88.

16. "Eight Preachers Suspended in Kuwait," *Kuwait al-Watan*, May 24, 1999, FBIS; in Arabic.

17. J. E. Peterson, "The Political Status of Women in the Arab Gulf Nations," *Middle East Journal*, Winter 1989, p. 39.

18. Mary Ann Tétreault and Haya al-Mughni, "Modernization and Its Discontents: State and Gender in Kuwait," *Middle East Journal*, Summer 1995, pp. 407–408.

19. Tétreault and al-Mughni, "Modernization," pp. 413–414.

20. "Retirement Age of Women: Cheers, Jeers for Draft Law," *Kuwait Times*, March 13, 2000.

21. Mary Ann Tétreault, "A State of Two Minds: State Cultures, Women, and Politics in Kuwait," *International Journal of Middle East Studies*, May 2001, pp. 205–206.

22. "Privatisation Law in the Offing," *Kuwait Times*, January 21, 1998, p. 1.

23. "People Pressure: A Survey of the Gulf," *Economist*, March 23, 2002, p. 5.

24. "The Aviators," *Middle East Economic Digest*, July 1–7, 2005, pp. 52–53.

25. See Mary Ann Tétreault, "Political Consequences of Restructuring Economic Regimes: The Kuwait Petroleum Corporation," *Millennium* 26, no. 2 (1997): 387–388.

26. Tétreault, "Political Consequences," pp. 392–401.

27. "Kuwaitis Grow Cynical over U.S. Motives in Gulf," *Wall Street Journal*, February 25, 1998, p. 14.

28. Anthony H. Cordesman, *Bahrain, Oman, Qatar, and the UAE: Challenges of Security* (Boulder, CO: Westview, 1997), p. 123.

29. An insightful account of Sultan Qaboos's efforts to modernize Oman and the hurdles that he faced is Calvin Allen Jr. and W. Lynn Rigsby II, *Oman Under Qaboos: From Coup to Constitution, 1970–1996* (London: Frank Cass, 2000).

30. Jeremy Jones and Nicholas Ridout, "Democratic Development in Oman," *Middle East Journal*, Summer 2005, p. 387.

31. Abdullah Juma Alhaj, "The Political Elite and the Introduction of Political Participation in Oman," *Middle East Policy*, June 2000, 97–110.

32. Marc J. O'Reilly, "Omanibalancing: Oman Confronts an Uncertain Future," *Middle East Journal*, Winter 1998, p. 75.

33. For the development of these consultative institutions, see J. E. Peterson, "Oman: Three and a Half Decades of Change and Development," *Middle East Policy*, Summer 2004, pp. 125–137.

34. Jeremy Jones and Nicholas Ridout, "Democratic Development in Oman," *Middle East Journal*, Summer 2005, p. 387.

35. Charles O. Cecil, "Oman's Progress Toward Participatory Government," *Middle East Policy*, Spring 2006, p. 67.

36. "Oman's Oil Yield Long in Decline, Shell Data Show," *New York Times*, April 8, 2004.

37. "Oman Relies Heavily on ESPs," *Oil and Gas Journal*, June 2, 2003, pp. 48–50.

38. "Charting a Clear Course," *Middle East Economic Digest*, June 10–16, 2005, pp. 43–44.

39. These developments are outlined in Moin A. Siddiqi, "A New Optimism," *Middle East*, November 1997, pp. 19–33.

40. Siddiqi, "New Optimism," p. 33.

41. Cordesman, *Bahrain*, p. 154.

42. "Sultanate Celebrates 23 July Anniversary," *Oman Daily Observer*, July 23, 1999.

43. Julian Taylor, "Finding Jobs for GCC Nationals," *Middle East*, November 1998, p. 19.

44. "Oman: Special Report," *Middle East*, November 1998, p. 24.

45. Peterson, "Political Status of Women," p. 40.

46. O'Reilly, "Omanibalancing," p. 75.

47. Gawdat Bahgat, "Security in the Gulf: The View from Oman," *Security Dialog*, December 1999, p. 450.

48. Bahgat, "Security in the Gulf," p. 454.

49. "Iran, Oman Discuss Strengthening Their Military Presence in Gulf," Agence France-Press, August 6, 1998. It is not clear if the exercise actually occurred because no further announcement followed. Both countries might have downplayed such an exercise, though, considering its strategic implications.

50. "Omani Minister on Gulf, MEPP Issues," *al-Hayah*, June 30, 1999, FBIS; in Arabic.

51. "Generation Rift Blamed for Cracks Within GCC," *al-Quds*, June 15, 1999; in Arabic.

52. O'Reilly, "Omanibalancing," p. 78.

53. The British had to mediate between the shah and three of the emirates, which had leased parts of the lands claimed by Iran to international oil companies. See Richard Mobley, "Deterring Iran, 1968–71: The Royal Navy, Iran, and the Disputed Persian Gulf Islands," *Naval War College Review*, Autumn 2003, pp. 107–120.

54. Cordesman, *Bahrain*, p. 292.

55. "No Taxation, No Representation," *Economist*, March 23, 2002, p. 12.

56. Interview, Abu Dhabi, March 2002.

57. "Who Needs Democracy?" *Middle East Economic Digest*, July 8–14, 2005, p. 32.

58. Cordesman, *Bahrain*, p. 295.

59. Peterson, "Political Status of Women," p. 37.

60. "Restructuring of Sixth Cabinet Sees First Woman Minister," *Gulf News*, November 3, 2004.

61. Fatma al-Sayegh, "Merchant's Role in a Changing Society: The Case of Dubai, 1900–90," *Middle Eastern Studies*, January 1998, pp. 87–102.

62. "In UAE, Tales of Paradise Lost," *Washington Post*, April 12, 2006.

63. One potential problem is the depletion of fish in the waters off the UAE, where the amount of fishing has increased by almost a factor of five since 1976. See Joanna Langley, "Gulf Marine Life Threatened by Lack of Legislation," *Gulf News*, April 26, 2000.

64. "Looking Bold and Talking Big: Dubai's Spending Binge," *Economist*, November 10, 2001, p. 46. These are in addition to the sail-shaped Burj al-Arab Hotel, one of the most lavish and expensive in the entire Middle East, where the least expensive rooms go for $800 per night.

65. "Blockbuster Emirates Order at Dubai Lifts Industry Spirits," *Aviation Week and Space Technology*, November 12, 2002, pp. 32–33.

66. Sharjah is home to small-scale industries, Ras al-Khaimah for new real estate developments, and education is booming in Sharjah, for example. Frauke Heard-Bey, "The United Arab Emirates: Statehood and Nation-Building in a Traditional Society," *Middle East Journal*, Summer 2005, pp. 365–366.

67. "Heading for the Peak," *Middle East Economic Digest*, July 8–14, 2005, p. 36.

68. Members of the Shiite faith constitute around 16 percent of the Muslim population of the UAE, but they do not hold any high-level positions in the government, due to concerns that Iran will attempt to infiltrate the UAE Shiites and use them for intelligence or sabotage. Interviews, Abu Dhabi, March 2002.

69. William A. Rough, "The Foreign Policy of the United Arab Emirates," *Middle East Journal*, Winter 1996, p. 58.

70. Louay Barry, "The Socioeconomic Foundations of the Shiite Opposition in Bahrain," *Mediterranean Quarterly*, Summer 2000, p. 133.

71. Interview, Manama, Bahrain, March 2002.

72. Gawdat Bahgat, "Peace in the Persian Gulf: The Shi'is Dimension," *Peace and Change*, January 1999, p. 83.

73. "Bahrain's Parliament Demands Real Power," *World Tribune*, January 27, 2003.

74. "Bahrain's Islamist Bloc Says Against Changing Political Associations to Parties," *Bahrain Tribune*, December 17, 2003.

75. "Playing by Unfair Rules," *Economist*, November 25, 2006, p. 46.

76. "Whitewash," *Economist*, January 23, 1999, p. 42.

77. "Bahrain Cleric Sentenced for Spying," Associated Press, July 7, 1999.

78. "Emir Grants Pardon to Jamri," *Bahrain Tribune*, July 9, 1999.

79. "Bahrain Respects and Protects Human Rights," *Bahrain Tribune*, April 20, 2000.

80. "Oasis of Hope: Bahrain's Bold Rebuff to Its Islamic Rebels," *Wall Street Journal*, October 25, 2001.

81. Interview, Manama, Bahrain, March 2002.

82. Peterson, "Political Status of Women in the Arab Gulf States," p. 38.

83. "Probe into Women's Situation in Bahrain," *Bahrain Tribune*, February 25, 2002.

84. "Shias Gain in Bahrain Polls," *al-Jazeera*, December 3, 2006.

85. Pamela Ann Smith, "Bahrain: Challenging Times Ahead," *Middle East*, May 1998, p. 24.

86. Cordesman, *Bahrain*, pp. 64–65.

87. "Bahraini Cabinet Approves of Privatization of Electricity Production," *Manama Gulf News*, December 29, 2003.

88. "Gulf Angered by Bahrain-US Deal," *al-Jazeera*, November 23, 2004.

89. Interview, Manama, 1989.

90. Crystal, *Oil and Politics*, p. 27.

91. For a discussion of Ottoman policy in Qatar, see Anscombe, *Ottoman Gulf*, esp. pp. 144–153.

92. Louay Bahry, "Elections in Qatar: A Window of Democracy Opens in the Gulf," *Middle East Policy*, June 1999, p. 119.

93. Interview, Doha, March 2004.

94. Interview, Doha, March 2004.

95. "Qatar Donates Land to Build First Church," *Gulf Times*, November 3, 2005.

96. Interview, Doha, March 2004.

97. Louay Bahry and Phebe Marr, "Qatari Women: A New Generation of Leaders?" *Middle East Policy*, Summer 2005, p. 116.

98. "Women to Vote in Landmark Qatar Elections," *Middle East Times*, January 27, 1999.

99. Bahry, "Elections in Qatar," pp. 122–123.

100. "World Leader Energy Plant for Qatar," *al-Jazeera*, October 20, 2003; "Exxon Mobil, Qatar Seal Gas Deal," *al-Jazeera*, October 15, 2003.

101. *Privatization and Deregulation in the Gulf Energy Sector* (Abu Dhabi: Emirates Center for Strategic Studies and Research, 1999), pp. 26–27.

102. "How to Continue Growth," *Middle East Economic Digest*, September 29–October 5, 2006, p. 45.

103. "Airbus Wins Huge Qatar Airways Order," *al-Jazeera*, December 9, 2003.

104. Crystal, *Oil and Politics*, p. 213.

105. Crystal, *Oil and Politics*, p. 220.

106. Interview, Doha, March 2004.

CHAPTER 7: YEMEN

1. The Queen of Sheba is named after the Hebrew word for the Yemeni land of Saba. While all three holy texts (the Christian Bible, the Jewish Torah, and the Muslim Quran) mention her, there is no other historical evidence for her existence.

2. These external players and their motives are discussed in Fawaz A. Gerges, "The Kennedy Administration and the Egyptian-Saudi Conflict in Yemen: Co-opting Arab Nationalism," *Middle East Journal*, Spring 1995, pp. 292–312.

3. W. Andrew Terrill, "The Chemical Warfare Legacy of the Yemen War," *Comparative Strategy* 10 (1991): 110–113.

4. Terrill, "Chemical Warfare Legacy," pp. 114–115.

5. Charles Dunbar, "The Unification of Yemen: Process, Politics, and Prospects," *Middle East Journal*, Summer 1992, pp. 457–459.

6. Dunbar, "Unification of Yemen," p. 460.

7. Dunbar, "Unification of Yemen," p. 469.

8. For a useful discussion of tribal formation in Yemeni history, see Paul Dresch, "Imams and Tribes: The Writing and Acting of History in Upper Yemen," in Philip S. Khoury and Joseph Kostiner, eds., *Tribes and State Formation in the Middle East* (Berkeley: University of California Press, 1990), pp. 252–287.

9. See Heinz Halm, *Shi'ism,* 2nd ed. (New York: Columbia University Press, 2004), chap. 5.

10. Jillian Schwedler, "Yemen's Aborted Opening," in Larry Diamond, Marc F. Plattner, and Daniel Brumberg, eds., *Islam and Democracy in the Middle East* (Baltimore: Johns Hopkins University Press, 2003), p. 97.

11. "Sanaa Radio Names Two Presidential Candidates," July 21, 1999, FBIS.

12. "Be Happy, Why Worry?" *Economist*, September 25, 1999, p. 52.

13. "Yemeni Leader's Poll Lead Challenged," *al-Jazeera*, September 22, 2006.

14. April Longley, "The High Water Mark of Islamist Politics? The Case of Yemen," *Middle East Journal*, Spring 2007, p. 244. Longley notes that Islah committed significant blunders in its electoral campaign.

15. "Yemeni President Accuses Opposition Media of Harming National Unification," *Yemen Times*, May 31, 2004, FBIS.

16. "Al-Khaiwani Still Detained, Authorities Ban Visits," *Yemen Times*, June 28, 2007.

17. Robert D. Burrows and Catherine M. Kasper, "The Salih Regime and the Need for a Credible Opposition," *Middle East Journal*, Spring 2007, pp. 263–280.

18. "Yemen Links to Bin Laden Gnaw at F.B.I. in Cole Inquiry," *New York Times*, November 26, 2000.

19. "One Sheik's Mission: Teach Hatred of West," *New York Times*, December 17, 2000.

20. "For Yemen, a Risk and an Opportunity," *Washington Post*, January 2, 2002.

21. Peter Kiernam, "Yemen: Surviving the Odds," *Middle East*, September 1998, p. 25.

22. "Constitutional Amendment at 3 Different Fronts," *Yemeni Times*, December 28, 1998–January 3, 1999.

23. Foreign observers monitored the elections and reported a number of irregularities, particularly cases where illiterate voters were persuaded to vote for Islah by "voter assistants" in the voting booths. However, the consensus among the election observers was that the elections were relatively free and fair. Mark N. Katz, "Election Day in Aden," *Middle East Policy,* September 1997, pp. 40–50.

24. Abdo Baaklini, Guilain Denoeux, and Robert Springborg, *Legislative Politics in the Arab World* (Boulder, CO: Lynne Rienner, 1999), pp. 212–213.

25. Schwedler, "Yemen's Aborted Opening," p. 93.

26. "Parliament Committee on Rights and Freedoms Inspects Taiz Central Prison," *Yemen Times*, September 23, 2003.

27. Baaklini, Denoeux, and Springborg, *Legislative Politics*, pp. 215–216.

28. "Key Behind Understanding Yemen Is Finding Out Who Is in Charge," *Wall Street Journal,* January 2, 2001.

29. Interview, Yemeni parliament, March 2005.

30. "Yemeni Judge Interviewed on Procedures, Outcomes of Dialog with Extremists," *London al-Quds al-Arabi*, December 30, 2003, FBIS; in Arabic.

31. "A Struggle for Peace in a Place Where Fighting Never Ends," *Washington Post*, December 19, 2005.

32. These examples of civil society are described in Sheila Carapico, *Civil Society in Yemen: The Political Economy of Activism in Modern Arabia* (Cambridge: Cambridge University Press, 1998).

33. Interview, Sanaa, March 2005.

34. "Civil Society Organizations," *Yemen Times*, November 2, 2005.

35. "Yemen Jihad Movement to Confront US Military Presence," *al-Quds al-Arabi*, June 7, 1998, FBIS-NES-98-158. The report that the Yemeni regime would grant the United States base rights on Socotra would be a significant departure from Yemeni policy.

36. "Yemen Kidnappings Were Revenge for Iraq Bombing," *London Daily Telegraph*, January 3, 1999; "War Against Terrorism Turns to Yemen," *Christian Science Monitor*, January 4, 1999.

37. "Yemen Sa'id Reviewing Extradition of Islamists to Ethiopia," *al-Hayah*, August 7, 1998, FBIS; in Arabic.

38. "Outside Aden, Clues, and Afghan Arabs," *Washington Post*, November 1, 2000.

39. See Maxine Molyneux, "Women's Rights and Political Contingency: The Case of Yemen, 1990–1994," *Middle East Journal*, Summer 1995, pp. 420–422.

40. Molyneux, "Women's Rights," pp. 423–427.

41. Janine Astrid Clark and Jillian Schwedler, "Who Opened the Window? Women's Activism in Islamist Parties," *Comparative Politics*, April 2003, pp. 293–312, esp. p. 301.

42. "Yemen: Islah Party Allows Women's Participation in 2006 polls," *Yemen Observer*, October 11, 2005.

43. Carol J. Riphenburg, "Gender Relations, Development, and the Democratic Process in Yemen" (paper presented to the 1998 annual meeting of the American Political Science Association, Boston, MA, September 3–6), p. 11.

44. "Women Candidates Exposed to Violations," *Yemen Observer*, September 29, 2006.

45. *Yemen Report on Human Rights Practices for 2007*, www.state.gov/g/drl/rls/hrrpt/2006/78867.htm.

46. *Yemen Report on Human Rights Practices for 2007*.

47. "Yemen's PCT Sells 45% of Yemen Mobile Shares in IPO," Arab Advisers Group, December 27, 2006.

48. Tom Owens, "No Upswing in Yemen," *Middle East*, October 2001, pp. 32–33.

49. "Yemeni Minister, Chinese Delegation Discuss Bilateral Cooperation," *Sanaa Saba*, December 11, 2005.

50. "WB Decreases Subsidies to Yemen," *Yemen Times*, December 15, 2005.

51. "Family Budget Survey: Dismal Picture of Economic Troubles," *Yemen Times*, April 5–11, 1999.

52. "Yemen," *Aquastat*, FAO, United Nations, March 1997.

53. "Food Security Yemen's Key Challenge," *Yemen Times*, August 20–27, 2001.

54. "One Killed, Three Wounded in Tribal Clashes in Ta'lzz," *al-Quds al-Arabi*, June 9, 1998, FBIS-NES-98-160.

55. Alan Richards, "Modernity and Economic Development: The New American Messianism," *Middle East Policy*, Fall 2003, pp. 64–65.

56. "Yemeni Population Will Double in 19 Years," *Yemen Observer*, July 1999.

57. "A Reading of Prince Nayif's Visit to Yemen," *Jeddah al-Madinah,* November 25, 1998, FBIS; in Arabic.

58. "Yemen Recovers Border Areas from Saudi," *al-Jazeera,* July 12, 2004.

59. Jillian Schwedler, *Faith in Moderation: Islamist Parties in Jordan and Yemen* (Cambridge: Cambridge University Press, 2006), pp. 205–206.

60. "U.S. Was Ambivalent About Yemeni Port," *Wall Street Journal,* October 16, 2000.

61. "Yemen, Long a Foe of U.S., Joins Anti-Terrorism Effort," *New York Times,* November 25, 2001.

62. "Yemen, U.S. Spar over al-Qaeda Leader," *al-Jazeera,* November 30, 2003.

CHAPTER 8: IRAN

1. See Vanessa Martin, *Islam and Modernism: The Iranian Revolt of 1906* (Syracuse, NY: Syracuse University Press, 1989). One consequence of this revolt was the establishment of Iran's first *majlis,* or parliament.

2. Janet Afary, *The Iranian Constitutional Revolution* (New York: Columbia University Press, 1996); Cosroe Chaqueri, *Origins of Social Democracy in Modern Iran* (Seattle: University of Washington Press, 2001).

3. For a history of this period, see Nikki R. Keddie, *Qajar Iran and the Rise of Reza Khan, 1796–1925* (Costa Mesa, CA: Mazda, 1999).

4. France apparently anticipated the future power of Muhammad Reza Pahlavi, giving him a hand-built 1939 Bugatti roadster on the occasion of his first wedding. The shah sold the car for around $275 twenty years later, but today it is valued at over $1 million.

5. On the Tudeh Party, see Ervand Abrahamian, *Iran Between Two Revolutions* (Princeton, NJ: Princeton University Press, 1982).

6. Unrest in the Azerbaijan region, directed at both the government in Tehran and the Soviet Union, was particularly strong. See Louise L'Estrange Fawcett, *Iran and the Cold War: The Azerbaijan Crisis of 1946* (Cambridge: Cambridge University Press, 1992).

7. For an analysis of the Soviet and American objectives in Iran, see Bruce Robellet Kuniholm, *The Origins of the Cold War in the Near East: Great Power Conflict and Diplomacy in Iran, Turkey, and Greece* (Princeton, NJ: Princeton University Press, 1980), chap. 3.

8. On the coup, see "Secrets of History: The CIA in Iran—a Special Report—How a Plot Convulsed Iran in '53 (and '79)," *New York Times,* April 16, 2000; Stephen Kinzer, *All the Shah's Men: An American Coup and the Roots of Middle East Terror* (Hoboken, NJ: Wiley, 2003). Pollack argues that the CIA (and their partners, the British intelligence services) could not have overthrown Mosaddeq had not significant elements of Iran's population lost faith in his leadership. Kenneth Pollack, *The Persian Puzzle: The Conflict Between Iran and America* (New York: Random House, 2004), chap. 3.

9. The shah wanted to execute Khomeini, but a member of his administration, Gen. Hassan Pakrauan, dissuaded him from doing so. Habib Ladjevardi, ed., *Memoirs of Fatemeh Pakrauan* (Harvard University: Harvard Iranian Oral History Project, 1980), preface.

10. See Jane Perry Clark Carey, "Iran and Control of Its Oil Resources," *Political Science Quarterly,* March 1974, pp. 150–151.

11. Quoted in Barry Rubin, *Paved with Good Intentions: The American Experience and Iran* (New York: Oxford University Press, 1988), p. 101. See also James Bill, *The Eagle and the Lion: The Tragedy of American-Iranian Relations* (New Haven, CT: Yale University Press, 1988); Mark Gasiorowski, *US Foreign Policy and the Shah: Building a Client State in Iran* (Ithaca, NY: Cornell University Press, 1991).

12. April Summitt said, "One of the most important lessons to learn from the Kennedy Administration is that the best-laid plans often fail because they lack a thorough understanding of regional interests and needs," a comment that applies to other administrations as well. April Summitt, "For a White Revolution: John F. Kennedy and the Shah of Iran," *Middle East Journal*, Autumn 2004, p. 575.

13. Amin Saikal, *The Rise and Fall of the Shah* (Princeton, NJ: Princeton University Press, 1980), p. 82.

14. Ali M. Ansari, "The Myth of the White Revolution: Muhammad Reza Shah, Modernization, and the Consolidation of Power," *Middle Eastern Studies*, July 2001, p. 3.

15. Cheryl Benard and Zalmay Khalilzad, "Secularization, Industrialization, and Khomeini's Islamic Republic," *Political Science Quarterly*, Fall 1979, p. 232.

16. Saikal, *Rise and Fall*, p. 75.

17. Mohammad Gholi Majd, *Resistance to the Shah: Landowners and the Ulama in Iran* (Gainesville: University Press of Florida, 2000).

18. Nikki R. Keddie, *Roots of Revolution: An Interpretive History of Modern Iran* (New Haven, CT: Yale University Press, 1981), p. 163.

19. A good study of the Iranian opposition and the difficulty it faced in organizing against the shah's government is Charles Kurzman, *The Unthinkable Revolution in Iran* (Cambridge, MA: Harvard University Press, 2004).

20. Lois Beck, "Tribes and the State in Nineteenth and Twentieth Century Iran," in Philip S. Khoury and Joseph Kostiner, eds., *Tribes and State Formation in the Middle East* (Berkeley: University of California Press, 1990), pp. 207–208.

21. Emory C. Bogle, *Islam: Origin and Belief* (Austin: University of Texas Press, 1998), pp. 121–124.

22. Bogle, *Islam*, pp. 125–126.

23. Keddie, *Roots of Revolution*, p. 240.

24. Nikki R. Keddie, *Modern Iran: Roots and Results of Revolution* (New Haven, CT: Yale University Press, 2003), p. 135.

25. For background on Iranian-Iraqi relations, see J. M. Abdulghani, *Iraq and Iran: The Years of Crisis* (Baltimore: Johns Hopkins University Press, 1984); and Tareq Y. Ismael, *Iraq and Iran: Roots of Conflict* (Syracuse, NY: Syracuse University Press, 1982).

26. Shahram Chubin and Charles Tripp, *Iran and Iraq at War* (Boulder, CO: Westview, 1988), p. 54.

27. Kamran Mofid, *The Economic Consequences of the Gulf War* (London: Routledge, 1990), p. 121.

28. Chubin and Tripp, *Iran and Iraq*, p. 71.

29. Chubin and Tripp, *Iran and Iraq*, chap. 7.

30. Geneive Abdo, "Electoral Politics in Iran," *Middle East Policy*, June 1999, pp. 128–129.

31. "Reform Win Is Major Step for Iranian Democracy," *Washington Post*, February 21, 2000.

32. Western-style rock and roll is illegal in Iran but highly popular among the young, and pirated CDs are available in large numbers for the right price. The official Iranian rock singer, Shadmehr Aghili, is Iran's most popular legal singer, and the government hopes that he will draw young rock consumers away from Western rock, which conservatives consider corrupt. Aghlili cannot give live performances, since the authorities find them difficult to censor. See "Roll Over, Khomeini! Iran Cultivates a Local Rock Scene, Within Limits," *Washington Post*, August 23, 2001.

33. "Reform Faction in Iran Is Hurt by 'Evil' Label," *Washington Post*, February 15, 2002.

34. "Ahmadinejad Calls for Iran's Unity," *al-Jazeera*, June 25, 2005.

35. "Western Leaders Condemn the Iranian President's Threat to Israel," *New York Times*, October 28, 2005.

36. Khamenei was even more conservative on the religious domination of the state than was Khomeini. See Maziar Behrooz, "Factionalism in Iran Under Khomeini," *Middle Eastern Studies*, October 1991, pp. 603–605.

37. Ladan Boroumand and Roya Broumand, "Is Iran Democratizing? Reform at an Impasse," in Larry Diamond, Marc F. Plattner, and Daniel Brumberg, eds., *Islam and Democracy in the Middle East* (Baltimore: Johns Hopkins University Press, 2003), p. 132.

38. Mohsen M. Milani, "Political Participation in Iran," in John L. Esposito, ed., *Political Islam: Revolution, Radicalism, or Reform?* (Boulder, CO: Lynne Rienner, 1997), pp. 81–85.

39. Shaul Bakhash, "Iran's Remarkable Election," *Journal of Democracy*, January 1998, pp. 80–94.

40. R. K. Ramazani, "The Shifting Premise of Iran's Foreign Policy: Towards a Democratic Peace?" *Middle East Journal*, Spring 1998, p. 180.

41. Joe Klein, "Shadow Land," *New Yorker*, February 18, 2002, p. 72.

42. Ray Takeyh, "Iran at a Crossroads," *Middle East Journal*, Winter 2003, pp. 42–56.

43. Hossein S. Seifzadeh, "The Landscape of Factional Politics and Its Future in Iran," *Middle East Journal*, Winter 2003, pp. 57–75.

44. "The New Populism," *Middle East Economic Digest*, July 1–7, 2005, p. 4.

45. The remainder of the population are Christian, Jewish, Bahai, and Zoroastrians. The Bahai, considered heretics by the Shiites, have been the target of considerable persecution.

46. Heinz Halm, *Shi'ism,* 2nd ed. (New York: Columbia University Press, 2004), pp. 48–49. Halm notes that the Shiite concept of *kalam* is closely tied to the Sunni concept of *ijtihad*, discussed in Chapter 3.

47. Olivier Roy, "The Crisis of Religious Legitimacy in Iran," *Middle East Journal*, Spring 1999, p. 202.

48. Roy, "Crisis of Religious Legitimacy," p. 207.

49. Roy, "Crisis of Religious Legitimacy," p. 209.

50. "Rebuke in Iran to Its President on Nuclear Role," *New York Times*, January 19, 2007.

51. "Iranian Clerics' Angling Stirs Worry on Absolute Rule," *New York Times*, September 25, 2006.

52. Farhang Rajaee, "A Thermidor of Islamic Yuppies? Conflict and Compromise in Iran's Policies," *Middle East Journal*, Spring 1999, p. 225.

53. Vali Nasr, "The Conservative Wave Rolls On," *Journal of Democracy*, October 2005, p. 12.

54. Elliot Hen-Tov, "Understanding Iran's New Authoritarianism," *Washington Quarterly*, Winter 2006–2007, p. 167.

55. Bahman Baktiari, *Parliamentary Politics in Revolutionary Iran: The Institutionalization of Factional Politics* (Gainesville: University Press of Florida, 1996), chap. 2.

56. Baktiari, *Parliamentary Politics*, chaps. 3–6.

57. See Khadija V. Frings-Hessami, "The Islamic Debate About Land Reform in the Iranian Parliament, 1981–86," *Middle East Studies*, October 2001, pp. 136–181.

58. "Advocate of Increased Freedoms Picked to Lead Iran's Parliament," *Washington Post*, May 31, 2000.

59. Ali Ansari, "Continuous Regime Change from Within," *Washington Quarterly,* Autumn 2003, p. 63.

60. "Shahroudi: Pressure on Iran on Nuclear Issue Promotes National Solidarity," Islamic Republic News Agency, October 11, 2005.

61. "Trial of 13 Iranian Jews Reconvenes," *New York Times*, May 3, 2000.

62. Robin Wright, "Iran's New Revolution," *Foreign Affairs*, January-February 2000, pp. 137–138.

63. "As Repression Lifts, More Iranians Change their Sex," *New York Times*, August 2, 2004.

64. "Iran Jails More Journalists and Blocks Web Sites," *New York Times*, November 8, 2004.

65. "Iran Exonerates Six who Killed in Islam's Name," *New York Times*, April 19, 2007.

66. "PKK Clashes with Iranian Troops," *Milliyet*, July 26, 2005, FBIS; in Turkish.

67. John R. Bradley, "Iran's Ethnic Tinderbox," *Washington Quarterly*, Winter 2006–2007, pp. 183–184.

68. Bradley, "Iran's Ethnic Tinderbox," p. 187.

69. See Eliz Sanasarian, *Religious Minorities in Iran* (Cambridge: Cambridge University Press, 2000).

70. "Omid Memarian Iran: Civil Society Feels Conservatives' Wrath," InterPress Service, June 2006, p. 1.

71. Hen-Tov, "Understanding Iran's New Authoritarianism," p. 174.

72. Mansoor Moaddel, "Religion and Women: Islamic Modernization Versus Fundamentalism," *Journal for the Scientific Study of Religion*, March 1998, p. 19.

73. Parvin Paidar, *Women and the Political Process in Twentieth-Century Iran* (Cambridge: Cambridge University Press, 1995), p. 303.

74. Paidar, *Women and the Political Process*, pp. 306–309.

75. Golnar Mehran, "Lifelong Learning: New Opportunities for Women in a Muslim Country," *Comparative Education*, June 1999, p. 3.

76. "Shorn of Dignity and Equality," *Economist*, October 18, 2003, p. 23.

77. "Women's Rights in Iran," *Tehran Times*, July 8, 2007.

78. Haleh Esfandiari, *Reconstructed Lives: Women and Iran's Islamic Revolution* (Washington, DC: Woodrow Wilson Center Press; Baltimore: Johns Hopkins University Press, 1997), chap. 1.

79. Farhad Kazemi, "Civil Society and Iranian Politics," in Augustus Richard Norton, ed., *Civil Society in the Middle East* (Leiden: Brill, 1996), p. 130.

80. See Shahra Razavi, "Islamic Politics, Human Rights, and Women's Claims for Equality in Iran," *Third World Quarterly* 27, no. 7 (2006): 1223–1238.

81. "Shorn of Dignity and Equality," *Economist*, October 18, 2003, p. 23. See also Keddie, *Modern Iran*, p. 286.

82. "Shorn of Dignity and Equality," p. 23.

83. "Iran's Women Win Boy Custody Rights," *al-Jazeera*, November 29, 2003.

84. "Fashion Police Get Tough in Iran," *al-Jazeera*, April 19, 2006.

85. Sanam Vakil, "Iran: The Gridlock Between Demography and Democracy," *SAIS Review of International Affairs*, Summer-Fall 2004, p. 47.

86. Olivier Roy, *The Failure of Political Islam* (Cambridge, MA: Harvard University Press, 1994), p. 139.

87. Roy, *Failure of Political Islam*, p. 139.

88. Jahangir Amuzegar, *Iran's Economy Under the Islamic Republic* (London: Tauris, 1993), p. 17.

89. Vali Nasr, *The Shia Revival* (New York: Norton, 2006), p. 134.

90. Nasr, *Shia Revival,* chap. 4.

91. Keddie, *Modern Iran,* p. 265.

92. "Iran: Khamene'i Announces Macro 20-Year Plan for Development," *Tehran IRNA,* November 3, 2003, FBIS.

93. "Iran Reformers Want U.S. to Tone It Down," *Los Angeles Times,* February 11, 2007.

94. *CIA World Factbook,* 2007.

95. Hen-Tov, "Understanding Iran's new Authoritarianism," p. 172.

96. "Will America Invoke Sanctions?" *Economist,* August 2, 2003, p. 57.

97. "Stepping on the Gas," *Middle East Economic Digest,* May 7–13, 2004, pp. 4–5.

98. "China to Look Abroad for Natural Gas," *Wall Street Journal,* June 23, 2004.

99. "Managing Director of the Oil Products Refining and Distribution Company: 'Gasoline Is Rationed in Three Provinces,'" *Hemayat,* January 28, 2007.

100. "Two Iranian Gas Stations Burned over Rationing," *New York Times,* June 28, 2007.

101. "Economy Could Do In Ahmadinejad," *Times of London,* June 27, 2007.

102. For an assessment of the impact of US sanctions on Iran, see Akbar Torbat, "Impact of the US Trade and Financial Sanctions on Iran," *World Economy,* March 2005, pp. 407–434; Ernest H. Preeg, *Feeling Good or Doing Good with Sanctions: Unilateral Economic Sanctions and the U.S. National Interest* (Washington, DC: Center for Strategic and International Studies, 1999), chap. 3; Hossein Alikhani, *Sanctioning Iran: Anatomy of a Failed Policy* (London: Tauris, 2000).

103. "The Price of Sanctions," *Middle East Economic Digest,* April 13–19, 2007, p. 4.

104. "Iranian Agro Sales Decline," *Tehran Times,* September 12, 2005.

105. "No State Can Claim Independence Without Production Ability," Islamic Republic News Agency, December 23, 2003.

106. "Listless Economy Drags Down Iran," *Washington Post,* September 15, 1999.

107. "Opiates of the Iranian People," *Washington Post,* September 23, 2005.

108. *AIDS Epidemic Update, December 2004* (Geneva: World Health Organization, 2004), p. 67.

109. "Iran's Diplomatic Moves Puzzle the U.S.," *Wall Street Journal,* March 19, 1998, p. 14.

110. Jalil Roshandel, "Iran's Foreign and Security Policies: How the Decisionmaking Process Evolved," *Security Dialog,* March 2000, p. 111.

111. Daniel Byman, "Should Hezbollah Be Next?" *Foreign Affairs,* November-December 2003, p. 61.

112. "Iranian Leader Urges Exchanges with U.S.," *Washington Post,* January 8, 1998, p. 1.

113. "Iran Exerts Sway on Afghan Border, Worrying the U.S.," *New York Times,* January 10, 2002. The charges, raised by the new US ambassador to Kabul, originally came from southern Afghan warlords, who may have resented Iranian efforts to curb their autonomy against the Northern Alliance, which both Iran and the United States supported. See "Back Into the Doghouse," *Economist,* January 26, 2002, p. 42.

114. "Iran Closes In on Ability to Build a Nuclear Bomb," *Los Angeles Times,* August 4, 2003.

115. "Iran Agrees to Inspection of Military Base," *New York Times,* January 6, 2005.

116. "Iran Reformists Want U.S. to Tone It Down," *Los Angeles Times,* February 11, 2007.

117. "World Atomic Agency Suspends 22 Programs of Aid to Iran," *New York Times,* February 10, 2007.

118. "Iranian Imbroglio Gives New Boost to Odd Exile Group," *Wall Street Journal,* November 29, 2006.

CHAPTER 9: IRAQ

1. For the argument that Britain should have remained, see Joel Rayburn, "The Last Exit from Iraq," *Foreign Affairs*, March-April 2006, pp. 29–41.

2. Yitzhak Nakash, "The Shi'ites and the Future of Iraq," *Foreign Affairs*, July-August 2003, p. 19.

3. Charles Tripp, *A History of Iraq* (Cambridge: Cambridge University Press, 2000), pp. 102–104.

4. For a first-person account of the British relationship with Nuri, see Waldemar J. Gallman, *Iraq Under General Nuri: My Recollections of Nuri Al-Sa'id* (Baltimore: Johns Hopkins University Press, 1964).

5. Iraq had intervened in Kuwait in 1938 to quell an uprising against the Kuwaiti ruler. See Nigel Ashton, "Britain and the Kuwaiti Crisis, 1961," *Middle Eastern Studies*, March 1998, p. 165.

6. Tripp, *History of Iraq*, p. 222; Reeva Simon, *Iraq Between Two Wars: The Creation and Implementation of a Nationalist Ideology* (New York: Columbia University Press, 1986), chap. 6.

7. See Eric Davis, *Memories of State: Politics, History, and Collective Identity in Modern Iraq* (Berkeley: University of California Press, 2005).

8. See Bruce W. Jentleson, *With Friends Like These: Reagan, Bush, and Saddam, 1982–1990* (New York: Norton, 1994).

9. The full scope of these attacks is discussed in Jeffrey Goldberg, "The Great Terror," *New Yorker*, March 25, 2002, pp. 52–75. According to Goldberg, Iraq launched chemical attacks against over 200 Kurdish towns and villages, killing thousands of civilians and leaving much of the surviving population with long-term effects that continue to claim hundreds of lives each year.

10. See Tim Niblock, *"Pariah States" and Sanctions in the Middle East: Iraq, Libya, Sudan* (Boulder, CO: Lynne Rienner, 2001), pp. 100–101.

11. "Iraq Now a Top Oil Supplier to U.S.," *Philadelphia Inquirer*, August 7, 2000.

12. "Iraq Won't Let Outside Experts Assess Sanctions' Impact," *New York Times*, September 12, 2000.

13. "Millions Spent on Camp Saddam," *London Times*, October 24, 2000.

14. "World-Wide Oil Shortage Grants Iraq Newfound Bargaining Power," *Wall Street Journal*, September 19, 2000; "Oil Price New Weapon for Warlike Saddam," *London Daily Telegraph*, September 19, 2000.

15. Niblock, *"Pariah States,"* pp. 189–190.

16. R. Jeffrey Smith, "Iraq's Drive for a Biological Arsenal," *Washington Post*, November 21, 1997, p. 1.

17. Smith, "Iraq's Drive," p. 1.

18. "Under Iraqi Skies: A Canvas of Death," *Washington Post*, June 16, 2000.

19. "Sunni Opposition to Iraqi Draft Constitution Intensifies," *New York Times*, August 30, 2005.

20. "Election Move Seems to Insure Iraqis' Charter," *New York Times*, October 4, 2005.

21. "Iraq's History Still Divides the Children of Mesopotamia," *Los Angeles Times*, December 29, 2005.

22. "Iraqi Death Toll Exceeds 600,000, Study Estimates," *Wall Street Journal*, October 11, 2006.

23. "Ethnic and Religious Fissures Deepen in Iraqi Society," *Washington Post*, September 29, 2003.

24. John Irish, "Marriage of Inconvenience," *Middle East Economic Digest*, November 24–30, 2006, pp. 4–6.

25. Ahmed S. Hashim, "Military Power and State Formation in Modern Iraq," *Middle East Policy*, Winter 2003, p. 39.

26. "In a Key Step on a Long Road to a New Iraq, Cabinet Assumes Office," *Los Angeles Times*, September 4, 2003.

27. "Bremer Returns to Washington amid Frustration in Iraq," *Washington Post*, November 11, 2003.

28. "Power Transfer in Iraq Starts this Week," *Washington Post*, January 4, 2004.

29. "Iraqi Shiite Parties Agree to Try and Unite Moderates," *New York Times*, June 29, 2007.

30. "Shiites Fall Short of Majority, Iraqi Election Results Show," *New York Times*, January 20, 2006.

31. "Three Set to Hang As Executions Return to Iraq," *New York Times*, August 17, 2005.

32. "Legal System in Iraq Staggers Beneath the Weight of War," *New York Times*, December 17, 2006.

33. "Vigilantes Target Iraqi Porn Surfers," *al-Jazeera*, June 29, 2007.

34. Victoria Stanski, "Linchpin for Democracy: The Critical Role of Civil Society in Iraq," *Journal of Third World Studies* 22, no. 2 (2005): 197–225.

35. Tripp, *History of Iraq*, p. 227.

36. Jan Goodwin, *Price of Honor* (Boston: Little, Brown, 1994), pp. 244–245. As Goodwin notes, the right to vote does little good in a country that does not hold elections.

37. Andrea Laurenz, "Iraqi Women Preserve Gains Despite Wartime Problems," *Washington Report on Middle East Affairs*, Special Report, July 1989.

38. Bengio, "How Does Saddam Hold On?" p. 94.

39. "Facing the Future," *Washington Post*, June 17, 2003.

40. "Iraq: Violence Against Women Increases Sharply," *Amnesty International*, March 31, 2004.

41. "Iraq's Fractious Kurds Have Reason to Fear an End to U.N. Sanctions," *Wall Street Journal*, January 6, 2000.

42. "Squeeze on Iraq Allows Its Kurds to Flourish," *Washington Post*, January 30, 2000.

43. "Iraqi Kurds, Flush with Aid, Lose Desire to Take On Hussein," *Wall Street Journal*, February 12, 2002.

44. "Kurds' Success Makes It Harder to Unify all Iraq," *Wall Street Journal*, May 19, 2004.

45. "Trouble Tempers Triumphs in Iraq," *Washington Post*, August 18, 2003.

46. Fareed Yasseen, "We Don't Want Oligarchs in Iraq," *Wall Street Journal*, September 30, 2003.

47. "U.S. Offers Iraqis Public-Works Jobs," *Wall Street Journal*, June 8, 2004.

48. "Child Malnutrition Doubles in Iraq," *Los Angeles Times*, November 23, 2004.

49. "Iraq's Oil Industry Pumps Away," *Wall Street Journal*, November 29, 2004.

50. "Iraq Economy Said Stable Despite War," *New York Times*, August 17, 2005.

51. "Missteps Hamper Iraqi Oil Recovery," *Los Angeles Times*, September 26, 2005.

52. "Petrol Pumps Run Dry in a City That Stinks of Oil," *London Times*, April 7, 2006.

53. "Billions in Oil Missing in Iraq, Study Finds," *New York Times*, May 12, 2007.

54. Nancy Birdsall and Arvind Subramanian, "Saving Iraq from Its Oil," *Foreign Affairs*, July-August 2004, pp. 77–89.

55. "Iraq's Ailing Banking Industry Is Slowly Reviving," *New York Times*, December 30, 2004.

56. "Dust Bowl Uncertainty Grows in Iraq," *Los Angeles Times*, April 15, 2006.

SECTION III: THE COUNTRIES
OF THE EASTERN MEDITERRANEAN

1. In November 1999 American Egyptologists found evidence of an earlier alphabet in the Western Desert of Egypt, which they dated to between 2000 and 1900 BCE. "US Experts Find Early Egyptian Alphabetic Writings," *Middle East Times*, November 26, 1999.

CHAPTER 10: EGYPT

1. Edward Said, "Farewell to Tahia," *al-Ahram*, October 7–13, 1999.

2. Virginia Louise Danielson, *The Voice of Egypt: Umm Kulthum, Arabic Song, and Egyptian Society in the Twentieth Century* (Chicago: University of Chicago Press, 1997).

3. Afaf Lutfi al-Said Marsot, *A Short History of Modern Egypt* (Cambridge: Cambridge University Press, 1985), p. 81. The anti-British sentiment had many causes, including summary executions of peasants who fired at British soldiers during a pigeon hunt.

4. An excellent discussion of this period may be found in Israel Gershoni and James P. Jankowski, *Redefining the Egyptian Nation, 1930–1945* (Cambridge: Cambridge University Press, 1995).

5. Fawaz Gerges, "Egypt and the 1948 War: Internal Conflict and Regional Ambition," in Eugene L. Rogan and Avi Shlaim, eds., *The War for Palestine: Rewriting the History of 1948* (Cambridge: Cambridge University Press, 2001), pp. 151–178.

6. The Baghdad Pact was formed in 1955 as a defense alliance between Britain, Turkey, Iraq, Iran, and Pakistan. The United States did not become a formal member because of Israeli opposition.

7. Alvin Z. Rubinstein, *Red Star over the Nile: The Soviet-Egyptian Influence Relationship Since the June War* (Princeton, NJ: Princeton University Press, 1997), p. 3.

8. See Barry Rubin, "America and the Egyptian Revolution, 1950–1957," *Political Science Quarterly*, Spring 1982, pp. 73–90. Other factors involved in the loan refusal included a general congressional disdain for foreign assistance and a particular concern from southern members of Congress about the possibility that Egyptian cotton crop increases from the Aswan dam irrigation would flood the export market and nudge out American-grown cotton.

9. Amin Hewedy, "Nasser and the Crisis of 1956," in William Roger Louis and Roger Owen, eds., *Suez 1956: The Crisis and Its Consequence* (Oxford: Clarendon, 1989), pp. 165–166.

10. The brief war also taught Nasser about the limits imposed by the Soviets on Egyptian forces, which were not allowed to use their newly acquired Soviet-built bombers against enemy targets. Soviet reluctance to support Egypt probably began the long deterioration in Egyptian-Soviet relations. See O. M. Smolansky, "Moscow and the Suez Crisis, 1956: A Reappraisal," *Political Science Quarterly*, December 1965, pp. 602–603.

11. These policies are discussed in John Waterbury, *The Egypt of Nasser and Sadat: The Political Economy of Two Regimes* (Princeton, NJ: Princeton University Press, 1983).

12. Interview, Cairo, July 1989. Many Jewish residents fled Egypt after Israeli agents recruited Egyptian Jews to spy and carry out sabotage against Egyptian targets.

13. Soviet pilots advising the Egyptian air force were contemptuous of Egyptian performance against Israeli aircraft. In an effort to show Egyptian pilots the presumed superiority of Soviet pilots, three Soviet flyers got into the cockpits of Egyptian fighters and rose up

against incoming Israeli planes. Israeli pilots quickly shot down all three, and reports claim that celebrations at the Egyptian air base lasted long into the night. Interview.

14. The standard interpretation was that the public still regarded Nasser as a hero, but another interpretation comes from an Egyptian peasant: "No, do you think you can throw us into the fire like this and then resign? Impossible. You are going to stay like this until you figure out how to rescue the country." Quoted in Reem Saad, "War in the Social Memory of Egyptian Peasants," in Steven Heydemann, ed., *War, Institutions, and Social Change in the Middle East* (Berkeley: University of California Press, 2000), p. 251.

15. While the Soviets had been Nasser's most important source of arms, they were also the source of pressure to engage in peace efforts, and their rebuilding of the Egyptian military after the 1967 was accompanied with a renewed effort to get Egypt to reach an accord with Israel. See Jerome Slater, "The Superpowers and an Arab-Israeli Political Settlement," *Political Science Quarterly*, Winter 1990–1991, pp. 557–577.

16. Patrick Seele, *Asad* (Berkeley: University of California Press, 1988).

17. A thoughtful analysis of Camp David may be found in Shibley Telhami, "Evaluating Bargaining Performance: The Case of Camp David," *Political Science Quarterly*, Winter 1992–1993, pp. 629–654.

18. Kirk J. Beattie, *Egypt During the Sadat Years* (New York: Palgrave, 2000), chap. 4.

19. Najib Ghadbian, *Democratization and the Islamist Challenge in the Arab World* (Boulder, CO: Westview, 1997), pp. 51–52.

20. Ghadbian, *Democratization*, p. 52.

21. "Egypt's Political Opening Exposes Frailty of Opposition," *Washington Post*, July 28, 2005.

22. "Out for the Count," *al-Ahram*, September 8–14, 2005.

23. Freedom House 2006 Egypt Country Report, www.freedomhouse.org/template .cfm?page=22&year=2006&country=6956.

24. Steven A. Cook, *Ruling But Not Governing: The Military and Political Development in Egypt, Algeria, and Turkey* (Baltimore, MD: Johns Hopkins University Press, 2007), p. 77.

25. "Apathy Marks Constitutional Vote in Egypt," *Washington Post*, March 27, 2007.

26. Robert Springborg, *Mubarak's Egypt: Fragmentation of the Political Order* (Boulder, CO: Westview, 1989), pp. 187–188.

27. See Byron Cannon, *Politics of Law and the Courts in Nineteenth-Century Egypt* (Salt Lake City: University of Utah Press, 1988).

28. See George N. Sfier, "Basic Freedoms in a Fractured Legal System: Egypt and the Case of Nasr Abu Zayd," *Middle East Journal*, Summer 1998, p. 405.

29. Steven Barraclough, "Al-Azhar: Between the Government and the Islamists," *Middle East Journal*, Spring 1998, p. 247. The professor, Nasser Hamed Abu Zayd, a faculty member at the College of Dar al-Uloum of Cairo University, fled with his wife to the Netherlands to escape a sentence of death or repentance. Commenting on the trial, one Cairo intellectual claimed that "Islamist thinking has penetrated the highest levels of the judiciary." See Mary Anne Weaver, "Revolution by Stealth," *New Yorker*, June 8, 1998, esp. p. 41. See also Sfeir, "Basic Freedoms," who notes that Abu Zayd's own writings were issued as a challenge to fundamentalist Islamic thought, pp. 411–412.

30. Eberhard Kienle, "More Than a Response to Islam: The Political Deliberalization of Egypt in the 1990s," *Middle East Journal*, Spring 1998, p. 222.

31. "Egyptian Rights Activist Charged with Bribery," *New York Times*, September 25, 2000.

32. "Egypt Sentences Sociologist to 7 Years in Quick Verdict," *New York Times*, May 22, 2001. The verdict came ninety minutes after lawyers summarized their arguments, indicating that the judges had not even read the thousands of pages of evidence submitted to them by the defense.

33. "Egypt Acquits Human Rights Activist," *Washington Post*, March 18, 2003. Ibrahim holds dual Egyptian-American citizenship, and the Bush administration threatened to withhold millions of American foreign aid dollars if Ibrahim was not released.

34. "Egypt Muzzles Calls for Democracy," *Washington Post*, January 6, 2004.

35. Imad Boles, "Egypt—Persecution," *Middle East Quarterly*, Winter 2001, pp. 23–30.

36. Kienle, "More Than a Response," pp. 231–234.

37. James Toth, "Islamism in Southern Egypt: A Case Study of a Radical Religious Movement," *International Journal of Middle East Studies*, November 2003, pp. 547–571.

38. Carrie Rosefsky Wickham, *Mobilizing Islam: Religion, Activism, and Political Change in Egypt* (New York: Columbia University Press, 2002), esp. pp. 7–8, 151–157.

39. This distinction was offered in Elie Podeh, "Egypt's Struggle Against the Militant Islamic Groups," *Terrorism and Political Violence*, Summer 1996, pp. 45–46, based on an article in the Egyptian paper *Sabah al-Khayr*.

40. Interview, Cairo, March 2006.

41. Ahmad Musa, "Scenario of the Muslim Brotherhood's Enablement Plan to Establish a Religious State," *al-Ahram*, January 20, 2007.

42. Musa, "Scenario," p. 46.

43. John Esposito and John O. Voll, *Islam and Democracy* (New York: Oxford University Press, 1996), pp. 177–178.

44. Salwa Ismail, "The Popular Movement Dimensions of Contemporary Militant Islam: Socio-Spatial Determinates in the Cairo Urban Setting," *Comparative Studies in Society and History*, April 2000, pp. 363–393.

45. See Patrick D. Gaffney, "Fundamentalist Preaching and Islamic Militancy in Upper Egypt," in R. Scott Appleby, ed., *Spokesmen for the Despised: Fundamentalist Leaders of the Middle East* (Chicago: University of Chicago Press, 1997), pp. 257–293.

46. For more on these policies, see David S. Sorenson, "The Dynamics of Political Dissent in Egypt," *Fletcher Forum of World Affairs*, Summer-Fall 2003, pp. 207–228.

47. Podeh, "Egypt's Struggle," p. 52.

48. Tamir Moustafa, "Conflict and Cooperation Between the State and Religious Institutions in Contemporary Egypt," *International Journal of Middle East Studies*, February 2000, pp. 4–5.

49. Barraclough, "Al-Azhar." Barraclough notes that al-Azhar has also moved independently from the government, and has grown in power such that "within a few years Al-Azhar may be controlling every mosque in Egypt, playing a major role in legal jurisprudence, and having the final say in media censorship," p. 249.

50. Barraclough, "Al-Azhar," pp. 5–7.

51. Gregory Starrett, *Putting Islam to Work: Education, Politics, and Religious Transformation in Egypt* (Berkeley: University of California Press, 1998).

52. Max Rodenbeck, "Is Islamism Losing Its Thunder?" *Washington Quarterly*, Spring 1998, p. 185.

53. Fawaz A. Gerges, "The Decline of Revolutionary Islam in Algeria and Egypt," *Survival*, Spring 1999, p. 117.

54. Fawaz A. Gerges, "The End of Islamist Insurgency in Egypt? Costs and Prospects," *Middle East Journal*, Fall 2000, p. 610.

55. Gerges, "End of Islamist Insurgency," p. 610.

56. Geneive Abdo, *No God but God: Egypt and the Triumph of Islam* (Oxford: Oxford University Press, 2000).

57. See Denis J. Sullivan and Sanaa Abed-Kotob, *Islam in Contemporary Egypt: Civil Society vs. the State* (Boulder, CO: Lynne Rienner, 1999), chap. 2.

58. Beattie, *Egypt During the Sadat Years*, chap. 3.

59. Yoram Meital, "The Struggle over Political Order in Egypt: The 2005 Elections," *Middle East Journal*, Spring 2006, pp. 316–318.

60. Selma Botman describes these struggles in *Engendering Citizenship in Egypt* (New York: Columbia University Press, 1999).

61. See Earl L. Sullivan, *Women in Egyptian Public Life* (Syracuse, NY: Syracuse University Press, 1986), pp. 22–23.

62. Sullivan, *Women in Egyptian Public Life*, p. 34.

63. "Winds of Change," *al-Ahram*, September 14–20, 2000.

64. Mona Khalifa, Julie DaVanco, and David M. Adamson, *Population Growth in Egypt: A Continuing Policy Challenge,* Rand Issue Paper (Santa Monica, CA: Rand Corporation, 2000), p. 4.

65. Abdo, *No God but God*, pp. 56–58.

66. See Kamran Asdar Ali, *Planning the Family in Egypt: New Bodies, New Selves* (Austin: University of Texas Press, 2002).

67. "New Law Grants Egyptian Women New Privileges," *Arabic News.com*, January 27, 2000. The new law did make one compromise to conservatives, though, in continuing a ban on travel by married women without their husband's permission.

68. "Egyptian Mothers Fight for Foreign Offspring's Rights," *New York Times*, May 14, 2001. Some supporters of the present law argue that it may help prevent the practice of wealthy Gulf Arab men taking poor Egyptian women as temporary brides and abandoning them after they become pregnant. This may be a dubious proposition, since almost 30 percent of the foreign marriages of Egyptian women are to Gulf Arabs. One observer notes that "you end up with entire villages where many of the kids are non-citizens."

69. "International: Surgery on Hardened Arteries; Egyptian Politics," *Economist*, October 4, 2004, p. 58.

70. Arlene Elowe MacLeod, *Accommodating Protest: Working Women, the New Veiling, and Change in Cairo* (New York: Columbia University Press, 1993).

71. "2 Million Girls a Year Mutilated," *UNICEF: The Progress of Nations 1996*, www.Unicef.org/pon/96/womfgm.htm, p. 1.

72. Nadia Wassef, "Masculinities and Mutilations: Female Genital Mutilation in Egypt," *Middle East Women's Studies Newsletter*, Summer 1998, p. 2.

73. Abdo, *No God but God*, p. 59.

74. Elizabeth Fernea, "The Challenges for Middle Eastern Women in the 21st Century," *Middle East Journal*, Spring 2000, p. 191.

75. "Marriage, Politics, and Jerusalem," *al-Ahram Weekly*, April 1–7, 1999.

76. Interview, Cairo, March 2007.

77. Khalifa, DaVanzo, and Adamson, "Population Growth in Egypt," p. 7.

78. "Unrest a Chief Product of Arab Economies," *Washington Post*, January 26, 2002.

79. Interview, Cairo, March 2006.

80. Iliya Harik, *Economic Policy Reform in Egypt* (Gainesville: University Press of Florida, 1997), chap. 4.

81. James Badcock, "Egypt: The Wheels of Change," *Middle East*, December 2003, p. 24.

82. "Egypt's Poor Untouched by Boom," *al-Jazeera*, September 1, 2005.

83. Matthew Gray, "Economic Reform, Privatization, and Tourism in Egypt," *Middle Eastern Studies*, April 1998, pp. 93–95.

84. "Is Egypt Backing Away from Economic Reform?" *Wall Street Journal*, February 17, 2000.

85. Interview, Ministry of Public Works and Water Resources, Cairo, March 2000.

86. "Egypt: Optimist for Future Projects," *Middle East*, July 1998, p. 41.

87. "Reclaiming the Desert," *al-Ahram*, December 17–23, 1998.

88. Ethiopia and Sudan signed an agreement in 1991 over joint use of Nile waters, raising fears in Cairo about efforts by the two countries to divert Nile water. Egypt has indirectly threatened both nations with military action should they separately or jointly restrict the flow of the Nile to Egypt. See Helga Haftendorn, "Water and International Conflict," *Third World Quarterly*, February 2000, p. 59.

89. Interview, Ministry of Water and Irrigation, Cairo, March 2000.

90. Making tanks is not the only economic activity carried out by the Egyptian military. They grow food for sale and manufacture a variety of things for commercial markets (plastic trash bags, for example). Their contribution represents 30 percent of the total industrial capacity of Egypt.

91. Interview, Cairo, July 1989.

92. Interviews, Cairo, March 2006.

93. "A Shift In USAID Focus," *al-Ahram*, November 8, 2004.

94. "Growing Gas Ambitions," *Middle East Economic Digest*, January 14, 2000.

95. For the background of the US-Egyptian relationship, see William B. Quandt, *The United States and Egypt* (Washington, DC: Brookings Institution, 1990).

96. "In Arab World Ally, Anti-American Feeling Runs Deep," *Boston Globe*, October 14, 2002.

97. "Good Night, Mr. Hamburger," *al-Ahram*, June 28–July 4, 2001. As a small bow to Egyptian tastes, if not to Egyptian culture, McDonald's offers McFelafel, based on a popular dish in the Middle East made from ground beans substituting for the traditional beef.

CHAPTER 11: TURKEY

1. See Berdal Aral, "The Idea of Human Rights As Perceived in the Ottoman Empire," *Human Rights Quarterly*, May 2004, pp. 454–482.

2. Suraiya Faroqhi, *Subjects of the Sultan: Culture and Daily Life in the Ottoman Empire* (London: Tauris, 2000).

3. Despite rejecting most aspects of the Ottoman Empire, modern Turkish officials are sensitive about what they consider ill-founded charges against it. So when the leading US official in post-Saddam Iraq used the term "Ottoman rule" over Iraq, Salih Kapusuz, deputy chairman of the Justice and Development Party (AK Party), stated, "I want to stress that the Ottoman Empire did not have any imperialist goals in its campaigns against other countries. In fact, the Ottoman Empire acted on behalf of the humanity. Therefore, its activities should be assessed objectively. If such an assessment is made, it will be seen that the Ottoman Empire was not colonialist in its geography at all and that it did not intervene in local cultures." *Ankara Anatolia*, October 27, 2003, FBIS.

4. The best history of modern Turkey remains Bernard Lewis, *The Emergence of Modern Turkey*, 3rd ed. (New York: Oxford University Press, 2002).

5. Lewis, *Emergence of Modern Turkey*, pp. 219–220.

6. Andrew Davison, *Secularism and Revivalism in Turkey: A Hermeneutic Reconsideration* (New Haven, CT: Yale University Press, 1998), pp. 153–154.

7. Sencer Ayata, "Patronage, Party, and State: The Politicization of Islam in Turkey," *Middle East Journal*, Winter 1996, p. 41.

8. Some argued that Ataturk, in an extreme effort to distance himself from Islamic morals, engaged openly in womanizing and heavy drinking, leading to his death from cirrhosis of the liver.

9. See Edward Weisband, *Turkish Foreign Policy 1943–1945: Small State Diplomacy and Great Power Politics* (Princeton, NJ: Princeton University Press, 1973).

10. Lewis, *Emergence of Modern Turkey*, pp. 315–317.

11. Douglas A. Howard, *The History of Turkey* (Westport, CT: Greenwood, 2001), pp. 139–140.

12. Tanel Demirel, "The Turkish Military's Decision to Intervene: 12 September 1980," *Armed Forces and Society*, Winter 2003, pp. 253–280.

13. Metin Heper and Aylin Guney, "The Military and the Consolidation of Democracy: The Recent Turkish Experience," *Armed Forces and Society*, Summer 2000, pp. 640–641.

14. Mehran Kamrava, "Military Professionalism and Civil-Military Relations in the Middle East," *Political Science Quarterly*, Spring 2000, p. 74.

15. The corruption charges became more strident as the result of a car crash in Susurluk in November 1996. A Mercedes carrying Abdullah Çathü, a gangster (involved in the jail escape of Pope John Paul II's attempted assassin), his girlfriend, the deputy police chief of Istanbul, and the only survivor, a parliamentary member of True Path who had ties to Tansu Çiller. The crash revealed that Çathü was working for the government, tarnishing both Çiller and Yülmaz. See Howard, *History of Turkey*, pp. 180–181.

16. Christopher Caldwell, "Bordering on What?" *New York Times Magazine*, September 25, 2005, p. 49.

17. On the social basis of the AKP and insights into the class basis of Turkish politics, see Jenny B. White, *Islamist Mobilization in Turkey: A Study in Vernacular Politics* (Seattle: University of Washington Press, 2002), esp. chap. 4 and postscript.

18. Soli Ozel, "After the Tsunami," *Journal of Democracy*, April 2003, p. 81.

19. Ozel, "After the Tsunami," pp. 82–91.

20. "Parliamentary Commissions Will Investigate Six Former Ministers," *Turkish Daily News,* December 11, 2003.

21. Survey taken by the Bosphorus University and reported in Gareth Jenkins, "Muslim Democrats in Turkey?" *Survival*, Spring 2003, p. 55.

22. "Turkey: Erdogan Issues Message for 29 October Republic Day," *Ankara Anatolia,* October 28, 2003, FBIS; in Turkish.

23. In August 2005 Turkish security forces arrested a Syrian national with alleged ties to al-Qaeda who is believed to have organized the 2003 bombings. When arrested, he admitted that he was preparing an operation to attack Israeli tourist ships off the Turkish coast. "Sakra Caught with 750 Kilograms of Explosives," Istanbul CNN TURK, August 11, 2005, FBIS; in Turkish.

24. "A Crescent That Could Also Wane," *Economist*, April 1, 2006, p. 41.

25. Ergun Ozbudun, "Turkey: Crises, Interruptions, and Reequiliberations," in Larry Diamond, Juan J. Linz, and Seymour Martin Lipset, eds., *Politics in Developing Countries: Comparing Experiences with Democracy* (Boulder, CO: Lynne Rienner, 1995), p. 220.

26. A captured Turkish terrorist later said, "In these friendly circles [his friends] people were talking about the explosions. People were saying that the people who did this could not

be Muslims." The speaker was portraying a common antiterrorist attitude in Turkey. "Al-Qaeda's Hand in Istanbul Plot," *Washington Post*, February 12, 2007.

27. Rusen Cakir, "The Rise and Fall of Turkish Hizb ut-Tahrir," in Zeyno Baran, ed., *The Challenge of Hizb ut-Tahrir: Deciphering and Combatting Radical Islamist Ideology* (Conference Report, Nixon Center, September 2004), pp. 37–40.

28. Jenny B. White, "The End of Islamism? Turkey's Muslimhood Model," in Robert W. Hefner, ed., *Pluralism, Contestation, Democratization* (Princeton, NJ: Princeton University Press, 2005), p. 109.

29. "Western Businesses Embrace Turkey As E.U.'s Resistance Grows," *Washington Post*, December 12, 2006.

30. "In Turkey, a Sign of a Rising Islamic Middle Class," *New York Times*, April 25, 2007.

31. A Turkish teenager assassinated Dink in February 2007, and Dink's funeral drew over 100,000 persons, including high-ranking Turkish officials.

32. "Demirel: Deep State Is the Military," *Turkish Daily News*, February 12, 2007.

33. For an excellent report on the crisis, see Carol Migdalovitz, *Turkey's 2007 Elections: Crisis of Identity and Power*, Congressional Research Service RL34039, June 12, 2007.

34. Cengiz Candar, "Ataturk's Ambiguous Legacy," *Wilson Quarterly*, Autumn 2000, p. 90.

35. An incisive analysis of the Turkish military in politics is in Steven A. Cook, *Ruling But Not Governing: The Military and Political Development in Egypt, Algeria, and Turkey* (Baltimore, MD: Johns Hopkins University Press, 2007), chap. 5.

36. Gareth Jenkins, *Context and Circumstances: The Turkish Military and Politics*, Adelphi Paper no. 337 (Oxford: Oxford University for the International Institute for Strategic Studies, 2001), pp. 42–43.

37. Jenkins, *Context and Circumstances*, pp. 46–47.

38. Heper and Guney, "The Military and the Consolidation of Democracy," p. 650.

39. Ersel Aydinli, Nihat Ali Ozcan, and Dogan Akyaz, "The Turkish Military's March Toward Europe," *Foreign Affairs*, January-February 2006, pp. 77–90.

40. See Michele Penner Angrist, "Party Systems and Regime Formation in the Modern Middle East: Explaining Turkish Exceptionalism," *Comparative Politics*, January 2004, pp. 229–249.

41. Ergun Ozbudun, *Contemporary Turkish Politics: Challenges to Democratic Modernization* (Boulder, CO: Lynne Rienner, 2002), p. 74.

42. Binnaz Toprak, "Islam and Democracy in Turkey," *Turkish Studies*, June 2005, p. 171.

43. See Suat Kiniklioglu, "The Democratic Left Party: Kapükulu Politics *Par Excellence*," in Barry Rubin and Metin Heper, eds., *Political Parties in Turkey* (Portland, OR: Frank Cass, 2002).

44. Ersin Kalaycioglu, "The Motherland Party: The Challenge of Institutionalization in a Charismatic Leader Party," in Rubin and Heper, eds., *Political Parties in Turkey*, p. 50.

45. See Umit Cizre, "From Ruler to Pariah: The Life and Times of the True Path Party," in Rubin and Heper, eds., *Political Parties in Turkey*.

46. M. Hakan Yavuz, "The Politics of Fear: The Rise of the Nationalist Action Party (MHP) in Turkey," *Middle East Journal*, Spring 2002, pp. 200–221.

47. Ziya Oni and E. Fuat Keyman, "Turkey at the Polls: A New Path Emerges," in Larry Diamond, Marc F. Plattner, and Daniel Brumberg, eds., *Islam and Democracy in the Middle East* (Baltimore: Johns Hopkins University Press, 2003), p. 183.

48. "Controversy over Independence of Judiciary Continues," Ankara TRT Net WWW-Text, December 12, 2003, FBIS; in Turkish.

49. Amnesty International Report, "Turkey," *Report 2006.*

50. "A General Look at Human Rights in Turkey in 2003," *Turkish Daily News*, December 13, 2003.

51. "Aksu: We are Determined to Eliminate Torture," *Turkish Daily News*, October 9, 2003.

52. For a useful discussion of civil society in Turkey, see Stefanos Yerasimos, Gunter Seufert, and Karin Vorhoff, eds., *Civil Society in the Grip of Nationalism: Studies on Political Culture in Contemporary Turkey* (London: Frank Cass, 2001).

53. Quoted in Henri J. Barkey and Graham E. Fuller, *Turkey's Kurdish Question* (Lanham, MD: Rowman & Littlefield, 1998), pp. 14–15.

54. Mia Bloom, *Dying to Kill: The Allure of Suicide Attacks* (New York: Columbia University Press, 2005), chap. 5.

55. Barkey and Fuller, *Turkey's Kurdish Question*, pp. 24–25.

56. "Turkey's Kurdish Spring Fading," *al-Jazeera*, September 27, 2005.

57. "Turkish Kurdish Rebels Disband," *al-Jazeera*, November 11, 2003.

58. "Turmoil Revisiting Southeastern Turkey," *al-Jazeera*, July 17, 2005.

59. "Clashes Steer Kurds and Turkey Back on a Rocky Path," *New York Times*, April 6, 2006.

60. Bedriye Poyraz, "The Turkish State and the Alevis: Changing Parameters of an Uneasy Relationship," *Middle Eastern Studies*, July 2005, p. 506.

61. Howard, *History of Turkey*, p. 142.

62. Turkey seems to have been the first country in the world to have a woman fighter pilot, Sabiah Gokcen, who joined the Turkish air force in 1938.

63. Sema Genel and Kerem Karaomanoglu, "A New Islamic Individualism in Turkey: Headscarved Women in the City," *Turkish Studies*, September 2006, pp. 473–489.

64. Asaf Savas Akat, "The Political Economy of Turkish Inflation," *Journal of International Affairs,* Fall 2000, pp. 265–282.

65. Philip Robins, "Confusion at Home, Confusion Abroad: Turkey Between Copenhagen and Iraq," *International Affairs*, May 2003, pp. 548–549.

66. See, for an example, "IMF Mission Visits NGOs in Istanbul, Tackles Lira Appreciation," *Turkish Daily News*, September 27, 2003.

67. Mark Johnson, "Turkish Turbulence," *Global Finance*, June 2003, p. 18.

68. "Forces for Change," *Middle East Economic Digest*, August 20–26, 2004, p. 28.

69. Marcie J. Patton, "The Economic Policies of Turkey's AKP Government: Rabbits from a Hat?" *Middle East Journal*, Summer 2006, p. 375.

70. "Turkish Economy on the Mend," *al-Jazeera*, October 4, 2003.

71. "U.S. Free-Trade Deals Include Few Muslim Countries," *Washington Post*, December 3, 2004.

72. "On the Rebound: A Stronger Economy Is Reviving Turkish Airlines' Privatization Plans," *Aviation Week and Space Technology*, October 27, 2003, p. 45.

73. "Investors in Turkey's Tupras Face Workers Opposed to Privatization," *Wall Street Journal*, September 3, 2003.

74. Some Armenian interest groups have strongly criticized the Bush II administration for supporting Israeli-Turkish ties and thus working, according to the allegations, to block resolutions at the state level condemning the 1915–1916 allegations of a massacre of Armenians by the Ottoman Empire. See David B. Boyajain, "The Turkish-Israeli Alliance and Genocide Denial," *Armenian Online Weekly*, April 2003.

75. "Thousands Mourn Slain Editor in Istanbul," *New York Times*, January 23, 2007.

76. Bruce Robellet Kuniholm, *The Origins of the Cold War in the Near East: Great Power Conflict in Iran, Turkey, and Greece* (Princeton, NJ: Princeton University Press, 1980), chaps. 5–6.

77. Interviews, Ankara, Istanbul, March 2004.

78. F. Stephen Larrabee, "Turkey Rediscovers the Middle East," *Foreign Affairs*, July-August 2007, p. 104.

79. "U.S. Aides Acknowledge Series of Missteps with Turkey," *New York Times*, November 10, 2003.

80. "Growing Bonhomie in Greek-Turkish Ties," *al-Jazeera*, October 29, 2003.

81. For a discussion of energy resources in the Caspian Sea basin, see Geoffrey Kemp and Robert E. Harkavy, *Strategic Geography and the Changing Middle East* (Washington, DC: Carnegie Endowment for International Peace in cooperation with the Brookings Institute Press, 1997), pp. 131–153.

82. Larrabee and Lesser, *Turkish Foreign Policy*, chap. 5.

83. Larrabee, "Turkey Turns to the Middle East," pp. 107–109.

84. See Graham E. Fuller and Ian O. Lesser, *Turkey's New Geopolitics: From the Balkans to Western China* (Boulder, CO: Westview, 1993).

85. On the F-16 Peace Onyx program, see Michael Robert Hickok, "Peace Onyx: A Story of Turkish F-16 Coproduction," in Pia Christina Wood and David S. Sorenson, eds., *International Military Aerospace Collaboration* (Aldershot, VT: Ashgate, 2000), pp. 153–182. TIA currently does not produce a complete aircraft but builds subcomponents for aircraft assembled in the United States and Europe.

86. F. Stephen Larrabee and Ian O. Lesser, *Turkish Foreign Policy in an Age of Uncertainty* (Santa Monica, CA: RAND Corporation, 2003), pp. 48–49.

87. Jenkins, "Muslim Democrats in Turkey?" p. 57. The announcement probably surprised NAFTA's membership since Turkey was hardly eligible for membership in a geographically bound organization.

88. For a discussion of the impact of the Copenhagen criteria, see Bertil Duner and Edward Deverell, "Country Cousin: Turkey, the European Union and Human Rights," *Turkish Studies*, Spring 2001, pp. 1–24; "Conclusions of the Presidency," European Council in Copenhagen, June 21–22, 1993.

89. Umit Cizre, "Demythologizing the National Security Concept: The Case of Turkey," *Middle East Journal*, Spring 2003, p. 225.

90. Interview, Ankara, March 2004.

91. Robins, "Confusion at Home," pp. 555–556.

92. Michael S. Teitlebaum and Philip L. Martin, "Is Turkey Ready for Europe?" *Foreign Affairs*, May-June 2003, pp. 97–111.

93. Birol A. Yesilada, "Turkey's Candidacy for EU Membership," *Middle East Journal*, Winter 2002, pp. 101–102.

94. "Turkey Needs More Work, Says EP Committee," *Enlargement News*, March 23, 2004.

95. "Turkey's Erdogan Makes Case for EU Membership," *Wall Street Journal*, May 21, 2004.

96. "Europe Asks Turkey to Hold Membership Talks Next Year," *New York Times*, December 17, 2004.

97. Interview, Ankara, March 2007.

98. Efraim Inbar, "Regional Implications of the Israeli-Turkish Partnership," *Turkish Studies*, Autumn 2002, p. 22.

99. "Israel Signs Water Deal with Turkey," *al-Jazeera*, October 3, 2003.

100. "Turkey Plans to Extend Gas, Oil, and Water Pipelines to Israel," *Haaretz*, January 16, 2007.

101. "Turkey's Cabinet Agrees to Contribute Troops to Iraq," *Washington Post*, October 6, 2003.

102. "Turkey's Cabinet Agrees to Contribute Troops."

103. Senol Demirci, "28 Percent Segregate Guests by Gender," *Istanbul Milliyet,* June 21, 2005, FBIS. The poll, conducted by Saban Kizildag, covered a number of items, including religious identity and practice. It was conducted only in Istanbul.

104. The poll results were announced by the Ari movement and the Infakto Research Workshop. Other results were that some 44 percent said they oppose the United States and President Bush but do not maintain a negative view of American popular culture. Some 1,244 respondents in fifteen provinces participated in the research. "It Is Bush Who Is Not Liked, Not the United States," *Milliyet*, July 6, 2005; in Turkish. See also David S. Sorenson, "Turkey and the United States: Exploring Change in a Hegemonic Relationship" (presentation to the First Global International Studies Conference, International Studies Association, Bilgi University, Istanbul, August 24–27, 2005).

CHAPTER 12: SYRIA

1. Eliezer Tauber, *The Formation of Modern Syria and Iraq* (London: Frank Cass, 1995), p. 25.

2. James L. Gelvin, *Divided Loyalties: Nationalism and Mass Politics in Syria at the Close of Empire* (Berkeley: University of California Press, 1998).

3. Philip S. Khoury, *Syria and the French Mandate: The Politics of Arab Nationalism, 1920–1945* (Princeton, NJ: Princeton University Press, 1987), chaps. 6–8. See also N. E. Bou-Nacklie, "Tumult in Syria's Hama in 1925: The Failure of a Revolt," *Journal of Contemporary History*, April 1998, pp. 273–290.

4. For a good discussion of Mardam Bey and Syrian nationalism in the immediate postwar period, see Salama Mardam Bey, *Syria's Quest for Independence* (Reading, UK: Ithaca, 1994).

5. A good discussion of the beginnings of Arab nationalism and Arab unity is found in Roger Owen, *State, Power, and Politics in the Making of the Modern Middle East* (London: Routledge), 1992, esp. chap. 4, "Arab Nationalism: Arab Unity and the Practice of intra-Arab State Relations."

6. See Joshua Landis, "Syria and the Palestine War: Fighting King Abdullah's Greater Syria Plan," in Eugene Rogan and Avi Shlaim, eds., *The War for Palestine: Rewriting the History of 1948* (Cambridge: Cambridge University Press, 2001), pp. 178–205; Kenneth M. Pollack, *Arabs at War: Military Effectiveness, 1948–1991* (Lincoln: University of Nebraska Press, 2002), chap. 6.

7. Patrick Seale, *The Struggle for Syria: A Study of Post-War Arab Politics, 1945–1958* (New Haven, CT: Yale University Press, 1986), p. 58.

8. For a discussion of this period, see Steven Heydemann, *Authoritarianism in Syria: Institutions and Social Conflict, 1946–1970* (Ithaca, NY: Cornell University Press, 1999).

9. Seale, *Asad*, chap. 6.

10. Bitar was assassinated in Paris in 1980.

11. Fouad Ajami, *The Vanished Imam: Musa al Sadr and the Shia of Lebanon* (Ithaca, NY: Cornell University Press, 1986), p. 174.

12. David Waldner, *State Building and Late Development* (Ithaca, NY: Cornell University Press, 1999), p. 83.

13. One account of the campaign against the Islamist militants is in Nikolaos Van Dam, *The Struggle for Power in Syria: Politics and Society Under Asad and the Ba'th Party* (London: Tauris, 1996), chap. 8.

14. David S. Sorenson, "National Security and Political Succession in Syria," *Mediterranean Quarterly*, Winter 1998, pp. 69–91; Glenn E. Robinson, "Elite Cohesion, Regime Succession, and Political Stability in Syria," *Middle East Policy*, January 1998, pp. 159–179.

15. Rumors spread in the Arab world that the death was really the work of Iraqi assassins, but Mercedes Benz engineers who examined the car estimated that Basil was going so fast that the car flipped at least seven times while still in the air before it hit the ground. Interview, Damascus, March 1994.

16. "Syria Bans Activities of Parties and Political and Legal Societies," *Arabic News*, June 8, 2004.

17. "Suicide by Syrian Interior Minister," *al-Jazeera*, October 12, 2005. The reported suicide was widely disbelieved in Syria, as one cynical joke of the time indicated: Asef Shawkat tried to commit suicide but the police could not find him at his office. "Fearing an Iraq in Post-Assad Syria," *New York Times*, November 6, 2005.

18. "For Syrians, a Siege Mentality Sets In," *Washington Post*, October 25, 2005.

19. Lisa Wedeen argues that this phenomenon reflects partially the need for the Baathists to gain obedience without having the capacity to reward it with resources. See Wedeen, *Ambiguities of Domination: Politics, Rhetoric, and Symbols in Contemporary Syria* (Chicago: University of Chicago Press, 1999).

20. Both Hafiz and Basil al-Asad reportedly hated Shawkat and prohibited him from marrying Bushra al-Asad. But after Basil's death in 1994, they eloped, and Mahar later shot Shawkat in the stomach. As one observer indicated, anyone who stole a daughter from Hafiz al-Asad was both clever and ruthless. See "A Syrian Tale: Power, Passion, and Assassination," *New York Times*, November 3, 2005.

21. See Hanna Batatu, *Syria's Peasantry: The Descendants of Its Lesser Rural Notables and Their Politics* (Princeton, NJ: Princeton University Press, 1999).

22. "Ba'th Party Command Discusses Activating Public Life in Syria," Damascus Syrian Arab Radio, November 29, 2000, FBIS; in Arabic.

23. "In First Meeting Since 50 Years, Syrian Socialist Party Leadership Meet in Damascus," *Arabic News.com.*, August 8, 2001.

24. Alan George, "In Syria, the Media is the System," *Middle East*, November 2000, pp. 38–40.

25. Najib Ghadbian, "The New Asad: Dynamics of Continuity and Change in Syria," *Middle East Journal*, Autumn 2001, p. 637.

26. "Syrian Activists Locked Up," *al-Jazeera*, September 25, 2003. Syria is one of the few Arab countries to actively discourage cigarette smoking, with billboards in Damascus and other cities comparing cigarettes and bullets.

27. "Syria, Long Ruthlessly Secular, Sees Fervent Islamic Resurgence," *New York Times*, October 24, 2003.

28. "Syria Pressing for Israeli Talks," *New York Times*, December 1, 2003.

29. See Volker Perthes, "The Political Economy of the Syrian Succession," *Survival*, Spring 2001, pp. 147–148.

30. "Syria Imposing Stronger Curbs on Opposition," *New York Times*, April 5, 2006.

31. "In the Fief of the Assads, Friends Melt Away," *New York Times*, November 2, 2005.

32. "President's Amnesty for Political Prisoners, Legal Penalties," *Syria Times*, November 17, 2000.

33. "Torture Ties May Exist," *Toronto Globe and Mail*, June 22, 2004.

34. "Syria Arrests Wives of Terror Suspects," *al-Jazeera*, September 27, 2005.

35. Raymond A. Hinnebusch, "State and Civil Society in Syria," *Middle East Journal*, Spring 1993, pp. 243–257.

36. See Alan George, *Syria: Neither Bread Nor Freedom* (London: Zed, 2003), chaps. 2–3.

37. "Syrian Opposition Groups Unite," *al-Jazeera*, October 17, 2005.

38. Joshua Landis and Joe Pace, "The Syrian Opposition," *Washington Quarterly*, Winter 2006–2007, pp. 45–68.

39. David W. Lesch, *The New Lion of Damascus: Bashar Asad and Modern Syria* (New Haven: Yale University Press, 2005), pp. 85–95.

40. Seale, *Struggle for Syria*, p. 77. Unlike men, though, women required a primary school certificate to be eligible to vote.

41. "Islamic Revival Led by Women Tests Syria's Secularism," *New York Times*, August 29, 2006.

42. "U.N. Study Finds that 25% of Married Syrian Women Have Been Beaten," *New York Times*, April 11, 2006.

43. Eyal Zisser, *Asad's Legacy: Syria in Transition* (New York: New York University Press, 2001), pp. 191–193.

44. Bassam Haddad, "Syria's Curious Dilemma," *Middle East Report*, Fall 2005, p. 11; Lesch, *New Lion of Damascus*, p. 222.

45. Volker Perthes, "The Syrian Economy in the 1980s," *Middle East Journal*, Winter 1992, p. 40.

46. Perthes, "Syrian Economy," pp. 51–52.

47. Fred H. Lawson, "Domestic Transformation and Foreign Steadfastness in Contemporary Syria," *Middle East Journal*, Winter 1994, p. 50.

48. Lawson, "Domestic Transformation," p. 50.

49. Haddad, "Syria's Curious Dilemma," p. 11.

50. Peter Kiernan, "Syria's Economic Dilemma," *Middle East*, March 1999, p. 35.

51. "U.S. Said to Weigh Sanctions on Syria over Iraq Network," *New York Times*, January 5, 2005.

52. James Bruce, "Lebanese Factions Begin to Challenge Syrian Domination," *Jane's Intelligence Review*, June 2001, p. 42.

53. Robinson, "Elite Cohesion," p. 162.

54. David W. Lesch, "Is Syria Ready for Peace? Obstacles to Integration in the Global Economy," *Middle East Policy*, February 1999, p. 103.

55. Ghadbian, "New Asad," p. 635.

56. "Production of Sham Car to be Started Next March," Syrian Arab News Agency, February 5, 2007.

57. "Syria Advances Cautiously into the Online Age," *Washington Post*, April 27, 2000.

58. "Syria Advances Cautiously."

59. Volker Perthes, "The Political Economy of Syrian Succession," *Survival*, Spring 2001, pp. 146, 149.

60. Judith Harik, "Syrian Foreign Policy and State Resistance Dynamics in Lebanon," *Studies in Conflict and Terrorism*, July-September 1997, p. 252. This became more important

after the election of Benjamin Netanyahu in 1996. See Patrick Seale, "Asad's Regional Strategy and the Challenge from Netanyahu," *Journal of Palestine Studies*, Autumn 1996, pp. 27–41.

61. Yahya Sadowski, "The Evolution of Political Identity in Syria," in Shibley Telhami and Michael Barnett, eds., *Identity and Foreign Policy in the Middle East* (Ithaca, NY: Cornell University Press, 2002), pp. 137–154.

62. Interview, Syrian Foreign Ministry, March 1999.

63. Jerome Slater, "Lost Opportunities for Peace in the Arab-Israeli Conflict: Israel and Syria, 1948–2001," *International Security*, Summer 2002, pp. 605–606.

64. Lesch, "Is Syria Ready," p. 105.

65. Henry Siegman, "Being Hafiz Assad," *Foreign Affairs*, May-June 2000, pp. 2–7.

66. Steven Simon and Jonathan Stevenson, "The Road to Damascus," *Foreign Affairs*, May-June 2004, pp. 110–119.

67. See Serdar Guner, "The Turkish-Syrian War of Attrition: The Water Dispute," *Studies in Conflict and Terrorism*, January 1997, pp. 109–110.

68. For a good discussion of the issue, see Robert Olson, "Turkey-Syria Relations Since the Gulf War: Kurds and Water," *Middle East Policy*, May 1997, pp. 168–193.

69. Olson, "Turkey-Syria Relations," pp. 176–177.

70. Guner, "Turkish-Syrian War," p. 110.

71. Alan George, "Syria Builds One of the Middle East's Biggest Dams," *Middle East*, March 1999, p. 34. Funding for the dam came from the Kuwait Fund for Arab Economic Development.

72. Patrick Seale, "Turkey and Syria: The War over Water," *Middle East International*, June 4, 1999, pp. 20–21.

73. "Historical Turkey Visit for Syrian Leader," *al-Jazeera*, January 5, 2004.

74. Observations, March 2002, Damascus.

75. "Senior U.S. Officials to Level Weapons Charges Against Syria," *New York Times*, September 16, 2003.

CHAPTER 13: LEBANON

1. See Leila Tarazi Fawaz, *An Occasion for War: Civil Conflict in Lebanon and Damascus in 1860* (Berkeley: University of California Press, 1994).

2. For a discussion of the decisions that led to US intervention, see Agnes G. Korbani, *U.S. Intervention in Lebanon, 1958 and 1982* (New York: Praeger, 1991), chap. 4.

3. See Naomi Weinberger, "How Peace Keeping Becomes Intervention: Lessons from the Lebanese Experience," in Milton J. Esman and Shibley Telhami, eds., *International Organizations and Ethnic Conflict* (Ithaca, NY: Cornell University Press, 1995), p. 239.

4. For a good discussion of UNFIL, see Bjorn Skogmo, *UNFIL: International Peacekeeping in Lebanon, 1978–1988* (Boulder, CO: Lynne Rienner, 1989).

5. Itamar Rabinovich, *The War for Lebanon, 1970–1983* (Ithaca, NY: Cornell University Press, 1984), pp. 124–125.

6. Rabinovich, *War for Lebanon*, p. 138.

7. Rabinovich, *War for Lebanon*, pp. 144–145.

8. See Korbani, *U.S. Intervention in Lebanon*, chaps. 5–6.

9. See Pia Christina Wood and David S. Sorenson, "Alliance Theory, Risk Assessment, and Peacekeeping Operations: The French and U.S. MNF to Lebanon, 1982–1985" (paper

presented at the International Studies Association annual conference, San Diego CA, April 1996).

10. See Pia Christina Wood, "The Diplomacy of Peacekeeping: France and the Multinational Forces to Lebanon, 1982–84," *International Peacekeeping*, Summer 1998, pp. 19–37.

11. See Samir Khalaf, *Civil and Uncivil Violence in Lebanon: A History of the Internationalization of Communal Conflict* (New York: Columbia University Press, 2002), pp. 241–242. On the formation of belief system of Hizbollah, see Hala Jaber, *Hezbollah: Born with a Vengeance* (New York: Columbia University Press, 1997). One of the best studies of AMAL is Augustus Richard Norton, *AMAL and the Shia: Struggle for the Soul of Lebanon* (Austin: University of Texas Press, 1987).

12. Daniel L. Byman, "Divided They Stand: Lessons About Partition from Iraq and Lebanon," *Security Studies*, Autumn 1997, p. 6.

13. "No Discussion of Article 49 Until President Asks for It, Says Berri," *Lebanon Daily Star*, September 15, 1998.

14. "Gen Lahoud has Great Chance of Becoming President, says Berri," *Lebanese Daily Star*, September 21, 1998.

15. "Hariri: Talk of Next Premier Is Premature, Election Victor Plays Down Prospects of Return to Office," *Daily Star*, September 6, 2000. Hariri required Syrian approval to regain the prime ministership, revealing Syria's political influence. See "Hariri Awaits Syrian Election Nod," *New York Times*, September 5, 2000.

16. Daniel Byman, "Should Hezbollah Be Next?" *Foreign Affairs*, November-December 2003, p. 60.

17. "Islamic Militants Behind Gemayel's Killing: Probe," *Bahrain Daily Tribune*, July 8, 2007.

18. "Parliament to Question Cabinet on Security Efforts," *Daily Star*, September 28, 2005. Murr survived a bombing in July 2005.

19. Fouad Ajami, "The Autumn of the Autocrats," *Foreign Affairs*, May-June 2005, p. 25.

20. See Paul Salem, "The Future of Lebanon," *Foreign Affairs*, November-December 2006, pp. 13–22, for details.

21. "Chaotic Lebanon Risks Becoming Militant Haven," *New York Times*, July 7, 2007.

22. Sarkis Naoum, a columnist for al-Nahar newspaper, quoted in "As Crises Build, Lebanese Fearful of a Failed State," *Washington Post*, June 5, 2007.

23. "A Nation with a Long Memory but a Truncated History," *New York Times*, January 10, 2007.

24. For a discussion of the origins of Lebanese clientalism, see A. Nazar Hamzeh, "Clientalism in Lebanon: Roots and Trends" (paper presented at the 1999 Annual Conference of the American Political Science Association).

25. "Hoss: New Electoral Law Needed to Rescue Democracy," *Daily Star*, December 29, 2004.

26. "Painful Glimpse of Home for Palestinians," *New York Times*, May 30, 2000.

27. "Palestinian Resettlement: Rhetoric Confronts Reality," *Washington Post*, January 12, 2001.

28. "Palestinian Resettlement."

29. "Waiting to Go Sparks Discussion on Palestinians' Return," *Washington Report on Middle East Affairs*, October 2004, p. 77.

30. Elizabeth Picard, *Lebanon: A Shattered Country* (New York: Holmes & Meier, 1996), pp. 66–67.

31. The mix in Beirut is reflected by its representatives: six Sunni, three Armenian Orthodox, two Greek Orthodox, two Shiite, one Greek Catholic, one Armenian Catholic, one Protestant, one Druze, one Christian Minority, and one Maronite.

32. Abdo Baakline, Guilain Denoeux, and Robert Springborg, *Legislative Politics and the Arab World* (Boulder, CO: Lynne Rienner, 1999), pp. 95–96.

33. "Mixed Messages," *Middle East*, August 1998, p. 14. The most common means of execution is public hanging, which has been carried out fourteen times since the law was passed.

34. "Berri, Hrawi Agree on Constitutional Change, Speaker Takes More Moderate Approach to Amendments," *Lebanese Daily Star*, January 1, 1998.

35. "Baabda Faces New Crisis Over Charges of Police State," *Daily Star*, August 9, 2001.

36. "Court Sentences 25 in Bombings," *Lebanon Star*, December 21, 2003.

37. For more on the origins of Hizbollah, see Hala Jaber, *Hizbollah: Born with a Vengeance* (New York: Columbia University Press, 1997).

38. See Martin Kramer, "The Oracle of Hizbollah," in *Spokesmen for the Despised* (Chicago: University of Chicago Press, 1996), pp. 83–181.

39. August Richard Norton, "Hizballah: From Radicalism to Pragmatism," *Middle East Policy*, January 1998, p. 148.

40. "To U.S., a Terrorist Group; to Lebanese, a Social Agency," *New York Times*, December 28, 2001.

41. Norton, "Hizballah," pp. 151–152.

42. "Hizbollah Is Rearing an Uncivil Society," *Financial Times of London*, September 1, 2006.

43. Paul Kingston, "Patrons, Clients, and Civil Society: A Case of Environmental Politics in Postwar Lebanon," *Arab Studies Quarterly*, Winter 2001, pp. 55–73.

44. Lamia Rustum Shehadeh, "The Legal Status of Married Women in Lebanon," *International Journal of Middle East Studies*, November 1998, pp. 501–519.

45. "Divorce Rules Stack the Deck Against Women," *Daily Star*, December 6, 1999.

46. "Lebanon: The Reform Movement," *Middle East Economic Digest*, July 8–14, 2005, pp. 4–5.

47. "State Finances Show Improvement," *Beirut Daily Star*, June 27, 2003.

48. "Paris III Aid Funds: Signed, Sealed, and Still Delayed," *Daily Star*, May 17, 2007.

49. "Banks Post Handsome Profits Despite Crises," *Beirut Daily Star*, February 7, 2007.

50. Sami E. Baroudi, "Continuity in Economic Policy in Postwar Lebanon: The Record of the Hariri and Hoss Governments Examined, 1992–2000," *Arab Studies Quarterly*, Winter 2002, pp. 73–74.

51. Giles Trendle, "Lebanon Looks to Industry," *Middle East*, September 1997, p. 26.

52. Trendle, "Lebanon Looks to Industry," p. 27.

53. "Back in the Black," *Middle East Economic Digest*, December 5–11, 2002, p. 33.

54. "Keeping the Lights On," *Middle East Economic Digest*, August 5–11, 2005, p. 32.

CHAPTER 14: ISRAEL

1. The West Bank is referred to by some Israelis as Judea and Samaria, and by most Palestinians as the Occupied Territories.

2. David Grossman, "Fifty Is a Dangerous Age," *New Yorker*, April 20, 1998, pp. 55–56.

3. Charles S. Liebman and Eliezer Don-Yehiya, *Civil Religion in Israel: Traditional Judaism and Political Culture in the Jewish State* (Berkeley: University of California Press, 1983), pp. 28–47.

4. See Idith Zertal, *Israel's Holocaust and the Politics of Nationhood* (Cambridge: Cambridge University Press, 2005).

5. When its founder, Abraham Stern, died in combat in 1942, Yitzhak Shamir became its leader, and eventually Menachem Begin. Both Shamir and Begin were later Israeli prime ministers.

6. For a history of the Labor Party in Israel, see Mitchell Cohen, *Zion and State: Nation, Class, and the Shaping of Modern Israel* (New York: Columbia University Press, 1992), pt. 2.

7. The ideology of Histadrut is discussed in Zeev Sternhell, *The Founding Myths of Israel: Nationalism, Socialism, and the Making of the Jewish State* (Princeton, NJ: Princeton University Press, 1998), chap. 4.

8. For an excellent discussion of this period, see Peter Y. Medding, *The Founding of Israeli Democracy, 1948–1967* (New York: Oxford University Press, 1990), chap. 1.

9. For a discussion of this shift, see Anita Shapira, *Land and Power: The Zionist Resort to Force, 1881–1948* (New York: Oxford University Press, 1992).

10. American financial support was critical to the new nation, since many of its refugees had arrived almost penniless. According to one study, private American contributions amounted to 25 percent of Israel's national budget during its first years of statehood. "From Infancy, a Helping Hand," *Washington Post*, April 29, 1998, p. 1.

11. A fascinating discussion of Ben-Gurion's role in directing the 1948 war and his relations with the new leaders of Israel's military forces is found in Eliot A. Cohen, *Supreme Command: Soldiers, Statesmen, and Leadership During Wartime* (New York: Free Press, 2002), chap. 5.

12. Roger Friedland and Richard Hecht, *To Rule Jerusalem* (Berkeley: University of California Press, 2000), pp. 27–28.

13. Future Prime Minister Menachem Begin was on the *Altalena* and reportedly threatened to "go down with the ship," until the captain explained that it was grounded and could not sink.

14. One unfortunate Jew was apparently instructed to carry a bomb into a cinema in Alexandria, but the bomb's fuse began to smoke prematurely as he was waiting in line to buy a ticket. The police arrested the bomber, who confessed that Mossad ordered him to carry out the act. The next day all of Alexandria's Jewish citizens were expelled from Egypt, and most went to Israel. Interview, Alexandria, June 1989.

15. Medding, *Founding of Israeli Democracy*, pp. 24–26.

16. Adam Garfinkle, *Politics and Society in Modern Israel: Myths and Realities* (Armonk, NY: Sharpe, 1997), p. 62.

17. Asher, *Second Republic*, p. 49.

18. A government of national unity is a coalition normally formed in the face of outside tension, usually consisting of both Labor and Likud plus a smattering of smaller parties. Sometimes the major party leaders take turns as prime minister; at other times the leader of the largest party becomes prime minister while rewarding the other large party with valuable cabinet portfolios like defense or foreign affairs.

19. One Israel is a party list; see below for an explanation of party lists.

20. Some held that Sharon took this action to gain public attention while he was waging a battle for Likud leadership with Netanyahu.

21. Alan Dowty, "Impact of the Aqsa Intifadah on Possible Resolution of the Israeli-Palestinian Conflict" (paper presented to the International Studies Association conference, Budapest, Hungary, June 2003), p. 12.

22. "Grind of War Giving Life to Opponents of Sharon," *Washington Post*, November 12, 2003.

23. "Unemployment Hit 11 Percent in February; 292,000 People out of Work," *Haaretz*, April 22, 2004.

24. "New Title Created for Peres," *Jerusalem Post*, December 29, 2004.

25. "Netanyahu to Challenge Sharon; Move Could Force Election," *Washington Post*, August 31, 2005.

26. Israeli demographics do not always recognize that the categories "Arab" and "Muslim" are not necessarily the same, as Israel has a small percentage of Arab Jews, though not all Jews who speak Arabic (or whose ancestors spoke Arabic) accept the term.

27. Jonathan Cook, "Sharon Stokes Israeli Fears of Arab Minority to Serve His Long-Term Interests," *Washington Report on Middle East Affairs*, October 2003, p. 16.

28. "Turtles Without a Shell," *Haaretz*, December 30, 2003.

29. "Study: Arabs May Be Poorer, but Jews Get More Welfare Funds," *Haaretz*, March 28, 2007.

30. See Omar Kamil, "The Synagogue as Civil Society, or How We Can Understand the Shas Party," *Mediterranean Quarterly*, Summer 2001, pp. 128–143.

31. Pretz, Kook, and Doron, "Knesset Election 2003," p. 600.

32. The kibbutzim have changed also, from rural collective farms epitomizing the early socialist ideal to modern strip malls. This provides yet another social division within Israel, and Orthodox rabbis objected strongly when they learned that some kibbutzim were open on the Sabbath and selling pork sausage. But, as one resident said, the problem is that "we practice our own kind of Judaism, Judaism without a synagogue. And that threatens the rabbis." See Zeev Chafets, "On the Kibbutz, Dirty Hands at Last," *New York Times Magazine*, September 27, 1998, p. 44.

33. See Eva Etzioni-Halevy, *The Divided People: Can Israel's Breakup Be Stopped?* (Lanham, MD: Lexington, 2002).

34. Asher Arian, David Nachmias, and Ruth Amir, *Executive Governance in Israel* (New York: Palgrave, 2002), p. 94.

35. Zeev Maoz, *Defending the Holy Land: A Critical Analysis of Israel's Security and Foreign Policy* (Ann Arbor: University of Michigan Press, 2007), p. 182.

36. This was in response to parties representing groups which believe that there can be no legitimate political state until the arrival of the Messiah. The prohibition of racist parties was in response to the activities of Meir Kahane's Kach Party, which took a strong anti-Arab stance.

37. "The Knesset Takes Command," *Haaretz*, November 24, 2004.

38. Arian, *Second Republic*, p. 104.

39. Alan S. Zuckerman, Michal Shemir, and Hanna Herzog, "The Political Bases of Activism in the Israeli Labor and Herut Parties," *Political Science Quarterly*, Summer 1992, pp. 318–319.

40. Another way to hold elections was to divide Israel into electoral districts, as in the case of other parliamentary democracies worldwide. It works reasonably well in places like the United Kingdom and Japan, where threshold rules limit the influence of small parties. However, barriers emerged to such an idea, partially because Israel was seen as too small to divide and because territorial division worked against ongoing efforts to cement national unity. For

more on the issue of territorial representation, see Nancy L. Schwartz, "Representation and Territory: The Israeli Experience," *Political Science Quarterly*, Fall 1994, pp. 615–646.

41. Don Peretz, Rebecca Kook, and Gideon Doron, "Knesset Election 2003: Why Likud Regained Its Political Domination and Labor Continued to Fade Out," *Middle East Journal*, Autumn 2003, p. 593.

42. Emanuele Ottolenghi, "Why Direct Election Failed in Israel," *Journal of Democracy*, October 2001, pp. 109–123.

43. Peretz, Kook, and Doron, "Why Likud Regained Dominance," pp. 596–597.

44. "Lapid Officially Resigns from Shinui," *Jerusalem Post*, January 25, 2006.

45. Interview, Israeli Democracy Institute, March 2006.

46. Ofer Kenig, Gideon Rahat, and Reuven Y. Hazan, "The Political Consequences of the Introduction and the Repeal of the Direct Elections for the Prime Minister," in Asher Arian and Michal Shamir, eds., *The Elections in Israel—2003* (New Brunswick, NJ: Transaction, 2005), pp. 33–62.

47. For an excellent discussion of Kook, see Gideon Aran, "The Father, the Son, and the Holy Land," in W. Scott Appleby, ed., *Spokesmen for the Despised: Fundamentalist Leaders of the Middle East* (Chicago: University of Chicago Press, 1997), pp. 294–327.

48. Kahane was an American-born Jew who immigrated to Israel and founded Kach in the early 1970s. He won a seat in the Knesset in 1984. However, the Knesset banned Kach in 1988 on the grounds that its anti-Arab platform was racist. Kahane was shot and killed in New York City by a Palestinian extremist in 1990.

49. Kach and Kahane Chai continue to organize anti-Arab demonstrations and disseminate anti-Arab literature, both in Israel and in New York. "Terror Label No Hindrance to Anti-Arab Jewish Group," *New York Times*, December 19, 2000. Kahane's son, Benjamin, was killed in an ambush in Israel in December 2000.

50. For two contrasting perspectives on Gush Emunim, see Ian S. Lustick, "Israel's Dangerous Fundamentalists," and Mordechai Nisan, "Gush Emunim: A Rational Perspective," in Ian S. Lustick, ed., *The Conflict with the Arabs in Israeli Politics and Society* (New York: Garland, 1994), pp. 166–198.

51. "Israeli Court: Army Must Hand Over Bodies of Jenin Dead to Palestinians," *Washington Post*, April 14, 2002.

52. The Bar Association is ultimately answerable to the High Court of Justice for policing the actions of representatives to the court selection committee. A July 1998 case found the High Court of Justice demanding that one of the two representatives be barred from the Court Selection Committee because he was under a charge of contempt of court. See "Bar Chief Barred from Judge-selecting Panel," *Haaretz*, July 23, 1998.

53. An April 2004 a High Court ruling took child custody and alimony out of sole purview of Druze courts. In allowing a petitioner a choice of religious or civil courts, it threatened to undermine the role of other religious courts in such matters. "Court Ruling May Transform Druze Family Law," *Haaretz*, April 11, 2004.

54. Friedland and Hecht, *To Rule Jerusalem*, p. 79.

55. "Tichon Against High Court," *Haaretz*, July 10, 1998.

56. Asher Arian, *The Second Republic: Politics in Israel* (Chatham, NJ: Chatham House, 1998), p. 268.

57. "Court Orders Review of Arab Marriage Policy," *Haaretz*, July 23, 1998. In July 2003 the Knesset passed a law suspending permits for marriage between Israeli citizens and residents of the Occupied Territories.

58. "Peres Defeated by Katzav in Israel's Presidential Election," *New York Times*, July 31, 2000.

59. Yael Yishai, "Civil Society in Transition: Interest Politics in Israel," *Annals of the American Academy of Political and Social Science*, January 1998, pp. 151–155.

60. Yishai, "Civil Society," p. 154.

61. A woman seeking an abortion must gain the approval of one of the forty-one abortion committees operating in a hospital or health clinic. In the 1980s, the Errfat Committee for the Encouragement of Higher Birth Rates tried to limit abortions by forcing women to view photographs of aborted fetuses or dead Holocaust victims, but the Knesset narrowly defeated the proposal. Simona Sharoni, *Gender and the Israeli-Palestinian Conflict* (Syracuse, NY: Syracuse University Press, 1995), p. 34.

62. See Esther Hertzog, "Women's Parties in Israel," *Middle East Journal*, Summer 2005, pp. 437–452.

63. "Violence: The Facts!" www.iwn.org/law/main.htm.

64. "Wife Jailed for Requesting Alimony Hearing," *Jerusalem Post*, March 27, 1998, p. 3.

65. "Petition Challenges Rabbinical Courts," *Haaretz*, August 12, 1998.

66. "Survey: 45% of Israeli Women are Feminists," *Haaretz*, July 13, 1998.

67. "Employment," www.iwn.org/law/main.htm.

68. Israel Aircraft Industries is Israel's largest single employer, with a workforce of over 13,000. It does over $1.5 billion in business, with over 80 percent of its total earnings from exports. One of the more lucrative exports for IAI is reconstructed military aircraft, including the Phantom 2000, an modernized American F-4 fighter, and reconstructed Soviet-built MiG-21s. Israel buys these aircraft, often in dilapidated condition, from a variety of nations, then rebuilds them with modern equipment. It is reported that some are sold to the People's Republic of China, and that around 10 percent of the sales price goes back to Russia in payment for using former Soviet aircraft. Interview, March 1999.

69. Yair Aharoni, "The Changing Political Economy of Israel," *Annals of the American Academy of Political and Social Science*, January 1998, p. 132.

70. Aharoni, "Changing Political Economy," p. 132.

71. "Why Histadrut Is Striking," *Haaretz*, November 3, 2003; "Israeli Court Limits National Strike," *New York Times*, November 3, 2003.

72. "Some Israelis Say Strings Attached to U.S. Aid Aren't Worth the Money," *Wall Street Journal*, October 26, 2000. For fiscal 2007, $610 million out of the $2.34 billion US military assistance may be spent in Israel.

73. See Duncan L. Clarke, "US Security Assistance to Egypt and Israel: Politically Untouchable?" *Middle East Journal*, Spring 1997, p. 25.

74. Yaron Ezrahi, "In Israel, Peace Means Prosperity," *New York Times*, January 21, 1997, p. 23.

75. "GDP Rises Only 1.7%," *Haaretz*, May 22, 2001.

76. "GDP Contracts 0.6% in First Half of 2001," *Haaretz*, August 15, 2001.

77. "1 in 5 Israelis—Below the Poverty Line," *Jerusalem Post*, October 30, 2003.

78. "Poverty Worsening in Israel and Palestinian Areas, 2 Studies Find," *New York Times*, November 24, 2004.

79. "600,000 Children Living in Poverty," *Jerusalem Post*, April 21, 2004.

80. "Intifadah Has Cost Israel $2.4 Billion, Mainly in Tourism," *Haaretz*, March 21, 2002.

81. "Report: Intifada Cost Israel $12b," *Jerusalem Post*, November 14, 2004.

82. "Caniel Opens Jordan Operation," *Jerusalem Post*, February 23, 1998, p. 1.

83. There are many sources on American foreign policy toward Israel, including Stephen L. Spiegel, *The Other Arab-Israeli Conflict: Making America's Middle East Policy, from Truman to Reagan* (Chicago: The University of Chicago Press, 1985); Abraham Ben-Zvi, *The United States and Israel: The Limits of the Special Relationship* (New York: Columbia University Press, 1993); A. F. K. Organski, *The $36 Billion Bargain: Strategy and Politics in U.S. Assistance to Israel* (New York: Columbia University Press, 1990); Isaac Alteras, *Eisenhower and Israel: U.S.-Israeli Relations, 1953–1960* (Gainesville: University Press of Florida, 1993); Michael G. Bard, *The Water's Edge and Beyond: Defining the Limits to Domestic Influence on United States Middle East Policy* (New Brunswick, NJ: Transaction, 1991); George W. Ball and Douglas B. Ball, *The Passionate Attachment: America's Involvement with Israel, 1947 to the Present* (New York: Norton, 1992); Camille Mansour, *Beyond Alliance: Israel in U.S. Foreign Policy* (New York: Columbia University Press, 1994); Dana H. Allin and Steven Simon, "The Moral Psychology of US Support for Israel," *Survival*, Autumn 2003, pp. 123–144; Bernard Reich, "The United States and Israel: The Nature of a Special Relationship," in David W. Lesch, ed., *The Middle East and the United States: A Historical and Political Reassessment* (Boulder, CO: Westview, 2003).

84. The poll noted that support for Israel dropped while sympathy for the Palestinians did not change from previous polls. A significant 43 percent answered both, neither, or had no opinion. The question read: "In the Middle East situation, are your sympathies more with the Israelis or more with the Palestinian Arabs?" and was conducted March 8–9, 2002. "Recent Middle East Violence Costs Israel Some U.S. Public Support." Poll Analysis, Gallup News Service, March 15, 2002.

85. See, for example, Edward Tivnan, *The Lobby: Jewish Political Power and American Foreign Policy* (New York: Simon & Schuster, 1989); Paul Findley, *They Dare to Speak Out: People and Institutions Confront Israel's Lobby* (Westport, CT: Lawrence Hill, 1985); Dov S. Zakheim, *Flight of the Lavi: Inside a U.S.-Israeli Crisis* (Washington: Brassey's, 1996).

86. Nicholas Laham, *Selling AWACS to Saudi Arabia* (Westport, CT: Praeger, 2002).

87. See Bernard Reich, "The United States and Israel: The Nature of a Special Relationship," in David W. Lesch, ed., *The Middle East and the United States: A Historical and Political Reassessment* (Boulder, CO: Westview, 1996), pp. 249–250.

88. Organski, *The $36 Billion Bargain*, chaps. 1, 5.

89. Scott Lasensky, "Paying for Peace: The Oslo Process and the Limits of American Foreign Aid," *Middle East Journal*, Spring 2004, pp. 210–235.

90. "Israel's Fence Mixes Security and Politics," *Washington Post*, September 23, 2003.

91. "Israel's Fence."

92. "Israel Urged to Reach Accord with PA to Reduce Damage from Premature US Pullout," *Yediot Aharonot*, FBIS, November 17, 2003, FBIS; in Hebrew.

93. "Former Israeli Security Chiefs: War of Catastrophe," *Washington Post*, November 14, 2003; "Israeli Army Engaged in Fight Over Its Soul," *Washington Post*, November 18, 2003.

94. "Yishai: 'Greater Israel' Outdated," *Jerusalem Post*, February 15, 2006.

95. Cleaning up government corruption and improper functioning is at the top, with a weighted grade of 31.5 (out of 100). After that come rehabilitating the IDF and Israel's deterrent capability (22.1), closing the economic gaps (20.1), countering violence and crime (15.4), and achieving a peace agreement with the Palestinians (10.8). "Peace Index/Corruption Hits Top Spot," *Haaretz*, February 8, 2007.

96. Alain Gresh, "Turkish-Israeli-Syrian Relations and Their Impact on the Middle East," *Middle East Journal*, Spring 1998, pp. 190–192.

97. Lee Hockstader, "Turkey, Israel Forge Deeper Strategic Alliance," *Washington Post*, December 23, 1997, p. 11.

98. Dietrich Jung and Wolfang Piccoli, "The Turkish-Israeli Alignment: Paranoia or Pragmatism?" *Security Dialog*, March 2000, pp. 96–97. As Turkey improves its human rights record and its relations with Greece, which are both AKP policy objectives, this advantage lessens.

99. The seminal work on the Israeli nuclear weapons program is Avner Cohen, *Israel and the Bomb* (New York: Columbia University Press, 1998). Cohen, an Israeli citizen, and other Israelis have been investigated and sometimes imprisoned for discussing Israeli nuclear programs. Aluf Benn, "Censoring the Past," *Bulletin of the Atomic Scientists*, July-August 2001, pp. 17–20.

100. The Israeli government released Vanunu in 2004, but he is forbidden to leave the country or talk to reporters.

101. "If Pushed to the Wall, Israel Could Fire Nukes," *Toronto Star*, September 15, 2002.

102. For details, see Zeev Moaz, "The Mixed Blessing of Israel's Nuclear Policy," *International Security*, Fall 2003, pp. 44–77; Maoz, *Defending the Holy Land*, chap. 8.

103. Lawrence Scheinmann, "Politics and Pragmatism: The Challenges for NPT 2000," *Arms Control Today*, April 2000, pp. 18–23.

104. "Background: Would Israel Ever Give up the Bomb?" *Haaretz*, December 26, 2003. Libya later abandoned its nuclear program, and Iran now restricts nuclear inspections.

CHAPTER 15: JORDAN

1. Not all Circassians reached Jordan this way; others came because of Russian discrimination against them.

2. See Chapter 5 for a discussion of Sheik Wahhabi and his influence on modern Saudi Arabia.

3. For various reasons, Abdullah considered Talal, his younger son Nayif, his grandnephew Faisal II of Iraq, and his grandson Hussein. See Robert B. Satloff, *From Abdullah to Hussein: Jordan in Transition* (New York: Oxford University Press, 1994), chap. 1.

4. Satloff, *From Abdullah to Hussein*, chap. 3.

5. Satloff, *From Abdullah to Hussein*, chaps. 5–6.

6. Uriel Dann, *King Hussein and the Challenge of Arab Radicalism, Jordan, 1955–1967* (New York: Oxford University Press, 1989), chap. 3.

7. Dann, *King Hussein*, chap. 4.

8. Dann, *King Hussein*, p. 102.

9. Philip Robins, *A History of Jordan* (Cambridge: Cambridge University Press, 2004), pp. 120–124.

10. Adam Garfinkle, "U.S. Decision Making in the Jordan Crisis: Correcting the Record," *Political Science Quarterly*, Spring 1985, pp. 122–123.

11. Robins, *History of Jordan*, p. 135.

12. According to the Jordanian constitution, the king must not be out of the country for more than three months at a time. Thus King Hussein had to periodically visit the Jordanian embassy in Washington, DC (technically Jordanian territory) to retain the Crown.

13. Jordan is full of stories about sightings of King Hussein, who loved to travel around the country and meet people, sometimes in disguise so that he could get an accurate portrayal of issues and problems. Almost all Jordanians report sightings of the late king, including one military officer who did not notice the motorcyclist next to him at a stoplight until

the rider briefly pulled up the helmet face shield and smiled at him, then roared off before the officer could salute his ruler.

14. "Pressure Builds Under Jordan's King," *Washington Post*, February 5, 2003.

15. King Hussein was married four times; in 1955 to a distant Egyptian cousin he divorced in 1956; in 1961 to a British woman, Antoinette Gardiner (the mother of King Abdullah II), whom he divorced in 1972; in 1972 to Queen Alia, a Jordanian, who died in a 1977 helicopter accident; and in 1978 to Lisa Halaby, an American, who took the name "Noor" after her marriage.

16. Glenn E. Robinson, "Defensive Democratization in Jordan," *International Journal of Middle East Studies*, August 1998, pp. 387–410.

17. Glenn E. Robinson, "Can Islamists Be Democrats? The Case of Jordan," *Middle East Journal*, Summer 1997, pp. 268–269.

18. Political Islamists won thirty-four seats in total, giving them the biggest single bloc in the Majlis al-Nuwaab.

19. Robinson, "Defensive Democratization," pp. 401–404.

20. *Economist*, November 8, 1997, p. 52.

21. "Tiff Among Islamists Is a Storm in a Teacup," *Jordan Star*, October 15, 1998.

22. "Shihan Rules Out Muslim Brotherhood Extremism in Jordan," Amman *Shihan*, December 13–19, 1997, p. 11, FBIS-NES–97–350, December 16, 1997; in Arabic.

23. "Centrists Capture Veteran's Seats on Brotherhood Shura Council," *Jordan Times*, July 14, 1998.

24. Jillian Schwedler, *Faith in Moderation: Islamist Parties in Jordan and Yemen* (Cambridge: Cambridge University Press, 2006), esp. pp. 204–205.

25. Yitzhak Reiter, "The Palestinian-Transjordanian Rift: Economic Might and Political Power in Jordan," *Middle East Journal*, Winter 2004, pp. 72–92.

26. "New Government Needs More Than a Few New Faces," *Jordan Star*, August 20, 1998.

27. "Jordan's Prime Minister Resigns," *Washington Post*, January 14, 2002.

28. Ellen M. Lust-Okar, "The Decline of Jordanian Political Parties: Myth or Reality?" *International Journal of Middle East Studies*, November 2001, p. 555.

29. "Political Islam's Opportunity in Jordan," *Washington Post*, April 13, 2006.

30. Abdo Baaklini, Guilain Denoeux, and Robert Springborg, *Legislative Politics in the Arab World* (Boulder, CO: Lynne Rienner, 1999), p. 151.

31. Baaklini, Denoeux, and Springborg, *Legislative Politics*, pp. 152–164.

32. "King's Allies Set to Sweep Jordan Polls," *Washington Post*, June 18, 2003.

33. Baaklini, Denoeux, and Springborg, *Legislative Politics*, pp. 164–167.

34. "Deputies Refer Press and Publications Draft to National Guidance Committee," *Jordan Times*, June 22, 1998, p. 1.

35. Quintan Wiktorowicz, "Civil Society as Social Control: State Power in Jordan" (paper presented at the meeting of the American Political Science Association, Boston, MA, September 3–6, 1998), p. 4.

36. Quintan Wiktorowicz, "The Limits of Democracy in the Middle East: The Case of Jordan," *Middle East Journal*, Autumn 1999, pp. 609–610.

37. Wiktorowicz, "Limits of Democracy," p. 9.

38. Stefanie Eileen Nanes, "Fighting Honor Crimes: Evidence of Civil Society in Jordan," *Middle East Journal*, Winter 2003, pp. 112–130.

39. "Experts Discuss Civil Society Integration," *Jordan Times*, March 14, 2007.

40. Mahmood Monshipouri, *Islamism, Secularism, and Human Rights in the Middle East* (Boulder, CO: Lynne Rienner, 1998), p. 80.

41. The following discussion draws heavily from Sherry R. Lowrance, "After Beijing: Political Liberalization and the Women's Movement in Jordan," *Middle Eastern Studies*, July 1998, pp. 83–102.

42. See the Jordanian National Committee for Women, www.nic.gov.jo/jncw/jncw_index.html.

43. Wiktorowicz, "Limits of Democracy," p. 610.

44. *Jordan Times*, February 8, 1998.

45. Janine Astrid Clark and Jillian Schwedler, "Who Opened the Window? Women's Activism in Islamist Parties," *Comparative Politics*, April 2003, pp. 293–312, esp. p. 301.

46. Interview, Amman, March 1999.

47. "Female Circumcision Still Haunts Jordanian Tribe in Southern Jordan," *Jordan Times*, August 13, 1999.

48. Robins, *History of Jordan*, p. 145.

49. Laurie A. Brand, *Palestinians in the Arab World: Institution Building and the Search for a State* (New York: Columbia University Press, 1988), p. 157.

50. Brand, *Palestinians in the Arab World*, p. 157.

51. The king dismissed Finance Minister Rifai in late April and promised to hold elections. See Riad al Khouri, "The Political Economy of Jordan: Democratization and the Gulf Crisis," in Dan Tschirgi, ed., *The Arab World Today* (Boulder, CO: Lynne Rienner, 1994), p. 105.

52. Interview, US embassy, Amman, March 1999.

53. "Building a Safe Haven," *Middle East Economic Digest*, July 22–28, 2005, p. 25.

54. Stephen Glain, "Jordan: The Consequences of Peace," *Survival*, Spring 2003, p. 173.

55. "Tensions Ease in Jordan-Israel Water Dispute, Officials Say," *Jordan Times*, April 7, 1999.

56. "Lack of Long-Term Solutions to Water Problem Will Lead to Catastrophe," *Jordan Times*, August 23, 1999.

57. Interview, US embassy, Amman, March 1999.

58. Author's observations, 2001.

59. Marc Lynch, "Jordan's Identity and Interests," in Shibley Telhami and Michael Barnett, eds., *Identity and Foreign Policy in the Middle East* (Ithaca, NY: Cornell University Press, 2002), pp. 26–57.

60. Laurie A. Brand, *Jordan's Inter-Arab Relations: The Political Economy of Alliance Making* (New York: Columbia University Press, 1994).

61. *Jordan Times*, January 5, 1998.

62. "Jordan's King Says Islam Must Embrace the U.S.'s New Way of Doing Business," *Wall Street Journal*, January 2, 2002.

63. The 1994 peace accord between Jordan and Israel allows Israel to extract 12 million cubic meters (mcm) of water from the Yarmouk River in the summer, reserving the remainder for Jordan. In the winter Israel extracts 33 mcm from the Yarmouk, storing 20 mcm in Lake Tiberias for Jordan to use over the summer. In 1997, both Jordan and Israel agreed to desalinate water from the Jordan River, and, pending completion of the plant, Israel agreed to supply Jordan with 25 mcm per year from Lake Tiberias.

64. The details of the treaty negotiations are in Abdul Salam Majali, Jawad A. Anani, and Munther J. Haddadin, *Peacemaking: The Inside Story of the 1994 Jordanian-Israeli Treaty* (Norman: University of Oklahoma Press, 2006).

65. "Jordan Sees an Opening for a Mideast Peace," *Los Angeles Times*, November 16, 2004.

CHAPTER 16: PALESTINE

1. "Painful Glimpse of Home for Palestinians," *New York Times*, May 30, 2000.

2. "United They Stand?" *al-Ahram*, December 17–23, 1998.

3. See "The Forgotten Arabs of Gallipoli," *al-Jazeera*, January 16, 2004; "Days of the Locusts," *Haaretz*, April 15, 2004.

4. Laurie A. Brand, *Palestinians in the Arab World: Institution Building and the Search for a State* (New York: Columbia University Press, 1988), pp. 115–122.

5. See Helena Cobban, *The Palestinian Liberation Organization* (Cambridge: Cambridge University Press, 1984), esp. chaps. 1–3.

6. Shaul Mishal, *The PLO Under Arafat: Between Gun and Olive Branch* (New Haven, CT: Yale University Press, 1986), pp. 7–8.

7. Cobban, *Palestinian Liberation Organization*, p. 13. For an incisive analysis of the impact of the battle of Karameh on Palestinian nationalism, see W. Andrew Terrill, "The Political Mythology of the Battle of Karameh," *Middle East Journal*, Winter 2001, pp. 91–111.

8. Itamar Rabinovich, *The War for Lebanon: 1970–1983* (Ithaca, NY: Cornell University Press, 1984), p. 40.

9. Cobban, *Palestinian Liberation Organization*, p. 47.

10. Interview with the author and others, Riyadh, Saudi Arabia, January 1989. He claimed that the United States "owed him" for numerous PLO actions, including saving Secretary of State Henry Kissinger's life by warning of a terrorist with a missile aimed at Kissinger's plane as it approached the Beirut airport. He also claimed that PLO warnings saved many American lives when the US embassy was bombed in Beirut in 1982. It is difficult to independently confirm these claims.

11. "Israel to Build 600 Homes in 3 Settlements, U.S. Officials Are Critical," *New York Times*, October 3, 2003.

12. Alan Dowty, "Impact of the Aqsa Intifadah on Possible Resolution of the Israeli-Palestinian Conflict" (paper presented to the International Studies Association Conference, Budapest, Hungary, June 2003), p. 7.

13. Judith Miller, "Arafat Was the Symbol of His People's Longing for Identity," *New York Times*, November 11, 2004.

14. "Abbas Wins Palestinian Vote by Strong Margin," *New York Times*, January 10, 2005; "Abbas Wins Election," *al-Jazeera*, January 9, 2005.

15. Interview with Palestinian official, Tel Aviv, Israel, March 2006.

16. "In the West Bank, Hamas Is Silent but Never Ignored," *New York Times*, June 28, 2007.

17. Khalil Shikaki, "Peace Now or Hamas Later," *Foreign Affairs*, July-August 1998, p. 30.

18. Shikaki, "Peace Now," pp. 31–32.

19. Results from a poll conducted by the Center for Palestinian Studies and Studies, reported in Shikaki, "Peace Now," p. 33.

20. Interview, Tel Aviv, March 1997.

21. Khalil Shikaki, "Palestinians Divided," *Foreign Affairs*, January-March 2002, p. 92.

22. "Jihadist Groups Fill a Palestinian Power Vaccuum," *New York Times*, May 31, 2007.

23. See Ziad Abu-Amr, "Sheik Ahmad Yasin and the Origins of Hamas," in R. Scott Appleby, ed., *Spokesmen for the Despised* (Chicago: University of Chicago Press, 1997), pp. 225–256.

24. David Remnick, "The Dreamer," *New Yorker*, January 7, 2002, p. 58.

25. "As Arafat Embraces Revolt, His Sagging Popularity Rises," *New York Times*, December 8, 2000.

26. "A New Mideast Battle: Arafat vs. Hamas," *New York Times*, December 6, 2001.

27. "In Chaos, Palestinians Struggle for a Way Out," *New York Times*, July 15, 2004.

28. "Arafat Names New Ministers," *Jerusalem Post*, August 6, 1998.

29. "Two Quit PA Cabinet over Corruption," *Jerusalem Post*, August 7, 1998.

30. "Arafat, Abbas Agree on New Palestinian Council," *Washington Post*, April 23, 2003.

31. "Abbas Steps Down, Dealing Big Blow to U.S. Peace Plan," *New York Times*, September 6, 2003.

32. "Arafat Taps Legislator as Premier," *Washington Post*, September 8, 2003.

33. "Emerging Question: If Not Arafat, Who?" *Washington Post*, December 20, 2001.

34. "Arafat Names New Cabinet and Declares an Emergency," *New York Times*, October 6, 2003.

35. Yezid Sayigh, "Arafat and the Anatomy of a Revolt," *Survival*, Autumn 2001, p. 47.

36. Sayigh, "Arafat," pp. 51–52. See also Ron Pundak, "From Oslo to Taba: What Went Wrong," *Survival*, Autumn 2001, p. 35.

37. "State for Palestinians and Peace with Israel Left Unrealized," *New York Times*, November 11, 2004.

38. Interview, Jerusalem, March 2006.

39. "Hamas Clears Way for Unity Government," *New York Times*, February 15, 2007.

40. "PA Police Break into Parliament, Firing into Air," *Haaretz*, October 3, 2005.

41. "C.I.A. Teaching Palestinian Police the Tricks of the Trade," *New York Times*, March 5, 1998, p. 1.

42. "Israel, Arafat Have Enemy in Common," *Washington Post*, June 11, 1998, p. A25.

43. "Early Warning," *Economist*, October 31, 1998, p. 48. A fourteen-year-old boy was killed in the attack.

44. For more on women's participation in the intifadah, see Nahla Abdo, "Women and the Intifadah: Gender, Class, and National Liberation," *Race and Class* 34 (1991): 19–34; Joost Hiltermann, *Behind the Intifadah: Labor and Women's Movement in the Occupied Territories* (Princeton, NJ: Princeton University Press, 1991); Adrien Katherine, "Custom, Religion, and Rights: The Future Legal Status of Palestinian Women," *Harvard International Law Journal*, Winter 1994; Julie Peteet, *Gender in Crisis: Women and the Palestinian Movement* (New York: Columbia University Press, 1991); and Rosemary Sayigh, "Encounters with Palestinian Women Under Occupation," *Journal of Palestinian Studies*, Summer 1981, pp. 3–26.

45. "Palestinian Women Throw off their Veils," *Economist*, April 4, 1998, p. 52.

46. "Palestinian Women," p. 52.

47. "Reformers for Women's Rights run into Palestinian Roadblock," *Calgary Herald*, August 8, 1998.

48. "Reformers for Women's Rights."

49. Amal Jamal, "Engendering State-Building: The Women's Movement and Gender-Regime in Palestine," *Middle East Journal*, Spring 2001, p. 261.

50. "Women, Secret Hamas Strength, Win Votes at Polls and New Role," *New York Times*, February 3, 2006.

51. "Gaza Adding More Children." The worldwide average and the Israeli average is 2.7 children per woman.

52. Salem Ajluni, "The Palestinian Economy and the Second Intifada," *Journal of Palestinian Studies*, Spring 2003, p. 68.

53. "Report: Intifada Cost Israel $12b," *Jerusalem Post*, November 14, 2004.

54. Sara Roy, "De-Development Revisited: Palestinian Economy and Society Since Oslo," *Journal of Palestinian Studies*, Spring 1999, p. 76.

55. Sara Roy, *The Gaza Strip: The Political Economy of De-development* (Washington, DC: Institute for Palestinian Studies, 1995), chap. 5.

56. "For Gaza, Peace Just Means More Poverty," *International Herald Tribune*, September 16, 1998, p. 2.

57. Roy, "De-Development Revisited," pp. 64–65.

58. Roy, "De-Development Revisited," p. 70.

59. "Gaza Adding Children at an Unrivaled Rate," *New York Times*, February 24, 2000.

60. Ilan Halevi, "Self-Government, Democracy, and Mismanagement Under the Palestinian Authority," *Journal of Palestine Studies*, Spring 1998, pp. 35–48.

61. "Arafat Hails Big Gas Find off the Coast of Gaza Strip," *New York Times*, September 28, 2000.

62. "Donors Pledge $3 billion to Palestinians," *Washington Post*, December 1, 1998, p. A14.

63. "Gulf Arab States Prepare a Bailout to Assist Arafat," *New York Times*, March 20, 2001.

64. "Arafat as Executioner," *Haaretz*, September 1, 1998.

65. "When Demography Affects Destiny," *Washington Post*, national weekly ed., August 24, 1998, pp. 14–15.

SECTION IV: THE COUNTRIES OF NORTH AFRICA

1. Governor Ubayd had ordered the slaughter of pregnant sheep so that he could send the soft wool pelts of unborn lambs to the Ummayyid Caliph. He also included Berber girls taken into slavery (even though they were Muslim) with those shipments. See Khalid Yahya Blankinship, *The End of the Jihad State* (Albany: State University of New York Press, 1994), pp. 204–208.

2. "France: Arab Maghreb Union Summit in Algiers Postponed Indefinitely," *Paris Le Monde*, December 24, 2003.

CHAPTER 17: TUNISIA

1. The French had been in Algeria since 1830. There is a long history of Algerians crossing into Tunisia seeking religious or political refuge. See Julia A. Clancy-Smith, *Rebel and Saint: Muslim Notables, Populist Protest, Colonial Encounters, Algeria and Tunisia, 1800–1904* (Berkeley: University of California Press, 1994), chap. 5.

2. Dwight Ling, *Tunisia: From Protectorate to Republic* (Bloomington: Indiana University Press, 1967), p. 1.

3. Kenneth J. Perkins, *A History of Modern Tunisia* (Cambridge: Cambridge University Press, 2004), p. 56.

4. Lisa Anderson, *The State and Social Transformation in Tunisia and Libya, 1830–1980* (Princeton, NJ: Princeton University Press, 1986), pp. 158–171.

5. Ling, *Tunisia*, p. 122.

6. Ling, *Tunisia*, pp. 146–147.

7. L. Carl Brown, "Bourguiba and Burguibism Revisited: Reflections and Interpretation," *Middle East Journal*, Winter 2001, pp. 44–57, esp. p. 55.

8. Stephen J. King, "Economic Reform and Tunisia's Hegemonic Party: The End of an Administrative Elite," *Arab Studies Quarterly*, Spring 1998, p. 3.

9. Anderson, *State and Social Transformation*, pp. 232–233.

10. Clement Henry Moore, *Tunisia Since Independence: The Dynamics of One-Party Government* (Berkeley: University of California Press, 1965), pp. 71–73.

11. Moore, *Tunisia Since Independence*, pp. 80–81.

12. King, "Economic Reform," p. 8.

13. Leon Carl Brown, "The Role of Islam in Modern North Africa," in Leon Carl Brown, ed., *State and Society in Independent North Africa* (Washington, DC: Middle East Institute, 1966), pp. 115–116.

14. John L. Esposito and John O. Voll, *Makers of Contemporary Islam* (New York: Oxford University Press, 2001), chap. 5.

15. King, "Economic Reform," p. 10.

16. L. B. Ware, "Ben Ali's Constitutional Coup in Tunisia," *Middle East Journal*, Autumn 1988, pp. 588–589.

17. Susan E. Waltz, *Human Rights and Reform: Changing the Face of North African Politics* (Berkeley: University of California Press, 1995), chap. 4.

18. "Tunisian Parliament Approves Election Changes," Tunisian Republic Radio, June 29, 1999, FBIS; in Arabic.

19. See Christopher Alexander, "State, Labor, and the New Global Economy in Tunisia," in Dirk Vandewalle, ed., *North Africa: Development and Reform in a Changing Global Economy* (New York: St. Martin's, 1996), pp. 177–202; Christopher Alexander, "Opportunities, Organizations, and Ideas: Islamists and Workers in Tunisia and Algeria," *International Journal of Middle East Studies*, November 2000, pp. 466–490.

20. Waltz, *Human Rights*, p. 71.

21. For more on these groups, see Douglas K. Magnuson, "Islamic Reform in Contemporary Tunisia: Unity and Diversity," in I. William Zartman, ed., *Tunisia: The Political Economy of Reform* (Boulder, CO: Lynne Rienner, 1991), pp. 169–192.

22. "Recent Events Producing Wear and Tear on Ben Ali Administration," *Paris L'Express*, June 8–14, 2000, FBIS; in French.

23. "En-Nahda Member Chair Reportedly Released," *al-Hayah*, August 31, 2000, FBIS; in Arabic.

24. Article 12 of the Tunisian constitution stipulates the presumption of innocence until establishment of guilt, departing from the French practice of presumption of guilt upon arrest. The accused has the right to be present at trial and to be represented by counsel. Both the accused and the prosecutor may appeal verdicts.

25. Perkins, *History of Modern Tunisia*, p. 135.

26. Waltz, *Human Rights*, pp. 175–176.

27. Waltz, *Human Rights*, p. 179.

28. Waltz, *Human Rights*, p. 183.

29. Deutsche Presse-Agentur, November 3, 1998.

30. Deutsche Presse-Agentur, November 3, 1998.

31. Country Reports on Human Rights Practices Released by the Bureau of Democracy, Human Rights, and Labor, March 8, 2006, www.state.gov/g/drl/rls/hrrpt/2005/61700.htm.

32. www.state.gov/g/drl/rls/hrrpt/2005/61700.htm.

33. "Tunisia's Tangled Web Is Sticking Point for Reform," *New York Times*, June 25, 2004.

34. Moore, *Tunisia Since Independence*, pp. 51–56.

35. Charles A. Micaud, with Leon Carl Brown and Clement Henry Moore, *Tunisia: The Politics of Modernization* (New York: Praeger, 1964), p. 145.

36. Mahmood Monshipouri, *Islam, Secularism, and Human Rights in the Middle East* (Boulder, CO: Lynne Rienner, 1998), p. 80.

37. "A Hundred Years of Fortitude," *Economist*, November 27, 1999, p. 43.

38. "Tunisia's Emerging Democracy," *Christian Science Monitor*, October 27, 1999.

39. For Bourguiba's thoughts on the role of women in society, see an address he gave in 1962, reprinted as "A New Role for Women," in Benjamin Rivlin and Joseph S. Szyliowicz, eds., *The Contemporary Middle East: Tradition and Innovation* (New York: Random House, 1965), pp. 352–355.

40. "Tunisia: Weekly Bulletin," *Africa News*, August 19, 1998.

41. *Tunisia Country Report on Human Rights Practices for 1997*, p. 11.

42. The 1950s figures are from Ghazi Duwaji, *Economic Development in Tunisia* (New York: Praeger, 1967), p. 24.

43. See Perkins, *Tunisia*, chap. 10, for details about the economy since 1956.

44. Eva Bellin, "Tunisian Industrialists and the State," in Zartman, ed., *Tunisia*, pp. 47–49.

45. Richard B. Parker, *North Africa: Regional Tensions and Strategic Concerns*, rev. and updated ed. (Westport, CT: Praeger, 1987), pp. 55–56.

46. Bellin, "Tunisian Industrialists," pp. 50–51.

47. For an incisive analysis of Ben Ali's reforms, see Emma C. Murphy, *Economic and Political Change in Tunisia: From Bourguiba to Ben Ali* (New York: St. Martin's, 1999), chaps. 6–8.

48. "Privatization Inspires Foreign Investments in Tunisia," *Corporate Location*, September 2000, p. 5.

49. "Africa's Model Economy," *Middle East*, July 2003, p. 33.

50. "Tunisia Shrugs off 9/11 Blues to Revive Tourism," *Gulf News*, February 10, 2007.

51. *La Presse*, December 15, 1998.

52. *La Presse*, December 15, 1998.

53. Mary-Jane Deeb and Ellen Laipson, "Tunisian Foreign Policy: Continuity and Change under Bourguiba and Ben Ali," in Zartman, ed., *Tunisia*, pp. 222–223.

54. Deeb and Laipson, "Tunisian Foreign Policy," pp. 223–224.

55. "North Africa Feared as Staging Ground for Terror," *New York Times*, February 20, 2007.

CHAPTER 18: LIBYA

1. Lisa Anderson, *The State and Social Transformation in Tunisia and Libya, 1830–1980* (Princeton, NJ: Princeton University Press, 1986), pp. 104–109.

2. The Sanusi Order was founded in the nineteenth century by Muhammad bin Ali as-Sanusi, who, like numerous other Islamist reformers, believed that Islamic leaders had led Islam away from its puritanical roots.

3. Ray Takeyh, "Qadhafi and the Challenge of Militant Islam," *Washington Quarterly*, Summer 1998, p. 162.

4. Dirk Vandewalle, *A History of Modern Libya* (Cambridge: Cambridge University Press, 2006), pp. 98–99.

5. Lisa Anderson, "Tribe and State: Libyan Anomalies," in Philip S. Khoury and Joseph Kostiner, eds., *Tribe and State Formation in the Middle East* (Berkeley: University of California Press, 1990), p. 297.

6. Anderson, "Tribe and State," p. 297.

7. After President Ronald Reagan's death in June 2004, Qadhafi remarked that he regretted Reagan died before he could be put on trial for murder.

8. "Middle East Split over Attack Reaction," *London Times*, September 13, 2001.

9. "Libyan Leader, in Europe, Makes His Case for Peace," *New York Times*, April 28, 2004.

10. Vandewalle, *History of Modern Libya*, p. 103.

11. John L. Esposito, *The Islamic Threat: Myth or Reality?* (New York: Oxford University Press, 1995), p. 83.

12. Esposito, *Islamic Threat*, pp. 81–82.

13. Esposito, *Islamic Threat*, p. 85.

14. Yahia Zoubir called this point to my attention.

15. Ray Takeyh, "The Rogue Who Came In from the Cold," *Foreign Affairs*, May-June 2001, pp. 64–65.

16. "Qaddafi's Modern-Sounding Son Is a Riddle to the West," *News York Times*, December 14, 2004.

17. Amnesty International, *AI Report 1999: Libya*.

18. "Libya: Time to Make Human Rights a Reality," Amnesty International press release, July 19, 2004.

19. "Libyan Journalist Possibly Killed by State Security," *Afrol News,* June 15, 2005.

20. "Libyan Court Orders Retrial in H.I.V. Case," *New York Times*, December 25, 2005.

21. "Militant Islamic Group Attacks Regime, Calls for Popular Uprising," *London al-Hayah*, June 11, 2000, FBIS; in Arabic.

22. This discussion of opposition groups draws on Mary-Jane Deeb, "Political and Economic Developments in Libya in the 1990s," in Yahia H. Zoubir, ed., *North Africa in Transition: State, Society, and Economic Transformation in the 1990s* (Gainesville: University Press of Florida, 1999), pp. 77–92.

23. Takeyh, *Qadhafi*, p. 168.

24. "Committee on Rights of Child Continues Consideration of Report Presented by the Libyan Arab Jamahiriya," United Nations press release, January 8, 1998.

25. "Committee on Rights of Child."

26. Delinda C. Hanley, "Women's Rights and Social Affairs Programs Vital to Libya's Progress," *Washington Report on Middle East Affairs*, March 2001, pp. 66–68.

27. *Libya: A Country Study* (Federal Research Division, Library of Congress, 1987), pp. 123–124.

28. Dirk Vandewalle, "The Libyan Jamahiriyya: Economic Liberalization in a Rentier State," in Azzedine Layachi, ed., *Economic Crisis and Political Change in North Africa* (Westport, CT: Praeger, 1998), p. 130.

29. Vandewalle, *History of Modern Libya*, p. 68.

30. Vandewalle, *History of Modern Libya*, p. 136.

31. For a discussion of US sanctions against Libya, see Meghan L. O'Sullivan, *Shrewd Sanctions: Statecraft and State Sponsors of Terrorism* (Washington, DC: Brookings Institution, 2003), chap. 5.

32. For an analysis of the impact of sanctions on Libya, see Tim Niblock, *"Pariah States" and Sanctions in the Middle East: Iraq, Libya, Sudan* (Boulder, CO: Lynne Rienner, 2001), chap. 8.

33. Takeyh, *Qadhafi*, p. 163.

34. "Libya Needs Economic Reform, IMF," *Afrol News*, March 22, 2005.

35. "Deal Clears Way for U.N. to Lift Libya Sanctions," *New York Times*, September 11, 2003.

36. "Libya Soon to Become a Huge Construction Hub Where Hundreds of Hotels Built, Roads Constructed, Office Buildings to Rise Up," *Tripoli Post*, March 6, 2007.

37. Gamal Nkrumah, "Tapping the Global Economy," *al-Ahram*, December 14–20, 2000.

38. Nkrumah, "Tapping the Global Economy."

39. Tarik M. Yousef, "The Effect of Sanctions on the Libyan Economy," *Policy Briefs: US Sanctions on Iran and Libya: What Have We Learned?* (Middle East Institute, 2001), pp. 3–7.

40. Vandewalle, "Libyan Jamahiriyya," pp. 129–131.

41. It is widely believed in most Shiite communities that Musa al-Sadr was murdered in Libya, though rumors sometimes place him in the desert praying, or in Italy, Amsterdam, or Syria. Libya claimed that officials put him on a flight to Rome after his visit to Qadhafi. See Fouad Ajami, *The Vanished Imam: Musa al Sadr and the Shia of Lebanon* (Ithaca, NY: Cornell University Press, 1986), chap. 5.

42. "Seeing a Plot, Saudis Recall Ambassador from Libya," *New York Times*, December 23, 2004.

43. See Kenneth M. Pollack, *Arabs at War* (Lincoln: University of Nebraska Press, 2002), chap. 4.

44. Ronald Bruce St. John, "Libyan Foreign Policy: Newfound Flexibility," *Orbis*, Summer 2003, pp. 463–478.

45. See Thomas C. Wiegele, *The Clandestine Building of Libya's Chemical Weapons Factory* (Carbondale: Southern Illinois University Press, 1992), for evidence of Libya's chemical weapons program.

46. Interview, Washington, DC, March 1991.

47. "CIA Can't Stop Libyan Chemical Weapons Plant," Reuters World Service, March 24, 1996.

48. "CIA Can't Stop Libyan Chemical Weapons Plant."

49. "German Intelligence Confirms Plans for Libyan Chemical Weapons," Deutsche Presse-Agentur, February 26, 1996.

50. "Libyan-Egyptian Summit Expected in Cairo," Deutsche Presse-Agentur, May 23, 1996.

51. "U.S. Concerned About Libyan Chemical Weapons Program," Associated Press, December 2, 1997.

52. "German Suspected of Libyan Chemical Weapons Connection," Radio Beirut, October 15, 1996; in Arabic.

53. "Atomic Agency to Make Nuclear Verification Visit to Libya," *New York Times*, December 22, 2003.

54. Wyn Q. Bowen, *Libya and Nuclear Proliferation: Stepping Back from the Brink,* Adelphi Paper 380, International Institute for Strategic Studies (New York: Routledge, 2006).

CHAPTER 19: MOROCCO

1. For details of the French military occupation of Morocco, see Moshe Gershovich, *French Military Rule of Morocco: Colonialism and Its Consequences* (Portland, OR: Frank Cass, 2000).

2. Douglas E. Ashford, *Political Change in Morocco* (Princeton, NJ: Princeton University Press, 1961), p. 28.

3. Dale F. Eickelman, *Moroccan Islam: Tradition and Society in a Pilgrimage Center* (Austin: University of Texas Press, 1976), p. 236.

4. For a discussion of one particular battle in this period, see Moshe Gershovich, "The Ait Ya'qub Incident and the Crisis of French Military Policy in Morocco," *Journal of Military History*, January 1998, pp. 57–73.

5. Ashford, *Political Change in Morocco*, p. 57.

6. Ashford, *Political Change in Morocco*, p. 79.

7. For details of the French deliberations on Moroccan independence, see Stephane Bernard, *The Franco-Moroccan Conflict, 1943–1956* (New Haven, CT: Yale University Press, 1968).

8. Ashford, *Political Change in Morocco*, pp. 94–95.

9. John Waterbury, *The Commander of the Faithful: The Moroccan Political Elite—A Study in Segmented Politics* (New York: Columbia University Press, 1970), pp. 146–147.

10. The Alawite dynasty's claim of decadency to the Prophet Muhammad's family is not widely recognized outside of Morocco. Note that the name "Alawi" comes from a family name and is not to be confused with the Alawi religious branch.

11. Abdellah Hammoudi, *Master and Disciple: The Cultural Foundations of Moroccan Authoritarianism* (Chicago: University of Chicago Press, 1997), p. 16.

12. Octave Morais, "The Political Evolution of the Berbers in Independent Morocco," in Ernest Gellner and Charles Micaud, eds., *Arabs and Berbers: From Tribe to Nation in North Africa* (Lexington, MA: Lexington Books, 1972), p. 278.

13. Morais, "Political Evolution," p. 281.

14. It has been revealed that the United States stored nuclear weapons at these bases without French knowledge or permission in the 1950s and 1960s. See Robert S. Norris and William M. Arkin, "Where They Were," *Bulletin of Atomic Scientists*, November-December 1999, p. 66.

15. The royal Boeing 727, flying in from France, was intercepted by four Moroccan fighter planes that repeatedly strafed the transport. The pilot, a Moroccan air force officer, falsely called out over his radio to the fighter pilots that they had killed the king, and thus there was no reason to down the 727. The fighter pilots landed at their air base, but their commander immediately ordered them into the sky once again, this time under strict instructions to down the 727. The crippled 727, with only two of its three engines still running, was just about to land when the fighters again attacked it, but the king and the plane made it safely to the ground. The next day the vice chief of the Royal Moroccan Air Force was shot and killed by security forces while playing golf with the American air attaché. A number of Moroccan fighter pilots were either executed or imprisoned for long terms.

16. Hammoudi, *Master and Disciple*, p. 27.

17. Agence Europe, November 1999.

18. "Local Hands Accused in Morocco Blast," *Los Angeles Times*, May 19, 2003.

19. See Adbellah Hammoudi, *Master and Disciple: The Cultural Foundations of Moroccan Authoritarianism* (Chicago: University of Chicago Press, 1997), esp. chap. 2.

20. Rahma Bourqia, "The Cultural Legacy of Power in Morocco," in Rahma Bourqia and Susan Gilson Miller, eds., *In the Shadow of the Sultan: Culture, Power, and Politics in Morocco* (Cambridge, MA: Harvard University Press, 1999).

21. Azzedine Layachi, "Economic Reform and Elusive Political Change in Morocco," in Yahia H. Zoubir, ed., *North Africa in Transition: State, Society, and Economic Transformation in the 1990s* (Gainesville: University Press of Florida, 1999), p. 49.

22. Article 19 in the 1992 constitution.

23. "Finding Religion at the World Bank," *Washington Post*, April 17, 1998, p. A28.

24. Abdo Baaklini, Gulain Denoeux, and Robert Springborg, *Legislative Politics in the Arab World* (Boulder, CO: Lynne Rienner, 1999), pp. 115–116.

25. "Laensar Critical of Youssoufi Government," *London al-Wasat*, August 17, 1998, FBIS; in Arabic.

26. "Morocco: All Eyes on Islamists," *al-Ahram*, October 3–9, 2002.

27. "Results Trickle in for Morocco Polls," *al-Jazeera*, September 13, 2003.

28. Susan E. Waltz, *Human Rights and Reform: Changing the Face of North African Politics* (Berkeley: University of California Press, 1995), pp. 189–190.

29. Waltz, *Human Rights*, pp. 190–191.

30. "King Mohamed Risks the Release of Islamist Leader," *Middle East Economic Digest*, June 2, 2000, p. 27.

31. "Shooting the Messenger in Morocco," *Economist*, December 9, 2000, p. 52.

32. "Feud with King Tests Freedoms in Morocco," *Washington Post*, February 12, 2006.

33. Halima El-Glaoui, "Contributing to a Culture of Debate in Morocco," *Journal of Democracy*, January 1999, p. 159.

34. El-Glaoui, "Contributing to a Culture of Debate," p. 159.

35. "In His Father's Shadow," *Economist*, April 8, 2006.

36. "Morocco Jails Three Journalists," *al-Jazeera*, November 4, 2003.

37. Bruce Maddy-Weitzman, "Women, Islam, and the Moroccan State: The Struggle over the Personal Status Law," *Middle East Journal*, Summer 2005, pp. 404–406.

38. "Islam's Pioneering Women Priests," BBC News, February 25, 2007. Officially Islam does not grant the title "priest."

39. M. Laetitia Cairoli, "Garment Factory Workers in the City of Fez," *Middle East Journal*, Winter 1999, p. 30.

40. Marvine Howe, "Fresh Start for Morocco," *Middle East Policy*, June 2001, p. 65.

41. Muhammad al-Sharqi, "The Moroccan Prime Minister to al-Hayah: Best Economic Performance Achieved in 2006," *al-Hayat*, February 15, 2007.

42. Interview, US Embassy, Rabat, March 1999.

43. Interview, American Club, Rabat, March 1999.

44. Cairoli, "Garment Factory Workers," p. 41.

45. Gregory W. White, "The Mexico of Europe? Morocco's Partnership with the European Union," in Dirk Vandewalle, ed., *North Africa: Development and Reform in a Changing Global Economy* (New York: St. Martin's, 1996), pp. 111–128.

46. "US Approves Free Trade with Morocco," *al-Jazeera*, July 21, 2004.

47. Abdeslam M. Maghraoui, "Depoliticization in Morocco," in Larry Diamond, Marc F. Plattner, and Daniel Brumberg, eds., *Islam and Democracy in the Middle East* (Baltimore: Johns Hopkins University Press, 2003), pp. 68–70.

48. Cameron Khosrowshahi, "Privatization in Morocco: The Politics of Development," *Middle East Journal*, Spring 1997, pp. 242–255.

49. Khosrowshahi, "Privatization in Morocco," p. 245.

50. *Morocco News*, February 9, 1998.

51. Andrew Album, "Moroccan Banking Sector," *Middle East*, December 1998, p. 31.

52. Khosrowshahi, "Privatization in Morocco," pp. 253–254.

53. "Moroccan Upper House Rejects Draft Law on Privatization," *Rabat MAP*, January 13, 1999, FBIS.

54. "Plan Azur Forges Ahead," *Middle East*, December 2003, p. 40.

55. "The Oil Club's Newest Member," *Economist*, September 16, 2000, pp. 54–55.

56. The Lone Star Drilling Company had found only three months' supply by the summer of 2001. Howe, "Fresh Start for Morocco," p. 62.

57. Alan Petzet, "Lightly Drilled Morocco Gears Up for More Exploration," *Oil and Gas Journal*, November 13, 2000, pp. 34–35.

58. Gulain P. Denoeux, "Morocco's Economic Prospects: Daunting Challenges Ahead," *Middle East Policy*, June 2001, p. 84.

59. Interview, Rabat, March 2001.

60. Interview, Moroccan Foreign Ministry, Rabat, March 1999.

61. "Moroccan Funeral Sets Stage for Peace Talks," *Washington Post*, July 26, 1999.

62. Interview, Ministry of Foreign Affairs, Rabat, March 1999. Algeria denies the claim. Interview, Ministry of Foreign Affairs, March 2005.

63. See, for example, "GIA Reportedly Infiltrates Moroccan Territory," *Algiers Liberte*, April 23, 2000, FBIS; in French.

64. Damis, *Conflict in Northwest Africa*, p. 15.

65. Damis, *Conflict in Northwest Africa*, p. 22.

66. "Polisario Front" is a shortened version of Popular Front for the Liberation of Saquia El Hamra and Rio de Oro.

67. Bruce Maddy-Weitzman, "Conflict and Conflict Management in the Western Sahara: Is the Endgame Near?" *Middle East Journal*, Autumn 1991, p. 595.

68. Maddy-Weitzman, "Conflict," pp. 595–596.

69. William J. Durch, "Building on Sand: UN Peacekeeping in the Western Sahara," *International Security*, Spring 1993, pp. 151–171.

70. "Morocco: Former Polisario Official on Mauritanians in Referendum," *Rabat MAP*, April 20, 1998, FBIS.

71. This statement was made by Abbas el-Fassi, secretary-general of the Istiqlal Party. See "Morocco: Official Says Sahara to Remain Moroccan Despite Referendum," *Rabat MAP*, April 20, 1998, FBIS.

72. "Morocco: Moroccan Diplomat Decries UN Envoy's Pro-Polisario Meeting," *Rabat MAP*, April 17, 1998, FBIS.

73. "Morocco: Moroccan Diplomat: UN Should Settle Voter Identification," *Rabat MAP*, April 17, 1998, FBIS.

74. "Western Sahara: Algiers Radio Interviews Saharan President," Algiers Radio Algiers Network, April 16, 1998, FBIS.

75. "He Tried, Hard," *Economist*, November 14, 1998, p. 47.

76. "He Tried, Hard."

77. "Morocco, UN Sign Agreement on Sahara Settlement Plan," *Rabat MAP*, January 29, 1999, FBIS.

78. "It's a Mirage," *Economist*, January 22, 2000, p. 47.

79. "Algeria: Western Saharan-Moroccan Talks in London Fail," Algiers Radio Algiers Channel 1, May 15, 2000, FBIS; in Arabic.

80. Charles Dunbar, "Saharan Stasis: Status and Future Prospects of the Western Saharan Conflict," *Middle East Journal*, Fall 2000, p. 525.

81. Dunbar, "Saharan Stasis," p. 538; "Triumph for Procrastination," *Economist*, November 4, 2000, p. 52.

82. Howe, "Fresh Start for Morocco," p. 62.

83. Yahia H. Zoubir and Karima Benabdallah-Gambier, "Western Sahara Deadlock," *Middle East Report*, Summer 2003, p. 11.

84. "Rabat Pushes W Sahara Proposal," *al-Jazeera*, March 27, 2006.

85. "Morocco Said to Abandon Hundreds of Migrants in Desert," *New York Times*, October 14, 2005.

CHAPTER 20: ALGERIA

1. Julia A. Clancy-Smith, *Rebel and Saint: Muslim Notables, Populist Protest, Colonial Encounters: Algeria and Tunisia, 1800–1904* (Berkeley: University of California Press, 1994), pp. 11–13.

2. Clancy-Smith, *Rebel and Saint*, p. 87.

3. Clancy-Smith, *Rebel and Saint*, p. 92.

4. David C. Gordon, *The Passing of French Algeria* (New York: Oxford University Press, 1966), p. 51.

5. William B. Quandt, *Revolution and Political Leadership: Algeria, 1954–1968* (Cambridge, MA: MIT Press, 1969), chap. 3.

6. Quandt, *Revolution and Political Leadership*, p. 51.

7. Gordon, *Passing of French Algeria*, chap. 2.

8. Robert Malley, *The Call from Algeria: Third Worldism, Revolution, and the Turn to Islam* (Berkeley: University of California Press, 1996), pp. 45–46.

9. Malley, *Call from Algeria*, pp. 52–57.

10. For more on the OAS, see Alexander Harrison, *Challenging de Gaulle: The O.A.S. and the Counterrevolution in Algeria, 1954–1962* (New York: Praeger, 1989).

11. "France Faces Its Demons for Algerian War Brutality," *Washington Post*, May 10, 2001.

12. The internationalization of the Algerian conflict is discussed in Matthew Connelly, *A Diplomatic Revolution: Algeria's Fight for Independence and the Origins of the Post–Cold War Era* (New York: Oxford University Press, 2002).

13. Martin Stone, *The Agony of Algeria* (New York: Columbia University Press, 1997), pp. 38–39.

14. Gordon, *Passing of French Algeria*, p. 69. The brutality of the French military during that period is graphically described by Henri Alleg, *The Question* (New York: George Braziller, 1958).

15. Keith Sutton, "Army Administration Tensions over Algeria's Centres de Regroupment, 1954–1962," *British Journal of Middle East Studies*, November 1999, pp. 243–272.

16. Matthew Connelly, "Rethinking the Cold War and Decolonization: The Grand Strategy of the Algerian War for Independence," *International Journal of Middle East Studies*, May 2001, p. 238.

17. John Damis, *Conflict in Northwest Africa: The Western Sahara Dispute* (Stanford, CA: Hoover Institute Press, 1983), p. 18.

18. Mohand Salah Tahi, "The Arduous Democratisation Process in Algeria," *Journal of Modern African Studies* 30 (1992): 397.

19. Robert Mortimer, "Islamists, Soldiers, and Democrats: The Second Algerian War," *Middle East Journal*, Winter 1996, p. 20.

20. Mortimer, "Islamists, Soldiers, and Democrats," pp. 25–26. As Mortimer notes, the FIS actually lost over a million votes from the 1990 election, a drop of 54 to 47 percent of the turnout. Only 24 percent of Algeria's electorate actually voted for the FIS in 1991.

21. Mortimer, "Islamists, Soldiers, and Democrats," pp. 26–27.

22. "A Farce, Again," *Economist*, April 17, 1999, p. 48.

23. "Bouteflika Names New President amid Fresh Violence," *Middle East News*, April 21, 1999. The six opposition candidates claimed a figure of under 23 percent. "While Refuting the Turnout Rate Advanced by the Interior Minister, the 'Six' Did not Recognize the Outcome of the Vote," *Algiers La Tribune*, April 16, 1999; in French.

24. "Militant's Murder," *World Press Review*, February 2000, p. 27.

25. "Boutiflika's Bid for Concord," *Economist*, January 29, 2000, p. 45.

26. Clement M. Henry and Robert Springborg, *Globalization and the Politics of Development in the Middle East* (Cambridge: Cambridge University Press, 2001), p. 120.

27. Ray Takeyh, "Islamism in Algeria: A Struggle Between Hope and Agony," *Middle East Policy*, Summer 2003, p. 72.

28. "Algeria President Re-Elected in Landslide," *New York Times*, April 9, 2004.

29. "Algerian Fighters to Surrender," *al-Jazeera*, April 22, 2004.

30. "Top Algerians Prefer Amnesia to Accountability for War," *New York Times*, September 26, 2005.

31. "Algerian Voters Approve Amnesty Plan in Civil War," *New York Times*, September 30, 2005. Turnout was much lower, around 11 percent, in some predominately Berber areas.

32. Simon Serfaty, "Algeria Unhinged: What Next? Who Cares? Who Leads?" *Survival*, Winter 1996–1997, p. 137.

33. Serfaty, "Algeria Unhinged," p. 137.

34. Quandt, *Revolution and Political leadership*, p. 5.

35. Susan E. Waltz, *Human Rights and Reform: Changing the Face of North African Politics* (Berkeley: University of California Press, 1995), p. 75.

36. Lahouari Addi, "Army, State, and Nation in Algeria," in Kees Koonings and Dirk Kruijt, eds., *Political Armies: The Military and Nation Building in the Age of Democracy* (London: Zed, 2002), p. 181.

37. William B. Quandt, *Between Ballots and Bullets: Algeria's Transformation from Authoritarianism* (Washington, DC: Brookings Institution, 1998), p. 84.

38. Waltz, *Human Rights and Reforms*, p. 186.

39. Waltz, *Human Rights and Reforms*, pp. 186–187.

40. Amnesty International, *AI Report 1998: Algeria*.

41. Amnesty International, *Unrestrained Powers: Torture by Algeria's Military Security*, MDE 28/004/2006, July 10, 2006.

42. John L. Esposito and John O. Voll, *Islam and Democracy* (New York: Oxford University Press, 1996), pp. 153–156.

43. Thomas Kamm, "U.S., EU Pressure Algeria to Quell Reported Violence," *Wall Street Journal*, January 7, 1998, p. 1.

44. Kamm, "U.S., EU Pressure Algeria," p. 1.

45. See Stathis N. Kalyvas, "Strategies or Preferences? A Study of Massacres in Algeria" (paper presented at the 1999 Meeting of the American Political Science Association).

46. Brynjar Lia and Ashild Kjok, "Sanctuary or Enemy Territory? The Strategy of Middle Eastern Islamist Insurgent Groups in Europe: The Case of the Algerian Armed Islamic Group (GIA)" (paper presented at the annual conference of the International Studies Association, Chicago, February 2001).

47. Fawaz A. Gerges, "The Decline of Revolutionary Islam in Algeria and Egypt," *Survival*, Spring 1999, pp. 119–120.

48. US State Department, "Middle East Overview," *Patterns of Global Terrorism*, April 30, 2001. In 2007 the GSPC changed its name to al-Qaeda in the Lands of the Islamic Maghreb.

49. Esposito and Voll, *Islam and Democracy*, p. 169.

50. Ed Blanche, "Violence and Discontent Worsen As Algeria Goes from Crisis to Crisis," *Jane's Intelligence Review*, August 2001, p. 36.

51. "Berbers Quit Algeria Government," *BBC News*, May 1, 2002.

52. "Clashes in Algerian Berber City," *al-Jazeera*, March 31, 2004.

53. "Algeria Forbids Efforts to Convert Its Muslims," *New York Times*, April 6, 2006.

54. "Seminar Held on Forms of Violence Against Women," *Algiers El Watan*, October 29, 2001, FBIS; in Arabic.

55. "Algeria to Adopt Progressive Approach to Women's Rights," *Africa News*, January 22, 1999.

56. Catherine Lloyd, "Organising Across Borders: Algerian Women's Associations in a Period of Conflict," *Review of African Political Economy*, December 1999, pp. 479–491.

57. "A Special Theme: Arab Women in Parliament," Symposium on Arab Parliamentary Development, www.pogar.org/publications/legislature/lcps1/section5.html.

58. Henry and Springborg, *Globalization*, pp. 105–106.

59. Paul Shemm, "Truce Masks Algeria's Real Problems," *Middle East Times*, June 17, 1999.

60. "Algiers Daily on Difficulties Ahead for Privatization Superminister," *Algiers Liberte*, August 30, 2000, FBIS; in French.

61. "Fewer Deaths, Lower Debt," *Economist*, February 14, 2004, p. 13.

62. United States Energy Information Administration, *Algeria*, February 1999, p. 2.

63. See Yahia H. Zoubir, "Conflict and Cooperation in North Africa: Algerian-Moroccan Bilateral Relations in the 1990s" (paper presented to the annual conference of the International Studies Association, Los Angeles, CA, March 2000).

64. "Morocco Delegation Hands Over Urgent Humanitarian Aid to Algeria," *Arabic-News.com*, November 13, 2001.

65. "White House Makes an Overture to Algeria," *Washington Post*, November 12, 1998.

66. "White House Makes an Overture." In the first two weeks of October, some 215 people died in Algeria from the violence, including 83 killed by government troops.

67. Bouteflika noted, "We, of course, refrain from gloating over the fact there are other peoples who, on their turn, knew the very misfortune from which the Algerian people have suffered for years." Address by Algerian President Abdelaziz Bouteflika to students at start of new academic year, Algiers Channel 1, October 7, 2001, FBIS; in Arabic.

68. Interviews, Criel, France; Paris, France, March 2001.

INDEX

Note: The index organizes by prefix, so the words beginning with "al" are grouped together. Technically this is incorrect—the word after the "al" should be indexed—but organizing by "al" should make words easier to locate.

1948 War, 22–25, 235
1956 War, 25–26
1967 War, 26–28, 237, 280
1973 War, 30–31, 238

Abbas, Mahmoud, 39, 119, 375–378
Abd ar-Rahmen, Uman, 245
Abduh, Muhammad, 56
Abdul Aziz ibn Abdul-Rahman al-Saud. *See* al-Saud, Abdul Aziz
Abraham. *See* Ibrahim
Abu Bakr, xiii, 47, 60
Abu Dhabi, 158
Abu Hanifa, 50
Abu Musa Island, 162, 208
Abul Huda, Tawfiq, 354
Abul Madg, Kamal, 62
ad-Din, Ahmad, 176
ad-Din, Muhyi, 412
ad-Din, Qadir, 412
Abdul-Radg, Ali, 339
Adalet ve Kalkynma Partisi (AKP), 62, 260, 261–262, 264, 265
Aden-Abyan Islamic Army, 184
Aflaq, Michel, 20, 278
ahl al-Sunna wa-l-jammaah, 48

Ahmadinejad, Mahmud, 197–201
Ajman, 158
al-Adawiyya, Rabia, 51
al-Afghani, Jamal al-Din, 56
Al-Aqsa Mosque, 47
Al-Aqsa intifadah, 353–354
al-Arabiyya, 109
al-Asad, Bashar, 53, 280–283, 287
al-Asad, Basil, 280
al-Asad, Hafiz, 31, 33, 106, 280–282, 351
al-Asad, Rifat, 280, 281, 282
al-Askari, Hassan, 49
al-Audah, Salman, 135
al-Azhar University, 51, 240, 245, 247
al-Bakr, Ahmad Hasan, 215
al-Banna, Hassan, 55, 143
al-Baqir, Muhammad, 49
al-Basri, Hasan, 51
al-Darzis, Hashtakin, 52
al-Daud, Ibrahim, 215
al-Din, Salah, (Saladin), 111
al-Durr, Shajarat, 112
al-Farabi, Abu Nassir, 4, 64, 65, 100
al-Ghazzaly, Muhammad, 62
al-Hadi, Ali, 49
al-Hakim bi-amr Allah, 52

al-Hamdi, Ibrahim, 178
al-Harithi, Muhammad, 49
al-Harrani, Muhammad, 4
al-Hashimi, Yasin, 213
al-Hawali, Safar, 135
al-Husri, Sati, 20
al-Hussein, Amin, 24
al-Husseini, Hajj Amin, 18
al-Illah, Abd, 214
al-Iryani, Amadi, 176–177, 181
al-Jafari, Ibrahim, 221
al-Jamaa al-Islamiyya, 244–245
al-Jawad, Muhammad, 49
al-Jazeera, 109
al-Jihad, 244, 245
al-Khaymah, Ras, 158
al-Khalifa, Hamad bin Isa, 164
al-Khalifa, Isa bin Salman, 163–164
al-Khaibi, Hussein, 53
al-Khattab, Umar, xvii, 47
al-Khoury, Bishara, 293
al-Kindi, Abu Yusuf, 6
al-Maktoum, Mohammad, 159
al-Maliki, Nuri, 221
al-Mowahidden. *See* Druze
al-Mulqi, Fawiz, 334
al-Nabhani, Taqiuddin, 58
al-Nabulsi, Sulayman, 335
al-Nahdah, 374, 375, 376, 380, 419
al-Nahyan, Zayid bin Sultan, 158–159
al-Nayif, Razzaq, 215
al-Qadir, Abd, 412
al-Qaeda, 57, 58, 61, 87, 132, 189
   in the Islamic Maghreb, 420
al-Qudsi, Nazim, 279
al-Quwwatli, Shukri, 277–278, 279
al-Rashidi family, 128
al-Razi, Muhammad ibn Zakariya, 6
al-Sabah, Nawaf al-Ahmed, 148
al-Sabah, Nasir al-Muhammad al-Ahmad,
   148
al-Sabah, Sabah al-Ahmed, 148
al-Said, Nuri, 212, 214
al-Sadiq, Jafar, 49

al-Sadr, Moqtada, 219, 221,
al-Sadr, Muhammad Sadeq, 217
al-Sadr, Musa, 53, 391
al-Sallal, Addallah, 176
al-Saud, Abdul Aziz, 127–129
al-Saud, Abdullah, 131, 133, 135
al-Saud, Fahd, 131–132
al-Saud, Khalid, 130
al-Saud, Nayef, 132
al-Saud, Turki, 136
al-Shabi, Najib, 180
al-Shafi, Muhammad, 50
al-Shara, Farouk, 283, 288
al-Sistani, Ayat Allah, 219
al-Sohl, Riad, 293
al-Sudayri, Hassa, 131
al-Tal, Wasfi, 336
al-Thani, Abdullah, 170
al-Thani, Ahmad, 169
al-Thani, Hamad, 169–170
al-Thani, Khalifa, 169–170
al-Thani, Muhammad, 170
al-Utaybi, Juhayman, 135
al-Wahab, Muhammad, 54, 128
Alawi, xiii, 53, 279–280. *See also* Alevi
Alevi, xiii, 53, 268
Algeria, 411–424
   Berbers in, 421
   economic performance of, 422–423
   foreign policy of, 423–424
   history of, 411–418
   judicial system of, 419–420
   legislature of, 419
   political parties in, 419
   relations with Morocco, 9, 423
   women's status in, 421–422
Ali ibn abi Talib, 47
Ali, Rashid, 214, 334
Ali, Salim Rubaia, 178
Aliya, 15, 310
Allah, xiii, 44–46
Allawi, Ayad, 219
Allenby, General Edmund, 16
AMAL, 297, 298, 302

Amazigh. *See* Berber

American Israeli Public Affairs Committee, 326

Anglo-Iranian Oil Company, 168, 191–192

Anglo-Egyptian Treaty, 234

Anglo-French Declaration, 277

Anglo-Iraq Treaty, 212

Annan, Kofi, 409

Ansar al-Islam, 224

Aoun, Michel, 296

aquifers, 90

Arab, definition of, ix

Arab country, definition of, ix

Arab Deterrent Force (ADF), 296

Arab Human Development Report, 101

Arab Land Party, 339

Arab League, 23–24

expulsion of Egypt from, 117

Arab Legion, 24

Arab nationalism, 20

Arab Revolt, 16, 212

Arab Socialist Party, 214

Arab Socialist Union, 236

Arabian American Oil Company (Aramco), 84, 139

Arafat, Yasir, 37, 38, 298, 350–351, 356

peace talks with Israel, 118–119

Arif, Abd, 214, 215

Armed Islamic Group (GIA), 420

Armed Islamic Movement, 420

Armenians, 271

Army of the Prophet Muhammad, 420

as Said, Nuri, 19, 25

Ashkenazi, xiii, 311, 316

Ashrawi, Hanan, 357

Assembly of Experts, 200

Aswan High Dam, 26, 236, 250

Ataturk, Kemal, 255–257, 262

Averroës. *See* ibn Rushd

Az-Zahrawi, Abu al-Qasim, 4

Baathist Party, xiii

in Iraq, 214–216

in Syria, 278–282

Baghdad Pact, 26, 192

Bahaullah, 54

Bahai, xiii, 54, 112, 203

Bahnini, Ahmed, 398

Bahrain, 162–167, 174

economic performance of, 166–167

history of, 163–164

judicial system of, 165–166

legislature of, 164–165

women's status in, 166

Baker, James, 409

Balfour Declaration, 17–18

Bani-Sadr, Abu al-Hassan, 195, 201

Barak, Ehud, 107, 118, 288, 313, 317, 325

withdraw from Lebanon, 33, 306

Baraka, 388, 406

Basic Law, 320, 321

as Israeli constitution, 317

Basij, 200

Battle of the Camel, 47

Bayar, Mahmut Celal, 257

Bazargan, Medhi, 194

Begin, Menachem, 32, 33, 117, 238, 297, 312

Beheshti, Muhammad, 195

ben Ali, Zine el Abidine, 372–373, 415

ben Bellah, Ahmad, 21

Bendjedid, Chadli, 409, 415, 416, 420

Ben Gurion, David, 23, 310–311, 316

Berber, 111, 366, 397, 403

Bernadotte, Count Folke, 24

Berri, Nabhi, 302

Besht, 66

bida, xiii, 50

bin Laden, Osama, 3, 39, 57, 60, 131, 136, 182

attacks on Saudi Arabia, 136

Bitar, Salah al-Din, 278, 279

Blum, Leon, 414

Boumedienne, Houari, 408, 418

Bourguiba, Habib, 62, 370–373

Boutiflika, Abdelaziz, 416–418, 424

Brahimi, Lakhdar, 221

Bremer, L. Paul, 219, 221

Brezhnev, Leonid, 33
Buraymi Oasis, 153
Bush, George H. W., 35
Bush, George W., 3, 39, 105, 119, 386
 attack on Iraq, 218
 axis of evil speech, 83, 209

Cairo Agreement, 38
Cairo Conference, 212
Camp David, 32, 117
Carter, Jimmy, 32, 195, 238
 Iranian hostage crisis, 195
 role in peace process, 117
Carthage, 369
Cedar Revolution, 299
Ceuta, Melilla, 406
Chalabi, Ahmed, 219, 274
Chaldean Christians, 70
Chamari, Khemis, 373
Chamoun, Camille, 294
Cheney, Richard, 35
Christianity in the Middle East, 68–70
Church of the Holy Sepulcher, 2, 25
Çiller, Tansu, 259
Circassian, 332
civil society, 108–109
Clemenceau, Georges, 277
Clinton, Bill, 348
Coalition Provisional Authority, 219–221
Cole, USS, 184, 188
colons, 370–371, 414–415
Committee for Defense of Legitimate
 Rights, 135
Committee of National Unity, 257–258
Compagnie Française des Pétroles' role in
 Iran, 193
Constitutional Democratic Rally Party
 (RCD), 373
Constitutional Union Party, 400
Consultative Council, 242
Consultative Council on Human Rights
 (CCDH), 402
Copenhagen criteria, 273
Coptic Christians, xiv, 69–69, 112, 244

Council of Chalcedon, 69
Council of Ephesus, 69
Council of Guardians, 198, 200
Cox, Percy, 212
Crusaders, 3, 12, 14
 reference by Osama bin Laden, 3
Cyprus, 272
Cyrenaica, 383

Damascus Declaration, 284
Dawa Party, 221
Dayan, Moshe, 26, 63
de Hautecloque, Jean, 370
Declaration of Principles, 362
Deir Yassin, 23
DeLesseps, Ferdinand, 15
Demirel, Süleyman, 258–259, 262
democracy, characteristics of, 98–105
Democrat Party (DP), 257–258
Democratic Constitutional Assembly, 373
Democratic Front for the Liberation of
 Palestine (DFLP), 349
Democratic Left Party, 260–261
Democratic Party of Iranian Kurdistan, 202
democratic transformation, 103–104
Derbala, Mohammed Essam, 61
Destour Party, 370
Destourian Socialist Party, 373
dhimmi, 65
diwaniyya, 96, 109
Dome of the Rock, 2, 25, 47, 118
Druze, xiv, 52–53
 in Israel, 321
 in Syrian politics, 282
Dubai, 158
Dulles, John Foster, 26, 236

Ecevit, Bülent, 260–261, 265
Egypt, 233–253
 agricultural development in, 250–251
 civil society in, 246
 economic performance of, 248–251
 foreign relations of, 251–252
 history of, 234–240

judicial system of, 242–244
legislature of, 241–242
political parties in, 241
women's status in, 246–247
elites, definition of, 106–107
Erbakan, Necmittin, 258–260
Erdoğan, Recep Tayyip, 260–261, 264,
   views on Islam and democracy, 63
Eshkol, Levi, 335
Étoile Nord-Africaine, 414
Evian Accords, 415
Expediency Council, 201

Fadlallah, Muhammad Hussein, 61, 303
Falasha, 68
Farouk I, 25, 234–235
Fatah, 351, 357, 358
Federation of Arab Republics, 391
Filali-Ansary, Abdou, 64
fitna, xiv, 42, 60
foreign debt, 79
foreign direct investment, 82
Franco-Tunisian Protocol, 371
Franjeih, Suleiman, 295–296
Free Life Party of Kurdistan, 202
Free Officers Movement, 25
Freedom House, xi, 100
   critique of, 100
   rating for Algeria, 418
   rating for Bahrain, 164
   rating for Egypt, 240
   rating for Iran, 198
   rating for Israel, 315
   rating for Jordan, 315
   rating for Kuwait, 148
   rating for Lebanon, 301
   rating for Libya, 387
   rating for Morocco, 399
   rating for Oman, 154
   rating for Palestine, 354
   rating for Qatar, 170
   rating for Saudi Arabia, 132
   rating for Syria, 281
   rating for Tunisia, 373

rating for UAE, 159
rating for Yemen, 180
Front de Libération Nationale (FLN), 414,
   415, 417
Front for the Defense of Constitutional
   Issues, 398
Front for the Liberation of South Yemen
   (FLOSY), 178
Front Islamique du Salut, (FIS) 415–416
Fujairah, 158
Future Movement Bloc, 302

Gallipoli, 16, 255
Gaza, 354, 356, 363
Gemayel, Bashar, 297
Gemayel, Pierre, 295
General Federation of Jordanian Women,
   341
General Federation of Women (Iraq), 223
General People's Congress, 384–385
Gesher Party, 318
Ghanem, Shukri, 387
Ghannouchi, Rachid, 63, 372, 380
Ghashmi, Ahmed, 178
Glaspie, April, 35
Glubb, John Bagot, 334, 335
Golan, 27
Grand Mosque, 130
Grand Mufti of Jerusalem. *See* al-Husseini,
   Hajj Amin
Great Britain, colonial policy of, 16–18
Great Green March, 408
Great Man-Made River Project, 390
Greater and Lesser Tunbs, 162, 208
Green Book, 387, 390
Guardians of Independence, 212
Gül, Abdullah, 260, 262
Gulf Cooperation Council (GCC), xiv, 77,
   143
Gulf Oil, 193
Guney Doğu Projesi (GAP), 91,
   potential impact on Syria, 288–289
Gürsel, Cemal, 257–258
Gush Emunim, 320

Habash, George, 29, 350
Hadad, Saad, 296
hadith, xiv, 46–47
Haganah, 23, 309
Halacha, 66
Hamas, 37, 353, 354–355, 358, 359
Hamidaddin, Yahya Muhammad, 176
Hamza ibn Ali ibn Ahmad, 52
Hanafi school of Sunni jurisprudence, xiv,
    50
Hanbali school of Sunni jurisprudence, xiv,
    50, 53, 58, 376
    influence in Saudi Arabia, 105–106
Hansah Society, 360
Haram al-Sharif, 36, 38, 70, 313. *See also*
    Temple Mount
Hariri, Rafiq, 298–299, 304
Hariri, Saad, 302
Hashemi-Shahrudi, Mahmoud, 201
Hasidism, 66–67
Hassan II, 397–399, 405, 408
Hattab, Hassan, 421
Hawatma, Nayef, 349
Helou, Charles, 295
Herzl, Theodor, 308
High Committee for Islamic Da'wa, 245
Histadrut, 311, 312
Hizb ut-Tahrir, 58
    movement in Turkey, 262
Hizbollah, xiv–xv, 56, 208, 289, 298, 302,
    314, 327
Holst, Johan Jurgen, 117
human rights, 110–111
Huss, Salim, 299, 300–301
Hussein, Abdullah I, 23, 332–334
Hussein, Abdullah II, 337–338, 339, 344
Hussein ibn Ali, xv, 16, 47, 128, 276
Hussein, ibn Talal 334–337
Hussein, Talal, 334
Hussein, Faisal I, 212
Hussein, Faisal II, 214–215
Hussein, Ghazi, 213–214
Hussein, Hajj Amin, 18, 24
Hussein, Saddam, 97, 106, 214, 215, 220

    attacks on Kurds and Shiites, 216
    invasion of Kuwait, 35–37, 216
    war with Iran, 196
Huwaidy, Fahmy, 62

Ibadi, xv, 54, 152–153, 154
ibn Battuta, 4
ibn Baz, Sheik Abd al-Aziz, 135
Ibn Firnas, 4
ibn Hanbal, Ahmed, 50
ibn Ibad, Abd Allah, 54
Ibn Khaldun, 4, 20
ibn Rushd, 6, 64
ibn Saud. *See* al-Saud, Abdul Azziz
ibn Saud, Muhammad, 128
ibn Sina, 6
ibn Taymiyya, 53, 55, 56
    critique of the Alawi, 53
ibn Taymur, Said, 154
ibn Zayid, Tariq, 6
Ibrahim, 211
Ibrahim, Saad Eddine, 243
Idris I, Mohammad as-Sanusi, 383–384,
ijtihad, xv, 50, 56, 57, 62
Ikhwan, 128, 129
Imamiyya, 49
Inonu, Ismet, 257
inport-substitution industrialization (ISI),
    77
International Monetary Fund (IMF), xv, 79,
    238, 249, 269, 338, 390, 405,
    422–423
intifadah, xv, 352–353
Iran, 190–210
    economic performance of, 205–207
    foreign policy of, 207–209
    history of, 190–198
    judicial system of, 201–202
    legislature of, 200–201
    minority groups in, 202–203
    nuclear question, 209
    support for Hizbollah, 208
    women's status in, 203–204
Iran-Iraq War, 34–35, 196

Iraq, 211–228
   civil society in, 223
   economic performance, 224–226
   foreign policy of, 226
   history of, 211–220
   invasion of Kuwait, 215, 216
   judicial system of, 222–223
   legislature of, 222
   women's status in, 223–224
Iraqi Petroleum Company, 212, 215
Irgun Zvai Leumi, 2–3
Islah, xv, 62
Islah Party of Yemen, 179, 182, 185
Islam, xv, 44–65
   and politics, 54–56
   and pluralism, 64–65
   beliefs and practices, 44
   reformation of, 61
Islamic Action Front (IAF), 342
Islamic Alliance, 239
Islamic Front in Syria, 280
Islamic banking in Bahrain, 167
Islamic Fighting Group, 388
Islamic Martyrdom Movement, 388
Islamic Revolutionary Party (IRP), 201
Islamic Salvation Army, 417
Islamic Tendency Movement (MTI), 372
Ismail, Abdul Fattah, 245
Ismaili, xv, 49, 152, 282
Israel, 307–330
   cabinet of, 317
   civil society in, 332
   economic performance of, 323–325
   foreign policy of, 325–328
   history of, 308–315
   judicial system of, 320–322
   Knesset (parliament), 317–318
   nuclear weapons program, 328–329
   political demographics of, 315–316
   political parties in, 319
   women's status in, 322–323
Istiqlal Party, 396
Izzedine al-Qassam Brigades, 355

Jadid, Salah, 279–280
Jahiliyya, 55
Jamahiriyya, 390
Javad-Bahonar, Mohammad, 195
Jerusalem, 2, 3, 16, 23, 24, 25, 27, 29, 36,
      38, 46, 60, 67, 70, 310
   as proposed Palestinian capital, 118
Jewish Agency, 23
jihad, xv, 59–61
Jordan, 331–346
   civil society in, 340–341
   economic performance of, 342–344
   foreign policy of, 344–345
   history of, 332–337
   judicial system of, 340
   legislature of, 339–340
   Muslim Brotherhood in, 338
   political parties in, 340
   women's status in, 340–341
Jordanian Islamic Action Front, 62
Jordanian National Committee for Women,
      341
Jumblatt, Kamal, 294, 295
Jumblatt, Walid, 302
Justice and Development Party (AKP), 260,
      264
Justice and Development Party (Morocco),
      401
Justice Party, 258

Kabbalah school, 67
Kach Party, 320
Kadima Party, 314, 319
Kadouri, Yitzhak, 67
Kahane Chai, 320
Kahane, Meir, 320
kalam, 49
Kanaan, Ghazi, 281
Karbala, Battle of, 48
Karrubi, Medhi, 201
Katsav, Moshe, 322
Khaddam, Hikmat, 283
Khadija, 46, 47
Khamene'i, Ali, 198–199, 206

Khan, Reza, 191
Kharijites, 54, 153
Khatami, Muhammad, 196–197, 208
Khomeini, Ruhollah, 34, 55, 193–196,
    206, 207–208.
Khrushchev, Nikita, 26
Kibbutz, 15
Kissinger, Henry, 31
Kitchener, Lord, 332
Kook, Avraham Yitzhak, 68
Kulthum, Umm, 234
Kurdish Freedom and Democracy Congress
    (KADEK), 267–268
Kurdish Regional Government, 220
Kurds, 111
    in Iran, 203
    in Iraq, 213, 216–217, 224
    in Syria, 281
    in Turkey, 267–268
Kuwait, 146–152, 174
    economic performance of, 150–152
    history of, 146–147
    iraqi invasion of, 35
    National Assembly, 149
    women's status in, 150

Labor Party of Israel, 311–312, 319
Lahoud, Elias, 298
Lapid, Yosef (Tommy),
Laraki, Ahmed, 398
Law of Return, 68, 311
Law of Shame, 239
Lawrence, T. E., 16
League of Islamic Awakening, 212
League of Nations, 18
Lebanese Arab Army, 296
Lebanese National Movement, 295
Lebanon, 292–306
    civil society in, 303–304
    economic performance of, 304–305
    foreign policy of, 305–306
    history of, 292–300
    judicial system of, 302–303

legislature of, 301–302
    women's status in, 304
Levy, David, 318
Liberal Party, 241
Liberty, USS, 27
Libya, 382–393
    civil society in, 388–389
    economic performance, 389–391
    foreign policy, 391–393
    history of, 383–386
    judicial system of, 388
    legislature of, 387
    WMD, 292–293
    women's status in, 389
Libyan Islamic Group, 388–389
Libyan Militant Islamic Group (LMIG),
    388
Likud Party, 312, 319
Livni, Tzipi, 323
Lochamei Herut Yisrael, (Stern Gang), 23,
    309–310

Mafouz, Naguib, 96, 234
Madrid Conference, 117
Mahir, Ali, 235
majlis, 63, 104
Majlis al-Shaab, 283
Majlis al-Shura-e-Islami, 200
Majlis al-Umma, 149, 349
Majlis al-Watani, 222
Majlis Oman, 155
Malik ibn Abnas, 50
Maliki school of Sunni jurisprudence, xv,
    50, 376
Mapai Party, 311
marabouts, 395
Mardam Bey, Jamil, 377
Mardom Party, 193
Maronite Christians, xv–xvi, 69
martyrdom, 61
McMahon, Sir Henry, 332
Mecca, xvi, 44, 46–47
Medina, 44,

Meir, Golda, 133, 322–323
Melliyun Party, 193
Menderes, Adnan, 257–258
Mendès-France, Pierre, 370
Meretz Party, 317, 319
Mesopotamia, xvi, 2, 4, 5, 6, 16, 17
Mitzna, Amram, 313
Middle East defined, ix
Milli Selamet Partisi (MSP), 258
Mirza Hussein Ali. *See* Bahaullah
Mission for the Referendum in Western
    Sahara (MINURSO), 409, 410
Mitzna, Amram, 313
Mohamed V, 395, 397
Mohamed VI, 399, 410
monophysitism, 69
Morocco, 394–410
    civil society in, 403
    economic performance of, 404–406
    foreign policy of, 406–410
    history of, 395–399
    judicial system of, 402–403
    legislature of, 401
    political parties in, 401
    Western Sahara issue, 407–410
    women's status in, 403–404
Mossadeq, Muhammad, 191–192
Motherland Party (ANAP), 259
Movement for an Islamic State, 426
Movement of Democratic Socialists, 373
Muawiya, 47
Mutazilism, 46
Mubarak, Gamal, 247
Mubarak, Hosni, 239
    role in Egyptian court system, 243
    role in Egyptian economy, 248, 249
Muhammad, xvi, 44, 46
    life of, 45–46
    nocturnal journey, 46–47
Muhammad Ali, 25, 75
Muhammad Ali Nasser, 178, 179
Mujahedin-e Khalq (MEK), 209
Murr, Elias, 299

Muslim Brotherhood, 234, 244, 338
Muslim National League, 212
mutawwa, xvi, 127, 128, 138
Muwahuddin, xvii, 128, 135. *See also*
    Wahhabi

Nablus-Gilboa Aquifer, 90
Naguib, Muhammad, 236–237
Napoleon, 14
Nasrallah, Hassan, 349
Nasser, Gamal Abdul, 26, 235–237
Nasserite Unionist Party, 180
Nation Party, 339
National Arab Socialist Baath Party, 180
National Bloc, 278
National Constitution Party, 339
National Democratic Party, 238, 239,
    241–242
National Democracy Party, 259
National Liberation Front (NLF) of Yemen,
    178
National People's Assembly, 419
National Progressive Front, 280, 282, 283
National Progressive Unionist Party, 241
National Rally of Independents, 401
National Religious Party, 313
National Responsibility Party. *See* Kadima
    Party
National Salvation Front, 258
National Union Party, 313, 319
Nationalist Action Party (MHP), 258, 264,
    265
Nationalist Democracy Party (MPD), 259
natural gas in the Middle East, 87
Neo-Destour Party, 372, 373
Nestorian Christians, 69–70
Netanyahu, Binyamin, 38, 288, 313–314,
    318, 325
New Wafd Party, 239
News Media in the Middle East, 109–110
Nicine Creed, 69
Nouria, Hedi, 378

Ocalan, Abdullah, 260, 267
Occidental Petroleum, 85
Olmert, Ehud, 314
Oman, 152–158, 174
  economic performance of, 155–156
  foreign policy of, 157
  history of, 152–154
  judicial system of, 155
  legislature of, 155
  women's status in, 156–157
One Israel, 313
Operation "Deny Flight", 37
Operation Desert Fox, 144
Operation Iraqi Freedom, 144, 219–220, 270
Operation Peace for Galilee, 297
Organisation Armée Secrète (OAS), 414
Organization for Democratic and Popular Action, 401
Organization for Economic Cooperation and Development (OECD), 77
Organization of Arab Petroleum Exporters (OAPEC), xvi, 84–86, 143
Organization of Petroleum Exporting Countries (OPEC), xvi, 84–86
Orientalism, 6–8
Orthodox Judaism, 66
Oslo Accords, 117, 313
Oslo II Agreement, 38, 345, 353, 362
Ottoman Empire, xvi, 14–15, 254–255, 293, 332
Ouyahia, Ahmed, 418
Ozal, Turgut, 259, 265, 289

Pahlavi Dynasty, 191–194
Pahlavi, Muhammad Reza, 191–194
Palestine, 347–364
  economic performance of, 360–362
  foreign policy of, 362–363
  history of, 350–354
  judicial system of, 359
  legislative council, 358–359
  women's status in, 359–360

Palestinian Authority (PA), xvi, 354, 356–359, 361–362. *See also* Palestine Liberation Organization
Palestinian Charter, 357
Palestine Liberation Organization (PLO), xvi, 28, 29, 37, 350–352. *See also* Palestinian Authority
Palestinian Islamic Jihad, 356
Palestinian National Council, 351
Partisans of Ali. *See* Shiites
Partiya Karkeren Kurdistan (PKK), xvi, 202, 267–268
Peel Commission, 18
People's Democratic Republic of Yemen, 179
Peres, Shimon, 312, 314, 322
Peretz, Amir, 314
petroleum, 83–87
Petroleum pipelines, 86
Phalange Party, 295, 297
Plan Dalet, 25
Polisario Front, 407–410
Popular Front for the Liberation of Palestine (PFLP), 29, 312, 336
Popular Movement (MP), 397, 401
population growth rates in the Middle East, 78
Populist Party (HP), 259
privatization, 79–80

Qaboos, ibn Said al-Said, 154–155
Qadhafi, Muammar, 379, 384–387
Qadhafi, Sief al-Islam, 387, 391
Qasim, Abd al-Karim, 21, 147, 147, 214–215
Qasimiyya-Hadawiyya school of jurisprudence, 179–180
qat, 187
Qatar, 168–173, 174
  economic performance of, 172–173
  history of, 168–170
  judicial system of, 171–172
  women's status in, 172
Qubaisiates, 285

Quran, xvi, 48
  as source of Islamic belief, 45–46
Qureia, Ahmed, 357
Qutb, Said, 55

Rabin, Yitzhak, 37, 107, 312, 327
Rabta chemical weapons plant, 392
Rafsanjani, Ali Akbar, 200, 203, 207
Reagan, Ronald, 195, 297
  role in Lebanon, 33
Rentier state, 82
  Libyan example, 390
  Saudi Arabian example, 139
  Yemen example, 181
Republican Peasant's National Party, 258
Republican People's Party (CHP), 257,
  260–261, 264
Resurgence Party, 193
Revolutionary Command Council (RCC),
  in Egypt, 235–236
  in Libya, 384
Revolutionary Guards, 195
Reza Khan. *See* Pahlavi, Muhammad Reza
Rida, Rashid, 56
Rogers Plan, 29

Said, Edward, 233
Sabra and Shatilla refugee camps, 33, 297
Sadat, Anwar, 21, 28–29, 237–239
  initiation of peace process, 117
Sadat, Jahan, 247
Sadqi, Bakr, 213
Sadr, Muhammad Sadeq, 217
Safavid Dynasty, 50
Salafist Group for Preaching and Combat
  (GSPC), 380
Salafiyya, xvi, 56–58, 399
Salalfi Group for Call and Combat, 421
salat, 44
Saleh, Ali Abdullah, 178, 180–181
Samuel, Herbert, 333
San Remo Agreement, 293
San Remo Conference, 277
Sarkis, Elias, 296–297

Saudi Arabia, 127–145
  civil society in, 134
  economic performance, 138–142
  foreign policy of, 142–144
  Supreme Council of Ulama in, 132
  women's status in, 137–138
Saudi Basic Industries Corporation
  (SABIC), 141
SAVAK, 192, 194
Sephardi, xvii, 311, 312, 316, 319
Shafii school of Sunni jurisprudence, 50
shahadah, 44
Shamir, Yitzhak, 37, 312, 318
Sharia, xvii, 43, 55, 56, 59, 61, 63, 165,
  268, 321, 341, 376, 387, 401
  as source of Egyptian law, 242, 244
  as source of Qatari law, 171
  as source of Saudi Arabian law, 133
Shariati, Ali, 194
Sharjah, 158
Sharon, Ariel, 33, 107, 297, 313–314, 328,
  357
  Election of 2003, 313
  incident in October 2000, 38, 313
Shas Party, 313, 319
Shatt al-Arab disagreement between Iran
  and Iraq, 34
Shawkat, Asef, 282
Shiites, xvii, 37, 47–49
  difference from Sunni, 47–48, 50–51,
  134
Shiite clerical structure, 48
Shiite sects, 48–49
Shihab, Fuad, 294–295
Shiniu Party, 313, 319
Shuqayri, Ahmad, 350
shura, xvii, 63, 104
Siniora, Fuad, 301
Siyam, 44
Social Democratic Movement, 401
Social National Front, 293
Socony Vacuum, 193
South Lebanon Army, 296–297
Soviet Union, 20–21, 27, 28

Spanish-Moroccan Treaty of 1861,
St. James Conference of 1939,
St. Maron, 69
Standard Oil of California, 84, 193
Standard Oil of New Jersey, 84, 193
Standard Oil of New York, 84
Sudan, 252
Sudayri Seven, 132
Suez Canal, 15, 26, 236, 251
Sufi, xvii, 51–52
Sunni, xvii, 47–51. *See also under* Shiite
Sunni Schools of Islamic Jurisprudence, 50
Supreme Council of Ulama, 132
Sykes-Picot Agreement, 16, 293, 332
Syria, 276–291
    civil society in, 284–285
    economic performance in, 285–287
    foreign policy of, 287–290
    judicial system of, 284
    privatization in, 286–287
    relations with Israel, 287–288
    women's status in, 285

Taif Accord, 298, 300
Takfir, xvii, 59
Takfir wal Hijra, 244
Talaq, 114, 185
Talfah, Adnan Khary, 215
Talibani, Jalal, 221, 224
Talmud, 66
taqiyya, 51, 52
tawhid, xvii, 50, 55, 57, 132
Temple Mount, 36, 38, 70, 313. *See also*
    Haram al-Sharif
Texaco, 84, 193
Third National Front, 194
Timman, Abu, 213
Tomorrow Party, 241
Torah, 66, 68
Treaty of Fez, 408
Treaty of Lausanne, 383
Treaty of Portsmouth, 214
Treaty of Sèvers, 176
Treaty of Sib, 153

Trevelan, Humphrey, 178
Tripolitania, 383
True Path Party, 259, 264
Truman Doctrine, 21
Trumbull, Richard, 178
tsaddik, 66
Tudeh Party, 191
Tunisia, 371–381
    economic performance of, 377–379
    foreign policy of, 379–380
    history of, 369–373
    judicial system of, 376–377
    legislature of, 375
    women's status in, 376–377
Tunisienne des Femmes Democrates, 376
Türke, Alparslan, 258
Turkey, 254–275
    civil society in, 266–267
    economic performance in, 269–270
    EU membership efforts, 272–273
    history of, 254–261
    Kurdish population, 267–268
    legal system of, 266
    legislature of, 265–266
    membership in NATO, 271
    membership in UN, 271
    political parties in, 264–265
    relations with Israel, 273–274
    role of military in, 263–264
    women's role in, 268–269
Turkish Petroleum Company, 212
Turkish Republic of North Cyprus
    (TRNC), 272
Tusi, Masiruddin, 4

Ubayd, Allah, 49
Ulama, xvii, 63
Umm al-Quwain, 158
UN Resolution 181, 23
UN Resolution 1701, 300
UN Resolutions 242 and 338, 116–117,
    337
Union Générale des Travailleurs Tunisiens
    (UGTT), 372, 374

Union of Social Popular Forces, (USFP), 401
United Arab Emirates, 158–162, 174
  economic performance of, 160–162
  foreign policy of, 162
  history of, 158
  women's status in, 160
United Arab List, 319
United Arab Republic, 236–237, 279
United Company of Jihad, 420
United Nations, 22, 36
United Nations Committee on Palestine (UNSCOP), 23–24
United Nations Disengagement and Observer Force, 32
United Nations Emergency Force (UNEF), 26, 27
United Nations Interim Force in Lebanon (UNFIL), 296
United Nations Special Committee on Palestine (UNSCOP), 23
United Torah Judaism, 319
Universal Declaration of Human Rights, 110
Usul al-fiqh, 56
Uthman ibn Affan, xvii, 47

Vichy French, 19
Vilayat-I Faqih, 55
Violet Line, 176
Virtue Party, 260, 264

Wafd Party, 19, 234, 239
Wahhabi, xvii, 57, 128, 132. *See also* Muwahuddin
War of Attrition, 28–29
water in the Middle East, 88–92
  rivers as sources of, 89
  shortages of, 89, 91
Weizmann, Chaim, 310
Welfare Party (Refah), 259–260
West Bank, 353, 355, 363
Western Sahara, 407–410

Western Wall, 25, 118
White Revolution, 193–194
women in Middle East society, 112–116. *See also under specific countries*
Woodhead Commission, 18
World Bank, 187, 405
World Values Survey, 63, 102, 114
World War I, 15–18
World Zionist Congress, 308
Wye Plantation peace talks, 287, 313

Yarmouk River, 344–345
Yarqon-Tanninim Aquifer, 90
Yassin, Ahmed, 314, 359
Yassine, Abdassalam, 403
Yassine, Nadia, 403
Yawar, Ghazi, 219
Yazdi, Muhammad Taqi Mesbah, 200
Yazid, 47
Yazidism, 70
Yemen, 175–189
  civil society in, 184–185
  economic performance of, 186–187
  foreign policy of, 188–189
  history of, 175–179
  judicial system of, 183–184
  oil and gas reserves, 186
  Parliament of, 182
  political parties in, 180–181
  women's status in, 185–186
Yiddish, 67
Yülmaz, Mesut, 259, 260, 261, 265
Yisrael Beieinu Party, 318
Yishuv, 310
Young Turks, 255
Youssef, Ben, 372

Zakat, xvii, 44
Zaydi, xvii, 49, 175
Zeroual, Liamine, 416
Zionism, 15, 94–95, 308, 316
Zuhdi, Karam, 61